'This engaging and lucid history of the Islamic world from its beginnings down to the advent of the modern age combines a clear theoretical framework with an up-to-date understanding of recent scholarship. The result is a readable history of pre-modern Islamic societies which avoids both excesses of names and dates and the conventional 'golden age' and 'decline' narratives in favour of more sophisticated explanations of historical change. It will be a very welcome addition to many university courses on Islam and Islamic History, and will also be genuinely useful to a wider general readership.'

Andrew Marsham, *University of Cambridge, UK*

'This clear and comprehensive summary will be a valuable addition to the literature and should find its place on all student reading lists. Indeed, all those interested in the history of Islamic civilisations will find much to enlighten them in this accessible volume.'

Esther-Miriam Wagner, *Woolf Institute, UK*

A History of the Islamic World, 600–1800

A History of the Islamic World, 600–1800 supplies a fresh and unique survey of the formation of the Islamic world and the key developments that characterize this broad region's history from late antiquity up to the beginning of the modern era.

Containing two chronological parts and fourteen chapters, this impressive overview explains how different tides in Islamic history washed ashore diverse sets of leadership groups, multiple practices of power and authority, and dynamic imperial and dynastic discourses in a theocratic age. A text that transcends many of today's popular stereotypes of the Islamic past, the volume takes a holistically and theoretically informed approach for understanding, interpreting, and teaching the premodern history of Islamic West-Asia. Jo Van Steenbergen identifies the Asian connectedness of the sociocultural landscapes between the Nile in the southwest to the Bosporus in the northwest, and the Oxus (Amu Darya) and Jaxartes (Syr Darya) in the northeast to the Indus in the southeast. This abundantly illustrated book also offers maps and dynastic tables, enabling students to gain an informed understanding of this broad region of the world.

This book is an essential text for undergraduate classes on Islamic History, Medieval and Early Modern History, Middle East Studies, and Religious History.

Jo Van Steenbergen teaches Islamic history at Ghent University, Belgium. He has published extensively on medieval Islamic history, including *Order Out of Chaos* (2006), *Caliphate and Kingship in a Fifteenth-Century Literary History* (2016), and *Trajectories of State Formation across Fifteenth-Century Islamic West-Asia* (2020).

A History of the Islamic World, 600–1800

Empire, Dynastic Formations, and Heterogeneities in Pre-Modern Islamic West-Asia

Jo Van Steenbergen

LONDON AND NEW YORK

First published 2021
by Routledge
2 Park Square, Milton Park, Abingdon, Oxon OX14 4RN

and by Routledge
52 Vanderbilt Avenue, New York, NY 10017

Routledge is an imprint of the Taylor & Francis Group, an informa business

British Library Cataloguing-in-Publication Data
A catalogue record for this book is available from the British Library

Library of Congress Cataloging-in-Publication Data
Names: Steenbergen, J. van, author.
Title: A history of the Islamic world, 600–1800 : empire, dynastic formations, and heterogeneities in pre-modern Islamic West-Asia / Jo Van Steenbergen.
Description: First edition. | New York : Routledge, 2020. | Includes bibliographical references and index.
Identifiers: LCCN 2020009899 (print) | LCCN 2020009900 (ebook)
Subjects: LCSH: Islamic countries—History. | Islamic civilization. | Islam—History. | Middle East—History.
Classification: LCC DS35.63 .S737 2020 (print) | LCC DS35.63 (ebook) | DDC 950—dc23
LC record available at https://lccn.loc.gov/2020009899
LC ebook record available at https://lccn.loc.gov/2020009900

ISBN: 978-0-415-66031-0 (hbk)
ISBN: 978-0-415-66032-7 (pbk)
ISBN: 978-1-003-05659-1 (ebk)

Typeset in Times New Roman
by Apex CoVantage, LLC

Contents

Maps

Dynastic tables

Illustrations

Acknowledgements

Writing a textbook such as *A History of the Islamic World, 600–1800* is a project of many years and of endless engagements of varying intensity with wide-ranging and dynamic fields of historical scholarship. It is also both an inspiring and a frustrating project of making sense of a past and a field of historical scholarship that are extremely diverse, and of trying to do this without losing track of the valuable complexity of both. It is finally a lifetime project of coming to terms with the fact that its outcome can only represent a snapshot in one's understanding of that past and scholarship, and that every rereading and every new engagement with that past and scholarship may yield new insights and understandings. Modesty and humbleness with respect to the claims that are presented in this book are therefore the only attitudes one can adopt when sending this project off into the world. Indulgence with the generalizing perspectives and grand narratives, which have been prioritized here, is all one can ask for. Any region or period specialist will undoubtedly be able to write with far more knowledgeability about his/her area of expertise than I have occasionally been able to do here. For a publication project such as the current one, however, and for its ambition to seek for meaningful coherence, for wider appreciations of premodern Islamic and West-Asian entanglement and connectivity, and for an explicit framework of interpretation that also didactically offers recurrent tools to hold on to, the challenge to fully acknowledge historical or historiographical particularity has occasionally appeared inevitably difficult to meet. I nevertheless sincerely hope that not only students and general readers, but also specialists and teachers, may yet find something useful in these wider interpretations, just as I myself, as a specialist of late medieval Syro-Egyptian social and cultural history, gained so many new insights in my many encounters with late antique, medieval, and early modern Islamic history.

Writing a textbook such as *A History of the Islamic World, 600–1800* is a project that above all owes a lot to a great deal of people and institutions that deserve to be mentioned. Words of gratitude should first and foremost be directed at Routledge, and at Routledge's Medieval and Early Modern History team in particular, from former commissioning editor Vicky Peters to current editors Laura Pilsworth and Morwenna Scott. Vicky deserves credit for suggesting the project to me now more than a dozen years ago, when I was still teaching at the School of History of the University of St Andrews in Scotland. Laura and eventually also Morwenna deserve equal credit for their enormous patience when I failed to meet innumerable deadlines, and for nevertheless keeping in touch, for allowing me to first publish a Dutch version of the book, and for thus keeping the project alive. I am also grateful to Laura and Morwenna for skillfully steering the manuscript through the peer review process, for allowing sufficient time for its revision, and for handling the new version and the many changes that I made to it with relentless support and enthusiasm. I am also grateful to Emma Brown for taking care of the all but evident process of obtaining the images and their permissions, and to Routledge more in general for enabling the latter, as well as the drawing of specific maps for the book and the provision of English proofreading facilities. A big word of thanks should also go to the two anonymous reviewers who read the manuscript for Routledge, providing me with many and highly constructive suggestions, which offered invaluable inspiration and incentives to substantially rewrite the text and transform it into a thicker but also a much better book. Furthermore, I would like to thank the four anonymous reviewers who back in 2017 already did the same for the earlier, Dutch version of the text (published in 2018 with the title *Een Nieuwe Geschiedenis Van De Islamitische Wereld. Rijks- En Identiteitsvorming in Islamitisch West-Azië (7de–18de Eeuw)* [Leuven, Den Haag: Acco]).

There are beyond these editorial contexts many people who over the past dozen years have contributed to my thinking about this book, consciously or not. These include many colleague historians, especially first at the University of St Andrews and for many years now at Ghent University, notably in the context of our institutional and collegial collaboration in the Henri Pirenne Institute for Medieval Studies. They also include many students that I have been working with over the past decade or so, at graduate level, but especially for this book at undergraduate level. Over the past years, different generations of the latter in particular have been confronted with various versions of the texts that eventually transformed into this book, in the context of my teaching an introductory course of premodern Islamic history at Ghent University to BA students of Arabic and Islamic studies, history, and various other subjects. Not all of them may have always equally appreciated the accumulation of texts and case studies from the field they had to study for their final exam, but I am grateful for their differing engagements with these texts and teaching materials nevertheless, and for enabling me to thus refine my argument and its formulation in direct communication with one of its main target audiences.

A final word of thanks, as always, goes to my family. Even though my four children, Jonas, Marie, Anna, and Elias, have mostly grown up with this project without really realizing it, their continued presence, friendship, and love reminded me above all that all good things have to be given their own time to sprout and thrive, that there is more joy and pleasure in this process than in the achievement of any outcome, and that missing yet another deadline may therefore well have been to the benefit of, if not the book then certainly its author. Last but not at all least my wife, best friend, and colleague Maya has, once again, endured this project among many other unfinished ones that eat away from our time together, or that generate my mental absence even when I was physically present. As always, I cannot begin to express my gratitude for her relentless support and inspiration, for continuing to be my first reader and audience, and simply for always being there.

Jo Van Steenbergen
Antwerp
30 October 2019

Introduction

Islamic West-Asia, Late Antique imperial and 'medieval'-early modern dynastic formations, and a new history of the Islamic world

> Know that history is a discipline of fine principles, manifold uses, and noble purpose. It informs us about man's past experiences—from the characters of peoples, over the lives of prophets, to the reigns and rules of monarchs—thus providing useful models for those who aspire to emulate them, in religious as well as worldly contexts. [To achieve this, the historian] requires many sources and wide knowledge; [he also requires] keen judgement and careful scrutiny to lead him to the truth and away from lapses and errors. If reliance is placed on simple narrative as transmitted, without studying the roots of custom, the basics of rule, the nature of civilization, and the circumstances of man's social organization, and without comparing what is invisible with what is visible or what is present with what is absent—then there will be danger of obtaining unreliable results and stumbling and straying from the road of truthfulness.[1]

This appreciation of the didactic value of history and of the absolute necessity of applying a sound historical-critical method are nearly obvious rules of thumb for every contemporary historian. However, in this excerpt, they do not appear as the exclusive achievements of a modern and 'enlightened' science of history. On the contrary. In this particular case, they are the product of a 'medieval' Islamic time and space that in popular discourse continue to be associated with terms such as socio-cultural stagnation, intellectual sclerosis, political incapacity, and the beginning of centuries of dark ages, which would continue to define being Muslim until today. In recent decades, historical research has slowly but surely outgrown such doomed imaginations of Islamic history's premodern trajectory. The author of this striking academic statement of intent, the 'medieval' North African scholar Ibn Khaldun (d. 1406 CE in Cairo), tends nevertheless still to be regarded by many modern scholars as an exception, someone who was far ahead of his time and whose immediate intellectual impact would therefore have remained rather limited.

One of the most important objectives of this book is to show that Ibn Khaldun's is not an exceptional case, that there are different trajectories to be imagined, and that it might even be long overdue to tell another, new story about the Islamic world's 'characters of peoples, lives of prophets, and reigns and rules of monarchs'. Therefore, this is not just yet another reconstruction of the Islamic World's 'past experiences' in which merely the technical rules of the historical discipline are taken as a guideline. This book wishes to go beyond that. It wishes to provide insight into one of the ways in which today a new history of the central lands of the Islamic world in West-Asia during the pre-modern period can be written. New findings and ongoing advances in historical research of these regions and this period certainly invite for this, as does a growing awareness of how being explicit about the many forms of stereotyping the past—in the form of the Islamic world's doomed 'medieval' dark ages, or in any other model that is used to represent that world's historical trajectories—can open new horizons of understanding. This book engages explicitly with those ongoing advances in scholarship as well as with the need to explain its framework of interpretation, in order to write a new story, a story that transcends many of today's stereotypes of the pre-modern Islamic past and that attempts to fully appreciate the memory of Ibn Khaldun, his 'medieval' contemporaries, and their many predecessors and successors.

In fact, in his time, Ibn Khaldun was anything but an isolated scholar living a disconnected life of limited impact. On the contrary, the world in which Ibn Khaldun lived stretched exceptionally far, from Iberian Granada in the west all the way to beyond Central Asian Samarqand in the east. Both cities were the far ends of active networks of personal experiences, adventures, contacts, and imaginations that took Ibn Khaldun to most major urban centers of North Africa and the Middle East, and granted him access to the court of many rulers—from Abu Inan's court at Fez, over Sultan Barquq's at Cairo, up to the itinerant court of Tamerlane, the Central-Asian conqueror from Samarqand who received Ibn Khaldun in audience outside Damascus. The wide geographical extent of the space in which Ibn Khaldun was active was, furthermore, all but exceptional in the Islamic world of the 14th century. For example, in the mid-1350s, he ran into a prominent fellow traveler in Fez: the religious scholar Muhammad Ibn Battuta (d. *c.* 1377), who had ended up there after several decades of wanderings that had taken him not only to Granada and Samarqand, but even to urban centers at much wider opposite ends, from Timbuktu in West Africa to Delhi in northern India.

The travel journal that Ibn Battuta had recorded in Fez and the autobiography left by Ibn Khaldun in Cairo are, as a result of the surprising vastness of their personal spaces, privileged testimonies of a 'medieval' Islamic world that proved to be both enormously wide and remarkably coherent. The latter is mainly reflected in two factors that appear as shared experiences from many stories in both writings. First of all, Ibn Battuta and Ibn Khaldun travelled everywhere in the company of other Muslims: pilgrims on their way to Mecca and religious scholars in pursuit of knowledge like them, but also others, such as merchants and craftsmen heading for lucrative horizons. Whether they travelled great or small distances in this vast Islamic world, all contributed to a kind of *perpetuum mobile* of regular flows of travelers by land and at sea, who interweaved urban and rural communities from Africa to Asia, and made this intensely connected world, among other things, home to some of the most important and prosperous trading systems of the 'medieval' world. Secondly, both scholars moved throughout this vast world as anything but total strangers. As a result of their particular scholarly origins, education, and reputation, they were received in most places with substantial respect and reverence. In addition, they usually found themselves in an environment in which being Muslim manifested itself through more or less recognizable social practices and customs. Thus, Ibn Battuta's travelogue includes reports of how even in young Islamic communities in remote areas—for example, on the Maldives Islands in the Indian Ocean—it was almost natural for him to enjoy authority and esteem and to assume, as an outsider, socially impactful roles such as that of religious judge (*qadi*).

Throughout the ages and through the extensive circulation of goods, people, practices, and ideas, a regular flow of migrants and travelers had clearly succeeded in creating not only intense physical and economic contacts but also a meaningful social and cultural connectivity between a great variety of local communities, from Timbuktu to Delhi and from Granada to the Maldives. Connecting factors in this immense cultural area between the Atlantic and Indian Oceans were indisputably Islamic rituals, practices, and ideas, which, as contacts became more intense, gained a recognizable degree of uniformity everywhere. In addition, an equally crucial role was played by the Arabic language and the Arabic script, which—together with religion—had spread from the 7th century onwards across the Afro-Eurasian zone, as a cultural idiom with a divine dimension and as a widespread *lingua franca* for practical and especially commercial use.

At the same time, however, Ibn Khaldun and Ibn Battuta were not immune to the diversity of the vast Islamic world in which they travelled. Despite all recognizability associated with Arabic Islam, in reality local practices, ideas, customs, and habits appeared to differ greatly from each other. For example, the judge Ibn Khaldun found himself the focal point of criticism more than once in Cairo because of his too 'Maghrebi'—i.e. too strict, according to dominant Egyptian standards—application of Islamic law. He himself noted in his autobiography that not all the stories that were told about Ibn Battuta were perceived as credible in Fez, precisely because they often seemed to deviate so much from accepted norms and values. The experiences of figures like Ibn Khaldun and Ibn Battuta make clear, first and foremost, the extent to which, under one and the same mantle of the Arabic prophet of Islam, the trans-regional interconnectedness of their time continued to go hand in hand with remarkably varied, multivalent, contested, and localized appreciations of what it meant to feel at home under that mantle. These experiences reflect the heterogeneous backgrounds

Figure 0.1 Al-Idrisi's world map

Source: Wikimedia, public domain, https://commons.wikimedia.org/w/index.php?curid=322447

of the many communities that the Islamic world actually consisted of, backgrounds that in many cases go back to equally diverse pre-Islamic, non-Islamic, and Islamic origins. The world Ibn Khaldun and Ibn Battuta travelled in during the 14th century was therefore also the product of a highly active, dynamic, and innovative process of continuous and endless interaction and cross-fertilization between Arabian, Mediterranean, Persian, Inner-Asian, and many other, more local, legacies and imaginations of belonging. Each of these continued to exist (and change) in its own way while actively participating in the formation of wider, regularly contested, distinctive modalities that became recognizably Islamic. Giving shape to a multicolored world of interconnected Islamic identities, this process of trans-regional interaction and integration would never be 'finished', and this world continued, and continues, to undergo profound transformations, well beyond Ibn Khaldun's and Ibn Battuta's 14th century.

This rich, intense, and endless process of the construction of Islamic discourses of belonging was to a large extent paralleled, and fueled, by equally complex processes of empowerment and leadership formation that made judges, scholars, courtiers, and travelers such as Ibn Khaldun and Ibn Battuta into men of prestige, influence, and power beyond local or regional boundaries, even at the courts of Abu Inan of Fez, Sultan Barquq of Cairo, Tamerlane of Samarqand, Sultan Muhammad of Delhi, and the ruler of the Maldives. Ibn Khaldun himself already understood this dynamic as an intense and determining interaction between the sociopolitical and the cultural, and he described it as one of the driving forces of human history. In a striking passage in the rather theoretical 'Introduction' to his major chronicle of that history, he summarizes the trajectory of this dynamic, and the rich roots of the primarily urban and multi-colored Arabian-Persian-Turkish Islamic culture of his time, in a constructive way that also aptly summarizes the approach and organization of the current book:

> The urban culture is passed on by the previous dynasty to the next. The Persian culture was passed on to the Arabian Umayyads and the Abbasids, and the culture of the Umayyads in Andalusia was passed on to the Almohads and the Zanata [Berbers], the present rulers of the Maghreb. The culture of the Abbasids was passed on to the [Iranian] Daylamites, then to the Turks and the Seljuks, then the Turks in Egypt, that is, the supporters of the Ayyubids, and the Mongols in Mesopotamia and north-west Persia.[2]

This dynamic and mutually constitutive interaction between dynastic reconfigurations and cultural efflorescence, and more in particular between practices of power and discourses of belonging, is also central to *A History of the Islamic World, 600–1800*. Together, so it is argued here, these two processes represent a particular type of history that, for all its top-down and elitist specificity and for all the doubts that modern historians in general have been raising about its value, continues to yield fundamental insights into the endless process of the circulation of power that lead to a better and even newer understanding of the worlds in which Ibn Khaldun and Ibn Battuta lived. This—for some an undoubtedly unfashionable—focus in Ibn Khaldun's footsteps on the dynamics and interactions of power and belonging, is not meant to overwhelm the reader with mere traditional summations and detailed descriptions of endless sets of powerful individuals and high-profile events. In fact, unless for some minor factual corrections and updates, those histories have already been written. This book's Khaldunian focus involves a deliberate choice to prioritize leadership narratives in new, more connected interpretative lights. Based on the critical assumption that such narratives, in historical practice and discourse, were constitutive of, and constituted by, many related processes of meaning making, cohesion, and distribution, it puts these assumptions and choices to work to reconstruct a particular, but also meaningful, macro-narrative of the Islamic World's heterogeneity and interconnectedness across time and space. Such a macro-narrative appears here above all as a grand, all-encompassing story about different waves in Islamic history's ocean of events, people and narratives. As will be detailed below, not only did these waves wash ashore diverse but related sets of leadership groups. They continued to do so carried by multifarious but equally related sets of practices of power and discourses of belonging. Reconstructing the story of these leadership configurations through an identification of these different waves of their imperial and dynastic practices and discourses represents one of the few meaningful analytical ways, we think, in which true justice can be done to both new insights of recent scholarship (and the arguably highly leadership-oriented nature of the available sources) and the role and meaning of historical figures such as Ibn Khaldun.

As Ibn Khaldun himself prescribed in this introduction's opening quote, it is indeed a necessary prerequisite for every serious historical project to first study "the roots of custom, the basics of rule, the nature of civilization, and the circumstances of man's social organization". It is necessary first to choose the above-mentioned—more or less hypothetical—interpretative framework in which one establishes specifically how one thinks analytically, in our case about man as a socio-political and cultural being. It is also necessary to define a framework of time and space in a similar fashion, to establish in an equally specific way how one thinks about man as a historical being. In the former case, this mainly concerns the way in which the interaction between configurations, practices, and discourses of power is conceptualized in this book. In the latter case, this involves making clear how, from such a conceptualization, the monolithic idea of *the* history of *the* Islamic world is exchanged for a consideration of more specific, diverse, and changing units of time and space.

In this book, the historical interaction between practices of power and discourses of belonging is interpreted through the lens of a conceptual framework that is in critical ways derived from the social theory of the German scholar Max Weber (1865–1920). As is well known, Weber's analytical writings on economy, society, culture, and history have had an enormous impact on the humanities and social sciences in general, on the historical discipline in particular, and to some extent also on the study of the Islamic world most specifically. Weber helps us think of specific manifestations of this book's central power-discourse nexus in more analytical ways. He enables this via his key conceptualization of this relationship through the lens of legitimate authority, and his famous proposition that legitimate authority's different manifestations in human history may be interpreted as particular instances of three ideal types of such authority, differing in the rational, traditional, or charismatic mechanisms by which they make their claims to power. Power is therefore not only materially (that is, by the level of control over or access to material resources) but always also discursively determined (that is, by the social meaning and relative value attributed to appeals to reason and the law, to tradition and kinship, or to charisma and related abstract qualities of specialty). For this book especially, Weber's tradition-bound patriarchal and patrimonial models of legitimate authority shall present a permanent point of reference. This basically concerns the organization, and explanation, of power relations in the patriarchal form of highly personal kin and kin-related bonds and dynastic identities on the one hand, and in the more complex patrimonial form of historical state apparatuses of wielders of violence and organizers of resource accumulation operating in the service of such kin relationships and dynastic identities on the other. Occasionally, the rational model will appear as relevant for this book, as an interpretative addition to the latter patrimonial one, especially when patrimonial appearances of power increase in complexity and scale and their components acquire greater autonomy as powerful cogs in a bureaucratic machinery with a logic and agency of its own. Finally, these highly insightful patriarchal, patrimonial, and patrimonial-bureaucratic models will often be combined with the charismatic one. On the one hand, this charismatic model helps to make sense of important moments of origin and transition, when power relationships and discursive frames change and suddenly appear to coalesce around the special qualities of one or more new particular leaders and kin groups. On the other hand, the rallying force of this charismatic quality of specialty and appeal enables us to also include in our interpretations the workings of the symbolic framework of power within which all actors operate. This relates to not just dynastic discourses of kin-related specialty and entitlement, but in particular to the hegemonic theocratic contexts within which all patriarchal and patrimonial leaders and elites in this expanded time and space imagined themselves to be operating. Their power relations were continuously being appreciated as ultimately deriving from divine sovereignty and their discourses of belonging were unfailingly being constructed in function of how they conceived of their participation in that theocratic order. In these complementary and overlapping ways, these three Weberian ideal types thus represent a highly insightful common grid to interpret and understand twelve centuries of practical and discursive continuity and change.

The more historical leadership formation logic suggested by the complementary and overlapping uses that will be made of these Weberian models is further conceptualized by also engaging the historical theories of Ibn Khaldun in this book's interpretative grid. In a manner announcing in remarkable ways Weber's thinking about legitimate authority, Ibn Khaldun, as suggested above, also developed his own theory of 'the circumstances of human society', in which, simply put, he sees constant historical movement between highly personal kin-based power constellations on the one hand and on the other the more distant functional ties that bind rulers and all kinds of experts in the management of wealth and cultural refinement. For Ibn Khaldun, this movement always occurs within a theocratic social order, and it takes on a moral quality of decadence and decline of that order when, in his reading, functional relationships make up in lesser, weaker ways for the dissolution of kin-based ones. For him, too, the special appeal of prophetic leadership and religious invocation can counter this human historical tendency towards decline and relative social disintegration. At the same time, however, he also maintains that this movement remains an inevitable one, because it basically is the changing material condition of resources' availability in scarce or abundant quantities that is an important causative factor for the alteration of human connectivity. This book will definitely try to avoid the latter linear, teleological, and deterministic readings. Nevertheless, it will include in its analyses the notion that power is never an absolute category, but always, as Ibn Khaldun also suggests, a relational quality constituted in the material and immaterial inequalities, and their explications, that bind and separate people. As will be explained below, the meta-narrative of this book will above all be heavily inspired by how Ibn Khaldun himself imagined not just the dynamic between dynastic reconfigurations and cultural history within the theocratic order, but above all this iterative social process of the binding and separating of people as occurring in a continuous and tense interaction between the martial qualities of nomadic environments and the many benefits of urban life.

This Khaldunian movement between nomads and urban dwellers adds a more specific dimension of change, transformation and, more in general, people's history to the Weberian analytical grid of different models of legitimate authority that is described above. At the same time, it invites a more explicit discussion of the book's time-space framework and the choices that were made there. The term Islamic world of course covers a long historical era beginning in the seventh century CE. As a space, this world mainly stretches from the West African and Iberian coasts of the Atlantic Ocean to beyond the Indian Ocean and the Hindukush in the east, and from the Inner-Asian steppes in the north to Sub-Saharan Africa in the south. This historical space is mostly characterized by an enormous diversity, both in its geographical-ecological characteristics as well as its peoples and cultures. As the experiences of Ibn Khaldun and Ibn Battuta in the 14th century illustrate, it is nevertheless not incorrect to consider this enormously vast space as a historical continuum as well. As suggested above, clearly recognizable Islamic cultures, closely connected (but not limited) to the appearance of Islam as a hegemonic monotheistic world religion and of Arabic as a *lingua franca*, emerged there and gave shape, in an endless dialogue with that local diversity, to a dynamic that makes the study of this vast space under a common denominator of meaningful connectedness relevant.

This vast space as well as the long time in which these complex processes of genesis, change and continuity are situated, are further limited in *A History of the Islamic World, 600–1800*, for practical as well as for more historical substantive reasons. The latter reasons obviously built upon the ways in which until today historical research has engaged with these questions of chronological and spatial coherence. Arguably, one of the most important moments in this has been the posthumously published total history of the Islamic world in three dense volumes by Chicago historian Marshall Hodgson (1922–1968), entitled *The Venture of Islam: Conscience and History in a World Civilization*. In spite of the fact that this book is now more than fifty years old—and therefore, in some places somewhat outdated—Hodgson's general approach and many of his interpretations and carefully crafted neologisms continue to stand as seminal sources of inspiration for many specialists. In fact, as a result of this seminal and even visionary status of Hodgson's text (and also of the implicitly Weberian outlook of some of its interpretations) many of the spatial and temporal (and also interpretative) choices that are made in the current book have direct or indirect links with Hodgson's writings, and deserve to be identified as such. One of these concerns this book's explicit spatial focus on a number of historical core territories within their wider globalizing context. These are the Arabian Peninsula, historical Greater Syria (consisting of today's states of Syria, Jordan, Lebanon, and Israel-Palestine), the diverse regions covered by the modern states of Iraq, Iran, Afghanistan, Pakistan, Turkmenistan, Uzbekistan, and Egypt, and the peninsula of Asia Minor including the historical regions of Anatolia and Armenia. All of these territories are actually identified in Hodgson's text as the coherent historical unit of the Nile to Oxus zone. Another choice concerns the decision to look only at the pre-modern history of these lands, between the 7th and the late 18th centuries CE (or rather, between the 1st and the 12th centuries of the Islamic Hijra era). This is an era that Hodgson identified as pertaining to the so-called 'pre-Technical age', also usefully referred to by him as the 'Agrarian age', and that—given the current book's choice to focus on configurations, practices, and discourses of power—will also be thought of here as a 'Theocratic age'. These somewhat simplified qualifications highlight in particular the unprecedented changes in the history of human organization that were announcing themselves by the turn from the 18th to the 19th centuries and that require very different explanations and interpretations.

As Hodgson himself also explained, his Nile to Oxus zone largely coincides with what is today commonly known as the Middle East, a spatial label of Eurocentric making that until now continues to determine the representation of this region. An Arabic, more endogenous, alternative to refer to the same space is the Mashreq ('the east'), with which a geographical-ecological divide is emphasized, as well as—certainly since the 11th century—a relative historical fault line, with the North African region of the Maghreb ('the West'). One of the deeper motives that connect the chapters of this history will indeed be the intense eastern,

Asian connectedness of the landscapes ranging from the Nile in the southwest and the Bosporus in the northwest to the Oxus (Amu Darya) and Jaxartes (Syr Darya) in the northeast and the Indus in the southeast. Because of the defining importance of this Asian factor, however, we shall not speak of the Mashreq or the Middle East, nor of Hodgson's somewhat reductive Nile to Oxus alternative (as though mainly these two rivers defined the Islamic history of this historical space), but rather consistently of Islamic West-Asia, as a deeply intertwined and especially eastward-, Asia-oriented distinct historical space. 'Middle East', and to a certain degree also 'Mashreq', are, moreover, labels that insinuate a mostly European-Western interpretative framework, and they inadvertently tend to install this bias in the analysis as well. As specific products of 19th-century imperialism and modernization theory, they are therefore also unsuitable to describe an era that was not yet in any way linked to these phenomena of Europe's colonial expansion and its allegedly exemplary progress towards modernity. The reorientation of West-Asia, as it were from its own Asian east to the strange European west, only started to happen from about 1800, and it was accompanied, as Hodgson's periodization also surmised, by a number of deep changes that should also be understood from an entirely different interpretative framework—including not least as informed by ambiguous concepts such as modernization, Westernization, secularization, and globalization. Many contemporary readings of the complex and long history of Islamic West-Asia are in fact all too often obscured by the subconscious choice for such a different, more global, and very modern view, for which all that precedes the 19th century appears easily as a mere precursor. So as not to fall into this trap, we have chosen to tell only the story of what Hodgson considered the pre-Technical age, and what we will define below in full detail as the Late Antique and 'medieval'-early modern periods of Islamic West-Asia. This history of the Islamic world is, therefore, one in which a conscious choice has been made to focus on Islamic West-Asia between the 7th and the 18th centuries, from a perspective that emphasizes a dynamic type of contingent distinctiveness rather than any sort of rigid strangeness expectant of modernity. Only at the end of the book will we look forward in the briefest of terms to the modern and contemporary periods (19th–20th centuries), suggesting how the history of the region until the 21st century can only be fully appreciated when approached from non-teleological *longue durée* perspectives.

In addition, concerning periodization and the particular structuring of this history of Islamic West-Asia, we work from the idea that for this long period of twelve centuries, two major historical waves in that Khaldunian movement of nomadic-urban interaction can be usefully identified as coherent time-space units of configurations, practices, and discourses of power. A first Late Antique imperial wave started swelling during the Arabian expansion from the early 7th century and lost momentum in the course of the complete disintegration of the Abbasid Islamic imperial formation in the 10th century. A second 'medieval'-early modern dynastic wave then took over in the polycentric form of a long series of invasions by Inner-Asian Turkic and Mongolian speaking leaderships from the early 11th century onwards, and its effects appeared to peter out only with the radical transformations of the region's early modern dynastic formations in the 17th and 18th centuries. These two historical waves are of course merely analytical constructions, externally imposed upon the historical material to allow for connecting the multitude of available facts and stories into a coherent and digestible history that pursues some broader insight and better understanding. Nevertheless, it is beyond dispute that both waves are separated by deep fault lines (which incidentally also applies to the third wave of the so-called 'Technical' and 'post-Theocratic' age that starts at roughly 1800 and, in a sense, continues to roll on until today). They are distinguished from each other by a high degree of discontinuity in leadership configurations, practices of power, and discourses of belonging. Although their exact beginnings and ends should not perhaps be pinpointed precisely, it is therefore still very enlightening to describe and understand them as separate historical units. Particularly for the second historical wave, which coincides with the period between the 11th and the 18th centuries, this is an important assessment. While the first wave, in which Islamic monotheism emerges and an Islamic theocratic order experiences a Late Antique imperial peak with the caliphate, is traditionally considered of enormous importance and relevance to study, this is all but evident for the period of the second wave. As also suggested when referring to modern receptions of Ibn Khaldun's theories, the second polycentric wave is often considered to represent only a 'post-classical' shadow of the first period, an age of stagnation and decay that is often looked upon, even in the Islamic world's own historiographical traditions, with pity and condescension. How one attempted to escape these dark times from the 19th century onwards to reconnect with the first period is more often than not considered to be the only relevant and interesting narrative. As indicated, one of the contentions of this book is that such a stereotype does not hold validity, and that therefore, this second period of dynastic polycentrism and creative heterogeneity also needs full attention and appreciation in its own right. Only when one understands the intensity, innovativeness, and decisive impact of configurations, practices, and discourses of power in this second period better, can one fully estimate their trajectories in the modern and contemporary periods.

Within every historical wave, of course, a number of changes take place that, while retaining an important degree of continuity, make it sensible to build in a further periodization to enable a meaningful representation of the whole. For the first Late Antique imperial wave between the 7th and 10th centuries, it is of utmost relevance to distinguish two shorter periods. In the formative period (610–750), the Arabian expansion took place, as well as a remarkable transformation from nomadic networks of Arabian leadership to a more complex and diverse political whole. As will be further explained in the introduction to this first wave below, this period is explicitly situated in this book as an intrinsic part of the wider Late Antique world, in which a remarkable set of networks of mainly Arabic-speaking leaderships managed to claim a Late Antique type of legitimate authority on an unprecedented territorial scale. In this period, we also situate the origins of Islam as a successful platform for religious meaning making, as a multiform discourse of legitimate leadership and theocratic order, and as a rich cultural identity of substantial integrative force. The so-called 'classical' period (750–945) subsequently coincided with the unique existence of a coherent patrimonial-bureaucratic empire that at its peak stretched from the Atlantic Ocean to the Indus River. Through the cultural cross-fertilization between east and west and between a diverse Late Antique heritage and new Arabian forms of creativity, this period boasted a very intense and highly regarded intellectual and cultural life among its mainly urban elites. In all, this period witnessed the formulation of a slowly interconnecting whole of self-conscious Islamic and other discourses in the wake of a highly successful trans-regional imperial formation process. This process involved the appearance of a diversely composed and dynamic Arabo-Islamic apparatus of power and its theocratic imagination, with substantial cultural and socio-economic effects across the entire Islamic world.

For the second 'medieval'-early modern dynastic wave between the 11th and 18th centuries, we again distinguish two periods. In the 'middle period' or the 'medieval' phase (11th–16th centuries)—adapting here a semantic and chronological reinterpretation of Europe's Middle Ages that was first proposed by Hodgson—Islamic West-Asia went through a period of renewed expansion of pastoral nomadic leaderships, this time from the Inner-Asian steppes. Out of the overall changes this brought about, only very slowly, new, more cohesive, and more stable post-nomadic trans-regional dynastic formations grew. Before that happened, however, continuously recurring phenomena of nomadic conquest as well as of dynastic fragmentation coincided with the intensive experimentation with heterogeneous Islamic discourses, within which creative reimaginations of Islamic theocratic order and the circulation of Arabo-Persian (and eventually also Turkish) cultural experiences generated an ambiguous type of social cohesion across much of Islamic West-Asia. Ibn Khaldun and Ibn Battuta were both privileged witnesses of and very active contributors to these dynamics of change and intertwining. Finally, in the early modern period as defined here (17th–18th centuries), trans-regional, patrimonial-bureaucratic organizations emerged again, which were to control the entire Islamic world in the form of only a handful of trans-regional dynastic formations. In each of them, Islamic practices and discourses of power, authority, and theocratic order underwent an accelerated process of stabilization and integration that included, not least, the prioritization of explicit variations of Sunni and Shi'ite identities, with a defining historical impact.

In the following two parts and fourteen chapters, these two waves, four periods, and many configurations, practices and discourses of power in premodern Islamic West-Asia will be discussed and interpreted chronologically, with the assistance of the Weberian ideal types of legitimate authority and of Ibn Khaldun's nomadic-urban interaction, and with abundant illustration from the highly diverse and multivalent sets of contemporary Arabic, Persian, and Turkish sources, as well as from a selection of inserted maps, dynastic tables, and images. In each chapter, a central theme will be the history of power, as a relational quality that can connect people in local, regional, and trans-regional configurations; that can time and again redefine, rescale, or destroy such entities; and that to an important degree relates to processes of cohesion, meaning making, and distribution. The latter social, cultural, and economic aspects of every historical wave's processes of imperial or dynastic formation, therefore, will also be discussed in many of these chapters, within the limiting extent of what is relevant for the argument of the book, what is known from the primarily elite-oriented extant sources, and what is practically feasible. A general short introduction at the start of every part, furthermore, reiterates and further explains the rationale, main features, and organization of this book's discussion of every wave, and of the fourteen chapters that make for these two parts. Selected readings per chapter and, at the end of the book, a glossary of key concepts and words are added for reference and further study purposes.

Notes

1 Ibn Khaldūn (d. 1406), *al-Muqaddima* ('The Introduction'), translation adapted from Lewis, *Islam from the Prophet Muhammad to the Capture of Constantinople. Volume I: Politics and War*, v.

2 Ibn Khaldūn (d. 1406), *al-Muqaddima* ('The Introduction') (Book 3, chapter 15).

Wave 1

7th–10th centuries

Late Antiquity and Arabo-Islamic imperial formation

Since a number of decades, historical research on the period from the 7th to the 10th centuries has increasingly accepted the fact that it is particularly enriching and meaningful to view the history of the Islamic world, and thus also of Islamic West-Asia, as a full-fledged partner, rather than an outsider or stranger, in the longstanding regional and trans-regional history of this period. This has to do with the fact that there is a growing understanding that this is not only the period of the European Early Middle Ages, but perhaps even more the era of Afro-Eurasian Late Antiquity.

Indeed, the emergence of Islam coincided with an era that experienced a gradual transition from a historical period dominated, in the global West, by the hegemony of the Roman Empire (Classical Antiquity) to a period commonly known as the Middle Ages in Europe and a large part of the Mediterranean. This period, which runs from the beginning of the 4th to about—in this book at least[1]—the 10th century, is first of all characterized by a gradual accommodation of that classical or antique legacy to changing historical circumstances in Europe, the Mediterranean, and West-Asia, without completely letting go of that legacy. Therefore, this period has been coined in historical scholarship since especially the 1970s as Late Antiquity. More than of any other historical period, it can be said that in Late Antiquity a set of political, cultural, and social modes of organization developed that have been playing a lasting role throughout world history, both for the direct heirs of the antique empires, as well as for the new players on the scene of history. The dominant and defining form in which the three monotheistic religions—Judaism, Christianity, and Islam—then slowly started to appear, is on a global scale without doubt one of the most striking legacies of this period.

As in Antiquity, in Late Antiquity we are still dealing with an important hegemony of trans-regional empires over Europe, the Mediterranean, and West-Asia. All of these empires—whether they were Roman, Persian, or Arabo-Islamic—had a number of characteristics in common that are distinctive to Late Antiquity: they were all somehow connected to Classical Antiquity; they claimed a theocratic and monotheistic destiny of universalism—a foreordained future of exclusive world domination—as well as highly individualized charismatic origins and achievements—from the deeds of Ardashir and Constantine to those of Muhammad and Charlemagne; they could pride themselves on a relatively efficient patrimonial-bureaucratic state apparatus that paired these ideological claims with effective military and fiscal action; and as a consequence of these claims and actions, they were destined to clash with one another at regular intervals.

As the centuries progressed, such claims, actions, and conflicts proved to be self-destructive or at least increasingly difficult to manage and control. From the 9th century onwards at latest, it became progressively clear that the last of these expansive organizations was losing much of its integrative and centripetal capacities, and the Late Antique period of the great monotheist empires would eventually come to an end. After emerging from the Arabian tribal expansions across Afro-Eurasia in the 7th century and transforming into the enormously vast and powerful empires of the Umayyads and the Abbasids, the late antique Islamic empire was forced to make ever more room for a multitude of new historical realities in the course of the 9th and 10th centuries. The complex Late Antique history of this process of the emergence, formation, and transformation of a particular Islamic empire and of the construction, in interaction with that process, of novel imperial and Islamic discourses of power and belonging—or identities—is central to the next seven chapters.

The first four chapters reconstruct the formative period (7th–8th centuries), first from a chronological perspective of different and changing late antique leaderships, and subsequently laying out the changing conditions of leadership in terms of their territorial and organizational transformations. Chapter 1 summarizes both the historical evolution of the two empires that initially dominated Late Antique West-Asia and the contemporaneous organization of leaderships on the Arabian Peninsula. Chapter 2 continues this by looking at how Arabic-Islamic history picked up this Late Antique thread. It moves chronologically from the two phases that are traditionally associated with Muhammad's life as a prophetic leader in Arabia to a general reconstruction of the defining issues that are generally believed to have determined leadership over his community of followers and supporters after his death. Chapter 3 delves deeper into the history and claims to power and authority of Arabian patriarchal leadership in Syria between the mid-7th and mid-8th centuries. The wider picture of the enormous expansion of the reach of Arabian leadership networks in the Late Antique east and west and of its patrimonial transformation into an Islamic Late Antique imperial formation is discussed in Chapter 4.

Chapters 5 to 7 follow up from these transformations by reconstructing the highly complex processes of integration and disintegration that different elites, claims, and infrastructures of Islamic Late Antique imperial power went through in the so-called 'classical' period of the 8th to 10th centuries. Chapter 5 surveys the three central and fundamentally different episodes in the leadership configuration of the Abbasid caliphal dynasty: in the middle and late 8th century, the first decades of the 9th century, and in the middle and late 9th century. The wider contexts of the formation and transformation of the Abbasid caliphate's patrimonial-bureaucratic apparatus between the 8th and 10th centuries are considered in detail in Chapter 6, looking in particular at the enormous impacts of the diverse chains of Abbasid authority and agency that emanated from the Abbasid center in Iraq and that interacted in mutually formative ways with different urban elites and imperial agents alike. Chapter 7 finally complements chapters 5 and 6 by exchanging their centering focus on imperial leaderships and elites in Abbasid Iraq for a much wider consideration of the enormous complexity of the Abbasid as well as the post-Abbasid trans-regional imperial order in the 9th- to mid-11th-centuries.

Note

1 For this chronology of Late Antiquity, this book follows especially Fowden, *Before and After Muḥammad*.

1 West-Asia in Late Antiquity

Roman, Persian, and Arabian leaderships (6th–7th centuries)

Introduction: between *jahiliyya* and Late Antiquity

This chapter lays out the general outlines of the West-Asian world in which in the early 7th century an Islamic history started to make something of an appearance. In particular, it discusses various defining components of that world which are a prerequisite for any understanding of the movement that crystallized around the Arabian figure Muhammad. These include both the historical evolution of the two empires that dominated Late Antique West-Asia initially and a sketch of the contemporaneous situation on the Arabian Peninsula. The next chapter will then discuss the way in which Arabic-Islamic history picked up this Late Antique thread.

Traditionally, Islamic history has been rather simply regarded as an outsider in a human history that tends to be equated with a particular trajectory that leads to, and explains, Christian Europe. The Arabian and Islamic turn of the 7th and subsequent centuries required then an explanation as something completely new and different from what one was used to, as a deviation even from a historical destiny that—with due assistance of Arabic-Islamic channels of transmission—would have only fully resumed its historical role from the late Middle Ages and Early Modern times onwards. Not just within this pervasive tradition of Eurocentric historical narratives, but also within the Islamic historiographic tradition itself, a lot of value has always been attached to the awarding of an entirely distinctive character to the history of Islamic origins. For the latter tradition, the aim was of course not to present this history as an exception, but rather to interpret it as the fulfilment of the miracle of God's special intervention in an otherwise doomed Late Antique or Early Medieval wasteland, which was identified in this spirit as the *jahiliyya*, the time of ignorance. In more popular histories of early Islamic history, many traces of both teleological perspectives tend to remain present, in conscious and unconscious ways. In the historical research of the last decades, however, an entirely different approach takes precedence, in which early Islamic history is regarded as a full and defining component of Late Antiquity. In this chapter and the next ones, it will be made clear why this has proven to be an especially enriching and significant re-examination in contemporary understandings of early Islamic history.

1 The Roman Empire on the eve of the Arabian expansion

In the early 4th century, Constantine the Great (r. 272–337), who managed to reunite the divided Roman Empire by concerted military action, was the first Roman emperor to recognize Christianity—until then heavily persecuted—and award it a publicly accepted status in his empire. Constantine is also remembered for accomplishing all this from a new capital

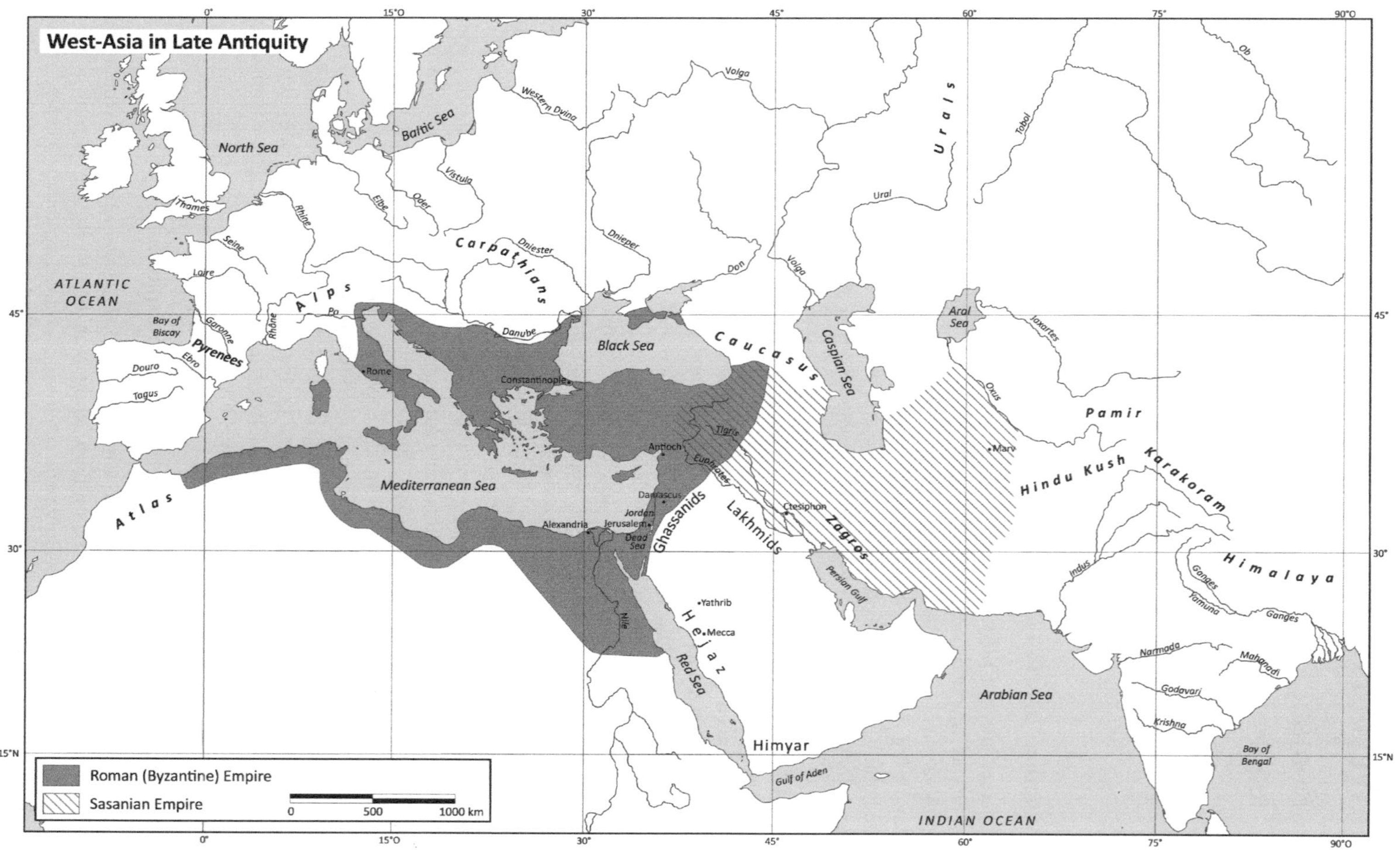

Map 1 West-Asia in Late Antiquity

that was strategically situated on the Bosporus, a clear indication for the shifting of the geographical center of gravity of the Empire to the east. This city, until then known as Byzantium, was aptly renamed Constantinople ('the City of Constantine'). It is in particular from the historical processes that originated here, and that culminated in the late 4th century in the proclamation of Christianity as the religion of the empire and in the final division of the imperial territories in a western and eastern part, that the so-called Byzantine Empire developed. This empire, with Constantinople as its capital, continued to exist in varying formats until the 15th century. Even though distinctly Christian, Greek, and organized around Constantinople, and despite the fact that in today's scholarship and common parlance it is almost always identified as the Byzantine Empire, its subjects (and most others, including their Arabian and Islamic contemporaries) continued to refer to the empire as the direct heir of Rome and they continued to call themselves, therefore, 'Romans' and their empire the Roman Empire. Under the leadership of a long and varied list of emperors, this Greek-Roman Christian Empire had a very eventful history. One important period in that long history—running from an absolute peak of imperial power and prosperity in the first half of the 6th century to an extreme low in the first decades of the 7th century—deserves more attention here.

More than any other emperor, Justinian I (r. 527–565) was a crucial figure in the geographical, political, military, and cultural organization of what modern historiography would dub the early Byzantine Empire. For the last time in history, he succeeded in turning the Mediterranean into an inner sea of the empire, with territorial expansions in South Europe and North

Figure 1.1 Istanbul/Constantinople: the former Roman basilica Hagia Sophia and the Ottoman mosque Ayasofya

Source: By Walter Mittelholzer—This image is from the collection of the ETH-Bibliothek and has been published on Wikimedia Commons as part of a cooperation with Wikimedia CH. Public Domain, https://commons.wikimedia.org/w/index.php?curid=50861064

Africa and on the Iberian Peninsula. At the same time, he provided for an efficiently centralized patrimonial-bureaucratic organization of this vast empire, including through a codification of Roman law and the installation of imperial governors where cities and regions had previously enjoyed a high degree of autonomy. Eventually, such a policy of centralization and integration around the legitimate authority of the emperor expressed itself in the organization of religion as well, when all non-Christian religions were barred from the empire, and when deviations from the Christian doctrine as coded under the auspices of the emperor—the orthodoxy—were resolutely and definitively rejected.

The latter would prove to be of great importance to the history of West-Asia. While the urban centers of Syria and Egypt, such as Antioch or Alexandria, traditionally were fully embedded into the cultural landscape of the empire—through the continued dominance of Greek and of antique traditions among those cities' elites—the local population of the smaller towns, villages, and rural areas had always continued to identify themselves above all with their own languages and cultural backgrounds. This relative cultural dichotomy between urban and rural environments, between the consciously 'Roman' elites and various other social elites and groups in Egypt and Syria, expressed itself particularly, and increasingly, in religious terms. As early as during the course of the 5th century, a theological dispute had grown between the eastern churches of Egypt and Syria (and Iraq) on the one hand and the central religious authorities under the so-called Caesaropapist leadership of the emperor on the other hand. This dispute, that would cause a permanent split between the two, had everything to do with an opposite view on the nature of Christ, which has been traced back to the dichotomy between a more humanistic and an absolutistic image of God. The eastern churches mainly subscribed to this last view, according to which Christ has only one, divine nature. The emperor and clergy, on the other hand, established in the Council of Chalcedon of 451 that the opposite position, which states that Christ has both a divine and a human nature at the same time, belonged to the official doctrine of the imperial Church. When, as mentioned, during the course of the 6th century, the latter doctrine was increasingly and often violently imposed as the sole acceptable, orthodox vision, this only increased the cultural gap between the orthodox center and its representatives in Egypt and Syria on the one hand and, on the other hand, the heterodox local populations there.

In retrospect, Justinian's expansion of the empire as a great power that was politically, militarily, economically, and culturally strongly centralized around the emperor and the imperial capital of Constantinople set in motion not only religious controversies, but also other transformations that would definitively alter the outlook of the Late Antique world. Crucial in this was the fact that the antique cities of the empire, which traditionally enjoyed substantial autonomy, now became fully dependent on Constantinople, the imperial administration, and the imperial army for their organization and defense. In the practice of the 6th century, this meant particularly that the tradition of relatively autonomous and prosperous major urban centers that had dominated the empire for centuries had come under severe pressure.

That process was exacerbated by the natural disasters that the empire's populations experienced in the course of the 6th century. In the middle of that century, the coasts of Syria, for example, were plagued by a series of earthquakes that largely destroyed a number of important antique trading cities there. Even more disastrous were the consequences of the bubonic plague that, from 541 onwards, regularly began to ravage the Late Antique world. This deadly infectious disease caused numerous casualties particularly in the densely populated urban territories of the empire, while it took far less of a toll in the more isolated small towns, villages, and rural areas of their 'hinterlands'. In the second half of the 6th century, furthermore, the empire began to experience serious political and territorial challenges with the loss of Italy to the Longobards, raids of Slavic and Avar steppe people in the Balkans, and the continuous competition with that other great power of Late Antiquity, the Sasanians, in Syria (see below). All of this inevitably meant that crucial changes were taking place in the organization of the empire, and that the integration of elites and territories into the empire's patrimonial center became increasingly difficult to manage. The territorial losses, the collapse of security, and the shifting of demographic balances went hand in hand, for example, with the nearly complete shutdown of the interregional and Mediterranean trade that had traditionally interconnected the antique world. This benefited a more local kind of commercial circulation in which particularly local food stuffs, pottery, and furs were traded and in which religious hotspots, such as pilgrimage sites, often also served as occasional marketplaces.

This process of 'ruralization' did not only manifest itself in economic contexts, but also gave shape to radical social transformations, especially regarding the political agency and military participation of rural social formations. As a consequence of the plague and due to the continuing military activities at all frontiers of the empire, the provision of manpower for the imperial armies also came under mounting pressure. One response to the latter problem took the form of a growing appeal to mercenaries who often belonged to population groups that lived in the margins of the empire, and who appeared, therefore, to have been less affected by the plague and the other difficulties of the 6th century. In Egypt and Syria, this meant, for example, that the Byzantine armies were largely composed of Arabian and Armenian mercenaries.

By the end of the 6th century, the empire had therefore undergone a remarkable transformation. It was simultaneously enormously centralized and ruralized, with the latter meaning that local populations, including 'marginal' groups such as the nomads of the Syrian Desert, had become of relatively larger importance, demographically, economically, and militarily. But at the same time, both in Egypt and in Syria, these local populations consistently maintained their own languages of communication, followed their own local churches and church doctrines, and became to some extent economically more isolated and therefore, almost self-sufficient. Centralization, ruralization, and the increasing participation of local elites and 'marginal' groups in the Late Antique world scene of events were not in any way accompanied by a process of acculturation and assimilation in a Greek-Roman West-Asia; quite on the contrary, a loosening and even disintegration of Constantinople's patrimonial-bureaucratic political order went hand in hand with a relative local empowerment of those elites and groups, or at least with a more volatile and tense relationship between the imperial center and many of its peripheries. In fact, this would have far reaching consequences for the 7th century, when an 'endgame' presented itself with that other great power of Late Antiquity: the Persian empire of the Sasanians.

2 The Sasanian Empire on the eve of the Arabian expansion

The origins of the Sasanian Empire date back to the 3rd century CE, and it continued to exist to the middle of the 7th century. The particularities of its history, and especially of its organization and of the integration of the Sasanian territories' diverse groups and elites into one dynastic political order, remain much debated in modern historiography. Given our main interest in 'post-Sasanian' Islamic history, the details of these debates need not directly concern us. Suffice to clarify that the current summary presentation of Sasanian history represents only one position in those debates, that there are, therefore, other explanations that may be equally valid, and that our choice here is certainly biased towards the macro-historical patterns that appear to meaningfully connect Sasanian history to that of its Greek-Roman counterpart as well as to 7th- and 8th-century post-Sasanian continuities.

Not entirely without justification, the Sasanians are also known as the last of the dynasties of the Ancient Near East. In the course of the 3rd and 4th centuries, this dynasty of regional rulers of the Persian land *par excellence*, the region of Fars in southern Iran, succeeded in gaining control over an area stretching across most of present-day Iraq, Iran, Afghanistan and Turkmenistan. They regarded themselves in this context of expansion and trans-regional empowerment as the direct descendants of the greatest—and most classic—of all Persian dynasties, the Achaemenids, whose reign had ended some six centuries before. Following the example of these illustrious predecessors, successive Sasanian rulers and their entourages built an extensive court ceremonial that aimed at consolidating the specialty, inaccessibility, and omnipotence of the dynasty. In addition, a related discourse of theocratic power emerged that confirmed the transcendent character of Sasanian power and in which the ruler and his family were given not only religiously defined legitimacy, but even divine status. This made for the absolute and universal nature of the Sasanian claims to legitimate authority and also helped to explain, and sustain, the Sasanians' trans-regional competition and repeated clashes with their Greek-Roman western neighbors. At the same time, however, not unimportant commercial and cultural contacts existed between the populations of both empires, which seem to have aided cross-fertilization and parallel transformations.

One such parallel transformation definitively revolved around the increasing patrimonial-bureaucratic centralization that marked the 6th century in both empires. According to at least certain interpretations in historical scholarship,[1] power in the Persian empire was continuously shared among various competing groups, including not just the Sasanians and their patrimonial apparatus of trans-regional power, but also longstanding dynasties of rulers of the empire's different regional units, and all kinds of local elites, most importantly the landed gentry, who were known as the *dihqan*s. In this view, the political history of the Sasanian dynasty between *c.* 300 and *c.* 600 is explained as an endless balancing act between regional families who wished to maximize or maintain their autonomy and the Sasanians who, often supported by the *dihqan*s, tried to safeguard and expand their sovereignty. In the 6th century in particular, this continuous balancing act experienced a number of very intense moments of change and renegotiation. The Sasanian 'king of kings' (*shahanshah*) Khosrow I Anushirvan (r. 531–579) is mostly identified as having been especially responsible for this. Just as his contemporary (and great rival) in the west Justinian I, Khosrow I was both militarily and administratively very active, resulting in an entirely new élan for the Sasanian empire in the second half of the 6th century. In addition to successful campaigns against the Greek-Roman empire (taking Antioch near the Syrian Mediterranean coast in 540), he undertook the reorganization of his own empire in an equally radical fashion, integrating or countering the power of the regional dynasts in the process. The empire now became formally subdivided in four large quarters, each under the leadership of a centrally appointed military commander, and each quarter in turn was subdivided into a number of provincial districts. One of these quarters was the empire's northeastern corner that was known as Khurasan, governed from the ancient city of Marv and destined to play a major role in much of later, Islamic history. In this way, the entire territory came more directly under the central control of the Sasanian ruler and his representatives. Moreover, the fiscal system was reformed and made more efficient, and the greater income that this generated was used to maintain and strengthen the central patrimonial apparatus, including the Sasanian standing army, which largely came to replace the troops that used to be delivered on more *ad hoc* bases by the regional elites.

This concentration of administrative, financial, and military means, largely inspired by the achievements of Khosrow's peer in the Greek-Roman west, enabled the Sasanian monarch to make his empire, and particularly the Sasanian dynasty, more powerful and more forceful than ever.

However, in this Sasanian case as well the costs and collateral damage of this success proved substantial. While Khosrow I Anushirvan had the personal charisma to maintain substantial control over this process of centralization, specialization, and expansion, this was far less the case for his successors. In particular, Khosrow II Parviz (r. 590–628) was regularly confronted with the uprisings of regional ruling families and the repeated dynastic turmoil that marked the end of the 6th and the beginning of the 7th centuries. When Khosrow II's reign ended in 628 as a result of defeat against external foes and loss of internal support (more about this below), another long-term succession crisis followed that ushered in no less than the end of both the Sasanian dynasty and the ancient Persian empire.

More even than was the case for the Greek-Roman empire, the Sasanian centralization process of the 6th century proved to not just upset ancient sociopolitical balances between the 'king of kings' and the diverse regional power elites. Historically, every region in the vast Sasanian Empire had always maintained its own particular social and cultural traits, so that the Persian culture of the Sasanian court was largely considered an outsider in many parts of the empire. The majority of the population had different customs, spoke a different language, and upheld a different religious tradition, and the long history of substantial autonomy under their own regional dynasties had certainly strengthened those different identities. To many of their own subjects, therefore—from regional dynasts to farmers who worked the land—the Sasanians and their representatives were perceived as uninvited strangers. Even charismatic Sasanian figures such as Khosrow I Anushirvan never really succeeded in bridging that gap.

By militarily calling upon a standing army of 'true' Persians from their own core lands of the Fars region, by administratively and fiscally relying on the expertise of Persian *dihqan*s first and foremost, and by trying to destroy the power of regional dynasts, the Sasanians in fact severed practically all ties between themselves—the center—and the many regions and local communities in their empire—the peripheries. This combined process of centralization and estrangement further manifested itself in Sasanian religious ideology and policies. The dynasty had linked its authority and fate closely to that of Zoroastrianism, the ancient Persian religion with dualistic and even—in this late antique period at least—monotheistic traits, which was led by a cast of priests, known as the *magi*, professed in fire temples, and aimed at ritual purity. Throughout the Sasanian empire, however, it was not this rigid and highly politicized Zoroastrianism but rather Christianity that was most widely professed during the 6th century, especially in the western parts of the empire and in the yet again 'heterodox' form of Nestorianism (which attributes two distinct 'essences'—the one divine, the other human—to the person of Christ). In a context of mounting tension with the Christian Greek-Roman empire in the west, these religious differences between local populations and the Sasanian dynasty meant that Nestorian Christians were often regarded as 'the enemy within'. This manifested itself especially in several persecution campaigns against the Nestorian populations of the empire, and towards the turbulent end of the 6th century, even the large Jewish population of Iraq, the Babylonian Jews, suffered the same fate on more than one occasion.

When in the course of the 6th century this increasingly tense relationship between the Sasanian patrimonial apparatus and the diverse elites and groups of the empire's different regions was further exacerbated by the same natural disasters that also affected the Greek-Roman empire, it may be clear that by the turn of the 6th to the 7th century the Sasanian empire was not so much a powerful antique empire, but rather an old colossus built on shaky foundations.

3 The clash of the Titans

This impression of Sasanian weakness was, however, certainly not shared by most of their contemporaries. Around 580, a historian in Constantinople at least noted down a very different assessment of the success and enormous impact of the Sasanian westward expansions of his time:

> cities [have been] enslaved, and populations uprooted and displaced, so all of mankind has been involved in the upheaval.[2]

Sasanian expansion and invasion continued also in the early 7th century. In 602, Maurice, the Greek-Roman emperor since 582, was murdered by dissatisfied troops in Constantinople. This rather local affair then triggered a whole series of events that would have far-reaching consequences for the entire Late Antique world. The reason for this remarkable impact needs to be sought in the close connection between Maurice and the Sasanian 'king of kings' Khosrow II. A decade earlier, the former emperor had assisted Khosrow II to regain his father's throne in Ctesiphon after an uprising of a regional dynast had briefly ended Sasanian rule. When Khosrow learned about the brutal murder of his patron in 602, he therefore considered it his duty (or at least an ideal opportunity) to intervene and avenge the murder. He started a long-term military campaign that after several years resulted in a number of truly historical successes. For example, in 613 and 614 his troops took Antioch, Damascus, and Jerusalem in historical Syria (and the relics of the Holy Sepulchre were transferred to the Sasanian capital of Ctesiphon in Iraq). Eventually, not only Syria was conquered in its entirety, but Egypt as well, and all were incorporated into the Sasanian Empire. The triumph of Khosrow II appeared absolute when his looting troops eventually crossed Anatolia and reached Chalcedon near the Bosporus.

However, nothing was further from the truth. The Sasanian investment of manpower and resources that was required to pursue these long campaigns of conquest turned out to come at a great cost and further strained the relationship between Khosrow II and various regional dynasts in Persia. Furthermore, one of the most important reasons for this Sasanian success had been the weakness of its opponent. In the aftermath of the murder of emperor Maurice, the empire had been plunged into a deep political crisis. General dissatisfaction with Maurice's successor had quickly led to new uprisings, which eventually resulted in the proclamation as emperor in 610 of a military commander who would turn out to become the savior of the empire. After several years, this capable strategist and politician, Heraklios, succeeded in bringing the political situation under control and reorganizing the army sufficiently to enter into a counter campaign. Against all expectations, rather than aiming for the reconquest of lost territories in Anatolia and the Levant, he decided to launch a direct attack on the Persian core territories. In 622, when the situation appeared hopeless, Heraklios led his troops via the Black Sea to the heart of the Sasanian empire in the region of Iraq. After various successes, he finally, in 628, managed to invade the Sasanian heartlands, capture their capital, Ctesiphon, remove Khosrow II from the throne, and restore his control over lost territories. Thus, Heraklios, at the peak of his career, was able to invade Jerusalem in 630 and restore the Church of the Holy Sepulchre to its ancient glory.

As stated, the consequences of this endgame were far-reaching. After more than twenty years of warfare and Sasanian occupation, the administrative and military organization in Syria and Egypt was at the very least in need of thorough restoration. The same applied more generally to the ties that connected the local populations to the Greek-Roman empire. For many, these ties were no more than a memory from a distant past so that, even in religious terms, the imperial troops and agents were as much considered strangers and invaders as the Sasanians had been before them. This destructive clash of the titans, fought in Syria, Egypt, and Iraq, accelerated in particular the 'upheaval' that had already been noted by Greek-Roman historians in the late 6th century, including in the form of the growing empowerment of peripheral social groups.

4 Arabia on the eve of the Arabian expansion

In view of the above-mentioned process of the increasing participation of groups from the imperial peripheries in the events of the Late Antique world, it is, in retrospect, surely no complete surprise that tribes from Arabia entered the limelight of history more forcefully than ever in the 7th century. The Avars and Slavs from the Inner-Asian steppes similarly exploited Constantinople's desolation in the early 7th century to obtain a place for themselves within the northern sphere of influence of the Greek-Roman empire, while the same process had previously taken place with Germanic tribes in the western part of the former Roman Empire. Nevertheless, to many contemporaries, the invasion of the Late Antique world from a desolate area such as Arabia did come as a surprise, and to many it remained, and remains, bewildering that Arabia's age-old tribes were suddenly capable of taking on a leading role on the Late Antique stage and that, moreover, this eventually generated the highly impactful addition of an entirely particular Arabo-Islamic layer to that stage. Current research on Late Antique Arabia, however, clearly demonstrates that the peninsula's different tribal leaderships were never entirely closed off from the wider Late Antique world, quite the contrary. In the last part of this chapter, as in the next chapters, these themes of Arabian tribal leaderships and their Late Antique participation and transformation will therefore be central issues.

4.1 From Nabataeans to Jafnids and Nasrids

There is, in fact, very little direct information about the historical circumstances in which the inhabitants of the Arabian Peninsula and its more northern extension, the Syrian Desert, actually lived. Most of the contemporary sources that we have are the products of outsiders, and they inform mostly about the less inhospitable fringes of this desert area, where ecological, commercial, or political opportunities made circumstances favorable for more complex forms of social organization to appear. Southern Yemen, unusually fertile because of monsoon rains and privileged by its central location on trade routes connecting the Indian Ocean and the Mediterranean, provided a home to various cultures and political formations since Biblical times. In the Syrian desert, there were for a long time similar commercial connections and interests that supported the rise and efflorescence of various petty Hellenistic polities. These included most famously those of the Nabataeans around Petra (4th century BCE–106 CE) and of Queen Zenobia and her family around Palmyra (3rd century CE). In the Late Antique era, however, particularly since the 6th century, it was no longer trade, but rather the competitive politics of the great imperial powers that stimulated the formation of more integrated and powerful local leaderships in this region. In their continuous struggle for hegemony, both the

Roman and the Sasanian emperors committed themselves to expanding their sphere of political influence as widely as possible. Combined with the previously sketched process where local communities and peripheral groups started to matter more, local leaderships that lived beyond the actual reach and frontiers of these two great powers started to attract more attention as well. More specifically, during the 6th century, both the emperor in Constantinople as well as his Sasanian peer entered into strategic alliances with two important leadership groups in the Syrian Desert. Constantinople's local allies are traditionally identified as the Banu ('clan of') Ghassan, or the Ghassanids, even though today's historical research prefers to identify them more specifically as one of this tribal group's leading clans, the Banu Jafna or Jafnids. Ctesiphon's allies are generally known as the Banu Lakhm, or the Lakhmids, though here too more specific reference to the Nasrids, one of the Lakhmids' leading clans, is increasingly preferred. In exchange for political and mainly financial support, these local dynasties in turn guaranteed to tie as many other clans and groups in Arabia to their leadership, and thus to their imperial patrons. In this manner, in the course of the 6th century, two expansive networks of tribal leaders, sometimes anachronistically referred to as 'confederations', developed in the region of Syria, Iraq, and northern Arabia around the Constantinople-oriented 'Ghassanid' Jafnid leaders on the one hand and the Sasanian oriented 'Lakhmid' Nasrid leaders on the other. As the following contemporary reference to two of their most famous and most successful leaders, al-Harith (r. *c.* 528–*c.* 569) and al-Mundhir (r. *c.* 504–554), suggests, these tribal networks derived their cohesion and authority mostly from active participation in the competition between the great powers and from the advantages provided by political, institutionalized relationships with these powers.

> Mundhir [the Lakhmid-Nasrid], holding the position of king, ruled alone over all the Saracens in Persia, and he was always able to make his inroad with the whole army wherever he wished in the Roman domain. Neither any commander of Roman troops, whom they call *duces*, nor any leader of the Saracens allied with the Romans, who are called *phylarch*s, was strong enough with his men to array himself against Mundhir, for the troops stationed in the different districts were not a match [individually] in battle for the enemy. For this reason, the emperor Justinian put in command of as many clans as possible Ḥārith [the Ghassanid-Jafnid], the son of Jabala, who ruled over the Saracens of Arabia, and bestowed upon him the dignity of king, a thing which among the Romans had never been done before.[3]

There are not, however, many details known about the histories of these two tribal formations. This holds true particularly for the Lakhmid-Nasrid leadership of al-Mundhir and his sons, whose center of power was Hira, a large settlement situated near the mid-Euphrates in present day Iraq. The situation is slightly better for the Ghassanid-Jafnid al-Harith and his offspring, who were active in the Damascus-Amman region, and who, in the course of the 6th century, became increasingly powerful in that region and also, simultaneously, influential at the imperial court in Constantinople. They seem to have used the growing wealth that came with this local and even regional empowerment to wage a very active dynastic propaganda (including through investments in monumental architecture and Arabic poetry) with far-reaching consequences for the development of a particular cultural identity.

This emergence of a distinctive local identity actually goes back to before the 6th century, as appears unmistakably from the few inscriptions (over time also recorded in a rudimentary but distinct Arabic script) that have been preserved from this Late Antique period, for these and similar local leaderships on the fringes of the Late Antique imperial worlds. One of the

Figure 1.2 Epitaph of Mara᾽ (Imru) al-Qays
Source: Photo © RMN-Grand Palais (musée du Louvre)/Franck Raux

most famous extant specimens of this practice is a 4th-century royal inscription on a tombstone from al-Namara in southern Syria, written in the Nabataean Aramaic script and one of the earliest known instances of a text in the Arabic language.

Whereas the reading and translation of this text remain hotly debated in modern scholarship, it does attest to the presence of particular political identities, connecting nomadic and settled communities from across Syria and Arabia and also tying them to the interests of the Late Antique empires. One of the most recent interpretations of this enigmatic inscription reads as follows:

> This is the funerary monument of Mara᾽ al-Qays, son of ʿAmr, king of all ʿArab, who bound on the crown
> and ruled the two Syrias [from Mesopotamia to Palestine] and [the tribes of] Niẓār and their kings, and who fought with Madhḥij until he struck
> with his spear on the gates of Najrān, the town of [the South Arabian King] Shammār. He ruled Maʿadd and gave his sons [rule over]
> the settled peoples, and they were made proxies for Persia and Rome (*al-fars wa-l-rūm*). And no king could match his achievements.
> Thereafter, he died, in the year 227, on the third day of Kislūl [= 332 CE][4]

Similar more complex political and cultural practices are suggested by the poetry that was produced in the course of the 6th century in the rivalling entourages of the descendants of al-Harith and al-Mundhir, and of which certain specimens have been famously preserved in later collections of Arabic poetry. They do not only illustrate the emergence of a distinctly Arabic literary culture, but also how—as in the following poem from the later 6th century, dedicated to one of these kings—Late Antique ideologies of legitimate authority, including notions of universalism and absolute sovereignty, had become part of that culture.

> Do you not see that God has granted you such a degree of power that you will observe every king trembling at your feet?
> For you are the sun, the [other] kings are stars; when the sun rises, no star will be seen.[5]

Like everything in this turbulent period of history, however, the situation between the Romans and Sasanians and these tribal political formations at the frontiers of their imperial reach was not always as unambiguous as suggested above. The majority of the population of Syria followed the Syrian Church, and so did the Ghassanid-Jafnids. The latent tension between the eastern Churches and imperial orthodoxy therefore certainly also—next to, according to recent research, their dangerously deep involvement in imperial politics in Constantinople—had a role to play in the arrests and exiles of a son and a grandson of al-Harith in the 580s and in the subsequent dissolution of this particular tribal leadership network. The Lakhmid-Nasrid leadership of Hira, in turn, had linked up with the Nestorian Church, and this may well have been part of the highly competitive relationship that they, just as various other regional dynastic rulers, had with the Sasanian dynasty and its claims to sovereignty. From the end of the 7th century, when the 'king of kings' Khosrow II had managed to consolidate his authority with Roman help and sought to increase his power, he targeted, among others, al-Nuʿman (r. 580–602), a son of al-Mundhir and the last of the Lakhmid-Nasrid Kings of Hira, who was executed in 602 and replaced with a Sasanian governor.

However complex, it is clear that the factors of military competition and identity politics that increasingly characterized the Late Antique period also enabled the very active participation of leaderships from the northern Arabian frontier regions in imperial events and transformations. When this participation backfired in the later 6th century and these imperial events became very chaotic in the early 7th century, those patterns of involvement seem to have offered new opportunities to leaderships from central and western Arabia. These eventually continued this process of Late Antique political and cultural transformations rather unexpectedly within an outspoken Arabian context.

4.2 From Arabian **ashraf** *to the Banu Quraysh*

Unlike these frontier regions of Arabia, the central and western parts of the peninsula never had sufficient resources to support more complex social and political organizational forms. From a very limited base of extant historical and archaeological material, it appears that since times immemorial such forms of organization there always remained limited to traditional patriarchal relationships determined by lineage and kinship, and that for many centuries, family clans and tent groups proved to be the only endurable socioeconomic reality. These groups all seem to have had a number of features in common, including with their peers in the Syrian Desert or the Yemeni south. These range from the closely related Semitic languages they spoke to religious, genealogical, and martial lore, memories, and mythologies that organized and gave meaning to live in and on the fringes of the desert. Inspired by these features, some shared imagination of social and cultural practices seems to have emerged. At least, it certainly seems to have done so with outsiders and observers mentioning or trying to identify these groups. For example, in the 8th century BCE, an Assyrian king is already reported to have referred to 'the Arabs who live far away in the desert and know no supervisors or officials'. As suggested here, perceptions such as these of a shared Arabian identity were never related to any more coherent political realities, and it actually remains an issue of academic debate to what extent before the 7th and 8th centuries CE any such common identity was actually meaningfully present at all among these groups. The scarcity of livelihood in the central Arabian steppes and deserts certainly made any kind of social integration on anything more than a very local scale very difficult. In fact, violent competition and struggle over these scarce resources, rather than integration and community formation, were the overwhelming normative principles on which life was, and continued to be, based there.

Survival in such barren and competitive circumstances, indeed, was a matter of belonging to a group that was large enough to ensure sufficient access to basic resources, but not too large to endanger this sufficiency. The tent group and clan, usually limited to a maximum of five generations of descendants of a (mythical) ancestor, therefore formed the basic units organizing daily life in Arabia. Larger tribal entities, such as those known from the historical records as the Banu Tanukh, the Banu Kinda, the Banu Azd, and the Banu Quraysh (and for that matter the Banu Ghassan and the Banu Lakhm), were also known and important, but they were always made up of a loose variety of largely self-sufficient groups and leaderships, and their integration continuously depended on the ecological conditions of the area in which they lived, remaining mostly very limited to various functional connections between their leaders.

As stated, violent competition for scarce natural resources was a constant in the life of these clans and groups, and therefore, all members without exception were experienced warriors. This competition expressed itself mainly in the form of regular raids and pillages (known as *ghazw*, literally 'razzia') against neighboring groups, primarily to seize cattle, foodstuffs, and slaves. Crucial in this context appears to have been a shared normative practice of internal solidarity that prevented such violent competition from resulting in total chaos. This practice, the blood feud, meant that a clan, a tent group, or even a larger tribal community was deemed to have the right to avenge violations of its own integrity (the killing or wounding of one of its members by another clan or tent group) in a proportionate fashion (by killing or wounding a member of the guilty clan or tent group). Because such a principle could, and did, cause endless cycles of reciprocal violence (threatening the weakening and even annihilation of a clan or tent group), minimizing bloodshed during pillages was desirable. In this way, this restrictive practice, as much as the practice of violent raiding and that of imagining tribal communal identities, participated in the construction of different social boundaries that defined social organization on the peninsula.

This organization of life on the Arabian steppes and deserts more in general was also highly egalitarian in nature, with responsibilities, benefits, and losses being equally shared among the members of a local group. Despite this egalitarianism, however, every tent group, clan, or even tribal community also had its leaders who were meant to defend the interests of the group as a whole. Especially in the context of more widely composed tribal communities, these positions of leadership always belonged to particular leading lineages that were identified as the tribal *ashraf* (as with the Jafnids and the Nasrids in the cases of the Ghassanids and the Lakhmids). Within and among these tribal *ashraf* dynasties, however, the actual assumption of positions of local or tribal leadership always remained defined by often fierce competition and by negotiating the consent and support from the tribal community or local group. Those most successful in this—potentially violent—competition and negotiation were responsible for the well-being and integrity of their community. They were supposed to act as a referee (*hakam*) and mediate conflicts within their group; they were responsible for finding sufficient resources, especially watering places and pastures for the herds, but also targets for raids, and partners to trade particular commodities with; they were to organize the group's defenses against raids and pillages by others; and they had to uphold the reputation of the group and receive travelers and other guests in a suitable fashion. In order to execute such tasks appropriately, certain advantages and privileges (for example, a larger herd), possibly also awarded in the form of a contribution paid by others, were a tribal leader's due. However, in most tribal communities, the continued need for negotiation, consent, and collective action meant that social differentiation remained rather limited.

Whereas this particular, egalitarian form of tribal organization applied without too much distinction to all who inhabited the Peninsula, there were significant economic differences between different groups and communities. Most were pastoral nomads who led a transhumant existence with their herds of camels, sheep, and goats. In order to support themselves and, in particular, to obtain access to non-pastoral resources, they either undertook the aforementioned raids or they entered into more stable relationships with local sedentary agricultural or trading communities; from those communities they received particular commodities, such as grain or dates, in exchange for hides or other pastoral products, or in exchange for certain services, such as protection from raids or guaranteeing a safe passage for trade caravans.

As the latter suggests, there were indeed tribal groups that had settled more permanently and provided for themselves in different, non-transhumant ways. In oases such as Khaybar, Yathrib, or Taif in the western Arabian region of the Hejaz, agriculture was actively pursued, and cereal crops and dates were cultivated. These more or less isolated agricultural communities, often consisting of different clans of varying tribal allegiances, also continued to be molded, in spite of their sedentary lifestyle, by the same violent competition and lineage-based patriarchal practices that organized the life of their transhumant peers. In fact, due to their lack of mobility, they often even ended up in a weaker and more dependent position compared to their more militant nomadic neighbors.

Yet another story is that of the clans that had settled to guard one of the many local sanctuaries on the Peninsula. The exact nature of these sacred spaces, and of the religious trends in pre-Islamic Arabia more in general, has been a topic of vehement academic debate for many years. Criticism is particularly and increasingly directed against an age-old vision that builds on the Islamic tradition itself and that assumes that there was a continuous dominance on the Peninsula of a polytheism in which every tribal community preferred its own deity to others. In the context of the above-mentioned religious dynamics in the Late Antique world, in particular the spread of monotheistic thought and the increasing weight of religious identity, it is not unlikely that this idea of a comprehensive polytheism, especially for the period after the 4th century CE, needs to be put in some new perspective. It is highly likely that Late Antique monotheism had gained a much firmer footing in Arabia than traditionally tends to be acknowledged. This can be connected to the impact of active networks of Christian northern Arabian leaderships, such as those of the Ghassanid-Jafnids and Lakhmid-Nasrids, and also to that of similar networks of equally influential and powerful Jewish and Christian South Arabian tribal communities and leaderships. Equally relevant factors are the centuries-long presence of Jewish groups in oases such as Yathrib in western Arabia, as well as merchants travelling across the peninsula, trading in the religious truths of their Late Antique surroundings as much as in all kinds of valuable goods. It remains impossible to establish to what extent the myths, ideas, and concepts of this omnipresent Late Antique monotheistic trend had affected the region's many modes of polytheism, but the mere speed with which monotheism was accepted as a common identity marker by various tribal communities in the 620s and 630s certainly supports the assumption that it had been for quite some time already among the most important substrates that informed religious experiences on the peninsula.

One strong tradition that is often considered a typical remnant of that other, polytheist substrate involves the presence on the peninsula of a variety of sacred places (*haram* or *mahram*). The belief in the divine character of, or in a divine presence at, certain places in Arabia is indeed very old. Wells springing up amidst barren lands, trees growing on infertile soil, rock formations and stones of unusual forms and shapes, or similar natural phenomena that defied easy explanations had traditionally been associated with the supernatural and the divine, and this association meant that such places often tended to be considered as protected by special powers. In the rough, conflict-ridden, and volatile conditions of life on the inhospitable Arabian Peninsula, these sacred places thus formed crucial oases of peace and stability where, under divine protection and in relatively safe circumstances, many activities could be pursued, including important rituals such as a pilgrimage or even the conclusion of agreements to settle conflicts.

The supervision of such a sanctuary was often performed by a special man, woman, or group responsible for safeguarding the sacred and inviolable character of the place, all those who dwelled there, and all the activities that took place there. These guardians were also responsible for the well-being of visitors, who gave them offerings or other gifts in return. The people or tribal groups who had settled at such sacred places and served as its supervisors and guardians enjoyed great respect from both nomadic and sedentary neighboring groups and lived off the income of the sanctuary. One such tribal community reportedly was the Banu Quraysh ('The Clan of Quraysh') whose mythical forefather Qusayy is said to have succeeded in the course of the 6th century in obtaining control over a sacred place in an inhospitable mountainous region in the western Arabian region of the Hejaz. Over time, the presence of a remarkable black stone and a freshwater source had generated there the appearance of a sanctuary with its own local myths, religious traditions, and practices of worship, and thus also with some opportunities for the accumulation of wealth and interests.

This ancient sacred place, known as Mecca, seems to have acquired an additional reputation of centrality beyond the Hejaz when in the 6th century, under the leadership of the Banu Quraysh, it is said to have become an increasingly important node in trade routes that connected the Peninsula's different parts as well as some Late Antique trading settlements at its frontiers. Another category of inhabitants of the peninsula was local groups and clans

Figure 1.3 Mecca and its surroundings in the early 20th century

Source: National Geographic Image Collection, public domain

that had organized themselves as trading communities who actively participated in these different commercial networks. As early as in the first millennium BCE, the importance of one trade route in particular, running across western and northern Arabia, was well established. Traditionally, this route was intensely used to connect the Indian Ocean and South Arabia with the Antique Mediterranean, and this transit connection was certainly also made possible by local groups who were involved in its organization. Again, there is hardly any information about the precise nature of these trade activities for most of this period. However, it is certain that, as a result of the above-mentioned collapse of urban economies in the Mediterranean region in the course of the 6th century, interregional transit trade came to a complete standstill to be replaced by a more limited, but on a local level perhaps no less lucrative, trade in hides, dates, and other local products between Arabia and the increasingly significant frontier zones of the great empires to the north and east. It is especially in this local trade that the Banu Quraysh of the *haram* Mecca was able to distinguish itself from the second half of the 6th century onwards. According to their own origin myths, it was the four grandsons of Qusayy, known as ʿAbd Shams, Hashim, Nawfal, and al-Muttalib, who managed to establish trade contacts between the Banu Quraysh in Mecca and the various parts and frontiers of the Peninsula. Whatever the reality of this, due to its strategic location and its *haram* status, the settlement of Mecca certainly turned out very successful in attracting trade and related activities. The leading Banu Quraysh also enjoyed sufficient prestige and authority to conclude the necessary agreements with tribal leaderships along the trade routes to ensure the safety and continued success of that trade. This was already illustrated around the mid-6th century, when a South Arabian army is reported by a variety of sources to have attacked Mecca, hoping to break the leading position of the Quraysh in West Arabian trade relations. When, as mentioned, the various powerful leaderships that had dominated the peninsula's northern and southern frontier zones for most of the 6th century disintegrated, it appears that it was more locally defined leadership groups such as the Banu Quraysh that managed to seize at least some of the opportunities this situation offered. Thus, from their West Arabian *haram* Mecca and based on an intense network of commercial activities across Arabia, the Quraysh leadership of the early 7th century continued to successfully connect with various tribal communities and settlements beyond the Hejaz in the pursuance of its interests. Even when the actual nature of those interests and of those relationships remains particularly vague from the historical record, it is clear that this kind of participation in the world of Late Antiquity would have transformative effects on the Quraysh leadership and its partners and competitors on the Arabian Peninsula as much as on that wider world, increasingly in disarray from the turn of the 6th to 7th centuries onwards.

Notes

1 See especially Pourshariati, *The Decline and Fall of the Sasanian Empire*.

2 Agathias (d. *c.* 594), "The Histories" (translation from Palmer, *The Seventh Century in the West-Syrian Chronicles*).

3 Procopius (d. *c.* 565), "The History of Wars" (translation from Hoyland, *Arabia and the Arabs*, 81).

4 See Michael C.A. Macdonald, "The Emergence of Arabic as a Written Language", in "Chapter 7. *Provincia Arabia*: Nabataea, the Emergence of Arabic as a Written Language, and Graeco-Arabica", in Fisher, *Arabs and Empires before Islam*, 405–9; a somewhat different, more traditional interpretation goes as follows: "This is the monument of Imru' al-Qays, son of ʿAmr, king of all Arabs, who ruled over both sections of [the Banu] al-Azd and Niẓār and over their kings, and who punished Madhhij, so he was successfully defeated, in the irrigated land of Najrān, the kingdom of [the South Yemeni King] Shammār. He ruled over Maʿadd. No king had matched his achievements the moment

he died, wealthily, in the year 223, the seventh day of Kislūl [328 CE]". (Hoyland, *Arabia and the Arabs*, 79).

5 al-Nabīgha al-Dhubyānī (d. 604), *Dīwān* ('Book of Poems'), translation from Hoyland, *Arabia and the Arabs*, 83.

Selected readings

al-Azmeh, A. *A History of Islam in Late Antiquity: Allah and His People* (Cambridge, 2014)
Bagnall, R.S. *Egypt in Late Antiquity* (Princeton, 1993)
Brown, P. *The World of Late Antiquity, from Marcus Aurelius to Muhammad* (London, 1976)
Clark, G. *Late Antiquity: A Very Short Introduction* (Oxford, 2011)
Daryaee, T. *Sasanian Persia: The Rise and Fall of an Empire* (London, 2009)
Fisher, G. (ed.). *Arabs and Empires before Islam* (Oxford, 2015)
Fisher, G. *Between Empires: Arabs, Romans, and Sasanians in Late Antiquity* (New York, 2011)
Fowden, G. *Before and After Muḥammad: The First Millennium Refocused* (Princeton, 2014)
Fowden, G. *Empire to Commonwealth: Consequences of Monotheism in Late Antiquity* (Princeton, 1993)
Haldon, J. *Byzantium in the Seventh Century: The Transformation of a Culture* (Cambridge, 1990)
Hawting, G. *The Idea of Idolatry and the Emergence of Islam* (Cambridge, 1999)
Hoyland, R.G. *Arabia and the Arabs from the Bronze Age to the Coming of Islam* (London and New York, 2001)
Hoyland, R.G. "Arabs", in *International Encyclopaedia for the Middle Ages* (Turnhout, 2004)
Iricinschi, E., Kotsifou, Ch. (eds.). *Coping with Religious Change in the Late-Antique Eastern Mediterranean* (Tübingen, 2016)
Kaegi, W.E. *Heraclius: Emperor of Byzantium* (Cambridge, 2003)
Lavan, L. (ed.). *Local Economies? Production and Exchange of Inland Regions in Late Antiquity* (Leiden, 2015)
Liebeschuetz, W. *East and West in Late Antiquity: Invasion, Settlement, Ethnogenesis and Conflict of Religion* (Leiden, 2015)
Palmer, A., Brock, S.P., Hoyland, R. *The Seventh Century in the West-Syrian Chronicles* (Liverpool, 1993)
Pourshariati, P. *The Decline and Fall of the Sasanian Empire: The Sasanian-Parthian Confederacy and the Arab Conquest of Iran* (London, 2008)
Retso, J. *The Arabs in Antiquity. Their History from the Assyrians to the Umayyads* (Abingdon, 2002)
Rosen, W. *Justinian's Flea: Plague, Empire, and the Birth of Europe* (New York, 2007)
Sarris, P. *Empires of Faith: The Fall of Rome to the Rise of Islam, 500–700* (Oxford, 2011)
Shahid, I. *Byzantium and the Arabs in the Sixth Century* (Washington, 1995–2009)
Sizgorich, Th. *Violence and Belief in Late Antiquity: Militant Devotion in Christianity and Islam* (Philadelphia, 2009)
Stroumsa, G.G. *The Making of the Abrahamic Religions in Late Antiquity* (New York, 2015)
Webb, P. *Imagining the Arabs. Arab Identity and the Rise of Islam* (Edinburgh, 2016)
Wickham, Ch. *Framing the Early Middle Ages: Europe and the Mediterranean 400–800* (Oxford, 2005)
Wickham, Ch. *The Inheritance of Rome: A History of Europe from 400 to 1000* (London, 2009)

2 The prophet Muhammad and the Arabian leadership of Medina (610–61)

Introduction: the challenges of early Islamic historiography

The available information about the early 7th-century life of the prophet of Islam, Muhammad, and about the history of the early community of supporters and followers that gathered around his leadership in Mecca, the Hejaz and Arabia, poses a number of specific challenges. The crux of this matter is that generally speaking there are two perspectives on Muhammad and his early community, which are inextricably connected, yet simultaneously very different.

On the one hand, there is the religious perspective, in which Muhammad and his early community represent a key moment in a narrative of human salvation linking the past with the present, and the present with the future. For this perspective, a detailed recollection of that past of Muhammad and his early community remains essential, as the key to giving meaning to life in the present and to achieving a specific destiny in the future. The aim of this recollection is to be able to follow continuously in the Prophet's footsteps in as authentic a way as possible. The means to that end is a belief in the capacity of collective transmission of authentic reports about those prophetic footsteps. A chronological chain of authoritative persons, their shared memories, and the written canonization thereof guarantee, for this perspective, the crucial link between the 7th-century reality of the life of the Prophet and his early community and the example to emulate (*sunna*) that may be derived from that life by successive generations of believers. A main concern of this perspective, therefore, is not so much the preservation of the past, which is considered a given, but rather the authenticity of the present on the road to a predestined future.

On the other hand, there is the perspective of modern historical scholarship, which, as a field of academic specialization within the humanities, has for a long time wished to neutralize the present as much as possible in its quest for a distant past. The by now somewhat outdated trend in this perspective, which, however, continues to reappear both in relevant academic scholarship and in popular discourse, treats the authenticity of that past as one of its main concerns, from an equally positive, optimistic belief in the preservation of a past that can be known in its immutable essence by digging as deeply as possible into the many layers of history that cover it. A search for sources and information contemporary or near contemporary to the life of Muhammad and his early community, therefore, has always been of primary importance for this positivist historical perspective. However, this is and remains a difficult and for many even frustrating search, in terms both of identification of relevant material and of its interpretation. As has been well established by now, the earliest source that can provide explicit information is undeniably the text of the Quran itself, given that coherent fragments and versions of it have been found on manuscripts that have in recent years been carbon-dated to the 7th century. This revelatory text, however, mentions Muhammad's name four times only, without providing any context, and it merely alludes to a handful of other historical persons, events, and places. From the critical historian's perspective, the historical information that may be culled from this very early source therefore remains rather vague, even though not without interest (see below).

In the absence of other written and non-written material that directly dates from this early period, reconstruction of this context needs to be derived primarily from a specific Arabic narrative tradition in which—driven by that other, religious perspective—the recollection

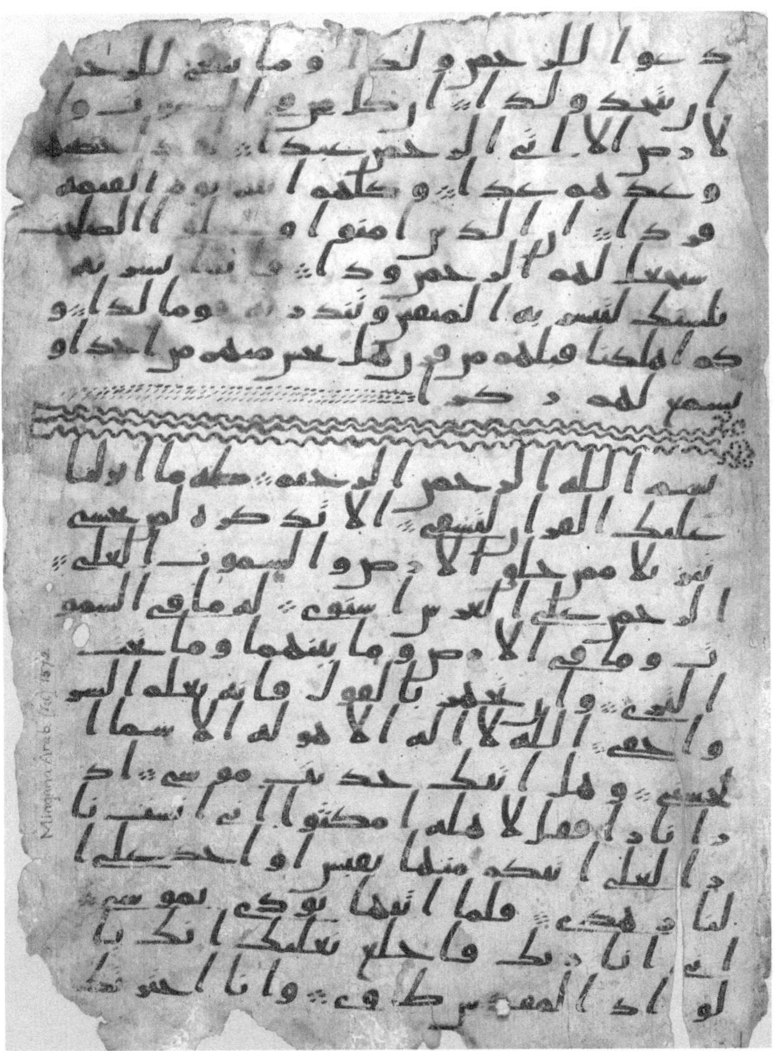

Figures 2.1 and *2.2* Quran fragment in Hijazi script, manuscript on parchment, carbon-dated *c.* 24 AH/645 (but dated *c.* 700 on the basis of style and decoration), conforming to today's standard text of the Quran (parts of chapters [surahs] 18 to 20)

Source: Cadbury Research Library: Special Collections, University of Birmingham. Arabic Islamic 1572a, Mingana Collection

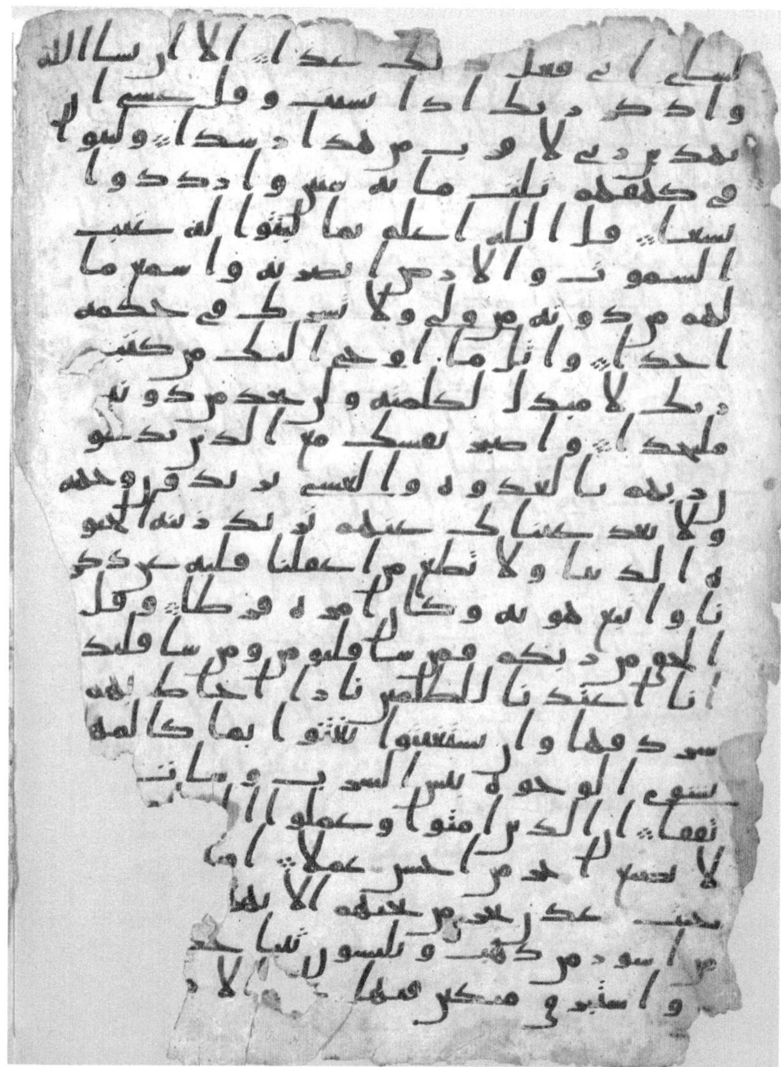

Figures 2.1 and *2.2* (Continued)

and memory of the Prophet and that earliest community has been kept alive by generation upon generation. The transmission of these stories (*khabar*s or *hadith*s) occurred at first mainly in oral form and started only to be written down in the course of the 8th century, particularly in structured collections of *hadith*s and in narrative biographies of the Prophet. The earliest biography of Muhammad, by the Iraqi scholar Ibn Ishaq (d. 770), is very explicit about the choices that were made in that orally transmitted material. Moreover, this first compilation only survives in a later edition, by the Egyptian scholar Ibn Hisham (d. *c.* 833). The six collections of *hadith*s that are considered authoritative by most Muslims all date to the 9th century, and are similarly the result of an editing process in which Islamic scholars, based on specific criteria, selected several thousands of *hadith*s as 'authentic' (*sahih*) from the vast number of stories in circulation at the time. It is clear, therefore, that throughout this complex history of transmission, deep interventions took place in the material transmitted, closely linked to the complex formation of a distinct Islamic community in the first centuries of Islamic history. The possible use of all this extant material to form an image of the historical person of Muhammad and his early community is therefore a source of continuing discussion. The general tendency in modern historical scholarship is that most material contains a 'kernel of truth', which can be unlocked in a variety of ways and which can lead to some historical reconstruction, the coherence and clarity of which depends on the position any modern historian takes in further discussions on where to situate those kernels' boundaries. At the same time, however, there are several voices in this ongoing debate that wish to go beyond this positivism and this traditional material entirely. They sometimes come to surprisingly revisionist conclusions, not all of which, however, have been deemed equally credible or convincing.

In this chapter, we will reconstruct what has been considered an authentic or truthful narrative of the life of the Prophet from both a religious as well as a positivist viewpoint. Also, we will present here in a similar way some crucial episodes in the life of Muhammad's new community of followers and associates after his death in 632. In spite of leaving more and more diverse traces, this early history has been contested in religious scholarship and modern historiography in the same way as Muhammad's life has been. The position that is pursued here for these reconstructions is, therefore, not so much that one of those two dominant perspectives is better or more authoritative, but rather that both of them appear to be based on an equally predisposed way of thinking, regardless of whether that way of thinking is geared towards the absolute value of the historian's past or the believer's future. This chapter actually works from the assumption that it is especially useful to accept that value judgement as a given and to try to understand how the memory of the lives of Muhammad and his early community, as a historically extremely powerful phenomenon, came to matter so much to those who support a religious perspective, to their modern positivist counterparts, and to many others who have made the history of the Islamic world ever since the 7th century into a highly impactful component of human history. The key question here is, therefore, not whether the lives of the Prophet and his early community can be sufficiently 'truly' reconstructed, but rather whether it can be sufficiently reconstructed in order to understand in the rest of this book, and beyond, to what extent for many people, groups, and social formations this life has been historically meaningful. The one thing that is undeniable is that as a meaningful memory, the narratives of the lives of Muhammad and his early community have had, and still have, an immense and wide-ranging significance. This significance merits a place in whichever historical understanding of both the processes that gave Late Antique times a remarkably new shape and the many changes that have subsequently occurred on a global scale. As a result, this chapter will consist of summary reconstructions of these prophetic and early community narratives, built around a kernel of truth according to some, existing as an authentic tradition (*sunna*) for others, interpreted as very different narrative constructions by others still, and considered as the starting point of meaningful late-antique, medieval, and early modern remembrances and history-making in this book.

As announced before, leadership and authority are central concerns for this book, and this will be no different in this chapter's brief engagement with this prophetic narrative. It will, therefore, chronologically move from the two phases that are traditionally associated with Muhammad's life as a prophetic leader in Arabia to a general reconstruction of the defining issues that are generally believed to have determined leadership over his community of followers and supporters after his death. The specifics of that leadership's remarkable expansion into the wider Late Antique world and of its organization will be integrated into Chapter 4, as that will allow for a longer, and therefore, more insightful, perspective of a first century of resilience, transformation, and entanglement of Late Antique and Arabian leaderships.

1 The life of Muhammad: an overview

1.1 Muhammad in the margins of Meccan leaderships

> It is alleged in popular stories (and only God knows the truth) that Amīna, the mother of God's messenger, used to say when she was pregnant with God's messenger that a voice said to her, 'You are pregnant with the lord of this people and when he is born say, "I put him in the care of the One from the evil of every envier; then call him Muhammad"'. As she was pregnant with him, she saw a light come forth from her by which she could see the castles of Buṣrā in Syria.
>
> Shortly afterwards, ʿAbd Allāh, the messenger's father died while his mother was still pregnant.
>
> The messenger was born on Monday, 12th Rabīʿ al-awwal, in 'the year of the elephant'.
>
> After his birth, his mother sent to tell his grandfather ʿAbd al-Muṭṭalib that she had given birth to a boy and asked him to come and look at him. When he came, she told him what she had seen when she conceived him and what was said to her and what she was ordered to call him. It is alleged that ʿAbd al-Muṭṭalib took him in the Kaʿba, where he stood and prayed to Allāh thanking him for this gift. Then he brought him out and delivered him to his mother, and he tried to find foster-mothers for him. Ḥalīma bint Abī Dhuʾayb of Banū Saʿd ibn Bakr was asked to suckle him.[1]

Islamic traditional accounts—such as the above one from Ibn Ishaq's prophetic biography in Ibn Hisham's early 9th-century recension—generally suggest that Muhammad was born in Mecca in the year 570, as a member of one of the four main clans of Quraysh, the Banu Hashim. At the time of Muhammad's birth, this is believed to have been the leading clan in Mecca, but after the death of its leader, Muhammad's grandfather ʿAbd al-Muttalib, it apparently had to forsake this leadership to the rival lineage of ʿAbd Shams (later better known as the clan of Umayya, named after a son of ʿAbd Shams) and their clan leader Abu Sufyan. Muhammad is believed to have become an orphan at a very young age, after which he grew up in the care of his uncle Abu Talib (d. 619), who succeeded his father ʿAbd al-Muttalib as the leader of the Banu Hashim. He eventually is said to have grown up to become active in the Meccan trading business, and at a certain moment he seems to have become involved, as a commercial agent, with the rich widow Khadija bint Khuwaylid (d. 619), whom he eventually also married.

Being a thoughtful and devout man, tradition has it that Muhammad regularly withdrew to a nearby cave at Mount Hira' for reflection and contemplation. At the highly symbolic age of forty years, in 610, so a particular strand of later biographies suggests, during one of his usual periods of withdrawal, Muhammad was visited by the angel Gabriel, who informed him about his prophetic calling and immediately communicated a first divine revelation. Versions of this matrix moment in Muhammad's life differ in their details, but most accounts traditionally claim that the words revealed during this 'Night of the Divine Decree' (*laylat al-qadr*) eventually ended up as the beginning of chapter 96 of the Quran, which goes as follows:

> Recite: in the name of thy Lord who created
> Created man of a blood-clot.
> Recite, and thy Lord is the most generous,
> who taught by the pen.
> He taught man that he knew not.

This is generally said to have been a traumatic experience for Muhammad, who would only gradually take peace with his destiny. In 612 it is said that he started to receive revelations from God via Gabriel again, and this then is believed to have continued to happen on a regular basis until his death in 632. Eventually, these snippets of the divine message, revealed over a long period of twenty eventful years, gave substance to the full text of the Quran's more than 6,000 verses, which were organized by his companions in the decades after his death in 114 chapters, or surahs, of unequal length.

The Islamic tradition always identifies Muhammad's first wife Khadija and his cousin ʿAli (d. 661), a son of Abu Talib, among the first to believe in his prophetic mission. Gradually, a handful of others—especially young members of his own clan—appear to have joined the limited flock of his followers in Mecca. Ultimately, inclusive ideas of general solidarity and equality which, as suggested also by the Meccan verses in the Quranic text, he preached in the first years of his mission are thought to have caused a few dozens of others to join as well. Apparently, most of these early followers were, in the first place, individuals who for various reasons were forced to live on, or beyond, the margins of Mecca's clan system. Aside from this social program, the themes of the earliest revelations involved advocating the omnipotence and mercy of the one and only god Allah, the obligation for all believers to perform good deeds, and the teleological certainty of God's Judgement on the Last Day.

At the same time, there also is said to have been resistance to the novel message that Muhammad preached, especially because the leaderships of the Banu Umayya and of the other clans of Mecca did not very much appreciate his pleas for social and religious reform. The protection Muhammad enjoyed within the tribal system, however, prevented problems at first, even though stories have been preserved that suggest that things were not as safe for some of his followers. This situation eventually changed for the worse when his wife and then also his guardian Abu Talib died in 619. After a difficult and long search for an alternative, Muhammad appears to have contacted the inhabitants of the oasis of Yathrib, in circumstances favorable to his needs and mission. Famously, the prophetic narrative explains how the practice of the blood feud had generated a highly destructive spiral of violence between the leading groups of Yathrib, the ʿAws and the Khazraj, and that this had also involved the three Jewish tribal communities of the oasis. Muhammad was therefore invited as an external leader and mediator to settle the conflict, to put a stop to the violence, and thus to ensure the survival of the oasis communities. In 622 several dozens of believers are traditionally believed to have migrated north from Mecca to Yathrib, where Muhammad himself, together with his closest companion and confidant Abu Bakr, arrived on September 24. The oasis settlement eventually became known with the new name of Medina (*Madinat al-Nabi*—'The Settlement of the Prophet'), and the moment of this migration (*hijra*) was quickly considered the beginning of an entirely new era of leadership and community building: the era of the community (*umma*) of Muhammad's followers, which had its own *hijri* calendar that coincided (and continues to coincide for all Muslims) with the era of the community's leadership and guidance by Muhammad and by those who follow in his footsteps.

1.2 Muhammad at the center of Medinan leaderships

Islamic tradition informs us that the different groups that lived in Medina and accepted Muhammad's charismatic leadership were integrated into a relatively new, particular communal identity between 622 and Muhammad's death in 632. The physical center of the new community was established in the home of the Prophet, often described as a building surrounded by walls that served as a place of prayer, a kind of *haram* sanctuary, and a dwelling for Muhammad and his family. The latter was formed by the daughters he brought from Mecca and by the wives who joined this family as a result of the eleven marriages that Muhammad is said to have concluded with members of various Meccan and Medinan leading families to support and consolidate his leadership. Hence, he came to be in charge of a new kind of supra-tribal group, the community of believers (*mu'minun*) or *umma*, in which both the migrants from Mecca—known as the *muhajirun*, 'those who undertook a *hijra*'—as well as the original inhabitants of Yathrib/Medina—known as the *ansar*, 'the helpers'—became full and equal partners, as long as they recognized Muhammad's leadership. This joining of forces and closing of ranks was allegedly ratified by agreements between the various stakeholders, a version of which has been preserved in Muhammad's biographies in the shape of a document that is today best known with the entirely anachronistic title of the 'Constitution of Medina'. This text explains how, through the identification of a common goal and a shared leadership, arrangements were made that helped to reduce internal tensions and contradictions. This formation of a new supra-tribal community is also believed to have interacted with the Quranic revelation, in which the verses that have been identified as having been revealed in this Medinan period are mainly concerned with the organization of the community, the religious and social practice of its members, and their joint action against outsiders. This also conforms with the image of Muhammad and his community that appears from some of the earliest extant non-Arabian textual references, stemming from the 660s and 680s. In such references, Muhammad appears as a strong religious leader and lawgiver of the community of his followers. This community—often identified as Ishmaelites (the descendants of Abraham's son Ismail), Hagarenes (the descendants of Ismail's mother Hagar), or Muhajirun (those who undertook a *hijra*)—is represented as closing ranks in a diverse apocalyptic movement that pursued divinely ordained violence for a religious cause that was an active partner in Late Antique monotheism.[2]

Despite the conclusion of agreements and the apparent closure of ranks, there are indeed many indications that this process of new community formation in Medina around Muhammad's charismatic leadership was far from self-evident and involved the wielding of substantial violence. It is believed, for instance, that the three Jewish groups of Medina could only accept Muhammad's leadership with difficulty. Eventually, the Islamic tradition explains how they were therefore all eliminated, by exile but also by capture and violent death. There apparently also were different local clan leaders in Medina who only reluctantly accepted the new situation. The success Muhammad nevertheless managed to achieve was closely connected to the increasingly successful raids and battles he is said to have led in the regional competition with neighboring groups and communities.

The prophetic narrative, therefore, insists on how the formation of a new community around Muhammad's leadership went hand in hand with turbulent developments outside Medina, in which the mounting tension with Mecca played a central role. For both economic and political motives—the need for income, control over the trade routes, and the affirmation of his leadership—Muhammad is said to have organized raids (*ghazw*) against trade caravans that passed through the region of Medina. Since it was the Meccan trade network that was dominant in the region, this appears to have resulted more than once in a violent collision with the Quraysh of Mecca. The first major confrontation is known as the Battle of Badr, in 624, where, against all odds, a prestigious victory is claimed to have been achieved by Muhammad and his associates. In March 625, according to Islamic tradition, there was the Battle of Uhud near Medina, where Muhammad himself was wounded and the Quraysh gained a close victory. March 627 is then said to have witnessed the great Battle of the Trench (*al-khandaq*) that involved tribal groups from almost the entire Hejaz and which the Meccans in the end had to forfeit without success. In June 628, a ten-year peace was famously concluded with Mecca at Hudaybiyya, after which, in the following year, Muhammad and his associates are said to have undertaken the pilgrimage to the Kaaba in Mecca. In the general malaise that followed in Mecca, most leaders of the Quraysh seem to have switched sides to join Muhammad, and the conquest of Mecca by his followers in January 630 is generally believed to have been substantially facilitated by this controversial integration of the majority of traditional Quraysh leadership. After 630 and a last famous battle, at Hunayn, against another alliance of Hejaz groups, most tribal communities on the Arabian Peninsula are believed to have allied with the new regional leadership of Medina. In the majority of cases, this is represented by referring to the reception of various tribal delegations in Medina, after which the reality of Muhammad's new authority was confirmed by the payment of a tribute (*sadaqa*).

In 632, the prophetic narrative explains how Muhammad took to Mecca for a last time, to perform the so-called 'farewell pilgrimage'. Upon returning to Medina, he fell gravely ill and died, reportedly on 8 June, 632, in the presence of his favorite wife ʿAʾisha and his cousin ʿAli.

Figure 2.3 Medina: mosque with grave of the Prophet (steel engraving, 19th century)

Source: Wikimedia CC BY-SA 3.0, https://commons.wikimedia.org/w/index.php?curid=517316

2 The leadership of Medina: succession and *fitna*

2.1 Authority and succession

The authority that is traditionally ascribed to Muhammad over different clans, groups, and tribal communities in Medina and the Hejaz and eventually even in other parts of the peninsula clearly must have been a multifaceted one, and the remembrance of its construction around both a new charismatic type of leadership and traditional relationships of patriarchal authority would become a crucial, but vexed, issue for those who followed in his footsteps. On the one hand, he is indeed remembered as a patriarchal leader in the ancient tribal tradition of the *ashraf.* He guaranteed the political and economic interests of his followers and organized a series of *ghazw* campaigns from Medina through which he eventually could take over the dominant role of the Quraysh of Mecca and their Meccan trade network, thus confirming the relevance of his leadership and its value for those groups who joined him. On the other hand, he is also remembered as the charismatic leader of a new supra-tribal community, in which individuals of various backgrounds were united around the banner of one and the same God, the powerful idea of Muhammad's God-given leadership, and a joint struggle against 'non-believing' others. He is therefore also considered as fulfilling an until that moment locally unknown—at least in the extant historical record—ideological and even religious role for all those who accepted his monotheist message, a role that was given its full significance for his followers in the framework of a specific imagination of his community's history as moving on an apocalyptic trajectory of salvation and divine guidance.

Muhammad's death in 632 thus occurred in an extremely successful and, at the same time, very complex context of the appearance of novel local and regional leaderships, movements, and ideas on the Arabian Peninsula. Therefore, it should hardly be considered a surprise that the continuation and consolidation of Muhammad's achievement was all but evident. In 632 and in subsequent years, local groups and leaders at various places on the peninsula appear to have attempted to emulate Muhammad's combination of charismatic and patriarchal success in their own, different, and autonomous ways. In the Hejaz, in 632 as well as at particular moments during the following decades, the succession to Muhammad remained an equally vexed issue, repeatedly opposing different groups and claims in ways that announced—or that at least have been explained as embryonic expressions of—Islamic history's future fault lines. It could even be argued that these many debates and conflicts about Muhammad's succession continued to define not just the formations and transformations of leadership in Islamic history, but also the formulation of political and wider cultural identities for varieties of stakeholders in those leaderships throughout the many centuries of that history.

The prophetic narrative explains how, according to most members of Muhammad's new community, no clear instructions appear to have been left for his succession and for the continuation of his very personal, charismatic authority. Whereas the sudden disappearance of the latter authority seems to have triggered the quick disintegration of the ties that bound tribal communities beyond the Hejaz to the new leadership of Medina, the lack of precedent and guidance is suggested to have generated a fierce debate within that leadership about the selection of Muhammad's successor. In hindsight, it turns out that, despite the lack of a clear regulation, a new consensus could time and again develop around the priority of a handful of widely respected 'migrants' (*muhajirun*) who belonged to the group of early converts. Thus, Muhammad is said to have been succeeded by his old companion Abu Bakr (r. 632–634), reportedly after long negotiations in the common space (*saqifa*) of one of the Medinan tribal groups, the Banu Sa'ida, between the leaders of Medina's original inhabitants—the *ansar*—and the Meccan migrants. Abu Bakr is especially praised in Islamic tradition for having been a prominent member of the Quraysh of Mecca, a successful merchant, and one of the first who accepted Muhammad's message and leadership. This special status in Muhammad's Meccan entourage was confirmed, according to that tradition, by the fact that in 622 Muhammad undertook the journey from Mecca to Medina together with Abu Bakr, that the Prophet married ʿA'isha, Abu Bakr's daughter and widely considered and represented as Muhammad's favorite wife, that Abu Bakr had led the prayer in Medina when Muhammad was too ill to perform this task, and that he was awarded the special epithet of *al-Siddiq*, the Veracious One. The short period of Abu Bakr's leadership, until his death in 634, is mainly remembered as a crucial moment of resetting Muhammad's achievement, with various raids and campaigns generating the coercive integration of most tribal communities on the peninsula into the new leadership networks that were brokered by Muhammad's entourage and his successor at Medina. In this context of tying together various groups and their *ashraf* elites, it is mostly Abu Bakr's knowledge of tribal traditions and genealogies that is praised as an important means to restore and elaborate this network.

The standard narrative of the early community suggests that Abu Bakr appointed his own successor shortly before his death, and that this was accepted without much discussion. This concerned another early companion, who also was the father of one of Muhammad's wives, and who served as the right hand of Abu Bakr during his short period of rule. Therefore, substantial continuity is claimed to have manifested itself in the leadership that this ʿUmar ibn al-Khattab (634–644) appears to have realized, not least in the format of the further trans-regional expansion—deeply into Roman and Sasanian territories in Syria, Iraq, and Egypt—of the networks of local leaders and resources that were somehow all bound to Medina. Amidst all of the enormous changes and challenges that this caused, it is clear that ʿUmar's political leadership remained a solid reality, primarily based on the effective charismatic qualities that were attributed to him and that are also alluded to by the fact that Islamic tradition remembered him as *al-Faruq*, the Redeemer. In 644, however, he died in Medina in unclear but violent circumstances, reportedly after being attacked by a dissatisfied Christian slave.

When the strong personality of ʿUmar was suddenly about to disappear in 644, the traditional narrative explains that on his deathbed he appointed a council of advisors (*shura*), consisting of six prominent 'migrants', to appoint a new leader to succeed him. This council is said to have eventually deliberated on two valid candidates: Muhammad's cousin and son-in-law ʿAli ibn Abi Talib and another son-in-law, ʿUthman ibn ʿAffan, who was also a member of the former leading clan of Mecca, the Banu Umayya. The choice of the council is said to eventually have fallen on the latter. The early community's narrative traditionally divides ʿUthman's long period of leadership, until 656, between six prosperous years and six difficult ones. These last years coincided with apparent attempts by ʿUthman to gain more direct control over the different networks of Arabic-speaking leaders and their followers that were now widespread across Arabia, Syria, Iraq, and Egypt, and especially over the substantial local resources that they now all had gained access to. This is reported to have led to vehement reactions, which eventually, in 656, are believed to have culminated in the murder of ʿUthman and the appointment by ʿUthman's opponents (and murderers) of ʿAli ibn Abi Talib as his successor. In 661, after a brief period of even more heavily contested leadership and of the disintegration and fragmentation of the ties and territories that had been bound to Medina by his predecessors, ʿAli was finally also murdered by political opponents, in the new settlement of Kufa in central Iraq.

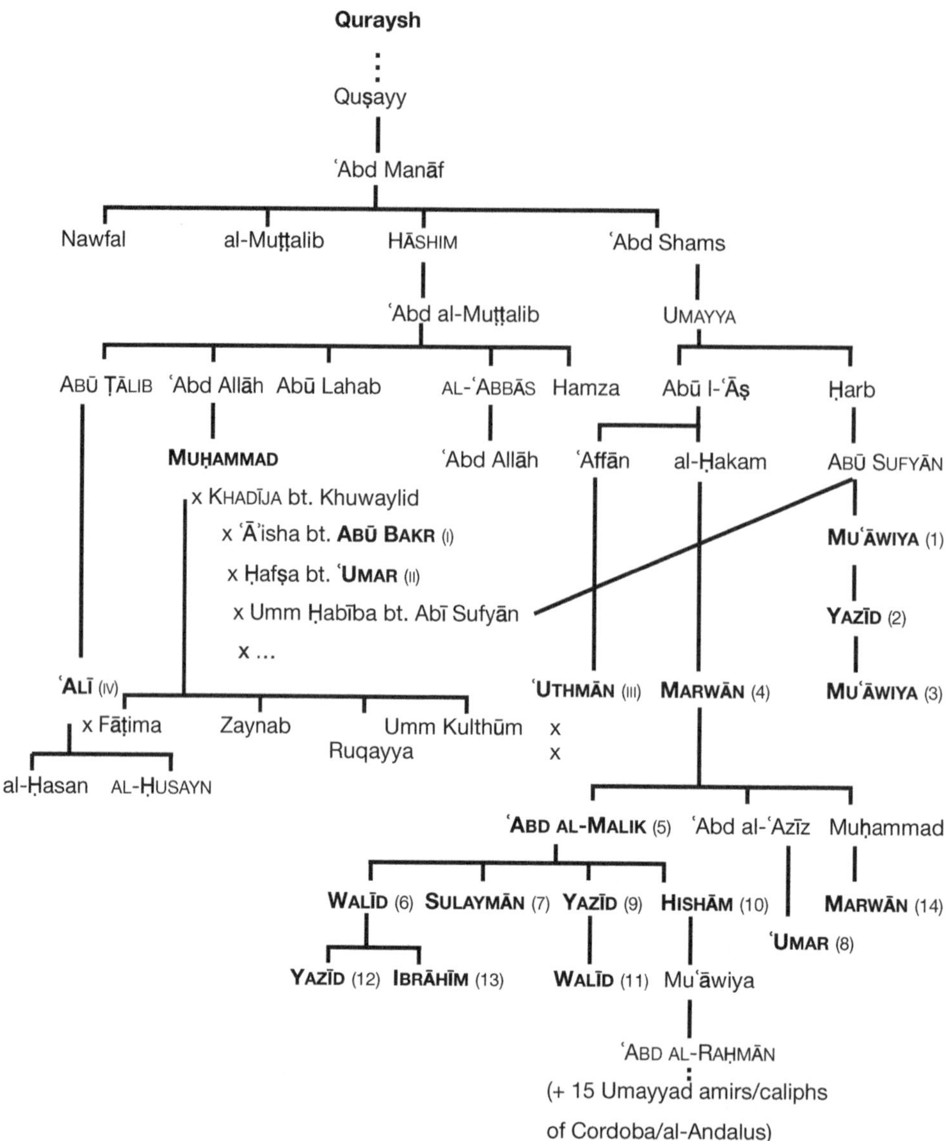

Bold = leaders of the early *umma*
SMALL CAPS = KEY FIGURES
Roman numbers = succession of the heads of the Arabian leadership of Medina
Arabic numbers = succession of Umayyad dynastic sovereigns

Dynastic Table 1 Simplified table of the Meccan leadership of Quraysh, including marital relationships in Muhammad's family and the Umayyads

With regard to the authority that was claimed by these four successors of Muhammad's centrality in expanding networks of Arabian leaders and their followers, a lot has often been derived from the rulership titles that were attributed to them by later generations. Each of these leaders are especially remembered in the standard narrative of the early community as *khalifat rasul Allah* ('successor of the messenger of God'). This Arabic title—and the derivatives 'caliph' and 'caliphate'—invokes claims to a sacral authority closely connected to the dominant salvation narrative that imagines Muhammad's community as progressing on a historical trajectory towards a predestined future in the hereafter, under the guidance of God, His messengers, and these prophetic substitutes. In the memory of later generations, this sacral authority of each of these four leaders—for most especially of Abu Bakr and 'Umar, for some (later imagined as Shi'ites, or rather proto-Shi'ites), however, only of 'Ali—started to acquire exemplary proportions nearly equal to that of the Prophet before them, which was reflected in the title eventually attributed to them of 'Rightly Guided Caliphs' (*al-khulafa' al-rashidun*), that is, people whose special leadership on God's straight path led their community to a certain monotheist future. Together with the generations of their children and grandchildren, they were (and are) also remembered by many in the same, normative sense as 'the Pious Ancestors' (*al-salaf al-salih*) whose lives are believed to represent a pure and ideal period of community building. The very few datable mid-7th-century sources that have in recent decades been retrieved, however, suggest that there are little to no good reasons to assume that well-known titles such as that of *khalifa*, which eventually—especially in the 9th and 10th centuries—became a central marker of legitimate Islamic authority, were already claimed in this authoritative fashion and with these particular meanings in the middle of the 7th century. Other, older, and far more personal names and titles—such as

Figure 2.4 Qāʿ al-Muʿtadil (Saudi Arabia): inscription of Zuhayr, referring to 'Umar's leadership and death in 24 AH/644, but without awarding him any titles

Source: 'A.I. Ghabban, "The inscription of Zuhayr, the oldest Islamic inscription (24 AH/AD 644–45), the rise of Arabic script and the nature of the early Islamic state", translation and concluding remarks R. Hoyland, Arabian Archaeology and Epigraphy 19 (2008): 209–36, p. 211.

al-Faruq, the Redeemer, for 'Umar or *al-Siddiq*, the Veracious One, for Abu Bakr—appear more prominently in the extant written record and, especially, in collective memories of their charismatic leaderships, informing at the same time, however, of a similar but more personal kind of sacral authority that was claimed for them.

In fact, the most important historical accomplishments of these prominent companions and successors of Muhammad do not so much include any conscious new interpretation of their claims to legitimate authority and theocratic order that would have announced and defined later conceptions of Islamic rule. Rather, they are important as those who realized first the continuation of their Arabian leadership after Muhammad's death, and secondly, its expansion on an unprecedented scale into the very heart of the Late Antique world while maintaining Medina's centrality. In this way, these new leaders and their local representatives gradually—and more than had ever been the case for the Hejaz—acquired a more prominent place in history through deeds and activities that left at least some written traces and that make it possible to say a bit more about their comings and goings than simply what later generations made of them. However, it remains a very difficult story to reconstruct and to interpret, apart from that, in particular, its outcome—the formation of a new Late Antique empire—has left its defining mark.

2.2 *Tension and* fitna

As far as that story is concerned, Muhammad's new 'community of believers' in fact went through a very turbulent history, which is also suggested by the violent death of three of its four first leaders. In 632, as mentioned, Muhammad's association with tribal communities beyond the Hejaz nearly immediately disintegrated. Thereupon, various campaigns were organized from the Hejaz to coerce these local leaderships across the Arabian Peninsula to again, or newly, accept Medina's leadership. These short but forceful and successful campaigns (632–634) entered history as the so-called *ridda* wars (the Wars of Apostasy), and they are inextricably connected to the rapid expansion of new networks of leadership beyond the peninsula, into Roman Syria and Egypt, and into Sasanian Iraq and Iran (see Chapter 4). The early community's narrative explains how the course and success of these campaigns had important consequences for the organization and stability of the new political formation around Muhammad's successors. The high and constant need for manpower made that recently subjugated Arabian leaders and their followers were deployed in new campaigns as soon as possible. Traditional practices and representatives of Arabian leadership were thus fully integrated in these expanding networks without much change, so that in practice two different generations of 'believers' (*mu'minun*) and two very different leadership arrangements were joined together in the new framework of the 'community'. On the one hand, there were the migrants (*muhajirun*), the *ansar*, and various other groups that had distinguished themselves already during the life of Muhammad by their early conversion to his message (a distinctive quality referred to as *sabiqa*—precedence in conversion) and by their closeness to his person (referred to as *sahaba*—companionship). These groups remained dominant by providing, as described above, the first four leaders, whose status and respect in the early community appear, therefore, mainly to have been based on the merits of their *sabiqa* and *sahaba*. On the other hand, there were the old tribal leaders (*ashraf*), including the Quraysh of Mecca, who are often depicted in the prophetic narrative as fighting Muhammad for years, or as renouncing his legacy after his death, and who often only seem to have been subjugated by coercive force. These *ashraf* appear to have continued to enjoy respect and authority on the basis of their traditional lineage-based claims, and their trans-regional experience and connections may even have proven very beneficial in the many campaigns that, after the *ridda* wars, took them all to the Late Antique regions of Syria, Egypt, and Iraq.

The inherent political tension that came with this mixture of old and new practices of leadership eventually appears to have culminated in the violent conflicts of the 650s. When ʿUthman ibn ʿAffan was appointed in 644, the choice seems to have been made for a consensus figure, since he, as described earlier, is not only remembered as an early convert and companion of Muhammad, but also as a member of the leading Quraysh clan of the Banu Umayya. In his attempt to take his leadership to a higher level and achieve a greater control over the different networks that met in Medina, he is said to have appealed to his ties with the traditional leadership of the *ashraf*. Thus, many *ashraf*, including most importantly ʿUthman's clansmen of the Banu Umayya, turn out to have received more opportunities to re-establish their old privileges, and particularly to obtain direct control over resource flows in the rich agricultural areas of Egypt and Iraq. In 656 the dissatisfaction about these changes among the original 'believers'—reportedly mainly in the previously relatively autonomous environments of Arabic-speaking leaders and groups of conquerors and migrants in post-Roman Egypt and post-Sasanian Iraq—caused some to move from Egypt and Iraq to Medina, where a lack of compliance to their pleas is said to have resulted in the murder of ʿUthman.

As referred to above, the Islamic tradition explains how, partly on the suggestion of these 'Egyptians' and 'Iraqis' who had murdered 'Uthman, Muhammad's cousin ʿAli was offered the vacant leadership. His acceptance is then said to have implied for many that he also gave his approval to the murder of his predecessor. This appears to have caused two reactions, the one more pernicious for the new political formation than the other. Both are remembered as fundamental to the further history of Muhammad's community and simultaneously as extremely destructive, to the extent that they are mainly identified as the first, grand *fitna*, the first in a series of moments in that community's early history when legitimate leadership was highly contested, when competition disrupted the community's cohesion, and when any trajectory of divine salvation seemed forfeited.

In Mecca, so the standard narrative goes, the protests against the murder of 'Uthman and the accession of ʿAli were led by three prominent companions of Muhammad (his widow ʿA'isha, and Talha and al-Zubayr), who moved to lower Iraq and a new settlement there, Basra, to seek support. ʿAli himself is said to have found support among the Arabic-speaking tribal groups in the central-Iraqi settlement of Kufa, and in December 656 the two armies of 'believers' are reported to have fought out their feud in the so-called 'Battle of the Camel'. Islamic tradition describes in much detail how this confrontation was won by ʿAli and his supporters, and how highly respected companions such as Talha and al-Zubayr fell on the battlefield.

That tradition reports in similar detail how, at the same time, there arose fierce protest against the murder of ʿUthman in the Syrian region, where the local leader of the Banu Umayya, Muʿawiya ibn Abi Sufyan (d. 680), demanded retribution for the murder of a member of his clan. When 'Ali refused this, the standard narrative continues, Muʿawiya gathered support among the tribal leaders in Syria to enforce justice, after which in 657 a confrontation took place near the Euphrates in northern Syria, at a place called Siffin. After three months of skirmishes, the Syrians famously requested to solve the conflict through a traditional tribunal, to which ʿAli complied. This is believed to have had fatal consequences for him, as in the meantime the tribal leaders of Iraq appear to have grown convinced of the advantages of supporting Muʿawiya, and another part of ʿAli's army is said to have also expressed their dissatisfaction with his decision by abandoning him and setting up their own camp near Nahrawan, east of the Tigris in Central Iraq. This last group entered history as the political movement (and ultimately also the Islamic sect) of the 'Kharijites' ('those who move away'). Despite the fact that ʿAli defeated these Kharijites, the standard narrative explains that he came out of this confrontation with a part of his own troops severely weakened. The tribunal eventually also proved not to bring any settlement, apart from the fact that it seems to have suggested that ʿAli had recognized Muʿawiya as his equal. Ultimately, in 661, ʿAli was allegedly murdered in Kufa by one of the Kharijites. In the meantime, Muʿawiya appears to have succeeded in obtaining recognition of his authority by the largest part of the tribal and other leaders that had first been bound to Medina and that were now widespread over Arabia, Egypt, Syria, Iraq, Armenia, and Iran. Subsequently, in 661, he seems to have managed to establish this authority in ʿAli's last stronghold, Iraq, as well. As a result, the center of power was definitively relocated to Muʿawiya's base in Syria, Damascus, and a new phase in the history of the expanding new leadership began.

Notes

1 Ibn Isḥāq (704–767), *al-Sīra al-Nabawiyya* ['The Life of the Prophet']; translation adapted from Guillaume, *The Life of Muhammed*, 69–70].
2 See Hoyland, *Seeing Islam as Others Saw It*.

Selected readings

Bowersock, G.W. *The Crucible of Islam* (Cambridge, MA, 2017)
Brown, J.A.C. *Muhammad: A Very Short Introduction* (Oxford, 2011)
Cook, M. *Muhammad* (Oxford, 1983)
Crone, P. *Meccan Trade and the Rise of Islam* (Princeton, 1987)
Crone, P., Cook, M. *Hagarism: The Making of the Islamic World* (Cambridge, 1977)
Donner, F.M. *Muhammad and the Believers at the Origins of Islam* (Cambridge, 2010)
El-Hibri, T. *Parable and Politics in Early Islamic History: The Rashidun Caliphs* (New York, 2010)
Guillaume, A. (transl.). *The Life of Muhammed: A Translation of Ibn Ishāq's Sīrat Rasūl Allāh* (Karachi, 1955)
Howard-Johnston, J.D. *Witnesses to a World Crisis: Historians and Histories of the Middle East in the Seventh Century* (Oxford, 2010)
Hoyland, R. *Seeing Islam as Others Saw It: A Survey and Evaluation of Christian, Jewish, and Zoroastrian Writings on Early Islam* (Princeton, 1997)
Hoyland, R. "Writing the Biography of the Prophet Muhammad: Problems and Solutions", *History Compass* 5/2 (2007): 581–602
Keaney, H.N. *Medieval Islamic Historiography: Remembering Rebellion* (New York, 2013)
Madelung, W. *The Succession to Muhammad* (Cambridge, 1996)
Motzki, H. (red.). *The Biography of Muhammad* (Leiden, 2000)
Rodinson, M. *Mahomet* (Paris, 1961)
Rubin, U. *The Eye of the Beholder: The Life of Muhammad as Viewed by the Early Muslims, a Textual Analysis* (Princeton, 1995)
Shaban, M.A. *Islamic History A.D. 600–750 (A.H. 132) A New Interpretation* (Cambridge, 1971)
Wansbrough, J. *The Sectarian Milieu: Content and Composition of Islamic Salvation History*. New Edition (New York, 2006)
Watt, W.M. *Muhammad at Mecca* (Oxford, 1953)
Watt, W.M. *Muhammad at Medina* (Oxford, 1956)
Watt, W.M. *Muhammad: The Prophet and the Statesman* (London, 1967)
Zeitlin, I.M. *The Historical Muhammad* (Cambridge, 2007)

3 The Arabian imperial formation of the Umayyads (661–750)

Introduction: *fitna* and the formation of a patrimonial empire

The first conflicts that within two decades after the death of Muhammad divided the community of his followers and successors, the *umma*, are also known as the first or great *fitna*—the first moment of chaos, division, and trial for the *umma*, and of its temporary loss of clear direction to follow in the prophet's footsteps on the divinely ordained road to salvation. As is suggested by this later remembrance of this episode as the first *fitna*, this represents a moment in the *umma*'s early history that was and continues to be laden with many powerful meanings. Just as in the religious perspective on the prophetic narrative, these meanings relate particularly to how the *umma*'s salvation narratives eventually were constructed, especially because the origins of the Sunni-Shi'ite split of that *umma* are traditionally situated in these mid-7th-century conflicts. From a strictly historical perspective, however, these conflicts' most important meaning is connected to the fact that eventually, and somewhat unexpectedly, centrality and priority among the diverse and widespread Arabic-speaking leaderships was now asserted by the former leading clan of Mecca, the Banu Umayya. Thus, this so-called *fitna* confirmed to a large extent the survival of the traditional social order of Arabia and of the *ashraf*, and especially of the Meccan leadership, albeit in an adapted form and on a hitherto unprecedented Late Antique scale.

The networks of Arabian and particularly Meccan leaderships outgrew indeed quite suddenly their early 7th-century boundaries. This remarkably swift process of restoration and trans-regional entanglement and empowerment was spurred by successful territorial expansion, first to Roman Syria and Egypt and to Sasanian Iraq, and later also beyond these adjacent territories. It benefited enormously from the resulting access to new resources and their mobilizing distribution among the Arabic-speaking leaderships of—especially—post-Roman Syria. At the same time, it remained strongly tied up with the rallying force of the monotheistic reorientation that was advocated by the prophetic revelation. This was increasingly invested in by this new Late Antique trans-regional leadership to fend off rival claims by Roman and Persian competitors and by other Arabian leaders and to keep the ranks of their followers and clients closed and tied up with a distinctive sovereign order of status, entitlement, and identity. More in particular, in the decennia that followed this renewal of the Umayyad-Meccan leadership and authority, this originally rather loose trans-regional network of Arabian leaders and their tribal-patriarchal entourages evolved quickly to a new level of organization. In this process, a more clearly defined and more explicitly promoted Islamic identity started playing a central political role, going hand in hand with, and also paving the way for, the further definition of that identity as a social and cultural system of specific practices, institutions, and discourses and of an expanding community of believers.

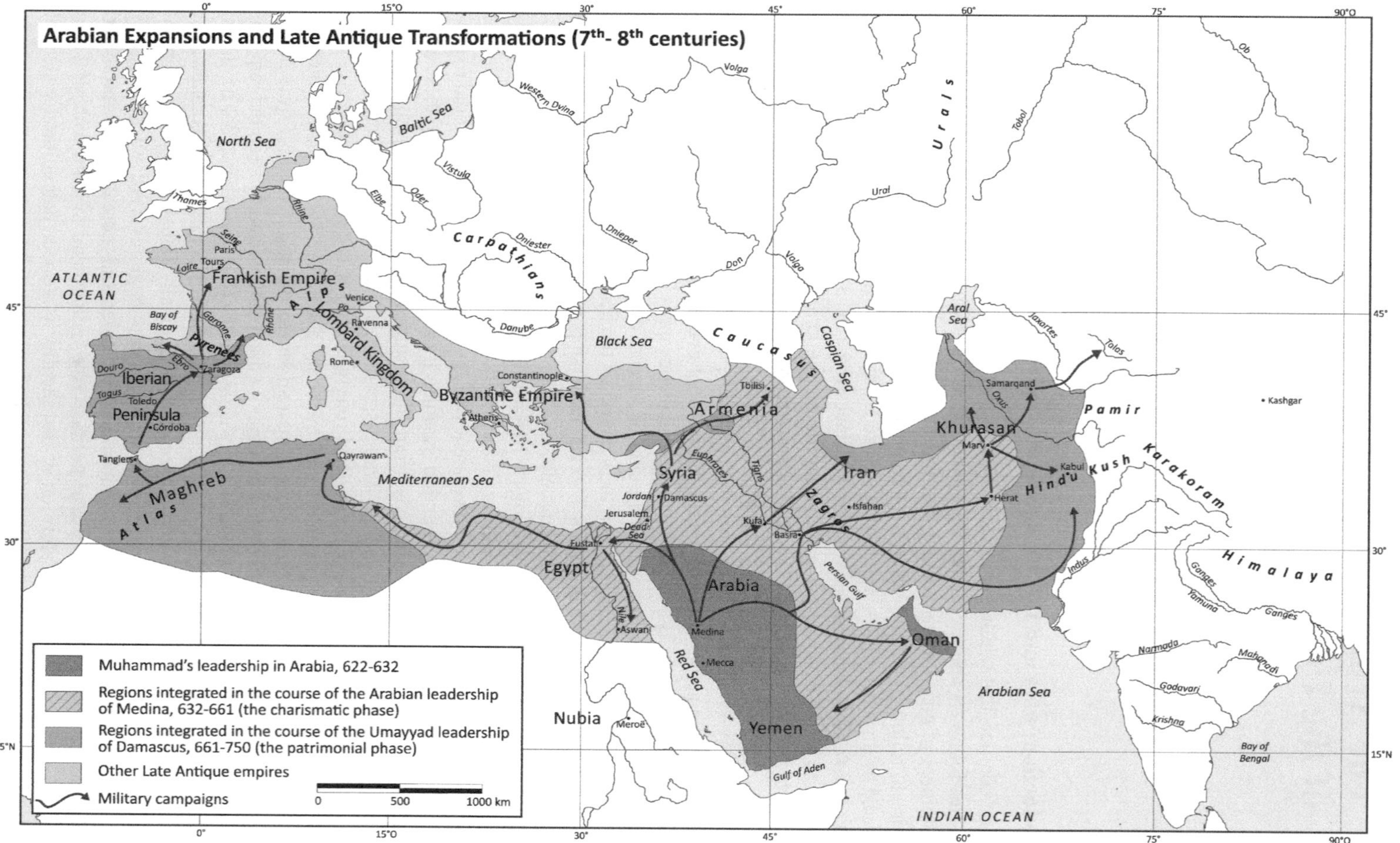

Map 2 Arabian Expansions and Late Antique Transformations (7th–8th centuries)

In the course of time, this new trans-regional leadership thus transformed into a full-fledged match of the Late Antique empires that it was to replace completely (the Sasanian empire) or partially (the Greek-Roman empire).

This transformation made the 7th-century contingency of the clustering of Arabian leaderships and new monotheism into a lasting and central factor in human history on a globalizing scale. It was achieved in the first place by the patriarchal leaders who, between 656 and 661, appear to have managed to position themselves from Syria at the center of the networks of leadership that had extended their power over many of the highly diverse local communities that populated the regions between the eastern Mediterranean and the Iranian plateau. Therefore, this chapter delves deeper into the history of this patriarchal dynasty of the Umayyads, focusing in particular on the whereabouts of their claims to power and authority in and from Syria. The wider picture of the enormous expansion of their and their predecessors' reach in the Late Antique east and west as well as of the Islamic imperial formation in this expansion's wake will be discussed in the next chapter.

1 The complexity of Umayyad authority

In 661, the Umayyad clan of the Banu Quraysh, led by a son of the Meccan leader Abu Sufyan, Muʿawiya, definitively achieved centrality among the Arabic-speaking leaderships in Arabia, Egypt, Syria, Iraq, and on the Iranian Plateau. Three decades after their loss of control over Mecca, the former Roman region of Syria had now become their new powerbase, with ancient Damascus and its fertile hinterland as its central location. This relocation

Figure 3.1 Damascus and the Umayyad mosque

Source: by Bernard Gagnon—Own work, , https://commons.wikimedia.org/w/index.php?curid=12267678

of the center of Umayyad activity to Syria turned out to offer the Umayyads many opportunities to acquire a powerful position within the radically changed leadership balances across the region, to consolidate that new political landscape around their authority, and to further its expansion east- and westward.

A telling and important factor in this process of finding new balances between change and continuity was the fact that with the empowerment of the Umayyads, the practices of *ashraf* leadership entered the many discussions about the thorny issue of the legitimate succession to Muhammad. This was a major cause for early Islamic history's conflict-ridden leadership trajectory, but it also contributed to the fact that, in the long run, dynastic forms of hereditary succession remained a dominant practice. Another important factor in this process is the fact that the leaders of this dynasty of the Umayyads started to profile themselves more explicitly than before as the rulers of an entirely new Late Antique political order, of which the Quranic message and Islamic monotheism were the distinguishing features. Despite the resultant framing in many, if not most, later sources and studies of the dynasty as that of the Umayyad 'caliphs', in recent decades, doubts have been raised about the uses in this period of Umayyad rule—as well as more in general, as hinted at in the previous chapter, in the wider period of Islamic history's first 200 years—of this specific title and its explicit assertion of divine representation or, as is more commonly suggested, of prophetic succession and emulation. Undoubtedly, already announcing the latter symbolically powerful and defining usage by the Umayyads' successors in the 9th century and beyond, the title of caliph seems to have been claimed for Umayyad rulers in specific contexts of political communication only, which were defined by particular audiences and moments of intense competition, especially with the Greek-Roman empire and its Late Antique idiom of theocratic and Caeseropapist power. For example, while it occasionally already appears in mid-7th-century court poetry, so far only one dated explicit assertion of this title is claimed to be known for this entire period, on a particular set of coins issued during the—in many respects particular—reign of the Umayyad ruler ʿAbd al-Malik (r. 685–705). Nevertheless, in the historiographic memory that was recorded from at least the 9th century onwards, various factors, including the growing need to assert direct continuity with the prophetic narrative, made this the preferred identification of Umayyad rule at the head of the Islamic empire too. As a consequence, even today, this dynastic leadership is usually referred to as the Umayyad Caliphate (661–750).[1]

In fact, not just the precise nature of Umayyad authority in the transforming and expanding networks of Arabian leadership appears today as more complex, volatile, and diverse than generally tends to be assumed, but also the Umayyads themselves were constituted from different groups that operated in changing and often unsteady constellations of power and interests. There were actually two leadership groups within the Banu Umayya who succeeded each other in the course of this formative process: the descendants of the Meccan leader and opponent of Muhammad, Abu Sufyan (d. 654)—known as the Sufyanids (661–683)—and the descendants of a later Umayyad leader in Mecca, Marwan ibn al-Hakam (d. 685)—known as the Marwanids (684–750). The transition of power from the former to the latter lineage was again characterized by a widespread and lengthy series of violent conflicts that once more revolved around the vexed issue of leadership over the *umma*. The fault lines now however ran between *ashraf* and prominent members of the *umma* as well as between different *ashraf* groups rallying around the former Meccan leadership.

2 Muʿawiya and the Umayyad-Sufyanids

Once his originally Syrian authority was recognized by most *ashraf* of the mix of Arabic-speaking tribal forces that were settling in Egypt, in Iraq, and beyond, Muʿawiya ibn Abi Sufyan (r. 661–80) successfully managed to maintain from the region of Damascus his priority and centrality in these continuously expanding networks of Arabian leaders, their followers, and the growing flows of resources they managed to tap into.

An important factor that enabled this has been credited to Muʿawiya's strong personal connections with the *ashraf* across these different regions. After all, Muʿawiya, as the son of Mecca's former leader and a close companion of the prophet, appears to have been able to build up both great political experience and an effective personal network of supporters and peers in the 630s, 640s, and 650s. After 661, this is generally believed to have translated into a remarkably broadly supported and barely controversial trans-regional sovereignty. It also seems that the Umayyad clan enjoyed longstanding close ties with the region of Syria, where already prior to the changes of the 620s it is likely to have possessed properties and to have been commercially active and highly respected among its Arabic-speaking Christian tribal groups. Thus, when after the retreat of the Romans from Syria in the 630s, Muʿawiya appeared there as the new regional leader, he and his entourage were anything but strangers in this new political context. During the course of the two decades in which Muʿawiya remained Medina's main representative and spokesperson in Syria, he appears to have strengthened his position in the rapidly changing and expanding Arabian networks by closely tying Syria's local Arabian leaderships and their manpower to his remarkably stable regional authority. That he eventually managed to gain a stronger grip over the full trans-regional set of those networks, therefore, had a lot to do with these specific Syrian

Figure 3.2 *Dirham* (silver coin) minted at Darabgird in name of Muʿawiya, 41 AH/661–2. Post-Sasanian decoration with Middle Persian (*pahlavi*) and Arabic inscriptions: one of the earliest dated references to the title 'commander of the faithful'. Central in Middle Persian (*pahlavi*): *Maawiya amir-i wruishnikan* ['Muʿāwiya, Commander of the Faithful']. In the margin in Arabic: *bismi llāh* ['In the name of God']

Source: J. Walker, A Catalogue of Muhammadan Coins (London: British Museum, 1941), 1.25–6, plate V.1; British Museum No. 35

circumstances and achievements. After 661, Muʿawiya's trans-regional authority was further strengthened and nourished by the organization of regular violent campaigns outside of Syria, in ways that parallel how the ancient *ghazw* tradition had been an intrinsic part of successful *ashraf* leadership on the Arabian Peninsula. In scale, direction, and impact, however, Muʿawiya's campaigns differed substantially from the latter Arabian practices. They targeted especially Greek-Roman assets and subjects in Asia Minor and Armenia. In addition, maritime campaigns were organized in the eastern Mediterranean, which culminated in a siege and blockade of the Greek-Roman capital Constantinople itself in the 670s, without, however, any lasting results (see also Chapter 4). As these maritime campaigns suggest, Muʿawiya's trans-regional leadership must have been much more than a simple copy on a grander scale of traditional Arabian leadership practices.

In the course of his relatively long reign of almost twenty years, Muʿawiya made the controversial decision to designate his own son Yazid as his heir apparent. This open appeal to patrilineal succession practices reminiscent of *ashraf* traditions added new fuel to the discussions about legitimate leadership over the *umma* that had, as explained above, caused tensions among the different Arabian leaderships since the Prophet's death. These now turned into increasingly vexed discussions between supporters and opponents of Umayyad-Sufyanid agnatic claims to leadership, with the latter opponents promoting different sets of rival claims. Just as had happened in 656, after Muʿawiya's death in 680, these discussions quickly transformed into violent conflicts. These fragmented the Arabian leaderships and divided their followers and dependents into different opposing camps, centered in Syria, the Hejaz, and Iraq. This complex whole of different violent confrontations, scramble for supporters and resources, and assertions and counter-assertions of trans-regional sovereignty over the *umma* is collectively remembered as the second *fitna* (680–692), and thus as another moment of temporary loss of clear direction for the community to follow in the Prophet's footsteps on the divinely ordained road to salvation.

In 680, Yazid succeeded his father in accordance with the latter's instructions, but his authority was immediately contested. Two distinct groups of Arabian leaders can be identified that, on different grounds, appear to have refused to recognize Yazid's claim. Each put forward their own leaders as more suitable. Those who supported the leadership of the direct descendants of Muhammad via his cousin and son-in-law ʿAli—often referred to with the Quranic notion of the *ahl al-bayt* or 'People of the [Prophet's] Household'—appear to have remained active in the region of Iraq after their disintegration in the course of the 1st *fitna*. These proto-Shi'ite movements of 'the party of ʿAli' (*shiʿat ʿAli*) are remembered as having seized the opportunity offered by Yazid's accession to close ranks once again behind the counter-claim of ʿAli 's son al-Husayn. When al-Husayn responded to their invitation to join them in Kufa and took his family and entourage from the Hejaz to Iraq, however, he was intercepted by Syrian troops near the Iraqi settlement of Karbala. In the infamous confrontation that followed, remembered in manifold later accounts and reports as having taken place on 10 October 680, the Prophet's grandson al-Husayn and his family and kin were all killed. After this moment of 'martyrdom'—as it is remembered in later, especially Shi'ite, accounts—the Iraqi proto-Shi'ite movements seem to have again fragmented in different local groups and leadership claims.

Simultaneously, in Mecca in the Hejaz, there were prominent local leaders who are similarly believed to have contested Yazid's succession. They are all recorded to have rallied around the cause of ʿAbd Allah ibn al-Zubayr (d. 692), the son of a prominent companion of the Prophet, al-Zubayr (who had died in the 1st *fitna*'s Battle of the Camel, see Chapter 2). This local renunciation of Umayyad-Sufyanid leadership generated violent action in the

Hejaz, with an extensive display of Umayyad coercive force, but without much political result. Upon the premature death of Yazid in 683, Ibn al-Zubayr appears to have proceeded quite successfully to proclaim himself on a wider regional and trans-regional scale as the sole legitimate 'commander of the believers'. His claims were based on the aforementioned notions of *sabiqa*—precedence in conversion—and *sahaba*—prophetic companionship—which gave him a clear advantage over any Umayyad or other Arabian leader of *ashraf* lineage. As again suggested by several coins that have been preserved and that were minted in Ibn al-Zubayr's name, he even succeeded in having those claims effectively recognized by most local leaders who had originally accepted or represented the authority of Muʿawiya and his agents, from North Africa in the west to Khurasan in the east, and even in Umayyad Syria. As a result, the default representation of Ibn al-Zubayr and his family and supporters in many accounts for this period as Umayyad rebels and insurgents is increasingly being questioned. Modern historical scholarship has actually started to acknowledge that this Zubayrid network of Arabian-Islamic leadership maintained trans-regional priority and authority during a large part of the 680s, and that the authority of the Umayyad-Sufyanids was therefore virtually nonexistent at that time.[2]

The apparent regionwide success of the Zubayrids was indeed not only due to the power and charisma of Ibn al-Zubayr. After the premature death of Yazid ibn Muʿawiya, the Umayyad clan and their Syrian-Arabian supporters became heavily divided themselves about Yazid's succession. This was closely linked, according to most accounts, to the tensions that had started to manifest themselves among the Syrian-Arabian leaderships. More specifically, a fault line had become visible between two tribal communities that appeared increasingly as two political factions in the Umayyad power constellation. On the one hand, there were those Arabian groups who all appear to have moved from the South Arabian region of Yemen (Yaman) to the Syrian desert long before the 630s, and who are, therefore,

Figure 3.3 *Dirham* (silver coin) minted at Darabgird in name of ʿAbd Allah Ibn al-Zubayr, 64 AH/683–4. Post-Sasanian decoration with Middle Persian (*pahlavi*) and Arabic inscriptions. Central in Middle Persian (*pahlavi*): *Apdula amir i-wruishnikan* [ʿAbd Allāh, Commander of the Faithful']. In the margin in Arabic: *bismi llāh* ['In the name of God']

Source: Silver drahm of 'Abd Allah Amir al-Mu'minin, DA, 683–84. 1951.148.3 American Numismatic Society

mostly referred to as the Yaman tribes. Consisting of different tribal lineages, they all linked their tribal genealogies to a shared mythical ancestor of South Arabian descent known as Kalb, which tied them to the comprehensive southern Arabian tribal community of the Banu Qahtan. On the other hand, there were also different Arabian groups of newcomers that had migrated to Syria much more recently, with and in the wake of the Arabian expansion. Most of these groups originated from the north of the Peninsula and they appear in 8th-century narratives to have begun identifying themselves since the 680s especially with their own lineage of mythical predecessors, especially Qays or Qays ʿAylan, who is imagined as the ancestor of one constitutive tribal subdivision in the comprehensive northern Arabian community of the Banu ʿAdnan. These two factions of various Arabian leaderships and their followers, branded as Yaman and Qays, are presented in later narrative sources as closing ranks behind different Umayyad branches (with Qays being closely linked also to the Sufyanids) and as becoming radically opposed when after 683 each advanced their own candidate for Yazid's succession. Against a background of mounting pressures from Zubayrid successes, this competition quickly seems to have erupted into violent confrontations between both Syrian groups, culminating in the so-called battle of Marj Rahit, a locality north of Damascus. Ending with the defeat of Qays' leaderships, this battle is said to have been followed in July 684 with the Yaman faction proclaiming their candidate the new Umayyad leader.

This candidate was Marwan ibn al-Hakam, descendant of a different line than the Sufyanid one within the Umayyad clan and a longstanding and respected leader of that clan in the Hejaz, until he had been forced to flee to Syria with the expansion of Zubayrid power. At the time of Marwan's accession in 684, indeed, Zubayrid empowerment had made the authority that Umayyad leadership could still claim substantially reduced, if not virtually non-existent, even in Syria. Upon his accession, therefore, the old Marwan and, particularly, the Yaman Arabian leaderships who had brought him to power, appear to have embarked on new violent campaigns to re-establish their trans-regional priority, to re-integrate the widespread networks of Arabian leaderships into their Syria-centered constellation, and to, as it were, reconquer their emerging empire.

3 ʿAbd al-Malik and the Umayyad-Marwanids

In April 685, Marwan died of old age and was succeeded without much opposition by his son ʿAbd al-Malik (r. 685–705). Generally, it is stated that it was thanks to ʿAbd al-Malik's political ingenuity and charismatic personality that Umayyad authority was re-established and that Arabian leadership started to take on the patrimonial shape that announced the formation of a new Late Antique empire. The restoration of Umayyad control over Syria and Egypt, the definitive victory over his rival Ibn al-Zubayr after the violent siege of Mecca in 692, and the suppression of further proto-Shiʾite rival movements in Iraq went hand in hand with remarkably novel—and increasingly better known—organizational features of Umayyad-Marwanid power. These organizational developments in turn stabilized ʿAbd al-Malik's own leadership and guaranteed his control over and management of the still expanding groups of people and resources in east and west that became connected with his Umayyad-Marwanid authority and order (see the next chapter for further details).

In the best of patriarchal and patrimonial leadership traditions, that authority was still primarily based on ʿAbd al-Malik's personal bond with members of his own Marwanid clan. These Marwanids were entrusted with regional rule over important local groups and resources, which thus remained closely tied up with the interests of the Umayyad center in Syria. This applied especially to Egypt, where for twenty years, from 685 to 705, ʿAbd al-Malik's brother, ʿAbd al-ʿAziz ibn Marwan, represented Umayyad authority and further expanded it. Moreover, ʿAbd al-Malik succeeded, through regular recruitment among Syrian groups and the re-integration of Qays leaderships, in further developing a more professional standing army around his person, which gave him greater clout in the confrontation with any remaining or new opponents, including rivals from the Greek-Roman north. Finally, in the establishment and exercise of his authority, ʿAbd al-Malik also called upon an important and loyal supporter, al-Hajjaj ibn Yusuf al-Thaqafi (d. 714). Originally a prominent member of the Banu Thaqifa, a powerful tribal formation from the town of Taif in the Hejaz, in 692 al-Hajjaj achieved for ʿAbd al-Malik the total victory over Ibn al-Zubayr in Mecca, confirmed by the death of Ibn al-Zubayr himself. Thereafter, al-Hajjaj was appointed as ʿAbd al-Malik's leading agent in the east, first in the region of Iraq, and eventually also in Iran and beyond. With the aid of Syrian Arabian troops and from the settlement of Wasit, established as the new center of Marwanid power in central Iraq, this talented commander and administrator succeeded in definitively restoring (or—depending on the narrative's perspective—finally imposing) Umayyad-Marwanid order in the period 694–995 in the Iraqi settlements of Kufa and Basra, thus unlocking the wealth of resources of the fertile ancient lands of Mesopotamia for the Syrian leadership. An infamous speech that was attributed to him in later Arabic literature vividly illustrates what kind of reputation of violence, loyalty, and powerful leadership this Umayyad-Marwanid representative managed to acquire (and how hostile an environment Kufa was and would remain to the Umayyad-Marwanids).

> Al-Ḥajjāj set out for Iraq as governor, with 1,200 men mounted on thoroughbred camels. He arrived in Kufa unannounced, early in the day. . . . Al-Ḥajjāj went straight to the mosque, and with his face hidden by a red silk turban, he mounted the pulpit and said, "Here, people!" . . . When the people were assembled in the mosque he rose, bared his face, and said:
>
> "I am the son of splendor, the scaler of high places. When I take off my turban you know who I am. By God, I shall make evil bear its own burden; I shall shoe it with its own sandal and recompense it with its own like. I see heads before me that are ripe and ready for plucking, and I am the one to pluck them, and I see blood glistening between the turbans and the beards.
>
> By God, O people of Iraq, people of discord and dissembling and evil character! I cannot be squeezed like a fig or scared like a camel with old water skins. My powers have been tested and my experience proved, and I pursue my aim to the end. The Commander of the Faithful emptied his quiver and bit his arrows and found me the bitterest and hardest of them all. Therefore, he aimed me at you. For a long time now, you have been swift to sedition; you have lain in the liars of error and have made a rule of transgression. By God, I shall strip you like bark, I shall truss you like a bundle of twigs, I shall beat you like stray camels. . . . By God, what I promise, I fulfill; what I purpose, I accomplish; what I measure, I cut off. Enough of these gatherings and this gossip and 'he said' and 'it is said'! What do you say? You are far away from that! I swear by God that you will keep strictly to the true path, or I shall punish every man of you in his body. . . ." Then he went to his house.[3]

ʿAbd al-Malik grew into a particularly powerful ruler, who successfully managed to claim a trans-regional authority at the head of a specific political, socioeconomic, and cultural order the contours of which were increasingly clearly and effectively imposed and defined in and beyond Syria, Egypt, and Iraq. As a consequence, during the second half of his reign, that Umayyad-Marwanid authority appeared ever more in organized formats that paralleled those of its late antique imperial peers, experiencing relative political stability, economic prosperity, and cultural development (see the next chapter). This was, moreover, reflected in ʿAbd al-Malik's largely uncontested succession by his four sons. At first, this involved al-Walid I (r. 705–715) and his brother Sulayman (r. 715–717), under whose reigns a similar stability and prosperity could be maintained. A factor in and illustration of this successful dynastic leadership at the Syrian Arabian head of one of the largest land empires in human history (see the next chapter) are certainly the monumental buildings which these Umayyad-Marwanid rulers left behind, such as the Dome of the Rock and the al-Aqsa Mosque on the Temple Square in Jerusalem, the Great Mosque in the center of Damascus, and the Great Mosque of Aleppo.

From the end of the second decade of the 8th century at latest, however, new frictions and tensions appear to have arisen around the Umayyad-Marwanid leadership, which would lay at the origin of its complete loss of power some thirty years later. Several factors actually played a part in this new buildup of tension. The expanding Marwanid clan itself gradually lost cohesion, not least due to the conflicting ambitions of

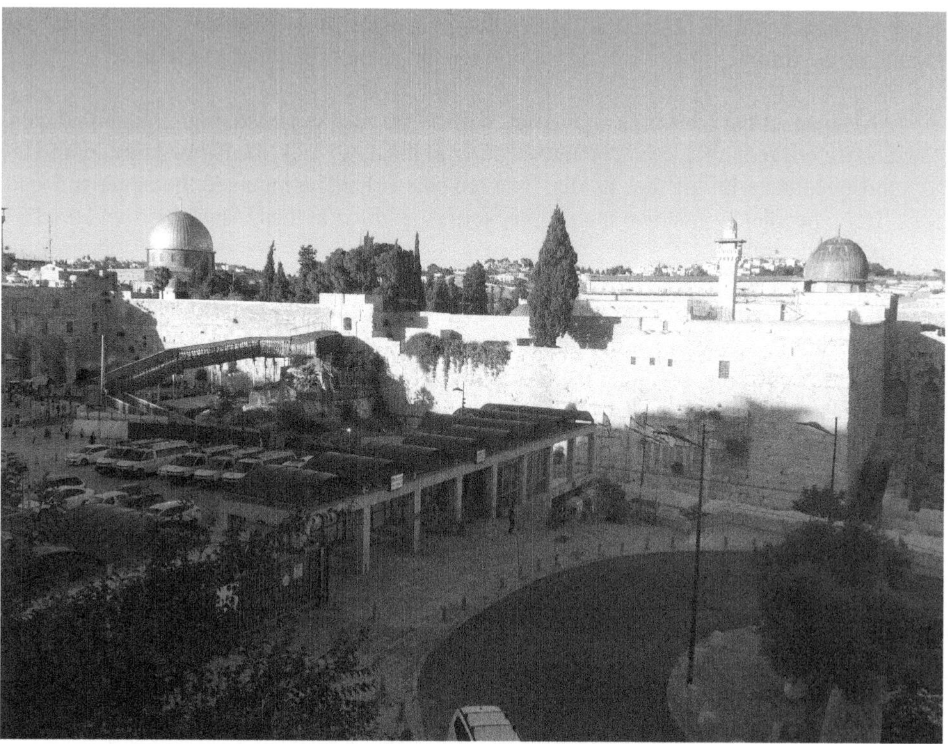

Figure 3.4 Jerusalem: view of the Temple Mount. On the left (behind the bridge giving access to the Temple square [*Ḥaram Sharīf*]) is the Western or Wailing Wall, as the only remaining part of the Second Jewish Temple; above that is the Dome of the Rock (covered with gold; before the mid-20th century it had always been covered in lead), originally built in 691; on the right can be seen a minaret and the lead dome of the al-Aqṣā ['The Farthest'] mosque, originally built in ca. 710

Source: Photo: Jo Van Steenbergen

different members and branches of the family. At the same time, the discord between Qays and Yaman groups in Syria resurfaced once more, and this factionalism may be read to have evolved over time again into a prominent matter of political tension and fierce competition. Finally, these growing internal pressures on central claims to authority allowed dissident voices in the many margins of Marwanid authority to be heard more loudly again. The novel argument that the Umayyad monarchs and their expanding courts were guiding the faithful away from the Quranic and prophetic path appeared especially forcefully in near-contemporary narratives about those dissident voices and their followers (even though in this context the particular framing of the Umayyads as un-Islamic by later narratives of the Umayyad successors' legitimate usurpation of their power should not be underestimated). In this volatile atmosphere, another social issue added substantially to these pressures: the situation of the so-called *mawali*. Members of non-Arabian Syrian, Egyptian, Iraqi, and other local communities who converted to Islam in increasing numbers in the course of the 7th and early 8th centuries had been able to participate politically, socially, economically, or culturally only if they linked themselves to one of the Arabian leaderships as their 'clients' (*mawali*, sg. *mawla*). Traditionally interpreted as resulting in social inequalities that became increasingly difficult to manage when *mawali* numbers grew, new understandings today rather stress the active participation of certain *mawali* in the Umayyad-Marwanid power constellation, even in very prominent positions of local or regional leadership. Nevertheless, the growing number of non-Arabian *mawali* participating in the formation and expansion of Umayyad-Marwanid authority certainly created not just new opportunities, but also new challenges for its traditional, Arabian leaderships, and this gradual transformation was never a straightforward process to manage for the Umayyad-Marwanid rulers and their growing numbers of representatives.

Initially, ʿAbd al-Malik's fourth son and successor, Hisham (r. 724–743), succeeded with his Syrian court and entourage in keeping at bay these old controversies and new fault lines, and thus in maintaining stability, coherence, and order for most of his reign of almost two decades. The price they—often literally—had to pay to preserve the support of the Syrian armies, to counter attacks in the northeast and in the Caucasus from various Inner-Asian Turkish peoples, and to deal with a major uprising of Amazigh—or Berber—leaderships in North Africa proved particularly high. When Hisham's cousin and successor Walid ibn Yazid (743–744) loosened his grip during his short period of reign, these latent tensions resurfaced immediately, with devastating effects for Umayyad-Marwanid control over the different regions and groups of the empire. The murder of this Walid in his palace near Palmyra in the Syrian Desert unleashed discord within the ruling family as well. When Marwan ibn Muhammad ibn Marwan (r. 744–750), an uncle of the competing offspring of ʿAbd al-Malik and an experienced Umayyad power holder in the frontier regions of Armenia and Azerbaijan, attempted to restore order in Syria with the help of local Qays leaders, this turned out to be only partially possible. Eventually, by the end of the 740s, Marwan proved incapable of dealing with an unusual combination of various anti-Marwanid groups in Syria, Iraq, and Khurasan, and the Umayyad-Marwanid leadership crumbled amidst violence. In January 750, Marwan and his Syrian armies were defeated in the Battle of the Great Zab in northern Iraq. A subsequent attempt to create a new power base in Egypt was ineffective, and eventually Marwan perished, together with a handful of his supporters, in a new confrontation near the Egyptian village of Busir, in the Nile Valley. This meant the definitive end of Umayyad-Marwanid leadership, at least in Islamic West-Asia.

Notes

1 See Marsham, "'God's Caliph' Revisited".
2 See especially Robinson, *'Abd al-Malik.*
3 From al-Jāhiẓ (781–869), *Kitāb al-Bayān wa l-Tabyīn* ['The Treatise of Clarity and Clarification']; as in the translation by Lewis, *Islam from the Prophet Muhammad to the Capture of Constantinople. Volume I: Politics and War*, 23–4.

Selected readings

(see next chapter)

4 Arabian expansions and Late Antique transformations (7th–8th centuries)

Introduction: *Ghazw*, *Futuh*, and Late Antique imperial formation

The enormous Afro-Eurasian empire over which the Umayyad-Marwanids could assert their sovereign authority in the early decades of the 8th century in no way resembled the local northwestern Arabian context in which Muhammad had been active a century earlier. The unprecedented territorial, social, and organizational changes that the Arabian leadership achieved in the 7th and early 8th centuries and that defined the future of these Afro-Eurasian territories and their inhabitants for centuries to come are the subjects of this chapter. It thus complements the preceding two chapters and adds to their narrow focus on successions of central Arabian leaderships a wider contemplation of the trans-regional reconfiguration of leadership networks and of the stabilization of the bonds and claims that tied them together.

The wider transformations that these leaderships brought about, and that they themselves also experienced, are often imagined as a violent process of conquest, which shows many parallels with the pre-Islamic tradition of tribal raids (*ghazw*). This is undeniably a relevant representation, not least because the many violent campaigns that brought about these changes are often identified in the narrative record of Arabic-Islamic memory in this way, as *ghazwat* or *maghazi*. The use of these related terms for pre-Islamic raids among tribal groups on the Arabian Peninsula, for the actions of the Prophet and his entourage against the Quraysh of Mecca and against other leaderships, and for the campaigns that his followers and successors after him organized across the Late Antique world is significant for the continuities in organization, aims, and results of these campaigns. At the same time, however, a new Arabic term, *futuh* (literally 'opening') appeared in Arabic-Islamic memory to express these territorial changes, as if to suggest that the Late Antique world was 'opened', or 'unlocked', for the network of Arabian leadership. *Futuh* suggests that there was much more at stake than simply the traditional violence and one-directionality of the tribal *ghazwat*. It hints at a much more complex whole of local, regional, and trans-regional changes that can be above all understood as a process of integration of new territories and local elites in a new political reality, with an enormous impact on both those territories and elites as well as on that new political reality itself. In other words, it alludes to a process of state and empire formation, which makes all those involved as well as the empire itself appear in a fundamentally new fashion.[1]

Whatever the case, the historical precondition for *futuh* is and remains of course the full set of *ghazwat* and violent campaigns that, ever since Muhammad's time in Medina, enabled the expansion of the networks of patriarchal leaders and their followers outside the traditional boundaries of the Arabian Peninsula and its Syrian extension. Traditionally, two phases are identified in the expansion of that Arabian leadership, closely connected to the wider changes to which *futuh* as a process of trans-regional political integration testifies. A first phase, which started with the *hijra* in 622 and continued until the mid-7th century, tends to be usefully framed in modern scholarship as the charismatic phase of the Arabian expansion. It involved an expansion that was mainly supported by the charismatic leadership of Muhammad, of Abu Bakr and ʿUmar after him, and of various Arabian leaders and their tribal manpower in Syria, Egypt, and Iraq. It also was an expansion that remained closely connected to the formation of a new political community around an equally charismatic imagination that—as suggested by aforementioned passages in the Quran and the 'Constitution of Medina'—connected the believers to each other by the 'struggle on God's path' against unbelieving others. It was finally not least also an expansion that, in the old *ghazw* tradition, consolidated itself by yielding new wealth, income, and economic possibilities for all campaigning groups—a socioeconomic reality that became painfully clear in the 650s when the slowing down of the expansion led to more competition for control over these new resources and income, and thus also to the 1st *fitna*. A second phase started after the ending of this 1st *fitna*, when this competition for socioeconomic control was forced into the tightening mold of the Syrian Umayyad leadership. This phase in the expansion, therefore, largely coincided with the reality of that Umayyad leadership and the process of patrimonial formation that the new Late Antique empire went through. Much more than before, it involved a systematically organized set of campaigns, executed by a coercive apparatus of power in full formation, driven by a trans-regional political order under Syrian Umayyad leadership, and, for these reasons, defined here as the patrimonial phase in the Arabian expansion and integration of the Late Antique world.

These two overlapping phases, the one mainly driven by charismatic and patriarchal authorities, the other by patrimonial authorities, will be considered here in their two related appearances in this period, the one territorial and violent, and the other organizational. First, the different moments in the rapid expansion from the Arabian Peninsula into and beyond the Late Antique world will be discussed to the limiting extent that the extant source material allows. Second, the parallel process of organizational integration and transformation of these territories and their diverse elites will be reconstructed, by presenting a handful of key examples and snapshots of this complex process of Arabian and then Islamic imperial formation.

1 Arabian expansions

1.1 The charismatic phase

Over the course of time, numerous propositions and scenarios have been formulated in modern historiography to explain the sudden historical reality and unrivalled success of the Late Antique scale-up of ancient Arabian leaderships. However, each of these propositions and scenarios is, and continues to be, primarily a hypothesis. Each of these hypotheses is, and continues to be, more or less convincing depending on the time spirit and the power of conviction or oratory talent of any of its 'believers' rather than by reference to old or new source material. Contemporary historical information about this expansion is after all particularly scarce, and the relatively rich later narratives continue to be especially difficult to interpret. The most coherent information can be found in the Arabic-Islamic literary heritage, where texts about violent campaigns (*maghazi*) and the expansion/integration (*futuh*) over time became a genre in its own right. However, just as in the case of the life of the Prophet and of his early community, many decades separate the earliest of these texts from these campaigns and expansion. They should, therefore, mostly be considered products of later social, political, and cultural realities, searching for justifications in hindsight that make sense of their own times and of how their own social and political order conforms to particular historical trajectories. Although these texts undoubtedly contain original and historically relevant material, the choices for that material, and the reconstruction of it in well-defined narrative wholes are determined by, and serve as, the social memory of later generations. In this process of the formation of a shared and meaningful imagination of these generations as one community, a lot of attention appears to have been attached to, amongst other things, recording the active participation in various campaigns of the Arabian ancestors of later prominent families. The emphasis in these historical reports, and in the social memory they mediated, therefore, was often on recording the names of participants rather than on reporting factual events. A telling example of this is the account of one of the most important battles of the Syrian campaign: while the participants on the Arabian side are named in detail, the course of the battle is reported in the vaguest terms, and it even remains unclear when exactly it took place.

> The battle of Ajnadayn ensued. In this battle, about 100,000 Greeks took part. . . . Against this army, the Muslims fought a violent battle, and Khālid ibn al-Walīd particularly distinguished himself. At last, by God's help, the enemies of God were routed and shattered into pieces, a great many being slaughtered. Those who suffered martyrdom on that day were ʿAbd Allāh ibn al-Zubayr ibn ʿAbd al-Muṭṭalib ibn Hāshim, ʿAmr ibn Saʿīd ibn al-Āsī ibn Umayya, his brother Abān ibn Saʿīd (according to the most authentic report. Others, however, claim that Abān died in the year 29), Ṭulayb ibn ʿUmayr ibn Wahb ibn ʿAbd ibn Kusay . . . and Salāma ibn Hishām ibn al-Mughīra.[2]

What is absolutely clear, in spite of this idiomatic nature of the mainly narrative Arabic source material and despite the paucity of other relevant sources, is the enormous historical impact of this charismatic phase. There can be no doubt that in the 630s and 640s two Late Antique empires became threatened to their very core, and that in the case of the Sasanian Empire this led to its complete annihilation in the 650s. Thus, in less than two decades, the centers of ancient Near Eastern civilizations, from the Egyptian Delta in the west across the Syrian plains and the Iraqi lowlands to the Iranian Plateau in the east, were overrun by men from the Arabian Peninsula and Syrian Desert, united under the banners of Arabian leadership and Quranic monotheism.

The origins of this quick and radical transformation of power relations in these ancient regions of Egypt, Syria, Iraq, and Iran clearly date back to the years in which the Prophet is believed to have been active in Medina. In particular, a first impetus was given, or at least a pattern of expectation seems to have been created for the new Arabian leadership, by the campaigns of the 620s, which are attributed to Muhammad and which targeted the Quraysh of Mecca and other Arabian leaderships of the Hejaz and, eventually, also beyond. During a subsequent episode of wielding violence from Medina, remembered in the later narratives of the early community's history as the 'Wars of Apostasy' (632–634), it is reported that Abu Bakr organized no less than a further eleven violent campaigns against these and other Arabian leaderships on the Peninsula. This followed some of these leaderships terminating their alliances with Medina upon Muhammad's demise, which was then later explained as an act of apostasy (*ridda*) (although the nature of religious conversion involved in these alliances with Muhammad remains an unresolved subject of debate). At the same time, this extensive coercive action from Medina revolved around the appearance of so-called 'false' prophets elsewhere on the Arabian Peninsula, among other tribal communities, keen to emulate, as it were, Muhammad's achievement. As this challenged the appeal and claims of Medina's leadership, a swift reaction was required. All of these violent campaigns were successful, yielding booty and new manpower and generating an unprecedented centrality and authority for Medina's leadership across the Arabian Peninsula.

When 'Umar assumed leadership in 634, it appears as if the success of these campaigns on the Arabian Peninsula generated a strong impetus to pursue further violent action and to acquire more booty and resources. The Arabian expansion into the Late Antique world of Romans and Persians can be explained, therefore, as an almost natural continuation of actions aimed at also integrating Arabian leaderships in, especially, the Syrian northern extension of the Peninsula, that is, in the unstable frontier areas with Late Antiquity's empires. The first wave of campaigns that thus snowballed out of the Arabian Peninsula and the Syrian desert continued unabated until the mid-650s and thereafter, with lesser intensity and territorial effects, into the 670s.

The first to be confronted with the armies of 'Umar outside the Arabian Peninsula were the Greek-Roman elites and troops in Syria. The exact chronology of confrontations and of victories and defeats remains unclear for lack of unambiguous source material. It is well established that several battles were waged with the Roman imperial armies between 634 and 637, among other places at Ajnadayn, in southern Palestine, and at the Yarmuk River, a tributary of the Jordan. It is also clear that the Romans were several times defeated and that as a consequence they kept retreating northwards. As a result, in this short period of only four years, Roman Syria's main ancient urban centers, such as Fihl (Pella), Damascus, Homs (Emessa), Qinnasrin (Chalcis), Antioch, and Aleppo, all fell to 'Umar's armies. Eventually, in 638, also Jerusalem in Palestine was taken. The enormous impact and symbolism of this final piece in the Arabian expansion into the historical region of Syria is reflected in the way in which this capture of Jerusalem is remembered in later narratives, which even suggest that 'Umar personally negotiated the surrender and then visited the city. In the early 10th century, one of the most important Arabic chronicles of early Islamic history reproduced the following version of the agreement that is claimed to have been concluded between 'Umar and the patriarch of Jerusalem at the occasion of the latter's surrender.

> In the name of God, the Merciful, the Compassionate. This is the assurance of safety (*amān*) which the servant of God, 'Umar, the Commander of the Believers (*'abd allāh 'Umar amīr al-mu'minīn*), has granted to the people of Jerusalem. He has given them an assurance of safety for themselves, for their property, for their churches and crosses, for the sick and the healthy of the city, and for all the rituals that belong to their religion. Their churches will not be inhabited by Muslims and they will not be destroyed. Neither they, nor the land on which they stand, nor their cross, nor their property will be damaged. They will not be forcibly converted. No Jew will live with them in Jerusalem.
>
> The people of Jerusalem must pay the poll tax (*jizya*) like the people of the [other] cities, and they must expel Romans and criminals. Those of the people of Jerusalem who want to leave with the Romans, take their property, and abandon their churches and their crosses, will be safe until they reach their place of safety. Those villagers (*ahl al-arḍ*) who were in Jerusalem before the killing of so-and-so may remain in the city if they wish, but they must pay the poll tax (*jizya*) like the people of Jerusalem. Those who wish may go with the Romans, and those who wish may return to their families. Nothing will be taken from them before their harvest is reaped.

> If they pay the poll tax (*jizya*) according to their obligations, then the contents of this letter are under the covenant of God, and are the responsibility of His Prophet, of the caliphs, and of the believers.[3]

It remains impossible to define to which extent precisely this later literary reproduction approaches the real text of the agreement, or if such an agreement ever was concluded, and even whether ʿUmar was at all personally involved. Nevertheless, a certain historical pattern that returns in all the stories about the Arabian expansion into Syria can clearly be distinguished here. This involves a pattern of violent threats and Roman incapacity, of negotiation, and of paying tribute and taxes to the new rulers in exchange for security and continuity. The same pattern can be found in the following version of the story about the conquest of Fihl:

> The inhabitants of Fihl took to the fortifications where they were besieged by the Muslims until they sought to surrender, agreeing to pay poll tax (*jizya*) on their heads and land tax (*kharāj*) on their lands. The Muslims promised them the security of life and property, agreeing not to demolish their walls. The contract was made by Abū ʿUbayda ibn al-Jarrāh, but according to others, by Shurahbīl ibn Ḥasana.[4]

The confrontation with the Sasanian Empire, and the expansion of Arabian leaderships into the regions of Iraq and then Iran, followed a similar pattern of violence, negotiation, and accommodation. Between 632 and 634, the so-called Wars of Apostasy are believed to have also directed a campaign to the frontier area with the rich and fertile lands of central Iraq, where local Christian Arabian groups and their settlements were thus integrated into Medina's leadership network. The Sasanian Empire itself was not targeted initially, but the standard narrative of this episode in the first phase of the Arabian expansion explains that the reconfiguration of Arabian power relationships in this area, however limited, did not remain unnoticed in Iraq. In 634, therefore, this is said to have led to a full-blown Sasanian military campaign. The subsequent confrontation, remembered as the Battle at the Bridge, with the famous Persian general Rustam and his heavily armed horsemen and elephants, is believed to have resulted in a major defeat for the local Arabian leadership. When the threat of the Sasanian great power continued to increase, the early community's narrative explains, new Arabian leaders and their followings, mainly from the Hejaz and Yemen, were sent under the general command of the famous Saʿd ibn Abi Waqqas (d. after 661), a close companion of the Prophet and a member of the Quraysh of Mecca. The subsequent build-up of tension led to an ultimate confrontation near the settlement of al-Qadisiyya on the Euphrates, where the Sasanian troops were unexpectedly and completely defeated and where many Sasanian leaders, including Rustam, perished. As is also the case for the many confrontations with Greek-Roman armies in Syria, there continue to circulate about this crucial battle in Iraq various heroic stories, which make any accurate reconstruction impossible and which even continue to hamper its exact dating (in 635, in 636, or—according to Armenian sources—in January 638). There is, however, no disagreement about the battle's outcome: Sasanian power over central Iraq disappeared rapidly, remnants of Sasanian resistance were hunted down and defeated or chased away—so that even the ancient Sasanian capital of Ctesiphon and its wider metropolis of al-Mada'in near the Tigris were captured—and local communities and elites quickly obtained guarantees for safety and protection in exchange for payments of tribute and taxes. A separate force, also sent by ʿUmar from Medina, is known to have succeeded almost simultaneously in achieving similarly successful results in southern Iraq. To establish some level of direct control over these rich and ancient lands of Tigris and

Euphrates and over their local elites, communities, and resources, two new regional centers of power were created. These were Kufa in central Iraq and Basra in southern Iraq, where the Arabian leaderships of ʿUmar's armies and their followers set up camp and established themselves as the region's new elites. After 638, these as well as new troops from the Arabian Peninsula advanced from Kufa and Basra further eastwards, across the Zagros mountains, and into the Iranian Plateau. There, the last Sasanian ruler Yazdagard III (r. 632–651) was pursued to the far eastern Sasanian province of Khurasan, where eventually he was murdered, and the dynasty came to its definitive end.

Finally, the Arabian expansion into Roman Egypt also seems to have followed a course of action that reflected the particular Egyptian situation. As may be gathered from later narrative reports, however, here too this particular course is remembered along the standard pattern of violence and local accommodation that also marked the Arabian expansion into Syria and Iraq. Arabian campaigns southwards after the expansion into Palestine appear to have benefited from longstanding tensions between Roman agents and local elites, the unexpected Arabian successes in Syria and varying Egyptian reactions to those successes, and possibly also earlier experiences of Arabian leaders in Egypt. After only three years of Arabian-Roman competition, these campaigns resulted in the Greek-Roman departure from Egypt and the Arabian leaderships of ʿUmar's armies and their followers setting up camp at a new Egyptian center, Fustat, located on a strategic locality between upper and lower Egypt. The main Arabian commander here was ʿAmr ibn al-ʿAs (d. 663), another famous Arabian leader, close companion of the Prophet, and prominent member of the Quraysh in Mecca. After a first successful campaign in 639 with a limited group of followers, extensive reinforcements are said to have been sent to him by ʿUmar from the Peninsula which, eventually, forced the Romans to abandon their province. This happened, among others, after a long siege of their fortified headquarters in Babylon-of-Egypt and a negotiated surrender of the Egyptian capital Alexandria. In September 642, ʿAmr reportedly entered Alexandria after the departure of the last of the Greek-Roman troops. By that time, he had established control over Egypt's main sites and local elites, allegedly again as a result of the successful application of the default practices of coercion and negotiation, guaranteeing local security and continuity in exchange for pledges of tribute and tax.

1.2 The patrimonial phase

After this first period of intense expansion from Medina and of victorious personal leadership by charismatic heroic figures such as ʿUmar, Saʿd ibn Abi Waqqas, ʿAmr ibn al-ʿAs, and Khalid ibn al-Walid, further campaigns and expeditions were organized from the new encampments of Fustat in Egypt and of Kufa and Basra in Iraq. These places served above all as central nodes in the expanding networks of Arabian leaderships that guaranteed some level of cohesion, integration, and control for these new elites amidst the diverse majorities of local communities with which they had to interact. The preservation and organization of the relatively sudden control over a vast territory and its enormous resources, in addition to its complex and very diverse socioeconomic and cultural realities, remained for a long time a great challenge. Both the cohesion of the expanding Arabian leadership networks and their local priority was therefore far from self-evident in the middle of the 7th century. In addition, in the unstable and turbulent context of the 7th century, where Roman and Sasanian power in some of these regions had been waxing and waning for decades, this new social and political order was all but considered a more permanent reality. A massive migration of Arabian formations and their leaders to Syria, Egypt, and Iraq filled the vacuum left by the disappearance there of the Greek-Roman and Sasanian political and military elites. On the densely populated canvasses of Egypt, Syria, and Iraq, however, these new Arabian leaderships represented no more than expanding spots of minority groups. Even though these quickly transformed into regional hotspots claiming centrality in many local and regional resource flows, their Arabian leaderships always had to work with majorities of local, mainly Christian, social elites, experts, and communities that had their own interests and assets to pursue.

From the new regional centers of Fustat in Egypt and of Kufa and Basra in Iraq, further campaigns and expeditions continued to be organized, driving with ups and downs the Arabian expansion ever further east- and westwards. In hindsight, as the narrative record suggests, the strategies employed on these campaigns and expeditions continued to aim at collecting booty and tribute and at participating in new forms of accommodation and local order that gradually pushed out for good, or at least marginalized, Greek-Roman, Sasanian, and other trans-regional elites. As a result, in the wake of these ongoing campaigns and expeditions, new spatial concentrations of leaderships, men, and resource flows continued to appear in the North African and Iberian west, in the Armenian and Azerbaijani north, and in and beyond the Iranian east, all generating and facilitating in their wake further migrations from the Arabian Peninsula. Between 651 and 671, different groups of Arabian leaders and tens of thousands of their followers are reported to have moved east from Iraq, setting up camp near the ancient urban settlement of Marv in the distant region of Sasanian Khurasan, which soon transformed into a new base for expanding control over the region and for campaigning further eastward. At about 670, Qayrawan was similarly set up as a new regional base in Roman Ifriqiya for further expansion westwards.

In this process of regional competition, local accommodation, and Arabian expansion from regional centers such as Fustat, Kufa, and Basra, and then also from places such as Marv in Khurasan or Shiraz in the southern Iranian region of Fars, or Qayrawan in today's Tunisia, coercive force and campaigning certainly continued to play an important role. In North Africa in particular, this further expansion is recorded to have happened in rather violent circumstances that were not easily pacified, involving the massive capture and enslavement of members of local Amazigh—or Berber—communities and the latter's use as additional manpower in campaigns further west. Some of these enslaved ones, however, were empowered by becoming successful commanders of expeditionary forces in their own right. The strategies that were employed on these campaigns and expeditions indeed appear to have further adapted to the rapidly changing realities, and to have been adapted by the process of imperial formation that marked Umayyad-Marwanid rule. As the years went on and the reality of Arabian leadership in, and migration to, these regions became ever more consolidated, the initial swift pace of endless campaigning dropped to a more regulated pattern of annual expeditions. In Roman North Africa and then on the Visigothic Iberian Peninsula, in Roman Asia Minor, in Khurasan and southern Iran, and then further east in the regions of Transoxania and Sind, ensuring regular flows of income in the form of booty and tribute remained for a long time more important than subjecting and integrating new local elites and territories. At the same time, however, and despite occasional setbacks, the recurring success of these regular plundering expeditions, the either violently or non-violently enforced transformations of previously minimal tribute agreements to more elaborate political relations with local elites, and the subsequent shift of campaign horizons further westwards and eastwards appear to have had no less of an impact. As is well attested in a great variety of sources, they resulted from the second half of the 7th century until the mid-8th century in the steady continuation of this nearly natural pattern of campaigning and raiding under Arabian and—increasingly also—other integrated leaderships, moving eventually into the heart of the 'Frankish' world in the west, into the Indus Valley in the east, and up to the Talas River in Inner Asia.

Although this appears as anything but a predestined, smooth, or clearly planned process of violent expansion, trans-regional empowerment and Arabian migration in westward and eastward directions, the fact is that over time, the organization of these campaigns assumed an increasingly organized form. Participants in the annual campaigns were each time recruited in the winter and spring seasons among the inhabitants of the regional centers. These troops, led by prominent leaders and commanders, departed every year at the beginning of the summer to return laden with spoils and tribute at the end of the season. Consisting of a variety of riches and commodities, including prisoners and slaves, these resources were subsequently divided among the participants in accordance with the role they had played in the campaigning and the social status they held. Yohannan bar Penkaya, a contemporary Nestorian monk who wrote a Christian history of the world, uniquely hints at how the structuration of these campaigns and expeditions was perceived in his community in northern Iraq:

> Their robber bands went annually to distant parts and to the islands, bringing back captives from all the peoples under the heavens. Of each person they required only tribute, allowing him to remain in whatever faith he wished.[5]

Especially after the end of the second *fitna* in the 690s, under the impetus of the Umayyad-Marwanid ruler ʿAbd al-Malik and the restoration of Syrian Arabian authority, the intensity of these regular campaigns increased again, with more direct territorial expansions as a consequence. However, here as well, it proves a difficult, if not impossible, task for modern historians to reconstruct the exact course of this second, patrimonial wave of expansion from the extant, mostly narrative and in hindsight constructed, source material. The broad lines of this course can, however, be clearly sketched, if only because of the gigantic territorial, socio-political, economic, and ultimately also cultural transformations that followed from these many campaigns.

In the west, the Umayyad-Marwanid impetus caused troops to cross the Strait of Gibraltar in 711 and to overrun the Visigothic kingdom on the Iberian Peninsula within a time span of only a few years. Strikingly, according to the dominant historical account, these campaigns were first led by Tariq ibn Ziyad, a commander of Amazigh, or Berber, descent who likely ended up in Umayyad-Marwanid service as a captive and a slave and then earned his manumission and promotion by military merit. His successful campaigns with several thousand Amazigh followers appear to have stimulated the Umayyad-Marwanid regional ruler in North Africa, the Arabian leader Musa ibn Nusayr (d. *c.* 716), to follow suit and move to Visigothic Iberia with a second, larger force of mainly Arabic-speaking origins. Both armies are then recorded to have crisscrossed the entire peninsula, defeated the Visigothic elites and ended their kingdom, and established Umayyad-Marwanid authority over most of Iberia, with the exception of a small area in the northwest. This marked the beginning of a centuries-long Arabian, Amazigh, and especially Muslim dominant presence in what came to be known in Arabic as al-Andalus. Eventually, during the greater part of the 8th century, Arabian and Amazigh leaders continued to advance further north of the Pyrenees, establishing local control and engaging especially in more campaigns. On many occasions, these campaigns brought them in confrontation with the leaders of Merovingian Francia, especially Charles Martel (d. 741) and his Carolingian successors. One of the most heroic and significant—according to later Latin generations at least—of these confrontations occurred in 732 between Tours and Poitiers. The latter, however, did not really affect the very fluid course of events here, nor did it prevent further haphazard campaigning and expansion from North Africa and the Iberian Peninsula over the next century towards Sicily, Sardinia, the Balearic Islands, the coastal towns and regions of the Italian peninsula, and various Trans-alpine areas.

In the northeast, between 705 and 715, similar campaigns appear to have departed from Marv and eventually crossed over the northeast boundary of Khurasan—the Oxus River—to the region of Transoxania, looking for new possibilities to collect booty and tribute. As a result of this, various tribute arrangements are reported to having been enforced from the populations of ancient urban crossroads on the so-called Silk Routes, such as Bukhara and Samarqand, and of adjacent prosperous regions, such as the Khwarazm oasis in the Oxus delta to the west and the Fergana valley to Transoxania's east. While many local elites in these regions were very gradually integrated more directly into the relationships of power and authority that emanated from Marv, Iraq, and Syria, Arabian and other leaders continued to campaign ever further eastwards, clashing on regular occasions (and with mixed results) with Turkic-speaking peoples of Inner-Asian origins and eventually even getting involved in a local conflict that, in 751 in the famous Battle of the Talas River, confronted them with the westward expansion of the Chinese Tang Dynasty (618–907). Although few details are known about this battle, the Tang army is known to have been routed, while Arabian-Islamic campaigning appears never to have continued beyond this easternmost point, separated by more than 7,000 kilometers from similar campaigning on the Atlantic coasts.

In the Iranian southeast, a similar pattern of regular violence and accommodation appears to have occurred in the first decades of the 8th century. In these regions of Fars, Kirman, and Makran, with their mountain ranges, fertile plains, sea ports, and deserts, Arabian and other leaders advanced with mixed successes further eastwards from new regional centers, such as Shiraz in Fars, eventually ending up in the region of Sind (today in Pakistan) and the Indus River. This pattern re-occurs, with similar ups and downs, in the regions of Armenia and Azerbaijan, and in the Caucasus, where another Turkic-speaking formation from the Inner-Asian north proved a tough foe. In Roman Asia Minor, finally, successful Umayyad-Marwanid expeditions and campaigns (including maritime ones), regularly led by members of the Marwanid clan itself, culminated in the period 716–718 in no less than a second siege of the Roman capital of Constantinople. Only with the help of another tribal formation on the march, the Bulgarians, did the Greek Romans succeed in averting this threat to the heart of the ancient empire and maintaining control over most of Asia Minor.

2 Late Antique transformations

The historical transformation of the *umma* that had first appeared on the Arabian Peninsula around Muhammad and the Quranic revelation, from trans-regional networks of Arabian leaderships to an empire of Late Antique ambition, organization, and magnitude, can be explained with a classic, yet particular, pattern of leadership formation. Irrespective of the historiographical reservation that needs to be made regarding what the available source material can or cannot reveal, this transformation lends itself very well to be understood as a structuring of sociopolitical relations along the line of the Weberian ideal types of charismatic, patriarchal, and patrimonial authority. The central issue is certainly the development of Islamic monotheism, from an inclusive and open call for equality in submission to the one and only God and in the active struggle against His enemies, to the formation of an ever more clearly defined and circumscribed theocratic social order, which was closely tied up with the questions of social identity and political authority that became ever more pressing issues in the Islamic Late Antique empire of the 8th century. This social and cultural transformation, however, still mainly only concerned the organization and nature of Arabian leadership, materializing especially in periods remembered as *fitna* in various sweeping developments in that leadership. Under the impulse of the enormous expansion and the accompanying local integration of a large variety of social groups, their leaders, and their expectations and habits, the networks of Arabian patriarchal leadership, more or less held together by charismatic qualities, personal relations, and *ashraf* traditions across ever-expanding distances, transformed into a more structured cohesive whole characteristic for a Late Antique patrimonial state apparatus, organized around a sovereign dynasty and its means of centralizing power and increasingly populated by numerous old and new groups of military and administrative specialists.

2.1 The charismatic phase

According to the prophetic narrative, in 622 Muhammad started organizing his *umma* as a kind of supra-tribal community of Meccan emigrants (*muhajirun*, 'those who undertook a *hijra*') and Medinan supporters (*ansar*, 'the helpers') closing ranks around his charismatic message and successful campaigning. As suggested before, this is also the image that appears from the earliest known sources for this particular aspect of that narrative: the Quranic text itself, the so-called 'Constitution of Medina' as preserved in later biographies, and non-Arabo-Muslim historical accounts from the mid-7th century.

The historical image that appears from the handful of explicit references to Muhammad in the Medinan verses in the Quran is that of a new leader sent by the one God ("a messenger" [Quran Surah (chapter) 3, verse 144], "God's messenger and the seal of the prophets" [33, 40], "the messenger of God" [48, 29]) who manages to unite his followers around the message that was revealed to him ("those who believe, and do righteous deeds and believe in what has been sent down upon Muhammad" [47, 2]) and to close their ranks against those who do not believe in it ("and those who are with him are forceful against the disbelievers, yet merciful among themselves" [48, 29]). In a related fashion, the so-called 'Constitution of Medina' represents a similar image of divinely ordained leadership and novel community formation. These agreements between *muhajirun* and *ansar*, preserved in a particular wording and a style that have been suggested to attest to this version's very early origins, include the following telling lines:

> A believer shall not take as an ally the freedman of another Muslim against him.
> The God-fearing believers shall be against the rebellious or him who seeks to spread injustice, or sin or enmity, or corruption between believers; the hand of every man shall be against him even if he be a son of one of them.
> A believer shall not shy a believer for the sake of an unbeliever, nor shall he aid an unbeliever against a believer.
> God's protection is one, the least of them may give protection to a stranger on their behalf. Believers are friends one to the other to the exclusion of outsiders.
> To the Jew who follows us belong help and equality. He shall not be wronged nor shall his enemies be aided.
> The peace of the believers is indivisible. No separate peace shall be made when believers are fighting in the way of God.
> If any dispute or controversy likely to cause trouble should arise it must be referred to God and to Muhammad, the messenger of God. God accepts what is nearest to piety and goodness in this document.[6]

The image that comes forth from these specific textual moments in the Quran and in the prophetic biography is one of a new community that transcends tribal fault lines, closes ranks around the primacy of the one God and the leadership of His messenger Muhammad, and—conforming with ancient Arabian practices—turns collectively against whomever threatens the integrity of this new supra-tribal community. This also resonates with how some of the earliest extant non-Arabian textual references, stemming from the 660s and the 680s, represent the origins and organization of the movement that, by that time, had swept across and transformed the Late Antique world. An untitled history of Armenia explains that Muhammad had preached to his Arabian followers—identified here with monotheist identifiers such as "Hagarenes" and "Ishmaelites"—to "go and take possession of your country which God gave to your father Abraham, and none will be able to resist you in battle, for God is with you", and that "he legislated for them not to eat carrion, not to drink wine, not to speak falsely and not to commit fornication".[7] The aforementioned Nestorian monk Johannes bar Penkaye suggests in his brief Syrian world history that the Arabian followers of Muhammad did not just have "a special commandment from God concerning our monastic station, that they should hold it in honor", but also that "they kept to the tradition of Muhammad . . . to such an extent that they inflicted the death penalty on anyone who was seen to act brazenly against his laws".[8]

In this diverse movement of Arabian believers, organized around Muhammad's charisma and a millenarian type of violence and composed of Medinan leaderships and their followers and Meccan outsiders and renegades, the aforementioned new qualities of precedence in conversion to Muhammad's message (*sabiqa*) and closeness to his person (*sahaba*) appear to have substantially contributed to the new community's social organization and, especially, to the differentiation of its leadership. The prophetic narrative also describes, however, how towards the end of the 620s, as a consequence of Muhammad's successful violent action and campaigning, other leaderships from the Hejaz started joining the new community. These famously included various Meccan *ashraf*, including prominent Quraysh members such as from the Banu ʿAbd Shams' Umayya clan (including the later Umayyad leader Muʿawiya ibn Abi Sufyan). Muhammad is mainly remembered as having pursued a pragmatic policy with respect to the integration of their traditional leadership in the particular Medinan context, his charisma proving capable of quelling any tensions that may have arisen from this combination of old and new leadership practices. In the longer term, however, when in the decades following 632 the charisma of Muhammad's leadership increasingly faded into abstraction, this divergence in the community's claims to legitimate authority between companions (*ashab*) and *ashraf* appeared ever stronger, and it would continue to fuel competition to rightfully step into his footsteps for a long time, not least in the highly disruptive form of *fitna*. For many other leaderships on the Arabian Peninsula, who joined Muhammad only after 630, a more traditional, functional type of relationship is remembered as having been preferred. They are therefore remembered as expressing their partnership in Medina-centered networks mainly by paying a tribute (*sadaqa*), collected at regular intervals by a representative of Muhammad.

When in 634, after the so-called Wars of Apostasy, the equally charismatic personality of ʿUmar took over leadership of Muhammad's expanding community, the early community's narrative explains that he tried to consolidate Medina's newly won, or re-won, Arabian priority by subordinating traditional leadership practices more forcefully to the new social order of the community of believers. Apparently, he was successful in maintaining this to some extent at least, but the narrative also has to concede that—as had been the case with Muhammad—reality eventually obliged ʿUmar to simultaneously pursue a pragmatic policy and to mediate between leadership networks that continued to be rather differently composed. This was obviously due to the Arabian expansion quickly progressing towards Late Antique Syria, Iraq, and Egypt, which created an urgent need for Arabian manpower and eventually forced ʿUmar to appeal to the assistance and resources of *ashraf* who had only recently and violently been integrated into the networks of power that were organized around Medina's centrality. Therefore, the divergence and competition between leadership practices of *ashab* and *ashraf* remained, and even deepened further. Only the recent memory of Muhammad's achievement and the success of the Arabian expansion seems to have kept at bay any serious tension that may have resulted from this ambiguity, as must have done the equally forceful charismatic personality that is generally ascribed to ʿUmar. As suggested above, it is at least very telling for his success to continue to bind different groups and communities to his authority amidst rapidly changing circumstances—and very suggestive of contemporary perceptions of that charismatic appeal and its success to overcome Romans and Persians—that ʿUmar is very often also referred to, including already in 7th-century Arabian poetry, in messianic terms as al-Faruq ('the Redeemer').[9]

This successful charismatic nature of ʿUmar's authority is also evidenced by an inscription on a rock in the north of the Hejaz, which is believed to contain the earliest datable reference to his leadership (see Figure 2.4). This inscription of three brief lines consists of the following passing statement:

> In the name of God
> I, Zuhayr, wrote [this] at the time ʿUmar died, year four
> And twenty.[10]

In spite of all political, territorial, and socioeconomic changes that must have been abundantly clear even at the time of ʿUmar's passing, in the Islamic year 24 (644 CE), ʿUmar's leadership continues to appear here in the first place as a very personal and charismatic one that could easily do without any title or other claim to legitimate leadership. At the same time, the new calendar that was used in this public text in a very self-evident way—even though only twenty-four years old at this moment—and its nearly ritual invocation 'in the name of God' simultaneously indicate that, at least in the Hejaz, the new community of believers and its basic organization around monotheism and around a shared sense of living in a new monotheist era was quickly establishing itself as referential, if not normative.

In the wake of the expansion of ʿUmar's networks, this increasingly organized and referential appearance of his leadership and of the community of believers also began to manifest itself in certain parallel practices of rule that the early narratives describe. In spite of the increasing physical distance that separated Arabian leaders and their raiding forces, ʿUmar and Medina appear to have maintained a remarkable degree of centrality, or at least some hierarchical notions of trans-regional priority and regional control. As mentioned above, instrumental in this were the new and strategically located regional centers of Arabian power that appear to have emerged from the encampments of ʿUmar's leaders and from the practice of keeping their followers, supporters, and anyone who joined them from Arabia concentrated in them. Most famous among these centers—referred to as *misr* (pl. *amsar*)—were Kufa in central Iraq, Basra in southern Iraq, and Fustat in Egypt. The long tradition of a strong presence of Arabic-speaking tribal groups in Syria appears to have forestalled any similar concentration of Arabian power in that region, even though depopulated quarters in formerly Roman urban centers are also thought to have served similar purposes, so that the region of Damascus quickly emerged with a similar centrality in the Syrian region.

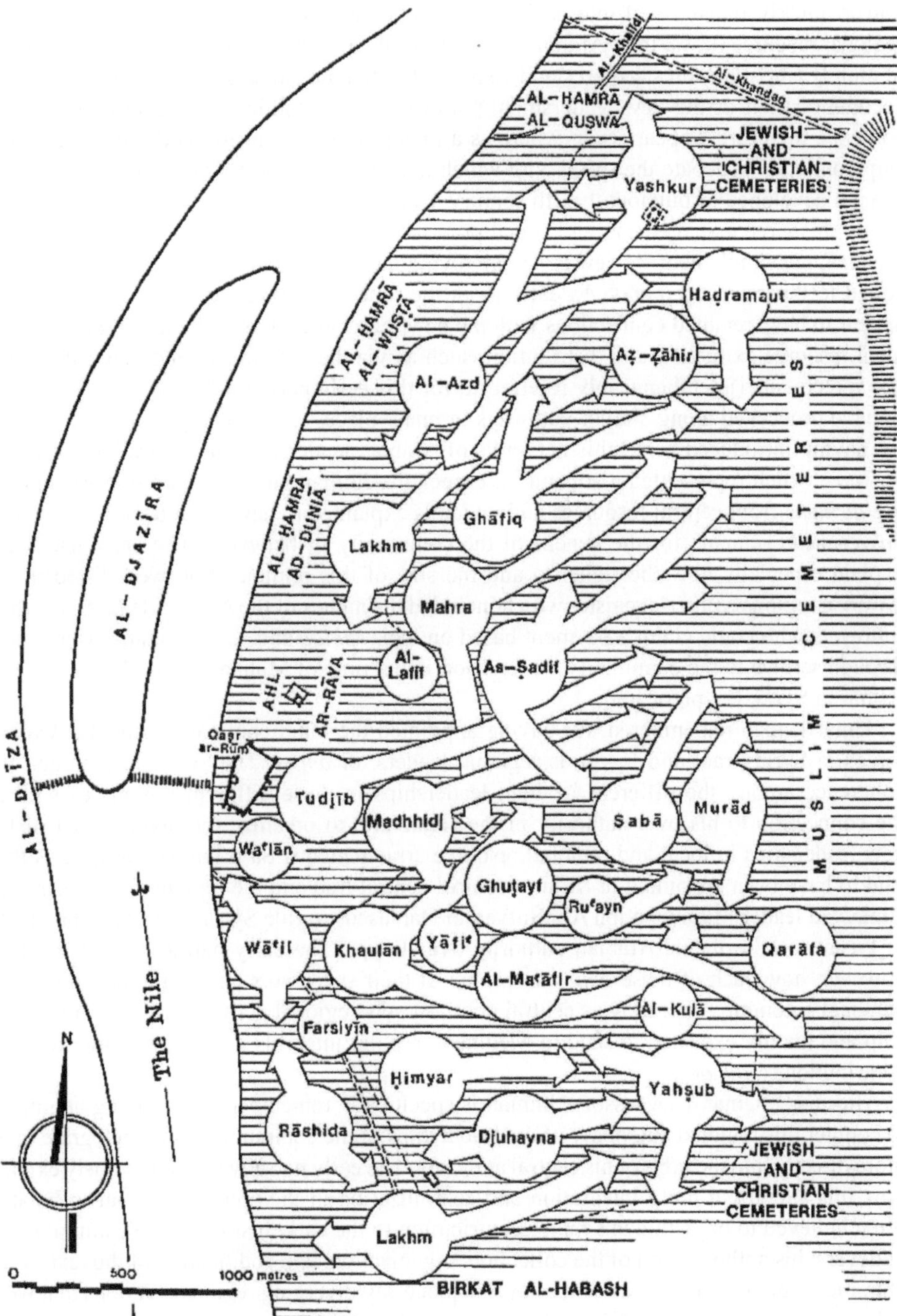

Figure 4.1 Reconstruction of the ground plan of the Egyptian center (*miṣr*) al-Fustat, with identification of the different Arabian leaderships and their camping sites

Source: From W.B. Kubiak, *Al-Fustat: Its Foundation and Early Urban Development* [Cairo: The American University in Cairo Press, 1987], p. 176, 'Plan 4. Ethnic Groups and Multi-Tribal Quarters'

As explained, even though each of these new nodal points in the networks of Arabian power quickly transformed into regional hotspots claiming centrality in many local and regional resource flows, their Arabian leaderships always had to work with local majorities of mainly Christian elites, experts, and communities that had their own assets to pursue. The accommodation of the new leaderships' political and economic interests to diverse local contexts, therefore, appears everywhere as a major issue of concern, and modern scholarship continues to debate the speed with which this process of organizational continuity and change developed throughout the 7th century. Everywhere, local arrangements of landownership, resource management, and social order are generally believed to have remained in practice, but simultaneously new layers involving the new leaderships and their agents were added to those arrangements. As early as in the time of ʿUmar, these new layers already appear to have retained connections with the new regional centers and with Medina, so that local resource extraction and distribution, such as via the aforementioned new tribute and tax agreements (interchangeably referred to for this early period as *kharaj* or *jizya*), seem to have proceeded along similar pathways in many places. In particular, ʿUmar is credited for having introduced across his networks of Arabian leaderships the centralizing practice of *ʿataʾ*, which represented a stipend in, especially, Roman golden *dinar*s or Sasanian silver *dirhams* from central resources and which is explained to have been awarded based on proven achievements for the benefit of the community of believers. The early narratives explain especially how the rights to and the size of this remuneration were listed in the *diwan*, a regional center's register which included the names of the Arabian leaders and their followers who could claim a payment based on their *sabiqa* and *sahaba* status, as acquired through service to the community's expansion in the time of Muhammad in the Hejaz or of ʿUmar in Syria, Egypt, or Iraq.

ʿUmar is also remembered, for having appointed the main commanders of the Arabian forces in Syria, Iraq, and Egypt as regional leaders, or *amir*s. They were to maintain the coherence among the different Arabian leaderships in these different regions as well as the connection to his own authority in the Hejaz and to organize the involvement of the new leaderships in local and regional resource arrangements. Saʿd ibn Abi Waqqas is thus said to have been appointed in Kufa to control central Iraq and the regions further east, the Umayyad leader Muʿawiya ibn Abi Sufyan in Damascus to rule Syria, and ʿAmr ibn al-ʿAs in Fustat to consolidate Arabian authority over Egypt. The early narratives also explain, however, how each of these *amir*s and some of their successors enjoyed a high degree of personal autonomy, operating as central nodes in new regional networks of Arabian leadership and mainly expected to send to Medina at regular intervals mostly symbolic tributary contributions (*sadaqa*).

After 644, ʿUmar's successor ʿUthman is specifically remembered for having attempted to counter this regional autonomy of the leaderships of the community and to integrate them more directly into the orbit of his central authority. The early narratives also famously explain how this attempt at more integration and centralization in the 650s played out in what is often believed to be ʿUthman's major contribution to the early history of the community of believers: his authorization of the collection, organization, and codification of the text of the Quranic revelation to Muhammad, so as to replace any diverging regional versions that were believed to be circulating. Given that the Quranic text appears—also from its extremely rich material record, with extant manuscript specimens that have been dated to this very early period—as extremely stable from the middle of the 7th century onwards, this undoubtedly suggests the reality of this mid-7th-century change in the ties that connected elites to Medina. At least it supports the impression that at that time, with the expansion reaching a challenging stretch and slowing down, an urgency was felt to replace extant centrifugal relationships of expansion with more centripetal ones of integration and centralization, if only to secure any reality of a community of believers and its monotheist cause. In ʿUthman's case, as the traditional narrative goes, his attempt to achieve this by prioritizing his personal network of followers and supporters, many of whom were close relatives, members of his Meccan Umayyad clan, and *ashraf*, backfired, and actually caused the dichotomy between new and old leadership practices to resurface in the format of violent competition, his murder, and, in its wake, the 1st *fitna*. However, just as the Quranic text proved sufficiently stable to maintain itself through this episode of the disintegration of Arabian charisma, so clearly had the notions of a monotheist community of believers and its trans-regional authority by then acquired the qualities necessary to maintain themselves and to eventually also be legitimately claimed by more traditional networks of Arabian leadership of Meccan origins.

2.2 The patrimonial phase

The local, regional and trans-regional leadership arrangements of the charismatic phase resurfaced from the 660s onwards, in ever more organized and centripetal dynamics, around Umayyad leadership, its center of power and resources in the region of Damascus, and its close alliance with the different Syrian *ashraf*. The Umayyad-Sufyanid leader Muʿawiya (r. 661–680) is remembered for having based his authority especially on his personal relations with these *ashraf*, also by integrating them more strongly through marriage relationships. But he also appears as coupling this with the further elaboration of a more specific apparatus of power, partly remolded from Greek-Roman and Persian precedents and partly emerging from the practical and discursive needs of the new leadership arrangements. This continued to manifest itself in the format of *amir*s, appointed to mediate between the Umayyad center and the regional Arabian leaderships, but now apparently chosen and sent out primarily from the ranks of *ashraf* that were closely related to Muʿawiya's entourage. As the aforementioned regular campaigns against especially Greek-Roman assets—including in the 670s Constantinople itself—suggest, Muʿawiya's trans-regional leadership must have been much more than a simple copy on a grander scale of traditional Arabian leadership practices. The mobilization of people and resources that such ambitious operations presuppose indicate in any case that he managed to develop more and more structured political and socioeconomic power relations outside of the patriarchal networks of Arabian leaders, often incorporating and building on existing local practices. This elaboration of a specific centralizing apparatus of power also emerges from how remaining traces of local administrative practices increasingly acquire their own coherent Arabic and Islamic forms. In the handful of inscriptions on coins and on papyrus documents that have been preserved from the time of Muʿawiya's reign, there appear for the first time datable references—in Middle-Persian (*pahlavi*), Greek, or Arabic—to the consistent use of well-known titles—'servant of God' (*ʿabd Allah*) and 'commander of the believers' (*amir al-muʾminin*)—to qualify Muʿawiya's name. These all represent conscious claims to legitimate and sovereign authority and the active participation—from Egypt's Nile delta to the Iranian highlands—in a particular, coherent, and monotheist discourse of theocratic power. References to the more cohesive practical organization of power appear explicitly for the first time as well, with Muʿawiya's leadership being represented as relating in parallel ways to diverse sets of agents and public works across the full territorial extent of his authority. A good example of this is the following Arabic inscription from his reign, which was left in the vicinity of Medina in the Hejaz and which combines Quranic discourse and Muʿawiya's claims to monotheist sovereignty with the public expression of a chain of personal authority and agency that strongly connects this locality in the Hejaz to the Umayyad-Sufyanid center in Syria:

> In the name of God the Merciful the Compassionate
> This dam is on behalf of the servant of God (*ʿabd Allāh*)
> Muʿawiya, commander of the believers (*amīr al-muʾminīn*).
> O God, bless him for it, Lord
> of the heavens and the earth.
> The one who built it was Abū Raddād, client (*mawlā*)
> of ʿAbd Allāh ibn ʿAbbās, by the power
> and strength of God,
> and it was overseen by Kathīr ibn al-
> Ṣalt and Abū Mūsa.[11]

Finally, the memory to this day of Muʿawiya's role as secretary to the Prophet, after the fall of Mecca in 630, and as an important figure in the editing history of the Quranic text itself support this impression that Muʿawiya's trans-regional leadership from Syria was not only effective, successful, and stable, but also of a growing complexity and layering, which included a powerful religious dimension.

This elaboration and organization of Umayyad authority and control in the format of a trans-regional patrimonial apparatus of power was furthered after the second *fitna*, from the reign of the Marwanid ruler ʿAbd al-Malik in the 690s onwards. Arabian leadership arrangements and local chains of authority, agency, and resources were further strengthened and expanded, and they circulated in increasingly coherent ways around Umayyad-Marwanid Syria. This included the emergence not just of administrative and courtly practices and experts, but also of a standing body of military commanders and their troops in Syria, Iraq, Egypt, and beyond, recruited from Syria's *ashraf* and their supporters, but also from the growing number of *mawali*, the diverse local groups of non-Arabian converts among the Arabian leaderships' followers. Furthermore, this included the elaboration and organization—not least in the interaction between Arabian and non-Arabian converts, and between them and other Late Antique monotheists—of monotheist discourse in claims to legitimate authority, in the pursuit of coherence and cohesion across the unprecedented expanse of Arabian, and—increasingly also—non-Arabian leadership networks in east and west, and in the search for knowledge about what it meant to be a Muslim monotheist.

In fact, in this widening process of patrimonial consolidation, the community of believers acquired its own distinct identity not just as a new Late Antique political and social order, but also as a specific monotheist movement. In the course of the second *fitna* between Syrian Umayyads and *ashraf*, Iraqi supporters of ʿAli's descendants and, especially, Meccan Zubayrids, the need arose to counter powerful appeals to *sabiqa* and *sahaba* that informed the claims to authority of the latter two groups. Simultaneously, re-intensification of the expansion in east and west and mounting competition with the Greek-Roman emperor Justinian II (r. 685–695, 705–711) contributed to this need to not just effectively organize recently won Umayyad-Marwanid power, but also make a strong case for its specialty and entitlement beyond the frameworks of 7th-century Arabian leadership. In this context of competing claims to authority and sovereignty, a notable uniformization and centralization of practices and discourses of power took place, which left clear traces in the full variety of extant documentary and other sources. As a result, Greek, Coptic, and Middle Persian were gradually marginalized in the remaining specimens of Umayyad-Marwanid administrative and political practice (tax receipts and other documents on papyrus, seals, coins, milestones, and other types of epigraphy), and the tradition of bi-lingual Arabic-Greek public texts and documents seemed to peter out. Arabic, which appears to have been used up to that point in the more specific contexts of an emergent court culture in Umayyad Syria and of that bilingual tradition that connected Arabian leadership arrangements to various local practices in east and west, clearly acquired a new status as the sole language of imperial communication and participation. Modern scholarship connects this to more explicit and self-conscious Umayyad-Marwanid formulations of political authority in distinctly monotheist and Islamic terms, with Muhammad's exemplary leadership, the Quranic text, and the community of non-Christian and non-Jewish Islamic monotheists becoming central poles for Umayyad-Marwanid claims to sovereignty. This manifested itself especially in an unprecedented set of articulations of Umayyad authority, remaining specimens of which have continued to refer ever since to those claims, their coherent and programmatic nature, and the Syrian patrimonial apparatus that must have been created for these complex forms of political communication to be realized.

As mentioned before, especially ʿAbd al-Malik and his entourage emerge from these specimens as great and successful innovators, experimenting with articulations of Umayyad sovereignty and Islamic identity on coins and in monument construction alike. This becomes apparent from the so-called 'Standing Caliph' gold and silver coins, minted in Syria between 694 and 697 and mostly thought to represent—for the first and only time in the young community's history—the ruler himself on the front or back. It also transpires from the self-references to ʿAbd al-Malik not just as 'God's servant' (*ʿabd Allah*) and 'commander of the believers' (*amir al-muʾminin*) on most extant public texts, but also exceptionally as 'God's deputy' (*khalifat Allah*) on some of these and a handful of other silver coins that were minted

Figure 4.2 *Dinar* (golden coin) minted in the name of ʿAbd al-Malik, in the course of the coin reform period (694–7); known as one of the 'standing caliph coins' (Damascus, 697). Around the margins of the obverse there is the Arabic inscription: *Lā ilāha illa llāh waḥdahu Muḥammad rasūl Allāh* ['There is no god but God alone; Muḥammad is the messenger of God']; in the middle of the obverse there is a standing human figure holding a sword or a papyrus scroll, mostly interpreted as a representation of ʿAbd al-Malik

Source: Ashmolean Museum, Oxford, HDC6573 (www.ashmolean.org/standing-caliph-dinar)

Figure 4.3 *Dinar* (golden coin) minted in the name of ʿAbd al-Malik, after the coin reform period, in Damascus, 81 AH/700–701; from this reform onwards, all iconic references and (remains of) Roman and Sasanian symbols disappear, making for a specifically Islamic form of entirely aniconic coins, on which the Arabic language and the Islamic profession of absolute monotheism and of Muhammad's prophethood are the central markers. Central on the obverse is the Arabic inscription: *Lā ilāha illa llāh waḥdahu lā sharīk lahu* ['There is no god but God alone; He has no companion']

Source: Ashmolean Museum, Oxford, HCR7446 (http://jameelcentre.ashmolean.org/collection/4/837/840/21973#)

in the same period.[12] It emerges most strongly from the outcome of this experimentation with coinage, when as of 697 only entirely aniconic coins were being minted, containing no images and just Arabic inscriptions that reproduce Quranic discourse and stress God's absolute unity. This was a total and explicit break from Late Antique monetary traditions, establishing a new numismatic norm for the remainder of Islamic history, and represented as an extremely powerful assertion of a distinct monotheist theocratic identity on one of the most important media for claims to sovereignty.

Another intervention from the period of ʿAbd al-Malik's reign, which bespeaks a similarly complex set of political meanings and monotheist discourse with long-term consequences, concerns the construction of the Dome of the Rock on the Temple Square in Jerusalem, commissioned by ʿAbd al-Malik just prior to this episode of monetary experimentation and to the conclusion of the second *fitna* (see Figure 3.4). Especially, the Arabic Quranic text that adorns the inside of this monument—one of the oldest clearly datable renderings of Quranic verses—undeniably testifies to the sovereign, distinct, and exclusive (non-Christian) position that the Umayyad-Marwanid leadership progressively started to appropriate for themselves and for their Islamic followers in the theocratic world of Late Antiquity.

> In the name of God, the Merciful, the Compassionate. There is no god but God. He is One. No associate has he. His is the Kingdom and his is the praise. He makes life and He gives to die; and He is powerful over everything. (Quran 6:163, 64:1, 57:2) Muḥammad is the servant of God and His Messenger.
>
> People of the Book, go not beyond the bounds in your religion, and say not as to God but the truth. The Messiah, Jesus son of Mary, was only the Messenger of God, and

His Word that He committed to Mary, and a Spirit from Him. So believe in God and His Messengers, and say not, Three. Refrain; better is it for you. God is only One God. Glory be to Him -That He should have a son! To Him belongs all that is in the heavens and in the earth; God suffices for a guardian. (Quran 4:171)

The true religion with God is Islam. Those who were given the Book were not at variance except after the knowledge came to them, being insolent one to another. And whoso disbelieves in Gods signs. God is swift at the reckoning (Quran 3:19)

These novel articulations of the nexus of Umayyad-Marwanid sovereignty and Arabo-Islamic identity were continued in similar and related forms by the expanding (and eventually also increasingly contested) patrimonial apparatus of ʿAbd al-Malik's successors in Syria and elsewhere. Surviving specimens of coinage, monument construction (including the Umayyad mosques of Jerusalem, Damascus, and Aleppo), and Arabic public texts (in epigraphic, documentary, and epistolary formats) speak not just of the widening penetration and appropriation of local arrangements and resource flows by Umayyad-Marwanid interests and agents. They also continue to appear amidst the extant record of Umayyad administrative and political practice as important and increasingly sophisticated media for those articulations of sovereignty and identity in the service of different Umayyad-Marwanid rulers. The growing ranks of experts who realized these complex forms of political communication are also increasingly more visible in the surviving documentary and literary record, as patrimonial clients who represented, pursued, and defined Umayyad-Marwanid political and economic interests in the empire's Syrian center as well as in many of its peripheries. This formative process is interestingly paralleled by the emergence of experts who operated on or beyond the Syria-centered margins of Umayyad-Marwanid authority, and who were involved in the articulation of more local, regional, or subversive varieties of the nexus of Arabo-Islamic identity and sovereignty, and thus in the embryonic construction of Islamic and other related knowledge practices.

The latter ranks, and this highly contested formative process from Arabian to Islamic leadership practices more in general, are best represented by the almost legendary, if not exemplary, *persona* of al-Hasan al-Basri (d. 728), who was allegedly born in Muhammad's entourage in Medina but lived most of his very long life in the new southern Iraqi center of Basra. He is remembered for having first, as one of the many followers of Arabian leaders, migrated to Basra and participated in military campaigns eastwards, and then, especially, for having settled in Basra and engaging with substantial authority, derived from his *sahaba* and *sabiqa*, in explanations of the Quranic text, formulations of Islamic identity, and also criticism of Umayyad-Marwanid leadership. The changing and professionalizing ranks of administrative experts in Umayyad service are similarly well represented by two rather different but equally legendary characters. One is known as John of Damascus (d. before 754), whose grandfather allegedly had been a financial expert in Damascus in Greek-Roman and eventually, in the later 630s, in Arabian service, and whose father is referred to in later renderings of early Umayyad narratives as a leading Greek-Christian scribe in Umayyad-Sufyanid and Umayyad-Marwanid service, until ʿAbd al-Malik's Arabization of administrative practice would have rendered his services at court useless. John is remembered for having succeeded his father as a leading scribe at the Umayyad-Marwanid court and then, in the later 710s, for succumbing to growing pressures on non-Muslims in Umayyad-Marwanid court service, so that he would have retired to a life of Christian scholarship in a monastery near Jerusalem and started earning his great fame as a Christian theologian and apologist. An entirely different character was ʿAbd al-Hamid ibn Yahya (d. 750), known by the nickname of 'the Scribe' (al-Katib). Born in Iraq to a Persian family that had converted to Islam, he was employed as a scribe in Umayyad-Marwanid Damascus in the early 700s, and he made his career at court until he became the personal letter writer of Hisham (r. 724–743). From the 730s onwards, ʿAbd al-Hamid entered the service of Hisham's uncle Marwan ibn Muhammad ibn Marwan (r. 745–750), whom he followed first to Armenia when Marwan was appointed *amir* there, then back to Syria when he took over Umayyad-Marwanid imperial rule, and finally to Egypt and into death in the fatal confrontation with anti-Umayyad forces near the village of Busir. As a powerful token of the elaboration and professionalization of the late Umayyad-Marwanid apparatus of power, ʿAbd al-Hamid is especially remembered as a pioneer of the Arabic epistolographic genre. Many of his letters, with their specific Umayyad-Marwanid formulas, style, and discourse of power that he creatively engaged with survived him through his apprentices and offspring, and they soon transformed into models of ideal Arabic administrative and wider literary practice.[13]

The cases of John of Damascus and ʿAbd al-Hamid ibn Yahya also demonstrate how these expanding ranks of administrative experts and agents in Umayyad-Marwanid service were always mostly composed of people who did not hail from the tribal and Arabic-speaking contexts of the peninsula and Syria. These agents and leaders, and ever more people of similar origins who operated on less visible platforms and scales of resource management, communication, and expertise, participated actively in the consolidation of Arabian leadership in east and west and in its transformation from charismatic networks of personal relationships to hierarchical chains of Umayyad-Marwanid authority and agency. Their diverse ranks also participated in, and were affected by, the gradual integration of these patrimonial chains in the increasingly vexed discussions on the nexus of Arabo-Islamic identity and Umayyad-Marwanid sovereignty. The latter process was allegedly personally experienced by the Christian John of Damascus and the Muslim ʿAbd al-Hamid, with the marginalization of the former's family and person tellingly coinciding with the professionalization and rise of the latter. It also speaks from the life story, and the rise to a novel type of prominence, of al-Hasan al-Basri, whose father is said to have been a prisoner of war from Sasanian Iraq, and who is remembered especially for participating in these discussions in subversive, anti-Umayyad ways that, from the later 8th century onwards, acquired an emblematic status and made for his *persona* being appropriated by different later Islamic groups as their intellectual forebear.

As mentioned before, throughout this era, from the time of al-Hasan al-Basri's migration from Medina to Basra to that of ʿAbd al-Hamid's death in the Egyptian delta in Marwanid service, these groups of non-Arabian participants to Arabian leadership practices and Umayyad-Marwanid arrangements of rule—especially the swelling numbers of free or formerly enslaved but freed converts to Islam among them—are identified in all contemporary and later sources as *mawali* (sing. *mawla*), 'clients'. Stressing the ties of clientage that connected them to Arabian leaderships—they are always identified as *mawla* of an Arabian leader—the notion of *mawali* and its continued use inform about the tribal, patriarchal organization of dominance that remained normative and about the creative solutions that were adopted from the very beginning to enable outsiders to that normative framework to actively participate. In fact, *mawali* appear not just as populating and leading local, regional, and imperial administrations and the networks of Umayyad-Marwanid experts that connected them, but freeborn and freed *mawali* were also active as military rank-and-file and as commanders and military agents of Umayyad-Marwanid power, as in the famous case of the freedman Tariq ibn Ziyad, the commander of Amazigh, or Berber, descent who was responsible for the crossing of the Strait of Gibraltar in 711. Furthermore, *mawali* emerge from the written record in the format of peasants converting to Islam or migrating to new urban centers and contesting local tax arrangements, and as scholars, teachers, and religious agents of—or against—Umayyad-Marwanid authority.

Traditionally the *mawali* arrangement of clientage to Arabian leadership has been interpreted as resulting in social inequalities that became increasingly difficult to manage when *mawali* numbers grew, and that as a result, contributed to the end of Umayyad-Marwanid rule. In view of the wide variety of contexts in which *mawali* appear from the expanding source record, however, today's understandings of this practice rather stress the diversity of social roles that seem to have been lumped together in different sources under this umbrella term, and the active participation of certain *mawali* in the Umayyad-Marwanid power constellation, even in very prominent positions of local or regional leadership. Nevertheless, the imperial context for this participation—even when marked by a substantial growth of complexity and of penetration of local resource flows and

Figure 4.4 Qusayr ʿAmra (Jordan): reproduction of the (heavily damaged) representation of six late antique rulers (incl. the Roman emperor, the Sasanian *shah*, the Visigothic king and the Ethiopian *negus*) in an Umayyad-Marwanid desert palace

Source: Alois Musil, Kusejr ʿAmra und Schlösser östlich von Moab [Wenen, 1907], Vol. 2, pl. XXVI. https://commons.wikimedia.org/wiki/File:Amra5.jpg.

arrangements—remained a patrimonial one, geared towards the interests of the Umayyad-Marwanid center and the competition with its rivals for local, regional or trans-regional power, the protection of its primarily Arabian clients and supporters, and the accumulation of sufficient resources—including manpower—to achieve success in these arenas of dynastic competition and protection.

While *mawali* increasingly appear side by side with Umayyad-Marwanid siblings and *ashraf* military agents in the remembrance of this era's social and political order, it was those siblings and their *ashraf* agents who continued to pull the strings that mattered most. This was obvious in the Syrian center of Umayyad-Marwanid power, where—as mentioned—ʿAbd al-Malik was succeeded first by four of his sons and a nephew, and in the 740s by three briefly reigning grandsons and then by another nephew, the aforementioned patron of the scribe ʿAbd al-Hamid, Marwan ibn Muhammad ibn Marwan. Umayyad-Marwanid centrality is equally obvious from the military leadership that was taken up by Marwanids in major campaigns, especially in Asia Minor against the Greek-Roman emperors, including the unsuccessful 716–18 siege of Constantinople, commanded by Maslama (d. 738), another son of ʿAbd al-Malik. Maslama reappeared slightly later with his personal Syrian troops in the regions of Armenia and Azerbaijan, as *amir* and successful challenger of invasions of Turkic-speaking formations from the north. ʿAbd al-Malik's nephew and eventual successor, Marwan ibn Muhammad ibn Marwan, also appeared in this context of effective Marwanid leadership in the north, first in the entourage of Maslama, and then as *amir* of Armenia and Azerbaijan in his own right. A parallel picture emerges from the rich region of Egypt, where after the second *fitna*, ʿAbd al-Malik's brother, ʿAbd al-ʿAziz, consolidated and safeguarded Marwanid interests. Upon his death in 705, ʿAbd al-ʿAziz was succeeded as *amir* by another son of ʿAbd al-Malik, ʿAbd Allah (d. 750), who is remembered especially for having embarked upon a campaign to increase Syrian control over Egypt and its resources. After 709, this campaign of Marwanid penetration was furthered, apparently more successfully, by Syrian Arabian agents of Marwanid power, including most famously Qurra ibn Sharik (d. 714), who hailed from one of the Arabic-speaking tribes of post-Roman Syria and whose period of regional leadership left substantial traces in the relatively rich documentary record of Egypt's early Islamic history. Parallel profiles of loyal and effective Marwanid service, military and political leadership, and Syrian centrality appear from many similar stories about Arabian commanders, including al-Hajjaj ibn Yusuf (d. 714) in Iraq, Musa ibn Nusayr (d. 717) in Ifriqiya and al-Andalus, and Qutayba ibn Muslim (d. 715) in Khurasan and Transoxania. They led campaigns east- and westwards, supervised the organization of Umayyad-Marwanid patrimonial rule everywhere, and occasionally turned from favored friends to disgraced foes when their interests and those of the Umayyad-Marwanid dynastic center got out of alignment.

Notes

1 Donner, "The Islamic Conquests".
2 al-Balādhurī (d. 892), *Futūḥ al-Buldān* ['The Conquest of the Lands']; adapted from the translation by Hitti, *The Origins of the Islamic State*, 174.
3 al-Ṭabarī (d. 923), *Tārīkh al-rusul wa-l-mulūk* ['The History of Prophets and Kings']; adapted from the translation by Friedmann, *The History of al-Tabari Vol. XII*, 191–2.
4 al-Balādhurī (d. 892), *Futūḥ al-Buldān* ['The Book of the Conquest of Lands']; adapted from the translation by Hitti, *The Origins of the Islamic State*, 177.
5 John bar Penkaye [*c.* 687], *Ktābā d-rīsh mellê* ['The Book of Salient Points']; translation from Hoyland, *Seeing Islam as Others Saw It*, 196; also in Donner, "The Islamic Conquests", 42.

6 Ibn Isḥāq (704–67), *al-Sīra al-Nabawiyya* ['The Life of the Prophet']; translation adapted from Guillaume, *The Life of Muhammed*, 232–3.
7 [Pseudo-]Sebeos, Bishop of Bagratunis (*c*. 660), *No Title*; translation from Hoyland, *Seeing Islam as Others Saw It*, 129, 131.
8 John bar Penkaye [*c*. 687], *Ktābā d-rīsh mellê* ['The Book of Salient Points']; translation from Hoyland, *Seeing Islam as Others Saw It*, 196–7.
9 Bashear, "The Title 'Fārūq' and Its Association with ʿUmar I".
10 Published in Ghabban, "The Inscription of Zuhayr, the Oldest Islamic Inscription (24 AH/AD 644–645)".
11 From Hoyland, "New Documentary Texts and the Early Islamic State", 416.
12 Marsham, "'God's Caliph' Revisited".
13 al-Qadi, "Early Islamic State Letters: The Question of Authenticity".

Selected readings

al-Qadi, W. "Early Islamic State Letters: The Question of Authenticity", in A. Cameron, L.I. Conrad (eds.), *The Byzantine and Early Islamic Near East* (Princeton, 1992), 1, pp. 215–75.
Bashear, S. "The Title 'Fārūq' and Its Association with ʿUmar I", *Studia Islamica* 72 (1990): 47–70
Borrut, A. *Entre mémoire et pouvoir: l'espace syrien sous les derniers Omeyyades et les premiers Abbasides (v. 72–193/692–809)* (Leiden, 2011)
Borrut, A., Cobb, P. (eds.) *Umayyad Legacies: Medieval Memories from Syria to Spain* (Leiden, 2010)
Crone, P. *From Arabian Tribes to Islamic Empire: Army, State and Society in the Near East, c. 600–850* (Aldershot, 2008)
Crone, P. *Slaves on Horses: The Evolution of the Islamic Polity* (Cambridge, 1980)
Crone, P., Hinds, M. *God's Caliph: Religious Authority in the First Centuries of Islam* (Cambridge, 1986)
Donner, F.M. *The Early Islamic Conquests* (Princeton, 1981)
Donner, F.M. "The Islamic Conquests", in Y. M. Choueiri (ed.), *A Companion to the History of the Middle East* (Chichester, 2005), pp. 28–51
Friedmann, Y. *The History of al-Ṭabarī, Volume XII: The Battle of Qādisiyyah and the Conquest of Syria and Palestine* (Albany, 1992)
Ghabban, A.I. "The inscription of Zuhayr, the oldest Islamic inscription (24 AH/AD 644–5), the rise of Arabic script and the nature of the early Islamic state", translation and concluding remarks R. Hoyland, *Arabian Archaeology and Epigraphy* 19 (2008): 209–36
Haldon, J.F. (ed.). *Money, Power and Politics in Early Islamic Syria: A Review of Current Debates* (Farnham, 2010)
Haugh, R. *The Eastern Frontier: Limits of Empire in Late Antique and Early Medieval Central Asia* (New York, 2019)
Hawting, G.R. *The First Dynasty of Islam: The Umayyad Caliphate AD 661–750*. Second Edition (London, 2000)
Hitti, P.K. *The Origins of the Islamic State, Being a Translation from the Arabic Accompanied with Annotations, Geographic and Historic Notes of the Kitâb Futûḥ al-Buldân of al-Imâm abu-l 'Abbâs Aḥmad ibn -Jâbir al-Balâdhuri* (New York, 1916)
Hoyland, R.G. *In God's Path: The Arab Conquests and the Creation of an Islamic Empire* (Oxford, 2015)
Hoyland, R.G. "New Documentary Texts and the Early Islamic State", *Bulletin of SOAS* 69/3 (2006): 395–416
Humphreys, R.S. *Mu'awiya ibn Abi Sufyan, From Arabia to Empire* (Oxford, 2006)
Judd, S.C. *Religious Scholars and the Umayyads: Piety-minded Supporters of the Marwānid Caliphate* (London, 2013)
Kennedy, H. *The Caliphate* (London, 2016)
Kennedy, H. *The Great Arab Conquests: How the Spread of Islam Changed the World We Live In* (New York, 2007)
Kubiak, W. *Al-Fustat: Its Foundation and Early Urban Development* (Cairo, 1987)

Marsham, A. "'God's Caliph' Revisited. Umayyad Political Thought in Its Late Antique Context", in A. George, A. Marsham (eds.), *Power, Patronage, and Memory in Early Islam: Perspectives on Umayyad Elites* (New York, 2016), pp. 3–37

Marsham, A. *Rituals of Islamic Monarchy: Accession and Succession in the First Muslim Empire* (Edinburgh, 2009)

Robinson, Ch. *'Abd al-Malik* (Oxford, 2005)

Sijpesteijn, P. *Shaping a Muslim State: The World of a Mid-Eighth-Century Egyptian Official* (New York, 2013)

5 The 'classical' period of the Abbasids

Late Antique imperial formation and the triumph of the east (750–908)

Introduction: *Fitna* and the formation of a patrimonial-bureaucratic empire

Just as *fitna* had ushered in the beginning of Syrian-Umayyad appropriation of trans-regional leadership, so too was the end of Umayyad-Marwanid rule heralded by a widespread series of conflicts that would be remembered as a period of social and political disintegration, apocalyptic chaos, and *fitna*. In the later 740s, the stakes of these conflicts—trans-regional rule of a powerful Late Antique empire and the recalibration of its local, regional, and trans-regional patrimonial relations in the service of the interests of the Marwanids' competitors—were more than ever before defined in religious, Islamic terms. Illustrating both the successful articulation since the 690s of a more consciously Islamic political identity for Marwanid leadership and its patrimonial apparatus, and the gradual marginalization of traditional Arabian leaderships and their practices, this *fitna* was now more explicitly than ever framed around the question of which 'precursor' (*imam*) was destined to lead that *umma* to its specifically Islamic destiny.

When this struggle for power was eventually settled in favor of another Meccan leadership group, descending from Muhammad's uncle al-ʿAbbas, ongoing discussions on the nature of legitimate authority and theocratic order acquired new levels of complexity and abstraction. In fact, the range of claims to, and practices of, authority to lead the community continued to stretch from appeals to distinct sets of patrilineal ties with traditional leadership—although now narrowed down to descendance from Muhammad and his clan of Hashim—to various ideas of meritocratic service to the community's benefit. Whereas these claims continued to oppose different groups of claimants and their supporters, they intersected ever more with equally vexed issues of consolidating the new Iraq-based trans-regional leadership and its regional and local representation, maintaining control over its many and widespread political and economic resources, and integrating and expanding formerly Marwanid organizational arrangements. In fact, these and other diversifying claims appear increasingly as being subsumed and integrated into—or also as firmly excluded from—those arrangements. They became part and parcel of the empowerment of alternative centers of power at the Abbasid court, in the imperial administration and army, and more widely along—as well as in the many grey zones of—the impressively complex chains of Abbasid authority and agency that were meant to tie the empire's many elites and resources together. When in 809, therefore, a succession crisis heralded another decade of fierce competition, violent disintegration, and apocalyptic chaos, again remembered as a time of division and trial for the *umma*, *fitna*, the main fault lines now turned out to run within the ranks of the Abbasid dynasty and its agents, and the outcome again radically changed those ranks, but not their Abbasid appearance.

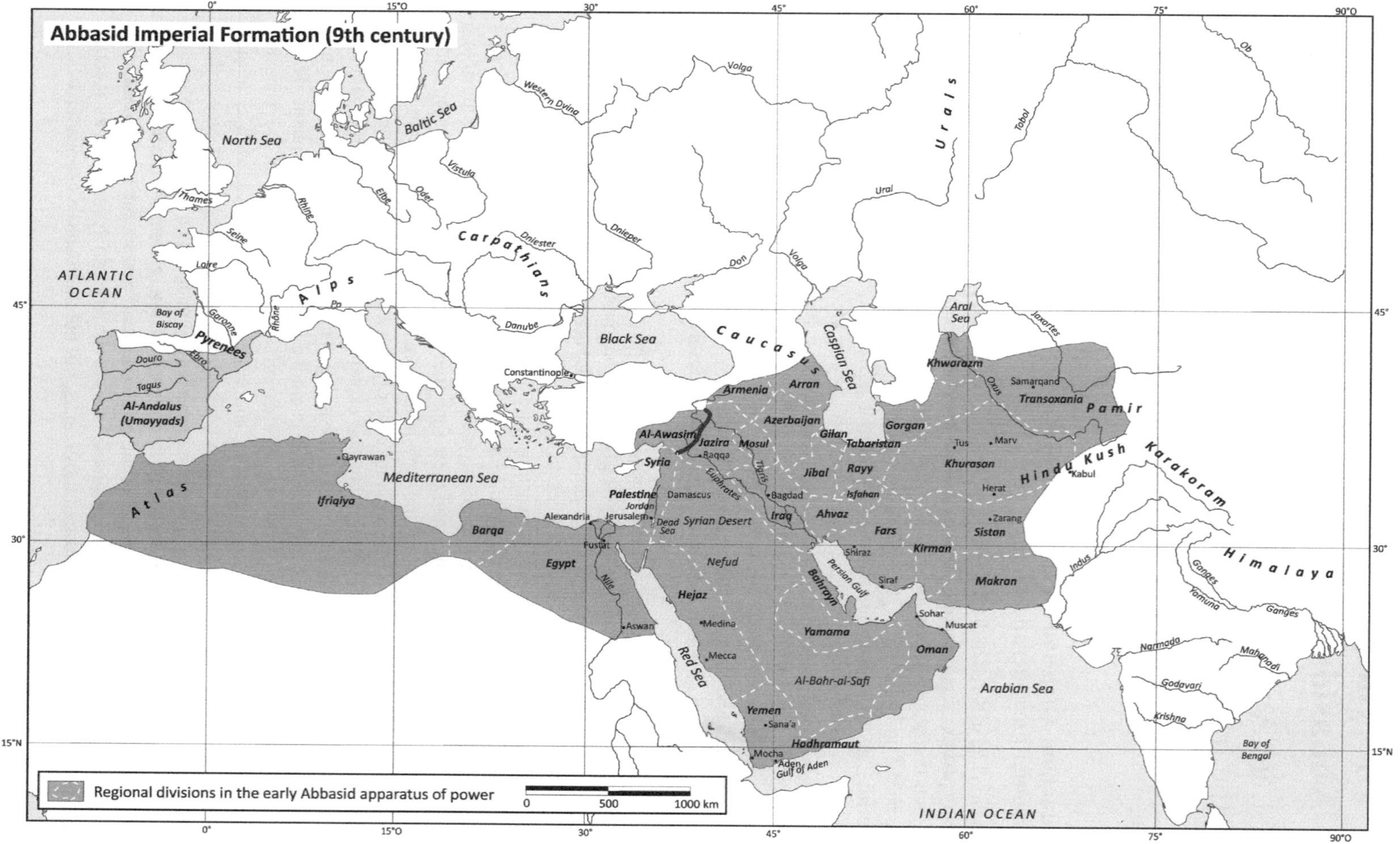

Map 3 Abbasid Imperial Formation (9th century)

This formation of a patrimonial-bureaucratic apparatus of power, and this expansion, diversification, and specialization of competition in the center and at the many peripheries of Abbasid authority also urged for dynastic claims to be articulated in more creative and distinctive ways. In the course of the 9th century, Abbasid caliphal authority actually became an ever more natural, evident, and abstract center piece, irrespective of whoever of the Abbasids actually performed it, of at least one dominant imagination of Islamic theocratic order. This is interestingly illustrated by the fact that no new apocalyptic *fitna*s are remembered to have occurred after the 810s, even though, at the same time, that Abbasid order's local, regional, and trans-regional realities were seriously contested by the multiplication of power centers, stakeholders, and centrifugal dynamics in, or against, the Abbasid patrimonial-bureaucratic apparatus. These contestants and rivals included emerging communities of Islamic legal experts, local and regional elites of varying backgrounds, and particular activist groups of Shi'ites. Their challenges had transformative effects, in political as well as very often also in territorial terms, and in the first decades of the 10th century they would herald the evaporation of Abbasid dynastic power. The fiction of an Abbasid theocratic order, however, would remain referential across much of Islamic West-Asia, even to those who wished to subvert it.

Before Abbasid power stumbled into abstraction, however, the protagonists and agents of the Abbasid dynasty still left their impressive mark on the Islamic world. According to many, this mark continues to reverberate to this day, not least as a result of the enormous cultural and intellectual achievements that from then on would continue to leave their traces on almost every formulation of what it means to be Muslim. These achievements were closely interconnected with the many shifts eastwards—in geographical but especially in social, political, and cultural terms—that were experienced by those Abbasid protagonists, agents, and participants. As the center of trans-regional power moved from Syria to Iraq and the rich former heartlands of the antique and late antique Persian empires, Abbasid power and authority were increasingly defined by new non-Arabian elites with local roots in eastern regions that stretched from Khurasan to, eventually, even the western fringes of the Inner-Asian steppes.

With this complex mix of Abbasid leadership, old locals and new 'easterners', and their diverse cultural and intellectual heritages successfully and definitively blending into active, creative, or also reluctant partners in the ongoing formation and transformation of this late antique patrimonial-bureaucratic empire, this Abbasid era's achievements quickly came to represent a permanent reference point in many readings of Islamic history, and to even be considered as uniquely efflorescent and therefore 'classical' by many. This linear and normative understanding has informed the reception of this empire and its achievements in modern scholarship for a long time. It has most certainly colored the increasingly richer contemporary written source base. These Arabic sources are predominantly of a narrative, literary, and didactic rather than strictly documentary nature, and they are conscious, purposeful, and tradition-bound constructions, reproductions, and representations of social memories and social conventions that are deeply determined by salvationist readings in hindsight of the *umma*'s history and its Abbasid caliphal leadership. They remain, therefore, difficult to interpret as historical sources, even despite—or perhaps not least because of—their returning tendency to engage in detailed storytelling.

Three central and fundamentally different episodes in the leadership configuration of this now explicitly caliphal dynasty—the middle and late 8th century, the first decades of the 9th century, and the middle and late 9th century—will be distilled from these particular contemporary and modern readings, and discussed in more detail in this chapter. The wider contexts of life along the chains of Abbasid authority and agency that made for the patrimonial-bureaucratic apparatus of Late Antique imperial power, in the imperial urban centers and at the courts of Abbasid Iraq between the 8th and 10th centuries, will be considered in more detail in the next chapter. Chapter 7 finally reconstructs the wider, trans-regional context of the Abbasid Late Antique imperial order, and introduces the political patchwork of different Islamic imperial leadership networks and their transformations from the 9th to the mid-11th-centuries.

1 Anti-Marwanid activism and Abbasid empowerment

1.1 The third fitna

The origin of the Abbasid dynasty and its seizure of power in the middle of the 8th century are generally situated in the Umayyad-Marwanid period, when various subversive movements and competitors for Marwanid power are believed to have closed ranks around the principle that legitimate leadership can be claimed for someone from the patrilineal family of Muhammad only (and therefore, not for someone from the wider group of Quraysh, as with the Umayyads). For this reason, these movements and competitors are all identified as proto-Shi'ite: they are closely related in leadership visions to what has been identified as the Shiʿat ʿAli ('the party of ʿAli'), with their repeated calls in the first and second Cf *fitna*s and thereafter to accept only the claims of Muhammad's son-in-law and his descendants, and also to the Shi'ite sectarian formations that later organized themselves around these calls; but theologically and intellectually these early movements and competitors did not partake in the systematized sets of ideas, beliefs, and practices that would later identify and distinguish those Shi'ite formations, nor were they necessarily destined to come to share in them. Moreover, among the multitude of these early proto-Shi'ite movements, no real agreement was ever reached about who exactly belonged to that family (descendants of ʿAli, the ʿAlids, only, or members of the wider clan of Hashim, the Hashimites, too?) or which one of the growing group of descendants within that family should actually assume leadership.

The rather controversial (because proto-Shi'ite) standard narrative of Abbasid origins refers to the importance of a particular transfer of authority among one of the most important proto-Shi'ite groups that, as explained in previous chapters, had emerged since the mid-7th century in Kufa. After the violent death of Muhammad's grandson al-Husayn near Karbala in 680, at the very start of the second *fitna*, deprived this group in central Iraq of its natural leadership, a movement within it is said to have rallied around the claims of another son of ʿAli, known as Muhammad ibn al-Hanafiyya. After the latter's death in 700, his son Abu Hashim played a leading role in this Iraqi movement, until he passed away by 716. At that moment, an important union of proto-Shi'ite movements operating in the margins of Umayyad-Marwanid authority took place, when the leading position of Abu Hashim was taken over by a certain Muhammad ibn ʿAli (d. 743), who claimed that Abu Hashim had designated him as successor for leadership within the 'family of Muhammad'. Like Abu Hashim, this Muhammad ibn ʿAli was related to the Prophet Muhammad through a paternal uncle. In the case of Muhammad ibn 'Ali, this was al-ʿAbbas (d. 653). As leader of the al-ʿAbbas clan Muhammad ibn ʿAli claimed leadership of the 'family of Muhammad', and consequently of the entire *umma*, from 717 onwards. However, because this remained a contentious issue, also among proto-Shi'ite movements, the standard Abbasid narrative explains how this claim was only made behind closed doors, and that to the outside world Muhammad ibn ʿAli's supporters and associates rather waged their subversive campaigns in the format of secretive and ambiguous anti-Marwanid calls for restoring the *umma* under the only legitimate authority of 'a chosen one from Muhammad's family' (*al-rida min al Muhammad*).

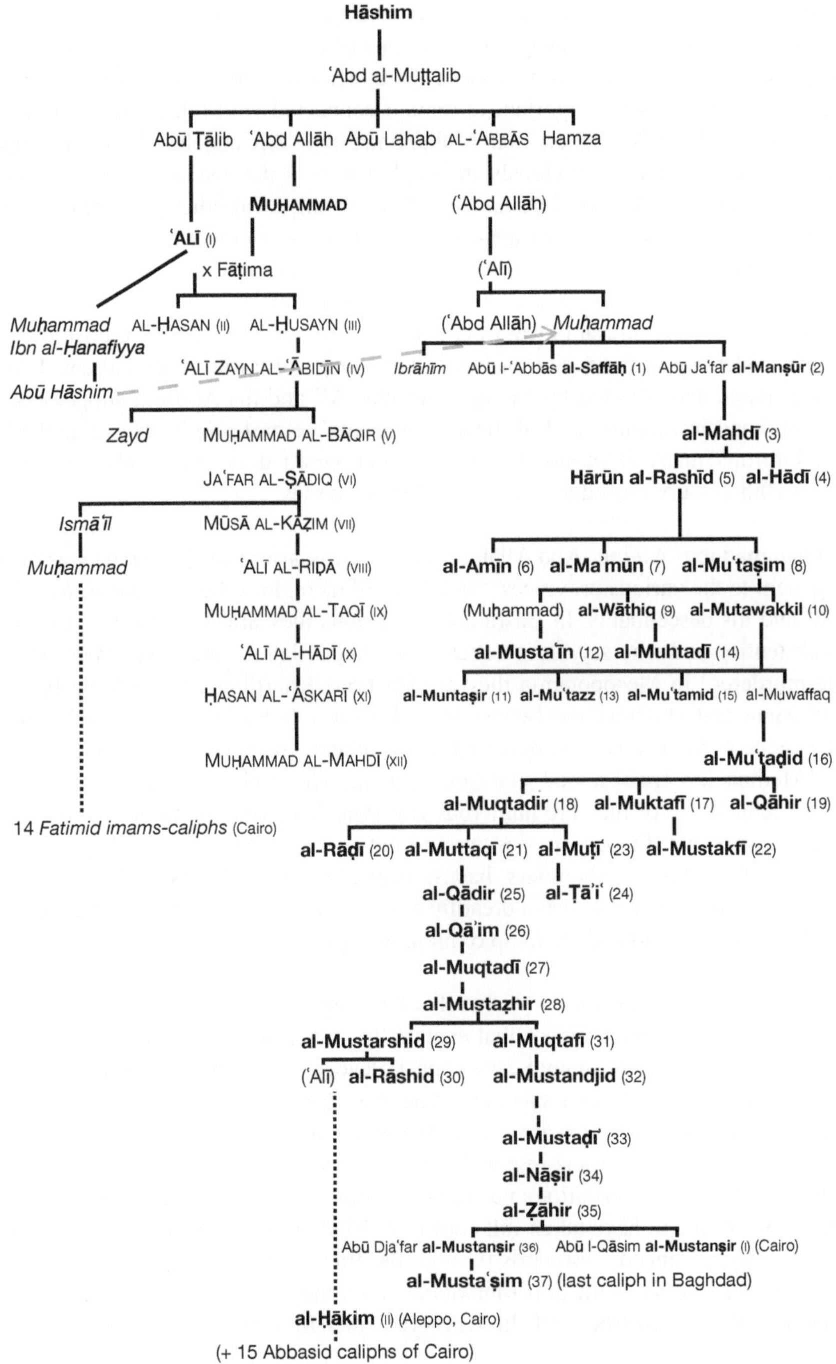

Roman numbers = succession of *imams as per* Imami/Twelver Shi'ite doctrine
Arabic numbers = succession of Abbasid caliphs
bold = leaders/caliphs of the (Sunni) *umma*

Dynastic Table 2 Simplified table of Muhammad's clan of Hashim, with specific focus on the descendants of Muhammad's nephew and son-in-law 'Ali ibn Abi Talib, the 'Alids, and of Muhammad's uncle al-'Abbas, the Abbasids, and on the respective lineages of Shi'ite *imams* and Abbasid caliphs among them in particular

The center of Abbasid subversive action is said to have been situated in Humayma, a remote site in southern Syria (today's Jordan), one of those many grey zones of Marwanid authority, but at the same time connected to the wider world by caravan routes that passed through. These routes were important to remain connected with other sites and groups of anti-Marwanid subversive action that Muhammad ibn ʿAli and his Abbasid supporters claimed to direct, including obviously in Iraq but also in the distant region of Khurasan, among descendants of Arabian leaders as well as among local elites and converts. Narratives about this formation of new trans-regional networks of power and political action all agree on the centrality in this of one Abu Muslim al-Khurasani (d. 754), who emerged in the mid-740s from disputed origins (a lowly Abbasid freedman, or *mawla*, sent to Khurasan according to some, a Khurasani local ruler according to other sources) to a position of anti-Marwanid leadership in the region of Marv. This image of a trans-regional anti-Umayyad network planned and directed by Muhammad ibn ʿAli and his Abbasid supporters, of its underground and just nature, and of these Khurasanis' central role in its eventual Abbasid success, informed many of the stories that were later recorded about it, as also appears in the following 10th-century reproduction of one of these stories.

> Muḥammad ibn ʿAlī ibn ʿAbd Allāh said to his emissaries [*dāʿī*] when he was dispatching them to the various provinces, "In Kūfa and its regions they are partisans [*shīʿa*] of ʿAlī and his descendants. In Basra and its regions they are ʿUthmāniyya who believe in abstention and who say, 'It is better to be ʿAbd Allāh the murdered than ʿAbd Allāh the murderer.' In Mesopotamia they are fractious Kharijites and Bedouin-like infidel barbarians and Muslims who behave like Christians. In Syria they know of nothing but obedience to the Umayyads, fierce hatred to others, and massive ignorance. In Mecca and Medina they are obsessed with Abū Bakr and ʿUmar. Give your attention to the people of Khurāsān, for they are numerous and steadfast, with strong breasts and uncommitted hearts, not divided by passions and not corrupted by discord. They are an army with terrifying bodies, shoulders, backs, heads, beards, whiskers, and voices, uttering fearsome sounds that issue from dreadful depths. I take good omen from the East, where the light of the world and the lamp of mankind rises."[1]

In reality, it is generally thought now that this later representation underestimates the multiplicity of movements and interests that eventually joined forces against the Marwanids in the 740s, as well as how for many years Abbasid leadership's competition for priority with various others had only limited success.[2] Whatever it may be, the empowerment of Abu Muslim in Khurasan clearly appears as a turning point, as does the weakening of Marwanid cohesion in the 740s, and a trans-regional agreement on joint violent action that appears to have aligned Marwanid opposition and Abbasid ambitions in 747. In 748 Abu Muslim and his followers are said to have taken full control of Marv and the wider region of Khurasan, after which they advanced westwards through the Iranian Plateau to Iraq, where, together with the Iraqi supporters of the anti-Marwanid cause, they managed to gain several further victories over the Syrian troops of the Umayyad ruler Marwan (r. 744–750) (see also the previous chapter).

In the meantime, Muhammad ibn ʿAli had been succeeded by his sons at the head of the Abbasid family, and in the autumn of 749, one of them, ʿAbd Allah, was formally proclaimed in Kufa the only legitimate leader of the *umma*, whereupon he assumed the ruling title of al-Saffah ('the shedder of blood'). Through further violent campaigning and confrontations (among others the major Battle at the Great Zab, in January 750), the initial success was consolidated and extended so that in the course of 750, nearly all regions of the former Umayyad-Marwanid empire were brought under the control of Abbasid representatives. Marwan and the entire Marwanid family were hunted down during these actions and captured, and most of them were eventually killed or executed.

This new, third episode of total fragmentation, apocalyptic chaos, and widespread competition for leadership, of *fitna*, at the core of the community of Muslims has been remembered in modern scholarship for a long time as a revolutionary moment, as 'the Abbasid revolution', and as bringing about substantial and sudden change in the political, social, cultural, and geographic balances of the Islamic empire. As suggested above, today this particular view of one revolutionary movement achieving success is no longer tenable, and many of the changes traditionally explained from this revolutionary perspective tend now to be explained as part of more slowly evolving processes of 8th-century change. Nevertheless, the rise to prominence and centrality of Arabian and non-Arabian Khurasani elites was undoubtedly boosted by the outcome of this episode of trans-regional violence, as was the swift change of fates for new Abbasid Iraq and for the old Umayyad heartlands in Syria. The sudden shift in dynastic power certainly also resulted in the very specific, negative framing of Umayyad-Marwanid leadership in extant, mostly Abbasid textual sources. This also transpires from the following 10th-century reconstruction of a story that explains the Umayyad downfall in the starkly moralizing and pro-Abbasid tone that has defined most hindsight literary representations of Umayyad-Marwanid rule.

> The [Abbasid] caliph al-Manṣūr (r. 754–75) had [ʻAbd Allāh, the son of the last Umayyad ruler Marwān] brought out of prison, and when he was in his presence he said to him, "ʻAbd Allāh, tell me the story of your encounter with the king of the Nubians." ʻAbd Allāh replied, "O Commander of the Faithful, I got to Nubia and I had been there for three days when the king came to me. He sat on the ground, although a valuable carpet had been spread for him, and when I asked him what prevented him from sitting on my carpet he replied, 'Because I am a king and it is a king's duty to humble himself before the might of God Who set him up'. Then he asked me, 'Why do you drink wine, when it is forbidden you in your Book?' I answered, 'Our slaves and followers have made bold to do this'. He asked me, 'Why do you trample the crops with your horses when such wrongdoing is forbidden to you in your Book?' I replied, 'Our slaves and followers did this out of their ignorance'. He asked, 'Why do you wear brocade and silk and gold when these are forbidden to you in your Book and in your religion?' I replied, 'We have lost our kingdom, and we have sought the help of foreigners who entered our religion and wear those clothes in spite of us'. The king bowed his head, sometimes turning his hand and sometimes rapping the ground and saying, 'Our slaves and our followers and foreigners who have entered our religion'. Then he raised his head and said, 'It is not as you have said, but you are people who have made licit what God has proscribed and have done what you were forbidden to do and oppressed where you have reigned. Therefore, Almighty God deprived you of power and clothed you in shame for your sins. God's vengeance against you has not reached its end, and I fear lest His punishment descend on you while you are in my country and it touch me together with you. The claim of hospitality is three days. Therefore, provision yourself with whatever you need and leave my country'. And so I did",
>
> Al-Manṣūr was astonished and sat for a while in silence. Then he took pity in him and thought of setting him free, but [someone from his entourage] reminded him that this man had received the oath of allegiance as heir apparent, so he sent him back to prison.[3]

1.2 The first Abbasid caliphs

In 754, the Abbasid ruler al-Saffah passed away. After a short power struggle within the leadership of the anti-Marwanid movements, in which Abu Muslim and some others were killed, a brother of al-Saffah, Abu Jaʿfar, succeeded him. Assuming the regnal title of al-Mansur ('the Victorious') (r. 754–775), this Abbasid managed to successfully further the integration of the formerly Marwanid apparatus of power and of the new leadership and its supporters, followers, and agents. In general, three factors emerged in this process as crucial sources of early Abbasid power and success. Firstly, there was the expanding network of the Abbasid family itself, soon remembered as 'the dynasty' (*al-dawla*); its new centrality was especially acquired by members who were sent out with their personal armies to establish and maintain control over different parts of the vast empire. Secondly, there were the Khurasani followers of Abu Muslim, many of whom descended from 7th-century Arabic-speaking migrants to Khurasan and, upon their victories over Marwanid forces and the eventual disappearance of Abu Muslim, remained in central Iraq in Abbasid service; they soon emerged as the hard core and new elite of Abbasid coercive force and, in due course, they came to be identified as the 'sons of the [Abbasid] dynasty' (*abnaʾ al-dawla*). And thirdly, there was central Iraq itself, strategically situated between Khurasan in the east and the empire's western regions and a rich and fertile agricultural landscape since the beginning of human history, which immediately transformed into the new territorial base of Abbasid power; this involved, between 762 and 777, the move of al-Mansur's new political, military, and administrative headquarters from Kufa to a newly constructed imperial settlement on the banks of the Tigris, which was called—with due reference to an apocalyptic imagination of the new Abbasid leadership—'City of Peace' (*Madinat al-Salam*) and which later became widely known by the ancient name of one of the villages it incorporated, Bagdad.

Al-Mansur's reign experienced a few difficult early years in which new balances of power and accommodation needed to be achieved between the new rulers, the agents and representatives of their new trans-regional authority and interests, and various new and old regional and local elites and communities. One of the most dangerous situations for the new rulership involved its relationship with the proto-Shiʿite groups that had been instrumental in the anti-Marwanid movement. When the Abbasid ascendance failed to meet the diverse Hashimite and especially ʿAlid expectations of these groups, many resorted again to resistance and violence. This happened especially in the early 760s, when two descendants of Muhammad's grandson al-Hasan, Ibrahim ibn ʿAbd Allah and his brother Muhammad (known under his nickname 'the pure soul'—*al-nafs al-zakiyya*) challenged the fresh authority and premature legitimacy of the Abbasid leadership from the southern Iraqi city of Basra and from Medina in the Hejaz, respectively. In the period 762–763, both brothers and their supporters were successfully defeated by al-Mansur and his Khurasani armies. This would turn out to be one of the last major proto-Shiʿite revolts that aimed to claim central authority in the Islamic empire, with many proto-Shiʿite leaders and their followers from now on tending to more quietist courses or at least pursuing their activist ambitions in the margins of Abbasid authority. From the mid-760s onwards, therefore, a quieter and prosperous reign is recorded to have followed for al-Mansur, who eventually died in October 775. Subsequently, he was succeeded, without any serious further questioning of the legitimacy of Abbasid authority, by his son and grandsons, who ruled under the titles of al-Mahdi (r. 775–785), al-Hadi (r. 785–786), and al-Rashid (r. 786–809).

Especially during the long and glorious reign of the latter, better known under his full name Harun al-Rashid, the dynasty, its imperial apparatus of power, and their many Muslim and non-Muslim subject communities between North Africa and Transoxania experienced a period of prosperity that would continue to captivate the imagination for a long time. At the same time, however, new problems arose that were closely connected to the further elaboration of the organization of political power and control and the rise of a complex patrimonial-bureaucratic apparatus of power. In this process ever more military and administrative agents along the expanding chains of Abbasid authority and agency promoted the interests of the dynasty, its regional and local elites, and increasingly also themselves, up into the furthest corners of the vast empire. The diverse effects of this remarkable process of imperial formation, in which new non-military and non-Arabian groups appeared as progressively powerful in the center of Abbasid authority, first emerged prominently within the context of the succession of al-Mahdi in the period 785–786, when his son al-Hadi is reported to having been murdered. According to most stories, the main protagonists in this dynastic drama were his and his successor al-Rashid's mother, Khayzuran, and the increasingly powerful leaders of the Abbasid palace administration, the family of the Barmakids.

Within this context of growing complexity and widening participation, a new fault line in the changing ranks of those that realized Abbasid power and authority actually started to acquire ever more prominence and impact. This line now ran between the leaders of the traditional, military agents of Abbasid success—especially the Khurasanis in central-Iraq and Bagdad—on the one hand, and new types of Abbasid leaders and power, on the other. The most important among the latter undoubtedly were those in charge of the ever more complex management of the dynasty's financial resources and political communication, collectively identified as the *kuttab* (the 'writers' or clerks). Their ranks at the Abbasid

Figure 5.1 Raqqa (Syria): remains of the palace of Harun al-Rashid

Source: Norbert Schiller collection, photo by Walter Fréres (https://commons.wikimedia.org/wiki/Category:Harun_al-Rashid#/media/File:Harun_al- Rashid_palace.jpg, Norbert Schiller/www.photorientalist.org)

court consisted largely of Iraqi and Persian families who derived their status and reputation from their involvement, often since pre-Islamic times, in local administrative and political practices and experiences. Under the efficient leadership of the family of the Barmakids, whose roots lay in Buddhist institutions in the Khurasani region of Afghanistan, there was realized a strikingly successful centralization, around the early Abbasid court, of political relationships and income flows from across the vast territory of the empire (see also the next chapter). This success, and the enormous authority and power that emanated from this court, can be measured by the fact that the names of the Abbasid governors of Basra, Kufa, and Egypt—transformed into mere cogs in a complex and rapidly rotating bureaucratic system—are even no longer known, and that the Abbasid representative in Egypt was reportedly summoned to the Abbasid court twice during this period to have his accounts checked. They also speak from the monumental remains of the imperial infrastructures and palaces that Harun had constructed for his court, army, and administration at the fortified extended settlement of Raqqa, on the left bank of the middle Euphrates, in the northern Iraqi region of the Jazira. In their meticulous planning and skillful construction these remains continue to attest to the impressive achievement, careful construction, and sheer wealth of early Abbasid authority, which was organized from there rather than from Bagdad between 796 and 808.

In 803 it appeared that the Barmakids had overplayed their hand when they fell out of Harun al-Rashid's grace and the centrality of Abbasid patrimonial interests—of Harun's in particular—amidst this bureaucratic apparatus was re-affirmed. This mythical moment of 'the fall of the Barmakids', the subject of numerous later literary imaginations, coincided with a mounting tension between the Abbasid court and the important region of Khurasan. The centralization process is explained to have caused growing unrest and opposition with local elites and regular refusal by Khurasani elites in particular to send locally collected tax revenues to Iraq. These increasing tensions led Harun al-Rashid to undertake, on several occasions, personal inspection tours to restore political and economic order in the east. In 809, however, during one of these tours he unexpectedly passed away near the urban settlement of Tus.

2 The great Abbasid *fitna* and the reigns of al-Maʾmun and al-Muʿtasim

2.1 The great Abbasid fitna

Harun al-Rashid's very active patrimonial leadership had obviously managed, although not without difficulty, to safeguard his Abbasid priority at court and in the empire's main regions. Upon his death, however, latent competition between various powerful groups in the dynastic center and at its many peripheries were integrated in the succession arrangement and soon led to violent confrontations that opposed his two eldest sons and their supporters and allies across most of the empire, once again in Iraq and Khurasan to begin with. As suggested, this new succession crisis, which both sons in turn failed to prevent from spiraling out of Abbasid control, heralded another decade of fierce competition, violent disintegration, and apocalyptic chaos. This was again remembered as a time of *fitna*, of division and trial for the *umma*. Unlike in preceding moments remembered as *fitna*, the main fault lines now mostly ran within the ranks of the Abbasid dynasty and its many competing groups of agents and allies. Whereas the outcome again radically changed those ranks, including those of the dynasty itself, it did not affect their appearance, which was to remain that of the Abbasid *dawla*. This is in fact a further illustration of the successful alignment of many trans-regional, regional, and local leadership relationships in the early Abbasid period and of the centralizing dynamic emanating from the Abbasid court in Iraq. Although it would be increasingly contested and fragile on various regional and local levels from the aftermath of this *fitna* onwards, this process remained ongoing, enclosing the Abbasids and their agents for another century in the bubble of their almost unchallenged trans-regional authority. The Abbasid succession crisis of the 810s is, therefore, the last of the four great *fitnas* that tend to be identified in this way in early Islamic history. After that, Abbasid dynastic politics and the violence that continued to accompany its late antique imperial transformations were never again remembered in the same total and religiously meaningful ways, as it is generally believed that within the patrimonial-bureaucratic order of Abbasid authority, the community, or *umma*, now began to acquire more than ever its own identity and leaderships. It did so in no less contested and political ways, but also in the format of autonomous formations that were pursuing their own paths in search for salvation and remained largely unaffected by any further dynastic transformations.

Harun al-Rashid left behind a handful of male descendants who each played their part in this so-called 4th and final moment of *fitna*. The traditional narrative records that, during a pilgrimage he undertook to Mecca in 802, he announced with much ado that upon his death he should be succeeded by his son Muhammad. At the same time, he pronounced his son 'Abd Allah as the second in line for the succession, while he also stipulated that the latter would be allowed to assume the position of autonomous Abbasid ruler in Khurasan during the reign of his brother. This arrangement—recorded in 9th- and 10th-century Arabic historiography in a remarkable anticipation and explanation of how events were subsequently to unfold—suggests, in dramatically plotted detail, how Harun continuously attempted to balance different power groups at his court and in his empire. In fact, it therefore mainly informs about the different labels that were used to identify the main players in this set of conflicts, framed in very traditional terms—another token of the successful patrimonial-bureaucratic formation of this late antique empire—as opposing the military *versus* the administrators, and at the same time the old powers *versus* the newcomers. Harun's son Muhammad is remembered, therefore, as having been brought up and trained in the traditional military ranks of Abbasid power in Bagdad, dominated by former Khurasani leaders who were identified as the *abna' al-dawla*, the sons of the dynasty. 'Abd Allah is traditionally attributed more of a 'palatial profile' that would have provided him with good relations with the ever more powerful camp of the *kuttab*. The following famous description of the ceremony that took place in Mecca in 802, to be found in one of the most important and influential Arabic chronicles of early Islamic history, represents these insightful leadership arrangements and the circumstances of their conclusion in the following foreboding detail:

> When [Hārūn al-Rashid] had accomplished the rites of Pilgrimage, he composed for his son 'Abd Allāh al-Ma'mūn two letters, over the composition of which the religious lawyers and judges had expended intensively their intellectual efforts. One of them comprised stipulations laid down upon Muḥammad setting forth the conditions which Hārūn had imposed on him regarding Muḥammad's faithful adherence to the arrangements in the document concerning the handing over of the administrative regions for which 'Abd Allāh was to assume responsibility, and he conveyed to him estates, sources of revenue, jewels, and wealth. The other was the documentary text of the oath of allegiance which the Caliph had extracted from the nobles and commoners alike, and that of the obligations due to 'Abd Allāh and incumbent upon both Muḥammad himself and those nobles and commoners. . . . Then he [Hārūn] thought it fitting to hang up the document in the

> Kaaba, but when it was lifted up in order to attach it for suspension, it fell down, and people commented that this arrangement would speedily be dissolved before it could be carried through completely.

The text of the document itself read as follows:

> In the name of God, the Merciful, the Compassionate One. This is a document composed by the Servant of God (*ʿabd Allāh*), Hārūn, the Commander of the Believers (*amīr al-muʾminīn*), which Muḥammad son of Hārūn the Commander of the Believers has written out in a state of soundness of mind and full exercise of his powers, willingly and unconstrainedly. The Commander of the Believers has appointed me as his successor after him and has imposed acknowledgement of allegiance to me on the whole of the Muslims. He has appointed ʿAbd Allāh the son of Hārūn the Commander of the Believers as his successor and as caliph and as the one responsible for all the affairs of the Muslims after myself, with my full agreement and freely conceded by me, willingly and unconstrainedly. He has given responsibility for Khurasān, its frontier regions and its districts, for the conduct of warfare there and its army, its land tax, its official textile workshops, its postal relay system, its public treasures, its poor tax, its religious tithe, the sums collected as tribute, and all its administrative divisions, both during his own (i.e. Hārūn's) lifetime and afterwards. I have accepted the obligation laid on me by the servant of God, Hārūn, the Commander of the Believers with my full agreement and a contented mind, that I will faithfully fulfil and hand over to my brother ʿAbd Allāh ibn Hārūn the right of succession, the executive power, the caliphate and the affairs of the whole of the Muslims, which Hārūn the Commander of the Believers has granted to him after me.[4]

When their father died in 809 in Tus, Muhammad and ʿAbd Allah are reported to have faithfully followed his instructions. The former was appointed Abbasid ruler with the regnal title of al-Amin in Bagdad, while the latter installed himself in the political center of Khurasan, Marv, as an autonomous regional ruler within the Abbasid trans-regional political order. Soon, however, the first problems are believed to have arisen when the *abnaʾ* leaders in Bagdad realized that this arrangement complicated their traditional, lucrative bond with Khurasan and its fiscal revenues. Therefore, they urged al-Amin to suspend the arrangement of his father, which in turn led to violent reactions among ʿAbd Allah's entourage and the elites of Khurasan, who saw their newly regained political and fiscal autonomy threatened. In the end, ʿAbd Allah's supporters in Marv therefore allegedly proclaimed him *imam*, or sacral leader of the *umma*, with the ruling title al-Maʾmun, which obviously was a direct contestation of al-Amin's claim to trans-regional authority. The further build-up of tension between these Iraqi and Khurasani groups led to a major confrontation between their supporters in 811 at Herat. Al-Maʾmun's Khurasani armies, led by the Khurasani leader of Arabian origin Tahir ibn al-Husayn, somewhat unexpectedly gained the upper hand, after which al-Amin and the *abnaʾ* leaders soon seemed to have been completely exhausted. In the period 812–813, Tahir besieged Abbasid Bagdad itself, eventually killing al-Amin and breaking the *abnaʾ*s resistance. As a result, in 813 al-Maʾmun was officially proclaimed Abbasid caliph in Marv, and the center of Abbasid power was moved further eastward, to this capital of the old Sasanian province of Khurasan.

Al-Maʾmun's moving of the center of Abbasid authority to Khurasan, as part of a conscious tactic to further dismantle traditional sources of Abbasid power in Iraq and Bagdad, was immediately met with great resistance, both in Bagdad and in the rest of the empire. The initiative in this resistance appears once again to have been taken by so-called proto-Shi'ite movements, who managed to return to the limelight especially in the region of Iraq. In 817, al-Ma'mun took conciliatory measures and appointed a certain ʿAli al-Rida as his heir apparent. As another direct descendant of the Prophet Muhammad through ʿAli and his son Husayn, ʿAli al-Rida was acknowledged by many of these movements as the eighth *imam*, the eighth descendant of Muhammad who had been appointed as sole divinely inspired and infallible leader of the *umma*. However, when this concession of al-Ma'mun did not generate the desired effect and most regions and groups in the empire remained difficult to control for his representatives, he decided to take more drastic measures. Al-Ma'mun had his main advisor, the chief of his court administration, killed and saw to it that ʿAli al-Rida was poisoned (his mausoleum can therefore still be found near Marv, in the East Iranian city of Mashhad). He then is said to have begun a long process of accommodation and reconciliation with various regional and local elites, which also included, around 819, the westward move of al-Ma'mun's court to Bagdad in Iraq. In this long process, al-Ma'mun himself and his other brothers, as well as the commander of al-Ma'mun's troops, the Khurasani leader Tahir ibn al-Husayn, and his descendants, are remembered to have played a central role. They provided al-Ma'mun with the necessary manpower to replace the traditional Abbasid force of the *abna'*, and through violent campaigning in east and west, these Tahirids made sure that, among other things, the majority of the empire eventually recognized the new caliph's authority.

Figure 5.2 Mashhad (Iran): complex surrounding the mausoleum of *imam* ʿAli al-Rida

Source: https://commons.wikimedia.org/wiki/Category:Views_of_Imam_Reza_shrine#/media/File:Imam_Reza_shrine_before_development.jpg, By Alborzagros—Own work, CC BY-SA 3.0, https://commons.wikimedia.org/w/index.php?curid=16743646

2.2 *The reigns of al-Ma'mun and al-Mu'tasim*

Al-Ma'mun emerged from the 4th *fitna* a victor and managed to restore his own version of Abbasid authority at the expense of traditional Abbasid power groups such as the *abna'*. In the eastern regions of that authority, well into Transoxania, and in Bagdad itself, mainly the Tahirids and their Khurasani troops remained his most important political and military supporters and representatives. Another brother of the caliph, Abu Ishaq, and his personal army simultaneously performed Abbasid authority in Egypt (see below). Any Abbasid control over the North African region of Ifriqiya, with its center at Qayrawan, in modern-day Tunisia, however, was definitively lost to a new regional dynasty of former Abbasid representatives, the Aghlabids (r. 800–909). In this substantially transformed political, territorial, and social constellation, stretching between Egypt and Transoxania, al-Ma'mun and his entourage succeeded in restoring the relationships of power and authority that made for Abbasid trans-regional rule in a relatively stable manner.

Al-Ma'mun eventually died in 833, on one of the campaigns that were again regularly organized against Roman Asia Minor. He was succeeded after only the briefest of opposition (in favor of one of his sons) by his brother Abu Ishaq, who reigned under the personal title of al-Mu'tasim (r. 833–842). Abu Ishaq had already played an important role in the accommodation of local and regional elites to the new Abbasid authority of his brother, especially in Egypt. He had achieved this in particular with his personal force of a few thousand men, which he had begun acquiring on the margins of Abbasid political and social order from around 815 onwards. This force basically consisted of a diverse collection of prisoners of war, former household slaves and freedmen, adventurers of all kinds, and numerous other 'marginal' individuals and groups without much meaningful social ties or established interests in the Abbasid context. They were mainly purchased on the slave markets in Bagdad, directly supplied by slave merchants from the booty of raids on the Inner-Asian steppes, or recruited in distant areas in the east, such as the remote Ferghana valley. In time, this rabble famously turned into a genuine and particularly efficient fighting machine around the person of their lord and master, Abu Ishaq al-Mu'tasim. When al-Mu'tasim ascended the caliphal throne in 833, these personal troops of his had become no less than the new military backbone of the Abbasid caliphate, definitely marginalizing the old Arabian and Khurasani *abna'* elites in the process. This army of only a few thousand so-called *ghilman* (sg. *ghulam*—'youths'), consisting mainly of *atrak* ('Turks', mostly enslaved individual horsemen of diverse Inner-Asian, Turkic-speaking origins) but also of Armenians, so-called *maghariba* from Egypt, and numerous other outsiders and *mawali* freedmen, ushered in the beginning of an entirely new era of leadership practices. *Ghilman* and *atrak* now came to provide personal coercive force to many a leader with sufficient resources, and very quickly these mostly Turkic-speaking fighters moved to the centers of dynastic chains of authority and agency and to positions of leadership in the apparatus of power of the Abbasids and of most of their dynastic competitors and successors.

This construction of a very effective instrument of coercive force around Abu Ishaq al-Mu'tasim's person was part and parcel of the unprecedented centralization of patrimonial-bureaucratic power relations and resource flows that this caliph, his brother al-Ma'mun before him, and their entourages of courtiers and administrators of especially eastern origins appear to have accomplished. This was achieved in particular with the assistance of the Turkic-speaking commanders of al-Mu'tasim's new *ghilman* troops, who also started to serve as caliphal representatives and administrators in different localities and regions of the empire—and thus also very often as ambitious and resourceful Abbasid powerholders in their own right. At the same time, different members of the Tahirid family remained another important, balancing pillar of Abbasid rule. Both in Bagdad and in the entire east, Tahirids continued to be relied upon as another well-integrated set of Abbasid administrators and commanders and, simultaneously, as powerful Khurasani regional leaders. This new era of effective Abbasid trans-regional power and authority was given physical expression as well through the creation of a new urban center for the organization and representation of al-Muʿtasim's effective and legitimate rule. Samarraʾ, on the east bank of the Tigris more than 100 kilometers to the north of Bagdad, proved another suitable location for a new imperial settlement. Its impressive remains, bringing to mind the monumentality of its caliphal palace, military quarters and hunting parks, congregational mosque, and markets, again continued to inform about the successful condition and achievement of the Abbasid central apparatus of power and powerholders in the mid-9th century. From the mid-830s onwards, the extensive Abbasid court, its new military leaders, and their mostly Turkic-speaking *ghilman* followers were stationed there rather than in the old quarters and palaces of Bagdad (see also the next chapter).

The success of these new arrangements became immediately clear from the many military victories that are reported to have been achieved in the many frontier zones of al-Maʾmun's and al-Muʿtasim's authority. This included the aforementioned regular campaigns against Roman Asia Minor, in which al-Maʿmun himself died in 833. They were also the result of efficient dealings with various local contestants of Abbasid authority in Azerbaijan, Khurasan, Iran, Iraq, and Syria. One of the most famous and most acclaimed exploits—included in the intense Arabic literary production of this era—of this new Abbasid power

Figure 5.3 Samarraʾ by the Tigris, with up front the Great Mosque of al-Mutawakkil and its spiral-shaped Malwiya minaret

Source: The National Geographic Magazine vol. 41 (1922), p. 530, aerial photo by A.T. Clay

undoubtedly concerns the retaliatory sacking of Ankara and Amorion in Roman Asia Minor, in 838, by an army commanded by al-Muʿtasim himself.

Al-Maʾmun's and al-Muʿtasim's personal, effective, and successful restoration and further elaboration of the Abbasid patrimonial-bureaucratic apparatus of power also speaks from the more explicit articulation of Abbasid authority's spiritual dimension that continues to transpire from the extant source material. Although this remains very much in line with what is known about preceding Umayyad, early Abbasid and wider Late Antique theocratic claims to sacral kingship, that spiritual dimension appears to have been enforced more clearly now in titles such as those of *imam* and caliph. Since these two titles became ever more central to Muslim identities in subsequent eras, their usage in and before the 9th century continues to be, as already surmised in preceding chapters, a subject of scholarly debate. Whatever these titles may have actually meant at the time, in the reigns of al-Maʾmun and his immediate successors, this articulation certainly involved the enforcement of a very explicit sacral and normative authority by this apparatus for itself and its caliph, in a particular context in which this wide-ranging claim to that authority was increasingly questioned and challenged (see next chapter).

3 The Abbasid 'middle period' (842–908)

3.1 Centralization and disintegration

After the death of al-Muʿtasim in 842 in one of his palaces in Samarraʾ, the centralizing formation of the Abbasid patrimonial-bureaucratic apparatus seems to have continued unabated under two of his sons, reigning under the titles al-Wathiq (r. 842–847) and al-Mutawakkil (r. 847–861). Simultaneously, however, once again tensions started to rise among the growing number of leaderships that were competing for power in the Iraqi centers of Abbasid authority. These included especially the different leaders of the new military backbone of Abbasid power, with the loyalty and functionality of the Turkic-speaking, Samarraʾ-based *ghilman* remaining closely connected to the personality and resources of the ruling caliph and of those whom the caliph had made their commanders. Especially during the reign of al-Mutawakkil, it transpired that a problem was growing right at the heart of the Abbasid power apparatus when longstanding *ghilman* and their commanders became an all too dominant power group that pursued its own interests rather than those of the new caliph and his supporters. Al-Mutawakkil tried to turn this situation to his advantage by relying on members of his own new entourage, especially two of his sons, to acquire more direct control over the regions of the empire and by recruiting new troops of his own and stationing them in another new imperial settlement to the north of Samarraʾ. However, this soon turned out to aggravate rather than solve the problem. The newly acquired power and interests of the *ghilman* of his predecessors turned out not to be easily challenged. In fact, the heightened competition that was triggered by al-Mutawakkil's creation of yet another group of contenders for caliphal resources eventually culminated, according to some reports, in December 861, in the caliph's assassination by a group of *ghilman*.

In 861, a period of political instability and chaos started that would last nine years and that was a consequence of this murder and of the subsequent disintegration of the dynastic center into numerous interest groups (Abbasid princes, *ghilman* commanders, *kuttab* leaders and various local strongmen) that fought each other over the caliphate and over the control of its political and economic resources. During this short period, no less than four caliphs assumed power, three of whom were murdered. Each one of these had the short-lived fortune to be represented by some political faction in the caliphal center of Samarra'. This was accompanied by a loss of cohesion and a severing of ties with different regional and local agents and elites. In Egypt and southern Syria, the Abbasid military leader Ahmad ibn Tulun declared himself autonomous; around Basra and in southern Iraq, a certain ʿAli ibn Muhammad inspired the Zanj, East African slaves working in the saltpeter mines, to partake in anti-Abbasid violence, causing irreparable havoc and destruction in the region; and in Iran and Khurasan, the regional Persian dynastic leaderships of the Saffarids and Samanids were able to maximize their autonomy, heralding the definitive disappearance of Abbasid power in these regions. This disintegration as a result of the internecine warfare at and around the court of Samarra' is known, furthermore, to have caused huge losses for the revenues of the caliphal court and its elites, presenting many new challenges for those in charge of the Caliphate's political economy (see Chapter 7).

3.2 New leadership and Abbasid restoration

In 870, the fragmentation and anarchy in Abbasid Iraq came to an end because, amidst the rivalries at the court, a victor arose, the *ghilman* leader Musa ibn Bugha (d. 877), and because once more a capable Abbasid ruler and experienced military commander, a son of al-Mutawakkil best known under his formal title al-Muwaffaq (d. 891), came to power. Al-Muwaffaq, however, never assumed the position of Abbasid caliph. Having emerged as the main Abbasid strongman from the internecine warfare of the 860s, he left that risky honor to his brother. While this brother reigned from Samarra' as al-Muʿtamid (r. 870–892), al-Muwaffaq appears from the written record to have placed him under his control ever more firmly thanks to his strong relations of mutual interest with Musa and with other leaders of the Samarra'-based *ghilman*.

As a result of the collaboration between Musa and al-Muwaffaq, their recruitment of new *ghilman* who were more uniformly of Turkic-speaking Inner-Asian origins, and the emergence of a new generation of efficient experts in the central administrative bureaus that were made responsible for the management of the dynasty's communication and political

Figure 5.4 *Dinar* (golden coin) minted in the name of caliph al-Muʿtamid (Sana'a, 271 AH/884–5), including an explicit reference in the last line of the obverse's center to his brother al-Muwaffaq

Source: Michel Écochard archive, courtesy of Aga Khan Documentation Center, MIT Libraries (AKDC@MIT)

economy, much of the former authority, territorial integrity, and resources of the empire could be restored. This affected in particular the regions and people of Iraq, Syria, and—eventually—Egypt, as a result of al-Muwaffaq's direct and sustained military operations. Eventually, also among the ever more autonomously operating regional elites in the east, a certain measure of Abbasid political order was reconstructed, even if only nominally. Moreover, this pursuit of restoration was concluded in 892 with the return of the court to the old Abbasid capital of Bagdad, where al-Muwaffaq had continued to reside and from where his son continued to pursue effective control over Abbasid resources from the middle of the 880s. When the caliph al-Muʿtamid died in 892 in Samarraʾ and was succeeded by this son of al-Muwaffaq, this automatically sealed the fate of this extended palatial and military settlement. During the next four centuries, from 892 to 1258, and in spite of all further changes and transformations, the center of the Caliphate would remain firmly located in Bagdad.

During the reign of al-Muwaffaq's son, the caliph al-Muʿtadid (r. 892–902) and that of his grandson al-Muktafi (r. 902–908), the more limited but again effective Abbasid political order in Islamic West-Asia was successfully maintained by a patrimonial-bureaucratic apparatus of Abbasid power and its diverse groups of dynastic, military, and administrative experts, agents, and leaders. It is, therefore, generally stated that during this last quarter of the 9th and the beginning of the 10th centuries, the Abbasid Caliphate experienced a new period of trans-regional control and prosperity, supported by a relatively efficient military and administrative organizational complex that was populated by *atrak* and *kuttab*, a flourishing cultural and economic life in the well-connected urban centers of the empire, and an Abbasid trans-regional political order that provided a sustained level of coherence to it all, especially in the regions of Iraq, Syria, Arabia, and Egypt.

Notes

1 Ibn al-Faqīh (10th century), *Mukhtaṣar Kitāb al-Buldān* ['Concise Book of Lands']; translation from Lewis, *Islam from the Prophet Muhammad to the Capture of Constantinople. Volume I: Politics and War*, 24.
2 Agha, *The Revolution Which Toppled the Umayyads: Neither Arab nor ʿAbbāsid.*
3 al-Masʿūdī (d. 955), *Murūj al-Dhahab* ['Meadows of Gold']; translation from Lewis, *Islam from the Prophet Muhammad to the Capture of Constantinople. Volume I: Politics and War*, 25–6.
4 al-Tabari (d. 923), *Tārīkh al-Rusul wa-l-Mulūk* ['The History of Prophets and Kings']; translation from Bosworth, *The History of al-Ṭabarī. Vol. XXX*, 183–6.

Selected readings

(see next chapter)

6 Late Antique patrimonial-bureaucratic formation in Islamic West-Asia

The construction of Arabo-Islamic urbanities, authorities, and courts (8th–10th centuries)

Introduction: norms, ideals, and discourses of power and belonging in a Late Antique context

The first few centuries during which the 'community of believers' expanded and acquired its shape as a distinct political and social order display an undeniable aura of continuity with Late Antique leadership practices and discourses. This continuity far transcends the many changes that followed the *fitnas* and dynastic upheavals of the 8th, 9th, and 10th centuries. For example, there was for much of this period the ongoing coherent reality of the imperial domain, connecting now many of the Mediterranean and Asian territories of its imperial predecessors. There also was the centered reality of the manifold local, regional, and trans-regional relationships that continued to organize this coherence. The majority of these all continued to revolve one way or another around a central dynastic leadership of Qurayshid Meccan origins that adopted Late Antique forms for their coherent organization. It was supported by an ever more integrated, elaborate, and powerful bureaucratic apparatus of military and administrative force. It was conceptualized and articulated from the perspectives of monotheist theocracy and sacral kingship. And it was fed by diverse but intensive agricultural systems in, mainly, the rich regions of the so-called 'fertile crescent' between Nile and Tigris, and also by various Afro-Eurasian commercial flows of commodities and people.

As always in history, important changes simultaneously took place in this Late Antique empire, not only regarding the impressive trans-regional scale of its imperial reach or the top-down dynastic *histoire événementielle* discussed in some of the previous chapters, but also on broader social and cultural levels. This concerned the many changes that were experienced by the ranks of those who participated in this empire and who made for its imperial appearances in the many local and regional arenas of their political action. Transforming from the Arabian leaderships of the turn of the 7th to 8th centuries to the multiple—including Persian- and Turkic-speaking—ones in the 9th and 10th centuries, these ranks' destinies did not just follow the fluid course of the Abbasid imperial venture, but also became intrinsically interconnected, even identified, with it, especially in the Abbasid heartlands between Nile and Tigris. As announced in Chapter 4, those changes therefore also involved the emergence of an increasingly distinct, shared, and contested notion of what it meant to be Muslim amidst the enormous sociocultural diversity of that new empire, for these changing leaderships and their followers, but also as time elapsed for many other groups and communities that were somehow affected by the expanding chains of Abbasid authority and agency. The confrontation with the rich set of Late Antique legacies played an important role in this context of Islamic discursive formation, both in its inclusion of Late Antique Greek-Roman, Perso-Sasanian, and wider Asian (including Indian) practices and ideas, and in its equally enriching process of searching for what distinguished this particular formation from those practices and ideas. In this process, as already announced by Marwanid monolinguistic measures, the Arabic language—even more than Islam's rendering of Late Antique monotheism—soon started to play a central role, as a *lingua franca* for all who needed, for a variety of reasons, to confirm their participation in the imperial enterprise. In modern historical research, emphasis is therefore usually put upon this process of transcending sociocultural diversity when considering what made Arabic into a distinctive and common language of communication across the Islamic empire. One of the most authoritative specialists in the study of these practices and discourses of Late Antique power and belonging, Robert Hoyland, summarizes this strongly integrative force that emanated from the process of Arabization in the following manner:

> Inevitably, the fact that the Holy Book was in Arabic and that the Prophet was an Arab born in Arabia meant that many a good Muslim, even if not of Arab ancestry, would acknowledge the link between matters Arab and Islam and even seek to strengthen that link. Thus the first comprehensive work on Arabian history and the life of Muhammad was by Ibn Ishaq (d. 150/767), whose grandfather was a prisoner-of-war from 'Ayn al-Tamr in Iraq. The earliest surviving [Arabic] Quranic commentary was by Muqatil ibn Sulayman (d. 150/767), who was born of Persian parents. And the first Arabic grammar was by Sibawayhi (d. 180/796), a native of Balkh in modern Afghanistan.[1]

Within the enormous diversity of ethnic, religious, linguistic, geographical, economic, and social landscapes that, in a very short time, were considered part of the new Late Antique empire and its theocratic order, the process of Islamization and particularly Arabization realized a continuously stronger connectedness and shared sense of belonging. This enabled the ever more complex social fabric of imperial leaderships to maintain a level of political cohesiveness that remained largely unaffected by the radical dynastic and elite transformations and re-alignments of the 8th and 9th centuries. In the process, an increasingly stronger and more consciously articulated imagination of a common sociocultural order and identity manifested itself as autonomous from the particular fates of these political and military leaders. In claiming this relative autonomy and these alternative forms of authority within the Abbasid theocratic order, it even left a lasting legacy, encapsulated in the writings and reputations of many of the era's eponymous scholars and intellectuals, such as Ibn Ishaq, Muqatil ibn Sulayman and Sibawayhi, and including Arabized Christians, Jews, and many others who had flocked to the imperial urban centers of Iraq.[2]

The formation of an Arabo-Islamic community, and more specifically the process of Islamization that shaped it, represent an altogether more difficult story to reconstruct. Especially the particular, mainly literary, and often formative, even normative, nature of the extant written source material—mostly only made by, for, and about the Ibn Ishaqs, Muqatils, Sibawayhis, and their elitist peers in this community—has proven an obstacle that is difficult to overcome when pursuing any more socially oriented research questions. Previous statistical research has suggested that conversion to Islamic monotheism of, especially, members of diverse local and regional elites reached a quantitative peak in the heydays of Abbasid imperial power and authority, approximately between 790 and 890. Because of the nature of that source material, however, these conclusions remain highly speculative and determined by the particular perspective of explaining later historical realities of Muslim majorities. They certainly seem to suggest how, after the Marwanid impetus, the relationship between the process of Islamization and the growing participation of local and regional elites in the expanding ranks of the imperial apparatus remained very close in the written record and inevitably

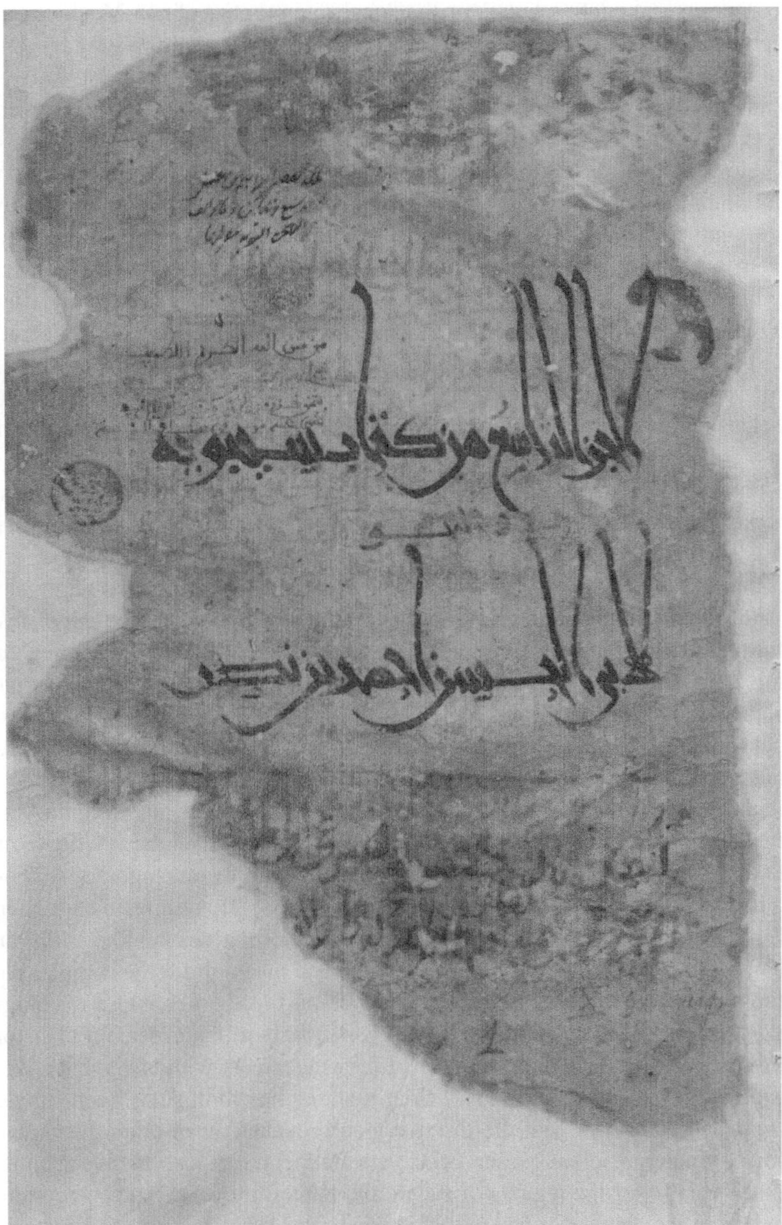

Figure 6.1 Heading of the ninth part of the one of the oldest extant copies of the *Kitab Sibawayhi*, manuscript on parchment (10th–11th century, Qayrawan)

Source: Ms. Milaan Bibliotheca Ambroziana X56sup

also in at least some of the social realities that that record represented. Whereas the expanding offspring of these converts undoubtedly continued to make the community grow—and to generate debates on its distinguishing features and boundaries—it has also been acknowledged, however, that these data do not allow for making much claims about how its changing size compared to that of other, non-Muslim groups and communities. There actually exists a general consensus in modern scholarship that local communities of non-Muslims remained a demographic majority throughout these centuries in most of the empire's regions and localities, from al-Andalus in the west to Khurasan and Transoxania in the east. This is said to also explain the relatively prosperous continuation of many of them to this day. Furthermore, what the extant data also suggest is that the appearance of new, first-generation converts gradually slowed down in the 10th century, as apparently did—with the contemporaneous disintegration of the Abbasid power apparatus and the growing priority of especially Shi'ite challenges—imperial incentives for the process of Islamization to continue in any similar fashion.[3] By that time, however, it was clear that all groups across these Afro-Eurasian lands, whatever their old or new discourses of power and belonging, had been deeply affected and altered by this imperial formation of a new Arabo-Islamic community and theocratic order. This manifested itself especially in how all had somehow become involved in the former process of Arabization that had mediated the imperial connections between all local and regional elites in east and west since the early 8th century, even when those connections had been of a mere nominal and symbolic or subversive nature.

These remarkable Late Antique changes and the relative trans-regional cohesion that simultaneously started to emerge as a result of these intertwined processes of imperial organization, Islamic discursive formation, and Arabization, made this period into a point of reference that would be remembered by many as a 'classical' ideal of trans-regional imperial majesty and Arabo-Islamic cultural efflorescence and as a historical moment of inspiration for the further articulation of Islamic identities and political formations as they continued to develop. This normative character of the period, along with a certain aversion among contemporary writers and historians to say anything about non-elite life, continues to pose substantial challenges to modern historians when they consult the extant textual material and try to understand not just processes of Arabization and Islamization, but also the period's wider social, economic, and cultural transformations. In fact, especially from the 9th century onwards, ever more texts that had a historiographical interest have been written, and quite a few of them have been transmitted through the ages. These contemporary Arabo-Islamic texts of a historical, literary, and legal nature are actually largely responsible for later memories of this period as a classical, if not ideal, and even normative one. They all share in the same ambition to create specific layers of cohesion and meaning for the complex times that their authors and their audiences experienced, writing these times into a teleological and traditionalist reading of the community's (and particularly of its leadership's) history as on the road to salvation, with little to no room for engagements with any subversive historical trajectories. In recent years, this particular material has fortunately been supplemented in increasingly useful ways with the discovery and revaluation of other documentary and archaeological material, often preserved in less deliberate and normative manners. This holds true especially for the regions of Egypt and Khurasan, where specific circumstances have enabled the accidental survival of many papyri, as also suggested in Chapter 4. But for most of period after the mid-8th century, the disclosure and study of this mass of material of a documentary and also of a more day-to-day nature remains in its infancy, something that applies even more to the interpretation of its value, significance, and impact, not only as historical witnesses but above all also as historical actors in the complex patrimonial-bureaucratic apparatus of late antique powers in their own right.

Nevertheless, it remains possible to make critical use of all this material to reconstruct a number of aspects of at least some key parts of this Late Antique 'classical' socio-political formation. Therefore, this chapter examines in more detail various social phenomena that are best known from the extant source material and that belonged to life along the chains of Abbasid authority and agency which made for that apparatus in the imperial urban centers and at the courts of Abbasid Iraq in particular.

1 Abbasid urbanities

1.1 Chains of imperial urbanization

> The creation of an Islamic empire, and then the development of an Islamic society linking the world of the Indian Ocean with that of the Mediterranean, provided the necessary conditions for the emergence of a chain of great cities running from one end of the world of Islam to the other: Cordoba, Seville and Granada in Andalus, Fez and Marrakesh in Morocco, Qayrawan and later Tunis in Tunisia, Fustat and then Cairo in Egypt, Damascus and Aleppo in Syria, Mecca and Medina in western Arabia, Mosul and Basra in Iraq, and beyond them the cities of Iran, Transoxania and northern India. Some of these cities had already existed in the time before the coming of Islam, others were creations of the Islamic conquest or the power of later dynasties. . . . By the tenth and eleventh centuries the great cities of the Islamic countries were the largest in the western half of the world.[4]

As one of the doyens of the study of premodern Islamic history, Albert Hourani, surmises here, the Late Antique Arabo-Islamic empire and the many groups and communities that were involved in or affected by its imperial practices of reproduction, competition, protection, and accumulation were to a substantial degree urban phenomena. Or rather, the many urban centers that are listed here and that tied together the regions between the Atlantic and Indian Oceans as junctions of trade routes, as nodes in sociocultural networks, and as centers of local, regional, and trans-regional control, were very much part and parcel of the processes of leadership formation and explanation that made for that empire and those groups and communities. At least, the particular nature of the currently available source material allows especially for retelling that urban side of these stories. It leaves scant opportunity to add any considerations of the organization, transformation, and differing scales of integration of the majorities of pastoralist and agrarian communities, and for that matter of the urban commoners and poor, who populated most of Islamic West-Asia's diverse landscapes and produced most of its resources.

As Hourani announces, there were different historical types of urban centers that came to matter so much in early Islamic history. Quite a few urban spaces, such as Damascus in Syria or Marv in Khurasan, had ancient or Late Antique roots. Many others derived their origins from the specific dynamics of the Arabian expansion and the organization of the new Arabian leadership. As explained before, for the deployment of tribal forces, the organization of Arabian migration, and the arrangement of power and control in new regions, the choice was always made to concentrate people and resources in new regional centers, *amsar*, such as Kufa and Basra in Iraq, Fustat in Egypt, and Qayrawan in Ifriqiya. This particular early practice was eventually also continued and reproduced in the phenomenon of new regional centers that new dynastic leaders or their regional representatives tended to create for the representation and organization of their freshly won authority. This was the case with Marwanid Wasit in Iraq, Abbasid al-ʿAskar in Egypt, and various palatial settlements created by Marwanid and Abbasid rulers in Syria and Iraq. In combination with the early leaderships' centralizing tributary and fiscal arrangements paid in goods, forced labor, and hard currency, many of these military settlements and political headquarters transformed into regional poles of rapid demographic and socioeconomic growth, and thus into full-fledged urban centers, where intense open market economies were enabled and stimulated.[5]

The most representative models of these novel imperial headquarters undoubtedly were the early Abbasid palatial centers of 8th-century Bagdad and 9th-century Samarra' in Iraq. As mentioned before, the former began in the 760s and 770s as a newly constructed imperial settlement on the banks of the Tigris and was first called 'City of Peace' (*Madinat al-Salam*). Only later, in the rapid process of its urbanization and transformation into a trans-regional metropolis, did it become more widely known by the ancient name of one of the villages it incorporated, Bagdad. Samarra' was similarly newly constructed in the 830s as an imperial settlement on the east bank of the Tigris more than 100 kilometers to the north of Bagdad. It

Figure 6.2 Ceramic bowl, probably from Samarra', 9th century
Source: Metropolitan Museum of Art, 1977.126

is claimed to have been formally named 'He who sees it is delighted' (*Surra Man Raʾā*), an Arabized version of its pre-Islamic name that was eventually adapted to Samarraʾ. As mentioned before, between 836 and 892, the Abbasid court and the heart of the chains of Abbasid authority and agency were organized here rather than in Bagdad, occupying a widely outstretched area along the Tigris with palaces, avenues, military quarters, hunting grounds, mosques, and markets.

As suggested, the strategies that informed the emergence of new imperial centers such as the 'City of Peace' or 'He Who Sees it is Delighted' were informed by political motives above all, with opportunities for and realities of further urbanization appearing as fortunate spill-over effects that were shared by many (but not all) of these settlements. These political and military leadership strategies behind the decision to build new imperial centers are certainly emphasized in most of the extant historiographical reports, as in the following unique anecdotal commentary in a contemporary geographical text that explains the transfer of Abbasid authority from Bagdad to Samarraʾ:

> When the rough and ill-mannered *atrāk* rode their horses [in Bagdad, they did so] at full gallop, knocking down people right and left. The urban toughs would seize hold of them, killing some, beating others. The blood of [the *atrāk*] was shed with impunity, while [the local authorities] did nothing to retaliate against those committing such deeds. This [state of affairs] weighed heavily on al-Muʿtaṣim, and he resolved [finally] to leave Bagdad.[6]

Just as, as suggested here, the move to Samarraʾ in the 830s was aimed at safeguarding and preserving the power and authority of al-Muʿtasim's new Abbasid elites, the Abbasid ruler al-Mansur is similarly related to have commissioned in 762 the construction of a new headquarters on the west bank of the Tigris for the backbone of the young Abbasid dynasty's military strength, the *abnaʾ* from Khurasan. Later historiographic memories place this foundation of Bagdad within the same pattern of the politics of leadership and military strategy, as in this passage from one of the most important chronicles of early Islamic and Abbasid history, which adds its own typical layer of exemplary leadership to the narrative:

> [Al-Manṣūr said:] "This is a good place for an army camp. Here's the Tigris, with nothing between us and China, and on it arrives all that the sea can bring, as well as provisions from the Jazira, Armenia and surrounding areas. Further, there is the Euphrates on which can arrive everything from Syria, al-Raqqa, and surrounding areas". The caliph therefore dismounted and pitched his camp on the Ṣarāt Canal. He sketched a plan of the city and put an army commander in charge of each quarter.[7]

Bagdad, or 'The City of Peace', was reportedly constructed between 762 and 777 as a round palatial settlement. Around a center with the palace of the caliph and the Friday mosque were several neighborhoods with small markets and residential buildings for the members of the Abbasid family, the court, and military leaders. Furthermore, the elite troops of the early Abbasids, the *abnaʾ*, were housed in a northwestern district, called al-Harbiyya. This well-organized city planning, which served both political-military and economic purposes, supposedly came under immediate pressure due to a swift influx of new inhabitants. Over time, numerous adjustments, therefore, had to be made, during which the original urban layout soon outgrew its closed, circular constraint. The rapid, pragmatic, and political nature of this process is beautifully suggested in the following stories, which were recorded in the early

10th century and which, at the same time, are illustrative of the complex, narrative nature of the most important historiographical source material that we still have today:

> ʿĪsā ibn ʿAli complained to [his cousin, the Abbasid caliph] Abū Jaʿfar [al-Manṣūr]: "O Commander of the Faithful, it is tiring for me to walk from the gate of the courtyard to the palace, for I have become weak," and he replied, "Have yourself carried in a litter," but he responded, "I am embarrassed because of the people". Al-Manṣūr said, "Is there anyone who continues to be embarrassed because of them?" but ʿĪsā continued, "Allow me, O Commander of the Believers, what is allowed one of the water-carrying camels". He said, "Does any water-carrying animal or riding animal enter the city?" Thus, he ordered that everyone move their doors to the intervals of the arcades and that no one should enter the courtyard except on foot. When al-Manṣūr ordered that the doors that led into the courtyard should be blocked and opened to the intervals of the arcades, the markets were established in the four arcades of the city, each one having a market. This continued until one of the Roman *patrikioi* [high officials] came as an ambassador, and [al-Manṣūr] ordered [his chamberlain] al-Rabīʿ to take him on a tour of the city and its surroundings to see the development and the building. Al-Rabīʿ took him on a tour, and when it was finished he asked, "What do you think of my city?" He had gone up on the walls of the city and in the domes of the gates, and he said, "I saw a beautiful building, but I saw your enemies with you in the city". The caliph asked him who they were, and he replied, "The market people". Abū Jaʿfar [al-Manṣūr] was silent about it and, when the *patrikios* had gone, he ordered that the market be sent out of the city. He appointed Ibrāhīm ibn Hubaysh al-Kūfī and attached Jawwās ibn al-Musayyab al-Yamanī, his freedman, and ordered the two of them to build markets in the Karkh area and ordered them to make booths and houses for every trade and hand them over to the people. When they had done this, he moved the market from the city and imposed rents on them according to size. When the number of people grew, they built markets on sites Ibrāhīm ibn Hubaysh and Jawwās had not sought to build on because they were unable [to construct] the booths from their resources. They were charged less in rents than was collected from those who settled in the buildings of the authorities.[8]

This flourishing urban center, in continuous expansion from its inception, is said to have already counted no less than one million inhabitants in the later 9th century. Although this undoubtedly is an overly optimistic estimate by contemporary authors, it does indicate that the Abbasid headquarters quickly became an unsurpassed metropolis and a central hub in Hourani's "chain of great cities running from one end of the world of Islam to the other", in political as well as in socioeconomic terms. This chain was indeed not just made up of political relationships that tied local elites to the regional and trans-regional urban centers of Abbasid authority. As also suggested in the fragment above, this chain also included the many economic connections that made urban spaces such as Bagdad into central nodes in diverse networks of locally, regionally, and trans-regionally circulating commodities and people. Among the anonymous mass of its different groups of inhabitants, Abbasid Bagdad therefore counted many merchants who—temporarily or permanently—made their living at this junction of trade routes. Regionally and trans-regionally oriented groups and networks of traders provided the court and the urban elites with many opportunities to spend their wealth, including especially on luxury goods, from textiles, precious stones, and metalwares to slaves. More locally oriented commodity chains and networks of traders ensured the necessary supply of food from Bagdad's fertile central Iraqi hinterland between the Tigris and

Euphrates, known as the Sawad ('the Black Land'). Here, experimentation with new crops and renewed investments in irrigation and land development are believed to have stimulated agricultural production and surplus income. Modern scholarship since the 1970s has even tended to consider this part and parcel of an Afro-Eurasian 'agricultural revolution'. This agrarian transformation is believed to have been generated by the Arabian expansion and trans-regional imperial formation of the 7th and 8th centuries and must have interacted favorably with demographic changes involved in Abbasid processes of urbanization and centralization. The regional and local particularities of this agrarian transformation, however, remain much debated and open for much further research and interpretation.[9] This certainly also goes for how this supposed transfer and spread of crops, such as wheat, sugar cane, or rice, and of related agricultural knowhow and technologies from east to west intersected with the period's commodity chains and commercial networks.

Another important group of urban inhabitants that defined everyday life in Bagdad, in all the other regional centers, and also in many of the agrarian hinterlands were the extremely diverse group of the unfree and slaves. These originated from non-Muslim populations that mostly lived beyond the many frontier regions of the empire—mainly central and northern Europe, eastern Africa, and Inner Asia. They were imported by specialist merchants and traded at specific, mostly urban, markets. These unfree were used by their masters in many capacities, including as labor forces on rural estates and plantations. In urban elite households, however, unfree men and women appear mostly as domestic servants, as guards and soldiers, as entertainers and concubines, and—if they were eunuchs—as guardians of the women of the household. In addition, unfree are regularly represented as obtaining their manumission, which in fact enabled active participation in social life, with access and connections mostly provided by their former masters, occasionally even becoming autonomous elite agents in their own right. Some of the most famous rags-to-riches stories that have been preserved about such fortunate former slaves include the stories about ʿArib al-Maʾmuniya (d. 890). This was an unfree woman of obscure origins as well as of great fame and many talents. She appears as a highly educated and widely admired courtesan and musician in caliphal and other households in Bagdad and Basra, before being manumitted by one of the mid-9th-century caliphs and acquiring legendary wealth, influence, and her own household of unfree servants and musical students.[10] Other stories concern the powerful leaders of the *ghilman* troops of caliph al-Muʿtasim, known as Ashinas, Itakh, and Wasif, who originally had served as cook, blacksmith, and in other capacities in Bagdad respectively before, from the later 810s and the 820s onwards, they—just as many *atrak* leaders in Samarraʾ after them—managed to embark on very different career paths of violence, power, and leadership.[11]

It was therefore not just the dynamics of imperial politics that made for the chain of Abbasid urban centers. Also the experiences and achievements of the anonymous masses of urban dwellers, including all kinds of unfree and merchants of whom only a very few—such as ʿArib, Ashinas, Itakh, and Wasif—entered the limelight of history, determined the process of urbanization across the Arabo-Islamic empire. That this was a remarkable process, which was experienced as central to Abbasid life, especially as far as Bagdad is concerned, is expressed in many a preserved literary account of people travelling there and admiring its urban qualities. This 11th-century version of a 9th-century homage to the merits of Bagdad attests to this as well:

> Have you seen in all the length and breadth of the earth
> A city such as Baghdad? Indeed, it is paradise on earth,

Life in Baghdad is pure; its wood becomes verdant,
While life outside of it is without purity or freshness.
The lifespan in it is long; its food
Is healthful; for some parts of the earth are more healthful than others.
Its Lord has decided that no caliph shall die
In it; indeed, He determines what He wishes for His creatures.[12]

1.2 Chains of imperial elite formation

Another important commodity that enabled Bagdad's connectedness to the wider world, not just in the format of political and economic relations, but also in the sharing of practices of knowledge production and community building, undoubtedly was paper.[13] Much as had been the case for the illustrious rags-to-riches careers of ʿArib, Ashinas, Itakh, and Wasif, or for that matter of the historian Ibn Ishaq, the Quran expert Muqatil ibn Sulayman, and the grammarian Sibawayhi, we know about life in Bagdad and in other regional centers mainly because many stories about it, and intellectual products of it, were committed to paper. This was done by and for the diverse milieus of urban elites, including people such as the former courtesan ʿArib and her many Abbasid patrons and admirers, who all appear from these papers and books as extremely interested in all manners of knowledge and beauty. From the early 8th century onwards, therefore—from al-Hasan al-Basri, mentioned in Chapter 4, over Ibn Ishaq, Muqatil ibn Sulayman, Sibawayhi, and their peers in the later 8th century, to the ever-expanding numbers of their successors in the 9th and 10th centuries—the process of the growth and diversification of the ranks of these artists and scholars continued. These *literati*, historians, theologians, philologists, jurists, philosophers, physicians, mathematicians, scientists of the stars, and polymaths appeared increasingly—admittedly especially from their own written records on paper—as diverse but very present and very active groups and networks of students, teachers, intellectuals, and practitioners in Bagdad as well as elsewhere along Hourani's "chain of great cities running from one end of the world of Islam to the other".

In fact, they did not just appear everywhere along this chain of urban centers, but also along the equally wide-ranging chains of Abbasid imperial authority and representation. This era's urban intellectual and cultural networks in formation benefited especially from their strong integration into the relationships that revolved around the Abbasid court and around the urban palaces and households of the Abbasid patrimonial-bureaucratic elites, especially in Iraq, but also elsewhere in the empire. Just as ʿArib, Ashinas, Itakh, and Wasif, they were actually all both products and agents of arrangements that made for the formation of that multivalent imperial apparatus, given that they were at least exposed to if not involved in many of its practices. The wide range of these practices included not just the subtle arts of fighting and courtesanship, but also of Arabic letter writing, bookkeeping and resource management, guaranteeing social justice and security, and articulating authority, all of which, and many more, connected in myriad ways with the blossoming fields of the arts and sciences.

A close interaction was actually established through the intense exchange of tangible and intangible resources between the growing ranks of Abbasid (and later in the 10th century also post-Abbasid) agents and leaderships and the diversifying ranks of Abbasid-era artists, *literati*, and intellectuals. From the many traces that remain of this interaction, it appears that the former had above all access to resources to offer, either within the expanding Abbasid power apparatus or somehow derived from that apparatus, especially in the format of stipends, appointments, rewards, connections, and reputations. The latter artists, *literati*, and intellectuals provided valuable tools—texts, performances, ideas, and expertise—to their patrons to quench a remarkable thirst for knowledge, education, and beauty, and at the same time to support claims to status, authority, distinction, and belonging. Abbasid leadership was thus soon measured by the quality of cultural and intellectual patronage and participation as much as by successes on the battlefield and political connections. The mutually beneficial and very personal interaction of courtly patronage and cultural clientage quickly became an essential part of the social hierarchies that, volatile as they were, marked elite urban life and leadership practices everywhere. Quite a few members of Abbasid power elite families are even remembered for their artistic and intellectual contributions rather than for any political role they may have played. Biographies of many of the most successful intellectuals and writers all invariably refer to this interaction to interpret in their narrative adaptations the life and fortune of their political and sociocultural protagonists. This is also the case for the following highly illustrative passage from a later compilation of biographies of renowned *literati*, which informs about the appearances of affluence and the complex set of social codes and arrangements that were believed to define the entanglement of men of culture and their political patrons in extended elite households.

> He [=Muḥammad ibn ʿAbd Allāh ibn Ṭāhir, Tahirid-Abbasid administrator of Bagdad,] gave me [= the grammarian and one of the *literati* Thaʿlab, 815–904] a separate apartment in his palace and a salary. I stayed with [Muḥammad's son] for up to four hours a day and would leave when he wanted to have lunch. His father was told about this so he had the hall and the arches of the courtyard redecorated and provided the rooms with fans and added to the variety of food. But I still left at the same time. When he heard this, he said to the servant who was assigned to us, 'I was concerned that he did not think there was enough food and that he did not find the place agreeable so we doubled what was served. Now I am told he still leaves as soon as his work is finished. Now you ask him yourself, "Is your house cooler than ours? Or is your food nicer than ours?" and tell him from me, "Your leaving at mealtimes puts us to shame"'. When the servant told me this, I stayed. I remained in this situation for thirteen years. As well as all this, he gave me seven rations of *khushkār* bread every day, one ration of *samīd* bread, three kilos of meat, and fodder for one animal. He also gave me a salary of 1,000 dirhams per month. In the year of the internecine warfare (865), flour and meat became difficult to get so the supervisor in charge of [Muḥammad's] kitchen wrote to him about the large size of the allowances. [Muḥammad] ordered that a register be drawn up so that rations could be restricted to what was essential. The secretary sent this and it comprised 3,600 people. Muḥammad read it and added some more people in his own writing. Then he dropped it and said that he was not going to deprive anyone of what he is used to, 'especially those who say, "Give me some bread to eat!" Distribute the provisions according to the register and keep up the supplies. We either live together or die together'.[14]

All kinds of knowledge practices, including not least teaching and advising the next generations of rulers and administrators, were very highly valued and, therefore, also intensely practiced in the Abbasid palaces and urban environments from as early as the 750s and 760s onwards. As suggested above, the expanding distribution and application at that time of the knowledge and technology required for the relatively cheap and easily repeated production of rag-paper was certainly one central factor in this. It is in fact no coincidence that quite a few writers and intellectuals that are known from this period are said to have made a

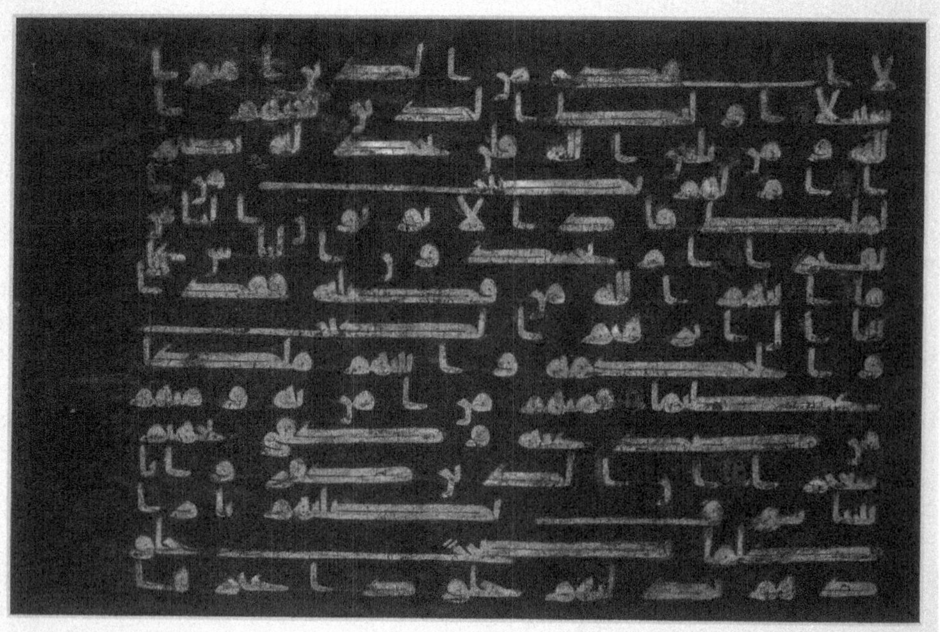

Figure 6.3 Folio from the 'blue Quran': manuscript with Kufic Arabic script in ink, gold and silver on indigo-dyed parchment (11 3/16 × 15 in. [28.4 × 38.1 cm] 9th–10th centuries, North Africa, Surah [chapter] 4: 56–9); the 'blue Quran' is considered to be one of the most luxurious manuscripts ever created

Source: Brooklyn Museum, Gift of Beatrice Riese, 1995.51a-b

primary living for themselves in the urban paper business. This was the case for the Bagdadi poet Mahmud al-Warraq (d. 845), author of ascetic verses and aphorisms, and known as an occasional slave merchant and as a copyist and bookseller (hence his name 'al-Warraq', the 'papermaker'). A similar example is that of Yahya ibn ʿAdi (d. 974), a famous Christian-Arabic theologian and polemicist and an important translator and commentator of the works of the ancient Greek philosopher Aristotle, who is also known to have been a copyist and bookseller, but then in 10th century Bagdad. A younger contemporary and colleague of this Yahya, Abu l-Faraj Muhammad Ibn al-Nadim (d. *c.* 995), who was a philosopher and a universal scholar, but of Shi'ite orientation, appears to have provided for most of his income from the same commercial activities. Both Yahya ibn ʿAdi and Ibn al-Nadim are said, moreover, to have been connected to one of the great households of Abbasid power from the first decades of the 10th century. Ibn al-Nadim's name, literally meaning 'the son of the courtier', certainly invokes the image of a family history of some form of Abbasid court service. According to Ibn al-Nadim himself, both men met in one of the social gatherings and cultural salons typical for Abbasid urban high culture that were organized by their patron, whom he praises for his interest in 'the ancient sciences'. Ibn al-Nadim's claim to fame is based especially on his *Fihrist*, his 'Catalogue' of all books in Arabic that were known to him, and for which he is reported to have made extensive use of his experiences as a copyist and a bookseller as well as of his friend Yahya's personal library with its many texts by Greek philosophers and their

Arabic translations. Collected in later 10th-century Bagdad, at a moment when the Abbasid patrimonial-bureaucratic apparatus of power had disintegrated, Ibn al-Nadim's text suggests how formerly Abbasid actors and practices had acquired sufficient autonomy to not necessarily disappear with that apparatus. Its thousands of book entries and biographical notices, furthermore, give detailed insight into how, by that time, that apparatus had left a lasting impact in fields of scholarship and specialization, the Late Antique riches and variety of which is suggested by the different subject areas covered by this Catalogue's ten sections: monotheist scripture, linguistics, historiography and prose writing, poetry, theology, jurisprudence, philosophy and 'ancient sciences', folklore, non-monotheistic religions, and alchemy.

1.2.1 Chains of Arabo-Islamic knowledge traditions

Next to all kinds of social and material conditions, such as Abbasid patronage, imperial formation, and paper production, the many discussions, expectations, and conflicts regarding the leadership over Muhammad's 'community of believers' and over the Arabo-Islamic empire appear as a central factor to stimulate the growth and intensification of knowledge practices and of the ranks of their practitioners. Starting with the ranks of Muhammad's contemporaries who had known him and experienced, even made, his early community's history, and succeeded by two generations of their successors who, as with al-Hasan al-Basri, upheld many of the early Arabian community's norms, values, and choices, these three successive groups—identified in previous chapters as 'the pious ancestors' (*al-salaf al-salih*)—are generally believed to have maintained an aural and oral tradition of preserving and transmitting the early community's memory and offering guidance on this basis on what it meant to be a member of the monotheistic community. Especially from the turn of the 7th to 8th centuries onwards, in the course of and after the second *fitna*, this question appears to have become increasingly pertinent and vexed, with answers being sought especially among supporters and opponents of Marwanid rule as well as amidst the—often overlapping—ranks of *mawali*, the various groups of non-Arabian converts in regions as far apart and as different as Ifriqiya and Khurasan.

In this context of exploration and confrontation, the relatively swift process of Arabization went hand in hand with a keen interest to master and understand the linguistic particularities of the new imperial language, and thus to fully participate in the imperial discourse and its written practices. Differences of opinion on these linguistic particularities soon gave rise to different regional traditions of Arabic grammar and philology, each organized around a handful of widely renowned specialists, such as the aforementioned Thaʿlab and his teachers in Kufa and Bagdad, and the great systematizer of Arabic grammar, the Persian-born Sibawayhi, and his peers and predecessors in Basra. In the much slower and far more diffuse process of Islamization, it was especially the understandings of the aforementioned nexus of Arabo-Islamic identity and sovereignty that continued to trigger debates and differences of opinion. These tended to be situated especially amongst anti-Marwanid movements, clustering around pious figures, such as al-Hasan al-Basri and his companions and students, or around various Iraqi and Khurasani competitors for leadership of the community, who required their anti-Marwanid claims to authority to be very carefully and convincingly staked. This clustering of people and ideas, mostly known in hindsight from later traditions only, somehow culminated in various theoretical positions—with practical political consequences—that were formulated, in an apparently vehement dialogue with each other, especially in the contexts of the 3rd *fitna* and the beginnings of Abbasid leadership, and of its recalibration during and after the 4th *fitna*. Key questions that were triggered by anti-Marwanid action and Abbasid ascendance to the position of 'commander of the believers' (*amir al-mu'minin*) revolved around the definition of what it meant be a member of the Muslim community (*umma*) and also what it meant to be its rightful leader (*imam*). They revolved especially around the status of sinners (such as the Umayyads were framed to have been) and more in general around different imaginations of the relationship between God and His creation, including apparent tensions emerging from Quranic discourses of divine omnipotence and human free will. These differing intellectual positions, discussions, and inquiries coalesced in formulations of bodies of knowledge (*'ilm*) about Islamic monotheism and its theoretical and practical particularities, constructed, written down, and transmitted by a growing group of specialists, referred to as 'people of knowledge'—*'ulama'*. Ibn al-Nadim's Catalogue actually provides insight into how this process of crystallization and specialization was perceived in 10th century Bagdad. It appears here as having clustered over two centuries and across multiple generations of *'ulama'*, patrons and scholarship into separate fields of religious knowledge practices that span the Catalogue's sections on monotheist scripture, theology, and jurisprudence, and that intersect also in many ways with its sections on linguistics, historiography and literature, poetry, philosophy and non-monotheistic religions.

The production and reproduction of the Catalogue's thousands of texts and of different bodies of knowledge by this diverse group of *'ulama'*, however, was far from as self-evident and clearly delineated a process as it appears *in hindsight* in surveys such as Ibn al-Nadim's. Different visions and views on religious truths, intellectual principles, and practical consequences were constantly under discussion, with repercussions that—in the hegemonic context of a theocratic order of all things—were never mere trivialities. An extremely complex episode that determined this formation of religious knowledge practices and its relationship with the fundamental discussions on the nexus of Arabo-Islamic identity and sovereignty concerns the religious authority debates that marked, especially, the 9th century. These involved debates on the position of the Abbasid ruler as an Islamic sovereign in particular, but also on the related authority of formally appointed religious judges (*qadis*) and of other local and regional leaders from the emerging ranks of the *'ulama'*. All of this concerned more vehement differences of opinion regarding the nature of human beings in their relationship with God. Between 833 and 849, these debates are reported to have culminated in Bagdad and other places in Iraq into an open authority conflict, known as the *mihna* ('inquisition'). Generally speaking, two groups opposed each other in this conflict. On the one hand, there were the Abbasid caliph al-Ma'mun (r. 811–833), his immediate successors, and their courts and entourages, who all more or less promoted the idea of the autonomy and sovereignty of Abbasid authority as God's caliph and the community's *imam*. A central figure in these entourages is said to have been the scholar Ahmad ibn Abi Du'ad (d. 854), who was chief judge under al-Mu'tasim and al-Wathiq and who is described—with a small group of other courtiers and *atrak* leaders—as kingmaker for al-Wathiq's brother al-Mutawakkil in 847. This remarkable powerbroker in the Abbasid patrimonial-bureaucratic apparatus is remembered for having been a strong advocate not just for Abbasid sovereignty, but also for so-called Mu'tazili teachings. This particular label, as explained later in Ibn al-Nadim's catalogue, was used to identify one of the earliest coherent traditions—or schools—of Islamic theology that had appeared around a set of rationalist doctrinal views, some of which became central stakes of contention in the *mihna*. On the other hand, there was a particular group of *'ulama'* who appeared as more attached to the sovereignty of the exemplary Tradition (*Sunna*) of the prophet Muhammad, as preserved and transmitted in the format of the aforementioned *hadith*, and as guarded and interpreted by specialist *ʿulamaʾ* (rather than the Abbasid ruler). These traditionalists soon transformed into the *mihna*'s main victims, and the natural leaders of groups and movements that opposed this violently enforced centralizing arrangement. The Bagdadi *hadith* expert and teacher Ahmad ibn Hanbal (d. 855) quickly came to be represented as these opponents' main protagonist who endured persecution, torture, and imprisonment but persevered, and thus moved from a position of ascetic aloofness and forced submission to a role of subversion, growing popular support, and increasing centrality. Eventually, Ahmad and his traditionalist peers are remembered as having emerged from this conflict as its moral victors. This became clear especially when in the period 848–849, Ibn Abi Duʾad and his fellow kingmakers disappeared from the Abbasid court, the *mihna* was revoked, and—at least according to later predominantly traditionalist accounts—the traditionalist position was fully embraced by the new caliph al-Mutawakkil (r. 847–861) and his new entourage of courtiers. The caliph is even reported to have tried to enlist the by then immensely popular Ahmad ibn Hanbal into this new entourage and to integrate him into his attempt to consolidate his newly won authority over the Abbasid patrimonial-bureaucratic apparatus. In 851, Ahmad was reportedly invited to the court in Samarraʾ, received with great pomp and circumstance, and offered a position to teach *hadith* to al-Mutawakkil's son. In the best of traditionalist traditions, however, he quickly forsook this close association with the court and returned to Bagdad for fear of the corrupting impact of power and wealth. When Ahmad died in Bagdad in mid-855, his funeral allegedly was attended by a great mass of people, high and low, so that its many representations in later texts were both understood as an ultimate token of the triumph of traditionalism and as a model by which to measure the popularity and success of many an ambitious Islamic scholar.

The strong impression of a mid-9th-century traditionalist victory and triumph, however, is above all a very popular, *in hindsight*, representation and simplification of a far more complex and multidirectional process. Just as in the case of Arabic linguistics with its Kufa/Basra antagonism, none of the different fields of knowledge that were catalogued by Ibn al-Nadim in the 10th century ever stopped being intensely pursued and at the same time heavily contested. The Catalogue's further subdivision of every field in different intellectual traditions and individual achievements is in fact far more revealing. For the third section of Arabic linguistics, therefore, the Catalogue speaks of 'three variations', from 'the Basran grammarians' over 'the Kufans' to 'a group of grammarians who mixed both traditions (*al-madhhabayn*)'. Similarly, the fifth and sixth sections on the major fields of Islamic theology and jurisprudence are tellingly subdivided into five and eight subsections, each identified in the Catalogue's introductory survey by a doctrinal signifier or by an individual's name around whom different groups of specialists are represented as having closed ranks:

> The Fifth Section, with five variations *(funūn)*, about rational theology (*al-kalām*—'the discourse' [on God]) and the rational theologians (*al-mutakallimīn*):
>
> - The first variation, about the beginning of the movement of rational theology and the rational theologians consisting of the Muʿtazilites ('those who maintain a neutral political position', *iʿtizāl—al-muʿtazila*) and the adherents of the doctrine of *irjāʾ* ('deferral of moral judgment', including political quietism—*al-murjiʾa*), with the titles of their books.
> - The second variation, with the reports about the theologians of the Imāmī Shi'ites, the Zaydī [Shi'ites] and other transgressive [Shi'ites] (*ghulāt*), and the Ismāʿīlī [Shi'ites], with the titles of their books.

- The third variation, with the reports about the theologians adhering to the doctrine of *jabr* ('compulsion', i.e. predestination—*al-mujbira*) and belonging to the Hashwiyya ('those that stuff [*ḥashw*] *hadith* in their argumentation', i.e. the traditionalists), with the titles of their books.
- The fourth variation, with the reports about the theologians of the Khārijites ('those who left [*kharaja*] ʿAlī's ranks during the 1st *fitna*', adhering to egalitarian and puritan doctrines—al-*Khawārij*) and their likes, with the titles of their books.
- The fifth variation, with the reports about the wanderers, the ascetics, the devotees, those adopting Sufi practices, and scholars of a theology based on hallucinations and deliriums, with the titles of their books.

The Sixth Section, with eight variations (*funūn*), about knowledge of Islamic law (*fiqh*) and the legal scholars and traditionists (*al-fuqahāʾ wa-l-muḥaddithīn*):

- The first variation, with the reports about Mālik [ibn Anas, d. 795] and his adherents (*aṣḥāb*), with the titles of their books.
- The second variation, with the reports about Abū Ḥanīfa al-Nuʿmān [d. 767] and his adherents, with the titles of their books.
- The third variation, with the reports about the *imām* al-Shāfiʿī [d. 820] and his adherents, with the titles of their books.
- The fourth variation, with the reports about Dāwūd [Ibn Khalaf, d. 884] and his adherents, with the titles of their books.
- The fifth variation, with the reports about the legal scholars of the Shi'ites, with the titles of their books.
- The sixth variation, with the reports about the legal scholars who are adherents of the *hadith* and traditionists, with the titles of their books.
- The seventh variation, with the reports about Abū Jaʿfar al-Ṭabarī [d. 923] and his adherents, with the titles of their books.
- The eighth variation, with the reports about the legal scholars of the *Shurāt* ('the vendors', 'those who have sold their soul for the cause of God', i.e. the Kharijites) the titles of their books.[15]

These introductory passages, with their attempts to classify Arabo-Islamic knowledge practices up to the later 10th century into distinct sets of categories and subcategories, represent only one moment in that long and winding process of the formation of more clearly delineated intellectual communities and 'traditions', or schools of thought (*madhhab*), among the wide and very diverse groups of the *ʿulamaʾ*. A handful of scholars from this period played a truly paradigmatic role in this process, and their thoughts and teachings would assume legendary pioneering proportions—as also announced in Ibn al-Nadim's Catalogue. Next to the aforementioned *hadith* scholar Ahmad Ibn Hanbal (d. 855), they are the legal specialists Abu Hanifa (d. 767) from Kufa, Malik ibn Anas (d. 795) from Medina, and Muhammad al-Shafiʿi (767–820), who was active in Bagdad, Mecca and Fustat, as well as the later theologians al-Ashʿari (d. 936) from Bagdad and al-Maturidi (d. 944) from Samarqand. From the wide variety of legal, theological, and practical disagreements, debates, and perspectives that marked the ranks of these *ʿulamaʾ* and their developing knowledge practices, the main Sunni branch of Islamic scholarship later crystallized, closing ranks around the teachings and practices of—especially—traditionalists and those who associated with interrelated legal and theological models attributed to Abu Hanifa, Malik, al-Shafiʿi, Ibn Hanbal, al-Ashʿari, and al-Maturidi.

As suggested above, however, in this period, this particular outcome in favor of the overarching perspective of Sunni traditionalism was all but predetermined. This also emerges from the remarkable unity of legitimate Arabo-Islamic knowledge practices, across sectarian and other doctrinal, political, practical, and epistemological boundaries, that transpires from the Catalogue and that thus continued to appear as a given for Ibn al-Nadim and for the many audiences that secured his text's circulation and survival beyond the later 10th century. All Arabic texts from each of the Catalogue's sections and subsections were clearly considered equally valid to be included among what Ibn al-Nadim defined as 'all kinds of knowledge' (*asnaf al-ʿulum*), even when some traditions obviously received a more favorable treatment from him than others.[16] This so to speak Late Antique and imperial Arabo-Islamic particularity of these knowledge practices, moreover, appears from the inclusion of quite a few traditions that would later disappear or be marginalized as legitimate fields or 'variations'. These include the legal traditions attributed by Ibn al-Nadim to the teachings of Dawud ibn Khalaf and to Abu Jaʿfar al-Tabari, neither of which survived for much longer after the 10th century. Dawud's many legal writings are actually only known from their listing in Ibn al-Nadim's Catalogue, as they disappeared when his and his followers' teachings of legal literalism lost all appeal among successive generations of *ʿulamaʾ*. A similar fate befell al-Tabari's legal teachings. In his case, however, the memory of his scholarly activities was very much kept alive by some of the other texts with which he contributed to other fields of knowledge and that thus also illustrate how polymaths such as al-Tabari and many, if not most, of his predecessors and peers did not necessarily operate within the disciplinary boundaries that classifications such as Ibn al-Nadim's tried to impose. Al-Tabari is said to have trained as a scholar in the 850s and 860s, moving from one urban center in Iran, Iraq, Syria, Egypt, and the Hejaz to another and from the study circle of one reputed specialist to that of another, and being employed also for some time as a teacher in an Abbasid elite household. This long immersion in trans-regional networks of scholarship and leadership made him into a polymath whose engagements with the fields of law, *hadith* scholarship, medicine, history, ethics, and poetry would secure his remembrance. At the same time, this career and diversity are in many ways emblematic, if not representative, for the boundless quest for universal knowledge (*talab al-ʿilm*) that came to be associated in Abbasid as well as in post-Abbasid times with a scholar's exemplary life. In al-Tabari's case, his timeless fame eventually derived above all from the enormous Quran commentary and the very detailed chronicle of universal history that he compiled. The latter reconstructs, along the traditionalist method of collecting and presenting all relevant traditions and earlier reports, human history from Creation to al-Tabari's own time, ending with the annals for the Hijri year 302 (915 CE). Both 'The Commentary' (*al-Tafsir*) and 'The History' (*al-Taʾrikh*) soon acquired a central status across the Islamic world as the main, canonical renderings of the Arabo-Islamic community's understanding of its revelatory experience as well as of the subsequent historical formation of its leaderships.

1.2.2 Chains of literary knowledge traditions

In the urban centers of the Late Antique Abbasid empire, Arabic literature and poetry (*adab*) were also held in high esteem as tokens of erudition, cultural refinement, and social status, both for the *literati* (*udabaʾ*) themselves as well as for their Abbasid patrons. These highly valued, socially effective, and politically relevant dimensions again also transpire from Ibn al-Nadim's listings of the Arabic literary agents and texts that were known to him in 10th-century Iraq. In this case, their diversity is assigned to two sections, one for prose writings, and the other for poetry. The close relationship with the Abbasid court and apparatus of power transpires especially from Ibn al-Nadim's organization of the former section on prose writing. Its subsections are structured as different performative aspects of leadership practices, ranging from engaging with history—as with al-Tabari's 'The History'—over directing arrangements of power to holding court.

> The Third Section, with three variations (*funūn*), about historical traditions, literary pursuits, biographies, and genealogies:
>
> - The first variation, with the reports about the compilers of historical traditions, narratives, and genealogies, and the authors of biographies and chronicles, with the titles of their books.
> - The second variation, with the reports about the scribes (*al-kuttāb*), the specialists of epistolography, the land-tax agents, and the members of the administrative departments (*al-dawāwīn*), with the titles of their books.
> - The third variation, with the reports about the courtiers (*al-nudamā'*), the attendants of literary salons (*al-julasā'*), the singers, and the buffoons, clowns and jesters, with the of their books.[17]

Ibn al-Nadim's separate section on poetry is subdivided in two chronological subsections, one for those earlier poets who followed pre-Islamic models and another for 'the Modernists' (*al-muhdathun*) of the Abbasid era. In this literary field, too, the link with Abbasid leaderships appears as an important driving force as well as—with the fates of many Abbasid agents, old and new, in continuous movement—a common subject to write about. Eulogies for patrons were particularly popular, produced by poets who, as reputed specialists of the Arabic language, vied with each other in applying all kinds of sophisticated old and new, 'modernist', poetic forms and techniques. The blossoming and diverse ranks of well-known and important poets from this period include such representative characters as Ibn al-Mu'tazz (d. 908), Ibn al-Rumi (d. 896), and Abu Nuwas (d. *c.* 814). Abu Nuwas was of Persian *mawali* origins and is generally considered one of the greatest and most versatile of all Abbasid 'modernist' poets; he was active in Bagdad in the entourages of the aforementioned Barmakid family of viziers and of the Abbasid ruler al-Amin; a 10th-century collector and admirer attributed no less than 1,500 poems to his pen, including all kinds of verses on wine, young boys, and hunting, and describing his own sensual experiences as well as those of others. Ibn al-Rumi was the son of a Greek-Roman convert to Islam who mainly lived off his panegyric poems to high-ranking patrons in 9th-century Bagdad and Samarra'. Ibn al-Mu'tazz, finally, was no less than an Abbasid prince and eventually, in 908, even an unsuccessful caliph for one day; in the field of poetry he is mainly known and remembered as yet another 'modernist', as a gifted composer of a great variety of aphorisms and verses, including wine poems and eulogies for some of his Abbasid relatives, and as the pioneering author of a more theoretical study of Arabic poetics, 'the Book of Innovations' (*kitab al-badi'*).

All kinds of preserved prose essays, produced especially by those Ibn al-Nadim identified as 'courtiers and attendants of literary salons', demonstrate how these too aimed to testify to the universal knowledge, creativity, sophistication, and refinement that were deemed to distinguish a man of culture, an *adib*. Just like poems or other types of texts, they were performed and discussed in literary salons at the court or in other exclusive urban meeting spaces, and thus represented an important medium of elite communication, of social distinction, and of competition for patronage and for cultural reputations. Characteristic of the elitist (and often deliberately shocking) nature and specific content of these essays is the (non-preserved) oeuvre of the 10th-century *adib* Ibn al-Shah al-Tahiri, a member of the distinguished family of the Tahirids. From this oeuvre, the following titles are known: 'The Superiority of the Comb to the Mirror', 'The Book of Bread and Olives', 'The War between Cheese and Olives', 'The War between Meat and Fish', 'The Miracles of the Sea', 'Adultery and its Enjoyments', 'Stories about Slave Boys', 'Stories about Women', and 'Masturbation'. One of the greatest and most influential of all *adib*s undoubtedly was an Iraqi scholar known as al-Jahiz (*c.* 776–869). This al-Jahiz apparently belonged to a family with *mawali* and Abyssinian origins. During his long and rich life, he was mainly active in Basra and Bagdad, and he is often claimed to have written more than 200 books, less than half of which have been at least partly preserved. These include in the best of the *adib*s' tradition bold titles such as 'The Book of Living', 'The Book of Misers', 'The Elegance of Expression and Clarity of Exposition', 'The Virtues of the Turks', and 'The Superiority of the Blacks over the Whites'. The differing contents of these many texts attest to the typical polymath nature of al-Jahiz' scholarship. They cover in highly erudite ways fields as diverse as Arabic rhetoric, rationalist theology, Aristotelian philosophy, and numerous other areas of specialization, and they confirm how al-Jahiz actively partook in many of the intellectual and political debates that were raging at his time. Very often this happened in close correspondence and relationships of patronage, intellectual exchange, and textual dedication with powerful members of the courts of al-Ma'mun and his successors, including the aforementioned Mu'tazili adherent, chief justice, and Abbasid kingmaker Ahmad ibn Abi Du'ad (d. 854).

1.2.3 Chains of ancient knowledge traditions

Al-Jahiz' readings into Aristotelian philosophy also connect him to the very intensely pursued knowledge practices that Ibn al-Nadim qualified as the seventh section in his Catalogue, "about philosophy and the ancient sciences". The width and Late Antique continuity of the latter common signifier are suggested in the introductory descriptions of its three very different subsections, with their range extending from logic over engineering and music to the theory and practice of medicine.

- The first variation, with the reports of the natural philosophers and the logicians (*al-falāsifa al-ṭabīʿīyīn wa-l-manṭiqīyīn*), with the titles of their books, their renderings (in Arabic), and the commentaries on them; which ones are extant, which ones are recorded but lost, and which ones were extant but later disappeared.
- The second variation, with the reports of the specialists of scientific trainings (*aṣḥāb al-taʿālīm*), the engineers, the arithmeticians (*al-arithmāṭīqīyīn*), the musicians, the calculators, the experts of the science of the stars (*al-munajjimīn*), the makers of instruments, and specialists of mechanics and dynamics (*aṣḥāb al-ḥiyal wa-l-ḥarakāt*).
- The third variation, about the beginning of medicine (*al-ṭibb*), with the reports of ancient and modern physicians, with the titles of their books, their renderings (in Arabic) and the commentaries on them.[18]

As these enumerations of different scientific fields of translation, commentary, and specialization indicate, in the various centers of 9th and 10th century Abbasid activities, considerable attention was paid to knowledge practices that pursued continuity with texts, teachings, and ideas from Greek and Hellenistic Antiquity. By that time, this attention focused especially on Late Antique renderings in Greek and Syriac of texts of philosophers such as Plato and Aristotle, of physicians such as Hippocrates, Galen, and Dioscorides, of mathematicians such as Euclid, and experts of geography and the science of the stars such as

Ptolemy. Genuine translation programs were deployed throughout the 8th, 9th, and 10th centuries as part of the formation, elaboration, and transformation of Abbasid imperial power. As with religious and literary knowledge practices and the Arabization process in general, these programs were mostly initiated and patronized by Abbasid rulers such as al-Mansur in the mid-8th century and al-Ma'mun in the first decades of the 9th century. They were also heavily sponsored by many other participants in the expanding Abbasid power apparatus, including not least families of *kuttab* and courtiers such as the Barmakids in the later 8th century or the 10th century post-Abbasid patron whom, as mentioned, Ibn al-Nadim praised for his special interest in 'the ancient sciences'. The pre-Islamic Greek or Persian origins of many of these power elites had a lot to do with this special interest, often connecting them in various ways with particular repositories, practices, and appreciations of ancient texts, insights, and ideas.

Practical and functional considerations, from organizing rituals of Arabo-Islamic identity and sovereignty to managing an empire, have long been identified as some of the main reasons for this programmatic quest for universal knowledge. So have been concerns and new opportunities for intellectual development and specialization. In recent decades, different leadership practices involved in the formation of an Islamic empire have been added as an important driving force. These would have developed from an 8th-century Perso-Sasanian revivalism in anti-Marwanid milieus, keen to reconnect with the Sasanian past and its appreciation of knowledge as an aspect of imperial sovereignty, to the aftermath of the 4th *fitna*, which witnessed the pursuit of what has been termed a 'new philhellenic imperial ideology' when caliph al-Ma'mun was faced with the challenge to build a new entourage and elite around his Abbasid authority in Bagdad and Iraq.[19] In this social and cultural dynamic between a Sasanian-inspired imperial discourse and a Greek and Hellenistic one, collecting, translating, and engaging with texts from 'the ancient sciences' remained a highly valued practice, which informed not only constructions of knowledge but also strategies of social distinction, elite membership, and political allegiance.

Contrary to what Ibn al-Nadim suggests, therefore, this practice, its diverse actors, and its social as well as cultural stakes revolved not only around textual specimens in Greek and Syriac, but took an equally intense interest in the Middle Persian (Pahlavi) and Sanskrit products of Sasanian and Indian knowledge traditions. It grappled with philosophical, scientific, technical, and medical texts and ideas, but also with other subjects such as ethics and history, from a variety of all these and many more traditions. The line that separated these knowledge practices and what was identified above as the sociocultural practice of *adab*, therefore, always remained extremely thin. Arguably, one could say that it was only with the growing preponderance of Greek and Hellenistic traditions in the course of the 9th century that such a division became clearer, culminating in Ibn al-Nadim's 10th-century separation of the categories of 'philosophy and the ancient sciences' and of 'historical traditions, literary pursuits, biographies, and genealogies'. Even so, as with the polymath al-Jahiz, scientists, *'ulama'*, and *adib*s, and also quite a few of their works, continued to pursue their practices across such categories of specialization.

An early central figure in the 8th-century Sasanian phase who illustrates this permeability very well was the Persian convert to Islam 'Abd Allah ibn al-Muqaffa' (*c*. 720–756). A *katib* in late Marwanid service he transferred his allegiance to the early Abbasids but is reported to have been tortured to death when he lost Abbasid favor. Ibn al-Muqaffa' is known especially for his many translations, including most notably a collection of Indian fables and moral tales known as *Kalila wa-Dimna* and some texts on pre-Islamic Persian history, all of which were translated from Pahlavi into Arabic. He is also known as the original author of two

Figure 6.4 Earliest dated Abbasid astrolabe (ca. 927, Bagdad, bronze), an instrument for using the positions of the stars to define routes, places, and directions

Source: © The al-Sabah Collection, Dar al-Athar al-Islamiyyah, Kuwait

pioneering literary prose texts in Arabic that identify him as an early *adib* and demonstrate his penchant for Zoroastrian and rationalist ideas. One of these texts was tellingly entitled 'The Great Work of Adab' (*Kitab al-Adab al-Kabir*), and eventually also inspired the abovementioned al-Jahiz. The other was a text of political council, advising the early Abbasid ruler al-Mansur on how to organize his court and establish central Arabo-Islamic sovereignty.

Central characters who contributed to the preponderance of a Greek and Hellenistic scientific discourse in the 9th century have been identified as three wealthy brothers from Marv in Khurasan, known as the sons of Musa ibn Shakir, the Banu Musa. They appear in the historical records as some of the foremost protegees of caliph al-Ma'mun, and acquired scholarly fame as mathematicians, experts of the science of the stars, and specialists of mechanics. After the 4th *fitna*, they moved to Bagdad with al-Ma'mun and became central agents of his construction of a new court and caliphal apparatus in the 820s and 830s, as well as of its many changes under al-Ma'mun's successors in the 840s, 850s, and 860s. Their major contributions as patrons of Greek and Hellenistic knowledge practices were later remembered as follows:

> Their noble intention was to master the ancient sciences and the books of the classical scholars and they devoted themselves to this project. They sent agents to the Roman Empire to bring them books. They attracted translators from distant lands and far off places by offering generous rewards. They made known the wonders of science.[20]

Most famous among the translation programs under al-Ma'mun are those associated with the Bayt al-Hikma ('the House of Wisdom') in Bagdad. This was the early Abbasid palace library and repository of ancient books that provided one of the material bases for these programs. Given that the origins of this practice of having a palace library, with its own staff and facilities for copying and storing texts, have to be sought in the Sasanian period, this early Abbasid palace library's original collection and functioning therefore evidently first revolved around preserving and transmitting that Perso-Sasanian heritage. In the reign of al-Ma'mun, however, members from his entourage, such as the Banu Musa, and their activities of collecting and translating in pursuit of the caliph's 'new philhellenic imperial ideology' are reported to have become attached to this Bayt al-Hikma as well.[21] The dynamic between a Sasanian-inspired and a Greek and Hellenistic imperial discourse thus materialized in the expanding manuscript collections of the Bayt al-Hikma, as well as in the diverse practices that emerged around this and similar elite libraries in the urban centers of Abbasid authority.

One of the foremost scholars whose scientific activities have been connected to the many opportunities offered by this palace library in the reign of al-Ma'mun is Muhammad ibn Musa al-Khwarazmi (*c.* 780–*c.* 847). Little is known about his background or about how he ended up in the entourage of al-Ma'mun, apart from the fact that his name suggests that he was somehow related to the eastern region of Khwarazm and, therefore, may have moved from Marv to Bagdad with al-Ma'mun. He is especially remembered for having authored a variety of pioneering writings in Arabic on geography, science of the stars, and mathematics. Some of these actually became standard works in the east and west for many centuries, including his 'Summary on Calculation by Reconstitution and Equation'. His significance as an important mathematician lingers on in modern methods, insights, and concepts, including the notions of 'algebra'—derived from the method of 'reconstitution' (*al-jabr*) explained in the latter book—and 'algorithm'—derived from a Latinized form of al-Khwarazmi's name. Illustrative of the hybridity of traditions that informed knowledge practices at this time, and for the mediating role of members from al-Ma'mun's entourage such as al-Khwarazmi, is the fact that he is credited with engaging actively not only with the Greek and Hellenistic tradition, but also with the Indo-Sanskrit one, both of which were integrated into his scholarship.

Amid the blossoming ranks of Abbasid scholars of the Greek and Hellenistic knowledge practices that became ever more dominant (but remained also continuously contested) across the 9th century and beyond, central and emblematic roles similar to that of al-Khwarazmi tend also to be awarded to the philosopher al-Kindi (d. *c.* 866) and the physician Hunayn ibn Ishaq (d. 873). In fact, not only their and their many peers' translation work but also their commentaries and textual scholarship—as also with al-Khwarazmi's many pioneering texts—played a central role in this period's ever wider variety of knowledge disciplines, practices, and traditions. A good example of these are the preserved works of Hunayn about the eye, especially his 'Book of the Ten Treatises on the Eye', compiled in about 860. It includes the following illustrative passage that informs about many continuities with antique scholarship as well as about that scholarship's actualization in an Arabic context and the theocratic framework of monotheism that loomed at the background of all of these knowledge practices:

> The first treatise on the nature of the eye and its structure:
>
> > Know that any one of the compound limbs [of the body] has its special function, which is particularly intended for it. Though it consists of many parts differing in their nature, that function is not performed by all those parts but only by one of them; the other parts are only there to serve that part which performs the function. So we find that the eye is consisted of many different parts, but that the vision is not in all the parts but only in that humor which resembles ice and which is called in Greek *krystalloeidès* or the ice-like. As for the other humors, tunics and similar parts, they are created, every one of them, only to be useful to the afore-mentioned ice-like humor. If it will be the will of the Most High God, we shall make this clear when we will now treat the function of each of the parts of the eye.[22]

Hunayn (808–873) was of Iraqi Christian origins, and never converted to Islam, although he continuously worked in close proximity of the Abbasid court and experienced a defining convergence of his and that court's Hellenistic interests. Hunayn dedicated some of his texts to caliphs such as al-Mutawakkil (r. 847–861) and al-Muʿtamid (r. 870–892) and is known to have received commissions and patronage from many other participants in the Abbasid apparatus, from the aforementioned Musa brothers to Yuhanna ibn Masawayh (d. 857). This Christian specialist of Greek and Hellenistic medicine and Arabic poetry was the Abbasid court physician of Harun al-Rashid (r. 786–809) and of many of his successors; in this capacity, he became another one of those scholars and practitioners whose interests significantly converged with those of al-Ma'mun's 'philhellenic imperial ideology', as also happened to one of his most important students, Hunayn ibn Ishaq. Together with his son and some other students, Hunayn is actually credited with producing very accurate and accessible translations of more than a hundred Greek texts on medicine, including almost the entire classical Galenic corpus, and thus with contributing substantially to the Hellenistic turn that medicine took in his and his peers' wake. At the same time, he appears as yet another typical polymath of the Abbasid era, who was not just active in the field of medicine, but also engaged with other areas of expertise. Translations of texts ascribed to Plato and Aristotle, and also of the Hebrew Bible, are equally attributed to him, and he is reported—in

Ibn al-Nadim's Catalogue—to have authored more than seventy texts of his own, including the above-mentioned 'Book of the Ten Treatises on the Eye', and also treatises in the fields of philosophy, rational theology, Arabic linguistics, and the natural sciences.

Hunayn's contemporary al-Kindi (*c.* 801–866), scion of an Arabian family, was perhaps one of the foremost agents of al-Ma'mun's "philhellenic imperial ideology". Similar to Hunayn, he also acted under courtly patronage in pursuit of making new translations, together with his own group of students and collaborators, and of authoring new texts and theorizations in most of the widening fields of scientific specialization that were eventually categorized by Ibn al-Nadim under the rubrics of philosophy and the ancient sciences. In Ibn al-Nadim's Catalogue, almost 250 titles of texts are listed as composed by al-Kindi. Specifically remembered as 'the philosopher of the Arabic-speakers' (*faylasuf al-'Arab*), it was above all in the field of philosophy that he is believed to have made the greatest difference. Al-Kindi is often credited with defining philosophy's turn to Hellenistic knowledge traditions in the Arabo-Islamic imperial world, as Hunayn had done for medicine. Many Abbasid intellectuals' fascination with Aristotle, and with texts and ideas ascribed to Aristotle's thinking, certainly owe a lot to al-Kindi's work of translation, commentary, and authorship. His own book 'On First Philosophy', dedicated to the caliph al-Mu'tasim (r. 833–842), shows many connections with the writings of Aristotle. This treatise has actually been explained as an advertisement for and a defense of the value of philosophical knowledge practices in an Islamic theocratic order of things at the time of the aforementioned *mihna* and the growing popularity of traditionalists such as Ahmad ibn Hanbal. Al-Kindi's strong connections with the entourages of al-Ma'mun and al-Mu'tasim also appear from his appointment as a tutor to one of the latter caliph's sons, to whom he also explicitly dedicated a number of his treatises. His temporary fall from favor under al-Mutawakkil (r. 847–861) is linked to this caliph's aforementioned campaign to free himself from the dominant clutches of the social and discursive apparatus of power that al-Mutawakkil's father and uncle had constructed. Despite this change of fortune, and the aforementioned empowerment of traditionalism in its wake, al-Kindi's textual and intellectual achievements had by then transcended the ups and downs of Abbasid court life and imperial ideology, or for that matter of his own life. In the later 9th-century, philosophical knowledge practices building on Greek and Hellenistic concepts, models and insights had become an established aspect of the Abbasid canon of universal knowledge, and were continued in many creative, and contested, ways by all kinds of scholars in and beyond Bagdad, including eventually also al-Farabi (*c.* 872–950), tellingly remembered as 'the second master' (*al-mu'allim al-thani*) after Aristotle, the Christian bookseller Yahya ibn 'Adi (d. 974), and his Shi'ite peer Ibn al-Nadim (d. *c.* 995).

When Ibn al-Nadim in the later 10th century captured all of these different chains of imperial knowledge traditions and tied them together into a greater whole of universal aspiration, the Abbasid patrimonial-bureaucratic apparatus of imperial power had all but disintegrated and continued to exist only in the virtual reality of the post-Abbasid trans-regional political order (see the next chapter). Nevertheless, most of these knowledge practices and traditions persevered and managed to accommodate to these changing circumstances. Ibn al-Nadim's text suggests, therefore, how formerly Abbasid actors, practices, and—more in general—urbanities had acquired sufficient autonomy to not necessarily disappear when the ties holding that apparatus together were cut. In fact, the intense entanglement of urban leaderships and of, especially, leadership practices and arrangements with the blossoming of the arts and sciences, and with the contested empowerment of their practitioners, ranging from the *'ulama'* over the *udaba'* to the philosophers, were to remain a dominant feature for many more centuries to come, preserving in the process the contested legacies of the thousands of texts which Ibn al-Nadim's Catalogue recorded. In very parallel ways, this perseverance and continuity also occurred with many of the urban centers of Abbasid imperial authority, including not least Bagdad. The metropolis Bagdad still proved an ideal setting for Ibn al-Nadim's bibliophilic activities in post-Abbasid times, and it remained a center of imperial sociopolitical, cultural, and intellectual aspirations well into the 13th century.

2 Abbasid courts, courtiers, and agents

The center that up to the early decades of the 10th century more or less held the many chains of the patrimonial-bureaucratic apparatus together was constituted not only by the Abbasid rulers themselves. The increasingly powerful but regularly changing entourages of relatives, supporters, agents, servants, and experts that these rulers gathered around them were at least equally central cogs in the Abbasid machinery of power. Together, they made for the complex social construction of the Abbasid court as well as for the centripetal social power that tied Abbasid elites—including *ʿulamaʾ*, *udabaʾ*, and philosophers—across the imperial territory to it, irrespective of where exactly this court was organized.

This trans-regional center of social gravity and complex social and ceremonial environment of the court was shaped and reshaped in the course of the later 8th and 9th centuries in the social and physical contexts of Bagdad and of the other imperial centers of Abbasid authority, such as al-Hashimiyya near Kufa in the 750s, al-Raqqa/al-Rafiqa in the days of Harun al-Rashid (r. 786–809), Samarraʾ during the reigns of al-Muʿtasim (r. 833–842), his son al-Wathiq (r. 842–847), and five of his grandsons (r. 861–892), and al-Mutawakkiliyya—also known as al-Jaʿfariyya—near Samarraʾ in the time of al-Mutawakkil (r. 847–861). Furthermore, the physical environment of central Iraq in which that court originated in the second half of the 8th century, dominated as explained above by a Sasanian-inspired imperial discourse and marked by a continuing presence of the ancient remains and memories of the Sasanian palaces, contributed substantially to the formation of that court. As in Sasanian times, it was completely organized around the authority of the ruler, whose elevated status was expressed in a complex set of palace rituals that combined Sasanian, Arabo-Islamic, and other traditions and that included the bestowal of robes of honor (*khilʿ*a) and of all kinds of other precious gifts along particular hierarchies of privilege and status. The effect of the ruler's distinction and specialty at the top of these hierarchies was further achieved by the complex practical and ceremonial organization of the increasingly extensive entourage of the caliph and by the ever more ingenious structural organization of the Abbasid palaces, which eventually came to resemble true labyrinths.[23]

Not only these courts and organizational traditions, but also these Abbasid palaces themselves have never stopped appealing to authors' imaginations. Until today, physical remnants, anecdotes, and descriptions indeed continue to stress their labyrinth-like appearances, as in the following 20th-century portrayal that stresses how they were "huge walled compounds with endless successions of apartments, courts, rooms, halls, and passageways, whose functions are not known".[24] In Abbasid Bagdad, where in the course of this Abbasid era various palaces were constructed, this generalizing description mainly applied to the so-called Golden Gate Palace. Although no physical remains have been preserved, literary references suggest that this first Abbasid residence indeed consisted primarily of elaborately decorated semi-open spaces, including a centrally located audience hall, accessible to those members of the palace or outsiders who were deemed important and privileged enough. In this hall, important guests were received, public declarations were made, and the caliph or his representatives performed justice, hearing and acting upon complaints against so-called bureaucratic malpractices, known as *mazalim*. At the same time, however, there were numerous closed living spaces in these palaces, only accessible to the happy few. This is reflected in the following anecdote about a visitor's astonishment when he was received by al-Mansur (r. 754–777) in a very sober environment.

> I was admitted by an entrance to the palace I had never been in before. Then I went into a little enclosure with one room in it and a portico in front of it, at the edge of the house and the courtyard, supported on teak columns. Over the front of the portico, curtains were hanging, as they do in mosques. I went in and in the room was a coarse carpet and nothing else except his mattress, his pillows, and his blankets, and I said, "O Commander of the Believers (*amīr al-mu'minīn*), this room is not worthy of you," and he replied, "O my uncle, this is the room I sleep in," and I asked if there was anything more than what I saw, and he said, "There is only what you see".[25]

Not only does this anecdote attest to how particular representations of these spaces were used to frame Abbasid rulers as exemplary Muslim leaders, it also leaves above all an impression of the seclusion as well as the multifunctionality of spaces such as these in the Golden Gate Palace. Many stories about both the austerity and the splendor of this palace are circulating, and in the absence of material remains, it continues to be difficult to distinguish fiction and ideal from reality.

The story is somewhat different for the many palaces that were constructed in the Abbasid imperial center of Samarra'. Until recently, ruinous parts of 'the Palace of the Caliphate' (*Dar al-Khilafa*) were still present, including its public part, the People's Palace (*Dar al-'Amma*), which opened onto a garden on the Tigris and where the caliph would regularly receive visitors in audience, and also its private part, the Khaqani Palace (*al-Jawsaq al-Khaqani*), where al-Mu'tasim and some of his successors with their families lived, amidst a remarkable maze of corridors, courtyards, and rooms. Furthermore, there are also many remnants of the more than twenty palaces that al-Mutawakkil had constructed for himself and for others in his new imperial settlement just to the north of Samarra', including his own palace, Friday mosque, and famous spiral-shaped minaret. Here, in the middle of the 9th century, extravagant material expression seems to have been given to the truly imperial grandeur, distinction, and specialty to which the Abbasid elites made claim. At least, later literary representations of this palatial building spray framed it very much as in line with Late Antique, especially Sasanian, traditions of kingship, and they tend to add an undertone of extravagance and vanity that demonstrates remarkable, and significant, contrasts with how al-Mutawakkil's forefather al-Mansur in 8th-century Bagdad was remembered.

> The caliph Mutawakkil had [his palace] decorated with great images of gold and silver and made a great pool whose surfacing inside and out was in plates of silver. He put on it a tree made of gold in which birds twittered and whistled. He had a great throne made of gold on which there were two images of huge lions and the steps to it had images of lions and eagles and other things, just as the throne of Solomon son of David is described. The walls of the palace were covered inside and outside with mosaic and gilded marble. 1,700,000 dinars were spent on this palace. He sat in the palace on his golden throne, dressed in a robe of rich brocade and he ordered that all those who entered his presence should be dressed in finely woven brocades.[26]

These representations, and the physical remnants that informed them, evince above all the Late Antique forms of specialty, authority, and legitimacy that the Abbasid dynasty and its

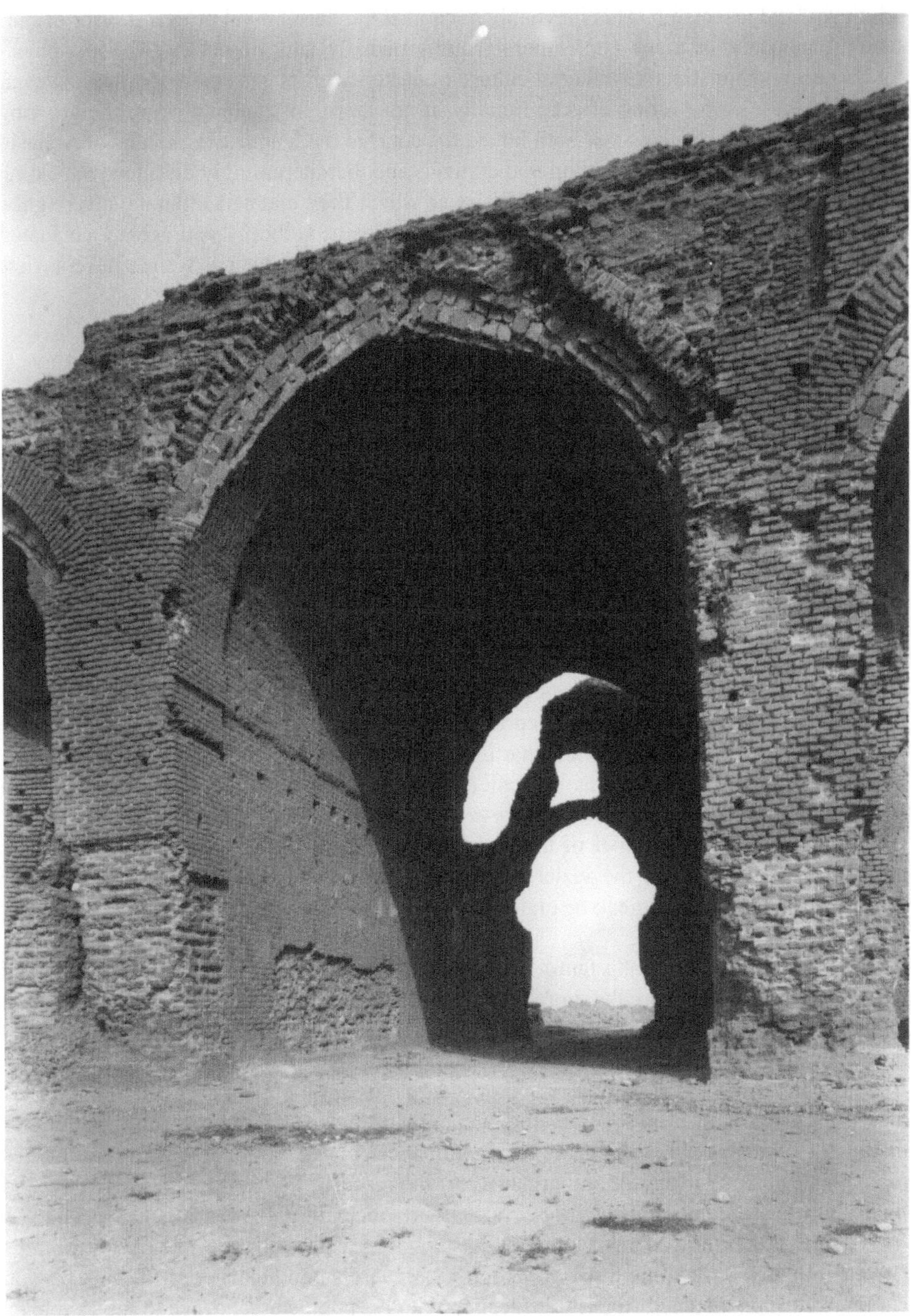

Figure 6.5 Samarra', remains of the Khaqani palace (*al-Jawsaq al-Khaqani*), Gate of the Common People (*Bab al-'Amma*) (*c*. 836–842)

Source: Photo by K.A.C. Creswell, early 20th century. © Creswell Archive, Ashmolean Museum, neg. EA.CA.6335, http://creswell.ashmus.ox.ac.uk/archive/EA.CA.6335-0.html

representatives claimed for themselves and for the arrangements that confirmed their power, privileges, and leadership. This inevitably generated the disapproval or even horror of outsiders, opponents, or many contemporary and especially later observers. Not just physical barriers and a distinctive material culture of austerity or its extreme opposite, however, generated these empowering effects. Equally, if not more, instrumental were the growing numbers of human shackles that both linked the court to the lengthening chains of Abbasid authority and agency across the imperial domains and that increasingly distanced the caliph and his entourage from the social worlds over which they claimed ultimate sovereignty. These human shackles from which the Abbasid chains of authority and agency emanated were the central administrative and military agents of Abbasid power as well as the courtiers and relatives that made for the Abbasid imperial household.

2.1 Shackles of Abbasid agents

In the entourage of Abbasid rulers, an important role was reserved for the aforementioned administrative experts or scribes, the *kuttab*. Together with the palace guards, harem eunuchs, and servants, they formed the core of the staff in the Abbasid palaces. Ibn al-Nadim in his aforementioned Catalogue's section on prose writing dedicated its 'second variation' to the writings of this group of 'the scribes', further identifying them and their activities as "the specialists of epistolography, the land-tax agents, and the members of the administrative departments (*al-dawawin*)".[27]

As suggested here by Ibn al-Nadim, and as already alluded to before, the *kuttab* mainly took care of the dynasty's wealth and political communication. They were in charge of organizing the court's resource flows, its correspondence and representation, and its reception of visitors, and were therefore arranged in different branches with different tasks and areas of expertise. These were the *diwan*s that Ibn al-Nadim also referred to, each of which was headed by a senior *katib*, such as 'the chief of the chancery' (*sahib diwan al-rasa'il*), 'the chief of the land-tax bureau' (*sahib diwan al-kharaj*), 'the chief of the relay postal network' (*sahib al-barid*), and 'the chief of the army bureau' (*sahib diwan al-jund*). All fell under the general supervision of the vizier (Ar. *wazir*), whose influence, resources, and power increased as the empire came to be organized in a more complex manner and the number of *kuttab* and *diwan*s grew.

One of the most fascinating families that controlled the Abbasid vizierate in the second half of the 8th century were the aforementioned Barmakids. The story of their rise and fall tells us much about the remarkable changes that the court and its leaderships experienced during this early Abbasid period. Originally connected to the management of a powerful Buddhist monastery in the eastern region of Balkh, the patron of the family, Khalid ibn Barmak (709–782), converted to Islam and became closely involved in the political changes of the 8th century. First, he appears as a commander of Khurasani troops during the 3rd *fitna*, then as an administrator and organizer of the resource flows of the new dynasty, and finally also as a regional agent ruling various provinces in the Abbasids' name. His son Yahya (733–805) followed in his father's footsteps at the court and grew into one of the most powerful figures of his time through his role as a guardian and teacher of the caliph's son Harun, who soon assumed Abbasid leadership with his pupil's ascendance to the caliphate. During the reign of Harun al-Rashid, Yahya became his most important vizier and counsellor, so that he, together with his two sons—who also acted as administrative leaders at the court—and other family members, largely controlled the balance of Abbasid power. In line with the sociocultural practices and dynamics that were sketched above, Yahya, as well as other Barmakids, were known during this period as the main sponsors and patrons of cultural and scientific knowledge production and exchange, taking a particular interest in the promotion and integration of Perso-Sasanian and Indo-Sanskrit traditions. The year 803, however, is known in Arabic historiography as the year of the fall of the Barmakids, when for unclear reasons Yahya and his supporters fell from favor, and Harun ordered the exile or execution of most of the Barmakids. This radical change of fortune for the Barmakids served many—especially in the Arabic literary imagination of *udaba'* and their audiences—as a telling example of the fickleness of power and the rapid turn of fate. Some Barmakid descendants nevertheless remained active as lower ranking *kuttab* and dynastic agents after that, but the era of Barmakid omnipotence was gone forever.

This did not at all, however, apply to the era of the powerful *kuttab* and viziers. In the process of patrimonial-bureaucratic formation and increasing centralization, many high-profile individuals and groups followed in the Barmakids' footsteps. These included the likes of 'Ubayd Allah ibn Yahya ibn Khaqan, who appears to have held the position of vizier for most of the time—despite the succession crises and internecine warfare of the 860s—from 850 until his death in 877, and of his less fortunate contemporary al-Fath ibn Khaqan (*c.* 817–861), who allegedly died defending the caliph al-Mutawakkil against his assassins in 861. Al-Fath's father, known as Khaqan 'Urtuj, was of Turkic-speaking Inner-Asian origins and is reported to have come to Bagdad as a free agent, with his own substantial following, in al-Ma'mun's entourage when the latter moved there from Marv after the 4th *fitna*. Khaqan 'Urtuj's son al-Fath never became vizier, but in the 850s he did become a central and, therefore, powerful character at the court of al-Mutawakkil, in whose service he is said to have performed supervisory duties that had to do with keeping the caliphal seal (*khatm*), with the collection of land-tax (*kharaj*), and with intelligence gathering and the relay postal network that connected various corners of the empire (*barid*). In the best of Abbasid traditions of patrimonial-bureaucratic leadership, al-Fath is also well known as an expert of Arabic poetry, as an author and a collector of books, and as a successful sociocultural patron for whom various texts were composed, including probably 'The Virtues of the Turks' by the aforementioned *adib* al-Jahiz. The vizier 'Ubayd Allah ibn Yahya ibn Khaqan's is a very different story, although the presence of the Turkish rulership title *khaqan* (later also used in the adapted format of *khan*) in the names of both 'Ubayd Allah and al-Fath seems to suggest parallel links to origins in some form of Turkic-speaking leadership in or beyond the Transoxanian northeast. In 'Ubayd Allah's case, however, the few things that are known of his family history hint at Khurasani origins, military action, transfer to Iraq during the 3rd *fitna*, administrative training and service in the entourage of the Barmakids, and eventually, after the 4th *fitna*, also in that of al-Ma'mun. 'Ubayd Allah and other *kuttab* members of his family are known to have thrived especially in the service of al-Mutawakkil, with whom 'Ubayd Allah is said to have had a special bond that gave him great power and authority. During his long term as vizier, he is reported to have continued to wield at least some of this aura of privilege and authority during the conflict-ridden reigns of al-Mutawakkil's sons. Some of the members of 'Ubayd Allah's family continued to be associated with terms of office as vizier up into the 920s.[28]

By the early 10th century, however, other *kuttab* families had emerged as central and powerful agents of Abbasid political action, most of them rising to prominence and power in the entourages of the Abbasid leader and restorer of social and political order al-Muwaffaq (d. 891) and his son and grandsons, the caliphs al-Mu'tadid (r. 892–902), al-Muktafi (r. 902–908), and al-Muqtadir (r. 908–932). Foremost among these are the al-Furat family (the Banu l-Furat) and the al-Jarrah family (the Banu l-Jarrah). The former hailed from a Shi'ite background, acquired administrative expertise and resources in the course of the 9th century, and was involved in the successful restoration of, and reorganization of resource flows to, the Abbasid court in the 890s. The latter al-Jarrah family had central Iraqi Christian origins, entered the palace administration in the 850s, and provided for different generations of Muslim viziers and *kuttab* in Abbasid service up to the 930s. The most well-known leaders of both families, ʿAli ibn al-Furat (d. 924) and ʿAli ibn ʿIsa ibn al-Jarrah (859–946), to a large extent dominated Abbasid court politics and the disintegrating Abbasid patrimonial-bureaucratic apparatus in the early decades of the 10th century (see the next chapter). As protagonists of these troubled times, who succeed each other on more than one occasion in the position of vizier, they have been framed in many literary representations as two extremes on a continuum of patrimonial-bureaucratic service, with ʿAli ibn al-Furat being scorned as a greedy self-serving tyrant who, when executed in 924 by order of the caliph, received his due, and with the octogenarian ʿAli ibn ʿIsa being praised as an exemplary model of virtuous *kuttab* behavior and loyal dynastic service.[29] The latter ʿAli ibn ʿIsa and his descendants certainly seem to have been rewarded for their memorable administrative track-record when they managed to retain the status and resources they had won in Abbasid service into post-Abbasid times. It was, therefore, no less than one of ʿAli ibn ʿIsa's sons who appears in Ibn al-Nadim's Catalogue, composed in the 970s, as the wealthy patron who was praised for his interest in 'the ancient sciences'.

The quickly growing socioeconomic, political, and cultural impact of the Abbasid *kuttab* brought them from the later 8th century onwards into direct competition with the other major agents of Abbasid power in the entourages of Abbasid rulers. These were the Abbasid military commanders who, with their troops, were mostly stationed as *amirs*, or military administrators, in Iraq and in the empire's different regions, from Ifriqiya to Transoxania, to represent Abbasid authority, wield Abbasid violence, and enforce Abbasid order everywhere. In fact, the boundaries between the leaderships of these two groups of administrative and military experts were always rather fuzzy, and perhaps even never meant to be very clearly drawn. This is also suggested by the cases of al-Fath and his father Khaqan ʿUrtuj, ʿUbayd Allah ibn Yahya ibn Khaqan and his Khurasani predecessors, and also viziers such as ʿAli ibn al-Furat and ʿAli ibn ʿIsa, each of whom occupied positions of Abbasid leadership that also required the build-up of substantial personal followings, the management of networks of supporters, allies, and resources of their own, and if necessary the wielding of violence and engagements in military action. The context of these two groups' leadership was not only one of administrative or military specialization and active participation in an ever more complex apparatus of power that integrated and penetrated in ever more strongly centripetal ways local and regional resource flows and leadership arrangements across the imperial territory. It also became even more a patrimonial-bureaucratic context, geared towards the contested interests of the growing ranks of the Abbasid center's dynastic, administrative, military, and other agents (including not least religious scholars appointed to act as Abbasid judges, or *qadi*s, in the different centers of the empire). Everywhere, these interests were above all defined by competitive strategies to confront their many external and internal rivals for local, regional, or trans-regional power and authority, to protect their clients and supporters along the expanding chains of Abbasid authority and agency, and to accumulate sufficient resources—including manpower—to achieve success in these arenas of dynastic and bureaucratic rivalry and protection.

As explained before, in the second half of the 8th century, the most important Abbasid troops were the former Khurasanis of the *abnaʾ*, who had won the 3rd *fitna* for the anti-Marwanid movement and had remained in Iraq in Abbasid service. They proved their unparalleled merits for the dynasty on many 8th-century battlefields, especially as infantry troops. In time, however, these *abna'* became particularly notorious for the disturbing roles they played in street fights in the rapidly urbanizing context of Abbasid Bagdad. Another important group that wielded violence as agents of the early Abbasids was made up of the so-called Khurasaniyya, who served as heavy cavalry. These *abna'*, Khurasaniyya, and many other groups of fighting men were all led by their own, relatively autonomous commanders (*qa'id*, pl. *quwwad*), who were usually confirmed in their commands by the Abbasid ruler. This meant that whereas they each organized the recruitment and deployment of their own troops, they were granted access to sufficient resources and privileges, including the right to carry an Abbasid banner, to enable this, and to lead their men in the pursuit, restoration, consolidation, or preservation of Abbasid local and regional order. These appointments were, therefore, above all determined by the human resources that these agents managed to muster and by the record of their and their relatives' relations with the Abbasid dynasty, rather than by any proven martial, strategic, or administrative qualities.[30]

The preserved stories about the rise and fall and Abbasid service of many of these commanders again illustrate in interesting detail the remarkable transformations that the dynasty, the court, and the elites of the Abbasid empire experienced between the mid-8th and early 10th centuries. Well-known and highly representative *qa'id*s and *amir*s from the later 8th century were the classical *abna'* leaders Khazim ibn Khuzayma al-Tamimi and his son Khuzayma. Khazim is known as a typical Perso-Arabian leader from the neighborhood of Marv, a descendant of the Arabian Tamim tribe that ended up in Khurasan by the end of the 7th century and became closely intertwined with local Persian families. Khazim earned his reputation especially by going to battle around 750 as commander of Khurasani troops in support of the Abbasid cause in Iraq. In the end, however, it was his son Khuzayma who gave this *abna'* family fame and glory. As the leading military commander in Bagdad, he and his army of about 5,000 Khurasani troops added the necessary military muscle to Harun's accession to the throne in 786. Thereafter, and until the 4th *fitna*, he continued to command his troops, with his relatives, from one of the palaces in Bagdad. Other well-known and highly representative *quwwad* during the early Abbasid period were the Arabian tribal leaders Ma'n ibn Za'ida al-Shaybani and his cousin Yazid ibn Mazyad. Ma'n was the leader of the Shayban tribal formation that was dominant in the northern Iraqi region of the Jazira and who, in the early 750s, appears as one of the last remaining opponents of the Abbasid takeover of Marwanid power. In 758, however, Ma'n and his tribal troops rescued the Abbasid ruler al-Mansur from the hands of local insurgents, after which he was actively integrated into the new context of the Abbasid apparatus of power, and sent with his tribal followers as an Abbasid *amir* to establish and maintain order in Yemen first and then in the Iranian region of Sistan. When Ma'n was murdered by a local anti-Abbasid movement in Sistan in 769–770, his cousin Yazid ibn Mazyad took over his position as a member of the Abbasid court and as a local leader in the Jazira, commanding an extensive force of Arabian and non-Arabian *mawali* fighters. Yazid and his men distinguished themselves mainly as important allies for Harun al-Rashid in the further deployment and consolidation of Abbasid leadership arrangements in the highly complex region of the Jazira. Simultaneously, in the transforming environment of Abbasid court culture, the fierce warrior Yazid appears also as having distinguished himself as a highly praised patron of Arabic poetry.

After the 4th *fitna* and the return of al-Ma'mun from Marv to Bagdad in the late 810s, the high-profile role traditionally ascribed to 7th- and 8th-century wielders of central violence, such as the Khurasani *abna'* and the Arabian tribes, came to an end. Under the incentive of al-Ma'mun's brother, the later caliph al-Mu'tasim (r. 833–842), from then on preference was increasingly given to fighters without any prior Abbasid history to make up the personal guard (*ghilman*) and the military power base of the Abbasid dynasty. In this first half of the 9th century, the core of the Abbasid military apparatus came to be dominated by a diverse whole of very different individuals and groups, identified as the 'Turks', or *atrak*—mostly (though not all, as in the case of Khaqan ʿUtruj) imported via commercial routes from the Inner-Asian steppes—, the *faraghina*—mainly consisting of the Ushrusaniyya and moving westward from the Fergana Valley and from the mountainous region of Ushrusana in particular in the wake of the 4th *fitna*—, Armenians, Arabian prisoners-of-war from Egypt identified as *maghariba* ('westerners'), and numerous other outsiders and *mawali* freedmen. As a result, the profile, and also the role, of the leaders of the Abbasid military muscle changed along, and the preserved biographies of some of these new leaders confirm the striking social change that took place in this period in the very center of the patrimonial-bureaucratic apparatus of Abbasid power and authority. Ashinas (d. 844), Itakh (d. 849), and Wasif (d. *c.* 867) are, as already mentioned, the most prominent names of the new leaders of al-Muʿtasim's *ghilman*, and the latter two are known to have been employed as a cook and a blacksmith in Bagdad before being sold to al-Muʿtasim and being destined for a whole new career and future. Other striking names of free agents and commanders are those of the aforementioned Khaqan ʿUrtuj and of al-Afshin (d. 841). The latter was an ambitious warlord who originally was a dynastic ruler of a remote mountain principality in Transoxania before appearing, in the course of the 820s, with his own Ushrusaniyya troops in the service of Abu Ishaq al-Muʿtasim when the latter re-established Abbasid control over Egypt for his brother al-Maʾmun. Just as in the latter case, these leaders of various origins also played an important role in the organization of Abbasid order across the imperial territories. For example, in the early 830s, Ashinas succeeded his master Abu Ishaq as the administrator of Egypt, a powerful and lucrative position that was soon to include all the Abbasid-controlled regions west of Iraq and in which he was in turn, upon his death in late 844, succeeded by Itakh. The strong patrimonial-bureaucratic centralization of the Abbasid power apparatus in this period, however, is evident from the fact that neither of them ever set foot in Egypt, and that both Ashinas and Itakh chose to rule through their own subordinates and representatives in order not to leave the center of Abbasid power and resources: the court in Samarraʾ.

These radical transformations in the social construction of the early 9th-century Abbasid military apparatus, which were paralleled—as already noted on various occasions above—by similar changes among most of the other groups that represented Abbasid authority, also connect in equally telling ways to al-Muʿtasim's aforementioned decision to leave Bagdad and to house his new entourage and troops in Samarraʾ. In this new imperial center, the new leaders—especially Ashinas, al-Afshin,. and Khaqan ʿUrtuj—and their different followers and troops are reported to have been allocated their own quarters, in which everything was done to preserve the military qualities and cohesive force that was meant to serve Abbasid interests. Contemporary literary renderings of these 9th-century transformations at the center of Abbasid authority at least suggest this course of social and urban planning, as in the following unique description of the organization of military life in al-Muʿtasim's Samarraʾ:

> [In Sāmarrāʾ] al-Muʿtaṣim isolated all the areas on which he settled the *atrāk* from those on which he settled the people, setting the one entirely apart from the other, so that the *atrāk* would not interact with any of the local populations nor would any but the *farāghina* live beside them. He allotted to Ashinas and his peers the area known as al-Karkh, and assigned to him a number of the *atrāk* commanders and troopers. He ordered him to build mosques and markets.

> He allotted to Khaqan ʿUrtuj and his peers the area adjoining the al-Khaqani palace, and ordered them to settle in one place all those who were assigned to him, that is, by forbidding them to mix with the townspeople. He allotted to Wasif and his companions the area adjoining [the hunting park of] al-Hayr; he had built a long wall which he called Hāʾir al-Hayr. He ordered that all of the distributed area on which the *atrāk* and the 'uncivilized' *farāghina* were settled were to be built far from the markets and everyday hubbub, on wide avenues and long side streets. In their allotted areas and along their streets, no townspeople, whether merchants or others, would be allowed to mix with them.
>
> Then al-Muʿtaṣim purchased [for the *atrāk*] slave women and married them to these women. He forbade them or anyone related to them from marrying into the local populace so that their offspring would marry only among themselves. He ordered that the slave women assigned to the *atrāk* be given fixed salaries and that their names be placed in the military registers. None of them would be allowed to divorce or abandon his wife.[31]

While these *ghilman* of al-Muʿtasim that were stationed in Samarraʾ were still a motley collection of leaders and men from all kinds of free or unfree backgrounds and origins, the repeated creation of fresh regiments in the Abbasid military apparatus via similar strategies throughout the 9th century realized a kind of competitive homogenization in the ranks of these new Abbasid elites. Especially after the purges and internecine warfare among the Samarraʾ-based leaderships that marked the 850s and especially the 860s, the reorganization of Abbasid power by al-Muwaffaq and his offspring manifested itself with the emergence of not only new *kuttab* families such as the aforementioned al-Furat and al-Jarrah, but also of yet another set of new *atrak* leaders in the Abbasid military apparatus. The *ghilman* of the Abbasid dynasty were actually recruited ever more exclusively from new imports of young boys who were transferred to Iraq from among the Turkic-speaking peoples of the Inner-Asian steppes. With the emergence of these more uniformly composed ranks of *ghilman*, their particular fighting techniques as mounted archers, resulting from the skills as horsemen most of them had acquired on the Inner-Asian steppes, also appeared ever more prominently as the key characteristic of how they now wielded Abbasid violence.

Whereas the last remaining leaders from al-Muʿtasim's entourage, especially Wasif (d. *c.* 867) and some of his peers, had somehow been involved in the struggles with and finally also the murder of al-Mutawakkil and a handful of his closest supporters, they finally disappeared from the Abbasid scene—in often equally violent circumstances—in the troubles of the 860s. At that time, some of their sons emerged in the sources as the new Abbasid powerbrokers and as the leaders of followings and networks that they and their fathers had managed to recruit. Most prominent among the latter undoubtedly was Musa ibn Bugha (d. 877), son of Bugha al-Kabir ('The Elder') (d. 862), who was himself one of al-Muʿtasim's Samarraʾ-based *atrak*, referred to especially in contemporary narratives as a tough commander leading Abbasid forces on various punitive campaigns between the 830s and the late 850s. His son Musa appears especially with his own *atrak* followers as one of the main supporters and henchmen of the caliph's brother al-Muwaffaq in the 870s. Another strongman of *atrak* background who acquired ever greater prominence from that time onwards, representing in many ways the new post-870 Abbasid elites and their whereabouts, was Muʾnis (d. 933), also known from one of the victories he won for his Abbasid overlord as Muʾnis al-Muzaffar ('the triumphant one'). Muʿnis first appears as one of the *ghilman* and commanders in the entourage of al-Muwaffaq's son. He is also referred to in that same capacity during this son's reign, as the caliph al-Muʿtadid (r. 892–902), which was now again performed and organized by and around new Abbasid agents such as Mu'nis from Bagdad. In the 910s and 920s, Mu'nis is described, with his *atrak*, as one of the main allies in Bagdad and Iraq for the aforementioned vizier ʿAli ibn ʿIsa ibn al-Jarrah, and thus as another powerbroker who dominated Abbasid court politics and the disintegrating Abbasid patrimonial-bureaucratic apparatus. By the turn of the 920s to the 930s, Mu'nis even emerged as one of the main Abbasid kingmakers. Eventually, however, parallel to what had happened to the leaders of al-Muʿtasim's entourage in the 850s and 860s, Mu'nis succumbed to the violent competition and internecine warfare among *atrak* leaders of similar resources and status that marked the 930s, and that—unlike in the 860s—soon heralded the arrival of Ibn al-Nadim's post-Abbasid times and realities (see the next chapter).

2.2 *Shackles of Abbasid courtiers and relatives*

In the aforementioned section on prose writing in Ibn al-Nadim's 10th-century Catalogue, he usefully identifies yet another set of shackles that both linked the Abbasid courts to the lengthening chains of Abbasid authority and distanced the caliph and his entourage from the world over which they claimed ultimate authority.

> The third variation, with the reports about the courtiers (*al-nudamāʾ*), the attendants of literary salons (*al-julasāʾ*), the singers, and the buffoons, clowns and jesters, with the names of their books.[32]

These are the court members who provided entertainment and counsel, including especially many of the *adib*s who have been described above, but also musicians such as the aforementioned courtesan ʿArib, and many others. The enormous extent and diversity of these Abbasid palace attendants, who by their very presence, activities, and opulence really made these Abbasid courts a paragon of Late Antique imperial splendor, are remembered in often fantastic and highly significant detail in various contemporary or later representations. One of these is the following detailed description of the complex organization and management of the court of the caliph al-Mutawakkil (r. 847–661) in an 11th-century anonymous text from Egypt, 'The Book of Gifts and Rarities':

> [When] al-Mutawakkil ʿalā Allāh was assassinated, the total sum in coin in his private treasury was a million [gold] dinars in cash and fifty million [silver] dirhams. He left eleven thousand unfree male and female servants, six thousand of these being eunuchs (*khādim*). He also left a personal guard of eight thousand unfree warriors (*al-ghilmān al-mamālīk*). As for his personal expenditures, [they amounted] to two million one hundred thousand [silver] dirhams every year, and for his mother Shujāʿ six hundred thousand dinars. The [other] expenses were two hundred thousand dinars for the kitchens; three hundred thousand dinars for construction and restoration; ten million dirhams in allowances (*arzāq*) for the entourage (*al-ḥasham*); five million dirhams for expenditure on his personal attendants (*dhawāt al-khāṣṣa*); three hundred thousand dinars for clothing (*kuswa*); a hundred thousand dinars for scents; a hundred thousand dinars for refurbishing the equipment in the treasuries, and for fabricating (*ṣiyāgha*) gold and silver [articles]; one million two hundred thousand dirhams for canvas (*al-khaysh*) and candles; two million dirham for ice; a hundred thousand dinars for furnishings (*farsh*); two million dirhams for beverage [storage] vaults (*khazāʾin al-sharāb*); five hundred thousand dirhams for the allowances of his courtiers (*nudamāʾ*); five hundred thousand

> dirhams for the wages of dog trainers (*kilābiziyyūn*), falconers (*bāzdāriyya*), and cheetah attendants (*fahhādūn*); five million dirhams for expenditure on light boats (*ḥarrāqāt*) and the like; a hundred thousand dinars for the purchase of slaves (*raqīq*); three hundred thousand dinars for the purchase of precious stones (*jawhar*); eight hundred thousand dinars for the wages of the house servants (*farrāshūn*); five hundred thousand dirhams for the wages of [entertainers such as] slapstick comedians (*ṣafā'ina*), jesters (*muḍḥikūn*), trainers of fighting rams (*kabbāshūn*), trainers of fighting dogs (*kilāb al-hirash*), and for the noisy breakers of wind (*ḍarrāṭūn*).[33]

These complex arrangements of courtiers, chamberlains, palace attendants, circulating gifts, and resources at the center of Abbasid power and authority overlapped in many ways between the later 8th and early 10th centuries with the arrangements that made for the fluid ranks of Abbasid military and administrative agents, as described in the previous section. They simultaneously intersected, as also suggested in Ibn al-Nadim's classification, with the diverse circles of *adib*s and of the many scholars and scientists who were active in the Abbasid urban centers. A case in point for this diverse profile of the Abbasid courtier is represented by the long and rich history, as Abbasid courtiers and much more, of the al-Munajjim family, the Banu l-Munajjim. Between the 8th and 10th centuries, its members were active as experts of the science of the stars, musicians and poets, bibliophiles, *kuttab*, specialists of Mu'tazili theology and followers of al-Tabari's legal teachings, patrons of the arts and sciences, recipients of Abbasid income, and brokers of power and status at the courts of Bagdad and Samarra'. This history of Abbasid court service reportedly began when the patron of this Munajjim family, a Zoroastrian of Persian origins and with Sasanian courtiers among his ancestors, allegedly was appointed by the Abbasid ruler al-Mansur to a position at his palace as expert of the science of the stars (*munajjm*), which earned the family its Arabic name. The family acquired prominence during the reigns of al-Ma'mun and his successors, with Yahya ibn al-Munajjim (d. *c.* 830), who was connected to the rich intellectual environment of the aforementioned Musa brothers, and his son 'Ali (d. *c.* 889), who received a position, influence, and substantial income at the courts of al-Mutawakkil and his sons and who engaged especially, as patron and compiler, with the fields of medicine, music, and Arabic poetry. The Munajjim family's history continued—as did the histories of numerous elite lineages of courtiers, *adib*s, and their likes in many parallel ways—along similar lines of connections, patronage, and intellectual and political agency in Samarra' and Bagdad with 'Ali's sons and grandsons, into the post-Abbasid 10th century. At that time, also Ibn al-Nadim's trajectory intersected with that of this longstanding family of scholars, scientists, *adib*s, courtiers, and men of culture, and his Catalogue benefited substantially from their longstanding experience with the Abbasid world of books and scholarship.

This permeability of, and diversity in, the ranks of Abbasid courtiers is similarly suggested by the stories of many others. One such story concerns that of the aforementioned Barmakid Yahya (733–805), who first appeared as a foster-father and tutor of Harun and then as a powerful vizier and counsellor during most of Harun's reign, until he famously fell from favor and was imprisoned, together with other Barmakids, at Harun's court in Raqqa, where one of his sons and assistants in the vizirate even was executed. Another story is that of the son of the commander Khaqan 'Utruj, al-Fath, who grew up in the caliphal palace of Samarra' with caliph al-Mu'tasim's son Ja'far, became—as detailed above—one of the latter's most trusted advisors and *kuttab* when Ja'far reigned as the caliph al-Mutawakkil, and died defending his lord and friend against his assassins. Yet another interesting and representative story is that of one of Ja'far's aforementioned kingmakers: the legal scholar and theologian Ahmad ibn Abi Du'ad (d. 854). Ahmad started his career in the historiographical spotlights as a courtier and advisor of the caliph al-Ma'mun. In the 830s and 840s, he appears, as explained above, as a very activist chief judge in Bagdad, as a cultural patron of *adib*s such as al-Jahiz, and as one of the main Abbasid power brokers. In these capacities, Ahmad is especially remembered for having enforced his views in favor of Abbasid sovereignty and Mu'tazili teachings in trials against his own and his Abbasid overlord's opponents. The latter's ranks included many traditionalists, in the context of the *mihna*, and also one of al-Mu'tasim's commanders, the princely warlord from Ushrusana al-Afshin, whom Ahmad convicted for apostasy and disobedience and who was consequently executed in 841. In the early days of al-Mutawakkil's reign, however, when Ahmad fell ill, the young caliph and his supporters managed to free themselves from his enormous influence, which reportedly and tellingly meant that they divested not just him, but also his sons and their enormous clienteles in Bagdad and Samarra', from their power and resources.

Finally, another immensely important, if not central, group that made up the Abbasid court and completed the entourages of Abbasid rulers in Bagdad, Raqqa, Samarra', or elsewhere was organized around that component of the family that was mostly identified as the *huram*. This specific term is directly related in meaning to the word *haram* that is used to denote the sacred and inviolable nature of the areas of Mecca and Medina in Arabia (*al-haramayn al-sharifayn*), and also of the Temple mount in Jerusalem (*al-haram al-sharif*). In post-Abbasid times the term *huram*, and especially its adapted, more well-known form harem (*harim*), referred to a separate female area in the royal palace or in an elite household, access to which was forbidden to (male) outsiders. This spatial dimension, however, seems not yet to have been similarly attached to these terms and their gendered practices in the 8th to 10th centuries. In these Abbasid times *huram* is used to denote especially the extensive social groups and entourages that coalesced around the wives, mothers, sisters, aunts, and minor children of the Abbasid rulers. Originally, they are known to have resided in their own palaces in Bagdad. With the extensive transformations of the 9th century, which also affected the Abbasid *huram*, however, they were more directly integrated into the complex caliphal palace compounds that arose in Samarra' and eventually again Bagdad, where they appear as confined to their own secluded quarters in the closed, private parts of the Abbasid palaces.[34] In both cases, the Abbasid harem also included among its ranks many others, who attended to the needs of these women, of their male relatives, especially the ruler, and hence also of the dynasty and its empire. These included female musicians and singers, female servants and housekeepers, and also courtesans and concubines, all of whom—such as the aforementioned 'Arib al-Ma'muniyya—entered the harem as unfree women, brought to Iraq from a wide variety of backgrounds and selected and purchased for dynastic service by the ruler's agents.

These ranks, furthermore, also included those female servants who were trained or favored to act as stewards and supervisors of the harem's daily organization, which allowed them more liberty of movement as well as direct access to the resources and allowances that were awarded to the Abbasid *huram*. A last group was that of the eunuchs, who—as a-sexual, unfree servants—could move between male and female worlds without violating the moral boundaries that were meant to keep both separated. They are mostly represented as acting as harem guardians and attendants, as intermediaries, and as teachers and tutors of harem children. In 9th and 10th century reports of these ranks of the Abbasid *huram*, the growth of these *huram* entourages to enormous, even gigantic, proportions is often stressed, as are the many strains this put on the dynasty's treasuries. In the above-mentioned 11th-century representation of al-Mutawakkil's mid-9th-century legacy, this is expressed in the phrase that

Figure 6.6 Samarra': reconstruction of a stuccoed image of wine-pouring dancing girls which once decorated one of the private rooms in the Khaqani palace

Source: From E. Herzfeld, Die Malereien von Samarra (Berlin, 1927) II (Djausaq, Harem, Bild der Tänzerinnen, teilsweis ergänzt)

"he left 11,000 unfree male and female servants, 6,000 of these being eunuchs (*khadim*)".[35] A parallel text from 11th-century Bagdad—a manual of Abbasid court ceremonial entitled 'The Protocols of the Caliphal Palace'—even states that "it is generally believed that in the [the 910s and 920s] the private palace contained 11,000 eunuchs (*khadim*)—7,000 blacks and 4,000 white Slavs".[36]

The role of the *huram* was not just one of sheltering and catering for the needs of Abbasid women. Rather, the *huram* was a central—if not the central—shackle in the politics of the dynasty, and thus of the imperial apparatus of power. On the one hand, there were many strategic marriages with the ruler or with members of his *huram*, which enabled the integration of women, and thus of their male relatives, and of men, with their families, followers, and local or regional resources, into the central orbit of Abbasid power and authority. On the other hand, there was the *huram*'s providing for the mothers of the ruler's male children, who thus ensured the reproduction of the dynasty, of the central apparatus of power and authority, and thus of the empire. This remarkable centrality in Abbasid court life of the *huram* also meant that its female leaders always wielded substantial power and influence, and that through all kinds of intermediaries, they continuously managed to have access to enormous resources and to set-up wide-ranging clienteles that secured their centrality within and without the *huram*'s, and even the court's, boundaries.

This agency and great impact of the *huram*—as with the already reported involvement of the mother of Harun al-Rashid in his accession, after the sudden demise of his brother al-Hadi in 786—was the imaginative subject of many literary renderings, many of which used this, as in a misogynous reflex, to explain the many troubles and moments of crisis that the Abbasid center endured. The interconnectedness of this heart of the Abbasid dynasty with the aforementioned deep sociocultural transformations of the 9th century is less well known. Between the 3rd and the 4th *fitna*, it was above all the women of the different Abbasid rulers who appear in this central role of *huram* leadership. This picture entirely shifts to the priority of the caliphs' mothers in the 9th and 10th centuries, when the *huram* were also ever more secluded in the caliphal palaces in Bagdad or Samarra'. The reason is that whereas in the later 8th century, marriages with, especially, Abbasid relatives were preferred to consolidate the family's fresh dynastic hold on Arabo-Islamic imperial power and agents, these Abbasid spouses entirely disappeared from the written record for the subsequent 9th and 10th centuries, when Abbasid centralization and the marginalization of more traditional elites was maximized even in the dynasty's core and its reproductive strategies.[37] From then on, concubines of Greek, Slavic, and various Inner-Asian origins acquired authority and power as the mothers of the ruler's male son, as *umm walad* ('mother of the boy'). This was a privileged status that legally guaranteed their automatic manumission upon their master's demise, permitted the accumulation of their own estates and resources, involved them deeply in Abbasid court politics at least for as long as their sons—and potential or actually appointed heirs apparent—continued to reside with them, and ensured unparalleled access and influence when these sons eventually succeeded their fathers and became caliphs in their own right.

A legendary and typical example of a powerful Abbasid spouse from before the changes of the 4th *fitna* is represented by the story of Zubayda (d. 831–832), wife of Harun al-Rashid, mother of his son and successor al-Amin, foster-mother of Harun's other son and successor al-Ma'mun, and, like Harun, grandchild of the Abbasid ruler al-Mansur (r. 754–777). Zubayda married her nephew in the early 780s and appears in many contemporary and later literary representations as an embodiment of Muslim rulership qualities that make her in many ways equal to Harun's reputation. This included references to her exemplary beauty—allegedly also expressed in the nickname by which she became most widely known, 'little bite of butter' (*zubayda*)—and its defining impact on the aesthetics of Bagdad's elites. This also derived from her renown for many acts of piety and patronage in Bagdad, to the benefit of scholars, poets, and musicians, and in Arabia, where she is reported to have invested in all kinds of provisions for visitors to Mecca, to the extent that the ancient pilgrimage route from Kufa in Iraq to Mecca, with its many facilities to provide food and drinking water for pilgrims, has for many centuries continued to be referred to as 'Zubayda's road' (Darb Zubayda). Another strong Abbasid spouse from this early Abbasid period was Zubayda's predecessor, al-Khayzuran (d. 789), mother of the caliphs al-Hadi and Harun al-Rashid. Her story, however, is remembered especially for being so exceptional in these early days of Abbasid power. Al-Khayzuran was of South Arabian origins. Captured and enslaved in Arabia, she was sold and added to the Abbasid *huram* when the Abbasid ruler visited Mecca, and eventually manumitted and married to the later caliph al-Mahdi. As the mother of al-Mahdi's two heirs and successors, she is especially remembered for having been actively involved in organizing a transition of power, after the sudden death of her husband in 785, that served best the interests and ambitions of the group of early Abbasid courtiers and agents that had rallied around her. A central power broker in this group is said to have been the aforementioned Barmakid vizier Yahya, who—as a tutor and even foster-father of her son Harun—appears as a very close associate of al-Khayzuran and hence also as her accomplice in generating, in 786, not just Harun's enthronement but also their power over him, until al-Khayzuran's demise in 789 and, eventually, the famous fall of the Barmakids in 803.

After the 4th *fitna* and the emergence in Iraq of entirely new Abbasid agents, including the *ghilman* and *atrak*, the caliphal *huram* followed suit, so that, as explained, women of diverse, mostly peripheral, unfree origins, and especially the manumitted mothers of ruling caliphs, started taking a leading role. Among the numerous women who were active in the Abbasid *huram* in all kinds of capacities concubines of Greek-Christian origins often occupied prominent positions. These women were all captured as booty during the ongoing regular military actions and expeditions at and beyond the northwestern frontiers with the Greek-Roman empire in Asia Minor, and a handful rose to become manumitted *umm walads* and powerful caliphal mothers in the *huram*, connected to the wider court and the outside world through their own agents and resources. This was the case with al-Mu'tadid's mother in the 890s and most famously perhaps with the mother of al-Mu'tadid's grandson, who began his reign as the caliph al-Muqtadir (r. 908–932) when he still was a minor (see next chapter). Al-Muqtadir's Greek-born mother, known by the slave name Shaghab, but mostly referred to in the sources as 'her Ladyship' (*al-Sayyida*) or as the 'Queen Mother' (*Umm Muqtadir*)—which says a lot about the role that tends to be attributed to her—is described in a variety of 10th-century and later sources as an even more powerful version of her predecessor Zubayda. This is related to the central role attributed to her in many acts of piety and patronage, using the abundant personal resources that her own estates and income provided, as also suggested in the following late-12th-century rendering of an anecdote about her:

> Shaghab is said to have devoted one million dinar each year from her private estates to the pilgrimage. She was devoted to the pilgrims' welfare sending water tanks and doctors and ordering that the reservoirs be prepared.[38]

This Queen Mother earned her name and fame above all, however, from the effective network of intermediaries and family members (including her own sister and brother, and the latter's descendants and troops), of her own *kuttab*, and of Abbasid administrative and military agents (including 'Ali ibn 'Isa, 'the good vizier', and for a long time also the *atrak* leader Mu'nis al-Muzaffar), which she, according to all reports, expertly managed throughout the 910s and 920s. This allowed her to partake actively in the ongoing competition with other rival power groups in Bagdad and Iraq for control over the court, the Abbasid apparatus of power and authority, and the diminishing resources of her son al-Muqtadir.[39]

Other groups of caliphal concubines in the extended *huram* ranks at the center of Abbasid power in the 9th and 10th centuries have been identified as clustering around women of Amazigh background, as Slavonic slave girls, and as many different easterners, whose origins stretched—just as those of al-Mu'tasim's and his successors' *ghilman*—from non-Muslim populations in Khurasan and Transoxania to all kinds of their peers in the vast Inner-Asian steppes. The mother of al-Ma'mun, who died long before he acceded to the caliphate, apparently had Khurasani roots, while al-Mu'tasim's mother is reported to have been brought over from Transoxania, and the mother of al-Mu'taṣim's son al-Mutawakkil—referred to above in the fragment concerning al-Mutawakkil's legacy as 'his mother Shujā'' and as the recipient of the enormous sum of 'six hundred thousand dinars'—[40] allegedly originated from the region of Khwarazm, west of Transoxania. With the assistance of their powerful and resourceful 'eastern' mothers and concubines, the Abbasid caliphs of the 9th and 10th centuries were, therefore, much more closely related to their *ghilman* and *atrak* leaders—from al-Afshin, Khaqan ʿUtruj, and Wasif to Muʾnis—than one would at first expect.

The Abbasid *huram*, the dynastic lineages that were birthed in its dynamic environment, and the courtiers and agents that operated around it were thus composed in parallel and highly interconnected ways of an enormous and regularly changing diversity of people, relationships, and interests. Despite this diversity and regular transformation, all of these factors somehow continued to share in very active and competitive ways in attempts to tie the intricate whole of chains of local, regional and trans-regional authority, agency, and patronage to the Abbasid specificity of the Late Antique Arabo-Islamic imperial order of things. When, in the course of the 10th century, this Abbasid specificity lost much of its centripetal appeal to many, if not most, along these chains, diversity, competition, and radical transformation were all that remained, even in the very center of the Abbasid order, and the caliph and this entourage of his would remain only as an abstraction, as it were—and as an ideal to be remembered and emulated—of their former selves, entirely separated from any realities of power or authority. In post-Abbasid times, these realities would first turn out to be occupied by many of the diverse sets of agents and courtiers that had grown autonomous along, or in the margins of, those shackles and chains of Abbasid authority, agency, and patronage.

Notes

1 Hoyland, *Arabia and the Arabs*, 247.
2 Fowden, *Empire to Commonwealth: Consequences of Monotheism in Late Antiquity*.
3 Bulliet, *Conversion to Islam in the Medieval Period*; Harrison, "Behind the Curve: Bulliet and Conversion to Islam in al-Andalus Revisited".
4 Hourani, *A History of the Arab Peoples*, 110.
5 Kennedy, "Military Pay and the Economy of the Early Islamic State".
6 al-Yaʿqūbī (st. 897), *Kitāb al-Buldān* ['The Book of the Lands']; translation from Gordon, *The Rise of Islam*, 131.
7 al-Tabari (d. 923), *Tārīkh al-Rusul wa l-Mulūk* ['The History of Messengers and Kings']; translation from McAuliffe, *The History of al-Ṭabarī. vol. XXVIII*, 238.
8 al-Tabari (d. 923), *Tārīkh al-Rusul wa l-Mulūk* ['The History of Messengers and Kings']; translation from Kennedy, *The History of al-Ṭabarī, vol. XXIX*, 7–8.
9 See Watson, "The Arab Agricultural Revolution and its Diffusion"; Watson, *Agricultural Innovation in the Early Islamic World*; Decker, "Plants and Progress: Rethinking the Islamic Agricultural Revolution"; Squatriti, "Of Seeds, Seasons, and Seas: Andrew Watson's Medieval Agrarian Revolution Forty Years Later".
10 Gordon, "Abbasid Courtesans and the Question of Social Mobility".
11 Gordon, *The Breaking of a Thousand Swords*.
12 al-Khaṭīb al-Baghdādī (1002–71), *Tārīkh Baghdād* ['The History of Baghdad'] quoting ʿUmāra ibn ʿAqīl (9th century), *Faḍāʾil Baghdād* ['The Merits of Baghdad']; translation from Lassner, *The Topography of Baghdad*, 47.
13 Bloom, *Paper before Print*.
14 Yāqūt al-Rūmī (d. 1229), *Irshād al-Arīb ilā Maʿrifat al-Adīb* ['Dictionary of Learned Men']; translation from Kennedy, *The Court of the Caliphs*, 246–7.
15 Ibn al-Nadīm (d. *c.* 995), *al-Fihrist* ['The Catalogue']; translation adapted from Dodge, *The Fihrist of al-Nadīm*, 3–4.
16 See Stewart, "The Structure of the Fihrist: Ibn al-Nadim as Historian of Islamic Legal and Theological Schools".
17 Ibn al-Nadīm (d. *c.* 995), *al-Fihrist* ['The Catalogue']; translation adapted from Dodge, *The Fihrist of al-Nadīm*, 3.
18 Ibn al-Nadīm (d. *c.* 995), *al-Fihrist* ['The Catalogue']; translation adapted from Dodge, *The Fihrist of al-Nadīm*, 4.
19 Gutas, *Greek Thought, Arabic Culture: The Graeco-Arabic Translation Movement in Baghdad and Early ʿAbbāsid Society*. Quote from Brentjes, "Sciences in Islamic Societies", 570.

20 Ibn Khallikān (1211–82), *Wafayāt al-Aʿyān wa anbāʾ abnāʾ al-zamān* ['Obituaries of Eminent Men and Accounts of the Sons of the Epoch']; translation from Kennedy, *Court of the Caliphs*, 254–5.
21 Balty-Guesdon, "Le Bayt al-Ḥikma de Baghdad"; Gutas, *Greek Thought, Arabic Culture*.
22 Ḥunayn ibn Isḥāq (d. 873), "The Book of the Ten Treatises on the Eye"; translation from Meyerhof, *The Book of the Ten Treatises on the Eye*, 3.
23 Kennedy, *Court of the Caliphs*.
24 From Ettinghausen, Grabar and Jenkins-Madina, *Islamic Art and Architecture, 650–1250*, 55.
25 al-Ṭabarī (d. 923), *Tārīkh al-Rusul wa l-Mulūk* ['The History of Messengers and Kings']; translation from Kennedy, *The History of al-Ṭabarī, vol. XXIX*, 118–9.
26 Shābushti (d. 998), *Kitāb al-diyārāt* ['The Book of Monasteries']; translation from Kennedy, *Court of the Caliphs*, 147–8.
27 Ibn al-Nadīm (d. *c*. 995), *al-Fihrist* ['The Catalogue']; translation adapted from Dodge, *The Fihrist of al-Nadīm*, 3.
28 Gordon, "The Khāqānid Families of the Early ʿAbbasid period".
29 Van Berkel, "The Vizier".
30 Kennedy, *The Armies of the Caliphs*.
31 al-Yaʿqūbī (st. 897), *Kitāb al-Buldān* ['The Book of the Lands']; translation from Gordon, *The Rise of Islam*, 131.
32 Ibn al-Nadīm (d. *c*. 995), *al-Fihrist* ['The Catalogue']; translation adapted from Dodge, *The Fihrist of al-Nadīm*, 3.
33 *Kitāb al-Hadāyā wa al-Tuḥaf* ['The Book of Gifts and Rarities']; translation from Qaddumi, *Book of Gifts and Rarities (Kitāb al-Hadāyā wa al-Tuḥaf)*, 208–9.
34 Kennedy, *Court of the Caliphs*.
35 *Kitāb al-Hadāyā wa al-Tuḥaf* ['The Book of Gifts and Rarities']; translation from Qaddumi, *Book of Gifts and Rarities (Kitāb al-Hadāyā wa al-Tuḥaf)*, 208–9.
36 Hilāl al-Ṣābiʾ (970–1056), *Rusūm Dār al-Khilāfa* ['The Protocols of the Caliphal Palace']; translation from Salem, *Rusūm Dār al-Khilāfa (The Rules and Regulations of the ʿAbbāsid Court)*, 14; El Cheick, "The Harem", 179.
37 Kennedy, *Court of the Caliphs*.
38 Ibn al-Jawzī (1116–1201), *al-Muntaẓam fī Taʾrīkh al-Mulūk wa-l-Umam* ['The Systematized History of Kings and Nations']; translation from El Cheikh, "The Harem", 172.
39 El Cheikh, "The Harem".
40 *Kitāb al-Hadāyā wa al-Tuḥaf* ['The Book of Gifts and Rarities']; translation from Qaddumi, *Book of Gifts and Rarities (Kitāb al-Hadāyā wa al-Tuḥaf)*, 208–9.

Selected readings

Agha, S.S. *The Revolution Which Toppled the Umayyads: Neither Arab nor ʿAbbāsid* (Leiden, 2003)

Ahsan, M.M. *Social Life Under the Abbasids* (London, 1979)

Ali, K. *Imam Shafiʿi: Scholar and Saint* (Richmond, 2011)

Balty-Guesdon, M.-G. "Le Bayt al-Ḥikma de Baghdad", *Arabica* 39 (1992): 131–50

Bernheimer, T. *The ʿAlids: The First Family of Islam, 750–1200* (Edinburgh, 2014)

Bloom, J. *Paper Before Print: The History and Impact of Paper in the Islamic World* (New Haven, 2001)

Bosworth, C.E. *The History of al-Ṭabarī, Volume XXX: The ʿAbbāsid Caliphate in Equilibrium. The Caliphates of Mūsā al-Hādī and Hārūn al-Rashīd, A.D. 785–809/A.H. 169–93* (Albany, 1989)

Brentjes, S. with Morrison, R.G. "The Sciences in Islamic Societies (750–1800)", in R. Irwin (ed.), *The New Cambridge History of Islam, Volume 4: Islamic Cultures and Societies to the End of the Eighteenth Century* (Cambridge, 2010), pp. 564–639

Bulliet, R.W. *Conversion to Islam in the Medieval Period: An Essay in Quantitative History* (Cambridge, MA, 1979)

Cobb, P.M. *White Banners: Contention in ʿAbbasid Syria, 750–880* (New York, 2001)

Cooperson, M. *al-Maʾmun* (Oxford, 2005)

Cooperson, M. *Classical Arabic Biography: The Heirs of the Prophet in the Age of al-Maʾmūn* (Cambridge, 2000)

Daniel, E. *The Political and Social History of Churasan under Abbasid Rule, 747–820* (Minneapolis, 1979)
De La Vaissière, E. *Samarcande et Samarra: élites d'Asie centrale dans l'empire abbasside* (Paris, 2007)
Decker, M. "Plants and Progress: Rethinking the Islamic Agricultural Revolution", *Journal of World History* 20/2 (2009): 187–206
Déroche, F. *The Abbasid Tradition: Qur'ans of the 8th to 10th Centuries* (New York, 1992)
Dodge, B. (ed. and transl.). *The Fihrist of al-Nadīm. A 10th Century AD Survey of Islamic Culture* (New York, 1970)
El Cheick, N.M. "The Harem", in M. van Berkel, N.M. El Cheikh, H. Kennedy, L. Osti (eds.), *Crisis and Continuity at the Abbasid Court: Formal and Informal Politics in the Caliphate of al-Muqtadir (295–320/908–32)* (Leiden, 2013)
Ettinghausen, R., Grabar, O., Jenkins-Madina, M. *Islamic Art and Architecture, 650–1250*. Second Edition (New Haven, 2001)
Fowden, G. *Empire to Commonwealth: Consequences of Monotheism in Late Antiquity* (Princeton, 1993)
Gordon, M.S. "Abbasid Courtesans and the Question of Social Mobility", in M.S. Gordon, K.A. Hain (eds.), *Concubines and Courtesans: Women and Slavery in Islamic History* (New York, 2017), pp. 27–51
Gordon, M.S. *The Breaking of a Thousand Swords: A History of the Turkish Military of Samarra, AH 200–275/815–89 CE* (Albany, 2001)
Gordon, M.S. "The Khāqānid Families of the Early ʿAbbasid Period", *Journal of the American Oriental Society* 121/2 (2001): 236–55
Gordon, M.S. *The Rise of Islam* (London, 2005)
Gutas, D. *Greek Thought, Arabic Culture: The Graeco-Arabic Translation Movement in Baghdad and Early 'Abbāsid Society (2nd–4th/8th–10th centuries)* (London, 1998)
Harrison, A. "Behind the Curve: Bulliet and Conversion to Islam in al-Andalus Revisited", *al-Masāq. Journal of the Medieval Mediterranean* 24/1 (2012): 35–51
Hourani, A. *A History of the Arab Peoples* (London, 1991)
Hoyland, R.G. *Arabia and the Arabs from the Bronze Age to the Coming of Islam* (London and New York, 2001)
Hurvitz, N. *The Formation of Ḥanbalism: Piety into Power* (London, 2011)
Kennedy, H. *The Armies of the Caliphs: Military and Society in the Early Islamic State* (London and New York, 2001)
Kennedy, H. *The Court of the Caliphs. When Baghdad Ruled the Muslim World* (London, 2004)
Kennedy, H. *The Early Abbasid Caliphate: A Political History* (London, 1981)
Kennedy, H. *The History of al-Ṭabarī. Volume XXIX. Al-Manṣūr and al-Mahdī* (Albany, 1990)
Kennedy, H. "Military Pay and the Economy of the Early Islamic State", *Historical Research* 75/188 (2002): 155–69
Lassner, J. *The Shaping of 'Abbasid Rule* (Princeton, 1980)
Lassner, J. *The Topography of Baghdad in the Early Middle Ages* (Detroit/Michigan, 1970)
McAuliffe, J.D. *The History of al-Ṭabarī. Volume XXVIII. ʿAbbāsid Authority Affirmed* (Albany, 1996)
Melchert, Chr. *Ahmad ibn Hanbal* (Oxford, 2006)
Melchert, Chr. *The Formation of the Sunni Schools of Law, 9th–10th Centuries C.E.* (Leiden, 1997)
Meyerhof, M. *The Book of the Ten Treatises on the Eye Ascribed to Hunain ibn Ishaq, 809–877 A.D.: The Earliest Existing Text-book of Ophtalmology* (Cairo, 1928)
Newman, A.J. *The Formative Period of Twelver Shīʿism: Ḥadīth as Discourse between Qum and Baghdad* (Richmond, 2000)
Northedge, A. *The Historical Topography of Samarra* (London, 2005)
Qaddumi, G.H. (transl.). *Book of Gifts and Rarities (Kitāb al-Hadāyā wa al-Tuḥaf). Selections Compiled in the Fifteenth Century from an Eleventh Century Manuscript on Gifts and Treasures* (Cambridge, MA, 1996)
Robinson, Ch.F. *A Medieval Islamic City Reconsidered: An Interdisciplinary Approach to Samarra* (Oxford, 2001)

Salem, E.A. (transl.). *Rusūm Dār al-Khilāfa (The Rules and Regulations of the ʿAbbāsid Court)* (Beirut, 1977)

Shaban, M.A. *The ʿAbbasid Revolution* (Cambridge, 1970)

Sharon, M. *Black Banners from the East. Vol. 1. The Establishment of the ʿAbbasid State: Incubation of a Revolt; Vol. 2. Revolt: The Social and Military Aspects of the ʿAbbasid Revolution* (Jerusalem, 1983–90)

Squatriti, P. "Of Seeds, Seasons, and Seas: Andrew Watson's Medieval Agrarian Revolution Forty Years Later", *The Journal of Economic History* 74/4 (2014): 1205–20

Starr, S.F. *Lost Enlightenment: Central Asia's Golden Age from the Arab Conquest to Tamerlane* (Princeton, 2013)

Stewart, D. "The Structure of the Fihrist: Ibn al-Nadim as Historian of Islamic Legal and Theological Schools", *International Journal of Middle East Studies* 39/3 (2007): 369–87

Tillier, M. *Les Cadis d'Iraq et l'état Abbasside (132/750–334/945)* (Beirut, 2009)

Tor, D.G. (ed.). *The ʿAbbasid and Carolingian Empires: Comparative Studies in Civilizational Formation* (Leiden, 2017)

van Berkel, M. "The Vizier", in M. van Berkel, N.M. El Cheikh, H. Kennedy, L. Osti (eds.), *Crisis and Continuity at the Abbasid Court: Formal and Informal Politics in the Caliphate of al-Muqtadir (295–320/908–32)* (Leiden, 2013)

Verkinderen, P. *Waterways of Lower Iraq and Khuzistan. Changing Rivers and Landscapes in the Early Islamic Middle East* (London, 2015)

Watson, A. "The Arab Agricultural Revolution and Its Diffusion, 700–1100", *The Journal of Economic History* 34/1 (1974): 8–35

Watson, A. *Agricultural Innovation in the Early Islamic World. The Diffusion of Crops and Farming Techniques. 700–1100* (Cambridge, 1983)

Wheatley, P. *The Places Where Men Pray Together: Cities in Islamic Lands, Seventh through the Tenth Centuries* (Chicago, 2001)

Zadeh, T.E. *Mapping Frontiers Across Medieval Islam: Geography, Translation, and the ʿAbbāsid Empire* (London, 2011)

Zaman, M.Q. *Religion and Politics under the Early ʿAbbasids: The Emergence of the Proto-Sunni Elite* (Leiden, 1997)

7 Abbasid imperial transformations and post-Abbasid fragmentation (9th–11th centuries)

Introduction: the end of Late Antique imperial formation

In the first decades of the 10th century, after the restoration of Abbasid power and authority in the core regions of Egypt, Syria, Arabia, Iraq, and western Iran by al-Muwaffaq and his supporters and successors, the complex and elaborate Abbasid patrimonial-bureaucratic leadership experienced a whirlwind of events and internecine conflicts. In the process, the shackles that had until then continued to bind at least some of the many chains of imperial agents, representatives, and resources to the Abbasid center were severely weakened. They further disintegrated under continued internal and external pressures in the 930s and 940s, until they collapsed and finally gave way everywhere to the highly fragmented, polycentric realities that had been encroaching upon the Abbasid imperial order since the early 9th century. This meant the definitive end of the Abbasid caliphate as an effective trans-regional power, of the patrimonial-bureaucratic apparatus that had sustained it, and of the final vestiges of Late Antiquity's period of trans-regional imperial centrality.

The Abbasid caliphal dynasty nevertheless continued to exist for many centuries, in Bagdad until 1258 and then (in a contested form) in Cairo until the early 16th century. Thereafter, the caliphate was formally continued in another dynastic format—and in often all but prominent ways—in Ottoman Constantinople, until it was officially abolished in February 1924, in the wake of the foundation of the modern, secular state of Turkey. This remarkable resilience followed from the fact that in the course of the 10th and 11th centuries, the Abbasid dynasty and the caliphal position—by then inherently interconnected—came to represent an entirely new kind of trans-regional authority. Abbasid caliphal leadership, remaining only as an abstraction, and as an ideal to be remembered and emulated, of its former imperial self and entirely separated from any realities of trans-regional power, was actually in due course reinvented as a symbolic and spiritual mediator who, as the only legitimate Successor of God's Messenger, continued to connect at least some of the diverse social, cultural, and political orders of the post-Abbasid world to the exemplary era of prophetic leadership and to integrate them, despite their diversity, into the community's united history of salvation.[1] The transition from an Abbasid to a post-Abbasid world, therefore, represented more than just the end of the era of Late Antique imperial formation. In addition, just as with the caliphate's eventual adaptation to the new contexts of 'medieval' Cairo and early modern and modern Constantinople, it involved the experimentation with and participation in entirely different and even new modes of Islamic authority and belonging by a great variety of old and new local, regional, and trans-regional actors and groups. This happened in highly contested and fragmented polycentric contexts that would, in fact, continue to define the great variety of Islamic leaderships and their claims to power and authority that will be discussed in the next, second part of this book.

The disintegration of the Late Antique Arabo-Islamic empire and the definitive end of the *umma* as one coherently centered trans-regional entity had many reasons, causes, and consequences. These are difficult to ascribe to one factor or to the reign of one single caliph, even though in both traditional as well as modern scholarship such simple explanations have certainly been contemplated. Most contemporary historians actually tended to put the blame on al-Muwaffaq's grandson al-Muqtadir (r. 908–932), on his lack of political acumen, and on the impact on the long reign of his personal entourage—especially the 'Queen Mother' (*Umm Muqtadir*) and her acolytes, discussed in the previous chapter. This general tendency is well illustrated in the following oft-quoted explanation by one contemporary observer of the violent death of al-Muqtadir in 932 and of the lack of effective Abbasid leadership in the subsequent decade, and of the quick disintegration of the imperial apparatus of power that turned out to be the result:

> [Al-Muqtadir] became caliph when he was still young, inexperienced and eager to indulge in luxuries. He did not concern himself with dynastic affairs, nor did he attend to the matters of the reign; instead, *amir*s, viziers and *kuttab* conducted the affairs of the dynasty, in which he did not have a say or influence, nor was he credited with the qualities of a ruler or administrator. Those who had power were women, servants and others, and this faulty leadership, which befell the empire, swept away whatever wealth or provisions were in the treasuries of the caliphate. This led to his blood being shed; affairs were unsettled after [his time] and many of the caliphate's ways were abandoned.[2]

Many modern historians have long followed these traditional views of 10th-century Abbasid decadence and decay in their descriptions and analyses. However, it is now generally accepted that deeper challenges with which the Abbasid apparatus of power was confronted should at least be taken into consideration as well, and that the trajectory of Abbasid imperial power was one of several ups and downs, rather than of any linear process of rise, efflorescence, decline, and fall.

Figure 7.1 Dinar (golden coin) minted in the name of caliph al-Muqtadir (Egypt, 311 AH/923–24)

Source: Harvard Art Museums/Arthur M. Sackler Museum, Bequest of Thomas Whittemore, Object Number 1951.31.4.2316

In the first place, it appears that the patrimonial-bureaucratic empire constantly had to, and mostly managed to, deal with a problem of insecure income from its main agricultural resources, but that, unlike before, in the early 10th century, no more solutions could be found. The fiscal revenues available to the caliph, most importantly from the extremely rich agricultural lands of southern Iraq, including especially the Sawad region south of Bagdad, but also from the many other regions of the imperial domain, came under pressure at several occasions throughout the 9th and 10th centuries. The destructions caused by the 4th *fitna* in and around Bagdad in the 810s, by the internecine warfare in and around Samarra' and Bagdad in the 860s, and by various anti-Abbasid movements in, especially, the 860s and 870s and again the 920s in southern Iraq were some of the main factors in this. The loosening of (fiscal) ties in the course of the 9th century—often related to the same moments of central disarray—with more distant imperial regions such as Ifriqiya in the west and Transoxania and Khurasan in the east (see below), as well as the unsuccessful experimentation with tax farming arrangements in less distant regions such as Egypt and Syria represent other, equally important factors. It is generally assumed that as a result, by the 10th century, the revenues of the Abbasid center in Iraq had dwindled enormously, increasing within the elaborate Abbasid apparatus of power the competition for control over and access to whatever was left, and putting any remaining coherence of this imperial infrastructure of dynastic agents and courtiers under extreme pressure. This unstable situation of the 920s and thereafter is well exemplified by the fact that according to one of today's leading Abbasid historians, Hugh Kennedy, "cross revenue yields from areas in the Sawad typically declined by between 85 and 97 percent" from what they had been in the middle of the 9th century.[3] A contemporary *adib* and courtier, renowned for playing chess with the caliph al-Muqtadir and with his son and successor al-Radi (r. 934–44), illustrated the sense of urgency and loss that prevailed as a result of this lack of resources with the following exclamation of despair and incapacity that he attributed to his pupil and eventual patron, the caliph al-Radi:

> This dominion has been thrust upon me, without my having done anything to attain it, without my having desired it. God knows that neither covertly nor openly have I made any move for it. It is not just that I would renounce the honor and the glory that rule bestows but simply that circumstances are not as in other times: the treasury is poor, the army insatiable and the country ruined.[4]

This unfortunate caliph al-Radi indeed reigned in the extremely violent and chaotic circumstances that marked Bagdad and the wider region of Iraq in the 930s and 940s. He had been put on the caliphal throne after his father al-Muqtadir (r. 908–932) and his uncle al-Qahir (r. 932–934) by one of the many Abbasid power groups who were in this period fighting among each other for control over the few remaining scraps of imperial resources and who were by this time mainly led by 'insatiable' military leaders and their personal hosts of *atrak* (see below). The longstanding challenges of the extreme lengthening of the many chains of Abbasid authority and agency that connected the caliph, the dynasty, and the court in Iraq to the rest of the empire, as well as the growing autonomy that many groups of *kuttab*, *atrak*, and others along these chains—whether or not in name of the caliph—acquired in the course of this process thus came to a head in ways that, *in hindsight*, proved impossible to reverse. This is often also related to the radical changes that occurred in the composition of central Abbasid elites in the course of the 9th century. With the growing predominance of Inner-Asian *atrak* and the preponderance of *kuttab* with Iraqi roots—such as the al-Furat and al-Jarrah families, discussed in the previous chapter—in the Abbasid apparatus of imperial power of the later 9th century, the Abbasid center became less than ever before connected to the networks and interests of local and regional elites outside Iraq. The fact that after the 4th *fitna* the Abbasid dynasty itself cut its bonds with local branches of the family in regions such as Syria, relied for its own reproduction on outsiders in the format of concubines, and limited its membership to particular agnatic lineages that were all born and raised in the palaces of Samarra' or Bagdad—first al-Mu'taṣim and his sons and grandsons (r. 833–992), then one of the latter, al-Muwaffaq, and his son and grandsons (r. 870–934)—did nothing to counter this total loss of trans-regional social cohesion and political integration. The strong leadership of al-Mu'tasim in the 830s and, especially, of al-Muwaffaq in the 870s and 880s—both also participating actively in successful military campaigns against internal and external foes—had time and again managed to restore central Abbasid power and authority and to rebuild at least the core imperial networks of elites and resources around their substantially transformed entourages. In the 930s, however, Abbasids such as al-Muqtadir and also al-Radi proved incapable of replicating these examples and especially of rallying around them sufficient men and resources to maintain any reality of political centrality in their imperial domains in Iraq, and eventually, even in Bagdad itself (see below).

This total loss of Abbasid political coherence that appeared especially in the 10th century, therefore, primarily was the outcome of a long-term historical process of change. This process was undeniably linked to the major social and political transformations that the Abbasid elites had already been going through since the early 9th century and that have been identified in previous chapters as part and parcel of the formation of a complex patrimonial-bureaucratic apparatus of centralizing power. In fact, this process of change unfolded among the diversely composed patrimonial-bureaucratic central elites in Iraq—as described in much detail in the previous chapters—and at the same time also among the local and regional elites in the many outlying areas of the Arabo-Islamic empire. How this not only empowered many of these elites but also enabled them as well as others to start acting in increasingly autonomous and post-Abbasid—outside of any effectively integrated reality of the Abbasid political order, but without necessarily relinquishing any fiction of its trans-regional continuance—ways will be further discussed in this chapter. This transition from an Abbasid to a post-Abbasid political and sociocultural order was not only a slow and haphazard process that happened simultaneously, and in deep interaction, with the formation of the patrimonial-bureaucratic empire since the 8th century. It was also a diverse process that never affected imperial regions and elites, from Transoxania over Iraq to al-Andalus, in similar ways and along similar trajectories. The chronological scope of the current chapter—the last one of this book's first part covering Islamic West-Asia's Late Antique period—will therefore not only have to incorporate, just as was the case for the previous chapter, the full scale of the Abbasid imperial timeframe from the 3rd and 4th *fitna*s onwards, but also the highly fragmented and contentious post-Abbasid order as that emerged in the course of the 9th and 10th centuries and as that prepared for new waves of nomadic migrations from the early 11th century onwards.

In this chapter, not just the central elites—discussed in much detail in the preceding chapter—and their loss of Abbasid cohesion will be described. The great diversity of 'peripheral' elites that also made for the Abbasid and especially for the post-Abbasid worlds will be equally discussed. This chapter will therefore serve as a complement to the previous chapters, not simply by reconstructing the next and final step in a chronology of Abbasid rise, decline, and fall, but rather by completing the far more complex picture of imperial ups and downs described so far with an outside perspective. This allows to explain the transition from the Abbasid to the post-Abbasid worlds as an equally complex and long process with many ups and downs. This process proceeded along many trajectories of elite formation and transformation that differed along regions and timeframes, from the appearance of an Arabian Umayyad as a virtually autonomous Abbasid *amir* in al-Andalus in the 750s to the assumption of power over Bagdad and its hinterlands, and of the title of Abbasid chief *amir* (*amir al-umara'*), by an equally autonomous Irano-Daylamite warlord almost two centuries later, in the 940s. Everywhere, these local and regional elites that appeared within or on the side of the Abbasid apparatus of power were of very diverse origins and backgrounds, and each operated according to dynamics and ambitions that were not necessarily linked to each other. The result was all the same, nevertheless. From the course of the 9th century onwards, the trans-regional cohesion of the Arabo-Islamic empire and its patrimonial-bureaucratic infrastructure of power gave way to an irregularly expanding mosaic of alternative leadership formations, which eventually even included the formerly central area around Bagdad. The intricate and complicated polycentric patchwork of post-Abbasid leaders and elites that emerged—often in circumstances of violence—in the regions between the Atlantic and the Indian Ocean from especially the 9th century onwards will be described and understood here in the generalizing format of a twofold typology of Abbasid and post-Abbasid elites, respectively originating first from within and subsequently also from without the Abbasid apparatus of power. This more schematic chronological representation of the political patchwork of Islamic leadership in the 9th to mid-11th centuries allows for a focus on the most well-known representatives that emerged for every type and in the most important regions, without getting lost entirely in the endless complexity of the many petty rulers, dynasties, claims, and practices of this post-Abbasid order.

1 Abbasid imperial transformations in the 9th and 10th centuries: the 'autonomization' of Abbasid agents and *amir*s

As suggested at the end of the previous chapter, in post-Abbasid times the realities of power or authority would first turn out to be occupied by many of the diverse sets of agents and courtiers that had grown autonomous along, or in the margins of, the shackles and chains of people and resources that made for local, regional, and trans-regional networks of Abbasid authority, agency, and patronage. These included especially various sets of Abbasid military agents and administrators, or *amir*s, with their personal followers and troops. Two regional types of these *amir*s in particular appear as relevant to be discussed together: Abbasid *atrak* leaders in 10th-century Iraq and Bagdad; and *atrak* leaders and dynasties with longstanding local and regional roots, especially in Ifriqiya, Egypt, Iran, Khurasan, and Transoxania, who had been operating as *amir*s in the 9th-century Abbasid patrimonial-bureaucratic apparatus.

1.1 Abbasid amirs *in Iraq*

As explained in much detail in the previous chapters, whereas the different military leaders from al-Muʿtasim's Samarra'-based entourage and then some of their sons after them continued to dominate and disturb the dynamics of Abbasid imperial and dynastic power with their *atrak* followers for most of the mid-9th century, an entirely new generation of *atrak* leaders rose to prominence by the turn of the 9th to 10th centuries. These included the likes of the aforementioned Mu'nis al-Muzaffar (d. 933), who, in the 910s and 920s, is described, with his approximately 9,000 *ghilman*, as one of the powerbrokers who dominated Abbasid politics at al-Muqtadir's court in Bagdad. By the turn of the 920s to the 930s, Mu'nis even emerged as one of the main Abbasid kingmakers, who in 932, after defeating al-Muqtadir in

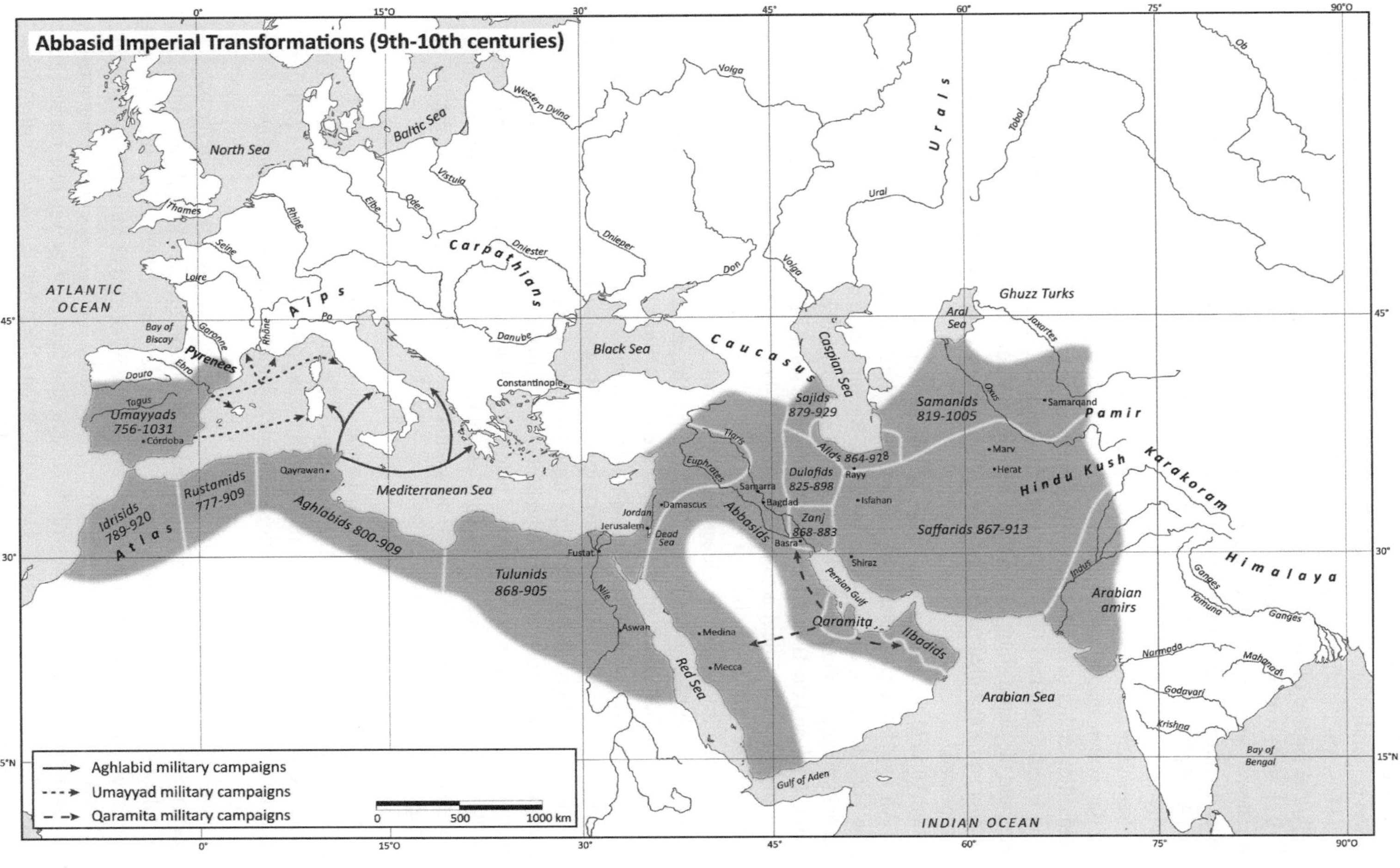

Map 4 Abbasid Imperial Transformations (9th–10th centuries)

Source: Redrawn from Hodgson, *The Venture of Islam. Vol. 1. The Classical Age of Islam*, p. 311

a battle that left the caliph dead, made the latter's brother al-Qahir the new caliph. Eventually, however, parallel to what had happened to the leaders of al-Mu'tasim's entourage in the 850s and 860s, Mu'nis succumbed to the violent competition and internecine warfare among Abbasid *atrak* leaders of similar resources and status that marked the 930s, as the caliph al-Radi (r. 934–944) with his despair over the 'insatiable' military also experienced.

The renewed empowerment of *atrak* leaders such as Mu'nis in the center of Abbasid power is often linked to the power politics of al-Muqtadir's aforementioned 'Queen Mother'. As explained in the previous chapter, she earned her name and fame above all from the effective network of intermediaries and family members (including her brother and the latter's descendants and troops), of her own *kuttab*, and of Abbasid agents such as Mu'nis al-Muzaffar, which she, according to all reports, expertly managed throughout the 910s and 920s. This allowed her to partake actively in the ongoing competition with other rival power groups in Bagdad and Iraq for control over the court, the Abbasid apparatus of power and authority, and the diminishing resources of her son al-Muqtadir. When Mu'nis went his own way and her son was killed in 932, however, Shaghab's network seems to have lost control and disappeared.

Another Abbasid agent who was linked to this network was the aforementioned "good vizier" 'Ali ibn 'Isa ibn al-Jarrah (859–946), whose lineage and resources would survive into post-Abbasid times, as suggested by Ibn al-Nadim's case of post-Abbasid patronage, referred to in the preceding chapter. In fact, by the early 10th century, *kuttab* families such as the Banu l-Jarrah and the Banu l-Furat had emerged as some of the most central and powerful agents of Abbasid political action. The most well-known leaders of both families, 'Ali ibn al-Furat (d. 924) and 'Ali ibn 'Isa ibn al-Jarrah (859–946), to a large extent dominated Abbasid court politics, as did the 'Queen Mother's agents and *atrak* leaders such as Mu'nis, in the second and third decades of the 10th century. The accession of al-Muqtadir in 908, still underage or at best barely of age, is often seen as a telling expression of how centrality in the power relations of the time in the caliphal palace had shifted from the strong dynastic personalities (and effective military leadership) of al-Muwaffaq and his son al-Mu'tadid (r. 892–902) to political groups and lineages from their entourages and dominated by *kuttab* and courtiers. A later Iraqi chronicle represented this remarkable collective and contested empowerment of the leaders of the Abbasid patrimonial-bureaucratic apparatus in the format of the following oft-quoted piece of wisdom, attributed to a discussion on the succession to the dying caliph al-Muktafi (r. 902–908) between the leading vizier at that time and one of his main advisors, 'Ali ibn al-Furat:

> For God's sake do not appoint to the post a man who knows the house of one, the fortune of another, the gardens of a third, the slave girl of a fourth, the estate of a fifth and the horse of a sixth; nor one who has mixed with the people, has had experience of affairs, has gone through his apprenticeship, and made calculations of people's fortunes.[5]

This is one of the ways in which the story is told of how the dominant figures in the palace, all *kuttab*, placed a young boy from the Abbasid harem on the throne and gave him the caliphal title al-Muqtadir. It is told especially, alongside many others about the continuous competition, intrigues, and violence that would have weakened al-Muqtadir's court and authority between 908 and 932, by later observers to make some sense of the continuously changing and ever more autonomous relationships and agents of power that marked the Abbasid court's history of this period. The rivalry among the powerful *kuttab*, furthermore, is often cited as an explanation for the striking inability of this collective Abbasid leadership to deal with the very real threats with which the core lands of the dynasty were confronted in the first decades of the 10th century. One of the most remarkable and disastrous problems was caused in the 920s by the so-called Qaramita. This referred to a militant anti-Abbasid Shi'ite movement whose leaders managed to march more than once with only a few thousand men from their headquarters in today's eastern Arabian region of Bahrain through Iraq, causing havoc and destruction and, in 927, even threatening Bagdad itself, without the far more sizeable Abbasid forces being able to repel them. All of this undermined the authority at the court and in Bagdad of the Abbasid *kuttab* leaders and their supporters and furthered the shift of power towards the only real wielders of protective violence, the *atrak* leaders and their *ghilman* troops, most prominently at this time Mu'nis al-Muzaffar. *Amirs* and their *ghilman* were thus able to take over power and, from the end of the 920s onwards, the position of caliph and the Abbasid family itself became subject to their rivalries and competition, which proved devastating and lethal for all. After al-Muqtadir died on the battlefield in 932, Mu'nis himself was murdered by a rival *amir* in 933, and the total loss of central power and authority that followed from this internecine warfare among Abbasid *amir*s, their *ghilman*, and their Abbasid supporters became complete when it transpired that the unwilling and frustrated caliph al-Radi (r. 934–44) and his few remaining representatives failed to command any further control over the remaining regions of the empire. Even the *amir* Muhammad ibn Ra'iq, the Abbasid military administrator of the nearby southern Iraqi regions of Wasit and Basra, so the infamous story of the Abbasid endgame goes, no longer wanted to send any revenues that were due to the palace. Al-Radi's attempt to organize a military campaign to rectify this situation is then reported to have led to nothing when it turned out that the caliph had no means or authority left to rally sufficient men.

Eventually, in 936, amidst warring *atrak* leaders and their *ghilman* in Bagdad, the caliph is said to have had no choice but to reverse the roles and invite the *amir* of southern Iraq to come with his own *ghilman*, protect the caliph, and restore order in Bagdad. According to this dominant storyline in traditional and modern historiography, this *amir*, Ibn Ra'iq, was then formally appointed by al-Radi as the new Abbasid chief *amir* (*amir al-umara'*), and he was given full authority over the Abbasid military and administrative apparatus in disarray. Subsequently, Ibn Ra'iq reportedly dissolved whatever remained of the formal features, responsibilities, privileges, and entitlements of the Abbasid power infrastructure, and worked only with his own *ghilman* and his own limited group of *kuttab* to try and establish some semblance of order and to organize his and his troops' and clients' access to whatever remained of local or regional resources in Iraq. In this way, as al-Radi exclaimed, the Abbasid treasury became "poor, the army insatiable and the country ruined",[6] the Abbasid dynasty lost its military and administrative mechanisms of power, and warlords of Abbasid provenance such as Mu'nis and Ibn Ra'iq (who was the son of a peer of Mu'nis and a former courtier of al-Muqtadir) and their violent and constantly shifting rivalries determined the swift transition to a new and highly unstable post-Abbasid regional order in Iraq.

This was an extremely messy and multivalent process of transition, in which many participated in varying capacities, and in which well-known and widespread stories, such as about Mu'nis' violent empowerment, al-Radi's total loss of control, and Ibn Ra'iq's redemptional intervention, should be considered as only one way in which especially later observers, writers, and historians tried to create some semblance of order and meaningfulness.[7] Further exemplifying the messiness of this process, the position of chief *amir* (*amir al-umara'*) appears to have remained fiercely and violently contested between various rivals of Ibn Ra'iq until 946, with further disastrous consequences for the fragile Iraqi ecosystem and including further episodes such as Ibn Ra'iq's murder in 942. Some more stability only emerged when, in January 946, a new, non-Abbasid warlord from western Iran, one Ahmad ibn Buya, established control over most of Iraq, entered Bagdad with his own Daylamite troops, and is said to have been recognized as Abbasid chief *amir*. This empowerment of Ahmad ibn Buya in Iraq in early 946 actually represents the end of this long and irregular process of the empowerment of Abbasid *atrak* leaders and *amir*s in southern Iraq, and of its increasing convergence with a very different but equally irregular process of the emergence of a post-Abbasid order elsewhere in the empire. Ahmad ibn Buya and his relatives, the Buyids—a family of mercenaries and warlords that had only recently moved south from their remote and mountainous homelands in the Daylam region near the Caspian Sea—would come to dominate the regions of Iraq and West Iran, as virtual representatives of a gradually re-invented Islamic order and as chief *amir* (*amir al-umara'*) and *amir*s of the Abbasid brothers and cousins who succeeded al-Radi to the now merely symbolic position of caliphal leadership of the *umma* in Bagdad (see below).

1.2 Abbasid **amirs** *outside Iraq*

The very different but equally real process of the emergence of a post-Abbasid order outside of the Abbasid imperial center actually meant that by the early 10th century, only the leaderships, elites, and resources of Iraq, most of western Iran, and the Jazira north of Iraq remained effectively integrated in the Abbasid power constellation, and that the Abbasid connection was tenuous at best among the highly diverse and dynamic leaderships of Arabia, Yemen, Egypt and Syria. Just as in the former Abbasid heartlands, which continued to be under effective Abbasid control until the violent and highly contested empowerment of Abbasid *amir*s in Iraq and in these other central regions in the 930s and 940s, in the lands of Yemen, Egypt, and Syria, as well as in quite a few other localities in east and west that had once been integrated into the chains of the imperial domain, a post-Abbasid order occasionally manifested itself around Abbasid *amir*s and their entourages, acquiring a state of permanent autonomy at various moments that differed from region to region. These *amir*s had all been sent from the Abbasid center in Iraq to maintain Abbasid control and secure flows of resources and services to the Iraqi center, but were variously inspired to minimize or even end those flows and claim local or regional autonomy for themselves and their offspring. As in the Abbasid center, in these Abbasid peripheries too the aftermaths of the 4th *fitna*, of the crises of the 860s, and of al-Muqtadir's reign proved important moments when those ties were severed, either temporarily or permanently. The dynamics in this process of transition and transformation within the Abbasid apparatus of trans-regional power display very specific differences between the Abbasid west and its east, both of which acquired in their own ways a new regional prominence and centrality after many decades, if not centuries, of Late Antique imperial integration. Each of these regions will therefore be presented separately here.

1.2.1 Abbasid amirs *and the Arabian west*

The western parts of the Abbasid imperial territory, ever more firmly Arabized in this period, were arguably the earliest to be confronted with the appearance of a diverse post-Abbasid order, especially on its most distant margins. When in the early 750s an Umayyad survivor, ʿAbd al-Rahman (r. 756–788), and his followers managed to craft a new space for their leadership in remote al-Andalus, they seem to have done so first by presenting ʿAbd al-Rahman as *amir* and representative of an imperial authority that was by then firmly coloring

Abbasid and Iraqi-centered. In reality, though, neither ʿAbd al-Rahman nor any of the more than a dozen Umayyads who succeeded him in Cordoba up to the end of Umayyad rule in al-Andalus in 1031 were ever really integrated in the Abbasid power apparatus. A sort of similar situation prevailed in the North African regions of the Maghreb and Ifriqiya, where mostly local, especially Amazigh ('Berber') and Amazigh-supported, leaderships remained dominant until the later 8th century. By that time, the *amir* Ibrahim ibn Aghlab (r. 800–812), originally a member of the Khurasani *abnaʾ* leadership of Bagdad, was confirmed as the leading Abbasid representative in Ifriqiya and set about restoring Abbasid order, and the collection of Abbasid tribute, across North Africa's fragmented landscape of leaderships. His descendants remained in power in the region until 909. From the 810s onwards, at the time of the 4th *fitna*, they maintained political order as a dynastic Aghlabid and autonomous one from the regional center of Qayrawan, only symbolically acknowledging their allegiance to the Abbasid center, and including the successful forceful deployment of Mediterranean ambitions towards Greek-Roman dominance over Sicily, southern Italy, and Sardinia.

Whatever these post-Abbasid realities on the 9th-century grounds of Ifriqiya and the Maghreb, both in outer regions such as these and in the Abbasid center in Iraq, the fiction of Abbasid sovereignty continued to be maintained by regional rulers who represented themselves as Abbasid agents and by caliphs who appointed regional administrators from Samarraʾ and Bagdad. This was no different for less distant regions such as Egypt and Syria or for that matter the Arabian Hejaz and Yemen. In fact, from the 820s onwards, the organization and management of power and authority in the regions stretching between Iraq and the Maghreb were delegated to particular members of the Abbasid family or, more frequently, even to Samarraʾ-based *atrak* leaders, who—as viceroys of the Abbasid west—appointed their own local and regional agents to represent the Abbasid center's (mostly fiscal-tributary) interests either virtually (in Aghlabid Ifriqiya) or effectively (in Syrian and Egyptian lands).

Until the 860s, the regions of Egypt and Syria thus remained firmly integrated through networks of *atrak* leaders and Iraqi-based administrators in the complex politics of the Iraqi center. Things changed, however, when in 868—during the period of internecine warfare in Iraq—Ahmad ibn Tulun (835–884), son of one of the Samarraʾ-based Abbasid *atrak*, arrived in Egypt as a local military agent for the newly appointed Abbasid ruler of the west. Until his death in 884, Ahmad ibn Tulun embarked on an endless and largely successful campaign of military and political action to maximize his and his own entourage's power and autonomy in and beyond Egypt, using the region's resources to build up his own military apparatus of *atrak*, blacks, and many others and to also be acknowledged as the legitimate Abbasid sovereign agent in Syria and southern Anatolia. Following the example of Abbasid Samarraʾ, Ibn Tulun built his own palatial infrastructure, al-Qataʾiʿ, to the north of Fustat, including a huge congregational mosque with a landmark spiraling minaret (after the model of al-Mutawakkil's minaret), an administrative center, and military quarters for the different components of his own military force.

Despite his military and political successes, Ibn Tulun and his son and grandsons, who succeeded him by dynastic designation rather than caliphal consent, continued to situate their authority within the Abbasid political order. This is suggested by the coins that Ibn Tulun struck and that—as one of the most important media used to articulate and project claims to sovereignty and Islamic leadership—continued to include explicit references to the caliph's name. It was reportedly confirmed in the treaties that Ibn Tulun's son and successor, Khumarawayh (864–896), consented to after violent confrontations with Abbasid forces. These confirmed the continuance of Tulunid rule over Egypt and Syria in return for a substantial annual tribute to be paid to the Abbasid center in Iraq. The descendants of Ahmad ibn

Figure 7.2 Cairo: mosque of Ahmad Ibn Tulun, *c.* 880

Source: Rare Books and Special Collections Library; The American University in Cairo, SC-1974-01-02-02-a08-pl43-a01, 'Aerial view of the Mosque of Ibn Tulun and its surroundings', http://digitalcollections.aucegypt.edu/cdm/ref/collection/p15795coll14/id/110

Tulun, known as the Tulunids, indeed remained in power in Egypt and Syria until 905, when this dynastic leadership and its main agents disintegrated in internecine warfare and Abbasid troops from Iraq razed most of al-Qata'i' to the ground.[8]

Between 905 and 935, Egypt and Syria again were more directly integrated into the politics of Bagdad, meaning that in theory at least regular tribute was again sent to Iraq and *amir*s were sent to Egypt and Syria to maintain order. Throughout this period, however, this proved all but self-evident, due to anti-Abbasid movements and various other problems in these regions as well as to the dissolution of power politics at al-Muqtadir's court in Iraq. Eventually, in 935, the *amir* Muhammad ibn Tughj (882–946) was delegated by the caliph al-Radi as his representative in Egypt, and in the messy context of the 930s he managed to emulate many of Ibn Tulun's achievements. As the son of a Tulunid *amir* originating from the Ferghana region east of Transoxania, Muhammad acquired a reputation as an effective Abbasid agent in Syria before being sent to Egypt, where he was eventually confirmed as an autonomous ruler in the west by caliph al-Radi, who allegedly awarded him the eastern title 'al-Ikhshid' ('the Servant'). Al-Ikhshid also moved northward from Egypt with his men, trying to expand his authority across Syria, but in northern Syria he was soon confronted with other Abbasid *amir*s, including the aforementioned chief *amir* Ibn Ra'iq, who all were similarly—from central and northern Iraq—attempting to carve out profitable spaces for themselves in the emerging polycentric order in these Abbasid heartlands. Al-Ikhshid died in the course of this scramble for influence over these regions, but his two young sons and successors—and especially his eunuch Kafur (d. 968), who continued to rule in their name—pursued the same policy of pragmatic expansion in a virtual context of Abbasid sovereignty. Eventually, in 947, they are reported to have settled for a formal division of the Syrian region between a northern part, connected to the Jazira and Iraq via the Shi'ite Arabian Hamdanid family of Abbasid *amir*s, known by honorary titles such as Sayf al-Dawla ('Sword of the Abbasid Dynasty') (r. 945–67, Aleppo) and Nasir al-Dawla ('Supporter of the Abbasid Dynasty') (r. 929–69, Mosul), and a southern part, controlled by Ikhshidid agents who were directed by Kafur from Egypt. Soon, however, both this Ikshidid reality of power—in the 960s, and especially after Kafur's death in 968, riven apart once again by internecine warfare among various competitors and dynastic agents—and the virtual Abbasid remnant to which it continued to relate—as with the official diploma that the caliph in Bagdad allegedly sent to Kafur in 966 to confirm him as 'Master' (*ustadh*) over the Ikshidid domains—would be replaced by a very different, and explicitly anti-Abbasid, sociopolitical order. This had been building in the west, had already swept away and replaced the Aghlabids in Ifriqiya and the southern Mediterranean in the early decades of the 10th century, and was intent on destroying any Abbasid remnants east of Ifriqiya, including any remaining branches of its *amir*s (see below).

1.2.2 Abbasid amirs *and the Arabo-Persian east*

Similar processes of 'autonomization' of Abbasid *amir*s and regional representatives marked the 9th-century history of the empire's east, in Transoxania, Khurasan, and eastern Iran in particular. In this eastern case however, the process appears as far more continuous and as far more connected to the local and regional histories of these regions' leaderships than in the west. As just explained, in the latter west, time and again, it had been outsiders who had managed to impose themselves and their entourages via the mechanisms of Abbasid and Arabo-Islamic power and authority. In the east, Abbasid order, and subsequently also post-Abbasid order, increasingly acquired local and regional colors that were basically articulated as continuous with the regions' wider Late Antique Perso-Iranian histories through the agency, empowerment, and patronage of several dynastic leaderships with local and regional roots and interests in eastern Iran, Khurasan, and Transoxania.

The aforementioned descendants of al-Ma'mun's most important supporter in the 4th *fitna*, the *amir* Tahir ibn al-Husayn, the Tahirids (r. 821–873), represented an important initial moment in this re-emergence to prominence of Perso-Iranian elites. They were not only put in charge of maintaining order in Abbasid Bagdad after their victory over the *abna'*. Parallel to what happened in the west, from the 820s onwards different generations of Tahirids also continuously appeared as Abbasid viceroys in the east, appointing other Tahirids or members of their own entourages and wider leadership networks—often themselves with deep roots in the region—to represent them in the many different localities and regions that made up Iran, their homeland of Khurasan, and Transoxania.

By their direct link with Abbasid order in Bagdad and Iraq, the Tahirids continued to have strong stakes in the interests of the Abbasid center, despite the great autonomy that they acquired in the east. However, when in 873 another group of local powerbrokers from the east, the Saffarids, broke the monopoly of Tahirid-Abbasid power in Khurasan through military action and took control of this region, this trans-regional bond with the Abbasid center became ever more tenuous. The Saffarids came from the southeastern Iranian region of Sistan, where they descended from a local family of coppersmiths (hence the name al-Saffar—'the coppersmith'). As early as the 860s, they had appeared as ever more powerful popular local leaders in Sistan, and after their appropriation of the Tahirid position in the region of Khurasan in the 870s, they were acknowledged and confirmed as Abbasid representatives in Sistan and Khurasan, even though their actual link with Bagdad remained highly strained. Eventually, around 900, they lost control over Khurasan, with ʿAmr ibn Layth al-Saffar (r. 879–901) being executed as an Abbasid rebel in Bagdad in 902. They nevertheless remained a leading family in Sistan for many centuries more, serving as local and regional agents and representatives for many of the dynasties who subsequently took control over the networks of leadership that dominated their homelands.

The Saffarids were driven out of Khurasan around 900 by another lineage of Perso-Iranian eastern origins, the Samanids. The Samanids originated from a family of major landowners with pre-Islamic roots in the region of Balkh. They earned their connections and reputation as Abbasid *amir*s who moved west in the entourage of al-Maʾmun and as loyal agents of the Tahirids in Transoxania, where they represented the Abbasid-Tahirid order from its main urban centers of Bukhara and Samarqand. In 875, however, one of these Samanids, Nasr ibn Ahmad ibn Asad ibn Saman (r. 864–892), who had retained his position as the ruler over Transoxania when his Tahirid sovereigns in Khurasan had been defeated, managed to have his Samanid power and authority over the region directly accepted by the Abbasid caliph al-Muʿtamid (r. 870–892) in Bagdad. The latter sent Nasr ibn Ahmad a caliphal banner and

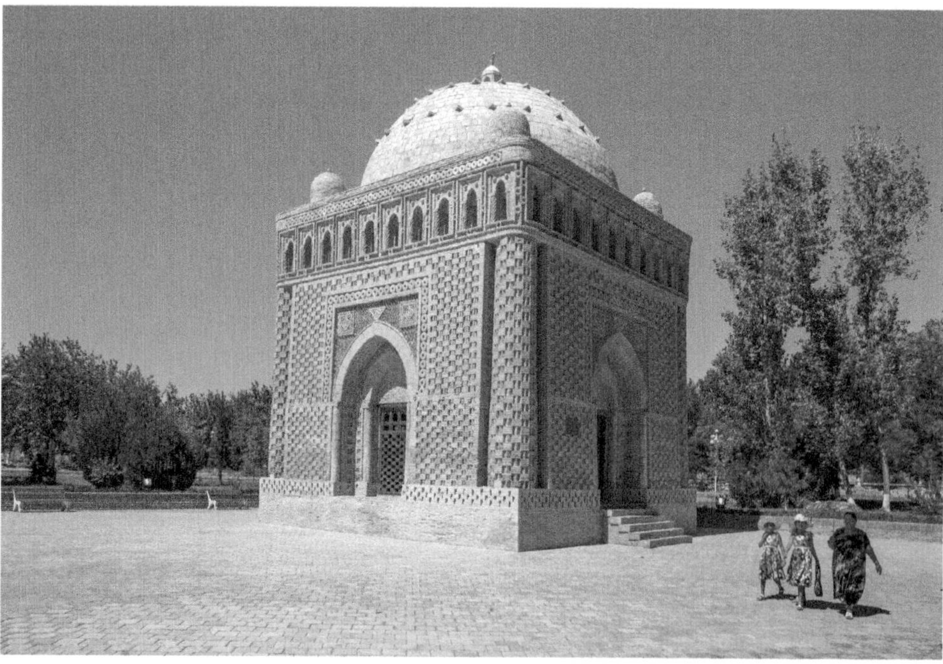

Figure 7.3a Bukhara (Uzbekistan): mausoleum of the Samanid ruler Ismaʿil ibn Ahmad (r. 892–907)
Source: Ismail Samani Mausoleum in Bukhara, Uzbekistan. iStock

robe, as honorific symbols of the delegation of Abbasid authority over Transoxania. The name of the caliph also continued to appear on Samanid coins, which thus projected an Abbasid-Islamic political order in which the Samanid rulers claimed their rightful place as Abbasid regional agents. However, the fact that the caliph in distant Bagdad did not, and could not, expect anything in exchange for this mutual recognition indicates that this was nothing but a symbolic relationship that helped to distinguish, above all, the Samanids and their claims from those of other local and regional leaderships in the east.

Around 900, Isma'il ibn Ahmad (r. 892–907) took Khurasan from the Saffarids and added it to his domains in name of his virtual Abbasid sovereign. In subsequent decades, amidst the violent dissolution of al-Muqtadir's court and its *amir*s in the west and Iraq, also most of eastern Iran came under Samanid control, especially due to the actions of the highly successful Samanid ruler and Abbasid *amir* Nasr (II) ibn Ahmad (r. 914–943). The Samanid dynasty continued to dominate in similar post-Abbasid capacities these eastern regions and their diverse local and regional elites until the later decades of the 10th century.

Throughout this long century of Samanid rule in the Islamic east, an elaborate administrative and military apparatus of dynastic power once again appeared around these new trans-regional rulers and around other leading members of the dynasty. With its reliance on the services of *ghilman* and of *kuttab* families of local or regional expertise, this Samanid patrimonial apparatus continued to be heavily inspired by the Abbasid power infrastructure that had preceded it and out of which it had quite naturally evolved. This also included many

Figure 7.3b *Dirham* (silver coin) minted in the name of the Samanid ruler Nasr (II) ibn Ahmad (r. 914–943) (Samarqand, 309 AH/921–2); the text on the central part (reverse) (re)confirms the Islamic theocratic order by representing the (new) hierarchy of the delegation of power in an explicit order of sovereignty:

l. 1 For God,
l. 2 Muhammad,
l. 3 —the Prophet of God,
l. 4 [caliph] al-Muqtadir bi-llāh,
l. 5 [the Samanid ruler] Naṣr ibn Aḥmad

of the practices that had defined the Abbasid courts and urban elites and that continued to engender a very active and intense cultural patronage of the arts and sciences. Combining this emulation of more recent Abbasid-Islamic practices of rulership and belonging with a revival of interests in these eastern elites' ancient Perso-Sasanian roots meant, furthermore, that also scholarship and literary production in an Arabized form of Persian began to be seriously pursued and encouraged.

One of the most famous and most important products, and agents, of both this Samanid apparatus and this practice of post-Abbasid cultural patronage in Samanid Transoxania undoubtedly was the physician, philosopher, and polymath Abu ʿAli Husayn Ibn Sina, also widely known with the Latinized form of his name as Avicenna (d. 1037). Ibn Sina was born before 980 near the Samanid political center of Bukhara, in a family of leading Perso-Iranian *kuttab* from Balkh. He followed in his family's footsteps, first in Samanid service in Transoxania and later—after the final disappearance of the Samanids from Transoxania in 999—in similar leading and highly appreciated courtly capacities, especially as a physician and vizier, in West Iran, with the post-Abbasid rulers of Hamadan first and of Isfahan eventually (see below). Building on the many opportunities that Samanid Bukhara offered him to acquaint himself with various sets of religious and scientific knowledge and their practitioners, Ibn Sina soon became a leading authority in his own right in most of these sets, especially in the fields of medicine and philosophy. Writing mostly in Arabic, Ibn Sina authored many dozens of books and treatises on these and many more subjects. Most famous among them are his 'Canon of Medicine' (*al-Qanun fi l-Tibb*) and his 'Book of the Healing [of the Soul]' (*Kitab al-Shifaʾ*). The former is considered the summa of all medical knowledge in his days and has remained seminal and referential in east and west, including the Latin West, for many centuries. In his 'Book of the Healing [of the Soul]', as in many others of his philosophical and scientific treatises, a similarly synthetic and original Islamic and Hellenic philosophical system of thought are brought together, representing in hindsight nothing less than a turning point in the Islamic field of philosophy (*falsafa*). Taking Avicenna's powerful and complex thinking as a new starting point for philosophical—and soon also theological—inquiry, in parallel ways to what Late Antique Aristotelian thought had meant for Abbasid thinkers, philosophical thought from this period onwards turned nothing less than consistently post-Avicennan. In fact, the career, scholarship, and legacy of Ibn Sina illustrate how, in the polycentric landscape of the post-Abbasid order of diverse and conflicting leaderships of the 10th and 11th centuries, new transregional centers of Islamic coherence and connectivity were to emerge, which were personal and intellectual rather than political and violent.

2 Post-Abbasid fragmentation in the 10th and 11th centuries: the emergence of new elites and discourses of belonging

As announced above, the polycentric patchwork of post-Abbasid leaders and elites that emerged in the regions between the Atlantic and the Indian Ocean from especially the 9th century onwards involved not only 'autonomizing' Abbasid elites whose origins lay somehow in the West-Asian Abbasid apparatus of trans-regional power and in their roles as *amir*s and wielders of Abbasid violence and patronage. The early Umayyads, the Aghlabids, the Tulunids, and the Ikshidids in the Arabian west, *amir*s such as Muʾnis al-Muzaffar, Ibn Raʾiq, and the Hamdanids in the Abbasid center, and the Tahirids and Samanids in the Persian east actually seem to have paved the way—much as the Tahirids had done for the Saffarids and the Samanids—for others to emerge and rise to local or even regional and trans-regional prominence and leadership in their wake. In the course of the 10th century, therefore, in the

Arabo-Persian east and Arabian west, each once more moving along very different trajectories, other post-Abbasid leaderships acquired local or regional priority without any direct involvement in any of the shackles and chains of Abbasid authority, agency, and patronage. Whereas they were, nevertheless, all forced to relate one way or another in the course of their dynastic histories to that virtual Abbasid framework of Islamic imperial authority—with its forms and meanings transformed by the 10th century into the dominant, if not natural order of things—they each did so in their own integrative or subversive ways, bolstering in due course novel discourses of power and belonging in a polycentric world.

2.1 Post-Abbasid amirs, *kings, and sultans in the Arabo-Persian east*

In the regions of Iran, Khurasan, and Transoxania, and also in Abbasid Iraq, this process of the formation of a truly post-Abbasid order manifested itself especially in the rise to power of two very different trans-regional dynasties. They dominated in competitive ways these regions' landscapes of multiple local and regional leaderships and authorities into the mid-11th century, and their choices, actions, and interactions substantially informed the gradual crystallization of distinctly Shi'ite and especially Sunni Islamic ideas and practices in these and subsequent centuries. These were the Buyids, the Daylamite relatives of the warlord Ahmad ibn Buya, who in 946 became chief *amir* in Bagdad, and the Ghaznavids, who expanded their power from the urban center of Ghazni in present-day Afghanistan. These Ghaznavids appeared by the later 10th century as the true heirs of the Samanids in the regions of Khurasan and eastern Iran, and eventually even, as a result of military expansion, in the northern regions of the Indian peninsula up to the Ganges valley, where they continued to exist until 1186.

The most important and successful leaders of the Ghaznavid dynasty were Mahmud (r. 998–1030) and his son Mas'ud (r. 1030–1041). The origin of these rulers lay with an *atrak* leader of the Samanid *ghilman*, Alptegin (d. 963), who led a failed uprising in 961 in Bukhara and then fled and hid with his followers and troops in the mountainous lands of southern Khurasan. In the later 970s, one of the *atrak* leaders of Alptegin's own *ghilman*, known by the name of Sebüktegin (d. 997), emerged at the head of the dominant force in this region. Sebüktegin's son Mahmud (d. 1030) then consolidated the achievements of his father, and through further military expansion built a new extensive and relatively stable power constellation—at the expense of the Samanids in Khurasan, among others—around his dynastic rule and elaborate court in Ghazni. In this way he connected once again local and regional leaderships in Khurasan with those of Iran in the west and of Khwarazm in the north, as well as with those of the Indian peninsula in the east. During the reign of this Mahmud, and also during that of his son and successor Mas'ud, once more an apparatus of patrimonial power was elaborated to represent the dynasty and secure its local, regional, and trans-regional interests. In the best of Abbasid and now also Samanid traditions, its ranks were populated by new and old Inner-Asian *ghilman* and Arabo-Persian *kuttab*, *udaba'*, and *'ulama'*, and embedded through practices, rituals, and political communication—including coinage, exchange of honorary robes and titles, and articulations of legitimate rule—in the symbolic aura of Abbasid-Islamic sovereignty and delegation of regional authority. Since the early 11th-century days of Mahmud, this allegedly included some experimentation with the novel rulership title of 'sultan' ('worldly power') for the Ghaznavid ruler in order to claim a clear and hierarchical distinction from 'ordinary' *amir*s and delegates who similarly claimed to inhabit the virtual universe of legitimate Abbasid-Islamic authority.

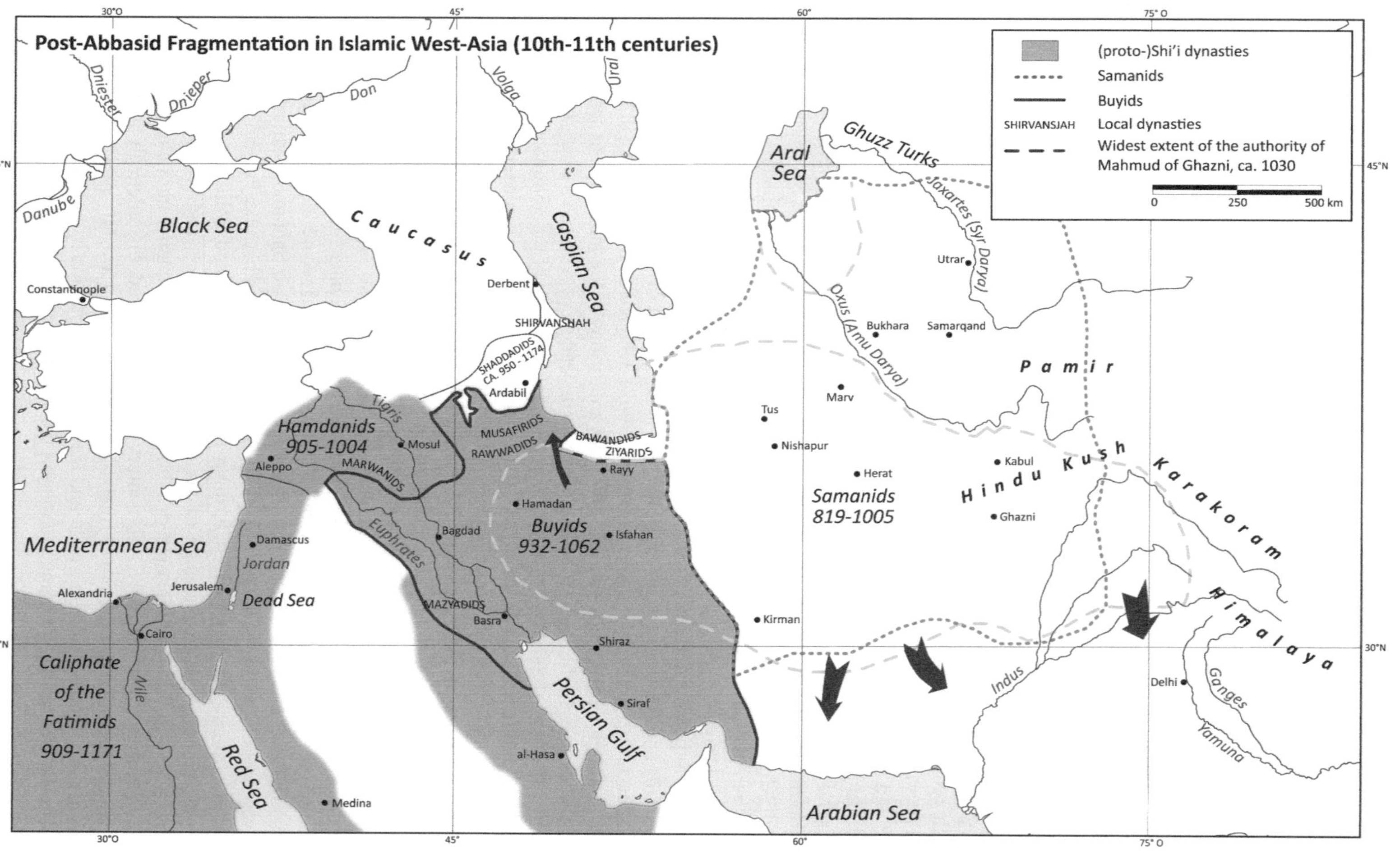

Map 5 Post-Abbasid Fragmentation in Islamic West-Asia (10th–11th centuries)

Source: Redrawn from Hodgson, *The Venture of Islam. Vol. 2. The Expansion of Islam in the Middle Periods*, p. 34

Figure 7.4 Miniature representing Mahmud of Ghazni receiving a richly decorated robe of honor from the caliph al-Qadir, from a manuscript of Rashid al-Din, *Jami' al-Tawarikh* (early 14th century) (Edinburgh University Library, ms. Or. 20, fol.121a)

Source: Picture from History/Bridgeman Images

This highly successful dynasty of unfree Inner-Asian origins and its diverse patrimonial representatives also furthered the Abbasid and Samanid practices of urban cultural patronage, cultivating in the process a particular Sunni-Islamic and Arabo-Persian identity. In this specific sociocultural context of elite membership and patronage, one of the quintessential books of Perso-Islamic literature and ideals of kingship came into being: the 'Book of Kings' (*Shahname*). This enormous epic of Persian history, written in Arabized New Persian, was composed by the poet Abu l-Qasim Firdawsi (940–*c*. 1020), member of an old Perso-Iranian family of landowners from Tus and famous for seeking reward and patronage for his poetic masterpiece from the court of sultan Mahmud. Ghaznavid expansion into northern India, the collection of enormous riches and booty from these campaigns, and the subsequent consolidation of Ghaznavid power in that region inspired Ghaznavid patrons and scholars at their courts to take active interest in Indian cultures. Especially the famous polymath Abu Rayhan al-Biruni (973–*c*. 1050), who was born and raised in Khwarazm and joined—apparently under duress—Mahmud's court in Ghazni after his conquest of Khwarazm in 1007, is remembered not just for the dozens of books in Arabic that he authored, including one on the science of the stars dedicated to Mahmud's son and successor Mas'ud, but especially for his Arabic 'Description of India', completed in 1030 after his participation in several Indian campaigns with Mahmud.

The main opponents and competitors for regional power in Iran, and for priority in the post-Abbasid trans-regional order, undoubtedly were the aforementioned Buyids. Their leadership origins, such as that of many other local and regional leaders in this timeframe, lay in one of the many almost inaccessible areas in Islamic West-Asia, such as the mountains of southern Khurasan, where the Ghaznavids had been able to organize themselves, or—in the case of the Buyids—the highlands of Daylam and Gilan around the southern coasts of the Caspian Sea. Around the turn of the 9th to 10th centuries, a sovereign local dynasty rose to power there in all but well-known circumstances, under leaders known in the historical record as the Shi'ite leader Hasan al-Utrush (d. 917) and Mardavij (d. 935), first ruler of the northern Iranian regional dynasty of the Ziyarids (931–1019), and in cultural contexts that combined strong embeddedness among local mountain leaderships with anti-Abbasid, Perso-Sasanian, and proto-Shi'ite political ideas. The Buyid family actually emerged from this same local context as military leaders and Ziyarid allies and competitors who commanded their own Daylami followers and fighters. They appeared especially in the early 930s in the southern Iranian region of Fars, where reportedly—as a reaction to the devastating internecine warfare of Abbasid *amirs*—local elites, mainly from Shiraz, hired their services to restore regional order. In this way, 'Ali ibn Buya came to power in Fars, and from 946–947 onwards, this 'Ali, together with his brothers al-Hasan and Ahmad and their Daylamite troops, succeeded in gaining military, and consequently, political control over central Iran and Iraq, including, as previously mentioned, over Bagdad, where the caliph accepted their authority and Ahmad was made chief *amir* (*amir al-umara'*).

Until the mid-11th century, the Buyids remained in power in this region, albeit with varying degrees of success. In addition, they subscribed in their own original way to the imagination of an Abbasid-Islamic theocratic order, with interesting consequences on the ongoing post-Abbasid reformulations of Islamic political theory. On the one hand, this new dynastic trans-regional leadership continued to honor their Daylamite, proto-Shi'ite, and Iranian background, for example by presenting themselves as a Perso-Iranian monarchy that claimed the old Persian title of *shahanshah* ('King of Kings'), and by managing the various territories they controlled through appanage practices, derived from their notion of patriarchal and collective Buyid leadership. In Bagdad and Iraq, this period of Buyid dominance, moreover, meant that a unique pro-Shi'ite climate appeared that would prove to be of fundamental significance for the intellectual and practical development of what would later become the most important and largest Shi'ite denomination, Imami or Twelver Shi'ism. This particular formulation of the Shi'ite vision on Islamic leadership and community membership organized itself in this period especially, both practically and intellectually, around a shared belief in the divine inspiration of a specific line of twelve *imams*, or descendants of Muhammad via 'Ali. On the other hand, the Buyids created their own, new dynastic place in the Abbasid political order that clearly continued to be normative. They did this, for example, by following the precedents and examples of their post-Abbasid peers and presenting themselves as agents and representatives of the caliph in Bagdad in the different Buyid localities and regions that were assigned as appanages to their leadership, actively using the Abbasid titles of *amir* and chief *amir*. They also all assumed Arabic ruling titles that testified to their special bond with the Abbasid imperial order, the *Dawla*, and organized their entourages increasingly along the well-known Abbasid patrimonial model, including with *ghilman* and Perso-Iranian *kuttab*.

One of the most important and forceful Buyid rulers undoubtedly was 'Adud al-Dawla ('Pillar of the Abbasid Dynasty'). From 949 to 983, this charismatic leader controlled the most important Buyid appanage of Fars. At the same time, he was recognized by his Buyid relatives who ruled elsewhere as the effective and powerful patriarch of the family, which thus allowed him to control the Buyid appanages of Iraq and northwestern Iran as well. After the death of 'Adud al-Dawla, however, none of the Buyid family members ever succeeded in claiming leadership over the family and their territorial possessions in an equally effective manner again. As a result, the real cohesion of the Buyid political order withered and, until the disappearance of the dynasty in the mid-11th century, members of the Buyid patrimonial apparatus, including Daylamites, *atrak*, and other military groups as well as local *kuttab*, regularly continued to maximize their rivalling influence on Buyid princes, their political ambitions, and their access to flows of resources.

This is, in fact, the post-Abbasid context in which the aforementioned Ibn Sina (Avicenna) (d. 1037) spent the final two decades of his life, first as a physician and vizier to the Buyid ruler of Hamadan, Shams al-Dawla (d. 1021), and then as a courtier and advisor of the Buyid-related ruler of Isfahan, ʿAla' al-Dawla (d. 1042). A telling example of the mixed Arabo-Islamic and Perso-Iranian environments in which Ibn Sina, originally from Samanid Transoxania, operated in West Iran is the fact that the only two texts in New Persian that he is known to have authored—one an introduction to his medicine, another an introduction to his philosophy—were written in this period, patronized by and dedicated to each of these two rulers. Another, different, proponent of this particular Buyid post-Abbasid context, whose writings became as referential as Ibn Sina's, albeit in his case mainly in subsequent discourses of Sunni jurisprudence and theocratic sovereignty, is the leading *qadi* of Bagdad Abu l-Hasan al-Mawardi (974–1058). Operating on various occasions as an advisor and representative of the Abbasid caliphs al-Qadir (r. 991–1031) and al-Qa'im (1031–1074), especially in negotiations of their complex relationship with Buyid leaderships, al-Mawardi left a wide range of texts in the fields of *adab*, linguistics, and jurisprudence. The latter texts included most famously al-Mawardi's seminal theorization of the post-Abbasid relationship between Islamic theocratic order, caliphal sovereignty, and polycentric claims to authority, such as those articulated for the Buyids. This text, entitled 'The Authority of Leadership Arrangements and the Sovereignty of Religious Ordinances' ('*al-Ahkam al-Sultaniyya wa-l-Wilayat al-Diniyya*'), actually formulated for the first time explicitly the doctrine of the delegation of sovereignty from the Abbasid caliph to his agents and representatives, from viziers over amirs to *qadi*s such as al-Mawardi himself, securing their status and authorities as integrative components of the Islamic theocratic order, whatever the realities of power.

2.2 *Post-Abbasid* imams *and caliphs in the Arabian west*

A parallel, but yet very different, far more subversive, and anti-Abbasid story is that of the rise of post-Abbasid leaderships in the 10th century in the Arabian west. This concerned especially the region of Ifriqiya, where the actions of another anti-Abbasid and pro-Shi'ite elite—almost simultaneously with Ziyarids and Buyids in the east—led to historical changes with equally far-reaching consequences. Around 909, no less than a new Shi'ite caliphal leadership over the Islamic *umma* was proclaimed in Ifriqiya, after a military victory by local Imazighen ('Berber') communities and their Arabo-Islamic leader, ʿUbayd Allah al-Mahdi (r. 909–934). ʿUbayd Allah, who had travelled from Syria to Ifriqiya and who was—at least ideologically—also related to the anti-Abbasid Shi'ite Qaramita movement in the region of present-day Bahrain, claimed direct descent from the Prophet Muhammad's daughter Fatima via a son of the sixth Shi'ite *imam*, who was known as Ismaʿil. ʿUbayd Allah and his supporters stated that he himself was no less than a divinely inspired *imam*, and he thus assumed the political and spiritual leadership of an Ismailite-Shi'ite movement that, through military action and active missionary work, wished to take over the place of the Abbasids at the head of the Islamic community. ʿUbayd Allah's successors and their supporters called themselves the Fatimids.

Figure 7.5 Cairo: interior courtyard and northeastern porticos of the al-Azhar mosque, the origins of which are Fatimid (974)

Source: Photo by K.A.C. Creswell, early 20th century. Rare Books and Special Collections Library; The American University in Cairo, SC-1974-01-02-02-a10-pl07-a04-c01, 'Courtyard of Al-Azhar Mosque' http://digitalcollections.aucegypt.edu/cdm/singleitem/collection/p15795coll14/id/112/rec/ 33

In their push towards the Abbasid east, these Fatimids, led by Caliph-Imam al-Muʿizz (r. 953–975) and with the support of Arabian and Imazighen nomadic leaderships from Ifriqiya, took the rich region of Egypt from the Ikhshidids in 969. There, north of Fustat, they founded an entirely new palatial center, as a new administrative, military, and spiritual headquarter that was to house the Fatimid dynasty and its military, administrative, and missionary forces. From this new urban center, named al-Qahira (after the planet Mars), allegedly for astrological reasons, the Fatimids subsequently succeeded in adding large parts of Syria, the Hejaz, and also Yemen to their North African, Mediterranean, and Egyptian possessions. At the same time, in their gradual elaboration of an infrastructure and apparatus to perform, expand, and maintain their power, the Fatimids too adopted many of the leadership traditions that had matured in recent Abbasid and related Tulunid and Ikshidid contexts, from the caliphal title itself, over the hiring of *ghilman* and *atrak*, to the reliance on experienced *kuttab* with diverse local and regional roots. Towards the end of the 10th and into the 11th centuries, this allowed for the emergence in the Fatimid west of another powerful and very prosperous patrimonial-bureaucratic apparatus, steering particularly Isma'ili-Shiʿite Islamic chains of agency, authority, and patronage from Ifriqiya to Syria and Yemen and encouraging some modern scholars of Fatimid history to identify that history as no less than that of the very last of the Late Antique empires.[9] Even though the coherence and territorial integrity of this specific Fatimid power constellation and infrastructure in the west faltered substantially and regularly from at least the mid-11th century onwards—along, indeed, patterns not dissimilar to what befell the Abbasid empire in the later 9th and 10th centuries—, the Fatimid dynasty and its supporters remained dominant in Egypt until the later 12th century (see Chapter 9).

In fact, in the 10th century, yet another Islamic leadership in the Arabian west took similar inspiration from the Abbasid example and from the apparent opportunities that were offered by the growing abstraction of Abbasid power. This at least deserves to be also mentioned here, despite this book's focus on West-Asian history, if not for its own history of brilliance, imperial formation, and transformative impact, then certainly for the way it confirms the tenacity and wide appreciation of the forms and practices of Abbasid trans-regional power and authority, as these had taken shape especially in 9th century Iraq and remained normative for many more centuries to come. This concerns the aforementioned Umayyad amirate of Cordoba, where in 929, the particularly successful Umayyad *amir* ʿAbd al-Rahman III (r. 912–961) proclaimed himself the only legitimate caliphal leader of the Islamic *umma.* In a local history written down many centuries later, this highly symbolic transformation and assumption of supreme Islamic sovereignty is explicitly linked to the simultaneous loss of central power and coherence in the east, in ways that confirm this centrality of the Late Antique Abbasid past in any subsequent imaginations of Islamic authorities and identities, in the Arabo-Persian east as well as in the Arabian west.

> Many, indeed, were the works of public utility which this just and enlightened monarch [ʿAbd al-Raḥmān III] caused to be erected in various parts of his extensive dominions. As to his capital, Cordova, he is well known to have embellished it and widened its precincts, so that it equaled, if it did not surpass, in size and splendor the proud metropolis of the [Abbasids][i.e. Bagdad]. His addition to the great mosque of Cordova, and the construction of the palace of al-Zahrāʾ in the vicinity of that capital, are two splendid erections, which will transmit the name of ʿAbd al-Raḥmān to posterity. . . .
>
> ʿAbd al-Raḥmān was the first sovereign of the Umayyad house in Andalus who assumed the title of 'Commander of the Believers' (*Amīr al-Muʾminīn*). The authors of the time say that when ʿAbd al-Raḥmān saw the state of weakness and abjectness to which the [Abbasid] caliphate had been reduced, and perceived that the *atrāk* freedmen in the service of the [Abbasids] had usurped all authority and power in the state—when he heard that the Caliph al-Muqtadir had been put to death . . . by one of his freedmen, called Muʾnis al-Muẓaffar—he no longer hesitated to assume the insignia of the caliphate, and call himself 'Commander of the Believers'.[10]

Notes

1 See Hassan, *Longing for the Lost Caliphate*.

2 al-Masʿūdī [st. 956], *Kitāb al-Tanbīh wa-l-Ishrāf* ['The Book of Admonition and Revision']; translation after Osti, "The Caliph", 50–1.

3 Kennedy, "The Decline and Fall of the First Muslim Empire", 13; Kennedy works with data culled from narrative sources and archaeological surveys that were presented in Waines, "The Third-century Internal Crisis of the ʿAbbāsids".

4 Al-Sūlī (d. 947), *Kitāb al-Awrāq* ['The Book of Papers']; translation from Waines, "The Pre-Buyid Amirate: Two Views from the Past", 345–6.

5 Miskawayh (932–1030), *Kitāb Tajārib al-Umam* ['The Book of the Experiences of Nations']; translation from Kennedy, "The Reign of al-Muqtadir", 18.
6 Al-Sūlī (d. 947), *Kitāb al-Awrāq* ('The Book of Papers'); translation from Waines, "The Pre-Buyid Amirate: Two Views from the Past", 345–6.
7 See Waines, "The Pre-Buyid Amirate: Two Views from the Past".
8 See Gordon, "Aḥmad ibn Ṭūlūn and the Politics of Deference".
9 See Brett, *The Rise of the Fatimids*.
10 From al-Maqarrī (st. 1632), *Kitāb Nafḥ al-Ṭīb min Ghuṣn al-Andalus al-Raṭīb* ['The Book of the Fragrant Scent from the Fresh Andalusian Twig']; translation from De Gayangos, *The History of the Mohammedan Dynasties in Spain*.

Selected readings

Bianquis, Th. "Autonomous Egypt from Ibn Ṭūlūn to Kāfūr, 868–969", in C.F. Petry (ed.), *Cambridge History of Egypt, Vol. I: Islamic Egypt, 640–1517* (Cambridge, 1998), pp. 86–119

Bosworth, C.E. *The Ghaznavids: Their Empire in Afghanistan and Eastern Iran, 944–1040* (Beirut, 1973)

Brett, M. *The Fatimid Empire* (Edinburgh, 2017)

Brett, M. *The Rise of the Fatimids: The World of the Mediterranean and the Middle East in the Fourth Century of the Hijra, Tenth Century CE* (Leiden, 2001)

Bulliet, R.W. *Cotton, Climate and Camels in Early Islamic History: A Moment in World History* (New York, 2009)

Busse, H. *Chalif und Grosskönig: die Buyiden im Irak (945–1055)* (Wurzburg, 2004)

de Gayangos, P. *The History of the Mohammedan Dynasties in Spain; Extracted from the Nafhu-t-tib min ghoshni-l-Andalusi-r-ratib wa Tarikh lisanu-d-din ibnil-Khatib by Ahmed Ibn Mohammed Al-Makkari* (London, 1840)

Fierro, M. *Abd al-Rahman III. The First Cordoban Caliph* (Oxford, 2007)

Gordon, M.S. "Aḥmad ibn Ṭūlūn and the Politics of Deference", in B. Sadeghi, A.Q. Ahmed, A. Silverstein, R. Hoyland (eds.), *Islamic Cultures, Islamic Contexts: Essays in Honor of Professor Patricia Crone* (Leiden, 2015), pp. 229–56.

Hassan, M. *Longing for the Lost Caliphate: A Transregional History* (Princeton, 2016)

Kennedy, H.N. "The Decline and Fall of the First Muslim Empire", *Der Islam* 81 (2004): 3–30

Kennedy, H. "The Reign of al-Muqtadir", in M. van Berkel, N.M. El Cheikh, H. Kennedy, L. Osti (eds.), *Crisis and Continuity at the Abbasid Court: Formal and Informal Politics in the Caliphate of al-Muqtadir (295–320/908–32)* (Leiden, 2013)

Mottahedeh, R.P. *Loyalty and Leadership in an Early Islamic Society* (Princeton, 1980)

Osti, L. "The Caliph", in M. van Berkel, N.M. El Cheikh, H. Kennedy, L. Osti (eds.), *Crisis and Continuity at the Abbasid Court: Formal and Informal Politics in the Caliphate of al-Muqtadir (295–320/908–32)* (Leiden, 2013)

Peacock, A.C.S., Tor, D.G. (eds.). *Medieval Central Asia and the Persianate World: Iranian Tradition and Islamic Civilisation* (London, 2015)

Raymond, A. *Cairo. City of History* (Cairo, 2003)

Sanders, P.A. "The Fāṭimid State, 969–1171", in C.F. Petry (ed.), *Cambridge History of Egypt, Vol. I: Islamic Egypt, 640–1517* (Cambridge, 1998), pp. 151–74

Tetley, G. *The Ghaznavid and Seljuq Turks: Poetry as a Source for Iranian History* (London and New York, 2009)

Thomson, K. *Politics and Power in Late Fatimid Egypt: The Reign of Caliph al-Mustansir* (London, 2015)

van Berkel, M., El-Cheikh, N.M., Kennedy, H.N., Osti, L. (eds.). *Crisis and Continuity at the Abbasid Court: Formal and Informal Politics in the Caliphate of al-Muqtadir (295–320/908–32)* (Leiden, 2013)

Waines, D. "The Pre-Buyid Amirate: Two Views from the Past", *International Journal of Middle East Studies* 8/3 (1977): 339–48

Waines, D. "The Third-Century Internal Crisis of the ʿAbbāsids", *Journal of the Economic and Social History of the Orient* 20 (1978): 282–303
Walker, P.E. *Caliph of Cairo. Al-Hakim bi-Amr Allah, 996–1021* (Cairo, 2009)
Walker, P.E. "The Ismāʿīlī Daʿwa and the Fāṭimid Caliphate", in C.F. Petry (ed.), *Cambridge History of Egypt, Vol. I: Islamic Egypt, 640–1517* (Cambridge, 1998), pp. 120–50

Wave 2

11th–18th centuries

Middle period, early modernity, and Turkish, Mongol, Turko-Mongol, and Turkmen dynastic formations

At the turn of the 10th to the 11th centuries, the Khaldunian movement of nomadic-urban interaction and social transformation identified in the introduction of this book as one of its interpretive frameworks experienced a radical shift. The polycentric and fragmented post-Abbasid world of Islamic West-Asia was confronted in this period with nothing less than a new wave of nomadic migrations from peripheral regions, this time from the Inner-Asian steppes to the north and northeast of the Caucasus, the Caspian, the Aral Sea, and Transoxania. Different waves of new pastoralist groups and leaderships, mainly identified as Turks and Mongols, entered the complex post-Abbasid world in a predominantly violent manner, substantially changed its political, economic, and social landscapes, and enriched and transformed its cultural dynamics. This process of nomadic migration, conquest, transformation, and accommodation actually continued to repeat itself in Islamic West-Asia for several centuries. More stabilized post-nomadic trans-regional leadership configurations emerged only haphazardly, and most successfully and permanently first only along West-Asia's western fringes, in the regions of Egypt, Syria, and western Asia Minor. In West-Asia's major central and eastern regions, from the banks of the Euphrates and the highlands of eastern Anatolia in the west to the banks of the Jaxartes and Indus rivers in the east, a different and more discontinuous pattern of regular iterations of nomadic conquest and dynastic formation remained a dominant determinant until the later 16th century. In the latter regions, it arguably even took until the later 18th century for the effects of this extended continuum of nomadic-urban interaction to slowly peter out.

Even though, as explained in this book's introduction, focus here is especially on West-Asian centers and processes of power, it is useful to also acknowledge that across the Islamic world's western regions of Ifriqiya, the Maghreb, and al-Andalus, in today's North Africa and the Iberian Peninsula, very similar processes of nomadic migration, conquest, transformation, and accommodation may be identified to have developed in the same period. Imazighen ('Berbers') and Amazigh leaderships from the southern Maghreb in particular repeatedly organized themselves, expanded their reach, and seized power across most of these territories from the 11th century onwards. This is actually a historical dynamic that appears to have directly inspired the 14th-century North African scholar Ibn Khaldun to develop his notion of a historically defining nomadic-urban interaction. It is, furthermore, also very clear that amidst these radical transformations, ideas, people, and commodities—as also experienced by the Tunis-born Ibn Khaldun and by his contemporary from Tangier, Ibn Battuta, both of whom, as mentioned in the introduction, spent considerable parts of their lives in Islamic Asia—continued to intensely circulate between these western lands of the Islamic world and their eastern counterparts, and to further expand even into Sub-Sahara Africa and South and Southeast Asia. Despite these highly relevant parallels and many connections, however, it is also clear that the regular moments of Amazigh regional and trans-regional empowerment from the 11th century onwards concerned rather specific 'western' histories of power and belonging that pursued their own trajectories in ways that were increasingly distinct—as already announced by the Fatimid and Umayyad anti-Abbasid caliphates of the 10th century—from what happened in West-Asia. The stories of the trans-regional dynastic formations of the Almoravids (*c.* 1035–*c.* 1150) and Almohads (*c.* 1120–*c.* 1275), of the regional dynasties of the Nasrids in Granada (1237–1492), the Marinids in Fez (1258–1465), the Hafsids in Tunis (1229–1574), the ʿAbdalwadids in Tlemcen (1236–1550), and the Malian *mansa*s of the West African kingdom of 'Takrur' (*c.* 1230–*c.* 1434), and of commerce, preaching, mystical leadership, *jihad*, and *reconquista*, therefore deserve their own framework and analysis and will only be included in this book's second part in a discussion of that circulation of people, ideas, and commodities. Ifriqiya and the Maghreb will, furthermore, reappear in this part only when from the 16th century onwards some of these regions again were more directly integrated into Asia-dominated landscapes of conquest, power, and dynastic formation.

As suggested in the introduction, the period covered by this second wave of Khaldunian movement is often considered to represent only a 'post-classical' shadow of the first wave, an age of stagnation and decline from Abbasid-Islamic imperial efflorescence that is often looked upon, even in these regions' own historiographical traditions, with pity and condescension. How one attempted to escape these dark times from the 19th century onwards to reconnect with the imperial achievements of the first wave is more often than not considered to be the only relevant and interesting narrative. As explained before, one of the contentions of this book is that such a negative frame does not hold much value, and even lacks validity, and that this second period also needs full attention and appreciation in its own right.

For this second wave between the 11th and 18th centuries, this book explicitly distinguishes two periods. The 'middle period' or the 'medieval' age (11th–16th centuries)—adapting and revising here a semantic and chronological re-interpretation of Europe's Middle Ages that was first proposed by the aforementioned Marshall Hodgson[1]—is the era that began with expansions and migrations of nomadic leaderships from the Inner-Asian steppes and that witnessed regularly recurring phenomena of Turkish, Mongol, Turko-Mongol, and Turkmen movement, conquest, and empowerment coinciding with diverse, heterogeneous, and contested articulations of theocratic order, dynastic specialty, and sociocultural belonging. The second, 'early modern' period (17th–18th centuries)—conforming to the more widely used notion of the globalizing age of early modernity—is marked by the substantial dynastic stabilizations and transformations at the turn of the 16th to 17th centuries of only a handful of Turkmen and Turko-Mongol dynastic leaderships and related theocratic identities—in West-Asia Sunni Ottomans and Shi'ite Safavids in particular—and by the increasingly structured and integrated circulating around them of all kinds of local and regional leaderships, resource flows, infrastructures, and discourses on a globalizing, early modern scale, with very distinct 18th-century effects.

Within the regularly changing 'medieval' and early modern West-Asian patchwork of more or, especially, less well-organized dynastic formations of Turkish, Mongol, Turko-Mongol, and related leaderships and their followers, new practices, discourses, and infrastructures of dynastic power, sovereign authority, and theocratic order simultaneously started to appear from the 11th century onwards, moving westward with these leaderships, from Transoxania to Egypt and Asia Minor. These both increasingly connected 'medieval' and early modern new and old elites across the many boundaries that had appeared in the post-Abbasid 10th century, and gradually integrated the wide diversity of post-Abbasid legacies and Inner-Asian traditions that shaped all of these elites. Most importantly, new formats of accommodation developed between new nomadic and longstanding urban elites, and between dynastic wielders of transregional power and local or regional leaderships, in the context of the formation, restoration, expansion, or elaboration of post-Abbasid or Inner-Asian mechanisms to eliminate rivals, protect clients, accumulate resources, and reproduce power. These formats of accommodation revolved especially around the cultural practices of elite households and their urban entourages. These cultural practices continued to be strongly related to Abbasid and post-Abbasid legacies but appeared now in non-Abbasid contexts of competition and belonging that pitted different dynastic courts and intellectual communities against each other, that offered opportunities to many groups and ideas to acquire and maintain prominence and authority, and that were only after many centuries again integrated into more coherent and stable patrimonial-bureaucratic apparatuses of dynastic power. This long process of recurring pastoralist migrations and nomadic conquests, and of the development of new formats of nomadic and post-nomadic accommodation that favored both ongoing symbiotic interactions between diverse elites and communities and the crystallization of particular Islamic discourses and agencies, is central to the next chapters.

First, this part's stage will be set by the opening chapter that surveys the main transformations induced by the West-Asian migrations and conquests of Turkic-speaking pastoral nomads and their leaders in the course of the 11th and 12th centuries, focusing on practices and realities of conquest and dynastic formation as well as of accommodation and local and regional integration. Subsequently, the description of the continuation of these two main subjects of conquest and accommodation will be split between different chapters, detailing first the many vicissitudes of conquest and dynastic-patriarchal as well as eventually dynastic-patrimonial formation between the 12th and 16th centuries. The discussion of these confusing vicissitudes is further divided, moreover, between four different chapters that each try to create some more analytical sense and unity in the period's confusing polycentric complexity of ever changing actors and configurations. This will be done by beginning with the post-nomadic stabilizing transformations that first started to occur from the 12th century onwards in the Euphrates-to-Nile zone, and moving from there back to the returning instabilities of nomadic and post-nomadic conquest that continued to mark the histories of West-Asia's major regions, from Anatolia to Transoxania, into the 16th century. Only after this 'medieval' complexity has been reconstructed in these four chapters, the penultimate chapter will turn to the identification and illustration of a further selection of some trends in the equally formative and defining accommodation and symbiotic interactions that especially diverse urban groups and communities experienced and participated in during these centuries. The final chapter will then close this part's, as well as this book's, macro-narrative of dynastic formation by surveying—in parallel with this second part's opening chapter—the main transformations induced by the diverse sets of stabilizing relationships and meanings of power and belonging that marked West-Asia's histories in the 17th and 18th centuries in the predominantly Sunni world of the Ottoman sultan in the west and in the mainly Shi'ite world of Safavid and post-Safavid leaderships in the east.

Note

1 Hodgson, *The Venture of Islam. Vol. 2. The Expansion of Islam in the Middle Periods.*

8 'Medieval' transformations across Islamic West-Asia

The Turkish dynasty of the Seljuks and networks of Perso-Iranian Viziers (1038–1194)

Introduction: Sunni Turkmen, Perso-Iranian Viziers, and their symbiotic relationships

In the early 11th century, the leadership landscape of Islamic West-Asia was strongly divided between Ghaznavid sultans, Buyid *amirs*, Fatimid *imam*-caliphs, many more local or regional post-Abbasid leaderships in the margins of or beyond the effective reaches of Ghaznavid, Buyid, or Fatimid power, and their highly competitive and very diversely articulated claims to power and authority. By the very end of that century, however, that same landscape of leaderships had entirely transformed with the disappearance of the Buyids, the pushing of Ghaznavids and Fatimids to the Indian and Egyptian margins of Islamic West-Asia, and the integration of even formerly Greek Asia Minor into one West-Asian dynastic political order, which, furthermore, once again, situated itself squarely within the virtual orbit of an Abbasid-Islamic sovereignty that was emanating from Bagdad. Even though this proved a rather short-lived dynastic order, the political reality of which was all but stable and well-integrated, it set a pattern of violence wielding and nomad-urban accommodation that determined the trajectories taken by various related and parallel West-Asian dynastic leaderships in its 12th- and 13th-century wake. This pattern revolved around particular social practices, articulations, and appearances of West-Asian legitimate leadership as well as the expansion and intensification of stakes in the Syrian-Anatolian frontier zone, with transformative effects. Whereas the Inner-Asian leadership of the Seljuk dynasty and its Turkic-speaking nomadic followers and associates were largely responsible for these radical transformations, novel Perso-Iranian and Arabo-Islamic power networks of men, expertise, and resources were equally central in the arrangements that determined the fickle stability of that political order. Each of these two groups and their mutual interactions in the course of the 11th and 12th centuries will be further discussed below. First, however, the wider pattern of violence wielding and nomad-urban accommodation that was set by these groups will need to be introduced as an intrinsic part of the contexts that defined their interactions and connected them to subsequent events and leaderships. This pattern, therefore, provides us with a useful tool for synthesis amidst the continuously changing 'medieval' landscapes of West-Asian power. It allows for interpretation through this book's common grid of Weberian ideal types of legitimate authority and for making sense of these landscapes' complex, if not simply confusing, diversity of leaderships. It is a pattern that actually reconsiders these diverse leaderships as part of the constitutive interaction between practices of power and discourses of belonging that was chosen as the backbone of this book's comprehensive framework of understanding.

As will be detailed below, from the early 11th century onwards, Turkic-speaking leaderships and their nomadic followers started entering Islamic West-Asia from their homelands in the southern steppes of Inner Asia. As explained in the preceding chapters, Turkic-speakers and related Inner-Asian elements were of course no strangers in the highly sedentarized, urbanized, and interconnected world of Islamic West-Asia. The migrations and expansions of the 11th century, however, were of a very different nature from what had happened before. Turkic-speakers eventually entered in the dominant forms of violence wielding leaderships, nomadic formations, and their pastoralist families and flocks, instead of as individuals and small groups offering their services to extant rulers. From the Inner-Asian steppes they brought with them traditions and practices of collective leadership and social organization, of nomad-urban symbiosis, and of subsistence that converged with, and at the same time transformed and redirected, the diverse sets of post-Abbasid relationships of power, belonging and land use in highly impactful ways. Of course, this impact had everything to do with the fact that especially the Seljuk leadership of the 11th-century migration flows westwards from Transoxania manifested itself—just like the Arabian Quraysh had done a few centuries

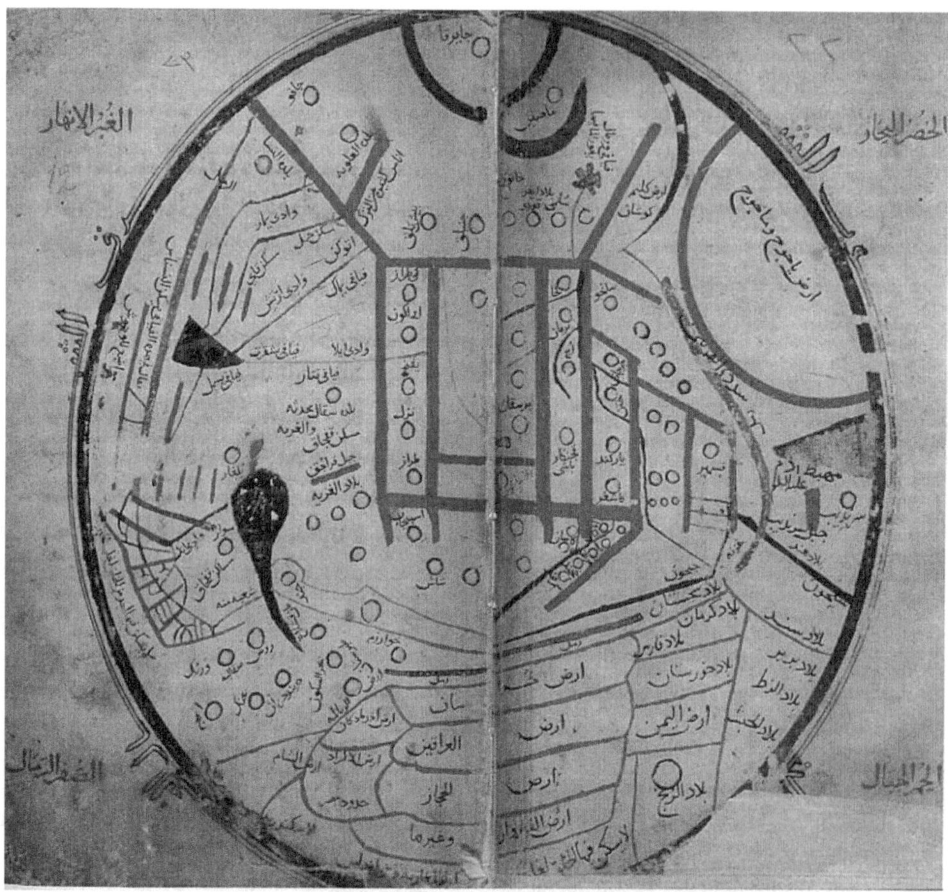

Figure 8.1 Cartographic representation of the Turkic-speaking world in the 'Compendium of the Turkish Tongues' (*Dīwān lughāt al-Turk*) by Mahmud al-Kashgari (1070s, Bagdad; illustration from the only remaining manuscript [1266], Millet Manuscript Library, Fatih Istanbul)

Source: The History Collection/Alamy Stock Photo

earlier—very quickly as a new dominant force and dynastic center of networks of power across most of Islamic West-Asia's different regions. Unlike in the Late Antique 7th century context, however, repeated similar migrations of nomadic groups from Inner-Asia and the practices of conquest and apportionment that defined Inner-Asian leadership traditions continued to give shape to predominantly patriarchal constellations and to keep more structural and patrimonial appearances of any apparatus of power to an *ad hoc* and transient degree. The sociopolitical primacy of leaders of nomadic and semi-nomadic origins, of their patriarchal and nomadic entourages, and of the unstable violence monopolies of their personal followers and troops therefore remained a returning and dominant phenomenon for several centuries in most of the regions of Islamic West-Asia.

At the very same time, the transformative impact of the 11th century also derived from the fact that quite a few local and regional urban elites in Islamic West-Asia—especially *kuttab* and *'ulama'* of Perso-Iranian and Arabo-Islamic background—quickly found opportunities to continue to play equally important roles in these unstable contexts of nomadic migration, expansion, and conquest. This in fact reflects how intense practices of exchange of resources and interests joined the latter urban elites and the former rulers in symbiotic alliances and networks of cooperation and competition that countered any unequal appearances in relationships of power and administrative or military service. In the later 11th and 12th centuries, in particular, this generated a particular kind of accommodation between Turkic-speaking trans-regional rulers and Arabo-Islamic and Perso-Iranian urban elites. This difficult balancing act between local, regional, and trans-regional leaderships and between nomad and urban elites would continue to determine the history of these regions deeply during the following centuries. Time and again it would also continue to relate actively and creatively with arrangements of Abbasid and post-Abbasid power and authority that had emerged in the 9th and 10th centuries. These ranged from the legitimating devices of caliphate and sultanate, over the infrastructural facilities and pomp of Islamic courts and royal households, of the amirate, and of the administrative *diwan*s and their leaderships, including the vizirate, to the increasingly prioritized mechanisms of cultural and intellectual patronage. Despite the persisting dynastic fragmentations and recurring violence, this symbiosis generated much more sharing of interests and coherence across political and other boundaries than one would expect. Sometimes interpreted from the perspective of post-Abbasid Islamic West-Asia's *a'yan-amir* system of symbiotic accommodation between autonomously operating urban elites (*a'yan*) and mostly Turkic-speaking wielders of violence (*amir*s), this interaction is now also occasionally understood through the prism of the 'military patronage state' model. Heavily inspired by the Weberian ideal type of traditional patriarchal and patrimonial legitimate authority that was briefly described in the introduction, this model is proving increasingly useful for modern specialists of this 'medieval' era to better comprehend the particular social and cultural histories of 'medieval' Islamic West-Asia. It shifts the focus from the integrative dynamics of any central apparatus of power—as in the Late Antique period—to the highly personalized politics of competing elite households, their leaders, and their creative re-uses of arrangements of Abbasid and post-Abbasid power and authority—including the caliphate, the sultanate, the amirate, and the vizirate—in the pursuit of their own reproduction, the elimination of rivals, the protection of clients, and the accumulation of sufficient resources in the urban-centered contexts of Islamic West-Asia. One of these modern specialists, Michael Chamberlain, even suggests that this was at the heart of the impact of the migrations, expansions, and transformations of the 11th century, ending the highly fragmented post-Abbasid order and generating the westward expansion of practices of accommodation that "permitted the ideal of the universal cosmopolitan [Abbasid-Islamic]

Figure 8.2 Ceramic bowl: representation of a Seljuk horseman-commander, 12th–13th century, Iran

Source: Metropolitan Museum of Art, Ceramics, Accession Number 51.53, 'Bowl with Prince on Horseback', Harris Brisbane Dick Fund, 1951, www.metmuseum.org/art/collection/search/451041

empire to survive within a political-economic context that tended towards fragmentation". "Although individual dynasties were short-lived", he concludes, "the practices that sustained them were enduring."[1]

As will be further illustrated in this and subsequent chapters, these practices built upon the mechanisms of cultural and intellectual patronage, social distinction, and belonging that had already marked Abbasid and post-Abbasid urbanities, but that now became even more central mechanisms of social and cultural order in the prolonged absence of truly stabilizing dynastic, patrimonial, or bureaucratic formations. In this capacity, these practices were the shared preserve of all urban elites, even when, especially from the 12th century onwards, they most often and most visibly coalesced around the priority of members of the ranks of *amir*s and their dynastic entourages. As particular, highly personalized, ways—often also defined as informal ways—of organizing the intense exchange of leadership resources and interests, they revolved especially around the highly profitable convergence of the management of rural and urban assets of elite households with the appearance of specific formats for the performance of Islamic rituals, for the preservation, creation, and transmission of Islamic and scientific knowledge, and—more symbolically—for the articulation of claims to sovereignty and legitimacy. These formats included the theoretical framework, communicative media, and symbolic forms and practices of the articulation of Islamic sovereignty, as these had been shaped at Abbasid courts and in the Abbasid-era debates on the nexus of Arabo-Islamic identity and sovereignty, and especially as these had been reshaped to reconcile the complexity of post-Abbasid contexts. In this era, however, to these Abbasid and post-Abbasid patrimonial formats to arrange the balancing of leadership resources and interests and the production of social order were added very novel ones, most emblematically represented by the physical infrastructures that became the central 'medieval' and early modern spaces for the construction, transmission, preservation, and performance of traditions of leadership, knowledge, and belonging—the *madrasa* and the *khanqah*—and that in the 11th and 12th centuries tellingly travelled with their patrons and practitioners from post-Abbasid Khurasan to post-Seljuk Syria and Egypt.

This intense exchange of resources and interests as well as the wider social and cultural dynamics that were part and parcel of this *modus vivendi* between various leaderships and elites created everywhere alternative forms of cohesion between distinct individuals, groups, and resources in the face of segmentation, fragmentation, disintegration, and violent competition, and in the absence of any more stabilized apparatus of central power. It has been generally acknowledged by now that *in hindsight* at least it appears that these alternative forms of cohesion even stimulated in most central spaces of power and patronage across Islamic West-Asia an intensification and re-orientation of debates and discussions about the ancient Islamic sovereignty and identity nexus. This happened most conspicuously from the 12th century onwards, when in the symbiotic accommodation between autonomously operating urban elites (*aʿyan*) and mostly Turkic-speaking wielders of violence (*amir*s), the latter increasingly pursued the integration of the former into their patrimonial apparatus of power through mechanisms of cultural and intellectual patronage mediated not just by their courts but also by the autonomous sociocultural and economic spaces of mosques, *madrasas*, *khanqah*s, and related infrastructures (see also next chapters). Before that closing of ranks became more evident, however, the 11th century mix of Turkmen migrations, Seljuk dynastic practices, and Perso-Iranian and Arabo-Islamic power networks set the scene for this to happen in the shared but heavily contested pursuit for convergence and accommodation amid radically changing local, regional, and trans-regional realities.

1 Turks and Seljuks between Turkmen and patrimonial transformations

1.1 Turkmen conquest practices and dynastic formation in Transoxania, Khurasan, and Iran

> When I saw that God Most High had caused the Sun of Fortune to rise in the Zodiac of the Turks (*atrāk*), and set their Kingdom among the spheres of Heaven; that He called them *turk*, and gave them the Rule; making them kings of the Age, and placing in their hands the reins of temporal authority; appointing them over all mankind, and directing them to the Right; that He strengthened those who are affiliated to them, and those who endeavor on their behalf; . . .

> [then I saw that] every man of reason must attach himself to them, or else expose himself to their falling arrows. And there is no better way to approach them than by speaking their own [Turkic] tongue, thereby bending their ear and inclining their heart.[2]

As this opening invocation in a book on Turkic languages, written in the 1070s for the Abbasid caliph in Bagdad, suggests, by the later 11th century, the centrality of Turkish leadership in Islamic West-Asia had become so evident that it inspired not only genuine interests in their origins and culture but also—as alluded to here—the incorporation of their centrality in imaginations of the Islamic theocratic order of the world and its history. On the Inner-Asian steppes, beyond northern Islamic regions such as Transoxania, Khwarazm, and Azerbaijan, and stretching from the northern shores of the Black Sea in western Eurasia to almost the Pacific in the east, that centrality of Turkic-speaking nomadic leaderships, their kinsmen, and herds, and their occasional wider associations into trans-regional formations of pastoralists had been a given since many centuries. This had always been well known in Islamic West-Asia as a result of various trade connections and military pressures on Umayyad and Abbasid military commanders in Azerbaijan and Transoxania. However, by the end of the 10th century, perhaps for reasons of climate change on the steppes,[3] these pressures increased to the extent that these tribal leaderships and their nomadic followers themselves now started to enter the substantially urbanized and settled world of Islamic West-Asia. This happened first, most prominently, with a trans-regional Inner-Asian network of tribal leaderships of Turkic-speaking chiefs (*khans*), organized around the authority of a great *khan* and referred to in modern research as the Turkish dynasty of the Qara-Khanids or the Ilek-Khans (r. 992–1211). Converting to Islam in the course of the 10th century, they eventually defeated the post-Abbasid dynasty of the Samanids in Transoxania and took their place. In the 11th and 12th centuries, they continued to impose their loosely organized Islamic, Turkish, and nomadic authorities over this and others regions further east, along the strategic commercial artery of the so-called 'Silk Roads' and up to the oasis town of Kashgar, today the westernmost city in the autonomous region of Xinjiang in the People's Republic of China. It was from these Qara-Khanid dominated lands that Mahmud al-Kashgari (d. 1102), the author of the above-mentioned book on Turkic languages, travelled westwards and produced his 'Compendium of Turkish Tongues' for the Abbasid caliph in Bagdad.

Simultaneously with the empowerment of the so-called Qara-Khanids, other so-called Oghuz (Ar. Ghuzz) Turkish leaderships (that is, 'western' groups among Inner-Asia's Turkic-speaking populations) also entered the Islamic spotlight, first as mercenaries in the military service of Samanid and then Qara-Khanid rulers in Transoxania and of the post-Abbasid Ghaznavid sultans in Khurasan, and ultimately also autonomously, aiming to create political spaces for themselves to dominate. The gradual pace with which this happened, and the rather open nature of Islamic identities that seems to have been dominant in these regions at the time, meant that this entry of new Turkic-speaking leaderships assumed quite smoothly and rapidly an Islamic appearance. Very early on, one leading kin group in particular played a central role in this entire process of migration, expansion, and integration. The following fragment from a later Arabic dynastic chronicle on the mythical origins of this kin group and its empowerment graphically refers to that particular context of Turkish contested leadership and violence wielding on the margins of Islamic West-Asia, of migration from the Inner-Asian steppes, and of conversion to Islam and integration into the symbolic universe of legitimate Islamic kingship, at the turn of the 10th to 11th centuries.

> Ṭuqāq means in Turkish 'iron bow'. He was a sharp and intelligent person, possessed of good judgement and the ability to handle affairs. The king of the [Ghuzz] Turks

> used to entrust the direction of affairs to him and used to derive illumination from the lamp of his judgement and the ability to handle affairs. The king of the Turks' name was Yabghu. It happened that, one day, the king prepared his military forces to march against the Islamic lands; Amir Tuqāq dissuaded him from doing that, but the king of the Turks Yabghu showed his opposition here. Tuqāq persisted in standing firm, and he struck the king of the Turks, who had ordered Tuqāq's arrest and being put in bonds, in the face. Amir Tuqāq showed his strength and sought security in the rope [of God]. They left him alone and bore the king to his residence [and he remained holed up like] a hyena in its den. He became perturbed regarding . . . his course of action and what plan he should adopt, and decided to go along to Amir Tuqāq's house and endeavour to conciliate him. The king of the Turks Yabghu was nevertheless concealing in his mind resentment and treacherous intentions (i.e. against Tuqāq) up to the time that Amir Tuqāq died.
>
> When Amir Seljuk, son of Amir Tuqāq, reached the age of maturity, the king of the Turks appointed him commander of the army, with the title of *sübashï* (amongst the Turks, this means 'commander of the army'). The wife of the king of the Turks was instilling into her husband fear and suspicion of Amir Seljuk ibn Tuqāq and was preventing him from freely exercising his authority, and she did not hide her feelings from him. One day she said to her husband, 'Kingly power recognizes no kinship bonds and it cannot tolerate sharing the rule; the successful exercise of power can only be achieved through killing Seljuk. The bright morning of your royal authority will not shine forth unless you give him to drink from the cup of death. For very soon, he will expel you from the seat of power and will plot your destruction'. Amir Seljuk was witness to all this and heard these words, so he rode off and set out with his entourage of horsemen and his troops, heading for the Islamic lands, and rejoicing in the Ḥanīfī [i.e. the Islamic] faith. He decided to make for the region of Jand, expelled from there the representatives and tax-collectors of the unbelievers and firmly established his power there. Amir Seljuk lived for a hundred years. One night in a dream he saw himself ejaculating fire, and its sparks blazed forth over the eastern and western lands of the earth. He consulted an onomancer about the significance of this, and the diviner said, 'There will be born of your seed monarchs who will rule over the remotest regions of the world'.[4]

As far as may be distilled from very particular later reports such as these, this Seljuk and his Turkic-speaking descendants and followers did indeed obtain a permanent place for themselves through military action and service, eventually even on the west side of the Oxus River. Around 1025, they were hired briefly and unsuccessfully by the Ghaznavid ruler of Khurasan. In the 1030s, they returned to Khurasan, where Ghaznavid power had come under increasing pressure due to fiscal disputes with local urban elites. Under the leadership of Seljuk's grandsons Tughril Beg (d. 1063) and Chaghri Beg (d. 1060), these Seljuk groups exploited this opportunity to rapidly take over Ghaznavid Khurasan. This occurred in the first place in the format of battles and great victories over Ghaznavid armies, first in 1037 at Marv and Herat, then in 1038 at Nishapur, and finally in 1040 again in the surroundings of Marv, at Dandanqan. Additional aggressive campaigns led by members of the Seljuk family and aiming at collecting booty for their nomadic associates and followers as well as checking rivals and opponents, secured Seljuk control over the region. In time, this regional dominance was mainly maintained from their new headquarters near Nishapur.

While Chaghri Beg continued to defend and consolidate the interests of the Seljuk patriarchal constellation and its nomadic followers in the region of Khurasan, Tughril Beg advanced further westwards with his followers and troops of, especially, Turkmen—the name most commonly used to identify the Turkic-speaking and Muslim nomadic pastoralists that came to roam across much of Islamic West-Asia in search of sufficient pasture for their herds. In Iran and Iraq, they pursued the confrontation with regional competitors, including Buyid and Fatimid agents as well as rival Turkmen. In 1055, after further military successes, among others in Isfahan in 1050, Tughril was asked by the Abbasid Caliph, al-Qaʾim (r. 1031–1074), to put an end to Buyid chaos and Fatimid pressures in Bagdad and central Iraq, which was secured without many problems. After the death of his brother Chaghri Beg in Khurasan in 1060, Tughril eventually appeared as sole head of the Seljuk leading kin group, their Turkmen followers and troops, and their newly conquered lands in Khurasan, Iran, and Iraq. Upon his death in 1063, this position of new patriarchal trans-regional leadership was taken over—and further consolidated and expanded in all directions—by Chaghri's son Alp Arslan (r. 1063–1073), even more forcefully by the latter's son Malik Shah (r. 1073–1092), and thereafter, in substantially changing and increasingly challenged regional and trans-regional contexts, by four more generations of Malik Shah's Seljuk descendants, until his great-great grandson Tughril III (r. 1175–1194).

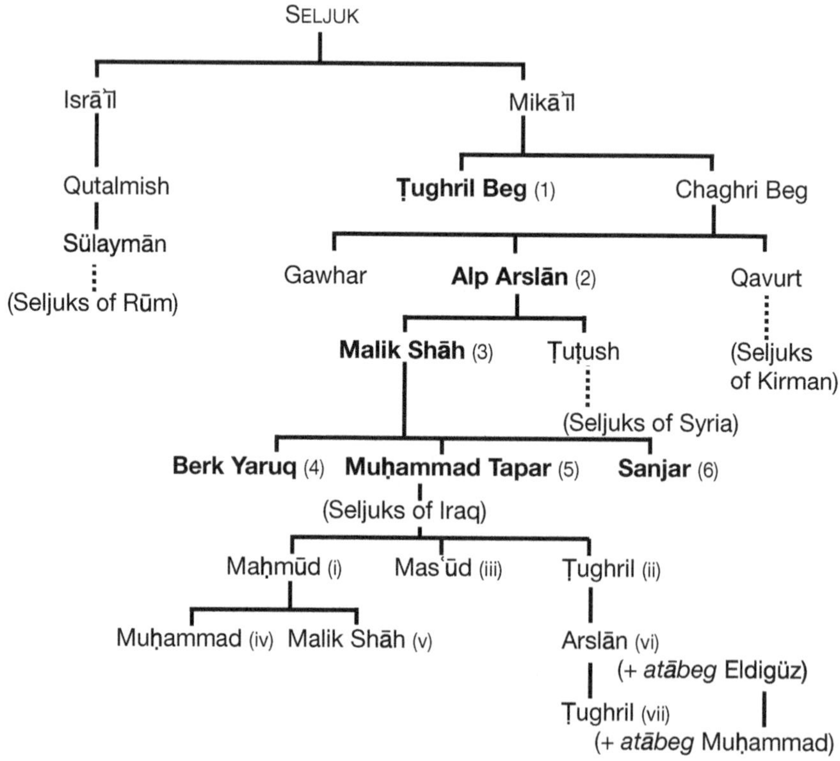

Bold = Great Seljuk sultans
Arabic numbers = succession of Great Seljuk sultans
Roman numbers = succession of junior sultans (sultans of Iraq)

Dynastic Table 3 Simplified dynastic table of the descendants of the Turkish leader Seljuk, the Seljuks

1.2 Seljuk dynastic and patrimonial transformations between Turkmen bands and post-Abbasid courts in the later 11th century

In the course of this expansion and consolidation of Seljuk power, Tughril and Chaghri Beg, and their Seljuk successors, all represented their actions and their leadership—despite its nomadic, Turkish, violent, and Inner-Asian origins—as part and parcel of the symbolic world of the post-Abbasid trans-regional order. As with the Samanids, the Buyids, and the Ghaznavids before, this happened by actively appealing to Perso-Iranian concepts of universal kingship—expressed in the active use of titles such as 'king of kings' (*shahanshah* or, in Arabic, *malik al-muluk*)—and, especially, through seeking confirmation of their newly acquired positions of power in Islamic West-Asia from the Abbasid caliph in Bagdad. This symbolic relationship with the caliphate was articulated through the awarding of honorary titles and privileges, and by explicit references to a theocratic order that involved God, the Prophet, and the caliphs, on most Seljuk coinage and in many other forms of dynastic communication and representation. Seljuk rulers and their entourages insisted especially on the caliphal bestowal of the distinguishing post-Abbasid titular form of *al-sultan al-mu'azzam* ('the supreme rule'). This explicit titular appeal to legitimate Islamic sovereignty became

Figure 8.3 *Dinar* (golden coin) minted in the name of sultan Malik Shah (484 AH/1091–92, mint place unclear). The text on the central part (obverse and reverse) (re)confirms the Sunni-Islamic theocratic order and its delegation of sovereignty, making also explicit references to the new title of *sultan* and to the ancient Persian title of *shahanshah* ('king of kings').

Obverse (left)

L. 1 There is no god but God

L. 2: Alone. He has no companion.

L. 3: [Caliph] al-Muqtadī bi-amr Allāh.

L. 4: Al-Sulṭān al-Muʿaẓẓam

Reverse (right)

L. 1 Muḥammad is the messenger of God.

L. 2 Shāhānshāh al-Aʿẓam

L. 3 Muʿizz al-Dunyā wa-l-Dīn

L. 4 Abū l-Fatḥ Malikshāh

Source: Classical Numismatic Group, Inc. www.cngcoins.com

now firmly established as the formal designation of the trans-regional authority that was claimed by Seljuk central leaders and by many who followed in their wake. When Iraq was added to the domains of Tughril Beg in the 1050s, the Seljuk sultan actually became the new patron and protector of the Abbasid caliphal leadership of the Muslim community, as also expressed by Tughril's adoption of the title of 'client of the commander of the believers' (*mawla amir al-mu'minin*). The precise nature of this unequal relationship—the Seljuks offering protection and resources in return for the delegation to them of Abbasid sovereign authority, and thus of legitimacy—and of its consequences remained, however, a vexed issue, regularly pitting ambitious caliphs, sultans, and their respective supporters against each other in recurrent pursuits to maximize their respective influence and impact on the other.[5] In fact, these complex but symbiotic relationships between Abbasid and Seljuk leaderships and claims to sovereignty are illustrative of the wider tension between the Turkmen social world and the post-Abbasid order that jointly continued to define the particular organization of Seljuk power and authority from the mid-11th to the later 12th centuries.

1.2.1 Turkmen patriarchal authority and Seljuk dynastic practice

Under Tughril Beg (d. 1063) himself, but mainly under his direct successors, his nephew Alp Arslan (d. 1073) and the latter's son Malik Shah (d. 1092), Seljuk trans-regional leadership was not only defined and explained in post-Abbasid terms. In line with Inner-Asian and Turkmen conceptions of collective leadership and family rule, all West-Asian lands in which the Seljuks acquired a dominant position were also organized as a vast dynastic network of diverse sets of people and resources, dominance over which was divided among the various male members of the leading clan and their entourages and followers. Personal merits of strength and charisma of the different dynastic members, if necessary demonstrated in violent competition and confrontation with dynastic peers, decided on the exact nature of this distribution as well as the leadership over the dynastic whole. This type of personal leadership, based on both charismatic and patriarchal strategies of power, certainly did not benefit the stability and resilience of Seljuk trans-regional rule. Especially when decisions about succession to the leadership of the Seljuk clan, and thus to the position of sultan, had to be made, this was always a source of rivalry, resource gathering, tension, and violent confrontations in which different members of the Seljuk family had to, or could, prove their equally legitimate claims, and in which all local, regional, and trans-regional leaderships and elites were forced to make uncertain political choices for or against various contenders for succession. This specific practice of violent dynastic succession, referred to in some areas of historical scholarship as 'blood tanistry'—succession as defined by the notion "that the most talented male member of the royal dynasty should inherit the throne, commonly by murder and war"[6]—countered any stabilizing and centralizing tendencies that the dynasty and any apparatus of power that emerged around its different leaders occasionally experienced. Seljuk tanistry actually enabled the continuous empowerment, from the turn of the 11th and 12th centuries onwards in particular, of a multiplicity of Seljuk, Turkmen, and other actors and rivals who all had different stakes in repeated moments of Seljuk succession, in the trans-regional Seljuk political order more in general, and thus in maintaining it while carving out and maximizing autonomous spaces within it, as sultans, as sultanic kingmakers, or as a variety of breakaway Seljuk agents whose reintegration by victorious rivals remained *ad hoc* or ephemeral only.

The succession of Tughril in 1063 and of his nephew Alp Arslan in 1073 had already been moments of great uncertainty, discord, and partisanship among the Seljuk and Turkmen leaderships, forced on each occasion to rally around two or more candidates for the succession, to engage in violent confrontations, and to respond to the need for a rapid rebuilding of the social and political cohesion and infrastructures of dynastic power around the victors, after their total disintegration during the transition. In 1073, Malik Shah thus only succeeded his father Alp Arslan after the victory over the followers and troops of his uncle Qavurt and the latter's capture and execution, and after the killing of their sister Gawhar Khatun, Malik Shah's aunt and allegedly a wielder of substantial Turkmen force. In 1092, after the death of Malik Shah, the pool of legitimate contenders seems somehow to have been limited, favoring his sons in particular and narrowing down—in contested ways—to a practice of competition among young royal sons and their supporters and kingmakers that was largely maintained by the next generations.[7] Nevertheless, internecine warfare continued for a long time after 1092 and no new member of this reshaped Seljuk dynasty—essentially re-centered and transformed into a Malikshahid lineage from 1092 onwards—emerged again that proved strong enough to entirely restore dynastic cohesion and centrality, even though many continued to situate themselves actively within the Seljuk trans-regional order. In fact, the dynastic domains from Transoxania to Asia Minor were gradually split between different members and branches of the family. Especially after the death of Malik Shah's son and sultanic successor Muhammad Tapar (r. 1105–1118) in 1118, and the transfer of the trans-regional authority of the sultanate to Muhammad's brother Sanjar (r. 1118–1157) in Khurasan, different branches within the Malikshahid dynastic dispensation started to go their own way, with Muhammad's descendants vying for the sultanate in Iraq and western Iran until the 1190s, and Sanjar struggling to uphold his sultanic authority in the face of Turkmen and other leaderships in the east until the 1150s (see below).

A related aspect that marked this highly personalized, patriarchal, and unstable dynastic leadership of Seljuks and Seljuk Malikshahids is the practice of appanage. This refers to the tradition of dividing Seljuk dominance over rural and urban resources and estates among male members of the Seljuk family and also among Seljuk supporters and followers, for the maintenance of their own entourages and often also in return for their continued support and loyalty. In the course of the 11th century, this practice contributed to the need for almost permanent territorial expansion. This proved essential to enable the Seljuk dynasty both to provide all its members with sufficient appanages and to continue to satisfy the Turkmen leaderships and their followers and kinsmen, who were the original power base of the Seljuks and primarily lived off spoils and sufficient pastures for their herds. This expansionist mode of Seljuk organization in, especially, the 11th century obviously caused continuous tensions with other local, regional, and trans-regional leaderships, including with other Turkmen in the west and eventually even with the Greek Romans in Asia Minor. In the latter case, this scramble for pasture and Turkmen leadership culminated in a major battle near the Armenian town of Manzikert (today's Malazgirt in eastern Turkey) in 1071, where the Greek Roman emperor and his armies were utterly destroyed by sultan Alp Arslan and his Turkmen forces.[8] Thus, different Seljuk and non-Seljuk groups of Turkmen were able to enter the Anatolian peninsula and push back its ancient Greek Roman dominance, quickly reducing it to a minor presence in Asia Minor's northwest only. In the wake of these Turkmen, a branch of the Seljuk clan, descending from a nephew of Tughril and Chaghri Beg and eventually known as the Rum ('Roman') Seljuks (r. 1077–1307), established itself there and organized its power and authority, in due course, especially around the South Anatolian regional center of Konya.[9] Chaghri Beg's aforementioned son Qavurt (d. 1092) established himself with his followers in the period 1049–51 as ruler of the southwestern Iranian region of Kirman, and his descendants continued to keep this region (and Oman on the other side of the Persian Gulf) as their appanage, and they are therefore known as the Seljuks of Kirman (r. 1051–1187). Yet another Seljuk clan, around Malik Shah's brother Tutush (d. 1095) and his descendants, ended up—albeit briefly—in Syria (1078–1117), at that time an unstable frontier zone with the Shi'ite Fatimids of Egypt.

Malik Shah's descendants, who continued to rule more and—increasingly—less effectively for most of the 12th century in the regions of Iraq, Iran, Khurasan, and Transoxania and who continued to vie with each other for presenting themselves as the 'supreme' sultan, or—from 1118 onwards—as 'the most supreme' sultan (*al-sultan al-a'zam*) in Khurasan and Transoxania and as a junior sultan in Iraq and western Iran, are identified in modern historiography as the Great Seljuks. This helps to distinguish their particular lineage and trajectory, and also their Malikshahid claims to superior patriarchal leadership and to Seljuk sovereignty, from those of the other branches of the Seljuk clan, which appeared ever more as autonomous regional dynasties in Asia Minor, in Kirman, and briefly also in Syria.

The consequences of Seljuk appanage practices included, however, not only territorial expansion and dynastic fragmentation. In the 12th century, Malikshahids considered too young to manage the dynastic domains assigned to them as an appanage—also often more formally referred to with the post-Abbasid Arabic term of an *iqta'* (a kind of prebendal allotment in return for military or administrative service)—were placed under the supervision of an *atabeg*. This Turkic title for a royal guardian or regent was mostly awarded, with concomitant local or regional responsibilities, to military leaders, or *amir*s, from the entourages of the fathers of these young Malikshahids. Enabling these Seljuk *amir*s and *atabeg*s the build-up of their own autonomous power bases in name of a young Malikshahid, this appanage practice, therefore, also generated a reality of even more devolved authorities and, in due course, the local and regional empowerment of *atabeg*s in the face of ever weaker dynastic cohesion and trans-regional leadership (see below).

1.2.2 Seljuk patrimonial households and post-Abbasid courts, courtiers, and agents

This 12th-century empowerment of Seljuk *atabeg*s was directly related to the emergence, from the mid-11th century onwards, of non-Turkmen agents and more organized mechanisms of Seljuk power and authority around the different members and branches of Seljuk regional and trans-regional leadership. The instable Seljuk dynastic networks of people and resources continued to be predominantly patriarchal constellations in which these more structural and patrimonial appearances were marked especially by the *ad hoc*, limited, heterogeneous, and equally unstable nature of these expanding chains of Seljuk authority and agency. In fact, what these constellations shared above all is the organization of dominance and leadership around individual Seljuks' extended families of male and female relatives, sworn associates, free and unfree servants, administrators, and warriors, around the urban and rural spaces that all of these occupied, around the diverse sets of resources that they needed for their households' maintenance, and around the many different relationships with other groups and similarly organized households or nomadic bands that they nurtured.[10]

'Power rested in the family', the modern historian of 'medieval' Islamic sociopolitical history Michael Chamberlain summarized one of the more recent and increasingly dominant understandings of Seljuk power constellations. For Chamberlain, this priority of personal ties and households actually means that:

> we should not think of the Seljuks as a unitary state, but rather as a collection of powerful households kept in check by the head of the most powerful among them. Seen in this light, the ruling household's adoption of monarchical and legal arguments for legitimate authority was one way of fending off the claims of the other households within the ruling family.[11]

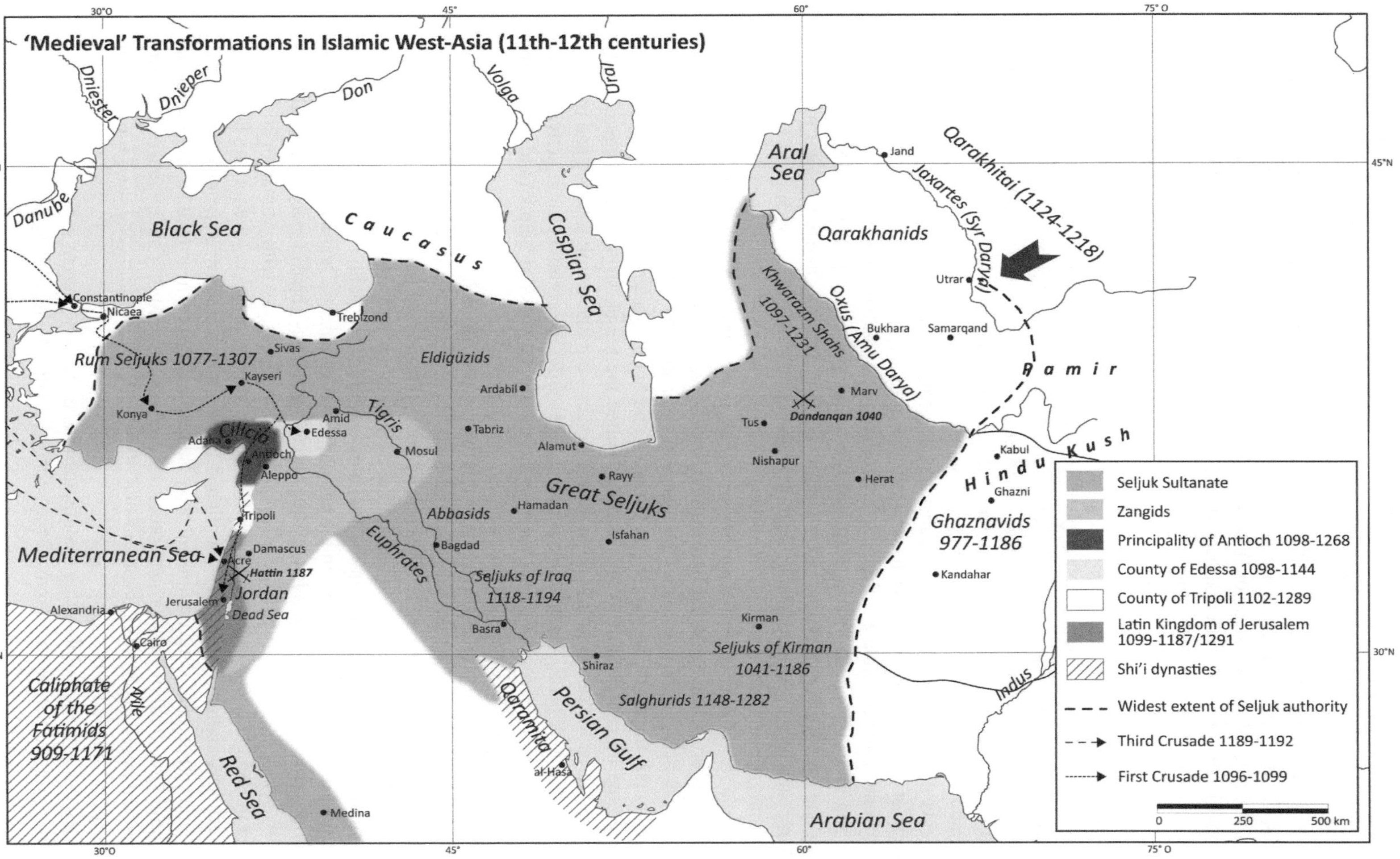

Map 6 'Medieval' Transformations in Islamic West-Asia (11th–12th centuries)

Source: Redrawn from Hodgson, *The Venture of Islam. Vol. 2. The Expansion of Islam in the Middle Periods*, pp. 40 + 263

More in general, patrimonial households and less formalized entourages of strongmen or warlords and their partners, supporters, and followers were the nodes that clustered into networks of Seljuk leadership and that competed for those networks' dominance, expansion, and local penetration in pursuit of the elimination of their rivals, the protection of their clients, the accumulation of resources, and the reproduction of their particular relationships of local, regional, or trans-regional power and authority. In fact, households and related personal forms of organization appeared and transformed in these central and competitive ways not just within 'the ruling family', but also as the main practical context of operation for rivalling or associated Turkmen leaderships and for non-Seljuk regional dynasts and all kinds of local wielders of violence and authority.

Nevertheless, different patrimonial apparatuses of amirs, *kuttab*, viziers, courtiers, privileges, and resources do make their appearance in the limited range of Arabic and Persian documentary and narrative sources that inform about Seljuk history. These patrimonial extensions of Seljuk households were at least represented along the post-Abbasid, especially Ghaznavid, models that were best known to the experts who populated them, or to the Persian and Arabic contemporary and later authors who tried to make sense of them. Above all, they gave shape to many of the mechanisms and agents of power that dynastic or any other brokers of Seljuk power used to the best of their abilities to eliminate their rivals, protect their clients, and accumulate sufficient resources to maintain the cohesion and autonomy of their and their households' participation in the Seljuk power constellation. These mechanisms and agents often came and went with the person, authority, and households of Seljuk leaders, such as Alp Arslan, Malik Shah, Muhammad Tapar, Sanjar, or Tughril III. At the same time, as suggested already, from the mid-11th century onwards, when non-Turkmen agents and more organized mechanisms of Seljuk power and authority around the households of different members and branches of Seljuk regional and trans-regional leadership started to appear, a gradual shift in the make-up and nature of these power elites occurred. In due course, therefore, no longer just Turkmen and Seljuk leaderships and their particular pastoral and nomad entourages and interests pulled the Seljuk strings—as predominantly continued to be the case until the reign of Alp Arslan—but also administrative and military agents of various local, Perso-Iranian, and unfree *ghilman* origins became active Seljuk partners and even leaders of their own households and networks of Seljuk (and eventually post-Seljuk) power (see also below).

The most important infrastructure for this expansion, transformation, and diversification of power elites, their households, and their networks at the center of Seljuk power and authority was—in the best of Abbasid and post-Abbasid traditions—the complex whole of spaces and people that rallied around the Seljuk sultan and made for the Seljuk court, the sultan's *dargah*. Originating in the Turkmen entourages of Seljuk leaders, Seljuk courts continued to relate in many ways to the encampments of pastoral nomads, even when they became ever more explicitly modelled after Abbasid and post-Abbasid precedents, and occasionally, even situated in veritable urban palace complexes, as with Muhammad Tapar's palace in Bagdad or Sanjar's at Marv in Khurasan. Mostly, however, even in the latter two cases, sultans and their entourages continued to reside in tented encampments outside the main urban centers of their dominions, near Bagdad and Marv, near Isfahan and Hamadan in central- and western-Iran, or near other regional centers, moving along general patterns of seasonal migration between locations that offered more favorable conditions for living in winter or in summertime.

As itinerant rulers, Seljuk sultans continued thus to be very present in the various central localities of their Seljuk dominions in ways that paralleled the residential patterns and habits of other Turkmen leaderships and their entourages and herds in 11th- and 12th-century Islamic West-Asia. When in due course different branches, members, and agents of the Seljuk dynastic order went their autonomous ways, many of them continued to organize their entourages in similar spatial ways around the splendor of their own royal tent enclosure and in tented encampments of freedmen *amir*s and their Turkic-speaking *ghilman* troops that included special training grounds for horsemen and for one of their favorite pastimes, the polo-game. Beyond the upholding of the appearance of post-Abbasid and Seljuk order through various sets of rituals, ceremonials, and hierarchies of proximity, distinction, and justice, these courtly encampments of Seljuk sultans, Seljuk minors and relatives, Seljuk amirs and *atabeg*s, and various local or regional others were organized around a specific series of royal activities. These ranged—as in pre-Seljuk times—from hunting over drinking parties to public demonstrations of largesse and benevolence, that joined the court and its members and visitors in shared experiences and expressions of leadership, partnership, hierarchy, and order. As a popular Persian text of rulership advice, 'The Book of Qabus' (*Qabusnamah*), authored in the 1080s by a Seljuk vassal for his son and successor, explains, a good ruler indulges in these courtly activities with sufficient restraint and moderation:

> Riding horses, going hunting, and playing polo are suitable occupations for powerful men, especially in youth: but everything should have a limit, measure and method. Do not go hunting every day for this is not methodical. The week has seven days. Go hunting two days, two or three days occupy yourself with drinking, and one day deal with affairs of state.[12]

As 'The Book of Qabus' also surmises, these activities that distinguish men of power from others—at least when they are not campaigning against rivals and competitors—were not the exclusive preserve of Seljuk royals and their entourages. Also, many non-Seljuk regional rulers such as the author of 'The Book of Qabus' and his designated successor, or other "powerful men", including non-Seljuk Turkmen leaders or 12th-century Seljuk *atabeg*s and *amir*s, or for that matter local lords and local wielders of violence of ancient Iranian, Transoxanian, Khurasanian, Arabian, or other leadership pedigrees (including the Abbasid caliph in Bagdad), participated in similar appreciations of these rulership practices.

Just as the pool of legitimate Seljuk competitors gradually narrowed down to Seljuk members of the household of sultan Malik Shah (r. 1073–1092) and their descendants, the novel non-Turkmen mechanisms and agents that would increasingly determine and dominate Seljuk power constellations in Islamic West-Asia in the 12th century stemmed especially from the ranks of experts and expertise that had enabled Malik Shah and his court to emerge victoriously over their Seljuk rivals and to indulge in horse riding, playing polo, and drinking wine. Building on the achievements and network of supporters of Tughril and, especially, Alp Arslan, there materialized around Malik Shah in particular a more professional, patrimonial apparatus of Seljuk dynastic power that directly related to Abbasid and post-Abbasid forms and meanings. On the one hand, as suggested, Turkic-speaking unfree *ghilman* from Inner Asia were again acquired to complement or even replace Turkmen forces as the ruler's personal bodyguard and, under the command of *amir*s that were often chosen from their ranks, as the forceful core of his violent manpower. On the other hand, a limited group of *kuttab* of Arabo-Persian origins was also again employed. These were organized in different *diwan*s, supervised by a vizier, and geared especially towards the organization of their leader's political communication and revenue management. This included not least the supervision of the awarding and reclaiming of the above-mentioned prebendal *iqta*ʿ allotments to *amir*s and Seljuk household members as well as occasionally to *kuttab* or allied local leaders. These allotments appeared in a variety of forms and sizes that ranged from the confirmation of a kind of virtual autonomy in the administration of Seljuk resources and authority in an appanage, region, or town over the negotiation of tax farms to the awarding of the temporary right to collect taxes in a particular rural area or village. More in general, these diverse groups of *amir*s, *kuttab*, and more structured mechanisms of power and representation that emerged around Malik Shah and his court connected particular networks of expertise and local leadership—especially from Khurasan and Transoxania, and from western Iran—to the sultan's household, expanding the interests they were meant to serve from those of Malik Shah and his relatives to those of many others—including themselves (which did not necessarily prove beneficial for the cohesion or coherence of the expanding whole) (see below).

These expanding ranks, mechanisms, and interests of power were certainly also complemented by the acts of cultural patronage that were recorded to emanate from Malik Shah's court. Whereas many achievements and accomplishments—especially in the fields of art and architecture—tend to be emphasized in discussions of Seljuk patronage, historian Andrew Peacock recently observed how "relatively little art can be securely dated and attributed to a Great Seljuk context" and "although many more examples of Great Seljuk architecture have come down to us, relatively few can be directly associated with sultanic patronage." Above all, therefore, Seljuk sultanic patronage appears in the traditional Abbasid and post-Abbasid court-centered formats of favoring and supporting *adib*s and scientists who were writing in Persian and Arabic and who specialized in particular in poetry, sciences of the stars, and medicine. One of the most famous among these recipients of Malik Shah's patronage was the Persian poet and scientist from Nishapur ʿUmar Khayyam (*c.* 1050–1123). Reportedly invited by Malik Shah to Isfahan as one of a group of leading scholars that worked at the royal observatory in the 1070s and 1080s, ʿUmar Khayyam penned a corpus of texts in Arabic and Persian on mathematics, science of the stars, Avicennan philosophy, mechanics, and music that also included a set of astronomical tables dedicated to Malik Shah, the *Zij Malik-Shahi*.[13]

This expansion of the networks of power and patronage around the personality of Malik Shah and his court is also reflected in how his leadership skills and accomplishments at the center of the Seljuk power constellation and patrimonial apparatus were consistently remembered and represented. An image of well organized, forceful, benevolent, and exemplary Muslim rule certainly emerges from the fragment below in one of the few Persian chronicles that are dedicated to the history of the Seljuk dynasty.

> The army which was always at the side of Malik Shāh and whose names were recorded in the muster rolls of the *dīwān* consisted of 45,000 horsemen. Their *iqṭā*ʿs were scattered in different parts of the realm so that wherever they went they should have fodder and expenses ready at hand.
>
> The justice and statecraft of Sultan Malik Shāh were such that during his time nobody suffered any injustice. And if any man appeared, claiming to have suffered an injustice, no one interposed to deny him access. He spoke with the Sultan face-to-face and demanded justice. As the proverb says, 'Whose zeal is great, his value is high'.
>
> Among the good deeds of Sultan Malik Shāh are the water reservoirs which he had constructed on the road to the Hejaz, the abolition of tolls and protection tax on the pilgrim road, and the granting of an appanage and revenues to the *amīr* of the two holy places, who previously used to take seven red *dīnār*s from every pilgrim. He showed

> much kindness to the desert Arabs and the sojourners of the mighty Kaʿba, and some of these revenues still remain. . . .
>
> Among sports and spectacles his favorite was hunting. I saw his hunt book, written by the hand of Abū Ṭāhir Khātūnī, in which it was recorded that in one day the sultan had hit seventy gazelles with arrows. It was his rule to give a Maghribi *dīnār* to the poor for every quarry he hit. In every hunting ground in Iraq and Khurāsān he made towers of hoofs of gazelles and wild asses. In the land of Transoxania, in the Arabian desert, in Marj, Khūzistān and the province of Iṣfahān, wherever there was plentiful hunting, he left memorials.
>
> As his seat of government and personal residence he chose Iṣfahān from all his lands, and there he erected many buildings, inside and outside the city, including palaces and gardens, such as the garden of Kārān, the House of Water, the garden of Aḥmad Siyāh, the garden of Dasth-i Gūr, and others. He erected the citadel of the city and the citadel of Dizkūh and kept his treasury there.[14]

However critical one should remain for this and similar idealizing later representations of the trans-regional extent, effectiveness, and exemplary nature of Malik Shah's rule,[15] they do conform to other sources in the general picture of the historical trajectory of Seljuk power that they put forward. This concerns the fact that in the 1070s and 1080s the members and agents of Malik Shah's Seljuk household and court—including especially his many 'horsemen'—achieved maximal priority in, and integration and expansion of, the networks of Seljuk power and authority, and transformed them in due course into a—regularly contested—Seljuk-Malikshahid centered relational whole that managed to sideline, ally with, or even incorporate rival groups and leadership households, from Damascus in Syria to Kashgar in the east, or for that matter from 'the mighty Kaʿba' over 'the hunting grounds in Iraq and Khurasan' to 'the land of Transoxania'. One of the main effects of this substantial integration and re-orientation of the Seljuk power constellation appears, furthermore, to have been the sustained pre-eminence of these Malikshahid patrimonial actors, agents, and mechanisms of power among Great Seljuk power elites between Syria and Transoxania from the turn of the 11th and 12th centuries onwards. Not only Malik Shah's direct descendants therefore prevailed, as with Muhammad Tapar (d. 1118) and Sanjar (d. 1157), each of whom transformed their personal bands of Turkmen followers and Seljuk households into their own sultanic courts, patrimonial apparatus, and centers of cultural patronage in Iraq and in Khurasan respectively. In addition, many others were simultaneously empowered in the formation of Malik Shah's court and patrimonial apparatus, and subsequently appeared with their own households in ever more autonomous ways in the ever more diverse and more intensely competing networks of Seljuk power and resources.

One of these was the mother of another one of Malik Shah's sons and potential successors, Mahmud (d. 1093). Mostly referred to as Terken Khatun ('The Queen Consort') (d. 1094), this daughter of the Qara-Khanid ruler of Transoxania is described in a later Arabic chronicle as commanding during the struggles over her husband's succession an army of no less than 10,000 men and as "the mistress of Isfahan, dealing with the wars while organizing and guiding the armies".[16] Among the other Malikshahid agents that were similarly empowered and became active—and in some cases eventually even autonomous—participants in the transformations of Seljuk order in and beyond the 1090s, Malik Shah's Turkish amirs, their *ghilman*, and their descendants represent an ever more dominant group. One of these amirs, who originally seems to have performed a position as 'gatekeeper' (*hajib*) in Malik Shah's royal household, was Aqsunqur (d. 1094). Appointed by

Malik Shah as his military administrator (*shihna*) of the region of Aleppo in 1087, he was killed in the competition over Malik Shah's succession, but his descendants, beginning with his son Zengi (d. 1146), became ever more powerful Seljuk and post-Seljuk leaders and regional rulers in Iraq, the Jazira and Syria (see next chapter). Another one of these Malikshahid amirs was Anushtigin (d. 1097), who allegedly began his career as 'keeper of the royal wash bowls' (*tastdar*) in Malik Shah's household and who ended it as titular administrator of the region of Khwarazm. Anushtigin's son joined the entourage and court of Malik Shah's son Sanjar in Khurasan and was appointed by him in the same capacity of regional authority as his father. However, receiving the additional privilege of adopting the ancient regional title of 'Khwarazm Shah', Anushtigin's son actually started organizing his own vassal Seljuk court in the region of Khwarazm and positioning himself directly in regional, especially Turkmen, and wider Transoxanian and Khurasani relationships of power. Anushtigin's grandson subsequently transformed from Sanjar's courtier and representative in the region of Khwarazm to one of his main competitors, so that from the mid-1150s onwards, Anushtigin's further descendants actually appear as the Khwarazm Shah successors of Sanjar's trans-regional power and authority, but then in their own, post-Seljuk, capacities (see below).

1.3 Malikshahid Fragmentation between the Great Seljuk west and east: sultans, **amirs, atabegs***, and others in the 12th century*

This process of the empowerment of courtiers and agents, and of their and their offspring's local or regional autonomization—in many ways reminiscent of the transition from an Abbasid to a post-Abbasid order—continued at the different courts and power apparatus that mushroomed in the 12th century around various Malikshahid successors. When different branches within the Malikshahid dynastic dispensation started to go their own way, with Muhammad Tapar's descendants vying for the sultanate in Iraq and western Iran until the 1190s, and Sanjar struggling to uphold his supreme sultanic authority in the face of Khwarazm Shahid and other leaderships in the east until the 1150s, this process of empowerment and autonomization actually seems to have intensified.

As suggested above, it was not only the formation of Seljuk courts and patrimonial military agents that enabled *amir*s and *atabeg*s to build-up their own autonomous households and courts, as Seljuk military administrators or in name of a young Malikshahid, and to organize their own regional power constellations in the gradually transforming trans-regional order. In addition, the aforementioned practice of appanage, even more intensely pursued amidst the 12th-century expansion of the pool of Seljuk claimants, contributed substantially to this disintegration of the Malikshahid household, court, and resources, to the abstraction of any dynastic relationships and dynastic leadership, and to the further weakening of Seljuk cohesion and trans-regional authority across Malik Shah's former territories between Transoxania and Syria. As also suggested above, this was, however, not a straightforward process. It concerned a diverse transformation that followed different trajectories when, also within the Malikshahid dynastic dispensation, different Seljuk branches started to go their own way. The main, heavily contested, divergence occurred from 1118 onwards, when Muhammad Tapar's sons and grandsons mostly continued to appear as Seljuk sultans—until the 1150s formally as junior sultans only—in Iraq and western Iran, while their uncle Sanjar upheld the trans-regional appearance of his father Malik Shah's "most supreme sultanate" from Khurasan until the 1150s.

1.3.1 The sultanate of Iraq and its Seljuk atabegs

This east-west divide within the so-called Great Seljuk Sultanate actually meant that the relationships of power that used to coalesce around it were now being re-oriented in various ways, especially around Sanjar and his household and court in the east and around Mahmud, Masʿud and their brothers, sons, nephews, and competing entourages in the west. The latter branch of descendants of Muhammad Tapar are referred to in modern scholarship as the Seljuk sultans of Iraq, and they actually continued to reign as sultans until 1194. Recurring rivalries and violent confrontations over the succession, especially in the 1130s after sultan Mahmud's death in 1131 and again in the 1150s after sultan Masʿud's death in 1152, not only enabled the rise to regional power and authority of different Seljuk amirs and *atabeg*s, such as the aforementioned Zengids (r. 1127–1233) in Syria and the Jazira—today's region of northern Iraq and northeastern Syria—or the Eldigüzids in and beyond the region of Azerbaijan (see below). These recurrent moments of competition for trans-regional authority also involved the renegotiation of relationships of power with many more stakeholders in that Seljuk authority and in the power it could effectively wield. This regular, if not constant, renegotiation with violent and non-violent means actually resulted in a reality of territorial losses for the western branches of the sultanate, seeing its actual claims reduced to some regions of western Iran and Iraq only—organized around the urban center of Hamadan—as well as in the further emergence of numerous new opportunities for all kinds of local and regional, formerly Seljuk or even non-Seljuk leaders, to expand their influence and power both within and beyond the crumbling Seljuk dynastic order. As one contemporary scholar and member of the post-Seljuk court of the Zengids in the Jazira explained, "affairs became difficult for sultan Masʿud and amirs demanded land without him having a choice [in the matter]. No land was left for him except the name of the sultanate, nothing else."[17]

This fragmentation and competition of claims, households, and courts around various Malikshahids and Malikshahid descendants that the 12th century witnessed, especially in Iraq and western Iran, actually stimulated the equally competitive further empowerment of several agents of these multiple households and courts, including especially several of the *atabeg*s ruling in the name of a young (occasionally even only virtually existing) Malikshahid descendant. An early representative case is that of the Burids of Damascus, rulers of Damascus between 1104 and 1154, and the descendants of the amir Tughtigin (d. 1128). Tughtigin came to power in this region of southern Syria as *atabeg* for the sons of Malik Shah's brother Tutush (d. 1095), retained and even expanded his position of Seljuk leadership when these sons died, and was succeeded by his son Buri (r. 1128–1132) and by Buri's sons and grandson who all—while maintaining their claim to being Seljuk *atabeg*s—acted as autonomous regional rulers. Another high-profile representative of this diversifying group of Seljuk and post-Seljuk amirs and *atabeg*s undoubtedly is the amir Eldigüz (d. *c*. 1176), who is mentioned first in the entourages of *ghilman* of Muhammad Tapar's sons and successors in Iraq and West Iran, the junior sultans Mahmud (r. 1118–1131) and Masʿud (r. 1134–1152). Eldigüz became Masʿud's virtually autonomous representative in the region of Azerbaijan, and after Masʿud's death he transformed into the main Seljuk strongman, kingmaker, and *atabeg* in the violent power struggles with other regional amirs and *atabeg*s that arose in western Iran. Two of his sons succeeded him as *atabeg*s of the Seljuk sultan and as central agents of the networks of Seljuk power in Azerbaijan and western Iran, and after the death of the last Seljuk sultan Tughril III in 1194, their Eldigüzid descendants remained dominant in these regions for another two decades.

Among the new regional leaderships that emerged from a non-Malikshahid context, that of the Salghurids in the southwest-Iranian region of Fars (r. 1148–1282) stands out. A clan of Turkmen leaders who, with their pastoral-nomadic followers, had migrated to Asia Minor in the later 11th century, they established themselves as a dominant and autonomous force in the region of Fars from the later 1140s onwards. Assuming the Seljuk title of *atabeg* (even though there was no minor Seljuk for them to guard), they participated actively in upholding the fiction of trans-regional order topped by the Seljuk sultan, while at the same time maintaining and expanding their autonomy vis-à-vis Seljuk and non-Seljuk rivals.

Another one of these non-Malikshahid regional leaderships was that of the Abbasid caliphs, who reappeared as ever more powerful regional strongmen in Bagdad and central Iraq, combining the strength of their unique claims to sovereignty with strong personalities, qualified agents, and sufficient resources to regain their autonomy and their centrality in regional networks of power, especially during the long reign of the charismatic caliph al-Nasir (r. 1180–1220). As suggested in the following contemporary assessment of the reign of the last Seljuk sultan Tughril ibn Arslan (r. 1175–1194), this great-grandson of Muhammad Tapar is indeed remembered as a referential abstraction of Seljuk dynastic power and legitimate order, and, at the same time, as stripped of any agency by the rivalries and competition that marked the Abbasid resurgence in Iraq and the autonomization of Seljuk *atabeg*s, such as the Salghurids in Fars, the Zengids in Syria and the Jazira, and, especially, the Eldigüzids in Azerbaijan and northwestern Iran.

> For ten years, the great lord, the mighty *atābeg*, the sun of the world and the faith Muḥammad ibn Eldigüz, may God have mercy on him, maintained well-being, security, and happiness in the dynastic domain, attending to affairs and procuring what was needful, while the Sultan was untroubled by the business of underlings. His loyalty to the Sultanate was such that the *atābeg*'s entire concern, in secret and in public, was devoted to one thing—the need to procure for this Sultan what Sanjar and Malik Shāh had never had. He sent envoys to different parts and had his name and titles inserted in the Friday prayer and on the coinage. At all times he proclaimed his sovereignty over Baghdad and sent a man there to require the rebuilding of the Sultan's palace. Now at that time the officers of the Caliphate were planning to use blandishments on the neighboring amirs and to create confusion in the land so as to establish their own rule and extend it over others, but they could not prevail against the *atābeg* Muḥammad. The *atābeg* said to a gathering of people, 'The Caliphs should busy themselves with sermons and prayers, which serve to protect worldly monarchs and are the best of deeds and the greatest of activities. They should entrust kingship to the Sultans and leave the government of the world to this Sultan'.[18]

After these first ten years of ephemeral rule and the death in 1186 of the *atabeg* Muhammad ibn Eldigüz, sultan Tughril is reported to have attempted with some success to regain his Seljuk agency and to free himself from the burdens of his caliphal and Eldigüzid rivals. Eventually, however, this turned out to be of little to no avail when shifting balances of power in the east and the emergence of a post-Seljuk sultanic order rapidly moved westward.

1.3.2 The Seljuk east between Sanjar and the Khwarazm Shahs

These eastern transformations were in many respects the legacy of Sanjar's Malikshahid rule over eastern Iran, Khurasan, and Transoxania during the entire first half of the

12th century, including—as repeatedly mentioned above—after the death of his brother Muhammad Tapar in 1118 as 'most supreme sultan'. Sanjar's long reign in the eastern half of the divided territories of the so-called Great Seljuk Sultanate is generally remembered as very effective, militarily successful, and efflorescent until the late 1130s—as also suggested in the fragment above with its reference to Sanjar's name as on a par with the name and reputation of his father Malik Shah. Sanjar's hold on the balances of power and leadership started to shift, however, from the later 1130s onwards. A turning point was especially the defeat of his armies by the Qarakhitai (r. 1124–1218), a nomadic dynastic leadership from Manchuria in today's People's Republic of China. This happened in 1141, when Sanjar unsuccessfully tried to stop the Qarakhitai 'Gurkhan' and his followers from invading Transoxania and from taking full control of its profitable commercial routes. This change of Sanjar's fortune coincided with further, related, challenges to his power and authority and with his subsequent growing inability to confront his local, regional, and trans-regional rivals, including the Qarakhitai in Transoxania, but especially his *amir* in the rich oasis region of Khwarazm, the aforementioned grandson of Malik Shah's *ghulam* Anushtigin, the Khwarazm Shah, as well as an ancient local dynasty from the mountainous areas of present-day central Afghanistan, the Ghurids (r. 1149–1215). In fact, from the early 1150s onwards, both the Khwarazm Shah and the Ghurid leadership would start claiming the title and authority of the sultanate for themselves and competing for what increasingly appeared as a post-Seljuk sovereignty over Khurasan and its adjacent territories. A post-Seljuk order thus gradually emerged in the 12th century east, in which any effectively integrated reality of Seljuk political order became ever more wanting, but a fiction of the trans-regional continuance of sultanic authority was somehow maintained.

This weakening of the networks of Seljuk power around Sanjar and his supporters, and these challenges to his authority from without as well as from within his own court and apparatus of power, were directly related—amongst many other causes and consequences—to the substantial transformation of the Seljuk power constellation in these eastern regions during his reign. Competition, rivalry, negotiation, and accommodation, and the constant scramble for scarce resources were accompanied—just as in the Seljuk west—by a loosening of that constellation's coherence and cohesion, or at least a lack of any sustained and substantial integration of leaderships and elites into the household, court, and networks of power that were revolving around Sanjar. The many cracks that thus remained, and also appeared anew, in these regions' landscapes of Seljuk power witnessed the rise or autonomization of rather different leaderships than in the west: not just descendants of Malikshahid agents such as the Khwarazm Shahs, but also only tenuously related Ghurid sultans, disruptive nomadic newcomers such as the Qarakhitai 'Gurkhans', and displaced Turkmen leaderships, in search with their pastoral nomadic followers and their herds for pasture and new living spaces amidst the substantially transforming political, social, and ecological landscapes of Transoxania, Khurasan, and Iran. As one of the few specialists of the history of this region and period, Jürgen Paul, explains, "Sanjar's empire emerges as a kind of framework in which, among other groups and individuals, nomad leaders and regional lords held a considerable measure of autonomy as long as they acted according to a given set of rules (and did not challenge the sultan openly)".[19]

From the 1140s onwards, Sanjar's link with most of these new, disruptive, and displaced local and regional leaderships indeed remained unstable and tenuous, and his Seljuk authority was actually increasingly challenged, including not least by Turkmen leaders whose migrations and expansions from Transoxania to Khurasan

Sanjar's agents proved incapable of accommodating. In 1152, Sanjar was confronted with a so-called 'great revolt' of Turkmen—specifically identified, just as the migrating bands of their Turkmen predecessors in the early 11th century, as 'the Ghuzz'—in the Khurasani area around the town of Balkh, in present-day northern Afghanistan. In subsequent violent confrontations, Sanjar himself was captured by the Ghuzz leadership, and while he remained a Ghuzz captive for three years, only a handful of his *ghilman* and amirs managed to retain a measure of Seljuk order in some parts of western Iran and Khurasan in the face of ongoing Ghuzz marauding and violence. When Sanjar eventually managed to escape in 1156, Seljuk order and authority were reduced to a fiction, and Sanjar found 'his treasury empty, his kingdom ruined, his people dispersed and his army lost', as a historian at the court of one of his Iraqi relatives later explained.[20] When he died shortly afterwards, in 1157, leadership in these disruptive, unstable, and volatile circumstances was left to those who would prove better equipped to these changed realities of leadership.

The Malikshahid dynasty of Sanjar's former agents in Khwarazm, the Khwarazm Shahs, eventually established themselves across these Khurasanian and adjacent territories as the centerpiece in the renewed transregional order of highly autonomous Turkmen leaderships and local or regional lordships. The Khwarazm Shahs Atsiz ibn Muhammad ibn Anushtigin (r. 1127–1156), his son Ilarslan (r. 1156–1172), and his grandson Tekish (r. 1172–1200) were instrumental in this remarkable expansion of Khwarazmshahid authority into and then across most of Sanjar's former territories. As the aforementioned expert of Seljuk history Jürgen Paul argues, this was especially due to this dynasty's radical but successful adaptation of their Seljuk context of representation and rule to the reality of Turkmen leaderships that had continued to prevail in the region of Khwarazm, and that returned to preeminence in most regions of Islamic West-Asia with the dissolution of Malikshahid order and the gradual disintegration of Seljuk authority in the east and then also the west. As Paul explains,

> [. . .] Atsız attracted nomad leaders, and . . . this was a cornerstone of his politics; he expanded his territory mostly by securing the allegiance of nomads. . . . Atsız can be presented as a "lord of nomads" not only because nomads were essential as Khwārazmian military manpower, but also because he had to adapt to nomad ways and accommodate them in and around Khwārazm.[21]

It was Atsiz's grandson, the Khwarazm Shah ʿAlaʾ al-Din Tekish, who eventually was responsible for the death of the last Seljuk sultan of Iraq, Tughril III, when their armies—largely composed of *ghilman* and Turkmen on both sides—met in battle near the Iranian urban center of Rayy in 1194 and Tughril was killed. Tekish was eventually formally recognized by one of his main allies in the west, the aforementioned Abbasid caliph and regional ruler of central Iraq al-Nasir, as the only true sultan of Iran, Khurasan, and Transoxania. Post-Seljuk order, in the making with the transformation and fragmentation of Malikshahid trans-regional networks of power and authority since the early decades of the 12th century, had definitely become the norm across Islamic West-Asia. Between Turkmen leaders and their roaming bands and herds on the one hand and *atabeg*s, caliphs, or sultans and their competing households and courts on the other, Seljuk forms and mechanisms of dynastic sovereignty, legitimacy, and patrimonial organization continued to represent the model for rulers and men of power to emulate.

2 Networks of Perso-Iranian viziers, urban elites, local resources, and Islamic infrastructures

2.1 The expansion of Seljuk actors between Transoxania and Iraq

As the restored centrality of the Abbasid caliph in and beyond 12th-century Iraq suggests, these forms and mechanisms of Seljuk and post-Seljuk power, and this story of the formation and many transformations of Seljuk and post-Seljuk power, were not the exclusive preserve of Turkmen leaders, of Seljuk sultans, amirs, and *atabeg*s, or of any other Turkic-speaking wielders of Seljuk and post-Seljuk violence. The changing local, regional, and trans-regional dynamics of the integration and disintegration of these 11th- and 12th-century men of power have traditionally been represented as the achievements and failures of, especially, these individual members and agents of the Seljuk clan, and as following a straightforward trajectory of 11th-century integration and 12th-century disintegration. Narrative renderings of these dynamics in the handful of Arabic and Persian chronicles of the time certainly preferred to employ clear-cut frames of heroic or ignoble leadership and of teleology to serve particular didactic, moralizing, and legitimating interests. Modern scholarship, however, is gradually coming to terms with how these frames represent at best only one part of a far more complex historical reality that involved many more actors than Seljuk and post-Seljuk leaders and their competing households and patrimonial courts only. Very much as with the Late Antique Abbasids discussed in part one, Seljuk power and authority were never a merely top-down achievement and never evolved along any linear trajectory of rise, efflorescence, decline, and fall. Seljuk history of the 11th and 12th centuries developed along a far more contingent and erratic pathway, involving many and diverse moments of ups and downs as well as the integration, agency, and empowerment of growing numbers of actors beyond the Turkmen and Turkic-speaking leaderships at the different centers of Seljuk dynastic power. One of the leading experts of Seljuk history, David Durand-Guédy, recently surmised one aspect of this ongoing revisionist imagination of the complexity of Seljuk power and its history as follows:

> Instead of a uni-dimensional struggle for power (one Saljuq, holding the title of sultan, challenged by other Saljuqs), the political and military life of the period was rather based on two levels of struggles: Turks against Turks on the one hand, Iranians against Iranians on the other hand, each level nurturing alliances outside of their field, as the control of local resources by [Saljuq] actors was only possible through the collaboration with local Iranian actors.[22]

The performance, consolidation, and accommodation of Seljuk trans-regional leadership involved the active involvement of numerous local and regional elites who, with their administrative as well as military knowhow, with their local and regional connections, and with their own rivalries and ambitions, actively contributed to the emergence of a new trans-regional political and social order in Islamic West-Asia. This order was awkwardly organized around the overlapping rivalries, interests, and practices of Seljuk (and post-Seljuk) leaders and households, of these urban elites and their own clients and followers, and undoubtedly also of many others.

Traditional imaginations of Seljuk power also tended to appeal to—as also alluded to in Durand-Guédy's distinction between 'Turks' and 'Iranians'—a functional division between Turkic-speaking "men of the sword" on the one hand and Arabic and Persian-speaking "men of the pen" on the other, and these two clear-cut categories of wielders of violence and of knowledge may well have been integral to the organization and representation—including in ceremonials and attire—of ruling households and courts. This ideal division of the labor of power was, however, continuously cut across by actual relationships of loyalty and obligation that secured the elimination of rivals, the protection of clients, the reproduction of status and power, and indeed 'the control of local resources' that were a central concern for all.[23] Similar segmentations of groups and identities were present, or at least represented, everywhere in the diverse urban and rural landscapes of Seljuk Islamic West-Asia, from Damascus to Kashgar and from Turkmen pastures in remote Asia Minor to densely populated urban centers such as Bagdad and Isfahan. Very often, the different markers of these segmentations provided for similar functional categories that divided different leaderships of potential strongmen, rivals, and allies along various and very real socioeconomic, cultural, intellectual, or ideological lines of divergence, and that clustered not just socially or symbolically but increasingly even spatially around different urban neighborhoods or rural territories. Besides Turks and Iranians, prominent further social dichotomies that were regularly appealed to in often very specific, locally determined combinations to rally, justify, or explain power constellations include those of nomad pastoralists versus agriculturalists and urban populations, Hanbali traditionalists versus Shi'ites as well as versus Ashʿarite rational theologians among Bagdad's urban elites, Hanafi jurists versus Shafiʿis in Nishapur's and eventually also Isfahan's urban leaderships, Iraqis versus Khurasanis among the Malikshahid *kuttab*, or Ismaʿili Shi'ites versus everyone else in Syria, Iraq, and Iran.[24] Realities, however, were always far more complex, and those men of power who proved most successful were often those who managed to transcend and reconfigure at least some of those apparent divisions, either in their own actions, or by mediating relationships that brought distinct groups and interests together in new power constellations.

2.2 *Nizam al-Mulk between Seljuk transformations and the Nizamiyya*

As Durand-Guédy insisted, Seljuk trans-regional leadership such as that was formed and transformed around Tughril, Alp Arslan, and Malik Shah in the 11th century or around Muhammad Tapar, Sanjar, and Tughril III in the 12th century, around their post-Seljuk peers, and around their different practices of conquest and court patronage, represented only one—albeit a dominant one—dimension in these complex local and regional realities. Another central, even exemplary, role in this mediation of relationships of local, regional, and trans-regional power is traditionally attributed to the brokerage of a remarkable convergence of later 11th-century elite interests by the Khurasani *katib*, courtier, and mighty vizier Nizam al-Mulk (1018–1092).

The historical record of Seljuk history remembered the central figure of Nizam al-Mulk not simply as a dominant patrimonial agent at sultan Malik Shah's court, but as another paragon of the ideal Muslim vizier in loyal service of the new format of Islamic sovereignty: the sultanate. This ideal representation includes attributing to Nizam al-Mulk a defining role as one of the aforementioned 'men of the pen' in the organization of the power apparatus of Alp Arslan and his son Malik Shah, and presenting his story thus as a prime example to be used in debates about the value of *kuttab* for Muslim men of power. This particular view on Nizam al-Mulk also derives from the book of royal advice that he composed in Persian shortly before his death, 'The Book of Administration' (*Siyasetnameh*), also known as the 'Conduct of Kings' (*Siyar al-Muluk*), and that soon acquired its own exemplary reputation and thus added to its author's fame as a highly talented vizier and courtier. An interesting specimen of this particular, functional hindsight representation of the figure of Nizam al-Mulk may be found in a 13th-century abridgement of a 12th-century Arabic chronicle of Seljuk history, written by one of these *kuttab*.

> [Niẓām al-Mulk] became vizier at a time when the order of the realm was weakened, and the decrees of religion had been altered at the end of the Daylamite dynasty [i.e., the Buyids] and the beginning of the Turks' dynasty [i.e., the Seljuks]. The lands had been destroyed by their toing and froing, and were impoverished and depopulated. Hostile hands took control of them and became strong, while mourners bewailed the territories and the calamities [that had befallen them]. [Niẓām al-Mulk] restored the realm to order, and religion to its proper state. He made the provinces flourish and he built constantly. The custom was that taxes were collected from the land and spent on the army; previously no one had held a land-grant [*iqṭāʿ*]. Niẓām al-Mulk realised that taxes were not being collected from the land owing to its poor condition, nor was revenue being realised for the same reason. He distributed land-grants [*iqṭāʿ*] to the soldiers and made them a source of income and property for them. They therefore had an incentive to make [the lands] prosper, and in the shortest time they returned to the best state of adornment. The sultan had relatives by marriage who prided themselves on their relationship to him, on account of which they continually claimed that they were his kinsmen. [Niẓām al-Mulk] clipped their wings and prevented them from causing harm. He ruled the masses with prudence and arranged their affairs with his policy. . . . With his pen he apportioned the kingdom which had been won by the sword in the best way, and carried out the most just assessment of the land. He investigated endowments (*waqf*s) and public works and established trustworthy men in their charge.[25]

What stands out from this fragment is not just its argument in favor of the centrality of *kuttab* and their appeal to 'just' procedures and 'trustworthy men' as opposed to 'the toing and froing' of the 'Turks' and of the sultan's relatives, but also the centrality and autonomous agency of Nizam al-Mulk. This is suggestive not simply of the heroic top-down framing of Seljuk power that determined many contemporary representations, but of the competitive parallels that can be drawn between this author's hero Nizam al-Mulk and the equally central role that was traditionally attributed to sultan Malik Shah himself, as in the afore-quoted representation in a Persian chronicle of the trans-regional extent, effectiveness, and exemplary nature of Malik Shah's rule, from 'the mighty Kaʿba' over 'the hunting grounds in Iraq and Khurasan' to 'the land of Transoxania'. What transpires above all from contemporary and later representations—beyond the narratives of exemplarity and *kuttab* specialty—is in fact this general picture of Nizam al-Mulk's empowerment not simply as a Seljuk agent, but as a man of trans-regional power and authority in his own right, whose own entourage transformed the landscapes of Seljuk power between Khurasan and Iraq and between the mid-11th and mid-12th centuries as much as Seljuks and Malikshahids did, and whose legacy was equally enduring, in discourses of power as much as in its practice.

Significant aspects of Nizam al-Mulk's own life story include his Khurasani origins in a local Perso-Iranian family that served as Ghaznavid *kuttab* and agents before the expansion of Seljuk power in the 1040s and his transfer to and active service in the entourage of the young Alp Arslan in Khurasan in the 1050s. He then became ever more actively involved in the rapid trans-regional empowerment of Alp Arslan's Khurasani leadership in the 1060s, which also included Nizam al-Mulk's active participation in the sultan's endless military campaigns and even his own successful command of military operations. This not only transformed him into much more than a mere 'man of the pen', but generated his centrality in the struggle for Alp Arslan's succession in the early 1070s, which was won by Nizam al-Mulk's Seljuk candidate Malik Shah and allowed him to secure the continuity in Seljuk power of Alp Arslan's household and entourage, as constructed by him.

Nizam al-Mulk is actually increasingly credited for the trans-regional networks of Khurasani *kuttab* and relatives, of his own military agents and *ghilman*, and of particular infrastructures and resources that he managed to construct around his own person and authority in parallel with the Seljuk networks of his overlords Alp Arslan and Malik Shah. This convergence in the person of Nizam al-Mulk of leadership of his own household and of centrality in trans-regional networks of power makes that this particular power constellation is often identified as the Nizamiyya. Although many of Nizam al-Mulk's peers and competitors in the entourages of Malik Shah and of other Seljuk leaders and rulers undoubtedly had similar clienteles to support them, it was Nizam al-Mulk's particular achievement to have made the Nizamiyya into a cohesive trans-regional set of networks of power that were uniquely spread across the main urban centers of Khurasan, Iran, Iraq, and the Jazira. The relative stability of Malik Shah's reign in the 1070s and 1080s, therefore, was not simply a function of this sultan's centrality in the expanding dynastic constellation and patrimonial apparatus of Seljuk family rule and of his sustained priority in its trans-regional wielding of Turkish violence. It was above all due to the symbiotic relationship that continued to tie the latter factors to the Nizamiyya, as represented by Nizam al-Mulk's double role both as Seljuk vizier and kingmaker of Malik Shah and as the patrimonial leader of his own network of power at the same time.

This stabilizing dual relationship always remained a highly competitive one, and it came under very high pressure in the early 1090s, from both dynastic and patrimonial rivals, especially from the aforementioned 'mistress of Isfahan', Malik Shah's powerful spouse Terken Khatun, and her main ally, Nizam al-Mulk's direct rival and peer Taj al-Mulk, with his own clientele of mostly non-Khurasani, particularly Iraqi, background. When this rivalry intensified, it not only culminated in the murder of Nizam al-Mulk in October 1092 and perhaps even in the death of Malik Shah shortly afterwards. The scramble for a new configuration of leaderships that followed opened opportunities for these competitors as well as for multiple other actors to try and emulate Malik Shah's and Nizam al-Mulk's powerful examples. The direct competitors and descendants of both—including not just Malik Shah's sons and amirs, but also at least nine of Nizam al-Mulk's sons and their progeny—started to appear from 1092 onwards in varying reconfigurations of their predecessors' alignments, especially from the 1120s onwards with Malik Shah's son and successor Sanjar in Khurasan.

2.3 The expansion of Nizam al-Mulk's infrastructures of power: **waqfs, madrasas, khanqahs,** *and the politics of knowledge*

What tends to be remembered as equally significant to explain Nizam al-Mulk's centrality and autonomous agency are the arrangements that enabled Nizam al-Mulk—just as many of his peers and competitors—to construct his Nizamiyya network of agents, resources, and ideas. These revolved in highly diverse and pragmatic ways around a specific set of infrastructures that originated in Abbasid and post-Abbasid contexts and that complemented in increasingly intensive ways the roles that—in Abbasid and post-Abbasid contexts, as well as in Seljuk and post-Seljuk contexts—elite households, royal courts, and apparatus of central power played as mediators of relationships of power, dynamics of integration, and flows of resources. These new mediating infrastructures became ever more central in the social, economic, and cultural lives of Islamic West-Asian elites from the time of Nizam al-Mulk onwards, and participated in arrangements that tied these elites together in all kinds of local, regional, and trans-regional circuits of resources, people, and articulations of Islamic sovereignty and identity and that did not necessarily overlap with parallel arrangements that were emanating from the era's dynastic courts. These multivalent infrastructures that operated as alternative platforms to arrange and structure relationships of power, patronage, and agency basically consisted of the built religious infrastructures of the *madrasa* and the *khanqah*, and the religio-economic infrastructure of the *waqf*. The *madrasa* refers to a mostly urban space that is entirely designed and equipped for education in and development of especially religious knowledge, primarily Sunni jurisprudence [*fiqh*], as well as for the employment and potentially even accommodation of the practitioners of these knowledge practices. The *khanqah* refers to another urban space that similarly caters especially for Sufi practices and the housing of Sufi adherents. The *waqf* is an Islamic legal instrument that allows for personal assets to be transformed into an inviolable and non-taxable religious endowment that provides for religious needs and services, including salaried positions, boarding facilities, and library collections for teachers and students in a *madrasa* or for Sufi masters and their followers in a *khanqah*. In their combination and insertion in the Seljuk world's urban and rural landscapes of elite membership and resources, these particular infrastructures actually enabled leaders such as Nizam al-Mulk to widely extend the access and control of their

Figure 8.4 Khargird (Iran): Remains of the main *iwan* (vaulted open hall) and courtyard of one of the first Nizamiyya *madrasas* (*c*. 1068)

Source: Photo by E. Herzfeld, 1925. Copyright © Herzfeld Papers, Freer Gallery of Art and Arthur M. Sackler Gallery Archives, Smithsonian Institution, neg. 2976.) https://archnet.org/sites/3867/media_contents/1066

personal networks of supporters, clients, and interests towards local communities, leaderships, resources, and discourses of power. These infrastructures, furthermore, appear to have allowed such networks of alternative arrangements to retain substantial power and autonomy while simultaneously also tapping into, and becoming entangled with, the different patrimonial apparatus of amirs, *kuttab*, viziers, courtiers, privileges, and resources. As suggested above, the latter apparatus came and went with the person and authority of Seljuk leaders such as Alp Arslan and Malik Shah. At the same time, these apparatus were constructed by Nizam al-Mulk and his peers along the post-Abbasid, especially Ghaznavid, models that they knew best, and they were used to the best of their abilities by Seljuk agents, Perso-Iranian viziers, and any other brokers of Seljuk power to eliminate their rivals, protect their clients, and accumulate sufficient resources to maintain the cohesion and autonomy of their empowering networks within the legitimating context of the Seljuk sultanate.

Nizam al-Mulk is especially remembered for setting up an extensive range of funded *madrasa*s across Khurasan, Iran, Iraq, and the Jazira, including in Nishapur, Marv, and Herat in the east, in the Seljuk center of Isfahan, in Basra and Bagdad in Iraq, and in Mosul in the Jazira. He appears to have been using these investments to promote his Khurasani and Transoxanian followers and supporters and connect them with local elites, patrimonial resources, and alternative networks of knowledge. The pattern that emerges actually suggests no less than a favoring of a particular—Shafiʿi legal and Ashʿari theological—vision on the ancient Islamic sovereignty and identity nexus by employing renowned Ashʿari and Shafiʿi scholars to teach at these *madrasa*s, to further develop and transmit their knowledge, and to actively participate in the many debates that continued to rage between traditionalists, Shi'ites, rational theologians, legal scholars, philosophers, Sufi master, and many others.[26]

Thus, the most famous of these Nizamiyya *madrasa*s, in Bagdad, allegedly opened in 1066, positioned Nizam al-Mulk and the Nizamiyya directly and actively at the center of Abbasid-Islamic authority and of that authority's complex relationship with the articulation of Seljuk power and legitimacy. At the same time, it enabled him and his entourage to take up position in the hotly debated—especially with traditionalists—articulation of Islamic legal and theological knowledge traditions by appointing one of the leading legal scholars of the time, Abu Ishaq al-Shirazi (d. 1083), and providing a powerful and stable forum for his Shafiʿi teachings. The equally famous Nizamiyya *madrasa* of Nishapur, in the region of Khurasan, similarly acted as a medium of social power and of active participation in highly vexed debates, in this case by appointing the leading rational theologian al-Juwayni (d. 1085) and giving him the opportunity to teach newly developing Ashʿari rational theology in opposition to—again—traditionalist teachings, which had also been actively espoused by Nizam al-Mulk's predecessor at the center of Seljuk power, Tughril Beg's vizier al-Kunduri (d. 1064). One of al-Juwayni's many students, Abu Hamid Muhammad al-Ghazali (d. 1111), undoubtedly stands as one of the most famous and most important products of these networks of Nizamiyya *madrasa*s and of the intellectual opportunities and political challenges that they represented. Born in Tus in 1058, al-Ghazali was integrated in the Nizamiyya network via his teacher in the Nizamiyya *madrasa* of Nishapur al-Juwayni. After the latter's death in 1085, he was reportedly invited by Nizam al-Mulk to Bagdad. Al-Ghazali taught at Bagdad's Nizamiyya *madrasa* until 1095, when after the murder of its patron, the Nizamiyya network was increasingly directly targeted by its opponents and rivals and al-Ghazali retired to an ascetic life of contemplation and study. Al-Ghazali returned to some Nizamiyya prominence in the period after 1106, when one of the sons of Nizam al-Mulk, vizier for Sanjar in Khurasan and heir to the Khurasani legacy of the Nizamiyya network, offered him a teaching post in the Nizamiyya *madrasa* of Nishapur. In the course of this long career of scholarship at the central spaces of the Nizamiyya in Khurasan and Iraq, al-Ghazali authored a substantial corpus of highly incisive legal, theological, philosophical, and Sufi Islamic texts in Arabic, and occasionally also in Persian. After his demise in 1111 in his own *khanqah* in Tus, these texts were to generate a central, authoritative, and transformative position for his visions in Sunni Islamic knowledge practices across the 'medieval' and early modern world of Islam.

The alternative infrastructures of power and of substantial penetration in and integration of local urban communities, leaderships, resources, and discourses of power that had given shape to the careers and textual legacies of scholars such as al-Ghazali acquired similarly central, authoritative, and transformative positions from the time of Nizam al-Mulk onwards (see next chapters). Already in the 12th century, with the multiplication of Seljuk actors and centers of power, they were increasingly intensely appealed to not just by Seljuk viziers and *kuttab*, but also by *ʿulamaʾ* who pursued positions of local leadership and prestige, by amirs and *atabeg*s with similar ambitions, and even by various Malikshahids in—especially—the Seljuk west.

One of the better studied representative cases of this dynamic of new local arrangements and local leaderships in this, as it were, post-Nizamiyya context is that of the Khujandis in Isfahan. Brought to Isfahan and western Iran from Marv in Khurasan by Nizam al-Mulk to locally represent his interests and lead his Nizamiyya *madrasa*, this family of Shafiʿi jurists transformed in the two decades following Nizam al-Mulk's death into a dominant and autonomous local and even regional Isfahani leadership in its own right. They managed this by combining their continued dominance in local Isfahani networks of landowning and Nizamiyya *waqf* management with a kind of dynastic prestige acquired through their monopolization of the position of Seljuk administrator (*raʾis*) of Isfahan. In the latter capacity, Khujandis mediated the Isfahani leaderships' local interests and the tributary demands of various Seljuk rulers until the 1190s, and they added to this different sets of relations of patronage and clientship with especially Shafiʿi jurists and students in Isfahan as well as in western Iran's and Iraq's major urban centers. The powerful reality of this unusually successful emulation of Nizam al-Mulk's example in western Iran and Iraq—even though in this particular 12th-century case tellingly achieved via relationships of scholarship and local leadership only—as well as the wider reality of the competitive multiplication of that example by various others stemming from within the Nizamiyya as well as increasingly from beyond its powerful clutches, is usefully summed up by David Durand-Guédy. In one of his detailed revisionist discussions of the history of what he calls an "emblematic family" of Isfahan and western Iran, he suggests that:

> The Khujandīs were not the only Khurasani family to have settled in Isfahan; however, they were the one whose fortune was the most enduring. Niẓām al-Mulk's family moved back to Khurasan, [the Hanafi leadership family of] the Khaṭībīs lost their influence [in Isfahan] at the beginning of the . . . 12th century, and the Ṣāʿids (a family from Bukhara who replaced the Khaṭībīs as *qāḍīs*) only became major actors in Isfahan towards the end of the Seljuk rule. The Khujandīs on the other hand played the leader role for over a century, and remained important actors up to the Mongol onslaught [in the 1230s].[27]

Amidst the many transformations of the 12th century, similar local reconfigurations of components of the Nizamiyya and of its different relationships with competing Malikshahid courts and patrimonial agents actually empowered all kinds of varieties of local and regional elites and their clienteles, at least up to the more disruptive changes in the Seljuk east and west from the 1150s onwards. Their success inspired many to pursue parallel practices of political integration of local—administrative and increasingly also religious—urban elites and resources. However, the relative stability that had characterized the symbiotic alignment of two very different but tightly knit sets of relationships and arrangements of power across much of Islamic West-Asia in the 1070s and 1080s—the one Malikshahid, the other as it were Nizamid—was never achieved again in similar centripetal ways by any of the 12th-century successors of Malik Shah or for that matter of Nizam al-Mulk.

Notes

1 See Chamberlain, "Military Patronage States and the Political Economy of the Frontier, 1000–1250" (quote from p. 152).
2 al-Kashgarī (1005–1102), *Dīwān Lughāt al-Turk* ['Compendium of the Turkish Tongues']; translation from Dankoff, "Qarakhanid Literature and the Beginnings of Turco-Islamic Culture".
3 See Bulliet, "Economy and Society in Early Islamic Iran".
4 (Pseudo)al-Husaynī (*c.* 1180–1225), *Akhbār al-Dawla al-Seljukiyya* ['The Reports of the Seljuk Dynasty']; translation from Bosworth, *The History of the Seljuq State.*
5 See Hanne, *Putting the Caliph in His Place.*
6 See Fletcher, "Turco-Mongolian Monarchic Tradition".
7 See Peacock, *The Great Seljuk Empire*, 131–4.
8 See Hillenbrand, *Turkish Myth and Muslim Symbol. The Battle of Manzikert.*
9 See Peacock and Yıldız, *The Seljuks of Anatolia.*
10 See Paul, *Lokale und imperial Herrschaft im Iran des 12. Jahrhunderts.*
11 Chamberlain, "Military Patronage States and the Political Economy of the Frontier", 142.
12 Kay Kā'ūs ibn Iskandar (fl. 11th c.), *Qābūsnāmah* ['The Book of Qābūs']; translation from Peacock, *The Great Seljuk Empire*, 172.
13 Peacock, *The Great Seljuk Empire*, 185–8.
14 al-Rāvandī (d. *c.* 1202), *Rāḥat-i Ṣudūr va āyat-i surūr dar tārīkh-i āl-i saljūq* ['The Gentle Beginnings and Words of Joy Pertaining to the History of the Family of Seljuk']; translation from Lewis, *Islam from the Prophet Muhammad to the Capture of Constantinople. Volume I: Politics and War*, 73–4.
15 See Peacock, "Court Historiography of the Seljuk Empire in Iran and Iraq".
16 Ibn al-Athīr (d. 1233), *al-Kāmil fī l-Tārīkh* ['The Complete History']; translation from Hanne, *Putting the Caliph in his Place*, 127; Peacock, *The Great Seljuk Empire*, 179.
17 Ibn al-Athīr (d. 1233), *al-Kāmil fī l-Tārīkh* ['The Complete History']; translation from Peacock, *The Great Seljuk Empire*, 97.
18 al-Rāvandī (st. *c.* 1202), *Rāḥat-i Ṣudūr va āyat-i surūr dar tārīkh-i āl-i saljūq*. ['The Gentle Beginnings and Words of Joy Pertaining to the History of the Family of Seljuk']; translation from Lewis, *Islam from the Prophet Muhammad to the Capture of Constantinople. Volume I: Politics and War*, 76.
19 Paul, "Sanjar and Atsız", 93.
20 Nishapuri, *Seljuknāme* ['The Book of the Seljuks']; translation from Peacock, *The Great Seljuk Empire*, 109.
21 Paul, "Sanjar and Atsız", 82.
22 Durand-Guédy, "New Trends in the Political History of Iran under the Great Saljuqs", 329.
23 See Paul, *Lokale und imperiale Herrschaft im Iran des 12. Jahrhunderts.*
24 See Bulliet, *Patricians of Nishapur*; Durand-Guédy, *Iranian Elites and Turkish Rulers.*
25 Al-Bundārī (fl. *c.* 1220s), *Zubdat al-Nuṣra wa-nukhbat al-ʿUṣra* ['The Quintessence of the *Nuṣra* and the Gist of its Extract'], an abridgement of ʿImād al-Dīn al-Iṣfahānī (1125–1201), *Nuṣrat al-Fatra* ['The Delivery from Weakness']; translation from Peacock, *The Great Seljuk Empire*, 69–70; Bosworth, "Towards a Biography of Niẓām al-Mulk", 302–4.
26 See Safi, *The Politics of Knowledge in Premodern Islam.*
27 Durand-Guédy, "An Emblematic Family of Seljuq Iran: The Khujandīs of Isfahan", 184.

Selected readings

Başan, A. *The Great Seljuqs: A History* (London, 2010)

Bosworth, C.E. *The History of the Seljuq State: A Translation with Commentary of the Akhbār al-dawla al-saljūqiyya* (London, 2010)

Bosworth, C.E. "Towards a Biography of Niẓām al-Mulk: Three Sources from Ibn al-ʿAdīm", in G. Khan (ed.), *Semitic Studies in Honour of Eward Ullendorf* (Leiden, 2005), pp. 299–308

Bulliet, R.W. *Cotton, Climate and Camels in Early Islamic Iran: A Moment in World History* (New York, 2010)

Bulliet, R.W. "Economy and Society in Early Islamic Iran: A Moment in World History", in V.S. Curtis, S. Stewart (eds.), *The Idea of Iran. Vol. 4. The Rise of Islam* (London, 2009), pp. 44–60

Bulliet, R.W. *The Patricians of Nishapur: A Study in Medieval Islamic Social History* (Cambridge, MA, 1972)

Chamberlain, M. "Military Patronage States and the Political Economy of the Frontier, 1000–1250", in Y.M. Choueiri (ed.), *A Companion to the History of the Middle East* (Chichester, 2005), pp. 135–88

Dankoff, R. "Qarakhanid Literature and the Beginnings of Turco-Islamic Culture", in H.B. Paksoy (ed.), *Central Asian Monuments* (Istanbul, 1992), pp. 73–80

Durand-Guédy, D. "An Emblematic Family of Seljuq Iran: The Khujandīs of Isfahan", in Ch. Lange, S. Mecit (eds.), *The Seljuqs. Politics, Society and Culture* (Edinburgh, 2011), pp. 182–202

Durand-Guédy, D. "New Trends in the Political History of Iran under the Great-Saljuqs (11th–12th Centuries)", *History Compass* 13/7 (2015): 321–37

Durand-Guédy, D. *Iranian Elites and Turkish Rulers: A History of Iṣfahān in the Saljūq Period* (London, 2010)

Fletcher, J. "Turco-Mongolian Monarchic Tradition in the Ottoman Empire", *Harvard Ukrainian Studies* 3/4 (1979–80): 236–51

Hanne, E. *Putting the Caliph in His Place: Power, Authority, and the Late Abbasid Caliphate* (Madison, 2007)

Hillenbrand, C. *Turkish Myth and Muslim Symbol: The Battle of Manzikert* (Edinburgh, 2007)

Hodgson, M.G.S. *The Venture of Islam. Conscience and History in a World Civilization. 2. The Expansion of Islam in the Middle Periods* (Chicago, 1974)

Lange, Ch., Mecit, S. (eds.). *The Seljuqs. Politics, Society and Culture* (Edinburgh, 2011)

Mecit, S. *The Rum Seljuqs: Evolution of a Dynasty* (London, 2014)

Paul, J. *Lokale und imperiale Herrschaft im Iran des 12. Jahrhunderts: Herrschaftspraxis und Konzepte* (Wiesbaden, 2016)

Paul, J. "Sanjar and Atsız: Independence, Lordship, and Literature", in J. Paul (ed.), *Nomad Aristocrats in a World of Empires* (Wiesbaden, 2013), pp. 81–129

Peacock, A.C.S. "Court Historiography of the Seljuk Empire in Iran and Iraq: Reflections on Content, Authorship and Language", *Iranian Studies* 47 (2014): 327–45

Peacock, A.C.S. *Early Seljūq History: A New Interpretation* (London, 2010)

Peacock, A.C.S. *The Great Seljuk Empire* (Edinburgh, 2015)

Peacock, A.C.S., Yıldız, S.N. *The Seljuks of Anatolia: Court and Society in the Medieval Middle East* (London, 2013)

Safi, O. *The Politics of Knowledge in Premodern Islam: Negotiating Ideology and Religious Inquiry* (Chapel Hill, 2006)

9 'Medieval' transformations in West-Asia's Euphrates-to-Nile Zone—Part 1

'Franks', Zengids, and Ayyubids (1095–*c.* 1260)

Introduction: situating post-Seljuk, post-nomadic, and 'medieval' western Islamic West-Asia

Among the handful of West-Asian regions where, in the 12th century, the political integration of, on the one hand, local resources and administrative and religious urban elites and, on the other hand, Seljuk and post-Seljuk amirs and *atabeg*s happened in stabilizing ways, the Jazira and Syria in the west certainly stood out. Between the Upper Tigris and Upper Euphrates in the north and the Jordan valley in the south the aforementioned descendants of Malik Shah's gatekeeper (*hajib*) Aqsunqur (d. 1094) and especially of the latter's son, the *atabeg* Zengi (d. 1146), managed to build up their own, increasingly autonomous, households and courts, eliminate rivals and expand their authority, and acquire centrality in most of these regions' local and regional networks of power.

From the mid-12th century and the collapse of Sanjar's Great Seljuk rule in the east onwards, this post-Seljuk Zengid order in the Jazira and Syria even appeared as an ever more central pole of attraction for diverse administrative and religious elites. These mostly urban elites not only had local roots in the Jazira and Syria, but also increasingly many of them stemmed from post-Malikshahid and post-Nizamiyya backgrounds in the east, or even from very different North African and Andalusian contexts. All found in these western regions of Islamic West-Asia ever more infrastructures of courts and of *waqf*-related *madrasa*s and *khanqah*s that could mediate their integration. All encountered here diverse groups of patrons, peers, and audiences ready to appreciate their skills, expertise, and knowledge, either in the limelight of Zengid and post-Zengid power and authority or in many of its margins. Many *'ulama'*, in particular, experienced in this dynastic limelight all kinds of opportunities to engage with ever more explicitly and more exclusively Sunni-oriented reformulations of the Islamic identity-sovereignty nexus. Many of them, indeed, participated actively in what used to be identified in 20th-century historical scholarship as the intellectual, religious, and ideological program of the 'Sunni revival' or the 'Sunni renascence', and what is today more modestly considered from a processual and centering perspective of a slow and contested closing of dominant political, intellectual, and cultural-religious ranks around a tradition-based and, at the same time, ambiguous consensus about both what it meant to be Muslim and how charismatic leadership in the Prophet's footsteps over a diverse but self-conscious and exclusively Sunni Islamic community should be realized.[1]

Others among the aforementioned main regional and trans-regional leaderships that dominated many of Islamic West-Asia's networks of power in the later 12th century, from the Rum Seljuks in Asia Minor, over the Eldigüzids in Azerbaijan, the Abbasid caliphs in central Iraq, and the Salghurids in Fars, to eventually also the Khwarazm Shahs in most of Iran,

Khurasan, and Transoxania, continued to be serious competitors for the Zengids and their networks of power, authority, and patronage, and from the 1170s also for the direct heirs of this Zengid centrality in Jaziran, Syrian, and ultimately even Egyptian networks, the originally Zengid *amir* Saladin (d. 1193) and different generations of his Ayyubid relatives. At the same time, these multiple Zengid and then also Ayyubid leadership networks acquired a post-Seljuk—defined by reconfigurations of Seljuk arrangements—cohesion and coherence and a 'post-nomadic'[2] urban centering that soon made them appear as pertaining to a new sovereign and explicitly Sunni Islamic trans-regional order. This was an order of power-holders and their elimination of rivals, protection of clients, accumulation of resources, and dynastic reproduction that, especially in the 13th century, more successfully than any other post-Seljuk leadership confronted the challenges of renewed westward Inner-Asian migrations on an unprecedented scale. The Seljuk and post-Seljuk trajectories of these Zengid and Ayyubid urbanizing leaderships in the Jazira, Syria, and Egypt, therefore, will be discussed in this chapter, whereas Chapter 10 will focus on the highly stabilized further 'medieval' trajectory of these leaderships' major legacy in these regions, the Cairo Sultanate. The renewed westward migrations of Inner-Asian nomadic leaders and their violence-wielding followers from the early 13th century onwards—this time in the format of Mongols and subsequently also of so-called Turko-Mongols—and their effects on other post-Seljuk leaderships in eastern and northern West-Asia will be the subject of Chapters 11 and 12. The interaction between all of these new post-Seljuk and Inner-Asian leaderships on the one hand and, on the other hand, diverse and equally mobile local resources and urban elites, mediated by Seljuk and post-Seljuk infrastructures and mechanisms of power and giving shape to trans-regional processes of 'medieval' identity formation such as the 'Sunni centralization', will be not only an important subtext for this and the next three chapters, but also the focus of more detailed reconstruction in Chapter 13.

The appearance of greater stability, coherence, cohesion, and urban integration in the trajectories of Zengid and then Ayyubid leaderships in the Jazira, Syria, and Egypt between the mid-12th and mid-13th centuries does not mean that these trajectories did not continue to face, as in the wider context of Seljuk and post-Seljuk West-Asian leaderships, substantial pressures. Here, too, the formation of Zengid and then again Ayyubid courts and patrimonial military agents enabled *amir*s and *atabeg*s to build-up their own households and networks of power, as Zengid or Ayyubid military administrators or in name of a young Zengid or Ayyubid, and, in due course, to even organize their own regional and trans-regional power constellations, as happened with the Zengid *amir*s whose descendants made for the Ayyubids and with the Ayyubid *amir*s who usurped Ayyubid rule. The Zengid and subsequently also Ayyubid emulation of the Seljuk practice of appanage contributed in these 12th- and 13th-century contexts too to the regular disintegration of Zengid and Ayyubid households, courts, and power constellations, to the repeated weakening of Zengid and Ayyubid cohesion and trans-regional authority across the regions of the Jazira, Syria, and Egypt, and to the regular appearance of opportunities for dynastic members, agents, or outsiders to rival their peers. In fact, the remarkable post-Seljuk pattern that continues to emerge in these regions, even all the way up to the early 16th century, is that of patrimonial military agents, amirs, who manage to seize exceptional opportunities and take over and transform, from within, their former patrons' contested dynastic leaderships and centrality in Syro-Egyptian networks of trans-regional power. This was the case with Saladin and the Ayyubids replacing their Zengid overlords in the later 12th century, and was most successfully repeated by the late Ayyubid *mamluk*, or military freedman, Qalawun (r. 1279–1290) and his Qalawunid successors from the later 13th century onwards, by the late Qalawunid amir Barquq (r. 1382–1389; 1390–1399),

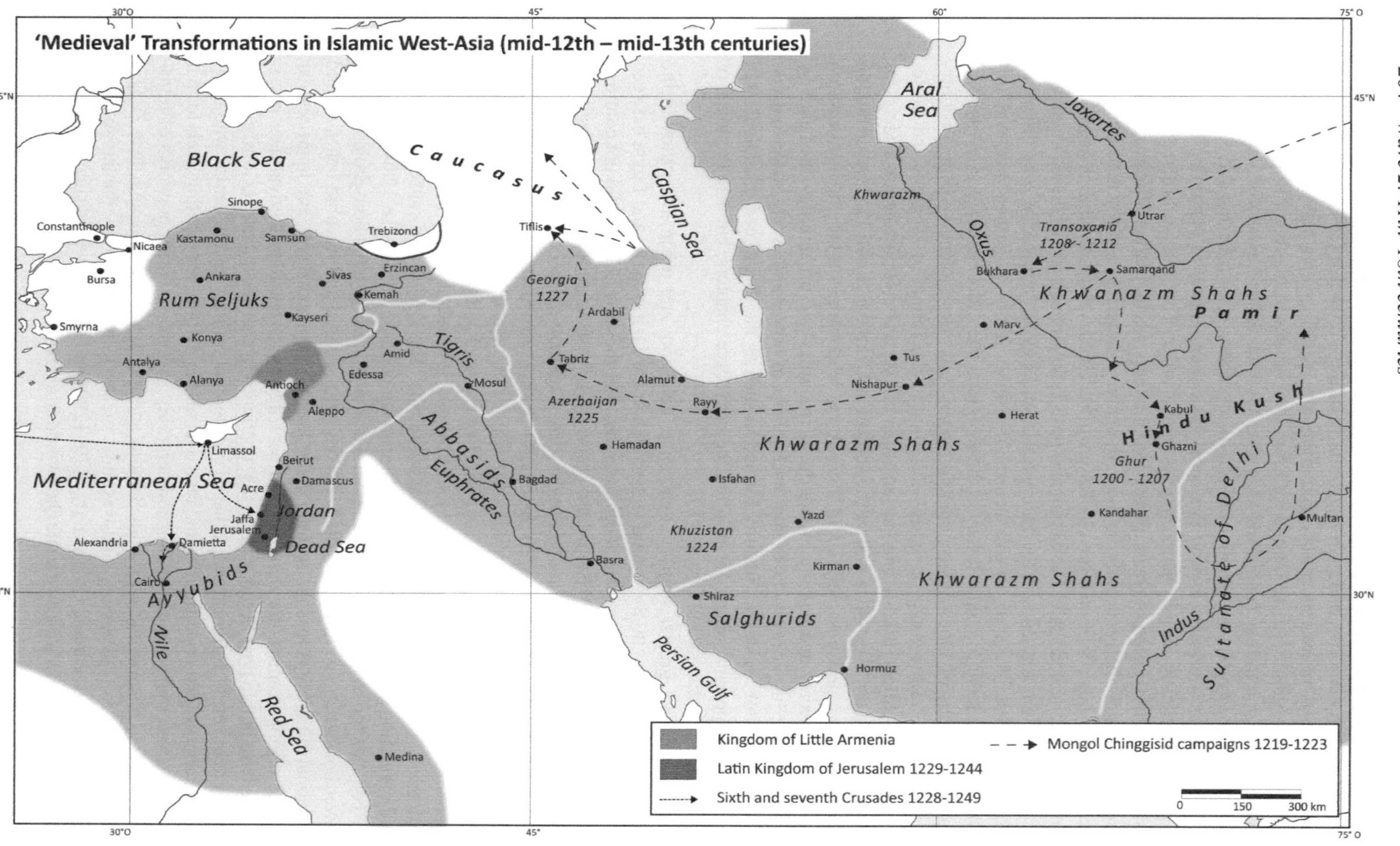

Map 7 'Medieval' Transformations in Islamic West-Asia (mid-12th–mid-13th centuries)

Source: Redrawn from Hodgson, *The Venture of Islam. Vol. 2. The Expansion of Islam in the Middle Periods*, p. 277

and the Barquqids in the 1380s, 1390s, and early 1400s, and then between 1412 and 1517 in dynastically far less successful ways by at least seven very powerful Syro-Egyptian sultans who all similarly rose to prominence as *mamluks*, amirs, and senior courtiers in the households, military apparatus, and courts of Barquq and of several of his successors—often their own predecessors in the sultanate.

As before, however, this post-Seljuk pattern of the repeated trans-regional empowerment of dynastic amirs never concerned any straightforward processes of first integration and then disintegration of patriarchal and patrimonial relationships of dynastic authority. It rather manifested itself in far more contingent ways, amidst a messy whole of regular iterations of both integration and disintegration, and often even occurring simultaneously, with some Zengid, Ayyubid, Qalawunid, Barquqid, or sultanic domains experiencing integration and others its opposite. Only very occasionally these ambiguous processes appear to have intensified and coalesced, mostly in the respective presence or absence of new or old charismatic central leadership. Even more occasionally, in the course of these 'medieval' centuries, this intensification seems to have generated truly transformative dynastic effects, as in hindsight turns out to have been the case for the contexts of trans-regional rivalry and violence that marked the 1170s, the 1250s, the 1380s, the 1400s, the 1420s and 1430s, the 1450s and 1460s, and the turn of the 15th to 16th centuries.

At the same time, in these particular dynamic cases and their highly revealing pattern of repeated dynastic and patrimonial transformation from within, many 12th- to 16th-century continuities in terms of people, practices, resources, values, infrastructures, and geographies of power actually contributed—despite endless moments of dynastic and patrimonial competition, confrontation, and fragmentation—to that above-mentioned appearance of an ever greater Syro-Egyptian stability, coherence, and cohesion. These ranged from the fact that many rose to prominence and power along the model of the *atabeg* Zengi and his father, the Malikshahid *ghulam* and Turkic-speaking amir Aqsunqur, over the remarkable centrality in these successive 'medieval' power constellations of Jaziran and Syro-Egyptian urbanities, eventually topped by the metropolis of Cairo and its court citadel, to Abbasid and Seljuk forms and mechanisms of power, with especially the amirate, the '*atabeg*-ate', the caliphate, and the sultanate continuing to embody the sovereignties, hierarchies, and privileges that were time and again claimed for those constellations.

These particular Jaziran, Syrian, and eventually also Egyptian cases of dynastic, patrimonial, and wider sociocultural changes as well as continuities interacted, moreover, in many constitutive ways with the threats, challenges, and opportunities that emanated from yet another series of violent migrations and expansions. At the end of the 11th century, an entirely new group of wielders of violence had appeared in the far west of the rapidly changing landscapes of Islamic West-Asia. These came from the Latin Christian northwestern margins of Eurasia, in pursuit of their own set of intrusive leadership ambitions, but acting on a much smaller scale and with far more limited success than Turkic-speaking leaders and their followers had been, and continued to be, doing across most of Islamic West-Asia.

The full scope and meaning of the popular migration and campaign of military conquest to 'the Holy Land' that occurred from the core regions of the Latin West in the later 1090s—later remembered as 'the first crusade'—and of many subsequent Latin campaigns and expansions into Islamic West-Asia's Far West should be understood first and foremost in the specific context of the history of the medieval Latin West. However, in the 12th and 13th centuries in particular, the local and regional effects of these campaigns in the western parts of Islamic West-Asia were substantial, in the form of Latin lordships that at one point in the 12th century held the region of Syria in a powerful Latin-dominated embrace, controlling its Mediterranean littoral and its points of contact with Fatimid Egypt in the south and with Turkmen Asia Minor in the north, and stretching from the Sinai in the south to Edesssa—al-Ruha in Arabic, later known as Urfa in today's southeastern Turkey—in the north. In fact, Latin lords became, from the early 12th century onwards, active partners in the fragmented and competitive Syro-Iraqi landscape of *amirs*, *atabegs*, sultans, caliphs, viziers, and many others, and their expansionist politics made them, in the second half of the 12th century in particular, into the main rivals for trans-regional pre-eminence of the Zengid ruler Nur al-Din (r. 1146–1174) and of the formerly Zengid *amir* Saladin (r. 1169–1193). This inevitably made a substantial impact on the formation and organization of these leaderships in the Jazira, Syria, and Egypt, and it also left many traces in the articulation of these and subsequent Syro-Egyptian leaderships' claims to sovereignty, and in the further convergence of elite interests and closing of elite ranks around practices, theories, and infrastructures of Sunni Islamic scholarship and identity. The multivalent presence of Latin lordships, as allies and foes, informed various equally competitive local and regional discourses that actually also contributed to the apparent stabilization of that complex Jaziran, Syrian, and Egyptian landscape of fragmented leaderships and contested identities. Therefore, before reconstructing the general trajectories of that stabilization under Zengids and Ayyubids in this chapter's second part, and by different Cairo sultans in the next chapter, a generalizing appraisal of these campaigns and expansions from the Latin West, and of their local and regional effects in particular, merits some attention in this chapter's first part. They represented after all another one of the different building blocks that defined the highly complex and dynamic landscapes of power, sovereignty, and identity that made for post-Seljuk, post-nomadic, and 'medieval' western West-Asia.

1 Frankish conquest practices and 'crusades'

1.1 The 'first crusade' (1095–1099), 'Frankish' conquest practices, and Arabo-Islamic memory

The campaign of pilgrimage, penance, and violent expansion that advanced from the heartlands of the Latin West to its so-called 'Holy Land' on the Syrian littoral in the later 1090s was undertaken in response to a widely spread call to arms from the Latin Pope Urban II (r. 1088–1099). Its particular design and course were defined by a much wider variety of spiritual, social and political concerns, interests, and contingencies that aligned and collided between the 1070s and early 1100s in the Latin West, in the Greek Roman world of the emperor of Constantinople, in Turkmen Asia Minor, and in Seljuk and Fatimid Syria.[3] In the spring of 1096, several armies—allegedly some 60,000 men strong—advanced from the core regions of the Latin West eastwards. Important leaders were figures such as Raymond of Toulouse (d. 1105), Bohemond of Taranto (d. 1111), Godfrey of Bouillon (d. 1100), and Baldwin of Boulogne (d. 1118). Between November 1096 and June 1097, these armies gathered near Constantinople, where—according to contemporary Greek reports—these so-called 'Franks' were welcomed with anything but open arms.

> [The Emperor Alexios I Komnenos (r. 1081–1118)] heard a report of the approach of innumerable Frankish armies. Now he dreaded their arrival for he knew their irresistible manner of attack, their unstable and mobile character and all the peculiar natural and concomitant characteristics which the Frank retains throughout; and he also knew that they were always agape for money, and seemed to disregard their truces readily for any reason that cropped up.[4]

In the summer of 1097, the combined Latin and Greek-Roman armies took the urban center of Nicaea from the Rum Seljuk leadership that had been establishing itself in the west of Asia Minor since the 1070s, and they returned it to the Emperor. Subsequently, in the Battle of Dorylaeum, they gained another hard-won victory over the Turkmen and their Rum Seljuk leadership. This turned out to be an important moment in the trajectory of this joint campaign, as a result of which it gradually began to claim some attention in Seljuk Syria. A contemporary from Damascus—similarly referring to these commanders and their armies from Latin Europe as 'Franks' [*firanj—ifranj*]—recorded the following account of this military confrontation:

> In this year there began to arrive a succession of reports that the armies of the Franks had appeared from the direction of the sea of Constantinople with forces not to be reckoned for multitude. As these reports followed one upon the other, and spread from mouth to mouth far and wide, the people grew anxious and disturbed in mind. The [Rum Seljuk] ruler, Dā'ud ibn Sulaymān ibn Qutulmish, whose dominions lay nearest to them, having received confirmation of these statements set about collecting forces, raising levies, and carrying out the obligation of Holy War. He summoned as many of the Turkmens as he could to give him assistance and support against them, and a large number of them joined him along with the troops of his brother. His confidence having been strengthened thereby, and his offensive power rendered formidable, he marched out to the fords, tracks, and roads by which the Franks must pass, and showed no mercy to all of them who fell into his hands. When he had thus killed a great number, they turned their forces against him, defeated him, and scattered his army, killing many and taking many captive, and plundered and enslaved. The Turkmens, having lost most of their horses, took to flight. The King of the Greeks bought a great many of those whom they had enslaved, and had them transported to Constantinople. When the news was received of this shameful calamity to the cause of Islām, the anxiety of the people [in Damascus] became acute and their fear and alarm increased.[5]

In spite of heavy losses due to hardships and skirmishes along the difficult journey through Asia Minor, around October 1097, these 'Franks' began the long and legendary siege of the Syrian urban center of Antioch, which was only successful in June 1098. Meanwhile, a small force (led by Baldwin of Boulogne) advanced to Edessa in the east, which was taken relatively easily in the course of 1098. The remaining 'Frankish' forces continued to roam around northern Syria somewhat aimlessly until, eventually, the march towards the south was undertaken and the heavily decimated armies—allegedly only 6,000 men strong by this time—took Jerusalem on 15 July 1099. The contemporary Damascene historian, *adib*, and *katib* Ibn al-Qalanisi (1073–1160) recorded the following stories he claims to have heard about this 'Frankish' marsh on and siege and conquest of Jerusalem—with its wider coastal hinterland a bone of violent competition between Seljuks and Fatimids since the early 1070s, and only recently returned to Fatimid control:

> Thereafter they proceeded towards Jerusalem, at the end of Rajab (middle of June) of this year, and the people fled in panic from their abodes before them. They descended first upon al-Ramla, and captured it after the ripening of the crops. Thence they marched to Jerusalem, the inhabitants of which they engaged and blockaded, and having set up the tower against the town they brought it forward to the wall. At length news reached them that [the Fatimid vizir] al-Afdal was on his way from Egypt with a mighty army

> to engage in the Holy War against them, and to destroy them, and to succour and protect the city against them. They therefore attacked the city with increased vigour, and prolonged the battle that day until the day-light faded, then withdrew from it, after promising the inhabitants to renew the attack upon them on the morrow. The townsfolk descended from the wall at sunset, where upon the Franks renewed their assault upon it, climbed up the tower, and gained a footing on the city wall. The defenders were driven down, and the Franks stormed the town and gained possession of it. A number of the townsfolk fled to the sanctuary [of David], and a great host were killed. The Jews assembled in the synagogue, and the Franks burned it over their heads. The sanctuary was surrendered to them on guarantee of safety on the 22nd of Shaʿbān (14th July) of this year, and they destroyed the shrines and the tomb of Abraham.[6]

Compared to later renderings in Arabic historiography of these events, this contemporary account represents a rather limited narrative that highlights in particular the violent change of leadership from Fatimids to Franks and the fate of the Jewish population of Jerusalem. From the later 12th and early 13th centuries onwards, under the impetus of the instrumental role that the memory of this event and of its effects on the political landscape of Syria would come to play, the same story is told rather differently. An early 13th-century Arabic chronicle of universal history, written at the court of one of the later Zengid rulers of Mosul and a seminal text for later understandings of 11th- and 12th-century history, contains a far more detailed version of the same narrative, full of symbolic and apocalyptic allusions. Most importantly, by identifying the protagonists as Franks and Muslims, the narrative as quoted below is newly framed as part of a wider confrontational relationship between Muslim and Latin Christian monotheists, and it is thus made to participate actively in the particular, negative imagination of that relationship as that became ever more central, and instrumental, in competing discourses of Islamic sovereignty and communal identity that marked the later 12th and early 13th centuries:

> After [the Franks'] arrival they besieged the town for some forty days. They constructed two towers, one on the Mount Zion side, but the Muslims burned it and killed all those inside it. After they had burned it, a call for help came as the town had been taken from the other side. They took it in the morning of Friday, seven days remaining of Shaʿbān (= 23 Shaʿbān/15 July). The population was put to the sword, and the Franks remained in the town killing the Muslims for one week. A group of Muslims barricaded themselves into David's Tower and fought on for three days. The Franks granted them safe-conduct and they surrendered it. The Franks honoured their word, and the group left by night for Ascalon where they remained. The Franks killed more than 70,000 people in the Aqṣā Mosque, among them a large number of Muslim imams and scholars as well as devout and ascetic men who had left their homelands to live lives of pious seclusion in this venerated place. The Franks stripped the Dome of the Rock of more than forty silver lanterns, each of them weighing 3,600 dirhams, and a great silver lamp weighing forty Syrian pounds, as well as a hundred and fifty smaller silver lanterns and more than twenty gold ones, and a great deal more booty. Refugees from Syria reached Baghdad in Ramaḍān, accompanied by the judge Abū Saʿd al-Ḥarawī. They held in the *dīwān* a speech that brought tears to the eye and wrung the heart. On Friday they went to the principal mosque and begged for help, weeping so that their hearers wept with them as they described the sufferings of the Muslims in this venerated town: the men killed, the women and children taken prisoner, the homes pillaged. Because of the terrible hardships they had suffered, they were allowed to break the fast.[7]

1.2 Latin lordships between West-Asian integration and confrontation

Around 1100, after this and a few more victories (especially at Ascalon, on 12 August 1099, against a Fatimid relief force from Egypt), about 300 Latin knights and their entourages are reported to have remained in the coastal lands of southwestern Syria to consolidate their hold of Jerusalem and its hinterland. Ultimately, four new Latin-Christian feudal lordships emerged in the regions between southeastern Anatolia and the Egyptian Sinai, often rather anachronistically referred to in modern scholarship as 'the crusader states'. These were led by the Latin Kingdom of Jerusalem (1099–1187 /1291), briefly ruled by the aforementioned Godfrey of Bouillon (d. 1100) and then by his brother Baldwin of Boulogne (d. 1118). The other lordships were the Principality of Antioch (1098–1268), the County of Tripoli (1102–1289), and the County of Edessa (1098–1144). Their 'Frankish' elites, mostly composed of Latin nobles and citizens, ruled various local populations who were active in trade and agriculture and consisted of eastern Christians and Jews as well as Muslims.

These Latin lordships soon became integral participants in the highly complex, unstable, and competitive Syro-Iraqi landscape of Seljuk and post-Seljuk leaderships. For many decades, they actually continued to appear as active local and regional partners as well as

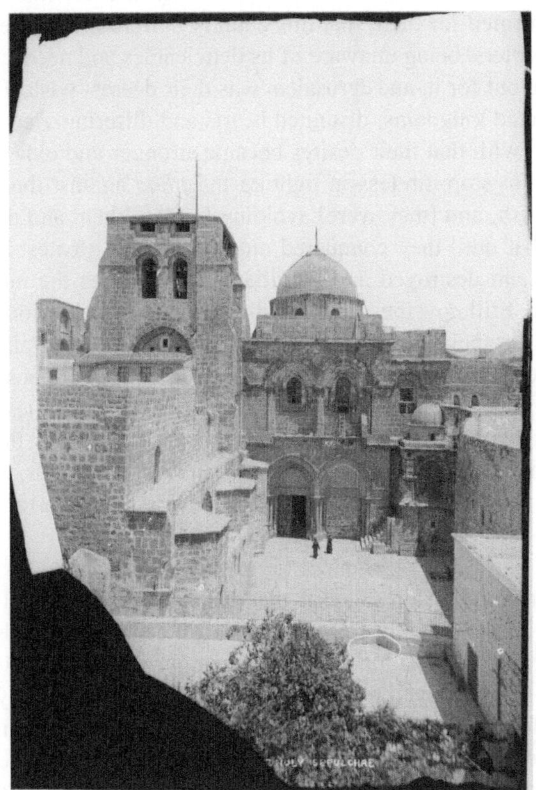

Figure 9.1 Jerusalem: Façade of the Church of the Holy Sepulchre

Source: Photo by American Colony Photo Department, *c.* 1900–20. Matson Photograph Collection, Call Number LC-M31–63, 'Church of the Holy Sepulchre and surrounding' www.loc.gov/pictures/collection/matpc/item/mpc2004000314/PP/

occasional opponents and rivals for trans-regional pre-eminence amid the complex webs of Syro-Iraqi relationships of power.[8] The latter was especially the case in the reigns of the kings Baldwin III (r. 1143–1162) and his brother Amalric of Jerusalem (r. 1162–1174), both born in the kingdom during the reign of their parents, king Fulc (r. 1131–1143) and queen Melisende (r. 1131–1161), herself the product of the mixed marriage of king Baldwin II (r. 1118–1131) with a local Greek-Armenian princess.

Despite all the partnerships, alliances, circulation, and deep Syro-Iraqi integration, however, in certain milieus the distinctly Latin identity of these lordships was not so easily forgotten, nor was the religious fervour and ambition that had brought their predecessors to the east, allowed them to take Jerusalem, and generated a new non-Muslim leadership in the Syrian heartlands of Islam. One of the best-known representatives of these milieus was a preacher from Aleppo, al-Sulami (d. 1106), who in his 'Book of Effort on God's Path' (*Kitab al-Jihad*) combined a wide-ranging apocalyptic analysis of his times with an appeal for closing Muslim ranks and formulating an adequate response to what he represented as an orchestrated Latin assault on Islamic leaderships in the entire Mediterranean.

> A number [of Franks] pounced on the island of Sicily while they disputed and competed, and they conquered in the same way one city after another in al-Andalus. When the reports confirmed for them that this country suffered from the disagreement of its masters and its rulers' being unaware of its deficiencies and needs, they confirmed their resolution to set out for it, and Jerusalem was their dearest wish. They looked out over Syria, on separated kingdoms, disunited hearts and differing views linked with hidden resentment, and with that their desires became stronger and extended to what they all saw. They did not stop, tireless in fighting the *jihād* against the Muslims. The Muslims were sluggish, and [they were] avoiding fighting them and they were reluctant to engage in combat until they conquered more than their greatest hopes had conceived of the country, and destroyed and humiliated many times the number of people that they had wished. Still now they are spreading further in their efforts, assiduous in seeking an increase [in their profits]. Their desires are multiplying all the time because of what appears to them of the [Muslims'] abstinence from [opposing] them, and their hopes are invigorated by virtue of what they see of their enemies' contentedness with being unharmed by them, until they have become convinced that the whole country will become theirs and all its people will be prisoners in their hands. May God in his generosity humble their ideas by bringing together everyone and arranging the unity of the people, for he is near, and answers [prayers].[9]

Traditionally, modern scholarship suggests that despite the efforts of al-Sulami and a handful of others after him, it was only from the mid-12th century onwards that a more coherent, effective, and explicitly Islamic counter-campaign—often identified as no less than a 'counter-crusade'—was deployed to confront this Latin presence in Syria and the Jazira.[10] However, the usefulness of this framing to represent a complex and multivalent set of 12th- and 13th-century actions and discourses revolving around Islamic leaderships and their vexed relationships with these Latin lordships has been seriously questioned in the recent decade (see also Chapter 13).[11] Nevertheless, it is clear that regional balances of power entered a new state of flux from the mid-12th century onwards, as a consequence of the empowerment of Baldwin III and Amalric and as also suggested by the conquests of Edessa in 1144 and of Jerusalem in 1187 by post-Seljuk amirs (see below).

In each of the latter two cases of substantial territorial transformations, however, successes of Muslim leaders brought about an enormous reaction in the Latin West, resulting in new campaigns of conquest that in scope and number of participants far exceeded the campaign of the later 1090s. These different sets of military campaigns are remembered as 'the second crusade', which took place between 1145 and 1149, and as 'the third' one, which ran from 1188 to 1192. The latter relatively successful set of campaigns, led by illustrious Latin royals such as King Richard I 'the Lionheart' of England (r. 1189–1199) and resulting in the treaty of Jaffa (2 September 1192) and a continued Latin presence in the east, was also the last to advance directly to the Syrian littoral. Subsequent major campaigns, especially between 1213 and 1229, under the leadership of Papal envoys and the Roman Emperor Frederick II (r. 1198/1215/1220–1250), and between 1248 and 1254, led by King Louis IX of France (r. 1226–1270), were all directed towards Egypt, signaling how, from the end of the 12th century, the balance of power and centrality in these regions shifted towards Egypt. This shift was of such a stabilizing nature that in the second half of the 13th century, it could put a definitive end to this dominant presence of Latin Christianity on the western fringes of Islamic West-Asia. In 1291, the last crusader towns on the Syrian coast once again fell into the hands of Islamic leaders—this time the Sultan of Egypt—and the last 'Frankish' lords were driven from Islamic West-Asia. In addition, by this time, the political climate in the Latin world had changed to such an extent that new reactions never again materialized in actual military campaigns to the Holy Land, and that the crusading idea—as far as such

Figure 9.2 Krak des Chevaliers / Hisn al-Akrad / Qal'at al-Hisn, a military stronghold in the western part of Syria. Originating from the middle of the 11th century, it was captured by Latin armies in the course of the first crusade, acquired and rebuilt by the order of the knights hospitallers in the 12th century, and taken by sultan Baybars of Egypt in 1271

Source: Syria, Crac des Chevaliers (Qal'at Al Hosn). iStock

campaigns were concerned—increasingly appeared as a functional political discourse rather than as a practically feasible enterprise.

2 From Seljuk *atabegs* to post-Seljuk *amirs* and sultans: Zengids and Ayyubids

2.1 Zengi and the Zengids

2.1.1 Zengi: from Seljuk atabeg *to post-Seljuk* amir

In the 12th century process of stabilization and centralization of what we will refer to in the remainder of this chapter as the Syrian frontier zone—at the beginning of the century divided and continuously contested among different 'Frankish', Seljuk, and Fatimid leaderships—a crucial role was reserved for the actual agents and heirs of Malikshahid power and authority in the regions around the ancient urban centers of Damascus, Aleppo, and Mosul: the *atabegs*. As suggested before, especially the *atabeg* of Mosul, ʿImad al-Din Zengi (d. 1146), and his descendants, the Zengids, played an ever more central role in this.

Zengi, like many others, was a local and regional powerbroker pursuing the greatest possible autonomy and dominance in the changing Malikshahid power constellations of the early decades of the 12th century. At the same time, however, as the son of one of Malikshah's favored *ghilman*, he remained a loyal representative of the Seljuk trans-regional order, accepting the sovereignty of the Great Seljuk sultan Sanjar and, especially, of his nephews in the junior sultanate of Iraq. Zengi began his career in full service of the latter, as an amir and a military administrator in urban centers such as Bagdad and Basra. In 1127, he was appointed in Mosul as *atabeg* for the young Seljuk to whom this urban center on the Tigris had been assigned. However, Zengi's own ambitions appeared more clearly when, in 1128, he also took control of Aleppo in northern Syria, and he subsequently gained recognition of his leadership over both urban centers from the Seljuk sultan in Iraq. In this period, Zengi appeared increasingly as one of the more successful examples of Malikshahid and post-Malikshahid *amir*s and *atabegs* who, as detailed in the previous chapter, continued to compete in various ways for control over, or access to, networks of power and resources in regional centers and across various territories in, especially, the regions of Azerbaijan, Iraq, Fars, the Jazira, and Syria.

From Aleppo and Mosul, Zengi actually began to expand his leadership in different directions, into the Jazira and Syria from Mosul and Aleppo, and also towards the region of central Iraq. In Syria, Zengi led his entourage and followers on various occasions in the

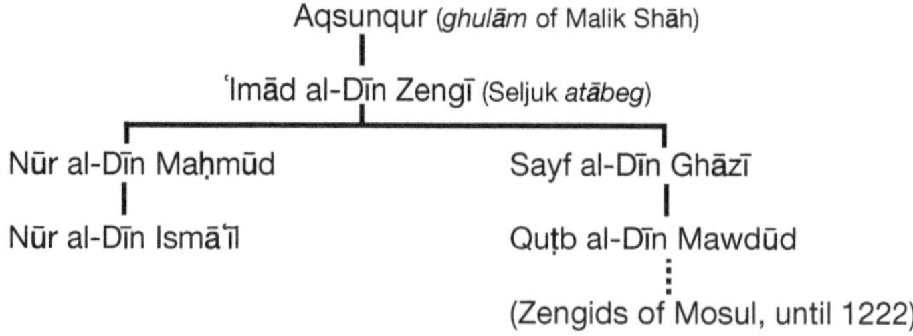

Dynastic Table 4 Simplified dynastic table of the descendants of the Seljuk *atabeg* Zengi, the Zengids

direction of the politically unstable urban center of Damascus, where power was in the hands of the aforementioned descendants of another *atabeg*, the Burids (1104–1154). Zengi's campaigns against Burid Damascus, however, never achieved any substantial results. From 1131 onwards, moreover, he became closely involved in the struggles for succession in the caliphate and the Seljuk sultanate of Iraq. In the end, however, Zengi's candidates and allies did not prevail, and when around 1140, sultan Mas'ud (r. 1134–1152) gained a steady control over relationships of power in Iraq, he appears to have considered Zengi's continued presence in the region of Iraq a liability.

It was, therefore, in the dissatisfying context of these Iraqi alliances, rivalries, and tensions with the Abbasid caliph and the Seljuk sultan that Zengi appears to have intensified his activities as a Seljuk agent in yet another direction and to have occupied himself especially with his 'Frankish' rivals in the region of the northwestern Jazira. In 1144, he was able to exploit the absence of the Count of Edessa, Joscelin II (r. 1131–1145), to take this Jaziran outpost of the Latin presence in West-Asia, and to put an end to the short-lived existence of the Latin County of Edessa. This success and the subsequent territorial expansion of Zengi's leadership—considered by many the first major Muslim victory over 'Frankish' lordships—turned out to offer many new opportunities for Zengi's regional leadership. It offered him above all a tremendous prestige as one of the first Muslim leaders to respond effectively and successfully to the call of al-Sulami and his audiences and peers to close ranks against Latin rule in Syria and the Jazira. It appears, furthermore, to have offered an additional opportunity to the Abbasid caliph in Bagdad, who now found in Zengi a powerful ally in his own competition with the Seljuk sultan of Iraq for sovereignty and for centrality in the region of central Iraq. This is at least the context that helps to explain the caliph's granting to Zengi the right to adopt the titles of 'The Ornament of Islam, Helper of the Commander of the Believers, Ruler under God's Care' (*Zayn al-Islam Nasir Amir al-Mu'minin al-Malik al-Mansur*). This new and highly symbolic titular privilege awarded Zengi his own autonomous position in the hierarchy of the Islamic theocratic order. As 'Helper of the Commander of the Believers', his authority was now represented as directly derived from God's representative on earth, the caliph, without any interference from the Seljuk sultan.

Zengi himself, however, never really benefited much from these changes in his relationships with caliph and sultan and in the territorial reach of his authority. He was reportedly murdered by one of his own domestic slaves in the night of 14 September 1146. In accordance with Seljuk practices, the succession to his leadership was heavily contested among his sons. Eventually, his domains and authority were divided among two of them: Sayf al-Din Ghazi (d. 1149) and Nur al-Din Mahmud (d. 1174). Sayf al-Din Ghazi took Mosul and its Jaziran hinterlands as his Zengid appanage, while the regions from the surroundings of Aleppo to Edessa were taken by his brother Nur al-Din Mahmud. In the further competition for new patriarchal leadership that ensued Zengi's death, it was the latter, Nur al-Din (r. 1146–1174), who eventually turned out to be most successful in stepping in his father's footsteps and expanding his power and authority across most of the Jazira and Syria.

2.1.2 Nur al-Din and the establishment of a Zengid trans-regional order between Egypt and the Jazira

This expansion actually did not only happen at the expense of his relatives in the region of Mosul, but also of the Burids in Damascus and of the sovereign order that continued to be claimed for the Seljuk sultanate of Iraq but that now lost all relevance in these Zengid-dominated regions. The eventual assumption by Nur al-Din of centrality in the Zengid patriarchal power constellation followed his successful campaigning in 1170–1171 against his Zengid rivals in the region of Mosul. This priority was then expressed first and foremost by the mentioning of Nur al-Din's name in the Friday prayer in Mosul's main mosque, which is one of the most important representations of Islamic sovereignty. It was further confirmed by his assignment of Mosul and of other appanages in the Jazira region to some of his nephews, a regional rearrangement of Zengid leaderships that was also confirmed by the caliph without any interference from the Seljuk Sultan. In Syria in the meantime, Nur al-Din had also been

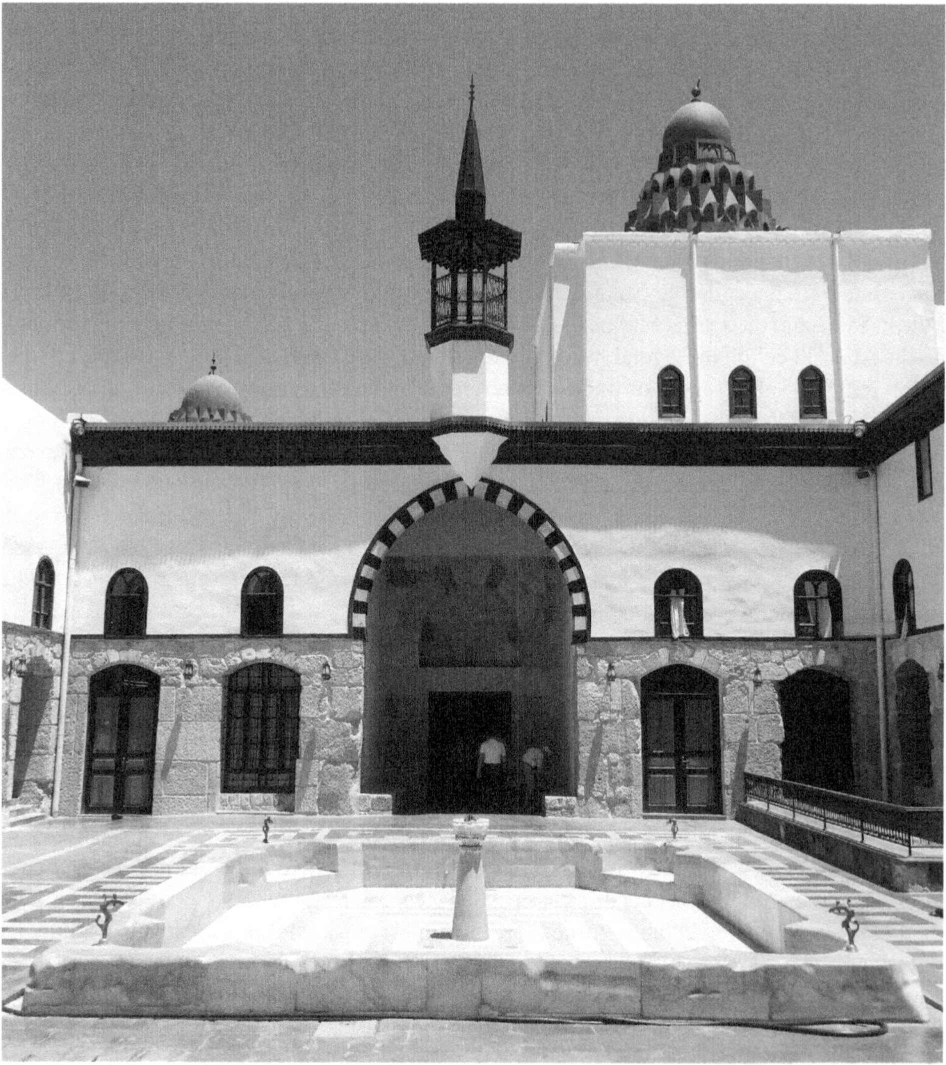

Figure 9.3 Damascus: courtyard and *iwan* of the Nuriyya, a *madrasa* for the teaching of Sunni jurisprudence, constructed by order of Nur al-Din in 1167, and which includes his own mausoleum (below the high dome on the right)

Source: By Bassel Khabbaz. This place is a UNESCO World Heritage Site, listed as Ancient City of Damascus. https://commons.wikimedia.org/w/index.php?curid=62449757

able to take over the role and prestige of his father, among other things, by confronting the so-called second crusade. The latter had attacked Damascus in 1148, but had not produced any real result, which was not least due to a victory won by Nur al-Din near Antioch in 1149. In 1154, this victorious aura finally allowed him to add, after a brief siege, the powerless urban center of Burid Damascus to his territories. Further consolidation of his now widely extended trans-regional leadership was pursued through the elaboration of Nur al-Din's own household and power apparatus, the integration of diverse local elites as active partners of his Zengid authority, and the marginalization or elimination of any remaining rivals, from Zengid competitors in the Jazira over Shi'ite groups and movements in Syria to Latin lords and their Frankish entourages between Antioch and Jerusalem. The relationships with the latter were actually marked by confrontations and violence as much as by the conclusion of agreements and treaties that allowed Nur al-Din to consolidate his dynastic leadership over Zengid and formerly Burid networks of power in the Jazira and Syria. In the best of post-Seljuk traditions, these pursuits were not only directed by different sets of dynastic and patrimonial agents from the vibrant courts—often organized in urban citadels—of Nur al-Din and of his Zengid relatives at Aleppo, Damascus, and Mosul and at the other appanages and towns of the Zengid trans-regional order. They were also mediated by the establishment in many of these urban centers of a number of *waqf*-related *madrasa*s, *khanqah*s, and related infrastructures (including a hospital in Damascus).

From the early 1160s onwards, furthermore, some of Nur al-Din's military agents appeared somewhat unexpectedly as active participants in a highly complicated competition among diverse groups of strongmen and their followers and allies in Fatimid Egypt. This power struggle at the court of the Shi'ite Fatimid caliph in Cairo took on trans-regional proportions when the Fatimid vizier Shawar (d. 1169) linked up on various, alternating, occasions with Nur al-Din as well as with the latter's ambitious Latin counterpart, king Amalric of Jerusalem (r. 1163–1174), to support him against his Fatimid rivals. Both Syrian rulers reportedly saw these invitations to become involved in Fatimid palace politics as excellent opportunities to try and extend the expanding reach of their Syrian authorities towards the region of Egypt and its rich resources. As these expectations were mutually exclusive, Amalric's and Nur al-Din's forces were bound to clash in Egypt.

When Shawar reached out a first time in the period 1163–1164, Nur al-Din actually called on a longstanding military supporter to represent his new interests in Egypt: a post-Seljuk amir of Kurdish Armenian origins known as Shirkuh ibn Shadhi (d. 1169). Together with his brother, Ayyub ibn Shadhi, Shirkuh and their entourages had served various Seljuk *atabeg*s in the 1130s and 1140s before joining the forces of Nur al-Din in Syria, where Ayyub in particular had been instrumental in consolidating and further shaping Zengid authority over formerly Burid Damascus in the 1150s. With his personal army of Kurdish and Turkmen followers and Turkic, Greek, and Armenian speaking *mamluk*s, Shirkuh undertook three expeditions to Egypt, in 1164, 1167, and 1169. These expeditions had varying degrees of success, closely linked to the ways in which Shawar tried to play Amalric and Nur al-Din against each other. In 1169, when Cairo was besieged by the armies of Amalric, Shirkuh returned to Cairo, where he gained an unexpected and final victory and executed Shawar. Subsequently, this military agent of Nur al-Din and new *de facto* strongman in the region of Egypt was promoted to become the new vizier of the Fatimid caliph. When Shirkuh died a mere two months later, his leadership and position as Fatimid vizier were taken over by the nephew that had accompanied him on these expeditions: Yusuf ibn Ayyub (1138–1193), better known by his own ruling title of Salah al-Din, or by its adaptation to Saladin.

After eliminating further rivals and competitors in Egypt—from Fatimid troops and their leaders, especially the so-called *Sudan* or regiment of the 'blacks', to further Latin and even joint Latin-Greek Roman attempts to reverse the new power balance in Egypt—Saladin formally ended the Shi'ite Fatimid caliphate and its longstanding claim to sovereignty and trans-regional Islamic order in September 1171. At that time, supposedly also by order of his Syrian leader Nur al-Din, Saladin deposed the caliph al-ʿAdid (r. 1160–1171), who died only a few days later, isolated any remaining members of his Fatimid family and forestalled their further procreation. At the same time, he actively re-oriented the region of Egypt and its now substantially transformed power constellations towards the symbolic transregional order of the post-Abbasid and post-Seljuk world of Nur al-Din in the Jazira and Syria and of

Figure 9.4 Jerusalem: pulpit (*minbar*) inside the al-Aqsa mosque. This pulpit was made in 1168 by order of Nur al-Din, following a decorative program that was geared towards *jihad* and the reconquest of Jerusalem; eventually, it was only brought from the great mosque of Aleppo to Jerusalem in 1187, by order of Saladin

Source: Photo by American Colony Photo Department/Matson Photo Service, first half of 20th century. Matson Photograph Collection, LC-M32-P-44, 'The Temple Area'. www.loc.gov/pictures/collection/matpc/item/mpc2004005787/PP/

the caliph in Iraq. This continued to be a world of power imagined around the sovereignty of the Abbasid caliph and his delegation of power, as well as around an ever more explicitly formulated anti-Shi'ite and anti-'Frankish' Sunni consensus, in which Saladin's entourage began to style their leader no less than 'the reviver of the dynasty of the commander of the believers' (*muhyi dawlat amir al-mu'minin*). All of this attests especially to how Saladin's empowerment in Egypt enabled him to acquire substantial autonomy and was actually quickly transforming his and his relatives' status from that of loyal Zengid agents and allies to that of formidable foes for Nur al-Din's leadership. This slowly intensifying competition and conflict of interests between Nur al-Din and Saladin seems only to have been resolved by the unexpected death of the former in 1174.

As a result of military actions in support of Shirkuh's Egyptian campaigns, large parts of the Latin territories in Syria had also fallen into the hands of Nur al-Din. In the course of this, a lot of attention had actually been paid to the active development of an ideological component to Nur al-Din's authority, in support of these military campaigns, and also of campaigns against Zengid and other rivals in the region, and calling to close ranks behind the leadership of Nur al-Din, heir of the 'champion of Islam' Zengi and leader in the *jihad* against the 'infidel Franks'. With the addition of Egypt to these territories in 1169, the unification of regional leaderships around this undisputed Islamic rule and the encirclement of the remaining Latin lands was completed. There are actually concrete indications—including a pulpit (*minbar*) that Nur al-Din had built in Aleppo for the al-Aqsa mosque in Jerusalem—that an attack on Jerusalem was indeed in full preparation.

Nur al-Din, however, died in Damascus in May 1174, before such possible plans could be carried out. His territories in Syria and the Jazira were then once again divided as dynastic appanages among a variety of his Zengid relatives. Saladin immediately seized this opportunity to consolidate his leading position and that of his own family over the rich region of Egypt, to formally declare himself autonomous, and to start representing himself accordingly. Again, the momentum and stability of a uniform Islamic leadership seemed lost.

2.2 *Saladin and the Ayyubids*

2.2.1 *Saladin and the reconfigurations of power in Egypt, Syria, and the Jazira*

From 1174 onwards, Saladin promoted himself as the actual successor of the politics and the ideological leadership of the Zengids. This manifested itself until the middle of the 1180s in the gradual conquest or subjugation of Zengid appanages and leaderships in Syria and the Jazira, and in the recognition of his Syro-Egyptian sovereignty by the Abbasid caliph in Bagdad. As early as in 1174, Saladin acquired control over Damascus, where the local Zengid amirs and urban elites had remained loyal to the family of his father and uncle, who, as mentioned, had been Zengid administrators there. In 1183, Aleppo and its Zengid leadership submitted after many years of campaigning and violent confrontations, and by 1186, Saladin's authority also extended to Zengid Mosul, when lasting peace was concluded, his name was mentioned in the Friday sermon, and Zengid military support for his campaigns against the 'Franks' was pledged.

At the same time, in the main urban centers of Syria and Egypt, a newly configured elite of *amirs* and *kuttab*/*'ulama'* was emerging around the household, court, and family of Saladin and his father Ayyub, benefiting both from the many opportunities created by the elimination of Shi'ite Fatimid elites and elite networks in Egypt and from the expanding patrimonial needs and demands of that family, court, and household in Egypt as well as in Syria. Both of these newly composed patrimonial groups of amirs and *kuttab/ʿulamaʾ* having mainly Syrian and Jaziran as well as post-Seljuk and post-Nizamiyya origins in common, they provided Saladin and his entourage with the necessary military force, expertise, authority, and cohesion to locally embed their new presence, to set up and extend new networks of leaderships, and to integrate remaining local elites and their access to diverse sets of local resources in Egypt, Syria, and elsewhere. This process of substantial regional and local transformation took the form, as with the competition with various Jaziran and Syrian Zengids, of endless campaigns of violent action and related threats and negotiations. In the best of post-Seljuk and post-nomadic traditions it also materialized in not only the continued set-up of royal courts, urban citadels, and a basic apparatus of power (including an Egyptian Mediterranean maritime force), but also in substantial investments in other urban infrastructures such as *madrasas*, *khanqahs*, and also economic facilities, and in the extensive personal patronage

Figure 9.5 Cairo: foundation inscription above the 'Gate of the Steps' (*Bab al-Mudarraj*), one of the gates of the citadel. This inscription announces that "the construction of this citadel was ordered by [...] our lord al-Malik al-Nāṣir Ṣalāḥ al-Dunyā wa-l-Dīn Yūsuf b. Ayyūb [=Saladin], restorer of the sovereignty of the commander of the believers [=the caliph], under the supervision of his brother and successor al-Malik al-ʿĀdil Sayf al-Dīn Abū Bakr [=Saphadin] [...] in the year 579 [= 1183–1184]

Source: (photo by Max van Berchem/Flury)8110 photothèque MVS (photo Flury) 1998 www.epigraphie-islamique.org/epi/picture_view_full.php?ref=2156/image/1.jpg

of relatives, amirs, and *'ulama'* more in general (see also Chapter 13). This was done at the new centers of Saladin's power, Damascus in Syria and Cairo in Egypt, as well as in all of the other dynastic appanages and regional centers that were gradually integrated into the orbit of his authority. These now ranged from the Zengid Jazira in the north to the Arabian region of Yemen in the south, where in 1174 one of Saladin's brothers violently established himself, in name of the Abbasid caliph and his brother, as a new regional leader.

By the mid-1180s, therefore, Saladin had acquired, with his relatives, a position of widespread trans-regional power, centrality, and authority—again explained, and performed, in many contemporary contexts from an anti-Shi'ite and anti-Frankish perspective of *jihad* leadership—that allowed him to take action against his last remaining major rival: the kingdom of Jerusalem. Tension between the two had been building up since the early 1180s, and in July 1187, after the death of Amalric's son, the so-called Leper King Baldwin IV (r. 1174–1185) and the disputed succession by his sister Sibylla (r. 1186–90) and her husband Guy of Lusignan (r. 1186–1192), Saladin and his allies and troops gained an overwhelming victory at Hittin, in northern Palestine. They destroyed the kingdom's main military forces and succeeded in capturing Guy and many of the kingdom's nobles with him, leaving its remaining leadership in full disarray. A few months later, in October 1187, Saladin succeeded in concluding this campaign with the successful siege and surrender of Jerusalem, soon followed by his acquisition of most of the kingdom's other towns, ports, castles, and lands. Just as had happened to Zengi and the Zengids with the conquest of Edessa in the 1140s, these victories and near annihilation of the Latin kingdom of Jerusalem awarded Saladin a widely acknowledged aura of immense political, military, and above all ideological prestige, which would continue to support his claims to sovereign power and authority, as well as those of his descendants, as the ultimate champions of Islam and the rightful leaders of its victorious armies.

The almost immediate Latin response to these substantial shifts in the Syrian balance of power gave shape to the so-called 'third crusade' (1188–1192), which was led by illustrious Latin royals such as King Philip II of France (r. 1180–1223), Frederick Barbarossa, king of Germany, Burgundy and Italy and Holy Roman Emperor (r. 1152/1155–1190), and King Richard I 'the Lionheart' of England (r. 1189–1199). This series of campaigns from the Latin West, especially those led by the latter King Richard I, confronted Saladin with the actual limitations of his patriarchal, charismatic, and therefore, highly devolved authority and power. Due to the renewed Latin military strength in the region, the destruction of Saladin's Egyptian Mediterranean fleet by the Latins, and the complex set of regional and local interests that regularly troubled relations with some of his main supporters and allies during these years, Saladin was eventually forced to enter into negotiations with Richard, which were concluded in September 1192. The main result of what has become known as the 'Treaty of Jaffa' was that the presence of Latin lordships in the Syro-Palestinian coastal region, from the reconquered coastal urban center of Acre to Jaffa, remained an inevitable reality. Even the decimated kingdom of Jerusalem continued to exist, albeit in this territorially reduced form and with Acre rather than Jerusalem as its new capital.

Saladin died after a brief illness in Damascus, in March 1193. Despite the setbacks and losses encountered in the years just before his death, his charisma and reputation proved powerful enough to continue to exist long after his death. This is evident from the way in which Saladin was represented in many contemporary and later writings, as an exemplary Muslim leader, both in his deeds and wisdom and in the responsible manner in which he, together with his family and entourage, supported Islamic ritual practices, the arts and sciences, and scholars and *'ulama'*. The following report on these final months of his life by a contemporary author and physician is an insightful representative of this exemplary image that, from very early onwards, came to be constructed around the immense and diverse achievements of Saladin and of his very personal politics of physical force, charismatic authority, family rule, and benevolent patronage.

> The news spread that Saladin had concluded a truce with the 'Franks' and had returned to Jerusalem. Out of necessity I had to go to him. I took as many books by Classical authors with me as I could carry, and left for Jerusalem. I made acquaintance with a great ruler, who stimulates feelings of fear and love with anyone nearby or faraway and who is easy-going and beloved. His companions follow his example and exceed each other in striving to do right. As the Almighty said: 'And We will have removed whatever is within their breasts of resentment' (Q 7: 43).
>
> The first night I spent in his company, I found myself in a big meeting with scholars who were debating different scholarly disciplines. [Saladin] truly excelled in his contribution to, and participation in, [this meeting]. He started [a discussion on] the nature of building walls and digging trenches, showing his expertise in this and [eloquently] presenting every aspect in an original way. At that time, he was occupied with building the walls of Jerusalem and digging its trench, which he himself supervised, carrying stones on his shoulders and making everyone—poor and rich, strong and weak, including even [his personal secretaries] ʿImād al-Dīn [al-Iṣfahānī] and al-Qāḍī al-Fāḍil—follow his example. Before sunrise he would ride to it [and remain] until the time of the noon prayer, when he would come to his residence, offer food, and then rest. He would ride again at the time of the afternoon prayer and would only return when the torches were lit. Most of the night he spent arranging what he had to do during the day.
>
> Saladin wrote [an order] for me [entitling me to] 30 *dīnār* every month from the *dīwān* of the Friday mosque in Damascus, and his sons assigned stipends to me. In this way there was fixed for me [an income of] 100 *dīnār* every month. I returned to Damascus and dedicated myself to studying and lecturing people in the mosque. Every time I devoted myself entirely to the books of the Classical authors, I wished to read them more, and the books of Ibn Sīnā [Avicenna] less. In this way, I was informed about the falsity of alchemy, and I got to know the true story of how it came about, and about who had brought it about and who had been lying about it [. . .]
>
> Eventually Saladin came to Damascus and he went out to bid farewell to the pilgrimage caravan. When he came back, he turned out to have a fever. Someone without any experience bled him, his strength dwindled, and he died before the fourteenth [of the month]. The people felt affected by his [loss] in the same way as they felt for the prophets. I have never seen people mourning a ruler's death in any similar way, because he was beloved by those who are innocent and by those who sin, by Muslims and by unbelievers.[12]

2.2.2 *Saladin's heirs and the contested stabilization of Ayyubid patriarchal authorities*

In accordance with the appanage and leadership practices that had become normative among post-Seljuk elites, in 1193, Saladin's trans-regional authority and territories remained divided and contested among members of his own extended family, henceforth known as the descendants of Saladin's father Ayyub, the Ayyubids. For the next seven decades, until the middle of the 13th century, Saladin's sons, brothers, nephews, and further descendants continued to represent the dominant power constellation in the regions of Egypt, Syria, and the Jazira, and

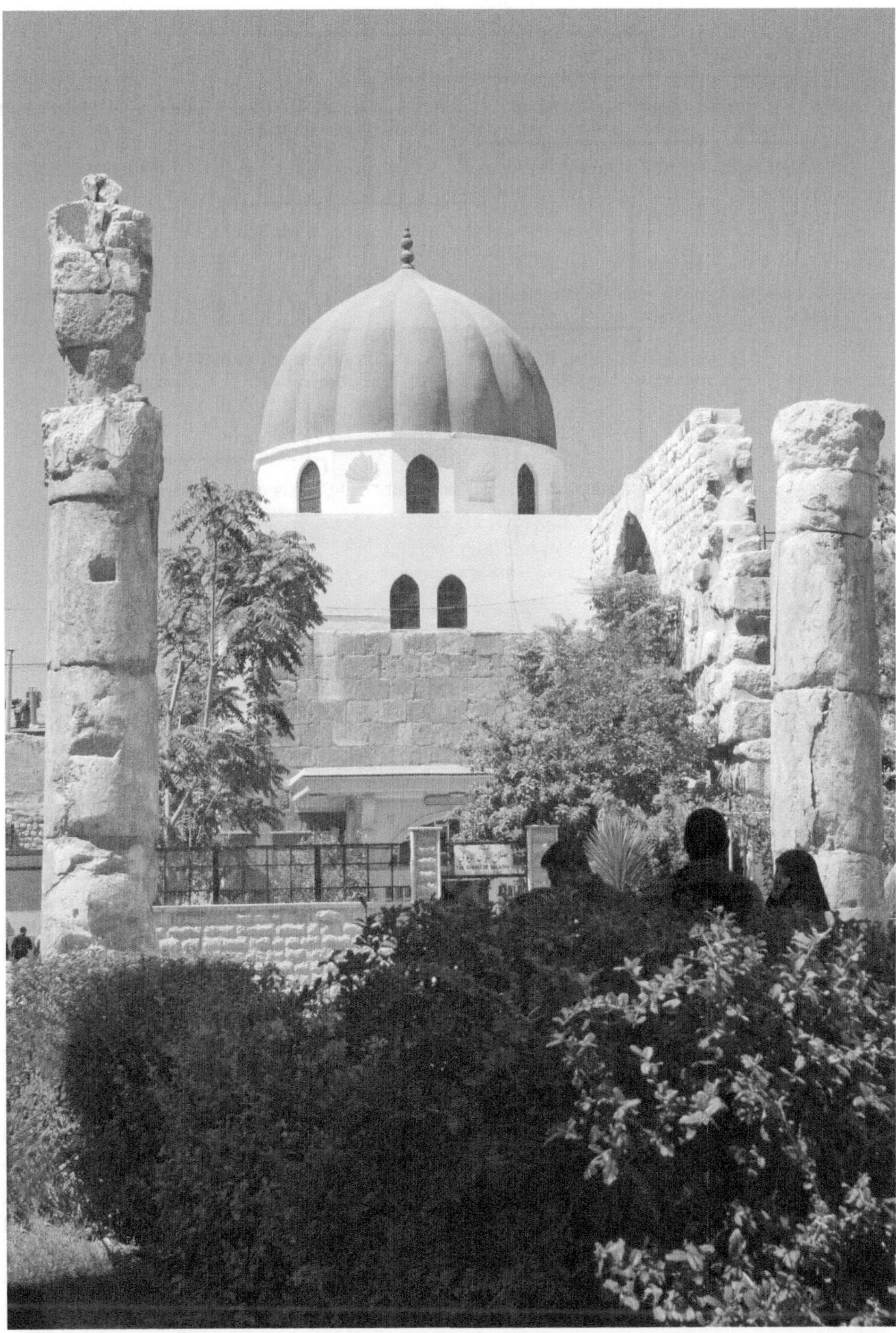

Figure 9.6 Damascus: Saladin's restored mausoleum (with dome), completed in 1195, and remains of the ʿAziziyya, the *madrasa* that Saladin's son al-ʿAziz ʿUthman had constructed next to the mausoleum

Source: Lil Lang/Alamy Stock Photo

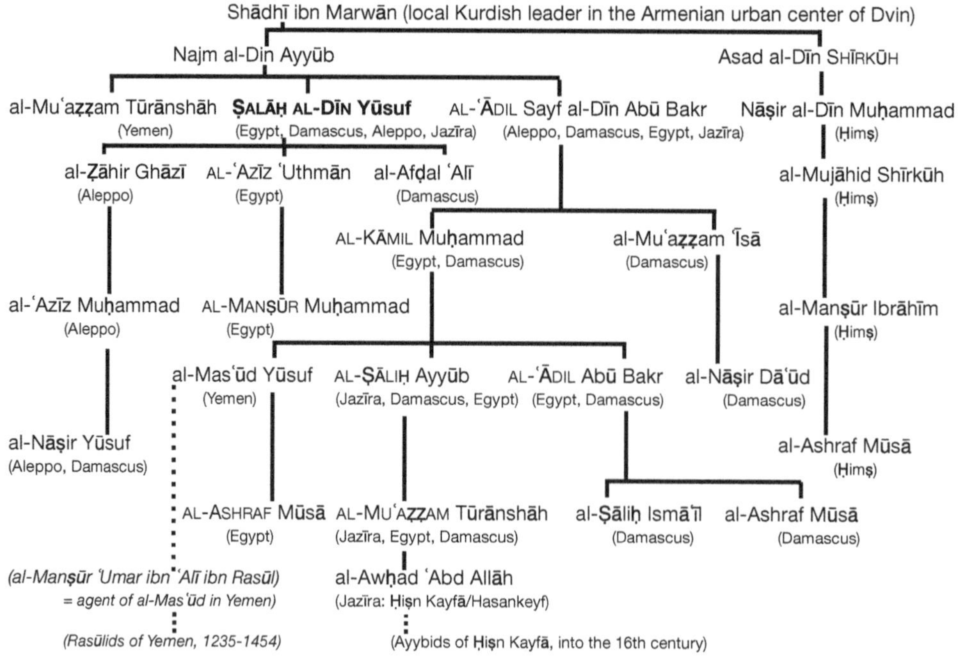

Dynastic Table 5 Simplified dynastic table of the descendants and relatives of Saladin, the Ayyubids (with reference to the region/s under their authority)

the hegemony and control over the networks of power and resources in these regions continued to be mainly divided and contested among the male members of this dynastic lineage.

In this particular Ayyubid power constellation, itself also resembling an expanding trans-regional network of regularly shifting dynastic members and their agents, the administrative and military apparatus of power that emerged around various Ayyubids and their households and courts always remained minimal, *ad hoc*, and very personal in nature. In fact, just as had been the case for Seljuk, post-Seljuk, and for that matter Zengid leaderships in the 12th century, each local or regional center with its hinterland had its own Ayyubid leader, who often was awarded his lands and titles as a dynastic appanage from a father, brother, or nephew, occasionally received assistance from a military *atabeg*, and remained bound to his peers and to the trans-regional Ayyubid order that they represented by complex webs of relationships of kinship, loyalty, obligation and, not least, rivalry and violence. Many Ayyubids (all distinguished with a particular royal title, beginning with 'al-Malik'—'the monarch') thus maintained their own households and royal courts in Cairo, Damascus, Aleppo, Hama, Homs, and in various other smaller towns or strongholds in Egypt, Syria, the Jazira and southeastern Anatolia, and in Yemen.

The practice and infrastructures of patronage that continued to flourish more than ever in this trans-regional context of widely devolved dynastic power and patriarchal authorities and resources made that every Ayyubid leader and his entourage remained closely linked—often in mutually constitutive ways—to many locally or regionally organized communities and networks and their often powerful urban leaderships. In the best of post-Seljuk and

Figure 9.7 Aleppo: citadel, majorly reorganized and reconstructed around the entourages and courts of Saladin's son al-Zahir Ghazi (r. 1193–1216) and his descendants

Source: Creswell Archive, Ashmolean Museum, University of Oxford, neg. EA.CA.5683

post-nomadic traditions, this local embedding and integration of unstable Ayyubid power relations was achieved in symbiotic, mutually accommodating, and often equally contested ways via the mechanisms of *iqta'* and *waqf*, via the mediating urban infrastructures of courts and of *madrasa*s and *khanqah*s, and via participation in ever more intensely pursued forms of Arabic intellectual and literary communication as well as of dynastic, charismatic, and religious reformulations of the Islamic sovereignty and identity nexus (see Chapter 13 for further details).[13]

As time progressed, patriarchal relationships of Ayyubid kinship stabilized to a certain extent around different branches of the family, with Saladin's son al-Zahir Ghazi (d. 1216) and his son and grandson dominating Aleppo and northern Syria until 1260, two lesser branches organizing their households and courts around the central Syria towns of Homs and Hama until 1260 and 1342 respectively, and Saladin's brother al-Malik al-'Adil Abu Bakr (d. 1218) and his sons and grandsons maintaining control over Ayyubid lands and claims to power in the northwestern Jazira and southeastern Anatolia, in southern Syria, in Egypt, and briefly also in Yemen. At the same time, dynastic rivalry and competition continued, focusing in due course in particular on gaining or maintaining control over Damascus and southern Syria, and continuing, therefore, especially to pit al-Malik al-'Adil's sons and grandsons against each other in regularly changing constellations and re-alignments of alliances and interests. In this continuous dynastic competition for access to local and regional networks of power and resources, eventually especially among or with al-Malik al-'Adil's descendants, Ayyubid dominance in the rich region of Egypt, moreover, appeared ever more regularly as an important factor and as a crucial symbolic constituent in any claims to trans-regional Ayyubid sovereignty. In the course of this, the very significant Seljuk title of 'sultan' even started to be used in increasingly formalized ways to distinguish the patriarchal authority claimed by al-Malik al-'Adil's offspring in Egypt from its regional peers, making Egyptian Ayyubid claims to superiority and direct delegation of caliphal authority very explicit and effective. Nevertheless, such claims always remained contested and highly qualified, moments of dynastic instability and disintegration persisted, especially among al-Malik al-ʿAdil's sons and grandsons, and for a long time the formation of more widely interconnected and stable trans-regional relationships of power, centered around the interests and patrimonial agents of the Ayyubid ruler of Egypt, appeared as an unfulfilled ambition of several Ayyubids.[14]

Only occasionally, mainly as a result of external threats such as various renewed campaigns from the Latin West in the early 1200s and again in the early 1220s, different, locally or regionally organized dynastic elites and their military forces closed ranks around the leadership of an Egyptian Ayyubid, and immanent rivalries and competition were—at least temporarily—transcended to deal with the common external rival. The standard situation, however, remained that of extremely complex and conflict-ridden patriarchal relations between Ayyubid households and courts in Cairo, Damascus, and Aleppo, as well as with various other, lesser, or more short-lived Ayyubid lineages, and with ever more brothers, nephews, and cousins keen to improve their and their entourages' appanages and prospects within these more stabilized territorial units of Ayyubid dynastic power. All of this required almost constant campaigning and wielding of violence between militarized households and their leaders, and enormous investments of manpower and resources. In due course—especially from the 1230s onwards—this also offered growing opportunities to those household members and military agents who were involved in the performance of those campaigns and in the management of those investments. As a result of the latter process of empowerment of patrimonial agents, Ayyubid control over the more distant region of Yemen was eventually lost to an Ayyubid military administrator, and his son and further descendants, who successfully adapted to local circumstances of leadership and continued to rule autonomously into the mid-15th century as the Rasulids (r. 1235–1454).[15] The different stabilizing branches of dynastic power and patriarchal authority in the Ayyubid heartlands of Egypt, southern and northern Syria, and parts of the Jazira and southeastern Anatolia proved more tenacious. In the mid-13th century, however, most of them—except in Hama in western Syria and in Hisn Kayfa on the upper Tigris, today's Hasankeyf in southeastern Turkey, where local Ayyubid branches remained in power until 1342 and the second half of the 15th century respectively—had to make way for increasingly powerful Egyptian Ayyubid military agents and representatives. In this the latter Ayyubid amirs were paradoxically supported in their own empowerment by the devastating effects of the Mongol invasion in the period 1259–1260 on the complex Ayyubid power constellation of the regions of the Jazira and Syria (see also the next chapters).

In the seven decades before that happened, however, the main protagonists in these strongly fragmented Ayyubid dynastic constellations were, as mentioned, the brother of Saladin, al-Malik al-ʿAdil Sayf al-Din Abu Bakr ('The Just Monarch, the Sword of the Religion, Abu Bakr'; also rendered in European texts and reports as Saphadin), and his sons and grandsons. This al-Malik al-ʿAdil (d. 1218) acquired centrality in the family and its Jaziran and Syro-Egyptian domains to the detriment of Saladin's sons, from 1200 onwards, at the time of a Latin campaign against Egypt. He is often considered the real organizer of what is also—anachronistically—referred to as the Ayyubid 'confederation'. Al-Malik al-ʿAdil succeeded to re-establish the cohesion of his brother's fragmented trans-regional legacy with the assistance of his three sons, who managed to gain control over the networks of power in the main Ayyubid centers of Cairo, Damascus, and Mayyafariqin in the northwestern Jazira, and by marrying one of his daughters to the descendants of Saladin who continued to control Aleppo and northern Syria. In the period 1218–1221, al-Malik al-ʿAdil's son and successor in

Egypt, al-Malik al-Kamil Muhammad (r. 1218–1238), appeared to be given the opportunity to repeat his father's achievement when a series of major Latin campaigns, later remembered as part of 'the fifth crusade' (1213–1229), inspired Ayyubid competitors for al-Malik al-ʿAdil's legacy to close ranks. In 1221, with the support of his brothers from Damascus and the Jazira and of his cousin from Aleppo, al-Malik al-Kamil prevailed, the Latin army was forced to surrender, and the strategic Mediterranean port of Damietta, in the eastern Nile Delta, was restored to Ayyubid control. Afterwards, however, and until shortly before his death in 1238, al-Malik al-Kamil continued to be forced to engage in a long series of conflicts and confrontations with his brothers and with other relatives in, especially, southern Syria and the Jazira about the actual nature and reach of his leadership over the Ayyubid family. This is one of the reasons why, in 1229, al-Malik al-Kamil agreed to a treaty, strongly criticized by many of his rivals and supporters, with the commander of the 'fifth crusade', the Holy Roman Emperor and king of Sicily, Germany and Italy Frederick II (r. 1198/1212/1220–1250), on the conditional and temporary return of Jerusalem to the Latins.

In 1238, when al-Malik al-Kamil passed away, the different territories in Egypt, southern Syria, and the Jazira that he had with difficulty gained control over were once again left divided as dynastic appanages and domains among, especially, his brothers and his sons. One of these sons, al-Malik al-Salih Ayyub (d. 1249), who had dominated with his personal entourage the region of Hisn Kayfa since 1230, prevailed in the rivalries and competition that ensued, when in 1240 he succeeded in conquering Egypt from one of his brothers. Persisting tensions and conflicts with one of his uncles in, particularly, southern Syria and the region of Damascus eventually culminated in 1245 in an ultimate military confrontation. With the help of groups of raiding Turkic-speaking mercenaries from the east, referred to as the 'Khwarazmians' due to their origins in the entourage of the last Khwarazm Shah (see next chapter), al-Malik al-Salih achieved the final, and reportedly very violent, retaking of Jerusalem from the Latins, and he subsequently defeated an alliance of Ayyubids from Damascus and Latin lords from the Kingdom of Jerusalem at al-Harbiyya (also known as La Forbie), northeast of Gaza. Al-Malik al-Salih thereupon managed to consolidate his power and authority in the regions of southern Syria, Egypt, and the Jazira, and at least symbolically appeared to emulate the achievements of his illustrious ancestor Saladin.

Al-Malik al-Salih's control over the Ayyubid territories that he gained control of from 1245 onwards was actually arranged somewhat differently from before, along more organized chains of authority, representation, and agency that emanated from his royal household and court in Cairo and that would prove a crucial springboard for some of his amirs to usurp Ayyubid power in Egypt, and eventually also in Syria. In the course of the 1230s and the early 1240s, al-Malik al-Salih managed to build up a forceful apparatus of wielders of violence around his person, that is generally credited with making him victorious in several confrontations with Ayyubid and other rivals in the Jazira and Egypt. This personal force of manpower seems to have been organized again, but reportedly in larger numbers than with any of his Ayyubid or wider post-Seljuk peers and predecessors, around several thousands of military slaves and their manumitted commanders. Identified in this context as *mamluk*s rather than as *ghilman*, in this period most of these men were made available as a rich source of manpower for Syria's and Egypt's leaderships by specialist merchants who brought them south from Qipchaq-Turkic-speaking pastoral nomads in the western, or Pontic-Caspian, parts of the Inner-Asian steppes—also often referred to as the Qipchaq steppes (*dasht-i Qipchaq*). This extended household guard of *mamluk*s was named the Salihiyya, after their master's official title of rule, al-Malik al-Salih ('The Virtuous Monarch'). Within the Salihiyya, a central and distinctive role was taken up by an elite corps of several hundreds of selected horsemen, referred to as the Bahriyya after their military headquarters on the island of Rawda in the Nile, locally referred to as *al-bahr* ('the Sea'). Supported by these Salihiyya and Bahriyya forces of horsemen and their commanding amirs, al-Malik al-Salih, moreover, pursued the establishment of greater personal control over his Ayyubid network of leadership and resources that was spread over Egypt, southern Syria, and the Jazira. To achieve this aspired centralization of his authority—an ambition that is also expressed by his formal adoption of the formerly Seljuk title of Sultan—he no longer mainly appealed to the practice of awarding appanages to his closest Ayyubid relatives to represent him locally, but rather increasingly relied on the personal services, expertise, and loyalties of the amirs from the narrow circle of—especially—his Salihiyya and Bahriyya supporters to maintain control over main urban centers, such as Damascus, for him. Amidst the divided and unstable Ayyubid balance of power between Egypt and the Jazira, so it would soon transpire, this combination of effective military organization, centralization, and prioritizing al-Malik al-Salih's amirs seems to have allowed a handful of these amirs and their supporters to be sufficiently experienced, connected, and empowered to start rivalling Ayyubid dynastic monopolies on their own terms, especially when new dynastic changes threatened their interests.

Such changes again announced themselves in the complex conditions and transformations that accompanied al-Malik al-Salih's unexpected death in November 1249, and the succession to his authority in Egypt, southern Syria, and the Jazira by his son al-Malik al-Muʿazzam Turanshah (r. 1249–1250). When al-Muʿazzam Turanshah tried to install, at the center of Ayyubid power in Cairo, his own household, court, and entourage—constructed around his person while he had been ruling Hisn Kayfa after his father, and in his father's name, during the preceding decade—the leading amirs from his father's entourage decided to act first. In May 1250, al-Muʿazzam Turanshah was assassinated, and his throne and authority over Egypt were awarded to a representative of his father's leading amirs. In Syria, moreover, his cousin and Saladin's great-grandson, the ruler of Aleppo al-Nasir Yusuf (r. 1236–1260), marched on Damascus and took control over southern Syria in July 1250. When he attempted to progress further south towards Egypt, however, he was defeated, in early 1251, by al-Malik al-Salih's former amirs. These rapid changes and violent encounters created the new division of power relations that would remain in place, despite ongoing rivalry, across the regions of Egypt, Syria, and the Jazira during the 1250s, with al-Nasir Yusuf ruling Aleppo and Damascus and their expansive and fertile hinterlands in northern and southern Syria, lesser Ayyubid branches—including a son of Turanshah in Hisn Kayfa—continuing to dominate various towns and dynastic appanages across Syria and the northern Jazira, and different amirs vying for post-Ayyubid power, authority, and the Sultanate in Cairo and Egypt.

When the patron of most of these amirs, al-Salih Ayyub, had died in November 1249, he had actually been encamped near the town of al-Mansura in the Egyptian Delta, in full preparation to confront the invading Latin armies of the French crusader King Louis IX (r. 1226–1270). The eventual victory of al-Malik al-Salih's forces, in the mere virtual presence of their recently deceased patron, in the absence of any successor, and followed by the capture of the French king, was in fact instrumental in the *de facto* usurpation of Ayyubid rule over Egypt by al-Salih's patrimonial agents, as well as in its subsequent explanation and legitimation. In direct communication with the remembrance of the successes of Zengi, Nur al-Din, and Saladin on the *jihad* front many decades before, similarly powerful notions of Islamic championship were derived from this victory in the creative representation of al-Malik al-Salih's leadership by his amirs, and in its highly functional reflection on their own agency, as his agents and successors (even though it is reported that their sultan had actually died in a rather unheroic fashion a few days before the final battle, bedridden and succumbing to

Figure 9.8 Cairo: inscription slab above the entrance to the mausoleum of sultan al-Salih Ayyub
Source: Photo: Jo Van Steenbergen

illness in his tent, and with his unwelcome death being kept a secret by his main advisors until after the battle). This creativity in the remembrance of sultan al-Malik al-Salih Ayyub is also suggested in the graphic allusions to his dynastic Ayyubid as well as heroic anti-Frankish leadership in the following memorial inscription, which can still be seen above the entrance to al-Malik al-Salih's mausoleum in the historical center of Cairo:

> In the name of God, the Merciful, the Compassionate. . . . This blessed tomb contains the grave of our lord the sultan al-Malik al-Ṣāliḥ Najm al-Dīn Ayyūb, son of al-Malik al-Kāmil Muḥammad, son of Abū Bakr, son of Ayyūb. He passed away in the grace of God while he was at the place of al-Mansura, confronting the Franks whose defeat was determined, presenting his throat to their swords, turning his face and chest towards the battle.

Notes

1 Berkey, "A Sunni 'Revival'?", in Berkey, *The Formation of Islam.*
2 Adapted from Wink, "Post-Nomadic Empires: From the Mongols to the Mughals" ("post-nomadic… the people who created them, while nomads in origin, had left their pastoral-nomadic lifestyle behind and no longer relied on pastoral nomadism for their subsistence" [p. 125]) to indicate the continued relationship between urbanizing arrangements of power and leaderships' pastoral nomadic origins and backgrounds in—especially—post-Seljuk western West-Asia.
3 See e.g. Bartlett, *The Making of Europe. Conquest, Colonization and Cultural Change, 950–1350.*
4 Anna Comnena (1083–1153), *The Alexiad*; translation from Dawes, *The Alexiad of the Princess Anna Comnena*, 248.
5 Ibn al-Qalānisī (*c.* 1070–1160), *Dhayl Tārīkh Dimashq* ['Continuation of the History of Damascus']; translation from Gibb, *The Damascus Chronicle of the Crusades*, 41.
6 Ibn al-Qalānisī (*c.* 1070–1160), *Dhayl Tārīkh Dimashq* ['Continuation of the History of Damascus']; translation from Gibb, *The Damascus Chronicle of the Crusades*, 47–8.
7 Ibn al-Athīr (d. 1233), *al-Kāmil fī Tārīkh* ['The Complete History']; translation from Hirschler, "The Jerusalem Conquest of 492/1099 in the Medieval Arabic Historiography of the Crusades", 39.
8 See Köhler, *Alliances and Treaties between Frankish and Muslim Rulers in the Middle East.*
9 al-Sulamī (d. 1106), *Kitāb al-Jihād* ['The Book of Effort on God's Path']; translation from Christie, *The Book of the Jihad of 'Ali ibn Tahir al-Sulami.*
10 See Sivan, *L'Islam et la croisade.*
11 Goudie, *Reinventing Jihād.*

12 ʻAbd al-Laṭīf al-Baghdādī (1162–1231) as mentioned in Ibn Abī Uṣaybīʻa (1203–1270), *ʻUyūn al-anbāʼ fī ṭabaqāt al-aṭibbāʼ* (ʻThe sources of information on the generations of physiciansʼ).
13 See Chamberlain, *Knowledge and Social Practice in Medieval Damascus*; idem, "The Crusader Era and the Ayyubid Dynasty"; Hirschler, *Medieval Arabic Historiography: Authors as Actors*.
14 See Humphreys, *From Saladin to the Mongols*.
15 See Vallet, *L'Arabie marchande. Etat et commcerce sous les sultans rasûlides du Yémen*.

Selected readings

(see next chapter)

10 'Medieval' transformations in West-Asia's Nile-to-Euphrates Zone—Part 2

The Cairo Sultanate and 'the reign of the Turks' (*c.* 1250–1517)

Introduction: from 'the Mamluk Empire' to the Cairo Sultanate

By the end of the 1250s, Egypt's leading amirs resolved their internal rivalries and disputes and successfully closed ranks behind the sultanate of one of them to confront their own major external enemy, the Mongols. When that happened, many of them acquired, and further invested in, a centrality in local and regional networks of power and resources across Egypt and across southern as well as northern Syria that soon appeared as far more cohesive, stable, and effective than had been the case with any of their Ayyubid, Zengid, and, for that matter, other post-Seljuk and post-nomadic predecessors in these and adjacent regions. Thus emerged, in the wake of these transformations of the mid-13th century, yet another, more stable, order of leaderships and elite interests in western Islamic West-Asia that continued to be of post-Seljuk and post-nomadic stock—deeply defined by ongoing reconfigurations of formerly Seljuk practical and formal arrangements, topped by the sultanate and *atabeg*-ate, and by an urbanization of these arrangements that simultaneously continued to relate to the pastoral nomadism of these leaderships' origins. The particular historical trajectory of this post-Seljuk and post-nomadic order soon appeared as organized around these late Ayyubid amirs, the regularly renewed ranks of their successors, and the urban military households that they all set up. It would be defined by the continued performance, by many different groups and generations of these household leaderships, of the hierarchies of agency and entitlement that, also inspired by Abbasid and Fatimid precedents, until the early 16th century, would continue to be derived from late Ayyubid forms of authority. This trajectory finally also would continue to revolve around these hierarchies' seats of power, at the citadel of Cairo and at its different local and regional offshoots, especially in formerly Ayyubid Alexandria, Damascus, Homs and Aleppo, in Ayyubid Hama, and eventually even in formerly Latin Syrian centers such as Tripoli, Safed, and al-Karak.

Due to this remarkable stabilization of post-Seljuk power relations around Cairo and its military elites, and given the continued, successful, and prosperous complexity of the centralizing organization of these relationships, an appealing appearance of an equally stable and autonomous administrative and military apparatus of power became dominant in representations and performances of these power relationships, as though a direct, sequential effect of, especially, al-Malik al-Salih's aforemenioned Ayyubid experimentation and its mid-13th-century violent transformations. Moreover, for more than two centuries thereafter, this apparent apparatus and the trans-regional order that it seemed to guarantee continued to be populated and dominated by particular sets of military elites and powerbrokers, many of whom began their Syro-Egyptian careers as household agents, military trainees and freedmen, and valuable merchandise supplied from non-Muslim pastoral nomadic peoples in the north.

Figure 10.1 Cairo: postal card (*c.* 1900) with a view of 'the Mauseolea of the Mamluks and the Citadel'

Source: "Caire: Tombeaux des Mamelouks et Citadelle." 3.5" × 5.4". From the collection of Dr. Paula Sanders, Rice University

As a result of the predominant sharing of this *mamluk* factor across different generations of amirs, both these diverse late Ayyubid, post-Ayyubid, and later groups of military elites and the relatively stable appearance of a Syro-Egyptian bureaucratic order and apparatus with which, and within which, they are presented as operating, are traditionally subsumed in modern scholarship by the notion of 'the Mamluk Empire', 'the Mamluk State', or 'the Mamluk Sultanate'. That scholarship, moreover, consistently tends to apply a 'Mamluk' periodization of this Sultanate's long history, in which regional shifts in the original nomadic-pastoralist identities of the majorities of these *mamluk* elites are prioritized as a parameter to capture some of the bigger changes that this order and its apparatus underwent in the course of the later 14th and early 15th centuries. In this traditional periodization, the year 1382 and the accession to the throne of a *mamluk* sultan of Circassian-Caucasian origins is considered a turning point. The period before 1382 is then identified as that of the Turko-Qipchaq, or Turkish, Mamluks—referring to shared majority origins from Qipchaq-Turkic-speaking pastoral nomads in the western, or Pontic-Caspian, parts of the Inner-Asian steppes—or, especially in earlier 20th century scholarship, also as the era of the Bahri-Mamluks, after the initially important role of the aforementioned Bahriyya of sultan al-Malik al-Salih Ayyub. The long period between 1382 and the violent elimination of the Sultanate's order and leadership by its northern rivals in the years 1516–17 is then defined as that of the Circassian—also, for unclear reasons, the Burji—Mamluks, referring to shared Circassian-Caucasian origins.

This particular imagination of this late 'medieval' Syro-Egyptian Sultanate as a particularly Mamluk and ethnogenetically defined bureaucratic one stems from ideas that certainly already circulated among some of its contemporaries, as with the North African scholar and historian Ibn Khaldun (d. 1406). In his introduction of the history of this Sultanate in his chronicle of Afro-Asian Islamic history, Ibn Khaldun described these *mamluk* origins of its elites in highly florid, appreciative, and defining terms, explaining them as part and parcel of divine providence and as the essence of the Sultanate's continued historical existence, which enabled a regular rejuvenation of its power elites and thus protected it—unlike other Islamic dynasties—from disintegration.

> The [Abbasid] dynastic reign had been immersed in sedentary culture and luxury, it wore the dress of decay and impotence, and it had been afflicted by the Mongol infidels who abolished the [Abbasid] Caliphate and wiped out the splendor of the land and replaced the True Faith by Unbelief. . . . [At this hopeless stage in the history of Islam] it was by the grace of God glory be to Him, that He came to the rescue of the True Faith, by reviving its last breath and restoring in Egypt the unity of the Muslims, guarding His order and defending His ramparts. This He did by sending to [the Muslims], out of his Turkish people and out of its mighty and numerous tribes, guardian *amir*s and devoted defenders who are imported as slaves from the lands of heathendom to the lands of Islam. This status of slavery is indeed a blessing . . . from Divine Providence. They embrace Islam with the determination of true believers, while retaining their nomadic virtues, which are undefiled by vile nature, unmixed with the filth of lustful pleasures, unmarred by the habits of civilisation, with their youthful strength unshattered by excess of luxury.[1]

This highly idealized representation of the Sultanate's dynamics of power and authority, as continuously determined by some redemptive moral qualities assumed to reside in its leaderships' slavery, actually appears as rather limited and particular to be useful to really understand the longevity and complexity of these dynamics. A certain trend in modern historical scholarship is certainly voicing increasing concerns about continued interpretations of the Sultanate's rich and long history merely from these moralizing *mamluk*, corporate, and ethnogenetic frameworks.[2] Rather than a nice and clean mid-13th-century break with preceding leaderships, followed by a long history of power that in its essence just changed once, in exactly 1382, and then in its ethnic appearance only, insightful continuities with Ayyubid and wider post-Seljuk and post-nomadic practices are emphasized. This revisionist trend, moreover, stresses equally insightful parallels with quite a few similar power elites in Islamic West-Asia, such as the aforementioned post-Abbasid Ghaznavids and the post-Seljuk Eldigüzids, Khwarazm Shahs, and for that matter Zengids, who all despite their unfree, Inner-Asian, and Turkic-speaking *ghulam* origins, do not tend to be reduced in modern scholarship to this one aspect among the great variety of factors that defined each of them. This new trend in the study of the Syro-Egyptian Sultanate—which will be foregrounded in the remainder of this and in subsequent chapters—therefore, also tries to understand what is yet different about this Syro-Egyptian Sultanate's leaderships and how, also beyond the mid-13th century, not only these leaderships but also the practices, strategies, and infrastructures of their power and authority continued to transform.[3]

The growing number of available contemporary historical, documentary, and related texts—actually even including by the above quoted Ibn Khaldun—in any case, hardly ever identify this Sultanate as exclusively determined by any *mamluk* property. They consistently speak of 'the Reign of the Turks' (*Dawlat al-Atrak*, *Dawlat al-Turk* or *al-Dawla al-Turkiyya*). By this double signifier, they refer to the more complex reality of a continuous Islamic order of leadership (*dawla*) that is populated by a power elite of diverse composition, the continuous making and remaking of which between the 13th and early 16th centuries involved processes of socialization and elite formation that revolved especially around particular forms and meanings of Turkish-ness. These forms and the Turkish meanings they embodied included leading membership of elite households that originated in amirs' personal histories of enslavement, long-distance transfer, manumission and Syro-Egyptian empowerment; appropriation and articulation of an inclusive and dynamic martial identity—expressed in practices associated with Turkish-ness and ranging from name-giving, over the wearing of precious furs, distinctive headgear, and weapons, to excelling in polo and related arts of horsemanship; and the ability to converse in Qipchaq-Turkic.[4]

Across West-Asia, North Africa, and elsewhere, the bustling metropolis of Cairo and the Sultan's court actually became one of the leading political, socioeconomic, and cultural hubs of the 'medieval' world. For this reason, this longstanding Syro-Egyptian order of the 'Reign of the Turks' will be mainly referred to here as the Cairo Sultanate. This choice is made consciously by analogy with the way in which today's historical scholarship refers to the contemporaneous Delhi Sultanate, on the northern Indian Peninsula, to identify five successive sultanic dynasties (r. 1206–1526), some of which similarly originated in the empowerment of amirs who began their careers as *mamluk*s, as with its first ruler, Aybak (r. 1206–1210), a *mamluk* and amir of the aforementioned post-Seljuk dynasty of the Ghurids, and as also with Aybak's granddaughter Radiyya bint Iletmish (d. 1240), whose father was a Turkic-speaking *mamluk* and one of Aybak's amirs and successors, and who reigned herself as sultana between 1236 and 1240.[5] An equally revisionist distinction will be further made in this chapter's discussion of this Sultanate and its different leadership groups between their reconfiguration in the Ayyubid transformations of the 1250s, their post-Ayyubid dynastic and patrimonial formation in a very long 14th century, and their Turko-Circassian and patrimonial-bureaucratic appearances in an equally long 15th century.

1 Ayyubid transitions and Salihiyya empowerment

As previously mentioned, in the 1230s and 1240s, the Ayyubid sultan of Egypt al-Malik al-Salih Ayyub (r. 1240–1249) had made abundant use of a steady supply at numerous local markets of human merchandise from the Qipchaq steppes north of the Black Sea to organize his military apparatus around the aforementioned personal guard of several thousands of royal *mamluks*, the Salihiyya, and the elite corps of several hundreds of selected horsemen from the Salihiyya, known as the Bahriyya. Moreover, with the support of their sultan and their own military entourages, new amirs, often themselves stemming from the ranks of the Salihiyya and the Bahriyya, had managed to considerably increase their share in the Ayyubid networks of power and resources. As a result, as detailed above and in parallel with many Seljuk and post-Seljuk precedents, from Eldigüzids to Khwarazm Shahs, these amirs from al-Malik al-Salih's entourage eventually managed to usurp Ayyubid power, and the sultanate, first after the victory near al-Mansura in the region of Egypt, and eventually also in the region of Syria, after another victory over a different but even more formidable host of external foes.

More specifically, this was a process that took about ten years of confronting rivals, rallying supporters, and accumulating human and other resources by various senior members of this post-Ayyubid Egyptian leadership. In this long process of the reconfiguration of Egypt's power elites, a major role was played by such particular characters as al-Salih's widow and former concubine of Turkic-speaking Inner-Asian origins, Shajarat al-Durr (d. 1257), and the amir and former food taster (*jashinkir*) and *mamluk* in al-Malik al-Salih's royal household, Aybak al-Salihi (d. 1257). Each of these two was even proclaimed sultan in the course of these years. In the case of Shajarat al-Durr, this concerned a very brief reign of some three months in 1250 only. Organized around the actual (female) strongman of her husband's royal household in Cairo, Shajarat al-Durr's reign was designed to both represent and secure continuity with the power constellation of al-Malik al-Salih Ayyub after the assassination of his son and heir, Turanshah. This is at least suggested in contemporary sources, such as the extant numismatic evidence. This confirms that the rulership privilege of *sikka*—the right to mint Islamic coins bearing the ruler's name and claim to sovereignty—was performed for Shajarat al-Durr, and that this was done by referring to her motherhood of al-Malik al-Salih's deceased son and to her Salihi identity, and also to an authority that was strongly asserted to derive directly from the Abbasid caliph in Bagdad, al-Mustaʿsim (r. 1247–1258). On the central parts of the obverse and reverse of one of the few remaining specimens of these particular coins, a dinar minted in Cairo, these combined Salihi-Abbasid claims and references were formulated as follows:

> The Mustaʿṣimī one, the Ṣāliḥī one (*al-Mustaʿṣimiyya al-Ṣāliḥiyya*);
> Queen of the Muslims; Mother of
> al-Malik al-Manṣūr Khalīl.
> The Commander of the Believers (*amīr al-muʾminīn*),
>
> The Imām al-Mustaʿṣim
> bi-llāh Abū Aḥmad ʿAbd
> Allāh, Commander of the Believers (*amīr al-muʾminīn*).[6]

The failure to get these claims accepted by the Ayyubids of Syria, and reportedly also by the caliph himself, resulted in further changes in Egyptian leadership arrangements.

Figure 10.2 Dinar (gold coin) minted in the name of Shajarat al-Durr (648 AH/1250)

Source: The Trustees of the British Museum. (British Museum: 1849, 1121.294, 'Gold dinar of Shajar al-Durr, Mamluk ruler') www.britishmuseum.org/research/collection_online/collection_object_details/ collection_image_gallery.aspx?assetId=135905001&objectId=1632390&partId=1

While Shajarat al-Durr remained one of the most powerful figures at the court in Cairo, further experimenting led to the enthronement of a young Ayyubid nephew of al-Malik al-Salih, al-Malik al-Ashraf Musa (r. 1250–1254), to the empowerment of the aforementioned Aybak as *atabeg* of this young Ayyubid sultan and also as the new husband of Shajarat al-Durr, and eventually to the assumption of the position of sultan by Aybak himself, adopting the royal style of al-Malik al-Muʿizz ('The Empowering Monarch'). In 1257, however, Shajarat al-Durr reportedly had Aybak assassinated when he threatened to overpower her, and she was then herself beaten to death in retaliation by some of Aybak's supporters. This rivalry between Aybak's personal entourage of household members and *mamluk*s, identified as the Muʿizziyya, and the entourages of his wife and of his former comrades of the Salihiyya household largely determined the course of events in these years, at first even obliging many of the latter to seek refuge with the Ayyubid ruler of Syria, the aforementioned great-grandson of Saladin, al-Nasir Yusuf. In the end, however, greater stability was only achieved when the balances of power shifted again in favor of the leaders of the Salihiyya.

Around 1259, this process was accelerated when the amir Qutuz (r. 1259–1260), one of the leaders of the Muʿizziyya and *atabeg* for Aybak's adolescent son and successor, al-Malik al-Mansur ʿAli (r. 1257–1259), claimed the sultanate of Egypt for himself. At about the same time, Qutuz also managed to enforce his authority over Ayyubid and Salihiyya leaderships and their bands of followers in Syria. This closing of ranks in Egypt and Syria around this new sultan and his non-Ayyubid amirs was in every way related to the raiding forces of the non-Muslim Mongols, which moved westwards from the regions of Iran and Iraq and swept through Syria in the period 1259–1260 (see the next chapter). These infamous Mongol armies were eventually confronted and defeated by these unified Syro-Egyptian forces in the late summer of 1260 at a place known as ʿAyn Jalut, in northern Palestine, and any remaining Mongol leadership subsequently quickly evacuated Syria to beyond the Euphrates. With most of the Ayyubid dynastic constellation swept away (including al-Nasir Yusuf, who had been captured, taken to Azerbaijan, and eventually executed in retaliation for the Mongol defeat at ʿAyn Jalut) and the new Mongol arrangements dissolved, the Egyptian sultan and his victorious amirs easily managed to expand their power, establish their authority, and renew local and regional networks of leadership and resources across much of the Syrian region, including in the former Ayyubid stronghold of Aleppo and in the bone of endless Ayyubid contention, Damascus.

It was not Qutuz, however, who was to reap the promising Syrian fruits from the victory at ʿAyn Jalut. In October 1260, in a final episode in the Salihiyya-Muʿizziyya competition for sovereignty, Qutuz was assassinated by some of his rivals and immediately succeeded in the sultanate by one of the main Salihiyya-Bahriyya leaders, al-Malik al-Zahir Baybars (r. 1260–1277). Baybars—in many modern readings the real organizer of the Sultanate and of the specific trans-regional order of the 'Reign of the Turks'[7]—and his remaining Salihiyya supporters and allies successfully managed to stabilize the by now substantially transformed relationships of power and local or regional leadership in Cairo and in the wider Syro-Egyptian regions. Eliminating any further rivals—including remaining Ayyubids, Latin lords, and Mongol agents in Syria, southern Anatolia, and the Jazira—they reconfigured this relational whole into a more coherent trans-regional political space, organized around the sultan's household and interests via the regular wielding of violence as well as via sustained investments in the post-Seljuk infrastructures of urban courts, *madrasa*s, and *khanqah*s.

2 Post-Ayyubid leaderships and patrimonial formation in the 13th and 14th centuries

2.1 Post-Ayyubid patrimonial formation and trans-regional integration

For most of the reigns of al-Malik al-Zahir Baybars and of his main successors, his Salihi peer al-Malik al-Mansur Qalawun (r. 1279–1290), and the latter's son al-Malik al-Nasir Muhammad (r. 1293–1294, 1299–1309, 1310–1341), the radically transformed Syro-Egyptian leadership of sultans, amirs, and their supporters and followers continued to face substantial external threats of violence and elimination, both from the Mongol-Hülegüid northeast (see Chapter 11) and from the Latin-'Frankish' West. For a long time, the Syrian lands, in particular, continued to be viewed from Cairo as an unstable frontier zone and a hotbed of competitors and rivals, potentially emerging from within—as dissident amirs, Frankish lords, bands of pastoral nomads and raiders, or Isma'ili-Shi'ite movements—as well as from the Latin shores of the Mediterranean and from Mongol territories across the Euphrates. Pragmatic defensive strategies that were given priority in response to these threats maintained and even strengthened the post-Seljuk organization of this leadership around the charisma and violence wielding of different generations of sultans, amirs, and their military households of imported *mamluks*, local *kuttab*, and relatives, friends, and associates of all kinds. This collection of amirs and their personal warbands of *mamluk* and other horsemen at the same time continued to transform—as in the reign of al-Malik al-Salih Ayyub—into a more coherent force of patrimonial violence. Organized in a Syro-Egyptian hierarchy of military leaderships topped by the sultan and the several thousands of his own freedmen, this patrimonial force was complemented at regular moments of military action by mercenary bands of Arabian, Turkmen, and other local leaders.

Thus, a new bundling of mechanisms and arrangements of trans-regional violence and centrality appeared from the reign of al-Malik al-Zahir Baybars onwards as a complex and ever more structured patrimonial order of clearly defined sets of ranks, status, privileges, loyalties, and obligations. These were organized around, and actually created, successive sultans' courts in Cairo's Citadel of the Mountain (*Qal'at al-Jabal*) or, especially in the 13th century, in mobile encampments and lesser royal urban infrastructures in Syria. The different military households of sultans and amirs that constituted this patrimonial apparatus in ever more hierarchical configurations continued to be supplied by regular flows of fresh manpower via commercial overland and maritime routes from, especially, the northern shores of the Black Sea. They also continued to be fed by longstanding mechanisms of resource and intelligence management, especially post-Seljuk *iqta'* and *waqf* for the former, and a Syro-Egyptian version of the Abbasid relay postal network of the *barid* for the latter. These mechanisms and related arrangements were supervised for these military households of sultans and amirs by their own sets of Syrian and Egyptian *kuttab*. The latter households, furthermore, remained locally and regionally connected via their active participation and investment in the parallel mediating circuits of urban courts, *madrasa*s, *khanqah*s, and related infrastructures, again topped in terms of urban effects, impact, and integration by those different sets of infrastructures that were associated with the most powerful among them, the sultan and his senior amirs. This particular stabilizing patrimonial order of conquest, power, patronage, wealth, and authority was finally also complemented by an equally ever more structured and interconnected social order of different converging networks of Sunni *'ulama'* and legal scholars, practitioners and students, of Sufi masters and their followers, and even of a new Abbasid caliphate, re-created in Cairo after the Mongol sack of Bagdad in 1258. Many of the latter groups' and movements' activities—including those that produced the exploding numbers of their diverse Arabic writings as well as many that were situated in, or even outside of, its social and ideational margins—actually provided this patrimonial order with a clear sense of purpose, meaning, and theocratic rightfulness, and a strong appearance of coherence and stability. This tended to happen in ways that were very often deeply intertwined with the dominant politics of military leadership via the parallel infrastructures of urban courts and of *madrasa*s and *khanqah*s (see also Chapter 13).

In the long run, this process of the bundling of patrimonial forces around the interests and ambitions of the military leaderships and households of the Cairo Sultanate proved successful on both 13th-century frontiers. From the 1260s onwards, what remained in Syria of the Latin Kingdom of Jerusalem, of the Principality of Antioch, and of the County of Tripoli was gradually confronted with, and annihilated by, the early Sultanate's formidable clustering of local and regional military forces. Eventually, in 1291, these 'Frankish' lordships' last remaining major urban center on the Syrian shore, Acre, was conquered by the Sultan and his armies.

Interestingly, among the many participants in the successful siege of Acre, there was an Ayyubid from Hama, who actively participated in this clustering of forces in Syria, and who later, in one of his many Arabic writings, reconstructed his impressions and memories of moments such as these in revealing personal detail. 'The Sultan al-Malik al-Ashraf [Khalil] marched on Acre with the Egyptian forces', this man of action as well as reflection, Abu l-Fida' (1273–1331), remembered:

> He sent to order the Syrian forces to come, and bring the mangonels with them. So al-Malik al-Muẓaffar, the [Ayyubid] lord of Ḥamāh, and [my father,] his uncle al-Malik al-Afḍal, with all the Ḥamāh contingent went to [the stronghold of] Ḥiṣn al-Akrād [Crac des Chevaliers]. There we took delivery of a great mangonel called 'al-Manṣūrī', which made a hundred cart-loads. They were distributed among the Ḥamāh contingent, and one cart was put in my charge. . . . Our journey with the carts was late in the winter season, and we had rain and snowstorms between Ḥiṣn al-Akrād and Damascus. We suffered great hardship thereby because of the drawing of the carts, the oxen being weak and dying from the cold. Because of the carts we took a month from Ḥiṣn al-Akrād to Acre—usually about an eight days' journey for horses. . . .
>
> The descent of the Muslim armies upon [Acre] was in [May 1291], and severe fighting developed. The Franks did not close most of their gates but left them open and fought in them. The contingent from Ḥamāh was stationed at the head of the right wing, as was their custom, we were beside the sea, with the sea on our right as we faced Acre. Ships with timber vaulting covered with ox-hides came to us firing arrows and quarrels. There was fighting in front of us from the direction of the city, and on our right from the sea. They brought up a ship carrying a mangonel which fired on us and our tents from the direction of the sea. This caused us distress until one night there was a violent storm of wind, so that the vessel was tossed on the waves and the mangonel it was carrying broke. It was smashed to pieces and never set up again.
>
> During the siege, the Franks came out by night, surprised the troops and put the sentries to flight. They got through to the tents and became entangled in the ropes. One of their knights fell into an amir's latrine and was killed there. The troops rallied against them and the Franks fell back routed to the town. . . .
>
> The troops tightened their grip on Acre until God Most High granted them its conquest by the sword on Friday, [17 June]. When the Muslims stormed it, some of its inhabitants

> took flight in ships. Inside the town were a number of towers holding out like citadels. A great mass of Franks entered them and fortified themselves. The Muslims slew, and took an uncountable amount of booty from Acre. Then the sultan demanded the surrender of all who were holding out in the towers, and not one held back. The sultan gave the command and they were beheaded around Acre to the last man. Then at this command the city of Acre was demolished and razed to the ground.[8]

This fall of Acre in 1291 heralded the end of the threats that had been perceived to emanate from the longstanding Latin presence in Syria, and no major Latin campaigns against Syria ever occurred again. Whereas the Mongol-Hülegüid danger from the northeast continued to exist and to occasionally materialize in new violent confrontations in Syria, by the second decade of the 14th century, the Sultanate gained the upper hand on this frontier too. Further negotiations resulted in a truce, and the Mongol-Hülegüid disintegration of the 1330s (see next chapter) meant that for at least six further decades, no new major West-Asian competitors for the Sultanate's claims to trans-regional sovereignty were to reappear.

The impression of trans-regional hegemony that the Sultanate's leadership therefore managed to uphold in the course of the 14th century led to no less than the emergence of Cairo as a new, more or less stable, point of reference for sovereign political authority in imaginations of Sunni-Islamic theocratic order, and as a central hub in Afro-Eurasia's flows of people, ideas, and commodities. More specifically, for many decades, a trans-regional centrality in networks of power and exchange—also beyond the Sultanate's core regions of Egypt and Syria—was achieved and maintained that benefited the interests of the Sultanate's military elites in their pursuit of the elimination of rivals, the protection of clients, the accumulation of resources, and the reproduction of their power. This relative balance of trans-regional, regional, and local relationships of power and exchange, organized in regularly adapted ways around the court and metropolis of Cairo as well as around those many trans-continental flows that converged there, was part and parcel of a much wider Afro-Eurasian order of connectivity and exchange that determined much of the 13th and 14th centuries.[9] One modern historian of the Sultanate's history graphically summarized this stable, unique, and formative 14th-century position of the Sultanate's leadership and patrimonial apparatus as follows:

> Its armies were triumphant, its cities were bursting with new construction, it was the linchpin between two flourishing trade zones in the Indian Ocean and the Mediterranean, and its centrality in the intellectual and religious life of the Arabic-speaking Sunnī world was uncontested.[10]

2.2 Post-Ayyubid dynastic leaderships: from the Salihiyya to the Qalawunids

Nevertheless, despite this stabilizing, integrative, and centralizing appearance of post-Seljuk and post-nomadic leadership, the cohesion of, and centrality in, networks of local, regional, and trans-regional power and authority remained as contested as they had been in Ayyubid, Zengid, and Seljuk contexts. More precisely, the demise of a sultan time and again continued to lead to the rallying of groups around different candidates for the succession, the recalibration and occasional disintegration of a particular power constellation that had emerged around the household and court of the deceased sultan, the emergence of possibilities for new protagonists and their entourages, the build-up of tensions culminating in displays of force and often violent confrontations, and—once the struggle was resolved—a complex search for accommodation and new balances between the interests of the victors, their supporters, and local and regional elites. Unlike before and elsewhere in post-Seljuk Islamic West-Asia, however, this remained a process of social rather than territorial reconfiguration. The earlier realities of repeated territorial fragmentations between members of the ruling dynasty were now mostly replaced by the centralizing spatial reality of the organizational and symbolic force that, since the middle of the 13th century, emanated from the sultan's court in Cairo's 'Citadel of the Mountain' (*Qal'at al-Jabal*). This manifested itself especially in the virtual disappearance of appanage practices, or at least in the strong ties that continued to connect Cairo with amirs in the towns, urban centers, and strongholds in Egypt or Syria that had been assigned to their care.

In this ongoing process of the fiercely fought social reproduction of power and status at the center of the Sultanate of Cairo, another parallel with Ayyubid and other post-Seljuk—and for that matter Seljuk—ideas and practices that continued to manifest itself concerned the prioritization of traditional patriarchal conceptualizations of authority and related dominant notions of dynastic specialty, entitlement, and distinction. The actual appearances of these dynastic tendencies in contexts of leadership transition remained the contingent outcome of the search for new balances among power elites, with succession by mostly young and often inexperienced sons continuing to be challenged by powerful—but equally dynastically empowered—others. This had been the case with the aforementioned contested succession to al-Malik al-Salih Ayyub in the 1250s, and re-occurred in the later 1270s, in the 1290s, and 1300s, between the 1340s and the 1380s, and again in the 1400s along similar patterns of amirs who were members of royal households and dynastic courts interfering actively in, or even contesting, patrilinear succession practices. At the same time, new post-Seljuk dynastic realities constituted themselves in the course of these contested reproductions, given that the offspring of one Salihi amir, who was a member of the royal households and courts of both al-Salih Ayyub and Baybars, managed to hold on to the sultanate for most of the later 13th and 14th centuries. No less than four generations of descendants of the *mamluk* sultan al-Malik al-Mansur Qalawun (r. 1279–1290), as well as three of his former *mamluk*s, succeeded him on the throne in Cairo and continued to reign as sultans between 1290 and the 1380s. Furthermore, in the 1380s and 1390s, an amir from the court of the last of these Qalawunid sultans—but of disputed, basically non-Qalawunid *mamluk* origins—tried to emulate Qalawun's dynastic achievement, but already in the 1400s the sons and successors of this sultan al-Malik al-Zahir Barquq (r. 1382–1389; 1390–1399) succumbed to rivalries and enormous violence in their and their father's entourage.

This post-Seljuk pattern of competitive transformation from within royal households, which meant the premature end of Barquq's dynastic enterprise in the first decade of the 15th century, had also been applied more than a century before by Qalawun himself. In the summer of 1279, with some of his Salihi peers, he had obliged the first son and successor of al-Malik al-Zahir Baybars to abdicate and had acted as *atabeg* for Baybars' second—minor—son and successor. Then, in the autumn of 1279, he had himself elected sultan, and thus a sort of first among competing equals, by his Salihi peers and their different military entourages and wider networks of longstanding Syro-Egyptian leadership. In the 1290s and 1300s, a handful of Qalawun's own *mamluk*s and amirs, furthermore, attempted to do the same to his sons and successors, first al-Malik al-Ashraf Khalil (r. 1290–1293)—the victor over the 'Franks' at the siege of Acre in 1291—and then the young al-Malik al-Nasir Muhammad (r. 1293–1294; 1299–1309)—confronted during his second reign with another series of devastating Mongol-Hülegüid invasions into Syria. As it happened, none of the veterans from the household and court of Khalil's and Muhammad's father, however, managed to construct a stable balance of leaderships and interests around their claims to sovereign authority, as

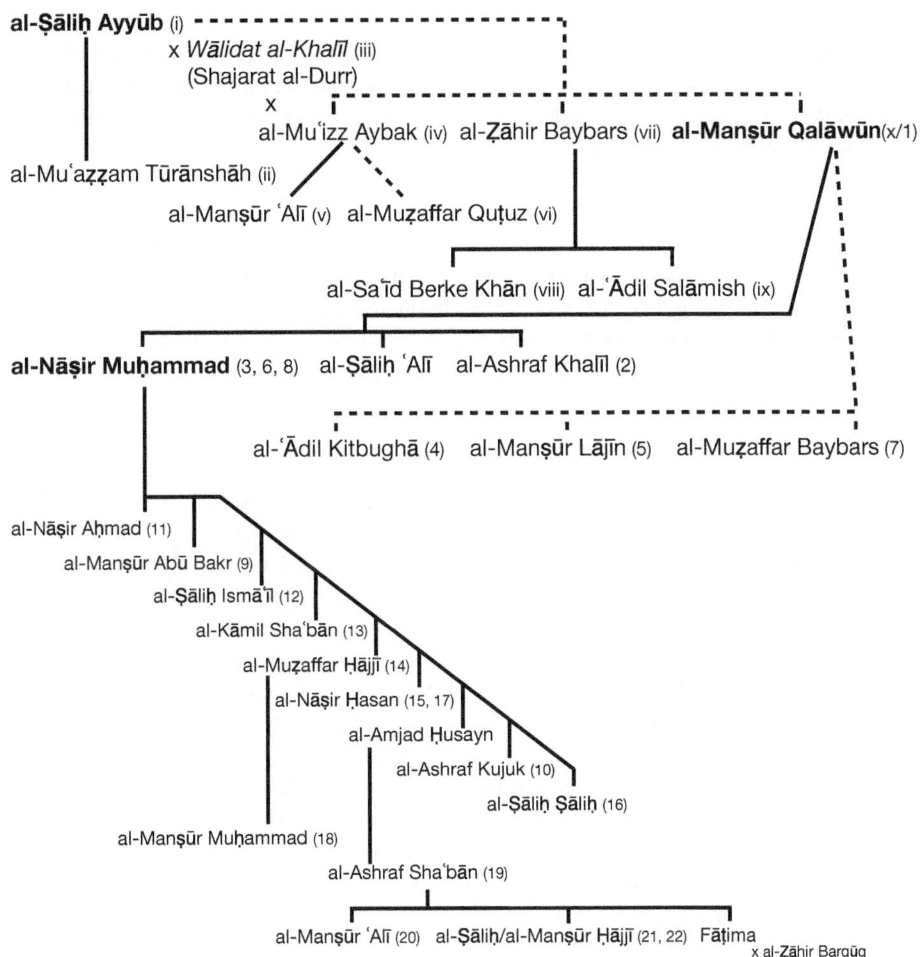

Dynastic Table 6A The Cairo Sultanate. Ṣāliḥiyya and Qalāwūnids

Baybars and then Qalawun had managed to do in the 13th century. Their dominance and leadership in the 1290s and 1300s, therefore, remained that of an unbalanced collection of competing military households, marred by violence and unchecked rivalries, and basically every constellation of power that appeared from this always proved a rather uneasily negotiated and short-lived enterprise. In the case of the last of the three *mamluk* amirs who became sultan in this period, al-Malik al-Muzaffar Baybars (r. 1309–1310), formerly a food taster (*jashinkir*) in al-Malik al-Mansur Qalawun's household and eventually one of the two strongmen behind the throne of al-Malik al-Nasir Muhammad, it turned out that his reign would not even last one year.

Throughout this timeframe of the 1290s and 1300s, moreover, competitive claims to power and authority, and to distinctive identities, often continued to be framed in relation to membership of the household of al-Malik al-Mansur Qalawun, and in terms of elimination of its rivals and protection of its interests, clients, and resources. This dynastic tendency explains the choice of the amir Baybars and his allies to return Qalawun's son al-Malik al-Nasir Muhammad to the sultanate in 1299, in the absence of other, similarly authoritative and stabilizing options. It especially accounts for many contemporaries' explanation of 14th century Syro-Egyptian leadership and its many transformations, even when *mamluk* amirs took the sultanate, in similarly dynastic terms. In one Arabic text of political advice, written in 1310 to be offered to the briefly reigning *mamluk* sultan al-Malik al-Muzaffar Baybars, this centrality of Qalawun's household and its competing members and this dominant narrative of the Qalawunid specialty of both his descendants and his *mamluk*s is tellingly framed as though culminating in this Baybars' reign:

> This blessed and prosperous dynastic reign of the 'Mansuriyya' (*al-dawla al-mubāraka al-sa'īda al-Manṣūriyya*) was built on justice and benevolence . . . for when God empowered our lord the sultan al-Malik al-Manṣūr Qalāwūn—may God bless his spirit and enlighten his grave—over Egypt and [when] he seized its multiple treasures, its exquisite supplies, its hidden resources, and its well-protected benefits, he distributed the wealth that [his predecessors] had taken [by force] in a correct, lawful and moderate way and he achieved an esteemed reputation by giving away freely what they had wasted by hoarding. God therefore rewarded him abundantly and gave him victory over the infidel enemy. . . . He manifestly proceeded in his demeanour along the path of the Truth and of the maintenance of God's Law, so that [the dynastic reign] after him remained firmly in the hands of his sons and *mamluk*s. They followed the pathway that had distinguished him, and God showed them His favour and benevolence.
>
> This was the case with his son al-Malik al-Ashraf [Khalīl], who was extremely generous, of noble character, and well-mannered. He besieged and conquered the coastal strongholds, he cleansed them from the [Frankish] polytheists, and he had them restored. . . . This is only one of God's favours and of what He has given to him.
>
> This was the case with al-Malik al-Nāṣir [Muḥammad], his second son, who encountered the forsaken [Mongol] enemy without hesitation. God made him victorious over them, so that they fled from before him as they were being beaten; they were 100,000 or even more.
>
> This was the case with those of the Manṣūriyya *mamluk*s who became sovereign, up to the point at which [the dynastic reign] arrived at the lion, the hero, our lord the sultan al-Malik al-Muẓaffar, the cornerstone of this world and the next, the lord of monarchs and sultans. He is their *pièce de résistance*, the star of their good fortune, whose generosity is boundless and whose benevolence is limitless.[11]

This remarkable aura of Qalawunid specialty, distinction, and entitlement, and thus of Qalawunid charismatic authority and royalty, only became more powerful as the 14th century proceeded, and as Qalawun's sons—beginning with al-Malik al-Nasir Muhammad, who began his third and longest reign when he chased Baybars from Cairo and eventually had him executed—his grandsons and their offspring, rather than any of his *mamluk*s, continued to reign. Irrespective of the ongoing and often equally violent competition and rivalry between different sets of amirs or between sultans and amirs, all relationships of power, authority, and patronage that mattered in, as well as beyond, the Syro-Egyptian lands were gradually connected to, or integrated as constitutive partners in, the succession of forms that the royal household and court of al-Malik al-Mansur Qalawun in Cairo acquired over this century. This Qalawunid stabilization and centrality in relationships, infrastructures, and identities of power between southern Anatolia and Upper Egypt was actually consistently stressed by articulations of these sultans' complete lineages on all kinds of media, including not least on their coinage. Eventually, this made that al-Malik al-Nasir Muhammad's great-grandson and twelfth and final successor, the minor sultan al-Malik al-Salih Hajji (r. 1381–1382; 1389–1390), had coins struck that uniquely detailed no less than five generations of

Figure 10.3 Cairo: façade (before restoration) of the mausoleum and the minaret of the complex of sultan al-Mansur Qalawun (1284–1285), consisting of a *madrasa*, a public hospital and a domed mausoleum, in which the remains of various Qalawunids were buried

Source: Photo by P. Dittrich, end 19th century. Rare Books and Special Collections Library, the American University in Cairo. K.A.C. Creswell Photographs of Islamic Architecture, SC-1974–01-02-a19-pl12-b02) http://digitalcollections.aucegypt.edu/cdm/singleitem/collection/p15795coll14/id/1663/rec/4 Identifier SC-1974-01-02-02-a19-pl13-b02, Original Identifier A19 Pl.13 B/2

Qalawunids, meaningfully connecting his 14th-century claims to sovereignty with those of his 13th-century ancestor al-Malik al-Mansur Qalawun.[12]

Qalawunid trans-regional cohesion and dominance was undoubtedly most effective and real in the long third reign of al-Malik al-Nasir Muhammad (1310–1341). In this era, rivalry with the Mongol-Hülegüid east subsided and fiscal reforms ensured Qalawunid priority in the accumulation of Syrian and Egyptian resources. At the same time, an expanding patrimonial host of amirs, *kuttab*, *ʿulamaʾ*, and their entourages competed to everywhere represent and perform the convergence of the sultan's and their own power, authority, interests, and patronage. This process was perhaps more than ever before mediated via the representational facilities and the lavish economies of exchange and patronage that marked the sultan's court and its many local or regional offshoots, as well as by a mushrooming of *waqf*-related *madrasa*s, *khanqah*s, and similar urban infrastructure. As a result, Egypt's and Syria's main urban centers and towns even acquired distinctively new layouts and skylines that would continue to define them and their inhabitants for centuries to come.[13] The specialty of this stabilization and centralization of power relationships in the wider post-Seljuk and 'medieval' West-Asian context is most strongly illustrated perhaps by the fact that al-Malik al-Nasir Muhammad was the first and only Islamic sovereign of trans-regional authority since the Abbasid caliph Harun al-Rashid (r. 786–809) to lead the main annual pilgrimage caravan to Mecca—and to remain absent from his court in Cairo for a prolonged period of time—more than once. This happened in 1312 and 1320, and then again, in a by all accounts most spectacular trans-regional display of the Sultanate's might, power, and benevolence, in 1332. One contemporary Arabic chronicle, dedicated to the commemoration of al-Malik al-Nasir Muhammad's long reign, left the following exalting description of the royal caravan that made the journey to Mecca:

> No narrator is capable of describing even some of the things that were present on this royal mission. . . . [Al-Nāṣir Muḥammad's royal caravan] took along fast racing camels, superb Bactrian camels, pack camels—carrying covered loads that damage the eye of anyone looking into them, because of the jewelry, precious clothes, gold, and silver in them—, highbred horses, grazing livestock, newly constructed carts, and camel-litters, as well as anything that can be [transported] on all this, including decorated objects inlaid with precious gems and rare stones. Even a summary of all this would take too long to explain. . . . The same is true if I were to mention only some of the gifts of our lord the sultan—may his victory be great—to all the lord commanders who proceeded in his royal caravan: the camels and dromedaries with brocaded camel saddles and gold and silver chains which he distributed among them, and all that one needs on the roads and in the deserts. . . . This was how things appeared to me and to other people like me, surpassing our comprehension. God the Exalted has favored this ruler with support and assistance, and he has enabled him to achieve all that he desired and wished for.[14]

It was these particular circumstances of stability, centrality, and prosperity of the long reign of al-Nasir Muhammad ibn Qalawun that especially allowed for the aforementioned complex whole of a formidable dynastic and patrimonial apparatus of power in endless formation to materialize. Continuously marred by ongoing rivalries among dynastic and patrimonial agents and competitors, this power constellation across Egypt and Syria appeared to have sufficiently stabilized to be able to absorb any internal competition, adapt to any sudden changes, and retain Qalawunid cohesion, centrality, and sovereignty when in 1341 al-Nasir Muhammad died. His descendants and their own regularly transforming entourages at least managed to retain that cohesion, centrality, and sovereignty for four more decades after 1341 in the form of three further generations of more and less powerful sultans. It was only in 1382 that an amir again emerged, first as *atabeg* of the above-mentioned minor sultan al-Malik al-Salih Hajji, who usurped the position of sultan in Cairo. However, until the early 1390s, this reorientation of social realities and explanations of leadership in Egypt and Syria, away from the by now centennial leadership frameworks of Qalawunid agents and agencies and towards the power and authority of the Qalawunid *atabeg* and then non-Qalawunid sultan al-Malik al-Zahir Barquq (r. 1382–1389; 1390–1399), remained fiercely contested. In fact, Qalawun's descendants reportedly continued to be identified as a dynastic group and to live at the court in the citadel in Cairo for many more decades, until 1433, when according to one contemporary chronicler

> they were all expelled from the citadel and scattered in all directions, much as their ancestor [al-Malik] al-Nāṣir Muḥammad ibn Qalāwūn had done to the royal descendants [living in the citadel and belonging to] the Ayyubid clan; likewise, God did to the Ayyubids as their ancestor [al-Malik] al-Kāmil Muḥammad ibn al-ʿĀdil Abu Bakr ibn Ayyūb had done to the descendants of the Fatimid Caliphs. 'And not one will thy Lord treat with injustice'.
>
> [Quran 18:49][15]

3 'Turko-Circassian' leaderships and patrimonial-bureaucratic formation in the long 15th century

3.1 The contested stabilization of patrimonial-bureaucratic leaderships

In the later 14th century, not just the Qalawunid dynastic configuration of Syro-Egyptian leadership gave way to substantial transformations. The devastating and long-lasting effects in Islamic West-Asia of the Black Death plague pandemic in the middle of the 14th century also generated a series of major crises that continued into the early years of the 15th century (see Chapter 13). Simultaneously, a new set of internal and external threats of violent elimination seriously affected the Sultanate's leadership. These threats manifested themselves especially in another sweeping campaign of Mongol and Turkmen raiding and violence in Syria by the Transoxanian Turko-Mongol ruler Timur Lank (r. 1370–1405) (see Chapter 12). They also emerged from a prolonged period of devastating rivalry and internecine warfare among the Sultanate's sultan and amirs, which played out especially again on Syrian battlefields.[16] These threats were maintained, furthermore, in the format of continued challenges, especially from Timur's allies and successors in the north and east, to the Sultan's claims to trans-regional power, authority, and centrality in networks of local and regional leadership in Syria and the adjacent regions of the Jazira and eastern Anatolia, as well as in the Hejaz.

The military leadership and patrimonial apparatus of the Sultanate, however, persevered, albeit in a substantially transformed constellation. In 1412, these radical new beginnings were actually graphically represented by the execution of sultan al-Malik al-Nasir Faraj ibn Barquq (r. 1399–1405; 1405–1412) on the walls of Damascus by some of the amirs from his own court and from his father's royal household, by these latter amirs' acclamation of no less than the Abbasid caliph of Cairo al-Mustaʿin (r. 1412) as an interim sultan, and by the virtual reconquest and reorganization of the Sultanate's apparatus of power and of resource accumulation by one of these amirs, soon to reign as sultan al-Malik al-Muʾayyad Shaykh (r. 1412–1421). In the 1410s and 1420s, this new sultan, as well as his immediate successors, managed to acquire, with their own household agents and military allies, renewed stabilizing forms of sovereignty and centrality in these substantially transformed Syro-Egyptian networks of power. When this happened, these diverse sets of networks began a new episode in which many of them continued to coalesce around the court in Cairo in ever more complex and empowering ways for many decades. In fact, this 15th-century process of renewed leadership formation increasingly integrated both new generations of sultans, amirs, and their military households as well as expanding ranks of mostly newly empowered local elites of Syrian and Egyptian *kuttab* and *ʿulamaʾ* and their entourages. Mediated via the court's mechanisms and arrangements of power, patronage, competition, and accumulation, and via the competitive interests of many of its members and participants, this process of patrimonial and even bureaucratic formation was fed, moreover, by varieties of new, especially commercial, resource flows. Furthermore, it coincided with the remarkable intertwining of some of the regions' main *waqf*-investments and related major urban religious infrastructures of power with these mechanisms and arrangements of the court in Cairo (see also Chapter 13).[17]

Figure 10.4 Cairo: funerary complex of sultan al-Ashraf Barsbay (the domed building with minaret on the left) (1432), consisting of a mausoleum for the sultan and his family and entourage, a mosque, a *madrasa*, a *khanqah* and a drinking fountain for passers-by, as well as some other 15th-century mausolea in this complex' vicinity, all situated in the desert area just north of the city (al-Sahraʾ), along the main route to Syria

Source: Photo by K.A.C Creswell, early 20th century; Rare Books and Special Collections Library; The American University in Cairo, SC-1974-01-02-02-a27-pl46, 'The Madrasa-Khanqah of al-Sultan al-Ashraf Barsbay and the Mamluk mausoleums in the Northern Cemetery'

This renewed courtly environment of an elaborate patrimonial-bureaucratic apparatus of trans-regional power and resources, and the hierarchies of household members and military and administrative agents who constituted it, with their various expertise and relationships, with their own families and networks, and with their competing claims to agencies, sovereignties, and resources, were actually reconstructed in highly illustrative as well as prescriptive and even performative detail in many Arabic texts from Egypt and Syria. The following is one among multiple examples that may be found in the era's contemporary annalistic chronicles. They all tend to inscribe the expanding 15th-century contours of this apparatus in one of the dominant theocratic readings of trans-regional order, as though continuing to emanate from not only the sultan and his major amirs-courtiers, but also from the Abbasid caliph residing in Cairo:

> At the beginning of this [annals'] year [1433–34] the caliph of the time is al-Muʿtaḍid bi-llāh Dāwud; the sultan of Islam in Egypt, Syria, the Hejaz, and Cyprus is al-Malik al-Ashraf Barsbāy [r. 1422–38].
>
> The grand amir is Sūdun min ʿAbd al-Raḥmān; the amir of arms is Aynāl al-Jakamī, the amir of the council is Aqbughā al-Timrāzī, the head of guards is the amir Timrāz al-Qirmishī, the amir of the horse is Jaqmaq, the executive secretary is Urkmās al-Ẓāhirī, and the grand chamberlain is Qurqmās.
>
> The vizier and major-domo is Karīm al-Dīn ʿAbd al-Karīm Ibn Kātib al-Manākh, the confidential secretary is Kamāl al-Dīn Muḥammad ibn Nāṣir al-Dīn Muḥammad Ibn al-Bārizī, the controller of the army is the *qāḍī* Zayn al-Dīn ʿAbd al-Bāsiṭ—he is the mighty effective manager of the resources of the reign (*dawla*)—, and the controller of the privy funds is Saʿd al-Dīn Ibrāhīm Ibn Kātib Jakam. The chief judges [of the four schools of law] remained [as before].
>
> The viceroys and the rulers of the different regions [in Egypt, Syria, the Hejaz, and beyond] are as they have been mentioned for the preceding year.[18]

In this Cairo-centric, trans-regional patrimonial-bureaucratic environment, even the sultanate itself began more than ever to appear as a bureaucratic prize to be won. Despite the renewed aura of stabilization in a patrimonial-bureaucratic structuring of relationships of power, post-Seljuk and post-nomadic forms of rivalry and competition between, especially, amirs, their military households, and their wider entourages remained a distinctive feature. They manifested themselves in their most violent and transformative guises whenever one of the seven more successful and long-reigning sultans of this long 15th century died, and succession to these sultans time and again proved a bone of fierce contention among the senior courtiers and commanders—as with the competition for sultan Barsbay's succession in 1438, only a handful of years after the above-mentioned snapshot was committed to writing, when Barsbay's 'amir of the horse' on this list, Jaqmaq, defeated his rivals, especially the 'grand chamberlain' Qurqmas, and assumed the sultanate. This situation not only occurred in the late 1430s, but also in the early 1420s, when Barsbay rose to the sultanate, and again in the early 1450s, twice more in the 1460s, and finally for a prolonged period at the turn of the 15th to 16th centuries.

In 1438, furthermore, Jaqmaq usurped the sultanate from Barsbay's young son and successor, al-Malik al-ʿAziz Yusuf (1424–1463, r. 1438), just as Barsbay had done from his predecessor's son in the early 1420s. Every time, indeed, some form of dynastic succession was prepared by each of these powerful 15th-century sultans along the 13th-century post-Seljuk model of Baybars or Qalawun. Every time too, however, it was the harsh reality of

Baybars' sons' prematurely ended reigns, rather than the centennial Qalawunid experience, that prevailed, with *atabeg*s or similar regent amirs, or their rivals, generating sufficient military muscle and peer support to usurp the sultanate and to generate new balances of power and authority around their own leadership. Between 1412 and 1517, therefore, it was mostly these former *mamluk*s who managed to rise from their positions as senior amirs and courtiers to that of sultan. In hindsight, it even transpires that they did so not only in intense and violent episodes of confrontation with competitors, but also after often long and sustained careers of military command, court service, accumulation of wealth, and network building (so that eventually a few of them reigned as septua- and octogenarians and died of very old age). These particular, patrimonial-bureaucratic strategies and tools—rather than their dynastic counterparts—now secured the loyalties and obligations necessary to gain access to the sultanate, to centrality in networks of power and authority, and to the top of hierarchies such as those reconstructed in contemporary texts. A key factor that very often decided this recurrent process of the substantial transformation of the court and its military household memberships, therefore, was represented by the practice of outbidding rivals with the resources one could afford to invest, the alliances one could afford to put to the test, and the fighters one could afford to muster—or more simply, to prevent from urban rioting, as especially turned out to be the major form of interaction between sultans and the violence wielding bands of their or their predecessor's young *mamluk* trainees, the *julban*.

3.2 The contested construction of Turko-Circassian leaderships

Between the 1410s and early 1460s, it actually was a series of Circassian freedmen from the late 14th-century household of sultan al-Malik al-Zahir Barquq—the aforementioned al-Malik al-Ashraf Barsbay (r. 1422–1438) and al-Malik al-Zahir Jaqmaq (r. 1438–1453), as well as al-Malik al-Mu'ayyad Shaykh (r. 1412–1421) before them, and al-Malik al-Ashraf Inal (r. 1453–1461) after them—who time and again, and in ever-changing constellations of households, courts, *amirs*, and other elites, succeeded in appropriating the sultanate along this post-Seljuk pattern of competitive transformation from within royal households. Throughout the 15th century, most of these sultans' young *mamluk* trainees, as well as many of their actual *mamluk* horsemen and of the amirs that served them, were similarly referred to as stemming from among (non-Turkic-speaking) Circassian peoples in the Caucasus. Only sultan al-Malik al-Zahir Khushqadam (r. 1461–1467) is reported to have had different, 'Roman' (*rum*, pl. *arwam*)—that is, Greek Christian Anatolian or perhaps even Southeast European—origins, as also explained in great detail in the following laudatory announcement of his accession by one of the mid-15th century's main court chroniclers:

> He is the 38th sultan of the rulers of the Turks and their offspring (*min mulūk al-Turk wa-awlādihim*) in the Egyptian domains, and the first of the 'Romans' (*Arwām*), after there had been thirteen rulers of the Circassians and their offspring who had been sultan, I mean, from the beginning of the reign of al-Ẓāhir Barqūq, who has initially established the dynastic reign of the Circassians (*dawlat al-Jarākisa*). As for those rulers who preceded [the reign of Barqūq] and who were Turko-Circassians (*al-Turk al-Jarākisa*) and [Turko-]Romans, there is much disagreement over them, due to the lack of precision of the historians over this issue and in what has been written by them. [However,] from the reign of al-Malik al-Ẓāhir Barqūq up to the present day, [it is certain] that the first of the Circassians was Barqūq and the first of the 'Romans' was Khushqadam, and that they are separated by 81 years to the day, as both of them assumed the sultanate on the 19th of the 9th month.[19]

B. Barqūqids and Turko-Circassians

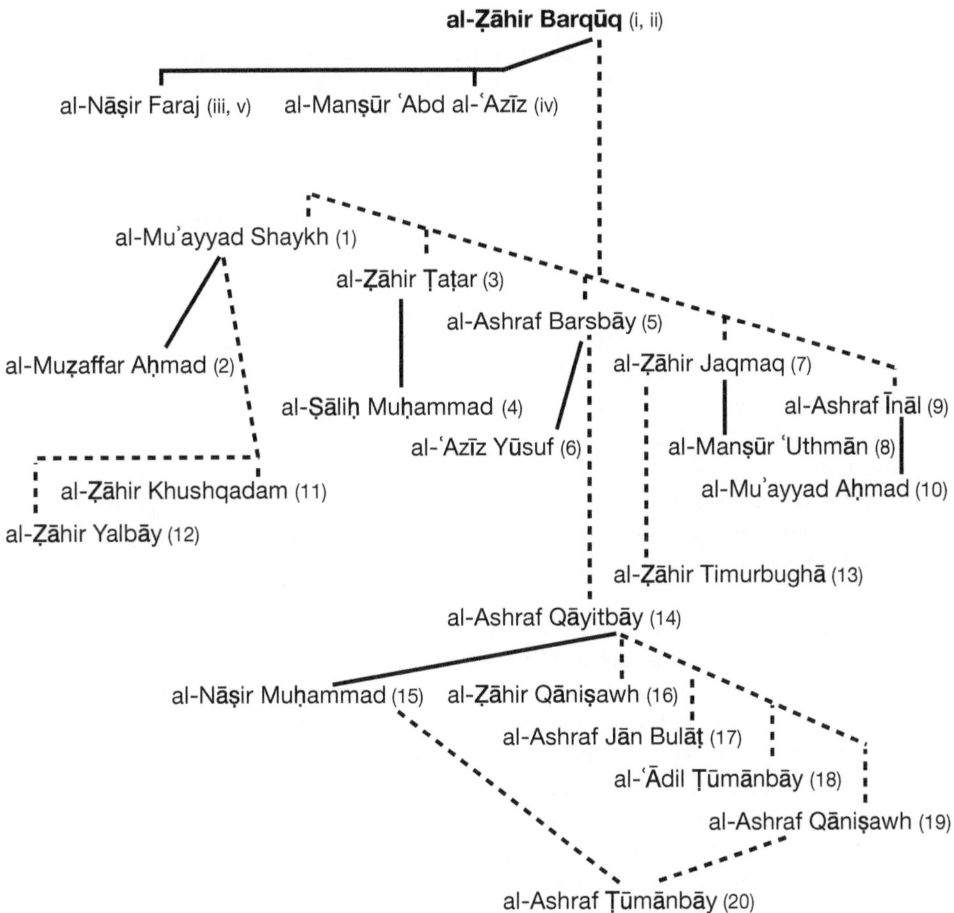

Dynastic Table 6B The Cairo Sultanate. Barqūqids and Turko-Circassians

The contested interruption of the dominance of one particular generation of so-called 'Turko-Circassian' veterans by 'Roman' newcomers—as it is framed in this contemporary report—did not last. At least, the two major sultans who dominated the remaining decades of the Cairo Sultanate's history—al-Malik al-Ashraf Qayitbay (r. 1468–1496) and al-Malik al-Ashraf Qanisawh (r. 1501–1516), as well as most of their main courtiers and amirs—once again all had Circassian *mamluk* roots in common, and are even reported to have nurtured active relationships with relatives in their Circassian 'homelands'. Typical commemorations of Qayitbay's leadership qualities by contemporaries, as in the following biography by another, later, court historian, certainly continue to stress not only his excellent patrimonial-bureaucratic skills and competences, but also this Turko-Circassian particularity:

> His career developed in glory and majesty. . . . He was serene and dignified, correct in decorum, invariably respected, projecting an aura of majesty to official ceremonies; highly intelligent, sound of judgment, skilled in affairs of reign, talented in administration; never indecisive, particularly when officials warranted dismissal. Yet he always reflected carefully before implementing a decision.
>
> Renowned for his bravery, adapt as a horseman . . . [he was] proficient in the martial arts, and yet obsessed with a lust for wealth.
>
> His lifestyle was correct. He never drank wine, nor indeed any inebriating substance. He was learned in religious science, widely read. He even authored pious litanies that are recited in mosques to this day. He had faith in Sufis, honored scholars, respected rights of the people—acknowledging the status each merited. He particularly admired the self-effacing life of ascetics.
>
> After violent fits of temper, he calmed rapidly. His fury always dissipated—an attractive trait.
>
> Overall, the good qualities outweighed the bad; he was the best of the Turkish monarchs, especially when compared with those who followed him. Although tainted by greed, he was the noblest of the Circassian rulers, their finest.[20]

In recent scholarship, this particular framing of the shared identity of the Cairo Sultanate's dominant power elite as not just Turkish, but above all Circassian, has actually been explained as a 15th-century 'ethnicization of power'.[21] The discursive awarding, or assumption of, this particular Turko-Circassian identity to, or by, the Cairo Sultanate's sultans, amirs, and further military elites may certainly have compensated for their recurrent fragmentation as a power elite and for the absence of—or recurrent failure to generate—any dynastic cohesion and any effective dynastic claims to sovereignty, as these had determined the Sultanate's long 14th century as well as all of its post-Seljuk predecessors. This Turko-Circassian ethnogenesis appears to have at least informed one of the more powerful formats that provided these many different and competing groups of former *mamluks* with a sense of Syro-Egyptian belonging and entitlement, and of active participation, despite all the rivalry, in a legitimate trajectory of leadership that—as also suggested in the above announcement, and in many other contemporary textual specimens—bound all of their successive generations together in one whole that supposedly originated with the late 14th-century Circassian sovereignty of al-Malik al-Zahir Barquq (r. 1382–1389; 1390–1399).

3.3 15th-century renegotiations of trans-regional integration

Between the 1410s and 1430s the sultans al-Malik al-Mu'ayyad Shaykh and al-Malik al-Ashraf Barsbay and their many agents also succeeded in restoring the coercive strength and trans-regional authority of the Sultanate. This happened first in Syria, especially in confrontations with rival amirs and their entourages and local allies, and then also—always with mixed successes and in the negotiated formats of what has also been defined as 'seasonal dominion'[22]—among the Turkmen of central and eastern Anatolia and among the Arabian leaderships of the Hejaz. This ambition to stabilize relationships of power and resources on a trans-regional and Cairo-centric footing also extended to the eastern Mediterranean. Three mostly successful maritime campaigns (1424, 1425, 1426) were undertaken against the Latin Kingdom of Cyprus, that was thus made a tributary vassal of the Sultanate, and the Latin elites who remained were thus strongly connected to the court in Cairo for several decades. This accomplishment was particularly celebrated in the following detailed contemporary chronicle report of one of these campaigns, once again—as in the 13th and 14th centuries—framed in particular narratives of leaders' displays of morally praiseworthy conduct (or its opposite) and of a theocratic order that gave meaning to it all.

> [After going to land near Limassol] the land-army proceeded in loose order [towards Nicosia]. . . . They were not in battle-array but like travelers. Some of them were armed but most of them were unarmed because of the heat. Each one of them went forward on his own without waiting for another. They thought that the lord of Cyprus would only encounter them outside his capital. The amirs lingered with the rear-guard as is usual with military commanders, and the men were pushing ahead to get to Nicosia, where they would halt and rest their horses until the troops were assembled and the squadrons were prepared for battle.
>
> While they were on the march, they were surprised by the ruler of Cyprus with his forces and troops, the Frankish rulers who had joined him, and others on every hand. The Muslims to whom the lord of Cyprus appeared were a very small detachment of the vanguard, mostly élite cavalry from the sultan's *mamluk*s. When they saw one another, the Muslims could not wait for those following them to join them, but they seized the opportunity and devoted themselves to martyrdom, one saying to another, "This is the spoils of war!" Then, true to heart, they spurred their horses against the enemy and made a mighty charge against the Franks, shouting "God is greatest!" They fought bitterly. Some of the company backed them up, others lagged behind—amongst them an important courtier, who stayed in the shadow of a tree there. . . . In spite of their fewness and small numbers, they remained steadfast until God gave the victory to Islam and abandoned the infidels to defeat. The ruler of Cyprus was captured in spite of his many followers and innumerably great forces, and the small force of the Muslims. There were fewer than 70 persons at the start of the battle. . . . When the forces of Islam came up, they rode after the Franks and put them to the sword, killing and capturing many. The rest of the Franks fled to the capital of Cyprus, Nicosia. . . . The sultan's *mamluk*s and other fighters in the Holy War who made their way to Nicosia continued slaying and making captives as they went until they reached the city and entered the king's palace, which they looted.[23]

This predominantly violently enforced restoration of the trans-regional power and authority of the Sultanate and its patrimonial-bureaucratic agents, and the renewed Cairo-centric stabilization of local, regional, and trans-regional relationships of power and interest that this restoration interacted with, became some of the most important characteristics of the Sultanate's history from the 1430s onwards. As a result, the contested accession of the—at least, as mentioned above, according to one of his biographers—highly qualified bureaucratic leader and Turko-Circassian sultan al-Malik al-Ashraf Qayitbay in late January 1468, and his subsequent long reign until his death in August 1496, represent by all accounts a renewed moment of cohesive trans-regional centrality and authority in multiple hierarchies and configurations of leadership and resources between the pastures of eastern Anatolia and the Jazira, the trade routes of the eastern Mediterranean and the Indian Ocean, and the dense networks of Syro-Egyptian urban communities.

Figure 10.5 Alexandria (Egypt): 19th-century illustration of the stronghold (with mosque) of sultan al-Ashraf Qayitbay, near the entrance to the eastern harbor; it was constructed in the period 1477–1479 on the exact location where until some decennia earlier the ancient Lighthouse (or Pharos) of Alexandria had been standing. (Victorian illustration modern lighthouse pharos Alexandria 1870)

Source: iStock

Mediated as ever via the urban infrastructures of the sultan's, his amirs', and agents' courts, *madrasa*s, *khanqah*s, and their likes—now, however, more than ever before, as suggested above, often appearing as closely intertwined and integrated mechanisms of patrimonial-bureaucratic power and resource accumulation—the Sultanate's centrality and authority coincided once more with moments of relative prosperity, abundance, and wealth emerging around these infrastructures of power and expressing themselves, amongst others, once again in substantial urban transformations. Much as in the 14th-century days of al-Malik al-Nasir Muhammad, this stabilization manifested itself once again in the highly symbolic and all but evident act of the sultan's personal performance in 1480 of the pilgrimage to Mecca, the Hajj, the enormous meaning and wider import of which were described in a recent study in the following terms:

> Sultan Qāyitbāy . . . would actually turn out to be the last sultan in history to achieve this personal participation and leadership during his tenure. As with al-Nāṣir Muḥammad's pilgrimages before, for Qāyitbāy's reign, too, this unusual royal [pilgrimage to Mecca] served as an impressive illustration of the accomplished nature of his long-lasting power and authority, to contemporary rivals for [trans-]regional supremacy such as the Turkman leader of Tabriz, to ambitious partners such as the Sharif of Mecca, and to

> modern observers. This image of supreme leadership and actual control was confirmed by Qāyitbāy's unprecedented patronage of endowed religious monuments in and near Mecca and in Medina, including the construction of an impressive *madrasah* adjacent to the Sanctuary Mosque and the reconstruction of the Prophet's Mosque after its complete destruction by a fire in [1481]. Since the thirteenth century, sultans of Cairo had continued to regularly invest in Meccan and wider Hejazi real estate, public services, and religious monument construction, but never in any similar quantities or qualities as those generated by Qāyitbāy's investments.[24]

As the reference in this assessment of Qayitbay's authority to 'rivals for trans-regional supremacy' suggests, in Qayitbay's case too, his achievement of trans-regional priority never was a given and continued to be challenged by many from within—as with the 'Sharif of Mecca', but also by many others in Egypt and Syria—and from without—as with 'the Turkman leader of Tabriz'. Regular changes of local, regional, and trans-regional leadership in the eastern and northern parts of Islamic West-Asia, involving especially the aforementioned Timur's descendants and successors as well as this 'Turkman leader of Tabriz' and various other Turkmen constellations of local or regional power (see Chapter 12), actually continued to leave as many marks on Qayitbay's reign as they had on the reigns of his 15th-century predecessors. As always, constant rivalries regularly culminated in violent confrontations, all fought out in the unstable frontier zones of Anatolia and the Jazira by some of the sultan's amirs and troops, who were always sent from Cairo and from Syria's main urban centers. This put a substantial strain on the resources of men and wealth available to the Sultanate's leaderships, as victories and defeats both were the sultan's share, and losses occasionally had substantial impact on the configuration of power at the court in Cairo. The latter certainly was the case with the amir Yashbak min Mahdi, Qayitbay's long-standing associate and in 1468 allegedly even his kingmaker, thereafter executive secretary and second-in-command at Qayitbay's court, and eventually also related by marriage to the sultan's household and its enormous resources and estates. By all accounts, Yashbak was widely feared as the effective and successful wielder of the sultan's violence in Egypt, Syria, and Anatolia against defiant Arabian Bedouin chiefs and, especially, Turkmen local and regional leaderships. When he was unexpectedly defeated, captured, and killed by a local Turkmen associate of 'the Turkman leader of Tabriz' during the siege of a town in the Jazira, in November 1480, it took until early 1482, when Yashbak's beheaded body finally arrived in Cairo and his death could no longer be denied, that his household was disbanded, his court positions were reassigned, and his estates were added to those of the sultan's.

In the case of Yashbak's murder, as the modern historian Carl Petry explains, 'the Turkman ruler of Tabriz', residing in Mardin on the Tigris at this time, both "rejoiced over such a humiliating defeat of the sultan's henchman and ordered [Yashbak's] head displayed on a lance throughout his kingdom" and "approached Qāytbāy humbly via emissaries, claiming that his vassal had acted improperly by ordering Yashbak's execution without prior consultation."[25] These confrontations with local and regional Turkmen leaderships in the Jazira and eastern Anatolia indeed always also involved a wider dimension of competition for Jaziran and Anatolian allegiances and resources with formidable, equally forceful rivals for 15th-century trans-regional authority, organized by the second half of the century especially around Azerbaijan and the Turkmen court of Tabriz, and around northwestern Anatolia and the southeastern Balkans and the Ottoman court of Constantinople (see Chapters 11 and 12). From the 1460s onwards, the latter in particular expanded most aggressively east- and southward and became as a result ever more actively and directly involved in violent confrontations in Anatolia with Yashbak and many of his peers. This continued when, in the early 16th century, al-Malik al-Ashraf Qanisawh became sultan in Cairo. In fact, further changes among the Turkmen leaderships in Azerbaijan—in the form of the rise to Turkmen power of the highly charismatic and ambitious Safavid ruler Isma'il (r. 1501–1524) (see Chapter 12)—had by that time materialized in an equally expanded challenge and threat, which only added to the many wider changes that sultan al-Malik al-Ashraf Qanisawh and his entourage were facing. From 1503 onwards, furthermore, these changes included totally unexpected but very real and unprecedented economic and military pressures in the Red Sea regions, after representatives of the Crown of Portugal and their enterprising seafarers

Figure 10.6 Portrait of sultan Qanisawh al-Ghawri by Giovio Paolo (1483–1552) from his 'Lives of Famous Men' (Pauli Iovii Novocomensis episcopi Nucerini Vitae illustrium virorum: tomis duobus comprehensae & propriis imaginibus illustratae, published at Basel in 1578)

Source: Pitts Emory University www.pitts.emory.edu/dia/image_details.cfm?ID=105626

had started to appear in the Indian Ocean, and 'the age of European discoveries' suddenly announced itself in the Cairo Sultanate's backyard.

While more and less successful campaigns of conquest, practices of accommodation, and renegotiations of relationships with old and new local, regional, and trans-regional leaderships and resources remained ongoing, the Sultanate and its Turko-Circassian leaderships eventually succumbed somewhat surprisingly—both in hindsight and to contemporary observers—to the Ottoman pressures from the north. In the ultimate confrontation with the belligerent Ottoman ruler Selim (r. 1512–1520), in August 1516, sultan al-Malik al-Ashraf Qanisawh was not only confronted with an unexpected military defeat, but he also died—according to one of his biographers, from the combination of old age, surprise, and apoplexy—on the battlefield of Marj Dabiq, near Aleppo, in northern Syria, and his body was allegedly never found again.

The Sultanate's Syrian domains and elites subsequently faced conquest and swift integration into the new trans-regional order of Islamic sovereignty that was now emanating from Selim's Ottoman-Turkish court at Constantinople. His march to Egypt and subsequent second confrontation with the Sultanate's remaining Turko-Circassian leadership, at al-Raydaniyya, in January 1517, ended with another defeat for the latter, and the equally swift Ottoman occupation of Egypt's major urban centers, including Cairo. The execution of Qanisawh's successor in Cairo, sultan al-Malik al-Ashraf Tumanbay (r. 1516–17), eventually not only marked the definitive end of the Sultanate, practically as well as symbolically, but it also concluded no less than the particular post-Seljuk and post-nomadic process of stabilization and transformation that had given shape to the Cairo Sultanate and its powerful but dynamic dynastic, patrimonial, and patrimonial-bureaucratic power apparatus and leaderships, from the Ayyubid Salihiyya, over different generations of the post-Ayyubid Qalawunids, to diverse groups of Turko-Circassians. This transformative event of the execution of Cairo's last sultan was, therefore, quite appropriately commemorated with substantial drama in the following contemporary Arabic chronicle report:

> When the Ottoman [sultan Selim] learnt that the people did not believe that Tūmānbāy had been taken, he was angered, and sent him across [to Cairo]. He went from [the port town of] Būlāq by way of al-Maqs, preceded by 400 Ottomans and arquebusiers. He went by way of Sūq Marjūsh and passed through Cairo, greeting the people along the way until he arrived at the Zuwayla Gate, unaware of what would befall him. When he came to the Zuwayla Gate, they dismounted him and loosened his bonds, and the Ottomans surrounded him with drawn swords. When he realized that he was to be hanged, he stood up at the Zuwayla Gate and said to the people around him, "Recite the Quranic opening chapter (*al-Fātiḥa*) three times for me". He spread out his hands and recited the *Fātiḥa* three times, and the people recited it with him. Then he said to the executioner, "Do your work". When they put the noose around his neck and raised the rope, it broke and he fell on the threshold of the Zuwayla Gate. It is said that the rope broke twice, and he fell to the ground. Then they hanged him. . . . When he died and his spirit went forth, the people cried with a great cry, and there was much grief and sorrow for him.[26]

Notes

1 Ibn Khaldūn (1333–1406), *Kitāb al-ʿIbar* ['The Book of Examples']; translation after Ayalon, "Mamlūkiyyāt: (B) Ibn Khaldūn's view of the Mamlūk Phenomenon", 345–6.

2 See Ayalon, "Baḥrī Mamlūks, Burjī Mamlūks – Inadequate Names for the Two Reigns of the Mamlūk Sultanate"; Van Steenbergen, Wing & D'hulster, "The Mamlukization of the Mamluk

Sultanate? State Formation and the History of Fifteenth Century Egypt and Syria: Part I – Old Problems and New Trends".

3 See Van Steenbergen, "'Mamlukisation' between Social Theory and Social Practice"; Van Steenbergen, "Re-reading 'the Mamluks' with Ibn Khaldun (d. 1406): *'Aṣabiyya*, Messiness, and 'Mamlukisation' in the Sultanate of Cairo (1200s–1500s)".

4 See Loiseau, *Les Mamelouks (XIIIe-XVI siècle)*, esp. Ch. 4: 'L'identité mamelouke' (pp. 143–205); Van Steenbergen, "*Nomen est Omen*. David Ayalon, the Mamluk Sultanate, and the Reign of the Turks".

5 See e.g. Fouzia F. Ahmed, *Muslim Rule in Medieval India: Power and Religion in the Delhi Sultanate* (2016).

6 See Schultz, "Mamluk Coins, Mamluk Politics and the Limits of the Numismatic Evidence".

7 See e.g. Thorau, *The Lion of Egypt. Sultan Baybars I and the Near East in the Thirteenth Century*.

8 Abū l-Fidā' (1273–1331), *Al-Mukhtaṣar Fi Akhbār al-Bashar* ['A Summary History of Mankind']; translation from Holt, *The Age of the Crusades*, 104; Holt, *The Memoirs of a Syrian Prince*, 16–7.

9 See Abu Lughod, *Before European Hegemony: The World System, A.D. 1250–1350*.

10 Humphreys, "Egypt in the World System of the Later Middle Ages", 445.

11 Al-Ḥasan ibn 'Abd Allāh al-'Abbāsī (d. 1310), *Kitāb Āthār al-Uwal fī Tartīb al-Duwal* ('The Book of the Pioneers' Traditions Regarding the Organization of Reigns') (translated from the edition Beirut 1989, 76–7).

12 See Schultz, "Mamluk Coins, Mamluk Politics and the Limits of the Numismatic Evidence".

13 On the latter point, see especially Raymond, *Cairo*, chapter 5: "The High Point of Mamluk Cairo (1250–1348)"; Kenney, *Power and Patronage in Medieval Syria: The Architecture and Urban Works of Tankiz al-Nāṣirī, 1312–1340*.

14 Ibn Aybak al-Dawādārī (d. *c.* 1335), *Kanz al-Durar wa-Jāmi' al-Ghurar. Vol. 9: al-Durr al-Fākhir fī Sīrat al-Malik al-Nāṣir* ['The Treasure of Pearls and the Collection of Excellent Things. Vol. 9: The Splendid Pearl: On the Life Story of al-Malik al-Nāṣir [Muḥammad]']; translation from Flinterman, Van Steenbergen, "Al-Nasir Muhammad and the Formation of the Qalawunid State", 95.

15 al-Maqrīzī (1365–1442), *Kitāb al-Sulūk li-Ma'rifat Duwal al-Mulūk* ['The Book Guiding towards the Knowledge of the Reigns of the Kings']; translation from Van Steenbergen, "The Mamluk Sultanate as a Military Patronage State: Household Politics and the Case of the Qalāwūnid *bayt* (1279–1382)", 211.

16 See Onimus, *Les maîtres du jeu: Pouvoir et violence politique à l'aube du sultanat mamlouk circassien*.

17 See Apellániz, *Pouvoir et finance en Méditerranée pré-moderne: le deuxième Etat mamelouk et les commerces des épices (1382–1517)* (2009); Igarashi, *Land Tenure, Fiscal Policy and Imperial Power in Medieval Syro-Egypt*.

18 Al-Maqrīzī (1365–1442), *Kitāb al-Sulūk li-Ma'rifat Duwal al-Mulūk* ['The Book Guiding towards the Knowledge of the Reigns of the Kings']; translation from Van Steenbergen, "Re-reading 'the Mamluks' with Ibn Khaldun (d. 1406)".

19 Ibn Taghri Birdi (1409–1470), *al-Nujūm al-Zāhira fī mulūk Miṣr wa l-Qāhira* ['Resplendant Stars among the Kings of Miṣr and Cairo']; translation from Van Steenbergen, "Re-reading 'the Mamluks' with Ibn Khaldun (d. 1406)".

20 Ibn Iyās (1448–1524), *Badā'i' al-Zuhūr fī waqā'i' al-duhūr* ['Marvellous Blooms among Events of the Times']; translation after Petry, *Twilight of Majesty*, 15–6.

21 See Loiseau, *Les Mamelouks*, 173–200.

22 Meloy, *Imperial Power and Maritime Trade: Mecca and Cairo in the Later Middle Ages*.

23 Ibn Taghri Birdi (1409–1470), *al-Nujūm al-Zāhira fī mulūk Miṣr wa l-Qāhira* ['Resplendant Stars among the Kings of Miṣr and Cairo']; translation adapted from Holt, *The Age of the Crusades*, 185–6.

24 Van Steenbergen, *Caliphate and Kingship in a Fifteenth-Century Literary History of Muslim Leadership and Pilgrimage*, 22–3.

25 Petry, *Twilight of Majesty*, 86.

26 Ibn Iyās (1448–1524), *Badā'i' al-Zuhūr fī waqā'i' al-duhūr* ['Marvellous Blooms among Events of the Times']; translation from Holt, *The Age of the Crusades*, 201–2.

Selected readings

Abu Lughod, J. *Before European Hegemony: The World System, A.D. 1250–1350* (Oxford, 1989)

Ahmed, F.F. *Muslim Rule in Medieval India: Power and Religion in the Delhi Sultanate* (London, 2016)

Apellániz Ruiz de Galarreta, F.J. *Pouvoir et finance en Méditerranée pré-moderne: le deuxième Etat mamelouk et le commerce des épices (1382–1517)* (Barcelona, 2009)

Ayalon, D. "Baḥrī Mamluks, Burjī Mamlūks: Inadequate Names for the Two Reigns of the Mamlūk Sultanate", *Tārīkh* 1 (1990): 3–52.

Ayalon, D. "Mamlūkiyyāt: (A) A First Attempt to Evaluate the Mamlūk Military System; (B) Ibn Khaldūn's View of the Mamlūk Phenomenon", *Jerusalem Studies in Arabic and Islam* 2 (1980): 321–49

Bartlett, R. *The Making of Europe: Conquest, Colonization and Cultural Change, 950–1350* (Princeton, 1993)

Berkey, J.P. "A Sunni 'Revival'?", in J.P. Berkey (ed.), *The Formation of Islam: Religion and Society in the Near East, 600–1800* (Cambridge, 2003), pp. 189–202

Chamberlain, M. "The Crusader Era and the Ayyubid Dynasty", in C.F. Petry (ed.), *The Cambridge History of Egypt. Vol. 1: Islamic Egypt, 640–1517* (Cambridge, 1998), pp. 211–41

Chamberlain, M. *Knowledge and Social Practice in Medieval Damascus, 1190–1350* (Cambridge, 1994)

Christie, N. *The Book of the Jihad of 'Ali ibn Tahir al-Sulami (d. 1106): Text, Translation and Commentary* (Farnham, 2015)

Christie, N. *Muslims and Crusaders: Christianity's Wars in the Middle East, 1095–1382* (London, 2014)

Cobb, P.M. *The Race for Paradise: An Islamic History of the Crusades* (Oxford, 2014)

Darrāg, A. *L'Egypte sous le règne de Barsbay, 825–841/1422–1438* (Damas, 1961)

Dawes, E.A.S. (transl.). *The Alexiad of the Princess Anna Comnena: Being the History of the Reign of Her Father, Alexius I, Emperor of the Romans, 1081–1118 AD* (London, 1928)

Eddé, A.-M. *Saladin* (Paris, 2008)

Ehrenkreutz, A.S. *Saladin* (Albany, 1972)

Flinterman, W., Van Steenbergen, J. "al-Nasir Muhammad and the Formation of the Qalawunid State", in A. Landau (ed.), *Pearls on a String: Art in the Age of Great Islamic Empires* (Baltimore and Seattle, 2015), pp. 101–27

Garcin, J.-Cl. "The Regime of the Circassian Mamluks", in C.F. Petry (ed.), *The Cambridge History of Egypt. Vol. 1: Islamic Egypt, 640–1517* (Cambridge, 1998), pp. 290–317

Gibb, H.A.R. (transl.). *The Damascus Chronicle of the Crusades: Extracted and Translated from the Chronicle of Ibn al-Qalānisī* (Mineola, 2002; London, 1932)

Goudie, K. *Reinventing Jihād: Jihād Ideology from the Conquest of Jerusalem to the End of the Ayyūbids (c. 492/1099–647/1249)* (Leiden, 2019)

Hawting, G. *The Ayyubid Empire* (Edinburgh, 2017)

Hillenbrand, C. *The Crusades: Islamic Perspectives* (Edinburgh, 1999)

Hirschler, K. "The Jerusalem Conquest of 492/1099 in the Medieval Arabic Historiography of the Crusades: From Regional Plurality to Islamic Narrative", *Crusades* 13 (2014): 38–76

Hirschler, K. *Medieval Arabic Historiography: Authors as Actors* (London, 2006)

Holt, P.M. *The Age of the Crusades: The Near East from the Eleventh Century to 1517* (London, 1986)

Holt, P.M. (transl.). *The Memoirs of a Syrian Prince: Abu 'l-Fidā', Sultan of Ḥamāh (672–732/1273–1331)* (Wiesbaden, 1983)

Humphreys, R.S. "Egypt in the World System of the Later Middle Ages", in C.F. Petry (ed.), *The Cambridge History of Egypt. Vol. 1: Islamic Egypt, 640–1517* (Cambridge, 1998), pp. 445–61

Humphreys, R.S. *From Saladin to the Mongols: The Ayyubids of Damascus, 1193–1260* (Albany, 1977)

Igarashi, D. *Land Tenure, Fiscal Policy and Imperial Power in Medieval Syro-Egypt* (Chicago, 2015)

Irwin, R. *The Middle East in the Middle Ages: The Early Mamluk Sultanate* (London and Sydney, 1986)

Kenney, E. *Power and Patronage in Medieval Syria: The Architecture and Urban Works of Tankiz al-Nāṣirī, 1312–1340* (Chicago, 2009)

Köhler, M.A., Holt, P.M. (transl.), Hirschler, K. (ed.). *Alliances and Treaties between Frankish and Muslim Rulers in the Middle East: Cross-Cultural Diplomacy in the Period of the Crusades* (Leiden, 2013)

Lev, Y. *Saladin in Egypt* (Leiden, 1999)

Loiseau, J. "De l'Asie centrale à l'Egypte: le siècle turc", in P. Boucheron et al. (eds.), *Histoire du monde au XVe siècle* (Paris, 2009), pp. 33–51

Loiseau, J. *Les Mamelouks: XIIIe–XVIe siècle. Une expérience du pouvoir dans l'Islam médiéval* (Paris, 2014)

Lyons, M.C., Jackson, D. *Saladin: The Politics of the Holy War* (Cambridge, 1982)

Madden, Th. F. *The New Concise History of the Crusades* (Lanham, 2006)

Mallet, A. *Popular Muslim Reactions to the Franks in the Levant, 1097–1291* (Farnham, 2013)

Meloy, J.L. *Imperial Power and Maritime Trade. Mecca and Cairo in the Later Middle Ages* (Chicago, 2010)

Mourad, S.A., Lindsay, J.E. *The Intensification and Reorientation of Sunni Jihad Ideology in the Crusader Period: Ibn 'Asakir of Damascus (1105–1176) and His Age* (Leiden, 2013)

Mouton, J.-M. *Saladin. Le sultan chevalier* (Paris, 2001)

Northrup, L.S. "The Bahri Mamluk Sultanate, 1250–1390", in C.F. Petry (ed.), *The Cambridge History of Egypt. Vol. 1: Islamic Egypt, 640–1517* (Cambridge, 1998), pp. 242–89

Onimus, C. *Les maîtres du jeu. Pouvoir et violence politique à l'aube du sultanat mamlouk circassien* (Paris, 2019)

Petry, C.F. *Protectors or Praetorians: The Last Mamlūk Sultans and Egypt's Waning as a Great Power* (Albany, 1994)

Petry, C.F. *Twilight of Majesty: The Reigns of the Mamlūk Sultans al-Ashraf Qāytbāy and Qānṣūh al-Ghawrī in Egypt* (Seattle, 1993)

Raymond, A. *Cairo: City of History* (Cairo, 2000)

Riley-Smith, J. *The Crusades: A History*. Third Edition (London, 2014)

Runciman, S. *A History of the Crusades* (Cambridge, 1951–54)

Schultz, W.C. "Mamluk Coins, Mamluk Politics and the Limits of the Numismatic Evidence", in Y. Ben-Bassat (ed.), *Developing Perspectives in Mamluk History: Essays in Honor of Amalia Levanoni* (Leiden, 2017), pp. 245–68

Setton, K.M., et al. *A History of the Crusades* (Madison, 1985)

Sivan, E. *L'Islam et la croisade: Idéologie et propagande dans les réactions musulmane aux croisades* (Paris, 1968)

Thorau, P. *The Lion of Egypt. Sultan Baybars I and the Near East in the Thirteenth Century* (London, 1992)

Tyerman, Chr. *The Crusades: A Very Short Introduction* (Oxford, 2004)

Vallet, E. *L'Arabie marchande. Etat et commerce sous les sultans rasulides du Yémen (626–858/1229–1454)* (Paris, 2010)

Van Steenbergen, J. *Caliphate and Kingship in a Fifteenth-Century Literary History of Muslim Leadership and Pilgrimage: A Critical Edition, Annotated Translation, and Study of al-Maqrīzī's al-Ḏahab al-Masbūk fī Ḏikr man ḥağğa min al-Ḫulafā' wa-l-Mulūk* (Leiden, 2016)

Van Steenbergen, J. "The Mamluk Sultanate as a Military Patronage State: Household Politics and the Case of the Qalāwūnid *bayt* (1279–1381)", *Journal of the Economic and Social History of the Orient* 56/2 (2013): 189–217

Van Steenbergen, J. "'Mamlukisation' between Social Theory and Social Practice: An Essay on Reflexivity, State Formation, and the Late Medieval Sultanate of Cairo", *ASK Working Paper* 22 (2015)

Van Steenbergen, J. "*Nomen est Omen*: David Ayalon, the Mamluk Sultanate, and the Reign of the Turks" (2013)

Van Steenbergen, J. *Order Out of Chaos: Patronage, Conflict and Mamluk Socio-Political Culture, 1341–1382 (The Medieval Mediterranean 65)* (Leiden, 2006)

Van Steenbergen, J. "Re-reading 'the Mamluks' with Ibn Khaldun (d. 1406): *'Aṣabiyya*, Messiness, and 'Mamlukization' in the Sultanate of Cairo (1200s–1500s)" (2020)

Van Steenbergen, J., Wing, P., D'hulster, K. "The Mamlukization of the Mamluk Sultanate? State Formation and the History of Fifteenth Century Egypt and Syria: Part I – Old Problems and New Trends; Part II – Comparative Solutions and a New Research Agenda", *History Compass* 14 (2016): 549–59

Wink, A. "Post-Nomadic Empires: From the Mongols to the Mughals", in P.F. Bang, C.A. Bayly (eds.), *Tributary Empires in Global History* (New York, 2011), pp. 120–31

11 'Medieval' transformations between Transoxania and Asia Minor—Part 1

Mongol and post-Mongol conquest practices and Hülegüid, post-Hülegüid, and Ottoman dynastic formations (13th–16th centuries)

Introduction: situating 'medieval' Islamic West-Asia between Transoxania and Asia Minor and its Mongol and post-Mongol leaderships

At the turn of the 12th to 13th centuries, the landscape of power in most of Islamic West-Asia was—as explained before—mainly dominated by various Turkmen leaderships and the particular interests of their Muslim pastoral nomadic followers. These Turkmen, furthermore, shared this landscape with local and regional rulers who had managed to adapt most successfully to these unstable realities. These included especially in eastern Islamic West-Asia the post-Seljuk dynasty of the Khwarazm Shah sultans, but also various others, such as the aforementioned Eldigüzids in Azerbaijan, the Salghurids in the Southwest Iranian region of Fars, and the Rum Seljuks in southern Anatolia. Other active participants in this landscape were those who had managed to carve out, or retain, their own particular spaces on its multiple Turkmen margins, including the Abbasid caliphs in central Iraq, the Khujandis and their many local peers and successors in Isfahan and in any of these West-Asian regions' other urban centers, Isma'ili communities scattered across strongholds in Syria and Iran, and for that matter the distinctive post-nomadic heirs of Saladin and their urbanized leaderships that were discussed in the preceding chapter.

In the course of the 13th century, all of these leaderships, their followers, and networks of power and resources, and even their diverse claims to authority and sovereignty, were deeply affected, transformed, and often even annihilated—as with the Ayyubids of Syria discussed in the previous chapter—as a result of a new wave of pastoral nomadic leaderships and their followers and associates sweeping over Islamic West-Asia from the Inner-Asian steppes. In hindsight these 13th century invasions from outside by so-called Mongol leaderships are actually considered to have had even greater transformative effects on Islamic West-Asia's peoples and lands than had been the case with any similar migrations in preceding centuries. This was certainly not only related to the fact that this basically concerned an invasion into the ancient Islamic heartlands by non-Muslim forces. These effects followed even more from the fact that this involved an expansion of leadership on an unprecedented spatial scale, transcending the landscape of Islamic West-Asia by far, transforming it into just one of the different peripheries of a much larger Eurasian whole, and simultaneously integrating it more closely and more meaningfully than ever in very active networks of power and resources that continued to emanate from the Inner-Asian steppes.

Moreover, this specific moment of Eurasian expansion from Inner Asia is remembered as having been characterized by a particularly brutal type of violence, which is considered to explain its enormous success, but which also left an enormous impact on many of the regions it passed through. One modern commentator summarized the widespread perception of 13th-century Mongols leaving only traces of extreme violence by graphically stating that "hundreds of thousands (perhaps millions) were killed; towns were devastated; sedentary agriculture suffered tremendously from pillage, plunder and heavy taxes".[1] This is not just a modern perception of the particularly destructive impact of Mongol violence. Accounts by many contemporaries of that violence, and of its consequences, allude to parallel understandings, as with a contemporary Persian historian and administrator, who explained that "every town and every village has been several times subjected to pillage and massacre and has suffered this confusion for years, so that even though there be generation and increase until the Resurrection the population will not attain to a tenth part of what it was before".[2] About a century later, in an Arabic chronicle from Damascus, its author similarly lamented that after its capture by the Mongols in 1258, "Bagdad, once the most civilized of all urban centers, became a ruin inhabited by only a few, who lived in fear and hunger and wretchedness and insignificance".[3]

The impact of Mongol violence, however, so contemporary scholarship has begun to suggest, may have been more complex and multifarious than prevalent images of utter destruction and of the arrival of West-Asia's dark ages tend to suggest. With the coming and the rise of the Turkmen in the 11th and 12th centuries, a process of nomadization and of the related development of new symbiotic relationships and of new spatial divisions between pastoralists, agriculturalists, and urban communities had already been set in various areas of Islamic West-Asia. This was especially the case in those areas that provided ideal circumstances for pastoral nomadism, as in Khwarazm, Azerbaijan, and eastern Anatolia. With the expansion of Mongol pastoral nomadic leadership into the Islamic heartlands, this process was certainly reinforced, due to their pastoral and nomadic interests as much as to the major damage done to various agricultural and urban communities and infrastructures in, especially, regions such as Khurasan and Iraq. At the same time, however, the integration in Eurasian networks of power and exchange created all kinds of new opportunities, including different forms of active participation in the intense circulation of substantial numbers of goods, ideas, and people between China in the east and England in the west that the period between the mid-13th and mid-14th centuries experienced.[4] As one 20th-century specialist of Islamic history, Bernard Lewis, suggested more than fifty years ago, in a revisionist paper about the effects of Mongol violence, "the dethronement of Iraq and the partial devastation of Persia are the significant exceptions in the general picture of gradual recovery and renewed activity in the Muslim Middle East". For Lewis, indeed, and for many specialists of Mongol history ever since, it was evident that

> Once the conquests, with their attendant horrors, were completed, the Mongols were quick to appreciate the advantages of peace and order, and the *pax mongolica* became a reality in their vast dominions.[5]

Unlike in the case of Ayyubid Syria, therefore, from which Mongol commanders and their followers were, as detailed before, chased in 1260 by sultan Qutuz and his combined Syro-Egyptian forces, everywhere else in Islamic West-Asia many of these new Mongol leaderships came to stay, with their mobile households, loyal personal guards, and enormous nomadic entourages, and with their politics of extreme violence, eclectic patronage, and dynastic sovereignty. After a first wave of destructions and displacements, these leaderships even created a rather novel, Mongol rather than post-Seljuk—and in the 14th and 15th centuries post-Mongol rather than Mongol—landscape of power in most of Islamic West-Asia that soon fully Islamized and that continued to agree well with Turkmen leaderships, but less so with most post-Seljuk formations. This landscape, therefore, continued to be dominated for a long time by nomadic and unstable Mongol, post-Mongol, and eventually also Turko-Mongol realities of local, regional, and trans-regional charismatic leadership, of violence, migration, and accommodation, and of dynastic and patriarchal formations and their regular disintegration as a result of endemic practices of conquest by outsiders. At the same time, very much as in the Seljuk case, the steadily widening integration of local urban elites happened not only via the infrastructure of Mongol courts, as these expanded to also cater for West-Asian arrangements and expertise of power, resource management, and articulations of sovereignty. Interestingly, in due course, this also happened via parallel post-Seljuk Islamic infrastructures such as *waqf*-related *madrasa*s, *khanqah*s, and mausolea. Only in the course of the 15th and 16th centuries did these diverse, eclectic, and highly dynamic realities of charismatic, dynastic, and patriarchal organization and nomadic centrality begin to stabilize into a remarkable set of extremely powerful and highly competitive configurations. In Islamic West-Asia, these emerged especially in the format of two very differently constructed post-Mongol Turkmen dynastic antagonists. At the turn of the 16th and 17th centuries, as will be detailed in Chapter 14, these two dynastic constellations—the one hegemonic in and beyond the western regions of Islamic West-Asia, the other in most of its eastern regions—began to present themselves in their most stabilized and most centralized elite configurations as the dynastic formations of the Ottomans (*c.* 1300–1922) and of the Safavids (1501–1722). Before that happened, however, both continued to be constituted by the same nomadic, and eventually also post-nomadic, practices, mechanisms, and heterogeneity that defined other 'medieval' leaderships, in the former Ottoman case in highly contested but very slowly stabilizing—even 'Ottomanizing'—ways, in the latter Safavid case in a very differently paced and far more imperfectly stabilizing and 'Safavidizing' rhythm.

All of these Mongol, post-Mongol, Turko-Mongol, and Turkmen leaderships' deeply integrated histories, and their shared but simultaneous heterogeneous trajectories of conquests and confrontations, of dynastic transformations, and of belated and highly contested stabilizations, will be summarily reconstructed in this and the next chapter. In both chapters they will also be presented as interestingly distinct from the Syro-Egyptian post-nomadic and patrimonial trajectories that were discussed in the previous chapters. The current chapter will introduce the complexity of Mongol and post-Mongol leadership and the nomadic as well as post-nomadic realities and dynastic consequences of their practices of conquest in 13th- and 14th-century West-Asia. It will also present a particular, extremely hybrid, specimen of post-Seljuk and especially post-Mongol practices of leadership and conquest, in this case even sustained into, and eventually also far beyond, the 16th century. This concerns the 'medieval' case of the Ottoman dynasty and of its transfer, as a result of these practices, from the 14th-century northwestern marches to the 16th-century center of Islamic West-Asia, or rather—especially with its violent integration in 1516–17 of the western Syro-Egyptian lands and their remarkably distinct post-nomadic and patrimonial trajectories, discussed in Chapter 10—its coercive transfer of that center to its own point of dynastic and increasingly post-nomadic gravitation in western Asia Minor.

1 Chinggisid conquest practices and dynastic formations in Islamic West-Asia

1.1 Mongol and Chinggisid conquest practices and dynastic formations in Eurasia

On the Inner-Asian steppes of Mongolia, at the turn of the 12th to 13th centuries, a local leader known by the name of Temüjin (1162–1227) succeeded via age-old Inner-Asian mechanisms of nomadic violence and alliance to gather a new, mainly Mongol configuration of pastoral-nomadic leaders and their followers around his charismatic authority and personal entourage. In 1206, this was famously confirmed and articulated as part of an ambitious program of universal sovereignty in an assembly of Mongol leaders, where all swore allegiance and Temüjin acquired his ruling title of Chinggis Khan ('Severe Ruler').

In the process of his empowerment, Temüjin engaged, much like similar strongmen operating on trans-regional scales before and after him, in what may be identified as a leadership practice of conquest. In this highly personalized practice of rule, the dynamics of sustained conquest and expansion allowed for the configuration around charismatic characters such as Chinggis Khan of new leaderships, new resources, and altering relationships of power without any need to directly challenge, subvert, or for that matter usurp from within extant leadership claims and arrangements. Most of the northwestern, central, and eastern

Figure 11.1 Portrait of Chinggis Khan, from an album with images of the Chinggisid Yuan emperors of China (14th century)

Source: GL Archive/Alamy Stock Photo

regions of West-Asia arguably witnessed this charismatic creation of central power from without becoming something of a returning 'medieval' pattern of Mongol and post-Mongol leadership. This occurred especially in the 13th and again in the later 14th centuries, and in ways of radical transformation that differed substantially from the post-Seljuk patrimonial transformations from within that, at the same time, continued to determine most of the itineraries of trans-regional leadership in the other, Syro-Egyptian parts of Islamic West-Asia, as discussed in the previous chapter. This creative Mongol and post-Mongol practice of conquest, therefore, informed not just recurring moments of destruction, violence, and nomadization. It also generated the regular West-Asian appearance of entirely new as well as newly configured Mongol, Turko-Mongol, and Turkmen leaderships that made for much of the 'medieval' histories of these regions between the 13th and 16th centuries. Thus, one of the leading historians in this field, Beatrice Manz, explains for one of the most formidable—in all respects—emulators of the charismatic models set by Chinggis Khan, the Turko-Mongol ruler Timur Lank (r. 1370–1405), that "like many other sovereigns, most notably Chinggis Khan, Temür promoted a new elite made up of his personal followers and the members of his family". "With these men he gradually displaced the tribal aristocracy from the center of power", Manz continues, adding that "in order to create this elite and to promote its power over that of the older ruling group, Temür needed to acquire additional wealth, manpower and political rewards to bestow on its members." A career of endless conquest, Manz concludes, turned out to represent the main mechanism to not just achieve this radical transformation, but also, paradoxically, to stabilize it, at least for as long as its charismatic centerpiece—Temür, or for that matter Chinggis Khan, and their direct military entourages, that is, their households and personal guards (*keshig*)—remained in charge.

> For the business of politics he now substituted that of conquest. . . . This transformation, changing an unruly tribal confederation into a huge army subordinate to one man, enabled Temür to embark on his unrivalled career of conquest and the conquests in their turn secured the change he had wrought, and enabled Temür to remain what he had first set out to be: sovereign over the [Turko-Mongol configuration of the] Ulus Chagha[d]ay.[6]

The apparatus of conquest that emerged around the charisma of Chinggis Khan was extremely effective, generating an entirely new Mongolian leadership around Chinggis Khan and his descendants. It secured their access to ever more and ever more widespread and diverse resources, and created a new trans-regional order of ever more extended ranks of their pastoral nomadic and violence-wielding followers, and of great varieties of local rulers and their troops. This apparatus of conquest, expanding from the Mongolian steppes and from Chinggis Khan's person, relatives, and commanders through violence, threats of violence, looting, and payments of tribute, was soon feared throughout the 13th-century Eurasian world. It proved, moreover, an excellent tool in the realization of a 'Chinggisid' adaptation of the ancient Inner-Asian notion of collective leadership and family rule. Successful conquest and expansion, especially westwards from the Mongolian steppes, supported the claims for Chinggis Khan's leadership—and subsequently that of his sons and descendants—as being blessed by 'good fortune' (*qut*) due to the intervention of the Mongolian divine entity of the 'sky' (*tenggeri*) and therefore, as endowed with universal sovereignty and the destiny to rule over the entire world. In the course of the 13th century, the success of these practices and claims shaped what is generally seen as the largest trans-regional formation on land that was ever dominated by a patriarchal dynasty, stretching from China to Russia and, at its greatest extent, even involved in the affairs of regions as wide apart as the Korean Peninsula in the east and the Hungarian Plain in the west.

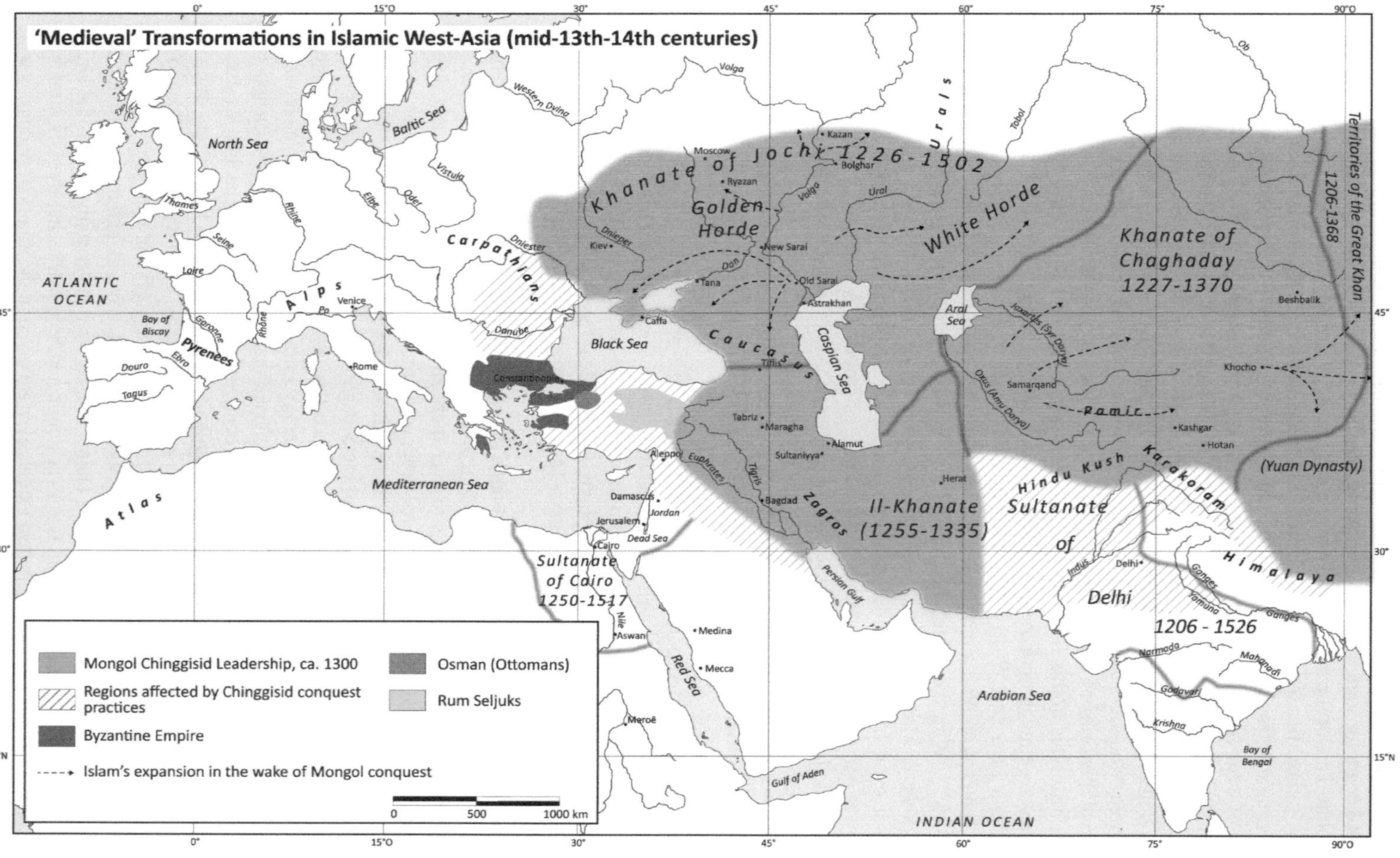

Map 8 'Medieval' Transformations in Islamic West-Asia (mid-13th–14th centuries)

Source: Redrawn from Hodgson, *The Venture of Islam. Vol. 2. The Expansion of Islam in the Middle Periods*, p. 411

In time, however, the apportionment and appanage practice that came with the patriarchal notion of corporate sovereignty caused this enormous Eurasian leadership network to fragment into a number of autonomous clusters dominated by separate Chinggisid branches and dynasties. Similar to what had happened, on a more reduced territorial scale, to the West-Asian Seljuks in the 11th and 12th centuries, the origins of this fragmentation lay in the territorial division of this vast network of leaderships and resources as dynastic appanages (*ulus*) among the four sons of Chinggis Khan. This coincided across, as well as within, these and subsequent Chinggisid appanages—especially within those beyond the Inner-Asian steppes—with pursuits as well as realities to stabilize relationships of power and structure them in more patrimonial and regionally integrated arrangements for the elimination of rivals, the protection of clients, the accumulation of resources, and the reproduction of Chinggisid power. For most of the 13th century, however, such transformations remained very partial, *ad hoc*, and diverse, depending on the time, the space, and the people involved. Above all, they continued to be obstructed by the rivalry and competition between these sons and their descendants for the maximization of their access to resources as well as for the position and nature of patriarchal leadership over the Chinggisid collectivity, as represented by the position of Great Khan (that is, depending on the transliteration, the *khagan* or *qaghan*) and his dominance of the Mongol homelands.

1.2 Chinggisid conquest practices in Islamic West-Asia

Mongols and Chinggisids represent highly complex and extremely rich historical phenomena that should be understood first and foremost from wide-scale and multi-disciplinary Eurasian perspectives. As far as the contribution of this much wider history to the leadership trajectories of 'medieval' Islamic West-Asia is concerned, the presence and impact of two distinct Chinggisid power constellations stand out, the one centered on the region of Transoxania and the other on that of Azerbaijan. A third appanage, of Chinggis Khan's eldest son Jochi (d. 1225) and his descendants, later known to historians as the constellation of 'the Golden Horde'—though more out of Islamic West-Asia's scope since it eventually was organized especially around the Pontic-Caspian, or Qipchaq, steppes (*dasht-i Qipchaq*) and the Khwarazm oases—is of some relevance too, and not only because, in the mid-13th century, it was the first Chinggisid leadership to Islamize. Jochi's descendants of the Golden Horde remained some of the main rivals of the two appanages in Islamic West-Asia in the ongoing Chinggisid competition for land and resources, which played out in particular in those same regions of Azerbaijan and Transoxania. In this context of endless violence and regular conquest, it even nurtured very close relationships of power and commerce—as a strategic ally against shared Chinggisid rivals and as a crucial source of *mamluk* manpower—with the Cairo Sultanate (as well as simultaneously and similarly—an example of one of those many unsuspected deeper connections and parallels of 'medieval' Eurasian history—with the latter's stabilizing namesake in the east, the Delhi Sultanate).

The region of Transoxania had originally been included in the western domains of the so-called Chaghadayid Khanate. Originally centered on lands further to the east, this Khanate was typically marked by a loose organization of Mongolian and Turkic-speaking nomadic leaderships around Chinggis Khan's second son Chaghaday (d. *c.* 1245), his descendants, and their Chinggisid rivals. In the course of the later 13th and early 14th centuries, this center of Chaghadayid leadership gradually moved westwards, towards the steppe areas of Transoxania and, eventually also, of Khurasan, in a process of nomadic conquest, confrontation, migration, infiltration, and Islamization (and of a territorial split with the regions and

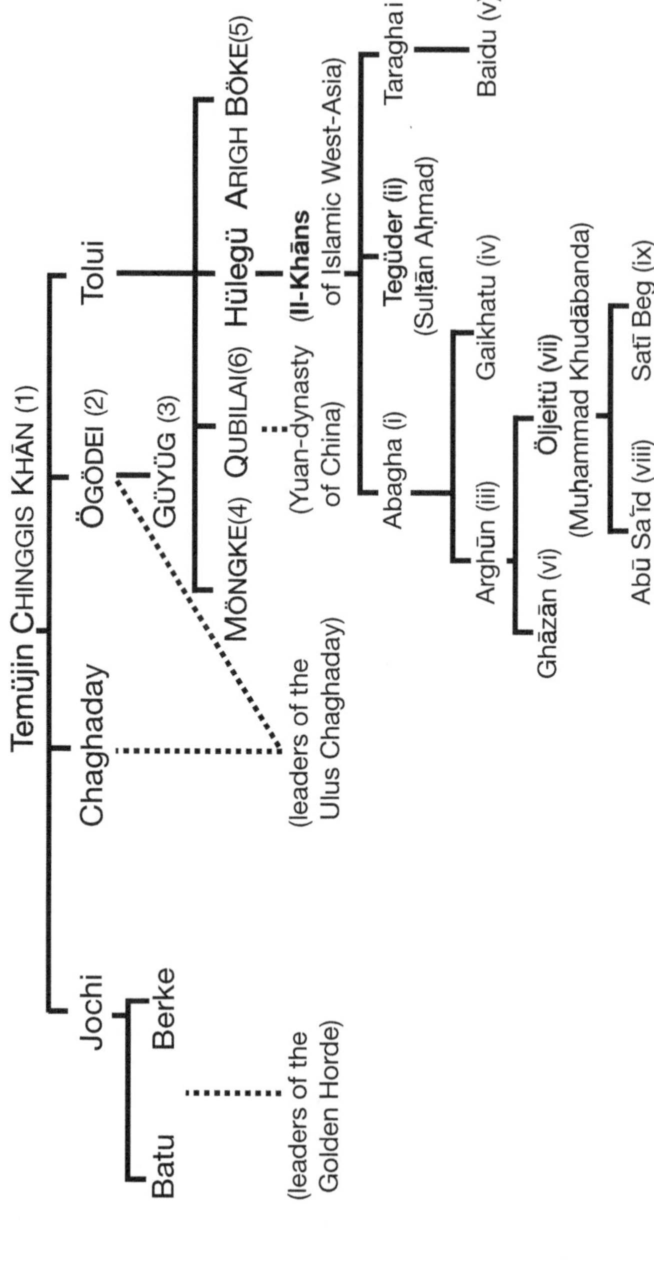

SMALL CAPITAL = GREAT KHANS
Arabic numbers = succession of Great Khans
Roman numbers = succession of Hülegüid Il-Khans

Dynastic Table 7 Simplified dynastic table of the descendants of Chinggis Khan, especially the Chinggisid Great Khans and the Hülegüid Il-Khans

leaderships of 'Mughalistan' in this Khanate's east). In this process, these West-Asian regions of Transoxania and Khurasan, and their Turko-Mongol leaderships—Turkic-speaking, adhering to Mongol and Chinggisid customs and traditions, pastoral and nomadic, increasingly Islamized, and symbiotically related to these regions' ancient urban centers and elites as well as to their rich commercial and agricultural resources—started to appear, or at least to be identified by contemporaries, as the distinct 14th-century configuration of the Ulus Chaghaday, from which eventually the Turko-Mongol leader Temür would arise (see the next chapter). In the regions of Azerbaijan, Iraq, and Iran, the so-called Il-Khanate ('The Sovereign Khanate')[7] (*c.* 1260–*c.* 1335) emerged from mid-13th-century campaigns of conquest by one of Chinggis Khan's grandsons, via his youngest son Tolui (d. *c.* 1233). In the continuation of this part of this chapter, the focus will be especially on the latter set of conquests and on the highly impactful transformation—including islamization and post-nomadic formation—of Chinggisid rule in these heartlands of Islamic West-Asia.

This diverse Chinggisid presence in Islamic West-Asia originated basically from two major campaigns of conquest, each with prolonged aftermaths, in the early 1220s and in the 1250s. The first in West-Asia to be confronted with these Mongol expansions, from 1218 onwards, were the leaders of the Qarakhitai in Transoxania and, especially, their rival and sovereign, the Khwarazm Shah sultan ʿAlaʾ al-Din Muhammad ibn Tekish (r. 1200–1220). In 1219, the unwise killing of Mongol merchant-envoys by the Khwarazm Shah's orders allegedly led to Chinggis Khan's punitive expeditions that caused, between 1219 and 1223, death and destruction throughout the regions of Transoxania and Khurasan, including in ancient urban centers such as Bukhara, Samarkand, Marv, and Nishapur. By 1231, the last Khwarazm Shah sultan, Jalal al-Din Mingburnu (r. 1220–1231) was defeated and dead, and the regions of Transoxania and Khurasan, as well as of Azerbaijan, Armenia, Georgia, and adjacent areas in Iran and Iraq had been the scenes of widespread violence, campaigning, and looting by Chinggisid commanders and their armies. In addition, these regions were witnessing the influx of new Chinggisid leaderships and, in their wake, of new groups of Mongolian and Turkic-speaking pastoral nomads. In June 1243, another major confrontation took place, this time in central Anatolia, near the mountain pass of Kösedagh, with the armies of the Rum Seljuk Sultanate, which at that time is reckoned to have been at the zenith of its power, ruling over most lands and elites of Islamic Asia Minor. This resulted in another major Chinggisid victory, the ignominious flight of sultan Kaykhusraw II (r. 1237–1246) from the battlefield, and further Chinggisid violent advances westwards. Representatives of the sultan, however, reportedly led by his vizier, managed to negotiate a new role for the Rum Sultanate and, especially, for its agents, as regional clients and safeguards of Chinggisid interests in Asia Minor. This allowed the Rum Seljuk dynasty in Konya to survive in an attenuated format—overpowered by viziers, amirs, and other courtiers, and eventually Chinggisid agents and warlords—into the early 14th century.

A decade later, Chinggis Khan's grandson and third successor in the patriarchal leadership of the dynasty, Great Khan Möngke (r. 1251–1260), sent his brother Hülegü from the Mongolian steppes to Iran. Hülegü's mission reportedly included the task to put an end to the specific threat that emanated from a particular leadership in Iran, the origins of which went back to a millenarian movement that had originated in, and split away from, the Fatimid Shi'ite Caliphate in Egypt in the early 1090s. These movements of the Nizari Isma'ilis—known in the west as the 'sect of the Assassins'—developed around particular remote areas and strongholds in Syria and Iran. They were infamous mainly for their various assassinations and attempted murders of Seljuk, post-Seljuk, and other rivals and opponents—including reportedly, without success, of Great Khan Möngke himself—and thus for representing another powerful, and subversive, player on Islamic West-Asia's landscape of leaderships. At the turn of the 11th to 12th centuries, these Nizari-Isma'ilis had successfully managed to carve out their own spaces of power, patronage, and leadership in the Alburz mountains south of the Caspian Sea, especially around the stronghold of Alamut, and in another mountainous region in the south of Khurasan, referred to as Quhistan. After Hülegü's troops had captured and destroyed these different Nizari strongholds, including Alamut, which was destroyed in 1256, they moved further westward, targeting first, especially, the regional leadership of the Abbasid caliph in Bagdad and central Iraq, and eventually also the rich and strategic lands of Syria and Egypt.

The ancient Abbasid center of Bagdad was besieged, captured, plundered, and ravaged in early 1258. In the course of this, the Abbasid Caliph al-Mustaʿsim (1242–1258) himself was executed by order of Hülegü, together with most remaining members of his family. As this event practically marked the end of the ancient Caliphate of Bagdad, it resonated widely as a token of Mongol wrath that left an enormous impact on many contemporary and, especially, later perceptions. The particular imagination of this non-Muslim Mongol destruction of the Caliphate and its ancient capital as a major disruption of the proper, theocratic order of Sunni-Islamic universal sovereignty and delegation of power—from God

Figure 11.2 Representation of a Mongol army besieging a city by a river (probably Bagdad by the Tigris, 1258); illustration from a manuscript of the first part of the Jamiʿ al-Tawarikh ['The Compendium of Histories'] by Rashid al-Din (Tabriz [?], first half 14th century) (Staatsbibliothek zu Berlin, Diez A fol. 70, S.04)

via the Prophet to the caliphs and their many representatives—soon surpassed the rather more limited actual significance of the annihilation of the 13th-century Caliphate, as only one among a wide spectrum of local and regional post-Seljuk power constellations that were being radically reconfigured in this timeframe. The oft-encountered framing of the Mongol siege and destruction of Bagdad, and of the execution of its last caliph, as a turning point and apocalyptic moment in Sunni-Islamic history—and in that history's relations with its many non-Sunni opponents—certainly also informed the following detailed reconstruction, recorded in an Arabic universal history chronicle from 14th-century Damascus:

> Then came the year 656 [1258], in which the Tatars [=the Mongols] captured Baghdad and killed most of its people, including the Caliph, and the dominion of the sons of ʿAbbās ended there.
>
> The arrival of Hülegü with all his troops, numbering nearly 200,000 fighting men, occurred on [January 19, 1258] . . . He came to Baghdad with his numerous infidel, profligate, tyrannical, brutal armies of men, who believed neither in God nor in the Last Day, and invested Baghdad on the western and eastern sides. The armies of Baghdad were very few and utterly wretched, not reaching 10,000 horsemen. They and the rest of the army had all been deprived of their *iqṭā*ʿs so that many of them were begging in the markets and by the gates of the mosques. Poets were reciting elegies on them and mourning for Islam and its people.
>
> All this was due to the opinions of the vizier Ibn al-ʿAlqamī the Shiite, because in the previous year, when heavy fighting took place between the Sunnīs and the Shīʿa, Karkh and the Shiite quarter were looted, and even the houses of the vizier's kinsmen were looted. He was filled with spite because of this, and this was what spurred him to bring down on Islam and its people the most appalling calamity that has been recorded from the building of Baghdad until this time. That is why he was the first to go out to the Tatars [=Mongols]. He went with his family and his companions and his servants and his suite and met Sultan Hülegü Khan, may God curse him, and then returned and advised the Caliph to go out to him and be received by him in audience and to make peace on the basis of half the land tax of Iraq for them and half for the Caliph. [. . .] But his clique of Shiites and other hypocrites advised Hülegü not to make peace with the Caliph. The vizier said, "If peace is made on equal shares, it will not last for more than a year or two, and then things will be as they were before". And they made the killing of the Caliph seem good to him so that when the Caliph returned to Sultan Hülegü he gave orders to kill him. . . .
>
> They came down upon the city and killed all they could, men, women and children, the old, the middle-aged, and the young. Many of the people went into wells, latrines, and sewers and hid there for many days without emerging. [. . .] But no one escaped them except for the Jewish and Christian *dhimmīs*, those who found shelter with them or in the house of the vizier Ibn al-ʿAlqamī the Shiite, and a group of merchants who had obtained safe-conduct from them, having paid great sums of money to preserve themselves and their property. And Baghdad, which had been the most civilized of all cities, became a ruin with only a few inhabitants, and they were in fear and hunger and wretchedness and insignificance.[8]

Upon these and similar acts of violence, most remaining leaderships in the Iraqi and Jaziran heartlands of Islamic West-Asia were either eliminated or integrated in the expanding southwestern branch of the Chinggisid power constellation. Further advances in the direction of the eastern Mediterranean brought Hülegü and his armies to Syria, where Aleppo was subjected to destruction and Ayyubid and Latin leaderships were made to submit or swept aside. These included the aforementioned direct descendant of Saladin al-Nasir Yusuf of Aleppo and Damascus, who was eventually captured, taken to Azerbaijan, and executed. In 1259, in the course of this spread of Chinggisid violence and power, and of their Mongolian wielders, across Syria, however, Hülegü received the news of the death of his brother, the Great Khan Möngke, and of the struggle for his succession in Mongolia between his two other brothers, eventually won by Qubilai (r. 1260–1294), the last Great Khan to appeal to some actual form of Chinggisid patriarchal sovereignty and trans-regional coherence. Whether to prepare for the outcome of his brothers' rivalry, or for reasons of shortage of grazing and foraging opportunities in Syria—as was suggested in a correspondence of 1262 between Hülegü's court and that of the French crusader King Louis IX (r. 1226–1270)[9]—Hülegü withdrew with the main force of his armies to the rich summer pastures of Azerbaijan, leaving Syria to a much smaller force led by one of his commanders (referred to as amirs in Arabic and Persian, but as *noyan* in Mongolian). Substantially reduced in manpower, new Chinggisid leadership in Syria was confronted head-on by the new sultan of Egypt and its diverse Ayyubid and related allies at ʿAyn Jalut, in Galilee, on 3 September 1260 (see the previous chapter). When Hülegü's commander fell and was killed, his troops were routed and most of them fled northwards. In December of the same year, another limited Chinggisid force invading from the north was overcome near the Syrian town of Homs, by a small combined host of local, Ayyubid, and Egyptian forces. After these two victories, for most of the next seven decades, the Cairo Sultanate and its different Syro-Egyptian leaderships proved more than capable to challenge Chinggisid rule in Islamic West-Asia, transforming the Syrian region's natural boundaries in the north and east, especially the Euphrates, into crucial barriers amidst occasionally heavily contested frontier zones.

2 Hülegüid dynastic formation in Islamic West-Asia

Hülegü and his royal household and extensive personal guard (*keshig*) established themselves as a consequence of these Chinggisid conquest practices as the new trans-regional rulers to the east and north of the Euphrates. He was succeeded by four generations of his descendants, and these Hülegüids acquired and maintained—often in fierce competition with their Chinggisid relatives in the north and in the northeast—priority in the trans-regional, regional, and local networks of Chinggisid, Mongolian, Turkmen, Kurdish, Persian, and various related kinds of power and resources that were spread across the high- and lowlands, the many towns and urban centers, the diverse agricultural estates, and the intricate webs of commercial routes and commodity chains in most regions of Islamic West-Asia. These regions stretched from the Hülegüid homelands in Azerbaijan—first with Maragha as its central point of Hülegüid gravitation, then, from the mid-1260s, Tabriz, and in the early 14th century, temporarily, the new urban settlement of Sultaniyya—to Anatolia in the west and to Khurasan in the east. Hülegü's descendants retained this West-Asian sovereignty and authority in increasingly structured and centralizing ways until the mid-1330s. At that time, the Hülegüid lineage came to an abrupt end and, as a result, its former cohesion soon gave way to various new—post-Mongol—realities of dynastic leadership in these regions, pitting non-Hülegüid Chinggisids, Hülegüid Mongolian amirs, and other local and regional elites against each other, very often in diverse but never entirely successful attempts to emulate Hülegüid claims to trans-regional sovereignty in Islamic West-Asia.

These particular claims to Chinggisid specialty are considered to having been articulated most coherently by the frequent use of the aforementioned Inner-Asian title of Il-Khan ('Sovereign Khan'), which is the main reason why this Hülegüid dynasty continues to be referred to in modern scholarship as that of the Ilkhanate, of the Ilkhans, or of the Ilkhanids. In fact, these claims to Hülegüid sovereignty in the region of West-Asia continued to be formulated in relation to wider, Chinggisid dynastic terms. Between the 1260s and 1290s, the first five Il-Khans and their entourages continued to position their rule actively within the larger context of a Chinggisid Eurasian order of universal power, emanating in these decades in ever more contested and ephemeral ways from the court of Great Khan Qubilai (r. 1260–1294) at the new imperial site of Khanbaliq, in present day Beijing. This coincided also with a period in which these Hülegüid rulers and their royal households and guards continued to experiment with different forms and practices of faith, including Mongol shamanism, varieties of Christianity, and especially Tibetan Buddhism, before in 1295, with the accession of the Muslim Il-Khan Ghazan (r. 1295–1304), collectively converting to Sunni Islam.

Among the factors that continued to connect Hülegü's descendants to their Chinggisid and Mongol origins were, however, not just their Chinggisid patriarchal ties and claims. Pastoral nomadic lifestyles, practices, and entourages remained for a long time predominant among the forms and groups that organized Hülegüid power, beginning with the centrality of the *keshig* or 'royal Mongol household'[10] and of its organization in royal tents and encampments that migrated between summer and winter pastures in, especially, the region of Azerbaijan. Engagements with these *keshig*s in the formative practice of conquest politics were another continued feature, targeting especially Syria—with three more major campaigns of violence being organized, without any lasting results, in the early 1280s, the turn of the 13th and 14th centuries, and the early 1310s—and also, on an almost continuous basis, Chinggisid rivals in the north—the so-called Golden Horde—and the Chaghaday east. The persistent appanage practices of distributive royalty and devolved authority, and subsequent realities of local and regional empowerment of Mongol amirs and their pastoral followers, made many of these amirs in the later 13th century—especially in Anatolia—regularly appear as autonomous warlords who engaged with their own *keshig*s and mostly pastoralist entourages in often violent competitions with peers, and especially with the Hülegüid center and its agents. A final connecting factor with Chinggisid and Mongol origins continued to be the corporate notion of sovereignty as a Chinggisid and more specifically Hülegüid dynastic privilege and subsequent realities of contested successions that transformed—as in the wider Chinggisid and Mongol case, and in parallel also with the Seljuk trajectory discussed before—dynastic relatives into rivals and their *keshig*s and entourages into active participants in often violent competitions. The conquest practice of the mid-13th century thus gave way to the equally destructive and creative practice of household competition and internecine warfare, basically opposing different Hülegüids and their allied Mongol amirs in the closing decades of the 13th century, and—after the elimination of rivalling Hülegüids and amirs in the centralizing efforts of the turn of the 13th and 14th centuries—the formers' patriarchal agents in the opening decades of the 14th century.

On several occasions in the 13th century, especially in the 1280s and the 1290s, competition for succession opposed uncles and nephews with their different groups of supporters and their followers. This remarkably generated not just violence and death and transitions of leadership, but also two generational shifts, from Hülegü's sons to his grandsons and from the latter to his descendants in the third generation. In both cases, the Il-Khan Arghun (r. 1284–1291) and his son, the aforementioned Muslim Il-Khan Ghazan (r. 1295–1304), reportedly had most of their active Hülegüid and Mongol rivals killed once they emerged victoriously from the power struggles with their uncles. Patriarchal tensions subsequently seem to have subsided and not to have returned in any similar manner. The succession of Ghazan in 1304 by his brother Öljeitü (r. 1304–1316) happened without much discussion, as the former left no living sons, and order and stability were similarly maintained when the latter was succeeded by his only son, Abu Saʿid (r. 1316–1335).

In the case of Abu Saʿid, however, only eleven or twelve years old at the time of his accession, Hülegüid amirs—much in the manner of the Seljuk and post-Seljuk *atabegs*—temporarily acquired greater centrality, demonstrating how, with Ghazan and his brother Öljeitü, a process of patriarchal formation and post-nomadic integration had been empowering non-Chinggisid military agents and representatives at the center of Hülegüid action, the royal household. These included especially the amir Choban (d. 1327), whose forefathers had been part of Chinggiz Khan's Mongolian entourage and who, with his own 'Chobanid' troops, had been a leading commander (*noyan*) in Hülegüid service since the 1280s. He eventually became senior commander (*amir-i ulus*) and was given one of Abu Saʿid's sisters as his wife, in which capacity he, together with his sons, controlled the young Il-Khan, his household and court, and key regions such as Anatolia and Azerbaijan. In 1327, however, Abu Saʿid managed to revert the balances of power in his own favor, had Choban and his sons executed, and their followers and assets reintegrated by marrying Choban's daughter. Thereupon, their positions were basically awarded by Abu Saʿid to another powerful amir and member of his household, known as Shaykh Hasan-i Buzurg ('the Elder') Jalayir (d. 1356). This Hülegüid amir descended from one of the leading Mongolian amirs in Hülegü's entourage and was himself the son of the sister of Abu Saʿid's predecessors, his father Ghazan and his uncle Öljeitü. Together with a handful of amirs of similar profiles, each with their own troops of Mongolian, Turkish, and other backgrounds and each deeply interconnected with Abu Saʿid's royal household as well as with the representation of his and their own interests in Azerbaijan, Anatolia, the Jazira, and Iraq, Hasan became one of the most powerful figures at Abu Saʿid's court. In 1335, upon Abu Saʿid's death without any direct heir, Hasan and his peers were therefore left to start pursuing their and their entourages' own interests amidst the breakdown of Hülegüid patriarchal bonds and growing Hülegüid dynastic irrelevance. Initially, however, all continued to frame their rivalling endeavors in Hülegüid or wider Chinggisid trans-regional terms. In one of the few historical reports of the confusing events that followed Abu Saʿid's death, reproduced in an early 15th-century Persian chronicle of Abu Saʿid's reign, Shaykh Hasan-i Buzurg, as Abu Saʿid's chief commander, is even presented as warning in a message to one of his main rivals and peers, in 1336, to not forsake their Mongol customs nor their shared Hülegüid dynastic cause and patriarchal constellation, as the alternatives may be detrimental to all.

> We have all been in one *ulūs* and we know one another. The custom of the fathers and ancestors is clear. It is better that we all agree and seat a ruler (*pādishāh*) on the throne who is deserving of the sultanate, and everyone stays on his own path and custom. Since that which you seek is that which brings discord throughout the land, in order that unlawful blood does not flow and the country remains flourishing and inhabited, the condition we give you is to either heed my words or suffer.[11]

In most 20th-century scholarship, the effects of Hülegüid and related leaderships on the West-Asian regions from Asia Minor to Khurasan is generally judged as another particularly negative specimen of the more general havoc caused by Mongol and Chinggisid conquest practices. Nomadization, exploitation of local communities and resources, decades of non-Muslim leadership, as well as continuous Hülegüid rivalries, regular campaigns of violence and plundering, and endless conflicts with other Chinggisid dynasties in the north and east as well as with the Cairo Sultanate in the south explain this rather negative assessment, by many contemporaries as well as in modern scholarship. At the same time, however, it is also true that, in the course of the 13th century, as new relationships of power between Anatolia and Khurasan stabilized around Hülegüid sovereignty, the dynasty increasingly integrated local and regional traditions of rule and developed its own solutions to generate more structured forms of interaction with local and regional elites, resources, and expertise. These included different, and oft-competing, forms of scientific, cultural, and religious knowledge practices and practitioners. In this process, enhanced by the dynastic centralization around Ghazan and his brother and nephew between the 1290s and 1330s, the 'royal Mongol household'—as the main Chinggisid and Hülegüid medium of integration, protection, distribution, reproduction, and even elimination—expanded and transformed, incorporating especially also post-Seljuk and post-nomadic courtly forms, functions, and arrangements. It became a place where the Mongolian and eventually also Turko-Mongol patriarchal leadership interacted on increasingly equal footing with Arabo-Persian *kuttab*, *'ulama'*, and other local elites and specialists of resource accumulation and of articulations of sovereignty and specialty. As a result, whereas already from the days of Hülegü the royal household and its itinerant tented encampment had appeared as yet another important patron of the arts and sciences, especially in the early decades of the 14th century it also became a courtly catalyzer of new urban forms of Arabo-Persian cultural expression (see Chapter 13).

However, in the best of Mongol traditions, Hülegüid households—including the courts of Ghazan and his successors in Tabriz and Sultaniyya—remained highly competitive environments, determined by personal bonds of kinship, trust, loyalty, and obligation and, at the same time, driven by difficult balances of interests and rivalries. Any changes in these fickle bonds or balances either quickly made one's fortune, or ended it, as in the aforementioned cases of the amirs Choban and Hasan-i Buzurg. As a result, quite a few *kuttab* and viziers in the 13th and 14th centuries—mostly identified as Persian speaking 'Tajiks', to distinguish them from the dynasty's Mongolian wielders of violence and Hülegüid patriarchal authority—seem to have been able, in this context of royal household and court service, to accumulate enormous wealth and personal resources, but almost none lived to benefit from them. In fact, another parallel that—to a certain degree—may be usefully drawn here with the Seljuk period concerns that between Nizam al-Mulk and the Nizamiyya in the 1070s and 1080s and the similarly stabilizing but contested 'Tajik' power and agency of one of the leading administrators of Ghazan and his successors, Rashid al-Din Fadl-Allah Hamadani (*c*. 1247–1318).

Rashid al-Din was a physician of Jewish origins from Hamadan, a Muslim convert, and a well-respected polymath, and his extremely wide-ranging chronicle of universal history—produced in both Persian and Arabic versions—represents one of the main sources for Hülegüid, Chinggisid, and, for that matter, Asian history. From the later 1290s onwards, Rashid al-Din became one of the most powerful, wealthy, and well-connected figures at the court in Tabriz, until in 1318 his rivals—reportedly led by another vizier of similar power, ambition, and resources—accused him of having poisoned the Il-Khan Öljeitü, and Öljeitü's young son and successor, Abu Sa'id, had the septuagenarian Rashid al-Din executed. Rashid al-Din's close relationship with Öljeitü's brother, the Il-Khan Ghazan—with whose father and uncle he had begun his career in Hülegüid household service, as their personal physician and steward—and, especially, his effective management of Ghazan's reorganization of central practices of resource accumulation, are generally identified as key factors in his empowerment. Equally important—just as in the Seljuk case of Nizam al-Din and the Nizamiyya—were Rashid al-Din's continuous personal investments in the development of his personal

Figure 11.3 Representation of a woman meeting a Chinggisid/H ülegüid ruler and his two companions; illustration from a manuscript of the first part of the Jamiʿ al-Tawarikh ['The Compendium of Histories'] by Rashid al-Din (Tabriz [?], first half 14th century) (Staatsbibliothek zu Berlin, Diez A, fol. 70, S.18)

Source: © 2019. Photo Scala, Florence/bpk, Bildagentur fuer Kunst, Kultur und Geschichte, Berlin

networks of *waqf*-related landed property and urban infrastructures, especially in Tabriz and also in Sultaniyya. The many opportunities for patronage generated by these infrastructures resulted in the emergence of Rashid al-Din's autonomous regional power constellation of family, friends, supporters, and resources in ways that strongly remind of the composition, role, and impact of the Nizamiyya in Iraq and Iran more than two centuries earlier.

Close ties with a Mongolian courtier and envoy from the Great Khan Qubilai, Bolod Chingsang (d. 1313), have been identified as equally important for Rashid al-Din's empowerment. These ties and their two very different but not dissimilar protagonists—the former, according to the specialist of Mongol history Thomas T. Allsen, "a Mongolian intellectual—literate, cosmopolitan, and a man of affairs",[12] the latter an Arabo-Persian and Jewish-Muslim administrator of similarly wide-ranging intellectual horizons and effective entrepreneurship—are in fact highly illustrative of the presence and entanglement of highly diverse groups, relationships of power, and interests at the Hülegüid households and courts, and of how protagonists of these groups appeared both as Hülegüid agents and representatives and as interconnected autonomous actors in their own right. Claiming descent from a Mongolian speaking tribal community of pastoralist nomads who were eventually made to join forces with Chinggis Khan, Bolod originally grew to become a prominent and highly respected member of Great Khan Qubilai's imperial guard and court in northern China. In the 1280s, he was sent westwards and came, as one contemporary observer noted, to "the court of Hülegü and his sons [as] a permanent amir who is held in great esteem".[13] Due to particular circumstances, he never made it back to Qubilai's court in China, but stayed in Hülegüid service until his death. He entered the royal household and its web of patriarchal bonds by marrying a Hülegüid royal concubine, became a central power broker in the many interactions between Mongolian and non-Mongolian groups at Ghazan's and Öljeitü's courts, and represented as such a crucial partner, ally, and advisor for Rashid al-Din.

The autonomy, strength, and resilience of Rashid al-Din's particular networks of resources and people—operating in parallel, if not in competition and collaboration, with those of various other dynastic agents, including patriarchal amirs such as Choban and Hasan-i Buzurg—is suggested by the fact that eventually one of Rashid al-Din's sons continued to be in charge of the vizirate and of his own networks of patronage for most of the reign of the Il-Khan who—paradoxically—had first had Rashid al-Din executed and his properties confiscated and looted. Upon Abu Saʿid's premature death in 1335, this vizier and son of Rashid al-Din even joined forces with a descendant of one of Hülegü's brothers in a joint attempt to maintain dynastic cohesion and occupy the dynastic center. Despite reports of their forces greatly outnumbering those of their opponents—led by one of Abu Saʿid's Mongolian amirs and relatives—they were defeated and summarily executed.[14]

3 Post-Hülegüid dynastic formations and conquest practices in Islamic West-Asia

3.1 Post-Hülegüid dynastic formations and conquest practices between Tabriz and Herat

With the premature death of Abu Saʿid in November 1335 and the absence of a generally acceptable heir, "the realm without a sultan became like a body without a soul and a flock without a shepherd", a Persian chronicler in the early 15th century noted.[15] The sudden disarray of the Hülegüid dynastic constellation indeed transformed 'Tajik' *kuttab* and Mongolian amirs—from Rashid al-Din's son to Shaykh Hasan-i Buzurg—from patriarchal agents into representatives of their own interests. With the Hülegüid aura and enforcement of trans-regional centrality and cohesion quickly disintegrating, the same was true for many local and regional dynasts in many of the towns, urban centers, and appanages that made for the regions between Anatolia and Khurasan. Between the mid-13th and early 14th centuries, these had been made, accepted, or newly risen to mediate both dynastic and local interests, as Hülegüid representatives or vassals of diverse origins and backgrounds and of equally diverse relationships of autonomy, of subversion, or—especially from the early 14th century onwards—of integration with the Hülegüid dynastic center. Soon after 1335, all of these formerly Hülegüid amirs, Chinggisid strongmen, local dynasts, as well as many Turkmen and other nomadic pastoralist leaders who had been operating in the margins of 14th century Hülegüid authority felt increasingly freed from the trans-regional bonds and coercive order that had so far determined them. All of these, as well as many others, embarked upon fierce competition to maintain their newly achieved forms of sovereignty and self-subsistence, or to expand them in fierce competition with rivals, from territorially ever more scattered power bases.

At first, this mostly happened—as with the above quoted call of Shaykh Hasan-i Buzurg to 'seat a ruler on the throne who is deserving of the sultanate'—by at least claiming to restore Hülegüid or wider Chinggisid trans-regional order and centrality, or by appealing to the authority and assistance of powerful outsiders, including especially the Cairo Sultanate in the southwest. From the middle of the 14th century onwards, however, such fictional ties and relationships, as well as any remaining Hülegüids and Chinggisids to represent them, quickly lost their symbolic relevance. Many new, post-Hülegüid, local and regional power constellations thus acquired ever more prominent autonomy and authority across most of Islamic West-Asia, in mostly overlapping and highly competitive ways, and appearing to emulate the 14th-century Hülegüid model from which many of them sprang especially in their multivalent pursuits of practices of conquest, apportionment, patronage, and internecine competition. Until the end of the 14th century, therefore, when most succumbed to new Turko-Mongol wielders of violence and Chinggisid practices of conquest from the east, these mostly dynastic constellations succeeded to stabilize relationships of power and resources in a handful of contested orders of regional sovereignty only.

Between the Caucasus and the Euphrates, these relationships clustered most prominently around Tabriz and Bagdad and around particular reconfigurations of Hülegüid patriarchal amirs, their households and military entourages, and their different Mongolian and Turkmen followers. In the neighboring regions of Iran, the Persian dynasty of the Muzaffarids (r. *c.* 1320–1393), formerly Hülegüid commanders and military administrators of Yazd, enforced and maintained a similarly fluid centrality between Shiraz, Kirman, and Isfahan in central and southern Iran. In the western parts of the region of Khurasan, highly complex and volatile sets of relationships of power and allegiance centered on Sabzawar and different local and spiritual leaderships. In the east of Khurasan, these relationships centered on Herat and on the long-standing Persian dynasty of Chinggisid making of the Kartids (r. 1245–1381). They emerged after 1335 as sovereign rulers between the Indus and the Oxus, until succumbing to different pressures from Transoxania, in the shape of, first, migrating Mongolian pastoral nomads and, subsequently, conquering Turko-Mongol amirs. In Asia Minor various regional centers of mainly Turkmen power emerged, first around Kayseri in the southeast, and subsequently especially around Sivas in the northeast, Konya in the southwest, and Bursa in the northwest. Most of these centers' dynastic leaderships, as well as many less prominent ones, were, by the turn of the 14th to 15th centuries, first coerced into the dynastic order of Ottoman rule, rapidly expanding from western Anatolia and Bursa, and subsequently released from this Ottoman bondage—mostly seeing their Turkmen leaderships restored to local or regional prominence—by the same conquerors from Transoxania that radically reoriented the landscapes of power everywhere in Islamic West-Asia (see next chapter).

One of the better studied specimens of these diverse and regularly changing regional leadership orders is the one that was dominated by the descendants of the aforementioned Shaykh Hasan-i Buzurg Jalayir (d. 1356). This Jalayirid leadership of Shaykh Hasan, his son, and his grandsons mainly operated, in conjunction with particular Mongolian groups of pastoral nomads, in Azerbaijan, the Jazira, and Iraq. Whereas Shaykh Hasan and his followers were first forced south, to the region of Bagdad and Iraq, by a grandson of his former peer Choban, known as Shaykh Hasan-i Kuchak ('the Younger'), in the 1350s the latter Chobanids were chased from this era's major bone of territorial contention, the former Hülegüid heartlands of Azerbaijan, and their position was eventually taken by Shaykh Hasan-i Buzurg's son, sultan Shaykh Uvays (r. 1356–1374), and his personal followers and nomadic allies.

With Shaykh Uvays, the Jalayirids obtained a new dynastic centrality in local and regional networks of power, resources, and patronage between Iraq and the Caucasus. In this capacity, they in fact continued to actively connect these regions' Hülegüid past with their own contested mid-14th-century present. This continuity was not least strongly appealed to in articulations of Jalayirid claims to sovereignty, as also expressed in the rulership titles that were attributed to Shaykh Uvays in an Arabic inscription on a water bowl attributed to his patronage. These titles represent Shaykh Uvays in mixed Chinggizid, post-Seljuk, and ambitiously Islamic terms similar to what had been done for the Hülegüid Abu Sa'id only a few decades earlier.

> Made on the order of the most supreme sultan (*al-sulṭān al-aʿẓam*)
> The supreme Ilkhan, the most just and noble Khan (*al-īlkhān al-muʿaẓẓam al-khāqān al-aʿdal al-akram*)

Master of the people of all obediences (*mālik riqāb al-umam*)
Shadow of God in the World (*ẓill allāh fī l-ʿālam*)
Invigorator of worldly blessings and religious ordinances (*muʿizz al-dunyā wa-l-dīn*)
Shaykh Uvays, may God preserve his realm and his power.[16]

These connections and continuities played out not only in particular leadership claims, but also in the continued symbiotic interaction via Jalayirid households and urban infrastructures with extant networks of administrators, scholars, spiritual leaders, and various forms of knowledge, expertise, and resources—occasionally still rooted in Rashid al-Din's earlier networks—as well as with profitable commodity chains on east-west as well as north-south trade routes.

Jalayirid dynastic centrality somehow continued to exist in the 1370s and 1380s, despite disruptive contexts of fragmentation and competition between Shaykh Uvays' sons and their supporters, and of external threats and incursions from the east. Eventually, one of Shaykh Uvays' sons and successors, Sultan Ahmad (r. 1382–1410), fought emphatically and with very mixed successes to retain and eventually to reclaim this centrality. In August 1410, however, he was defeated in battle and executed in Tabriz by the new Turkmen leadership of Azerbaijan (see next chapter), and other surviving Jalayirids were eliminated or marginalized. As one of the few experts of this period's history, Patrick Wing, concludes, the defeat

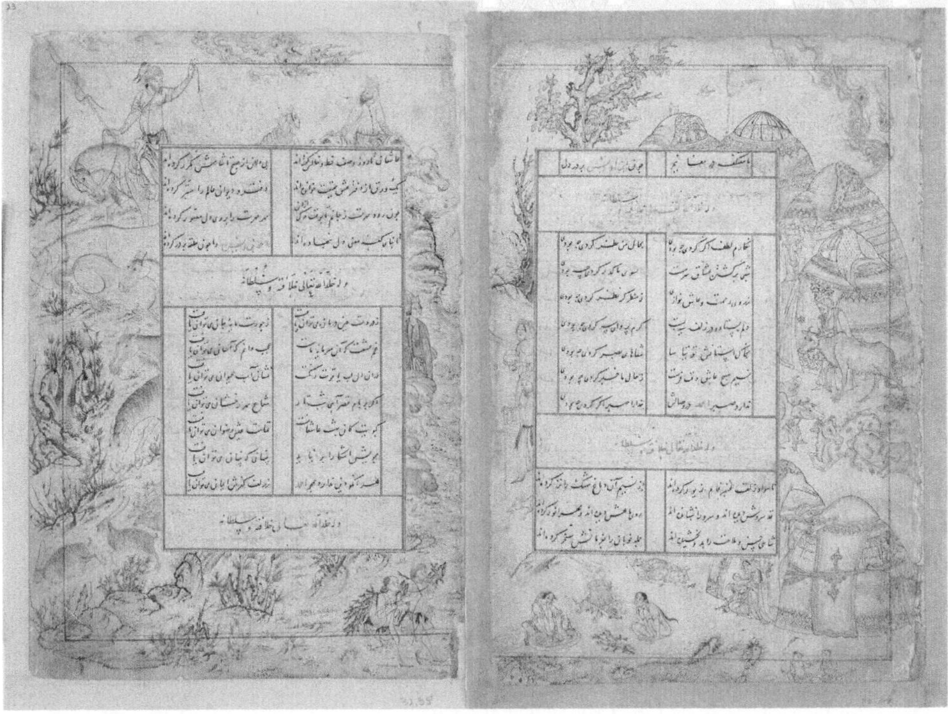

Figure 11.4 Illustrated bifolio from a *divan* (collection of poems) of sultan Ahmad Jalayir, representing a nomadic encampment (painting by Junayd, calligraphy by Mir ʿAli Tabrizi, 1405) (Freer Gallery of Art)

Source: ART Collection/Alamy Stock Photo

of Sultan Ahmad in 1410 not only "signalled the end of effective Jalayirid claims to the old centers of Tabriz and Baghdad". Above all it represented the final severing of these regions' "link to the Ilkhanid legacy, which served as ideological capital with which to make claims to legitimate authority in Azerbaijan and Iraq [until] the early fifteenth century".[17]

3.2 *Post-Hülegüid conquest practices and dynastic formations in and beyond Asia Minor: the complex case of Ottoman stabilization in Islamic West-Asia's northwestern marches*

This Hülegüid legacy, and especially its mid-14th-century evaporation, determined also, as suggested above, the emergence, or rise to prominence, of various regional centers of mainly Turkmen leaderships in Asia Minor. Asia Minor's landscape of Turkmen and other strongmen, warlords, and nomadic power elites originated in various, mostly obscure, realities of ongoing pastoralist migration and multivalent pursuits of practices of conquest, rivalry, and resource accumulation since the later 11th century. This landscape was also defined by post-Seljuk dynastic practices of collective leadership, apportionment, patronage, and internecine competition, which all continued to be strongly tied up with these practices of migration, conquest, and volatility, if not fluidity, of leaderships. The more successful among these 14th-century configurations of power—*beylik*s in Turkic—actually appear as constructed around complex post-Seljuk, and eventually especially post-Hülegüid, amalgams of violence-wielding and charismatic leadership, of Turkmen pastoralist traditions, and of the many local and regional legacies of performances of power and authority across the Anatolian complex. These derived especially from the achievements of the Persianate Sultanate of the Rum Seljuk dynasty of Konya (1077–1307) and of the Mongolian-Hülegüid overlordship of the latter Sultanate in the later 13th century, followed in the early-to-mid-14th century by its direct administration by Chobanids and by Shaykh Hasan-i Buzurg and his Jalayrid followers and representatives. These 14th-century configurations were also defined by the remnants, or even continued presence, of two competing Roman-Greek Christian Empires in Asia Minor, resulting from the—temporary (1204–1261)—Greek loss of Constantinople to Latin participants in, and beneficiaries of, the so-called fourth 'crusade', which had been diverted to the Bosporus in the period 1203–4. One of these two self-proclaimed continuations of the Greek Roman Empire was briefly centered in Asia Minor's northwest on Nicaea (1204–1261). The other in the northeast remained organized for more than two centuries around Trebizond (1204–1461). The eventual mid-13th-cenury restoration of the Greek-Roman empire of Constantinople (1261–1453) by the Nicaean leadership actually translated into a renewed Anatolian connectedness to the other side of the Bosporus, and in an ever more direct interconnectedness, and even integration, of the renewed empire's elites and leaderships with the different *beylik*s and lordships operating in Asia Minor's northwest.

One of these 14th century *beylik*s was that of the descendants of the Turkmen leader Ertughrul and his son Osman (a Turkified version of the Arabic Muslim name 'Uthman), both referred to—and simultaneously identified as formally articulating local claims to dynastic sovereignty—on a surviving Islamic coin that declares on the center of the obverse to having been 'struck by 'Uthman son of Ertughrul'.[18] These Turkmen leaders' exact origins, whereabouts, and wanderings in late-13th and early 14th century western Asia Minor remain difficult to reconstruct, however. This is due to a lack of detail in contemporary written sources as well as to the powerful agenda of an Ottoman destiny of trans-regional empowerment in the making that determined many later renderings of these early Turkmen beginnings. What is clear, however, is that Osman and his father belonged to the group of Turkmen leaders who had moved—probably as a result of Hülegüid pressures in the Anatolian east—with their pastoral followers and their flocks into the western Anatolian frontier zone with Christian, especially Greek Roman, communities and groups, their by then mostly autonomous leaders and urban lords, and their urban, rural, and commercial resources, often strongly tied to events across the Bosporus and Sea of Marmara. In very pragmatic ways, after the recentering of the Greek Roman empire on Constantinople at the other side of the Bosporus, all of these Turkmen and Greek leaderships in this unstable western Anatolian space of the later 13th century continued to be looking for new local and regional balances of power and interests for their personal entourages and for their ever-changing scores of supporters and allies. In this volatile context of local competition for manpower and resources between local leaderships of various origins, capacities, and connections, over time numerous overlapping locally and regionally oriented networks of Turkmen *beylik*s and their pastoralist and urban allies and resources emerged from endless practices of conquest, plunder, and tribute and their occasional clustering around particularly successful Turkmen, Greek, or related individuals and their personal bands of followers (*nöker*). One mid-15th-century reference to these paramount practices of conquest, and to their Turkmen wielders of violence, describes them both in the following explicit terms:

> The Turkish raiders are called in their language *akandye [sic. akıncı]* which means "those who flow," and they are like torrential rains that fall from the clouds. From these storms come great floods until the streams leave their banks and overflow, and everything this water strikes, it takes, carries away, and moreover destroys, so that in some places they cannot quickly make repairs. But such sudden downpours do not last long. Thus also the Turkish raiders, or "those who flow", like rainstorms, do not linger long, but whatever they strike they burn, plunder, kill and destroy everything so that for many years the cock will not crow there.[19]

The actual nature, motivations, and effects of these raids and empowerments in the Muslim-Christian frontier zones of 13th and 14th century Asia Minor have remained objects of long discussion in modern Ottomanist scholarship. For most of the 20th century, different positions in this discussion have revolved around two types of explanations. The one has always foreground ideas of Islamic religious fanaticism, in which a specific form of Islamic *jihad* and warfare against religious others—referred to as *ghazw*—would have yielded a political advantage and a mobilizing legitimacy for the leader and champion of *ghazw*, portrayed as the ultimate *ghazi*. The other explanation has rather tended to emphasize concepts of a Turkish proto-nationalism in which this kind of advantage was assumed to have existed within the essence of the Turkmen, or Turkish pastoralist, identity. In recent years, new voices in the debate have emphasized the remarkable, even unique, ability of the Ottoman *beylik* to transcend, connect, operationalize, and perpetuate the fluidity of 'medieval' boundaries in and beyond the Anatolian frontier zone between diverse groups and leaderships. In this view, there were numerous local groups and many of them were connected, despite their cultural or socioeconomic diversity, by a leadership that could continue to rally around its claims to centrality diverse groups of *ghazis* and so-called 'marcher' lords, of Turkmen nomadic leaderships, of their Greek peers and other Christian urban lords, and of numerous other spiritually and materially inspired parties, both in Anatolia and soon in similar territories on the other side of the Bosporus, in the Balkans (and eventually, in the 16th century, even far beyond these Ottoman heartlands).[20] As the modern Ottoman historian Cemal Kafadar explained, all of these groups of raiders and of otherwise motivated leaders were tied together in a complex and regularly changing whole of bonds of loyalty, obligation, kinship, service, benefit, fear, and fervor. As others have subsequently explained, this web of leadership networks originated from "the melting pot that was Ottoman Bithynia", equally defined by Christian as well as by Islamic identities, and with the latter having been claimed, furthermore, to appear from these 13th- and 14th-century nomadic margins of Islamic West-Asia as "strongly Turkish and [only] tentatively Islamic".[21] In hindsight, Kafadar therefore argues, the Ottoman *beylik* and its particular claims to dynastic sovereignty can be seen to have emerged from this complex relational amalgam as one of the more stable leadership configurations, while at the same time, groups and ideas—including Greek warlords as well as Turkic-speaking marcher lords and other *ghazis*—that had also been pivotal for this amalgam's successes but eventually proved less amenable to the priority and centrality of Osman's descendants and their agents, were gradually marginalized, and eventually even entirely excluded from active participation in the Ottoman center, if not entirely eliminated. "The gazis are discernible as a social group during the first two centuries of Ottoman history", Kafadar concludes, emphasizing further that

> they represented a specific segment of the medieval Anatolian frontier society with their own customs and lore, interests and alliances, within a coalition that had so much success that it eventually devoured some of its members. Like so many other elements of that coalition, such as the pastoralist tribes and the eventually heterodox dervishes, the gazis, too, represented a concrete social group which was eventually left out of the ruling stratum as an imperial, centralized polity emerged under the leadership of the House of Osman, who had once been of their kind, one of the gazi begs.[22]

As in the Chinggisid case described above, and as in the Turko-Mongol and Turkmen 15th- and 16th-century cases that will be detailed in the next chapter, this process of the stabilization and centralization of relationships of power around "the House of Osman" was first and foremost the result of highly personalized practices of sustained conquest and expansion. These generated the transfer and acquisition of the charismatic authority that allowed for the configuration around Osman's descendants of new post-nomadic leaderships, new post-nomadic resources, and altering post-nomadic relationships of power without any need to directly challenge, subvert, or for that matter usurp from within extant leadership claims and arrangements. In the particular Ottoman context, this was a slowly developing process of social and cultural transformation, that began in the 14th century and assumed its defining, stabilizing shape only in the course of the 16th century. As another modern Ottoman specialist, Heath Lowry, argues, this was actually a process of heterogeneous dynastic formation 'in which Christians and Muslims (many of whom themselves were converts), worked together to spread the Ottoman banner initially westwards into the Balkans and then later east to the heartlands of Islam'. Only in due course—from the turn of the 15th to the 16th centuries onwards—this process of both expansion and integration was, Lowry suggests, "religiously Islamicized, linguistically Turkified, and culturally Ottomanized".[23]

What the Ottoman dynasty benefited from before that final stabilization definitely transformed and 'Ottomanized' the heterogeneity of its leadership networks, is therefore especially the charismatic, flexible, and integrative persuasiveness that almost uniquely continued to emanate from many successive generations of highly successful Ottoman leaders. Until the end of the 16th century, the dynasty enjoyed the remarkable fortune of powerful and often exceptionally long-reigning Ottoman fathers bringing forth equally capable sons and successors. Successful violent action and, not least, ongoing charismatic conquest

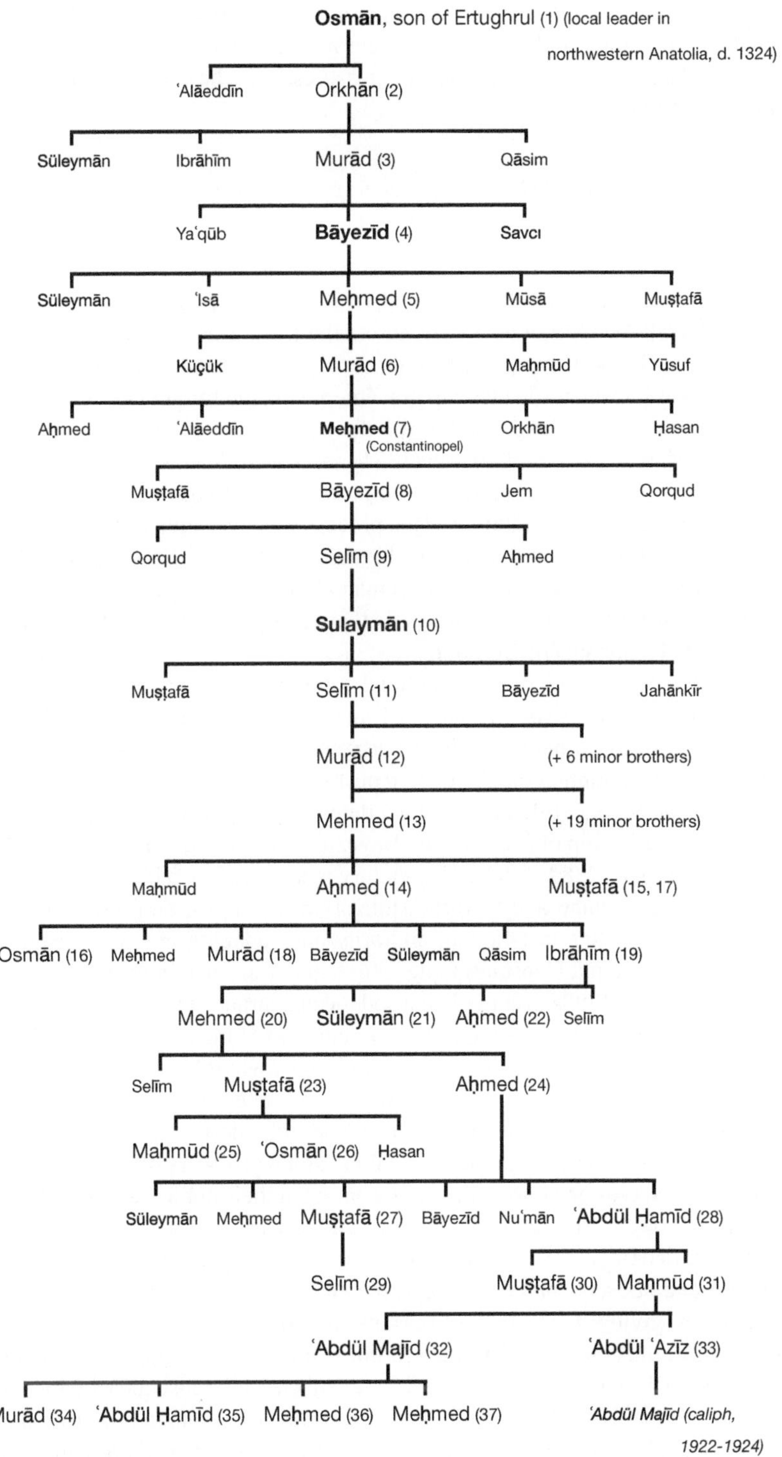

Arabic numbers: succession of Ottoman sultans and/or caliphs

Dynastic Table 8 Simplified table of Ottoman dynastic leadership

practices on a gradually expanding Eurasian scale, northwestwards as well as southeastwards, contributed substantially to the fact that time and again between the 14th and the 16th centuries these sons managed to transcend returning moments of dynastic fragmentation, internecine warfare, and internal or external pressures from the ever-changing ranks of both Muslim and Christian rivals.

*3.2.1 Twelve generations of Ottoman conquest practices and charismatic leaderships (*c. *1290–1595)*

The early 14th century leadership of Osman (r. *c.* 1290–1324) and his son Orkhan Bey (r. 1324–1362) was one that fully exploited rivalries and opportunities on two fronts: in Turkmen and Greek Asia Minor as well as across the Bosporus, the Sea of Marmara, and the Dardanelles in the Greek, Venetian, Albanian, Serbian, Bulgarian, and Hungarian dominated lands of the Balkans. Osman's leadership first emerged in the former Greek-Roman province of Bithynia. It subsequently expanded in the direction of the neighboring urban centers of Bursa (conquered in 1326) and of Nicaea (1331) and was followed by further expansion and campaigns, taking the shape especially of alliances with or raids against neighboring rivals and local West-Anatolian communities. This process was very much carried on by Osman's son Orkhan, whose presence in the historical record fared somewhat better than his father's. In the 1350s, Turkmen, as well as Greek-Roman alliances and raids, brought his followers to the central-Anatolian town of Ankara as well as, on the Balkan side of the Bosporus, the strategic town and peninsula of Gallipoli.

These charismatic, formative, and beneficial conquest practices in the Christian Balkans were continued by Orkhan's son Murad I (r. 1362–1389). Eventually, in June 1389, this culminated in a decisive confrontation with the Serbs and Bosnians, at Kosovo Polje. Murad—no longer styled *beg* but adopting the distinctive post-Seljuk title of sultan—died on this battlefield, but so did the Serbian ruler. Reportedly, defeat was especially inflicted upon the Serbs due to the heroic leadership of Murad's son Bayezid, who subsequently succeeded his father as Bayezid I Yildirim (r. 1389–1401). This victory made that Bayezid's forces could advance further towards the Danube and towards Hungarian territories, subjecting most Christian leaderships of the Balkans to Ottoman authority and reducing the Greek-Roman Empire to a mere city-state around Constantinople. This violent expansion of the Ottoman sultan's reach in the 1380s and 1390s eventually caused the appearance in the region of a huge Latin Western force, led by, mainly, French, Burgundian, and Hungarian royals and nobles, and marching eastwards without much opposition until the town of Nicopolis (present day Nikopol in Bulgaria), on the right bank of the Danube. In September 1396, Bayezid confronted these so-called crusader forces head on near Nicopolis, utterly destroying and decimating their ranks, looting their encampments, and taking some prisoners of war, with the prospect of selling them as slaves or of obtaining a ransom from their noble Latin families. Amongst the latter was the future Burgundian duke John the Fearless (r. 1404–1419), who earned his name on this battlefield and who spent considerable time in Anatolia as Bayezid's captive.

This battle and subsequent victory represented yet another important turning point in Bayezid's career, giving him sufficient reasons to first move against recalcitrant Turkmen allies across most of Asia Minor and then to inflict a crushing defeat on the flower of Hungary's and Latin Christianity's knighthood, with substantial consequences for the forceful reality—as well as on Latin Christianity's imagination—of Ottoman power on the Balkans. All of this has actually been described in some detail by an unsuspected eyewitness, a religious scholar from Damascus who had ended up at the court of Bayezid in Bursa, attended various military operations of Bayezid in 1396, including his aborted siege of Constantinople, and also joined him on his march to Nicopolis. In this Arabic historiographical report, Bayezid is described in familiar post-Seljuk dynastic and Islamic terms as 'the sultan Bayezid, whose justice spread far and wide afterwards, son of the Monarch of the Holy Warriors Murad, son of the Monarch of the Holy Warriors Orkhan, son of Osman'. This familiarity also transpires from how this well-connected author refers to Bayezid's use of the mediating and redistributive capacity of his court in Bursa to connect with scholars such as himself, when he explains that 'he had heard of me before and gave me slaves and concubines from what God had endowed to him from the conquests of the Wallachian people, and exceeded in his benefaction and benevolence. He asked me to stay in his capital [Bursa] and provided for me abundantly'. The following excerpts from the actual description of the engagement at Nicopolis is, furthermore, highly illustrative for what is known about Bayezid's practices of conquest on the Balkans and in Asia Minor, and simultaneously for how very personal and fickle dynastic and patriarchal relationships tied together his dominions.

> [Bayezid] heard of the designs of the infidels against his domains and of their arrival together with whoever accompanied them from among the soldiers. They had gathered in a number unheard of in this time. He rushed to face them before they devastated his lands. The same [news] reached me [as well], so I followed him and caught up with him two or three days before the incident. The infidels had crossed the Danube, which is a very wide river, with around 2,000 ships, and they shored there for several days. This river is the farthest border of [Bayezid's] realm, which he conquered beyond the Anatolian Sea [that is, the Sea of Marmara] for about a month's [distance]. We reached them at the town of Nicopolis. They had been trying hard to lay siege to it, and all that was left [to do] was taking it. This town was among those which he [that is, Bāyezīd] had conquered about three years earlier. . . . When they heard about the arrival of the sultan, they mounted their horses against him and attacked him fiercely in order to capture him before his arrival. When they arrived I was there with him, talking to him about the merits of holy war (*jihād*) and what God promises to holy warriors and to those of them who die in battle [as martyrs] and to those who have the patience to wait. . . .
>
> According to the first news, their number was 200,000 cavalry, though the highest number that was mentioned was 400,000. The truth is that nobody knows their number other than God most high. However, what I [personally] witnessed is that the vanguards who were preceding them amounted to 30,000 southern 'Franks' (*al-faranj al-janūbiyya*), of whom it is said that they are the bravest group of all the infidels. In my opinion, the truth is that he [eventually] seized twelve from among their leaders. It [that is, the battle] occurred on 2 October 1396 (28 Dhū al-Ḥijja 798). I witnessed a fierce battle which had no equal in this time. The astonishing thing is that the above-mentioned son of Osmān (that is, Bāyezīd) had sent a message to his soldiers so that they come from all his dominions, and to the appanages of his sons (*jamāʿat awlādihi*) to come with their own soldiers, but only one of his sons arrived a day before the battle. With him there were only 12,000 cavalry and foot soldiers. The upshot was that this godforsaken enemy was defeated in no time. [At the end] there remained no honour to them other than their great sultan who was the King of Hungary, who escaped together with approximately 50 souls. He [that is, Bāyezīd] kept as prisoners some of those who had escaped the massacre unharmed. The son of Osmān ordered the slaughter of all except for the children who had not yet reached puberty [and who could therefore be sold in slavery].[24]

Six years after this total victory, in July 1402, however, Bayezid himself succumbed to Turko-Mongol pressures that had been on the rise from the regions of Transoxania and Khurasan for several decades. During his endless campaigns of conquest across West-Asia, the Turko-Mongol ruler Temür (r. 1370–1405) (see next chapter) had become increasingly aware of the impressive Ottoman empowerment in Asia Minor and eventually confronted Bayezid's forces near Ankara, in central Anatolia. The unexpected defeat and capture of Bayezid, who subsequently died as Temür's captive, Temür's division of the remnants of the Ottoman domains among three of Bayezid's sons, and his restoration to regional power—as Timurid vassals—of many former Turkmen *beyliks* in Anatolia heralded the disintegration of the Ottoman dynasty and its networks of power, patronage, and resources. This manifested itself in both substantial territorial losses and prolonged internecine warfare among Bayezid's sons, their households, and their regional entourages over dynastic leadership and the sultanate. It was, therefore, mainly due to Temür's disinterest in consolidating his victory and his eventual departure eastward, with his full army, that the Ottomans were saved from total elimination.

The competition for Bayezid's succession was eventually settled in 1413 in favor of his son Mehmed Çelebi (r. 1413–1421). Under the leadership of Mehmed, dynastic cohesion was restored in the wake of an intense renewal of conquest practices, territorial expansions, and coercive or voluntary reintegration of local and regional elites. The territories lost in 1402, in both Anatolia and the Balkans, were mainly reconquered during the long reign of Mehmed's son Murad II (r. 1421–1451). As the trans-regional charisma and authority of Ottoman leadership were thus restored, Murad's son Mehmed II Fatih (r. 1451–1481) could pursue new conquests and further territorial expansion to the Danube and the Adriatic Sea in the west and to the Turkmen of the eastern Anatolian highlands in the east, as well as the final submission and annexation of remaining Greek Roman leaderships and resources around the Black Sea. A strategically as well as symbolically important moment in this was obviously represented by Mehmed II's famous conquest of Constantinople, on 29 May 1453. One of the most detailed contemporary reports, in an anonymous Turkish chronicle from the later 15th century, remembers these events in the following highly personalized terms of Mehmed's heroic leadership and his efficient deployment of Ottoman practices of siege warfare, conquest, and plunder.

> The padishah of Islam came auspiciously to Edirne and stayed there. The winter passed and spring came. With the arrival of the year 857 [AH, 1453–54], at a most auspicious time, the padishah of Islam [Mehmed II] gave the order to his viziers for the army to assemble. Right away, couriers went out to Anatolia and Rumelia [=the Balkans], and the entire army came and gathered at Edirne, perfectly armed and prepared for battle. All ships to be found at Gallipoli and elsewhere were filled with fully armed *azab*, and they set out to attack Istanbul. . . . So, at an auspicious time, he attacked Istanbul. . . . He had several large cannons dragged there, and his army assaulted Istanbul, occupying itself with royal battle day and night. But the ships were unable to enter the harbor in front of Galata [=the Golden Horn]. So the padishah ordered three trunks to be spread out along the ground, and the ships were thus dragged over dry land. They were then launched into the sea across from the resting place of his holiness Ayyub Ansari (may God be pleased with him). At that time, the padishah's army battled against some Frankish cogs and was able to sink one of them, firing on it with a cannon. Then the crews on board the Frankish ships fled and entered the city walls.
>
> . . . The next day, they dug trenches and fired stones with those large cannons, with which they began to demolish the city walls. When the fortifications had been ruined on all sides, the *tekfur* of Istanbul [=the emperor] summoned [his main advisor] and held counsel with him. He recommended surrendering the city, but the Frankish infidels were displeased and showed opposition. . . .

> The next day, the padishah mounted his horse with royal fortune. Giving encouragement to the infantry and other fighters, he praised them and urged them on. Right away, the army boiled up like the sea. Drums and kettledrums were sounded, and banners were raised. Cannons and guns were fired, the trenches advanced toward the city walls, and there was a royal battle beyond description. Ships advanced from the sea, on which ladders had been made ready. The *gazi*s brought them out and placed them on the fortifications, advancing all together with cries of 'God is great!' Meanwhile, the infidels had become exhausted from the constant warfare. The Franks fled defeated, boarded their ships, and went their own way. Then the army of Islam entered the city and plundered it. They captured the *tekfur* of Istanbul [=the emperor] and cut off his head. There was also a pretender there, who would go around saying, 'I am of the lineage of Osman'. He was also killed, and [the emperor's main advisor] was captured with his sons and dependents. The padishah of Islam entered the city with fortune and felicity, accompanied by the pillars of his government and the people of his Porte [=the leading members of his court and household]. Surveying the situation, [he understood that] there had been plundering beyond description. No one before had ever borne witness to such enrichment on the part of the *gazi*s.[25]

In fact, ever since the 7th century, and the recollection of the Arabian expansion—including its two unsuccessful sieges of Constantinople in the 670s and 710s—as a defining feature of Islamic identities, this conquest of one of the world's largest cities had always been

Figure 11.5 Portrait of sultan Mehmed II, probably by the Venetian painter Gentile Bellini (1429–1507), 1480 (National Gallery, London)

Source: incamerastock/Alamy Stock Photo

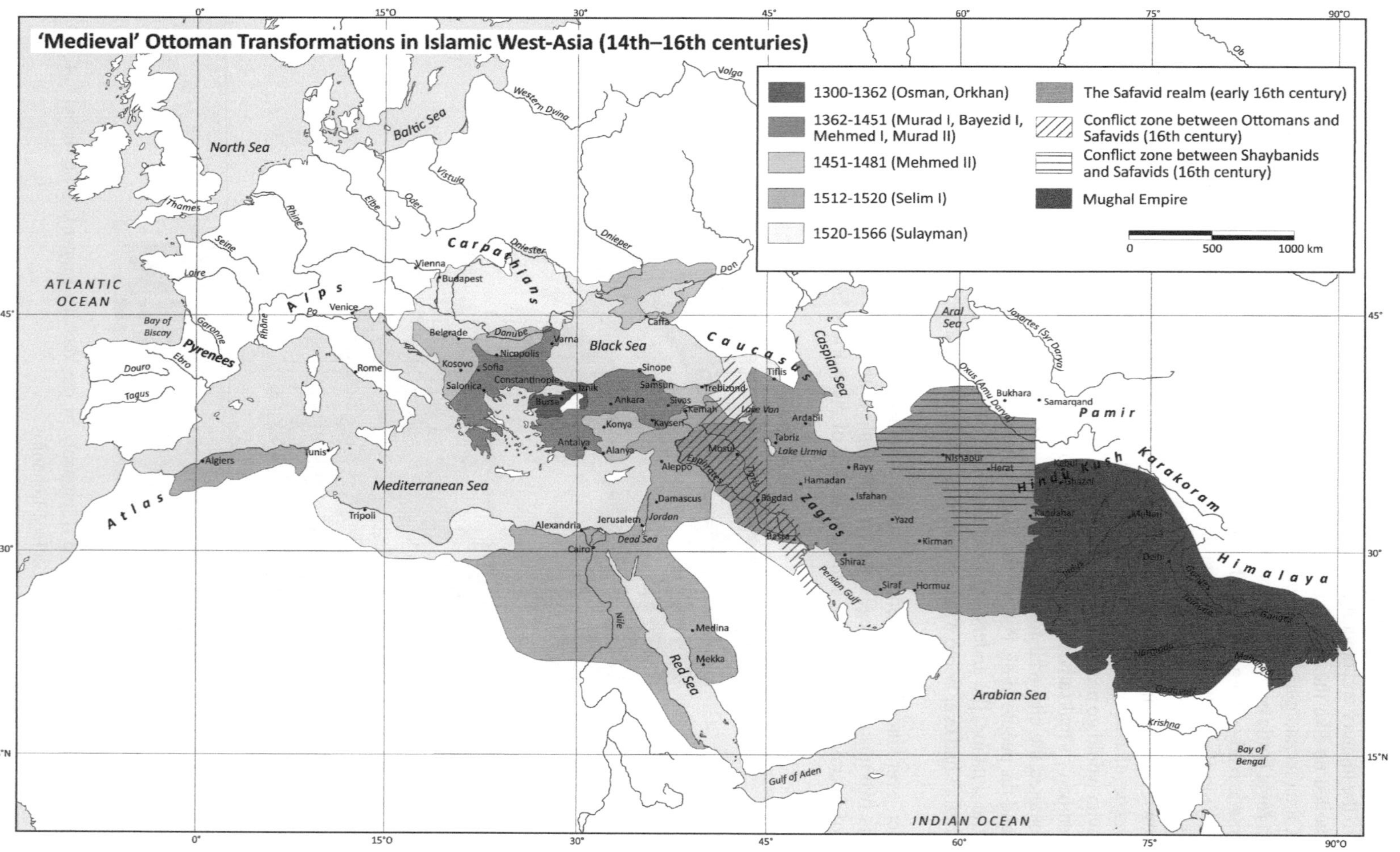

Map 9 'Medieval' Ottoman Transformations in Islamic West-Asia (14th–16th centuries)

considered a long-awaited achievement, carrying an immense eschatological significance. The events of May 1453, therefore, had far-reaching consequences for articulations of the trans-regional authority and claims to sovereignty of the sultan, which were as of now cast in much wider and more ambitious formats of messianic and universal rule. As a powerful token of these claims—and of the heterogeneous legacies from which they stemmed—Mehmed now began to style himself with both the Arabo-Turkic title of *Hakhan ul-barreyn vel-bahreyn* (Khan of the Khans of the Two Continents and the Two Seas—meaning Anatolia and Rumelia [the Balkans] and the Mediterranean and Black Sea) and the Perso-Greek title of *Kayser-i Rum* (Emperor of Rome). Mehmed, who eventually died of poisoning in 1481 and was succeeded by his less belligerent son Bayezid II (r. 1481–1512), was known in early modern Europe—just like many sultans after him—as 'el Gran Turco' (the Great Turk). In the Ottoman and West-Asian context, he was mainly remembered as Fatih or Ebu'l Feth (the Conqueror), that is, as a champion of the 'medieval' practices that had continued to generate his and his entourage's forceful and continuously expanding trans-regional leadership.

The constitutive practices of 15th-century conquest and expansion, of ever more stable Ottoman centrality in patriarchal and eventually also patrimonial relationships of power, authority, and violence-wielding agency, and the long and successful terms of four generations of Ottoman leadership very much continued on even wider trans-regional scales in the 16th century. Bayezid's son sultan Selim I Yavuz (r. 1512–1520) is especially remembered for his major victories in the east and south, won in a series of violent confrontations with the new and highly charismatic Turkmen power of Azerbaijan in 1514 (see next chapter) and especially, in 1516 and 1517, with the aforementioned Cairo Sultanate, the substantial territories, elites, and resources of which were subsequently fully integrated into the Ottoman dynastic order. The Ottoman Sultan thus, as the result of one highly successful campaign of conquest in a new, southward direction, gained control over a vast array of rich West-Asian territories. Dominating the eastern Mediterranean and the Red Sea trade routes, these lands were inhabited by various non-Muslim and, especially, Muslim populations, and included ancient and highly significant urban centers such as Mecca, Medina, Jerusalem, Cairo, and Damascus. This sudden violent expansion of Ottoman power and authority—and virtual doubling of the sultan's domains—into regions that stretched from the upper Euphrates to the Hejaz and upper Egypt, ending and replacing the longstanding Cairo Sultanate and bringing to Constantinople the last surviving Abbasid caliph of Cairo, therefore, added substantial, and particularly Sunni Islamic, prestige and dynastic charisma to the universal sovereignty that was now more than ever claimed for the Ottoman Sultan.

In hindsight, many of these processes of ongoing Ottoman expansion, integrative centrality, and trans-regional sovereignty culminated in the equally grandiose achievements of Selim's son and successor, Suleiman the Magnificent (r. 1520–1566). In line with the example of nine generations of Ottoman sultans before him, Suleiman also regularly assumed personal leadership of the military campaigns that continued to leave Constantinople annually in eastern or western directions, in search of booty, tribute, and enforcement of the authority of the sultan. In the east, especially in four different campaigns between the 1530s and 1550s, the Turkmen frontier zone stabilized following both a number of failed invasions of Azerbaijan and the effective integration of Iraq and the ancient urban centers of Bagdad and Basra, and also by the further opening up of the Persian Gulf for Ottoman commercial activities. In the west, the Ottoman battlefields in southeastern Europe and in North Africa became mainly determined by the rivalry and competition with the Spanish and Central-European dynasty of the Habsburgs. In the Mediterranean, the 16th-century Ottoman battlefield was also largely determined by the imperial maritime power of Venice, which was not only one of the most important economic actors of the time, but due to its control of numerous

Figure 11.6 Portrait of sultan Suleiman, by the Italian painter Titian (1490–1576), *c.* 1530 (Kunsthistorisches Museum Wien)

Source: Wikimedia, Public Domain, https://commons.wikimedia.org/w/index.php?curid=2646041

Mediterranean trade settlements, ports, and domains (including Cyprus between 1489 and 1573), also a formidable rival for trans-regional power and authority.

A crucial moment in this western competition was the crushing Ottoman victory, on 29 August 1526, over the Hungarians at Mohacs and, in the following decade, the definitive incorporation of most of the lands of the historical regions of Hungary. Competing Habsburg and Ottoman claims for the vacant Hungarian throne then put both great powers into direct opposition. In 1529, after the capture of Buda, the Ottoman troops, about 120,000 men strong, even advanced to before the walls of Habsburg Vienna. However, the siege remained without real results and retreat was sounded after just three weeks, due especially to extremely bad weather conditions. In regular campaigns along both sides, both dynastic leaderships continued to confront each other over the issue of Hungary, with the Ottoman troops of Suleiman usually gaining the upper hand. In 1547, after years of negotiations, a peace treaty with Suleiman—the so-called Treaty of Adrianople (or, in Turkic, Edirne)—was signed in which the Habsburgs were allowed to call a strip in the west and north of Hungary their territory in exchange for the payment of an annual tribute of 30,000 ducats to the sultan. The Ottoman sultan's control over Hungarian local and regional elites and resources had thus become an established fact, even though the relationship with the Austrian Habsburg house remained anything but peaceful, and invited for occasional further campaigns of conquest and reassertion of Ottoman local, regional, and trans-regional centrality. The last great Ottoman campaign westwards, in 1566, was again not only particularly impressive as a logistic operation, but also as a successful reaffirmation of Ottoman power beyond the Danube. It also meant the end, after more than four decades, of the reign of Sultan Suleiman, when he died in his royal tent in the night of 5 to 6 September, during the siege of the rebellious Hungarian fortress of Szigetvár.

Throughout the 16th century, and parallel to the long years of annual campaigns, regular open battles, and eventual stabilization of the Ottoman frontier zones in the Turkmen east and the Habsburg-Hungarian west, Suleiman was also closely involved, via various local and Ottoman representatives, in an enormous power struggle for control over routes and ports of the Mediterranean. Apart from the Venetian Republic ('La Serenissima'), the Habsburg kings of Spain were among the main players there. Major and strategic ports, fortifications, and urban centers on the North African coasts came under Habsburg control in the course of the first half of the 16th century. This fate befell, among others Tripoli, from 1510 to 1551, and Tunis, after a maritime campaign in 1535, in the form of a so-called crusade that ended with the looting of the town and a massacre among its population. On the Ottoman side, it was first of all the maritime experience, expertise, and resources of a number of seamen and privateers (the so-called 'Barbary pirates') that made the difference. These maritime strongmen first succeeded to develop a maritime counterweight from their headquarters Algiers, with Ottoman logistical and military support, and were soon also fully integrated in the structures of the emerging Ottoman patrimonial apparatus of power (see below). In time, the entire eastern Mediterranean area and North Africa up to Algiers were thus, via maritime agents, representatives, and violence, integrated in the Ottoman dynastic order. Eventually, in October 1571, under Suleiman's son and successor Selim II (r. 1566–1574), a defeat was suffered in a famous sea battle at Lepanto, off the Greek west coast, against an impressive fleet of the so-called Catholic Holy League (consisting of the Spanish Habsburgs, the Pope, and the republics of Venice and Genoa). As early as 1573, however, when the League had disintegrated and the destroyed Ottoman fleet had been rebuilt, Cyprus was conquered from its Venetian overlords, the coasts of southern Italy and Sicily were attacked, and shortly afterwards, in 1574, Tunis was permanently withdrawn from Spanish-Habsburg control. In these diverse but equally violent and coercive ways in the Mediterranean area as well, a clear-cut frontier zone stabilized between Ottoman centrality and interests in the east and south on the one hand and European priorities in the northwest on the other. Spheres of influence were definitively divided, overly ambitious expansionist plans were no longer up for discussion, and certainly after an Ottoman-Spanish treaty, concluded in the period 1580–81 during the long and stable government of Murad III (r. 1574–1595), further competition for control of Mediterranean maritime routes and resources tended to be left to the competition between all kinds of local forces, whether or not in the name of one of the era's great powers.

3.2.2 Twelve generations of dynastic practices and patrimonial formation

3.2.2.1 OTTOMAN DYNASTIC PRACTICES OF REPRODUCTION

The charismatic leadership that continued to be vested in twelve generations of Osmanids, or of Ottomans, and that time and again managed to command royal households and wider entourages of followers, agents, representatives, and allies at the center of enormously expanding networks of power, violence, patronage, and resources, was never the outcome of any static or self-evident process of the reproduction of a fortuitous and blessed dynastic lineage. Notions of collective leadership and corporate sovereignty, and the centrifugal tendencies inherent in practices of appanage and of distant integration—mainly via tributary arrangements and acknowledgment of overlordship—of longstanding local and regional dynasts and elites made the continued coherence of the Ottoman trans-regional dynastic order all but self-evident. Every generation had to—as it were—work hard to generate the transfer of dynastic charisma from its predecessors as well as from its rivals to consolidate transitions of power and maintain Ottoman cohesion and centrality.

A central mechanism that appears in this context of succession and transition as a well-known early Ottoman practice to secure the integral reproduction of dynastic power is the tradition of internecine warfare, transforming eventually into the more structured practice of so-called fratricide. In this Ottoman tradition, a violent struggle for life and death between the sons of the preceding sultan determined who was the legitimate heir to Ottoman leadership and, at the same time, completely eliminated all dynastic rivals. The narrative of Ottoman internecine warfare and fratricide between the 14th and 16th centuries in fact reconstructs an interesting alternative version of Ottoman dynastic leadership's long history of empowerment and expansion.

Osman's grandson Murad (r. 1366–1389) allegedly stepped into this tradition of internecine warfare and fratricide, when, in the poetic version of one early 15th-century Ottoman dynastic history, "his brothers became enemies to him/The affairs of all of them were ended at his hands/They were all destroyed by his sword".[26] In 1389, Bayezid I reportedly disposed of his brother Yaʿqub on the battlefield of Kosovo Polje, after their father Murad I had been killed there. Only from 1413, after many years of the aforementioned internecine warfare between the sons of Bayezid and after the death of his brothers Suleiman and Musa, Mehmed I appeared as the new Ottoman sultan. Mehmed's son Murad II acquired his authority only in the confrontation with the armies of his uncle and his brother, after he had the former hanged in Edirne in 1422 and the latter strangled in Iznik a year later. Mehmed II got rid of his rival, a minor son of his father Murad II, by ordering his execution immediately upon assuming power in 1451. At that time—so later reports at least claim, though seeking justification for later atrocities of Ottoman fratricide may also have to do with these claims—he allegedly even promulgated a formal regulation that transformed fratricide into a just and legitimate practice, decreeing that "to whomsoever of my sons the Sultanate shall pass, it is fitting that for the order of the world he shall kill his brothers. Most of the *ulema* allow it. So let them act on this".[27] In 1481, Mehmed's son Jem was defeated with his troops and supporters by his brother Bayezid, but Jem succeeded in escaping, first to Egypt and eventually to Europe, which in turn led to many years of Ottoman instability and uncertainty. Already in the course of their father Bayezid's life, Selim and his brothers engaged in military conflicts over the succession, which were won by the young Selim at the expense of his father (who was forced to resign in 1512) and his brothers Ahmed and Korkud and their descendants. In 1520, Suleiman was Selim's only male descendant, but when Suleiman grew old and weak, from the early 1550s onwards, the struggle for succession similarly broke out in his entourage. Suleiman himself took control of the situation and had his sons Mustafa, in 1553, and Bayezid, in 1562—only after various armed confrontations and a flight to the rival Turkmen court in Tabriz—executed, leaving only Selim II to succeed his father at his death in 1566. In subsequent succession issues, upon the deaths of Selim II in 1574 and of Murad III in 1595, it turned out that each time only one suitable male candidate was available for the succession due to the premature death or the minority of his brothers. Therefore, from Selim II onwards, by sheer coincidence, every time it was the oldest surviving candidate

Figure 11.7 Istanbul: mausoleum (*türbe*) of sultan Selim II (r. 1566–1574), on the courtyard of Hagia Sophia. Next to Selim's this mausoleum also contains the remains of his favorite wife Nurbanu (st. 1583) and of the five sons who were murdered at the accession of their brother Murad III in 1574

Source: B.O'Kane/Alamy Stock Photo

who ascended the throne, without any repetition of the campaigns, battles, and intrigues that had so much disrupted the dynasty and its power in the past. In 1574 and 1594, however, all minor brothers of the new sultans Murad III and Mehmed III (respectively five and nineteen princes) were still taken from the harem at Constantinople, executed as potential rivals, and buried together with their deceased father. It was not until the early 17th century that this tradition of fratricide was finally abandoned for the principle of primogeniture.

3.2.2.2 OTTOMAN PATRIMONIAL FORMATION IN THE DYNASTIC CENTER

The remarkable fact that Ottoman cohesion, centrality, and authority were successfully achieved by at least twelve generations of Osmanids between the 14th and 16th centuries, and then maintained by many more generations into the early 20th century, is, however, not only the result of the charismatic achievements of twelve heroic survivors of the violent and unstable 'medieval' realities of internecine warfare and Ottoman fratricide. Various other practices, strategies, and tools were also developed, or emerged along the way, to strengthen that charisma and enable not just the Ottoman dynastic center's continued elimination of rivals, protection of clients, and accumulation of sufficient resources, but also the stabilization and reproduction of its central relationships of power and resources. This occurred in highly interrelated ways that generated the dynastic center's slow transformation from a patriarchal into a patrimonial apparatus of central power, of conquest, of redistribution, and of patronage. Such a transformation manifested itself above all in the traditional mediating infrastructures of the royal household and court—first organized in the northwestern Anatolian urban center of Bursa, after 1402 especially in Edirne (Adrianople) in Thrace, and from 1453 onwards in Constantinople on the Bosporus—and of *waqf*-related urban infrastructures, which all experienced enormous transformations from being the arenas of traditional post-Seljuk Turkmen and Turkmen-related leaderships and their constituencies in the 14th century to those of Ottomanized 'new Turks' in the 16th century (see also Chapter 13).

Throughout the 14th and 15th centuries, royal marriages with the daughters of Turkmen *beys* or with Serbian and Greek-Roman princesses appear as preferred tools to integrate friendly or rival leaders in Anatolia or in the Balkans into the Ottoman dynastic order. In the 16th century, however, these mechanisms of patriarchal authority disappear, and instead privileged personal concubines of varying unfree origins—beginning with Suleiman's favorite wife Hürrem Sultan (*c.* 1502–1558), also known as Roxelana—acquire prominence in the household. This coincided with substantial changes in appanage practices. In fact, from the age of ten, royal sons used to be sent to one of the central Ottoman regions to set up their own households and courts, to gain their own leadership experience and charismatic reputation, and to basically prepare for the struggle that was to decide on their father's succession. This was also suggested in the above-quoted description of the late 14th-century battle of Nicopolis, where the Arabic eyewitness report suggests that sultan Bayezid I (r. 1389–1402) "sent a message to . . . the appanages of his sons (*jamāʿat awlādihi*) to come with their own soldiers", but also that these patriarchal bonds of loyalty and obligation could be rather fickle, so that in the end "only one of his sons arrived a day before the battle". Under Suleiman, this patriarchal practice too—since long abandoned as a more general practice to retain trans-regional cohesion in the Ottoman core lands between, as far as West-Asia is concerned, the Bosporus and the Nile—was definitely abandoned, and royal sons started to spend their time at their fathers' court rather than dangerously far removed from it. Succession struggles, therefore, were eventually fought out—and fratricide eventually only occurred—at the court palace among opposing groups of household and court members, rather than in the sultanate's core regions among different configurations of royal sons, regional leaders, and—especially—formerly Turkmen frontier lords.

These dynastic transformations, in fact, suggest how the Ottoman dynast evolved from being a first among Turkmen equals, whose support he continuously needed to renegotiate, to becoming a superior patrimonial ruler, empowered by his reliance on an ever stronger Ottoman patrimonial power apparatus, with new groups of 'Ottomanized' agents and servants gradually emerging—especially between the mid-15th and mid-16th centuries—in the center of dynastic power. A fundamental distinction was thereby installed in the discourse of the Ottoman order by considering all military, administrative, and other specialists who belonged to this expanding apparatus as the *ʿaskeri*, the 'military' who received an income from the sultan in exchange for their services, primarily conceptualized as services to the formative Ottoman conquest practices. In fact, as suggested above, in the course of the later 15th and early 16th centuries, the different groups and families who had shared in shaping the Ottoman dynastic order in Anatolia and on the Balkans gradually lost their privileges, status, and access as this central militarized organization of dynastic power grew in size and complexity. Traditional Turkmen and Turkic-speaking Anatolian families—including former Turkmen *beylik* leaderships, so-called marcher lords (*uç begs*) or frontier warlords, and other types of *ghazis*—in particular came into direct competition with the new, specifically Ottoman, groups of the *kapi kullari* (the 'servants of the Palace') in the higher ranks of the Ottoman military and administrative apparatus. The latter new elites among the unfree manpower of the sultan also became the core of the sultan's personal infantry guard and an important military innovation and addition to the more traditional cavalry force supplied by the Turkish-Ottoman landed gentry of the *sipahi*s.

Many of these new elites of 'servants of the Porte' were acquired and selected from the highly diverse ranks of prisoners-of-war or as tributary payments, selected and collected via an ever more regular practice of child levy (*devshirme*). From at latest the 1430s, the Ottoman mechanisms of the *devshirme*—of the collection and selection of young boys from among Christian communities on the Balkans and in Anatolia—played an increasingly important role in the recruitment of these new administrative and especially military elite forces. In one of the earliest Ottoman chronicles, the legendary origins of this particular recruitment arrangement are creatively reconstructed as a function of the process of Ottoman empowerment, patrimonial transformation, and integration into the Sunni fold of Islamic law and scholarship. At the same time, the new manpower thus put to benefit Ottoman interests is framed as a substantial improvement of the services traditionally provided by longstanding Turkic-speaking families, most prominent among whom were the Candarli:

> One day a scholar called Kara Rüstem came from the [Southanatolian] land of [the *beylik* of] Karaman. This Kara Rüstem went to Candarli Halīl, who was military judge (*qāḍī ʿasker*), and said: "Why do you let so much state income go waste?" The military judge Halīl asked, "What income is this that is going waste? Tell me at once". Kara Rüstem said, "Of these prisoners that the warriors in the holy war bring back, one-fifth, according to God's command, belongs to the Pādishāh (=the Ottoman sultan). Why do you not take this share?" The military judge Halīl said, "I will submit the matter to the Pādishāh!" He submitted it to Gāzī Murād (=Murad I), who said, "If it is God's command, then take it". They called Kara Rüstem and said, "Master, carry out God's command". Kara Rüstem went away and stayed in Gallipoli and collected twenty-five *akçe* (= 'aspers', the Ottoman silver coinage) from each prisoner. This innovation dates from the time of these two men. To collect a tax from the prisoners in Gallipoli has become the practice since Candarli Kara Halīl and Kara Rüstem. After that he also instructed Gāzī Evrenos to take one out of every five prisoners captured in the raids and, if anyone had only four prisoners, to take twenty-five *akçe* from him. They acted according to this rule. They collected (*devshirme*) the young men. They took one in every five prisoners captured in the raids and delivered them to the Porte. Then they gave these young men to the Turks in the provinces so that they should learn Turkish, and then they sent them to Anatolia. The Turks left these young men to work in the fields for a while and made use of them until they learned Turkish. After a few years they brought them to the Porte and made them janissaries, giving them the name 'New Troops' (*Yenī Ceri*). Their origin goes back to this time.[28]

The power of these notorious 'new troops' (*yeni çeri*), better known as the Janissaries, lay mainly in the regulated discipline that limited their loyalty to nothing but the interests of the Ottoman dynasty and patrimonial apparatus. In the so-called 'Rules of the Janissaries', this is explained as follows:

> From time immemorial it has been unlawful for janissaries to marry; only officers married and also private soldiers who were old and definitely unfit for service and then only on application to the Sultan. The state of a janissary is a state of celibacy, and for that reason barracks were built for them.[29]

As suggested in these fragments, both these selected, collected, and unfree young men from within the Ottoman territories, and many equally selected prisoners-of-war from outside, thus not simply joined the elite ranks of the Janissary foot soldiers and their likes, or of the palace service more in general. They were actually "religiously Islamicized, linguistically Turkified, and culturally Ottomanized".[30] This forced socialization and acculturation in an utterly Ottoman and Sunni environment, and this thorough preparation to enter into military and administrative service of the sultan and the palace, made these young men the ultimate products, and later also producers, of the ever more forceful and powerful Ottoman apparatus. Known by newly acquired political identities as 'Ottomans' or even as 'Romans', this social group made from the ever newly replenished ranks of Ottoman-Turkic-speaking converted Sunni Muslims of various origins eventually became the main central post-nomadic elites of the Ottoman household, court, and Sultanate.

Some of the most captivating examples of these new 'Ottomans' are Mesih Pasha (d. 1501) and Has Murad Pasha (d. 1473), Pargali Ibrahim Pasha (d. 1536), and Sokollu Mehmed Pasha (d. 1579). Mesih and Murad Pasha were actually two cousins of the last Greek-Roman emperor, who had been captured in 1453. Eventually, after conversion and training, they both managed to rise to the highest positions in the dynastic apparatus, as the highest Ottoman representative in the Balkans and as grand vizier in Constantinople respectively. In modern historical research, they are also seen as illustrative of the surprising way in which Greek-Roman and Balkan elites were massively and actively integrated, and even assumed a leading role, in the new and eclectic Ottoman sociopolitical and cultural order in the course of the 15th century. In the 16th century, when the role of such elites finally played out, completely different types of new 'Ottomans' came to the fore. Pargali Ibrahim Pasha was of Greek Orthodox origin, and around the year 1500 he

Figure 11.8 Bifolio from the Quran of Sokollu Mehmed Pasha (1506–1579) (manuscript on paper, Istanbul 1561) (Royal Library of Belgium, Hs. II 1256, fols. 2v-3r)

Source: Brussels, Royal Library of Belgium

had been taken from a small fishing community on the Ionian Sea during an Ottoman raiding party. He was subsequently selected for palace service where he grew up together with the future Sultan Suleiman. Eventually, Ibrahim Pasha gained so much military and diplomatic success, power, and prestige as Suleiman's grand vizier that he was considered a threat to the sultan himself and executed. Sokollu Mehmed Pasha was of equally modest Serbian Orthodox origin, and in 1516 he was selected as a 10-year-old boy for the Janissary corps in the context of the *devshirme*. As a talented warrior, he steadily rose in the state apparatus until he became Admiral of Sultan Suleiman's widely feared fleet, chief military leader of his armies in the Balkans and on the Persian front, and finally omnipotent grand vizier, who was the de facto leader of the Sultanate, especially during the short reign of Selim II—whose daughter Mehmed married. Under Selim's son Murad III as well, Mehmed remained the strong man of the dynastic center, but in a context of increasing tension with Murad and his much younger entourage, he was eventually killed in unclear circumstances.

As these different high-profile examples demonstrate, over time, these new and 'true' Ottomans not only occupied almost all key positions of military leadership at the court and at its different regional offshoots between the Balkans and Egypt. They also increasingly appeared as viziers and grand viziers who shaped and led their sultan's apparatus of power, authority, and administration, and whose fates thus were and remained closely connected with the effectiveness of the claims to trans-regional sovereignty that were articulated by that apparatus.

As suggested above, even these Ottoman dynastic claims to sovereignty transformed over time and adapted to the rapidly changing contexts, agencies, and audiences that they were meant to appeal to. Imaginations and narratives of Ottoman dynastic order continued to be informed by the ideal of holy war (*ghazw*) at the frontiers of Islam, whether in tales of early Ottoman actions in Christian Anatolia or on the Balkans, or in their 16th-century versions involving Habsburgs and Venetians. Extensive references also continued to be made to specific Turkmen genealogies that supported claims to a local or regional dynastic priority for the Ottoman lineage, appealing to kinship ties with the Seljuks of Rum or with the legendary Inner-Asian Turkish leader Oghuz Khan. Finally, similar claims to dynastic specialty, distinction, and entitlement were articulated by the adoption of a wide range of other Turkmen, post-Seljuk, post-Chinggisid, Islamic, and Late Antique titles and qualities. These included the titles of bey and later of sultan and of padishah, but also—from the mid-15th-century onwards—that of 'Caesar of Rome' and—from the early 16th-century onwards—of 'Guardian of the Two Sacred Sanctuaries' (Mecca and Medina), of caliph (as the appointed prophetic successor of the last Abbasid Caliph of Cairo), of Roman 'Caesar of Caesars' (as sovereign of the Habsburg Holy Roman Emperor), of Mongol 'khan of khans' (as sovereign of any Chinggisid claimants), and of Persian 'Khosrow of Khosrows' (as sovereign of the rulers of Iran). The amalgam of this symbolic arsenal of titles betrays a remarkable mix of traditions, a cross-pollination of leadership legacies, and an enormous diversity of interests in east and west, increasingly explicitly situated within the theocratic and dynastic orbit of one coherent trans-regional order topped by the Ottoman ruler and his Ottoman patrimonial agents. In 1568, a treaty text (*ʿahdname*) was drawn up by the Ottoman chancery of sultan Selim II (r. 1566–1574) for the Austrian Habsburgs and it opened in a powerful manner with a very telling evocation of this dynastic order. It gives insight into not only the eclectic richness and diversity of Ottoman claims to sovereignty in the 16th century, but also the enormous complexity of the trans-regional configuration of people, regions, urban centers, and local dynastic constellations over which Selim II and his court claimed power and authority after more than two centuries of Ottoman conquest practices, dynastic transformations, and 'Ottomanizing' adaptations:

> I, who am the sultan of sultans of the Roman, Arabian and Persian lands, khan of khans of the Chinese, the Khitai, the Khitan and the Turks and the Daylamites, . . . the padishah and sultan of the cities around the White Sea [=the Mediterranean], of the forts and fortresses around the Black Sea, of Egypt, Port Said, Aleppo, Damascus, Jeddah, Mecca, Medina, Jerusalem, Yemen, Aden, Sana, Ethiopia, Basra, al-Ahsa, Kurdistan, Georgia, Luristan, Van, the Qipchaq Steppe, the lands of the Tatars, as well as the totality of Anatolia, Zulkadria, Karaman and generally of Rumelia, Wallachia, Moldavia and of many other regions conquered with my victorious sabre.[31]

3.2.2.3 OTTOMAN PATRIMONIAL FORMATION IN THE DYNASTIC DOMAINS

The performance and maintenance of this ever more centrally and patrimonially organized Ottoman dynastic authority in these expanding territories was characterized by a great degree of diversity and local or regional accommodation. This had everything to do with the enormous variety of violent and non-violent ways in which many urban centers and regions in east and west continued to be integrated into the charismatic reach of Ottoman dynastic authority. Usually, the integration of new territories and populations in the Ottoman dynastic order took place very gradually, through the practice of *istimalet*, of 'reconciliation' and coexistence. At first, at a local or regional level, everything was left as much as possible as it had been before a place or region's conquest. Only a selection of relevant local or regional leaders and elites were included, in locally accommodating ways, in the network of Ottoman relations and possibly also in the dynastic apparatus of representation. The extent to which such integration into the Ottoman order continued depended on numerous local and central conditions. Beyond the more centrally located Ottoman regions, this was often limited to the on-site stationing of a (limited) Ottoman military force, such as a regiment of Janissaries, and some Ottoman administrators, who had to look after the Ottoman interests locally. In the Balkans and eastern Europe, where populations and elites mainly were Christian, such a pragmatic policy towards the preservation and continued existence of local and regional identities and practices was also often guaranteed in a more formal way, among other things by their confirmation in specific orders, the so-called 'capitulations' (*ʿahdnāme*). One of the oldest preserved Ottoman capitulation treaties, known as the *ʿahdname* of Milodraž, dates back to 1463 and was issued by sultan Mehmed II (r. 1451–1481) for a Franciscan abbey in the Bosnian region that he had just conquered.

> I, Sultan Mehmed Khan, hereby declare to the entire world that those who have this edict (*fermān*) in their possession, the Bosnian Franciscans, are under my protection. Therefore, I command the following:
> Let nobody bother or bring damage to these Bosnian Franciscans and their churches.
> Let them dwell in peace under my authority.
> Let those who have fled return safely and let them settle down without fear in their monasteries, which are in the peripheries of my territories.
> Nobody from my personal guard, from my viziers and servants, or from my subjects shall insult or hurt them.
> Let nobody attack, insult or endanger their lives, their properties, or the properties of their Church.

Even the things and the people they bring in from outside my territories enjoy the same rights.

As, thus, I have graciously issued this imperial edict, hereby take my oath:

I swear by my sword, in the name of God almighty who created the earth and heaven, in the name of God's prophet Muhammad, and in the name of 124,000 preceding prophets, that nobody who obeys and is loyal to my command will act or perform contrary to this edict.

28 May 1463[32]

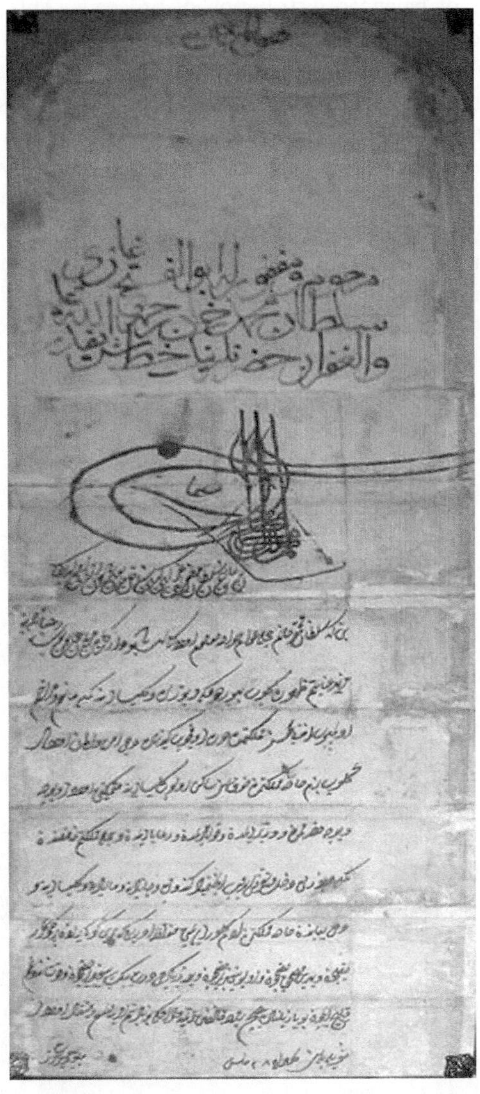

Figure 11.9 Transcript of the *ʿahdnāme* of Milodraž, 1463 (Franciscan convent of Fojnica, Bosnia-Hercegovina)

Source: Public Domain, https://commons.wikimedia.org/w/index.php?curid=13207054

Already at an early stage, the more central parts of the Ottoman territories in Anatolia and the Balkans were divided into more uniformly organized patrimonial units (*eyalet*). Initially, in the course of the 15th century, there appeared four central units (Rumeli in southeastern Europe and Anadolu, Rum and Karaman in Anatolia), administered in the sultan's name by Ottoman military officials with the high court rank of *pasha*. They were the *beylerbeyi*, had extensive military and administrative powers and responsibilities, and were always appointed by the grand vizier. Most *eyalets* were further subdivided into smaller units, the *sanjaks*, each headed by a local commander (*sanjak beyi*), whose authority was limited to land that was formally owned by the sultan (*miri*). The usufruct of this land was given to local farming communities, with reciprocal rights and duties organized around the household of a farmer (*hane*) and a principle of balanced distribution of proceeds. This *çift-hane* arrangement, which was mainly used for the agricultural and fiscal organization of the many *miri* lands in Rumeli and Anadolu, formed an important pillar of the political economy of the dynasty, and of its organization around the court and its annual conquest practices in particular. After all, the revenues and resources that pertained to the sultan were mainly used for the remuneration of the military service of the local landed gentry, the *sipahi*s, who, despite the expansion of the sultan's personal infantry regiments such as that of the Janissaries, continued to make up more than two thirds of the Ottoman forces. In exchange for limited, revocable, and rotating rights to the surplus of agricultural yields from clearly defined territories—the revenue apportionment mechanism of the *timar*, related to the post-Seljuk *iqta*ʿ arrangements

Figure 11.10 Fully equipped Ottoman cavalryman (*sipahi*) (*c.* 1550)

Source: Photo (C) Paris—Musée de l'Armée, Dist. RMN-Grand Palais/Emilie Cambier

mentioned before—these members and followers of the traditional Turkic-speaking Anatolian and Rumelian local leaderships and marcher lordships, the *beys*, had to provide military services and cavalry troops to the sultan and his apparatus of power. Official estimates, derived from many extant official tax registers (*defter*) that were drafted between the later 15th and early 17th centuries and that, on the basis of detailed cadastral surveys, were meant to update the taxable conditions of a *sanjak* every twenty years, provide also some numerical information for the early 16th century. At that time, a *sanjak* typically consisted of 100 *timar*s, representing some 100,000 villagers, and there were some 35,000 *timar*s in Anatolia and on the Balkans, representing half the revenue of the sultan's treasure.[33]

In this way, in the 15th and 16th centuries, the organization of the central Ottoman domains remained largely determined by the need to support the charismatic, and highly centralizing, practices of conquest and expansion, which continued to appear therefore—just as among most other leaderships in Islamic West-Asia—as a core dimension of the 'medieval' Ottoman configuration of elites, interests, and resources. In early 16th century Europe, very much aware of the forceful dynastic presence of the Ottoman sultan—*el Gran Turco*—and of the confrontational nature of the Sultanate's organizational practices, one famous and influential text of royal advice, *The Prince* by the Florentine diplomat Niccolò Machiavelli (1469–1527), introduced his contemporary reading of this military configuration of Ottoman leadership networks in the formulation of a thesis about the two distinct forms in which, in Machiavelli's version, dynastic sovereignties and conquest practices interacted throughout human history to pursue stabilizations of power.

> [A]ll principalities known to history have been ruled in one of two ways: either by one ruler, who is helped to govern the kingdom by others, who are in reality his servants, acting as ministers through his grace and favour; or else by a ruler and barons who hold that rank by hereditary right, not through the favour of the ruler. . . . The whole Turkish Kingdom is governed by one ruler, the others' all being his servants; and his Kingdom is divided into sanjaks, to which he sends various administrators, whom he changes and moves as he pleases. But the King of France is placed amidst a great number of hereditary lords, recognized in that state by their own subjects, who are devoted to them. They have their own hereditary privileges, which the King disallows only at his peril. If these two kinds of state are considered, then, it will be found that it is difficult to overcome a state of the Turkish type but, if it has been conquered, very easy to hold it. On the other hand, in some respects it is easier to conquer a state like France, but it is very difficult to hold it.[34]

This contemporary representation by an outsider such as Machiavelli undoubtedly should be critically examined as a highly simplified and 'orientalized' portrayal, with the 'medieval' realities of 16th-century Ottoman patrimonial leadership beyond the direct reach of its dynastic center never entirely escaping from the centrifugal regional and local logics of Machiavelli's second type. Nevertheless, this representation is at least indicative of the coercive, centripetal, and 'Ottomanizing' practices that tried to organize the trans-regional networks of Ottoman leadership and conquest, capturing the imagination of observers and opponents across and even beyond the sultan's many domains in highly empowering ways.

Notes

1 Katouzian, *The Persians*, 106; as quoted in Jackson, *The Mongols and the Islamic World*, 3–4.
2 ʿAṭā Malik Juvaynī (d. 1283), *Taʾrīkh-i Jahān Gushā* ['History of the World Conqueror']; translation from Boyle, *The History of the World Conqueror*, 1: 96–7; Morgan, *Medieval Persia. 1040–1797*, 82.

3 Ibn Kathīr (d. 1372), *al-Bidāya wa l-Nihāya fī l-tārīkh* ['History from the Beginning to the End']; translation adapted from Lewis, *Islam from the Prophet Muhammad to the Capture of Constantinople. Volume I: Politics and War*, 84.
4 Abu Lughod, *Before European Hegemony: The World System, A.D. 1250–1350.*
5 Lewis, "Mongols, the Turks and the Muslim Polity", 55.
6 Manz, *The Rise and Rule of Tamerlane*, 66–7.
7 See Jackson, *The Mongols and the Islamic World*, 139.
8 Ibn Kathīr (d. 1372), *al-Bidāya wa-l-Nihāya fī l-tārīkh* ['History from the Beginning to the End']; translation adapted from Lewis, *Islam from the Prophet Muhammad to the Capture of Constantinople. Volume I: Politics and War*, 81–4.
9 Meyvaert, "An Unknown Letter of Hulagu, Il-Khan of Persia, to King Louis IX of France", 258.
10 Melville, "The *Keshig* in Iran: The Survival of the Royal Mongol Household".
11 Ḥāfiẓ-i Abrū (d. 1430), *Dhayl-i Jāmiʿ al-Tavārīkh* ['The Continuation of the Compendium of Chronicles']; translation from Wing, "The Decline of the Ilkhanate", 83–4.
12 Allsen, *Culture and Conquest in Mongol Eurasia*, 79.
13 Al-ʿUmarī (1301–49), *Masālik al-Abṣār fī Mamālik al-Amṣār* ['Paths of Discernment into the Realms and Urban Centers']; translation from Allsen, *Culture and Conquest in Mongol Eurasia*, 73.
14 Wing, "The Decline of the Ilkhanate".
15 Ḥāfiẓ-i Abrū (d. 1430), *Dhayl-i Jāmiʿ al-Tavārīkh* ['The Continuation of the Compendium of Chronicles']; translation from Wing, "The Decline of the Ilkhanate", 81; Wing, *The Jalayirids*, 74.
16 Godard, "Bassin de cuivre au nom de Shaikh Uwais", 371; translation after Wing, *The Jalayirids*, 133.
17 Wing, *The Jalayirids*, 147, 175.
18 Imber, *The Ottoman Empire, 1300–1650*, 96.
19 Stolz, Soucek, *Konstantin Mihailovic, Memoirs of a Janissary*, 177; quoted from Lowry, *The Nature of the Early Ottoman State*, 47.
20 See Barkey, *Empire of Difference*.
21 Imber, *The Ottoman Empire, 1300–1650*, 8; Lowry, *The Nature of the Early Ottoman State*, 132.
22 Kafadar, *Between Two Worlds: The Construction of the Ottoman* State, 150.
23 Lowry, *The Nature of the Early Ottoman State*, 132–3.
24 Ibn al-Jazarī (1350–1429), *Jāmiʿ al-Asānīd* ['The Compendium of the Chain of Authorities']; translation from Binbaş, "A Damascene Eyewitness to the Battle of Nicopolis: Shams al-Dīn Ibn al-Jazarī (d. 833/1429)", 168–9.
25 Translation from Kastritsis, *An Early Ottoman History: The Oxford Anonymous Chronicle*, 177–9.
26 Ahmedi (fl. 1400), *Tevārīh-i Mülūk-i Āl-i Osman* ['The Chronicles of the Monarchs from the House of Osman']; translation from Imber, *The Ottoman Empire, 1300–1650*, 97.
27 Quataert, *The Ottoman Empire. 1700–1922*, 91.
28 *Anonymous Ottoman Chronicle*; translation from Lewis, *Islam from the Prophet Muhammad to the Capture of Constantinople. Volume I: Politics and War*, 226–7.
29 *kavanin-i-Yenicheriyan* ['The Rules of the Janissaries'].
30 Lowry, *The Nature of the Early Ottoman State*, 132–3.
31 Translation from Işıksel, "Ottoman-Habsburg Relations in the Second Half of the 16th Century", 55.
32 Translation after E. Ihsanoglu, "A Culture of Peaceful Coexistence: The Ottoman Turkish Example".
33 See Barkey, "The Ottoman Empire (1299–1923): The Bureaucratization of Patrimonial Authority", 110.
34 Niccolò Machiavelli (1469–1527), *Il Principe* ['The Prince']; translation from Skinner, Price, *The Prince*, 15–6.

Selected readings

(see next chapter)

12 'Medieval' transformations between Transoxania and Asia Minor—Part 2

Turko-Mongol and Turkmen conquest practices and dynastic formations (15th–16th centuries)

Introduction: situating 'medieval' Islamic West-Asia and its Turko-Mongol and Turkmen leaderships of Timurids, Qara and Aq Qoyunlu, and Safavids between Transoxania and Asia Minor

This chapter will continue the reconstruction of the recurring pattern of nomadic conquest, dynastic formation, and patriarchal or occasionally even patrimonial transformation that had entered Islamic West-Asia more forcefully than ever with the Chinggisids of the 13th century. In the central and eastern lands of Islamic West-Asia, from the Euphrates to the Jaxartes and Indus river basins, this pattern was emulated in highly intense, transformative, and only slowly stabilizing ways in the course of the 15th and 16th centuries by particular Turko-Mongol and Turkmen leaderships, clustering mostly around the charismatic ambitions and transformative practices of conquest of a handful of successive leaders and their close-knit entourages. These included especially the likes of Timur (r. 1370–1405) and his son Shah Rukh (r. 1405–1447), of the Turkmen rivals Jahan Shah (r. 1439–1467) and Uzun Hasan (r. 1453–1478), of the Safavid *shaykh* Isma'il (r. 1501–1524), and of the Uzbek warlord Muhammad Shaybani (r. *c.* 1500–1510).

The starting point for this chapter, and for its continuation with the previous chapter, is obviously represented by the aforementioned most formidable emulator of the charismatic models set by Chinggis Khan, the Turko-Mongol ruler Timur Lank (r. 1370–1405). As suggested before, Timur embarked upon a career of endless conquest not simply because he may have reveled in the experience of campaigning and violence wielding, but because it represented the main mechanism to construct and consolidate his new charismatic leadership and its patriarchal entourage of household, personal guards, and strong bonds of loyalty and obligation (*keshig*). As in the case of Chinggis Khan, the apparatus of conquest that emerged around the charisma of Timur was extremely effective and generated an entirely new dynastic—Timurid—leadership around his person, around his descendants and commanders, and around their access to and integration of West-Asian elites and resources, as mediated via the by now well-known courtly and urban infrastructures of power. A new, post-Mongol and Timurid trans-regional order of Turko-Mongol wielders of violence, great varieties of more or less integrated local and regional rulers and their followers, diverse Arabo-Persian networks of experts and expertise, and powerful mixes of ideas and articulations of authority and sovereignty actually emerged between the Euphrates in the west and the Jaxartes and Indus Rivers in the east. This trans-regional order proved highly charismatic and, therefore, not just unstable and constantly wavering between territorially dispersed polycentric realities and the coercion of these realities into more coherent frameworks, but also a blueprint for successful West-Asian rulership the emulation, even restoration, of which was pursued by at least a handful of Timurid and Turkmen leaders in the course of the 15th and 16th centuries. This gave rise between Transoxania in the east and Azerbaijan in the west to nothing less than a competitive co-existence, expansion, and succession of different Turko-Mongol and Turkmen dynastic enterprises in the 15th century. It culminated in the establishment of equally unstable and rivalling Safavid and Shaybanid trans-regional sovereignties in the early 16th century. Each of these recurrent moments of conquest and dynastic formation will be discussed in some detail below, focusing in particular on the Turko-Mongol Timurids, on their Turkmen and Safavid successors in the later 15th and early 16th centuries, and on the mid-16th century relative—and only temporary—stabilization and post-nomadic transformation of all these and many more relationships and imaginations of power and authority in, especially, Safavid Iran.

1 Turko-Mongol conquest practices and dynastic formations

1.1 Timur's Chaghadayid conquest practices

As suggested on various occasions, the radical transformations in the former Hülegüid lands and leadership networks between Anatolia and Khurasan were the result of new practices of conquest pursued, in the spirit of Chinggis Khan, from the eastern parts of his descendants' appanages in Islamic West-Asia. As suggested in the previous chapter, in these eastern parts of Islamic West-Asia, in the regions of Transoxania and Khurasan in particular, different mid-14th-century Turko-Mongol leaderships—Turkic-speaking, adhering to Mongol and Chinggisid customs and traditions, pastoral and nomadic, increasingly Islamized, and symbiotically related to these regions' ancient urban centers and elites as well as to their rich commercial and agricultural resources—had started to relate to each other in a particular constellation of shared interests and balanced relationships of power that was collectively identified by contemporaries as the Ulus Chaghaday.

In this Turko-Mongol configuration of devolved Chinggisid authority, one Timur ibn Turghay Barlas (d. 1405)—also known as Temür Lank, Tamerlane, and Timur the Lame—rose to prominence and priority in the course of the 1360s. Timur stemmed from one of the minor branches of the Mongolian Barlas leadership in Transoxania, which descended from one of the four senior commanders who had been tranferred, with their followers, by Chinggis Khan from his own entourage to his son Chaghaday's appanage more than a century earlier. Timur and his close-knit group of personal followers uniquely managed to rise in the ranks of Barlas and wider Chaghaday leadership until being confirmed in a formal gathering of his peers in April 1370 as a first among equals, or 'amir', of the Ulus and as a guardian of its Chinggisid order. Thereupon, he embarked on a spectacular career of more than three decades of strengthening and expanding his power and authority, eliminating old and new rivals, protecting the expanding ranks of his clients, and accumulating and distributing resources in ways that were to transform both the Ulus Chaghaday and post-Hülegüid Islamic West-Asia beyond recognition. The remarkable extent of this power and authority was based on Timur's charismatic personality and the longevity of his leadership. It also derived from his relentless and therefore, equally charismatic wielding of violence on an ever wider, Asian scale, until his death in 1405, at the beginning of his campaign to conquer Ming China and his thus frustrated attempt to reintegrate it—after the disappearance from the Chinese scene of leadership of the successors of the aforementioned Qubilai in the 1360s—in the Chinggisid order.

Figure 12.1 Head of Timur (reconstruction based on forensic research performed on the remains of Timur by Sovjet archaeologist and anthropologist M. Gerasimov in 1941–1942)

Source: Wikimedia Commons https://commons.wikimedia.org/wiki/File:Timur_reconstruction03.jpg

The sustained expansion of Timur's power and authority also related to the particular formation of his personal household. This involved, in the 1360s, his marrying into a branch of the Chinggisid line—which distinguished him from his Turko-Mongol peers as a 'royal in-law' (*güregen*). From the 1370s onwards, this particular formation of Timur's power also manifested in his construction of a new trans-regional network of leadership around his patriarchal authority by assigning conquered regions and towns to his sons and his personal supporters (mostly referred to as his *nöker*s, tied to him after many years of personal service through relationships of loyalty and obligation rather than kinship), their descendants, and their essentially Chaghadayid armies. Finally, Timur's power and authority also followed from his intense use of more structured arrangements. These included the courtly organization of his highly mobile royal tent and military encampment and its highly personalized distributive mechanisms to deal with the spoils of war. They also consisted of his investment in urban infrastructures—especially in Transoxania—such as mosques and *madrasa*s, bazaars, and garden palaces. The latter offered opportunities both for his patronage of local and regional elites, including *ʿulamaʾ* and spiritual masters, and their diverse knowledge

Figure 12.2 Samarqand (Uzbekistan): remains of Timur's Bibi Khanum mosque (1399–1405) (before its reconstruction in the course of the 20th century)

Source: Photo by Sergei Mikhailovich Prokudin-Gorskii, 1907, www.loc.gov/pictures/resource/prokc.21835/

practices, and for splendid articulations of his claims to sovereignty, skillfully executed by specialists and experts most of whom had been taken under duress from their hometowns across West-Asia to the new urban center of Timur's universe, Samarqand.

The mix of these and related factors of personal, coercive, Chinggisid, and Islamic charisma allowed Timur and his entourage to claim his own mixed forms of dynastic as well as Islamic sovereignty over a diverse group of nomadic and urban elites, first in Transoxania and subsequently in the whole of Islamic Asia. An impressive record of conquest and violence became the most important characteristic of this claim, and of its eventual formulation in novel, Timurid—instead of Chinggisid—terms of dynastic good fortune and divine blessing by many of those who claimed to be his successors. Endless practices of conquest throughout many of West- and Central-Asia's regions—with some localities even more than once conquered, looted, and then abandoned again—left many local and regional communities in disarray and made trans-regional networks of power and resources radically recalibrate around Timur's interests and concerns, and around their center of gravity in Transoxania. Campaigning in the 1370s took him mostly further east, against other Chaghaday contenders, as well as to the Khwarazm oases in Transoxania's northwest. The 1380s, however, were marked by major campaigns westwards, especially in Khurasan and Sistan as well as in Azerbaijan, and this was repeated in the mid-1390s with the more permanent effect of the establishment of Timur's representatives as regional rulers. The early 1390s also witnessed Timur engaging head-on with a Chinggisid rival in the Pontic-Caspian steppes north of the Caspian and Black Sea, ending in victory, Timur's troops' advancement all the way up to Moscow, and the general spread of havoc and looting in the Don and Volga regions. In 1398, he engaged in a campaign southward, towards the Indian peninsula, which culminated in the sack of Delhi in December 1398, and the departure of his armies back to Transoxania, loaded with Indian spoils. Between 1399 and 1402, another major campaign westward brought Timur's armies once again in Azerbaijan, and from there in Syria and Anatolia, which were eventually also retreated from, after the sacking of rich urban centers such as Aleppo and Damascus in the former region, and after putting a temporal end to Ottoman territorial expansion in the latter region. In 1404, he embarked upon his final China campaign, reportedly with an enormous army, but this came to a premature end with Timur's death in his encampment near the oases of Otrar, east of the Jaxartes, or Syr Darya.

Endless campaigning beyond the Chaghaday homelands, especially from the 1380s onwards, made above all that shared interests and benefits stabilized Timur's relationships with the diverse Chaghaday leadership, and kept their ranks closed around his commands and around the revenues from tribute and looting that flowed richly towards their home bases and entourages in Transoxania. Endless campaigning also forged the nature and composition of Timur's own leadership household and made it into a new trans-regional elite of commanders and relatives. Thus, a new dominant trans-regional order appeared very rapidly across most of Islamic West-Asia, emanating from the mobile encampments of Timur, of his commanders, and of his sons and grandsons, as well as from his Transoxanian headquarters in Samarqand, and connecting in entirely new networks of violence wielding and resource circulation Delhi in the east with Damascus in the west, and Moscow in the north with Hormuz in the Iranian south. Throughout Islamic West-Asia, the violent passage of Timur and his armies meant that power balances were redrawn, that the constellation of leaderships and communities changed in function of their varying relationships with Timur and his entourage, and that trans-regional connections and configurations were revised.

Whereas by default local arrangements and configurations of power across Islamic West-Asia were not really interfered with, or were left to quickly recover, especially the regional leaderships in the former Hülegüid lands between Anatolia and Khurasan appear to have become the object of Timur's remarkably selective wrath. The persistent perception of these dynastic formations as the only genuine rivals for his power and authority resulted above all in the aforementioned eliminations of the Kartids of Herat, the Muzaffarids of Shiraz, and the Jalayirids of Tabriz and Bagdad, and in the defeat and substantial weakening of the Ottoman Sultanate in Anatolia, the Cairo Sultanate in Syria, and the Delhi Sultanate in northern India. The region of Azerbaijan on the other hand, and in particular the Turkmen leadership that had only recently risen to prominence there in a context of Jalayirid internecine warfare, remained a more complex story. Neither Timur nor his commanders and local allies ever entirely managed to reorganize Azerbaijan's leadership arrangements as they did elsewhere, despite repeated campaigns and regular successful confrontations. In fact, from these days of Timur until the later 15th century, the former Hülegüid heartlands of Azerbaijan and its adjacent regions would remain one of the main frontier zones of the new West-Asian stabilizations of power relations that followed Timur's death. Unlike in Khurasan and Transoxania, in western Anatolia, and in Egypt, on the rich pastures and in the intense web of commercial routes of Azerbaijan loyalties would remain in flux for many decades after 1405. As also

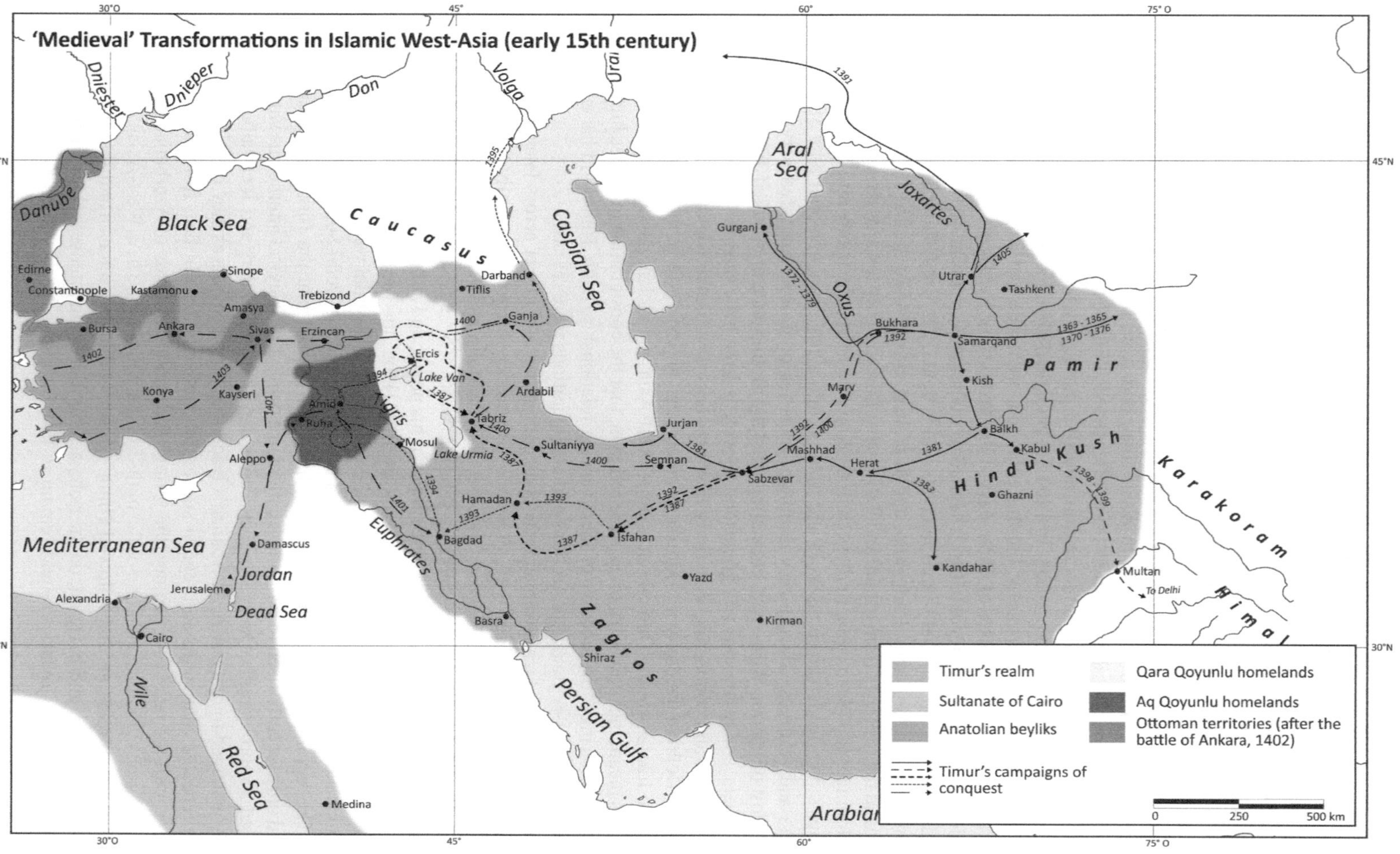

Map 10 'Medieval' Transformations in Islamic West-Asia (early 15th century)

Source: Redrawn from Hodgson, *The Venture of Islam. Vol. 2. The Expansion of Islam in the Middle Periods*, p. 431

announced by the aforementioned defeat and execution of the Jalayirid Sultan Ahmad in 1410 by his Turkmen rival and former ally, in this frontier zone, pastoral nomadic Turkmen would remain dominant in unstable configurations of local, regional, and trans-regional power and urban symbiosis, and an ideal stage of volatile leadership constellations would continue to be set for Timur's example of charismatic conquest and personal trans-regional rule to be emulated.

This emulation was actually pursued most ambitiously by at least three of these charismatic Turkmen leaders in the course of the 15th century (see below). Their cases, however, simultaneously marked a reversal of the dominant trend in Timur's—and for that matter Chinggis Khan's—practices of conquest, this time moving eastwards rather than westwards, from eastern Anatolia, the Jazira, and Azerbaijan to Iran and Khurasan. Seen in hindsight from this West-Asian perspective, Timur's spectacular career of conquest at the turn of the 14th to 15th centuries, affecting especially dynastic leaderships between the Euphrates and the Oxus and Indus, brought to shore yet another wave of destruction, fragility, and fragmentation of West-Asian networks of power that would take yet another century to stabilize. It also represents the final moment in the long range of Inner-Asian migrations and expansions that since the 11th century had continued to regularly transform West-Asia's landscapes of leadership and claims to authority and sovereignty. Even though greater trans-regional stability took a long time to reappear, no further substantial interferences from elsewhere were similarly to affect the entirety of West-Asia's landscapes of power for several more centuries. In the long course of the 15th and 16th centuries, when Timur's Turko-Mongol and Turkmen legacy joined the West-Asian ranks of the heirs of the Seljuks and the Hülegüids, including the Cairo Sultanate in the southwest and the Ottoman Sultanate in the northwest, the elites, ideas, and ideals that were to dominate West-Asia's history in subsequent centuries were finally settling in.

1.2 Timurid dynastic formation and post-nomadic conquest practices

In the 15th century, stabilization of relationships of power and resources in Timur's former, more directly administered, West-Asian territories occurred especially in the eastern regions of Khurasan and Transoxania. This stabilization now clustered around Timur's sons, his many grandsons, their further descendants, and their particularly Timurid claims to corporate sovereignty. The occurrence of this new dynastic stabilization, as well as the contested and fragile ways in which it nevertheless continued to appear, originated in Timur's apportionment of all his western and central Asian domains among his four sons and their descendants. This application of the standard practice of dynastic appanage by Timur was reportedly formalized in 1403. Former Jalayirid lands in the west went to one son and his family and former Muzafarrid lands in Iran were divided among grandsons via another son, who had died many years before. A grandson via yet another predeceased son received his portion in southern Khurasan, and his youngest son Shah Rukh (1377–1447) and Shah Rukh's two sons were awarded the regions of Khurasan, Transoxania, and the Chaghaday lands to their north and east. When Timur died in 1405, his sons and grandsons and their households and entourages, together with Timur's senior commanders and their armies, embarked on several years of internecine warfare for expansion of their apportionments, for acknowledgment as patriarchal leaders in their regional appanages, and for succession at the head of the Timurid constellation and trans-regional order. As the leading modern biographer of Timur, Beatrice Manz, concludes, Timur's succession was

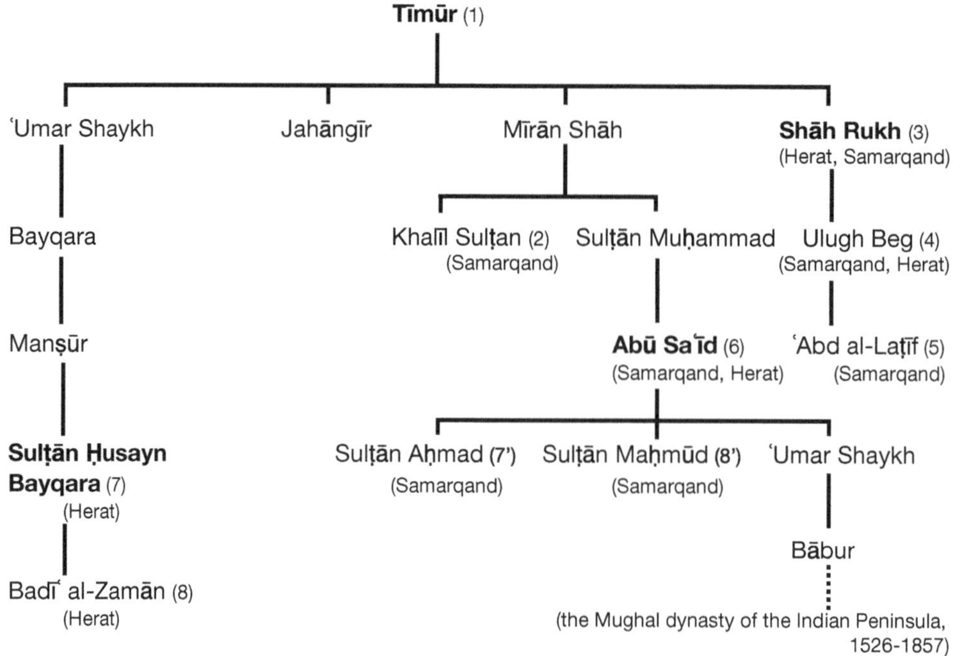

Dynastic Table 9 Simplified dynastic table of the descendants of Timur (Temür), the Timurids (with reference to the centers of their authority in the regions of Transoxania [Samarqand] and Khurasan [Herat])

a complex affair, affecting West-Asia's further configurations of power almost as much as his reign had transformed them.

> Temür had given his dynasty sufficient power and charisma to maintain their rule, but when the question of succession was finally decided, the realm his successors inherited was a smaller and poorer one.[1]

Executions, confrontations, warfare, and combat considerably purged the ranks and resources of Timur's family, commanders, and armies until, by 1409, Timur's only surviving son Shah Rukh emerged as one of the strongest. Eventually—after another decade of maneuvering, wielding violence, and campaigning from Transoxania to Iran, and even into Azerbaijan—he re-established Timurid coherence in many of the West-Asian regions that had once been conquered by his father. Shah Rukh, however, organized this dynastic coherence in his turn around his own configuration of family members and Timurid amirs and around his own court in Herat, in his original appanage of Khurasan, leaving the former Timurid center of Samarqand in Transoxania to one of his sons to administer.

As Beatrice Manz in a detailed study of Shah Rukh's long reign explains, Shah Rukh's was not exactly the same type of centrality that his father had once enforced. Shah Rukh's trans-regional leadership rather appeared in more limited, less coercive, and more locally negotiated formats, that involved multiple and diverse sets of actors, groups, and networks—including in fact quite a few millenarian, apocalyptic, spiritual, and intellectually subversive ones—who all operated with multivalent degrees of local, regional, or trans-regional autonomy. Timurid dynastic leadership, furthermore, had definitely entered a post-nomadic phase and became most effectively and most explicitly organized in the urban contexts of West-Asian power and resources. "Major cities contained centrally appointed governors and garrison troops, but not in numbers large enough to dominate the area", Manz even suggests, proposing a powerful metaphor to imagine the post-nomadic urbanity and polycentricism of Timurid trans-regional power and authority.

> The towns from which the Timurids ruled their dominions were rather like an archipelago within a sea of semi-independent regions, over which control was a matter of luck, alliance and an occasional punitive expedition. Some major cities remained under their own leaders, as vassals of the higher power. All of the local rulers, of cities, mountain regions and tribes, had their own political programs.[2]

Among the expanding ranks of actors who participated in the very long reign of Shah Rukh, which were especially stabilizing in the urban centers and hinterlands of Iran, Khurasan, and Transoxania, particular networks of urban elites once again stood out. Their integration in Shah Rukh's patriarchal household, as well as in those of other Timurids, and of major Turko-Mongol power brokers, were mediated by the by then traditional infrastructures of dynastic courts and of *waqf*-related *madrasa*s, mosques, and in particular different sets of

Figure 12.3 Samarqand (Uzbekistan): Registan square, including the *madrasa* built for Shah Rukh's son Ulugh Beg (1417–1420) (on the left)

Source: Alamy

shrines and mausolea for a variety of Sufi, Sunni, and Shi'ite personalities and their followers. As ever, this went hand in hand with the appearance of more structured leadership arrangements and with the expansion of the apparatus of power at the main urban centers of Timurid dynastic authority in the form of more patrimonial arrangements to engage with rivals, clients, resources, and reproductive strategies. Shah Rukh's household and court in Herat integrated once again—ever more prominently than had been the case in the predominantly Turko-Mongol entourage of his constantly campaigning father—various local and regional networks of 'Tajik', or Persian-speaking, experts and expertise. These networks tied Shah Rukh's court, as well as the entourages and courts of many other Timurids, to these regions' long-standing traditions of not only administrative organization (including again in *diwan*s, or *divan* in Persian), resource management, and apportionment of fiscal and tributary obligations and privileges, but also of articulating sovereignty and cultivating relationships of redistribution and patronage. As the Russian scholar and pioneer of Timurid studies, Vasiliy V. Barthold (1869–1930) already posited, these particular arrangements generated not least a remarkable, Timurid efflorescence of the arts and sciences. "The descendants of Timur . . . stand out in Islamicate history for their high personal cultivation and their patronage of arts and letters", modern historian Marshall Hodgson also noted, and this rise of Timurid scholarly and cultural efflorescence has more recently also been interpreted as an—often highly experimental and creative—extension of the many tools and strategies that were deployed in the endless competition between Timurid and other rivals and their households and courts (see next chapter).[3]

Shah Rukh's very long reign was never entirely free, however, from the violent realities of Timurid rivalry and competition, as Shah Rukh's nephews as well as his own sons and amirs continued to pursue the maximization of their and their personal entourages' interests. When Shah Rukh eventually died in 1447, these rivalries once again transformed into fiercely fought and highly destructive internecine warfare between various Timurids. Operating ever more as trans-regional warlords, each of these later Timurids engaged with their own military entourages of unstable sizes in their own formative practices of conquest against strategic urban centers of Timurid power and resources. This put further pressures on the reality and cohesion of the Timurid trans-regional power constellation as it had been reconstructed and maintained for many decades around Shah Rukh.

Eventually, especially Shah Rukh's nephews prevailed in the internecine warfare that followed his death. They did so, however, in ever more circumscribed and reduced territorial contexts, centered above all on Herat in Khurasan and on Samarqand in Transoxania. A grandson of Shah Rukh's brother, Sultan Abu Saʿid (r. 1451–1469), first fought and negotiated his way to Timurid priority and trans-regional centrality until he was defeated in an unsuccessful engagement in westward conquest practices, in particular in an attempt to reclaim Timurid power and authority over the Turkmen in Azerbaijan, which actually culminated in Abu Saʿid's execution by one of his own Timurid rivals. These dynastic rivals thereupon continued to fight for control over Khurasan and Transoxania, with Abu Saʿid's cousin Sultan Husayn Bayqara (r. 1470–1506) as the most notable among them. After more than ten years of roaming, plundering, and fighting his Timurid relatives and opponents in Khurasan and Khwarazm, in the late 1460s this Sultan Husayn eventually managed to take Herat with his small entourage of loyal Turko-Mongol followers and to consolidate his Timurid power in most of the region of Khurasan. Sultan Husayn subsequently once again organized his household and court and its investments in mostly urban religious infrastructures as new mediating and stabilizing infrastructures of his power, authority, and ever-expanding centrality in the region. This proved a relatively successful endeavor and another moment of

Timurid stabilization of relationships of power in Islamic West-Asia's east. This renewed moment of Timurid 'renascence', however, came to a definitive end with Sultan Husayn's death of old age in 1506, the subsequent succession dispute between his sons, and the capture of Herat by the newly rising Transoxanian leadership of the former Timurid amir, Uzbek nomadic warlord, and Chinggisid descendant Muhammad Shaybani (r. *c.* 1500–1510). Sultan Husayn's only remaining Timurid peer of some regional prominence at that time was Babur (1483–1530), a grandson of Sultan Abu Sa'id who was for most of the 1490s and 1500s active as a Timurid warlord in and near the regions of Transoxania and 'Moghulistan' farther to the east, with mixed successes, mostly frustrated by Muhammad Shaybani. Eventually, this Babur and his entourage and followers moved to northern India, where he and his descendants proved more successful in carving out a space for, and stabilizing relationships of power and resources around, their Timurid leadership, soon to be portrayed and remembered as the Mughal Empire (1526–1857).

The defeat of Babur's grandfather, Sultan Abu Sa'id, in Azerbaijan in 1469, by the hand of the Turkmen ruler Uzun Hasan (r. 1453–1478, see below), demonstrated that Timurid force and leadership had shrunk to a mere shadow of its former self, especially in the regions to the west of Khurasan. Abu Sa'id's defeat and subsequent execution confirmed that Turkmen power and authority were on the rise in Islamic West-Asia's trans-regional order of sovereignty. At this junction of mounting Timurid incapacity to generate any trans-regional power and cohesion, Uzun Hasan even began styling himself the actual upholder of a Chinggisid, Islamic, and dynastic sovereignty that had originally been claimed for Temür and Shah Rukh. At least, such Turkmen claims to Timurid sovereignty—reminiscent of the aforementioned Jalayirid claims to the sovereignty of the Hülegüid Il-Khans—are believed to have been explicitly articulated in a Persian letter that had reportedly been sent by Uzun Hasan, together with Abu Sa'id's severed head, to formally announce not only this Turkmen victory to Uzun Hasan's virtual overlord, the Cairo sultan, but also even more boldly Hasan's intention to displace the latter in West-Asia's theocratic order of shifting sovereignties and delegations of authority. This letter, therefore, introduced in an extant copy as "a letter from [Uzun] Hasan Padishah Bayandur to the Sultan of Egypt [Qayitbay] on his victory over Sultan Abu Sa'id" and also preserved in an almost word by word copy addressed to the Ottoman sultan Mehmed II (r. 1451–1481), presents a highly representative and remarkably direct insight into the complex world of 15th-century West-Asian claims of sovereignty and trans-regional authority, of related relationships of loyalty, obligation, and friendship, and of the widely shared verbal and non-verbal idioms that were used to articulate these claims and bonds. At the same time, this letter to the Cairo sultan as well as its parallel copy to his Ottoman peer explicitly allude to the fragile realities of shifting Timurid, Turkmen, and Turkish alliances and rivalries, of patriarchal entourages and calculating patrimonial agents, and of warfare, looting, and conquest practices, which all substantially and similarly defined and determined West-Asia's 15th-century leaderships, from Cairo to Samarqand. This is certainly graphically suggested in the following selected fragments that report about the course of this confrontation's events in early 1469, at least as seen from the Turkmen victor's perspective.

> After . . . annexing the territory of Azarbayjan together with all its strongholds, messengers . . . brought word that Sulṭān Abū Sa'īd Mīrzā together with his sons, the Chaghadayid amirs (*umarā' Çaghātāy*) and the leaders (*a'yān*) of Samarqand and Khurasan had assembled an army drawn from all of Turkistan and the farthest reaches of Hindustan, from Kashgar, Badakhshan and Kabul, from Sistan, Iraq, Kirman, Tabaristan

and Mazandaran, and were on the march, indeed, had reached Sultaniyya on the border of Iraq and the environs of Miyana. Given that we had always shown subservience in all sincerity and concord toward His Majesty, my blessed *khāqān* [Shāh Rukh] and *amīr* Tīmūr [before him], and consistently observed all dictates of reverence and honor toward them in the form of gifts and correspondence as well as acknowledgement in the Friday sermon and mention on all minted coin, we sent a letter [to Sultan Abu Saʿid] by the hand of our noble son Niẓām al-Dīn Murād Beg to reason with him to abide by the longstanding bond of friendship and concord between us and withdraw. He rejected this proposition, marching on Ardabil and taking it [by way of reply]. We then sent as envoy the elect of the elect, pride of the people of Ṭaha and Yasin, best of the Prophet's descendants, Sayyid Murshid al-Dīn ʿAlī, one of the foremost teachers and ascetics of the age, and charged him to reiterate our message. But [Sultan Abu Saʿid] again refused [and issued an edict (*yarligh*)] demanding instead that we return to our original holdings in Diyarbakr and relinquish Azarbayjan inasmuch as it is properly a Timurid patrimony. He will repair to his winter encampment at Qarabagh, then come spring set out with his troops for Anatolia (*Rūm*), Syria (*Shām*) and Egypt (*Miṣr*) and when he has taken them he will grant us [governorship over] them in return for Azarbayjan. [We sent reply] that as the bonds of our mutual affection and regard toward those [dominions] are strong we cannot entertain such a plan, doomed as it is to failure. In short, his egotistical caprice having inflamed the nostrils of his mind and the smoke from his feverish greed having belched forth he departed his borders intent on expropriating the lands we have won by force of our flaming sword. Once the lightning bolts of greed began striking, rationality and self-restraint could no longer contain him . . . and with an army larger than thought can comprehend and with such irresistible force as staggers the mind he decamped from Ardabil in the direction of Mughanat, and intending war pitched camp there. . . .

For four months our brave and steadfast warriors surrounded his troops' encampment, cutting off all points of access; all the enemy's attempts to resupply with arms, equipment and provisions were intercepted and his soldiers killed. [Sultan Abu Saʿid], having grown daily more aware of the inexorable victoriousness flowing from our felicitated forelock and favored brow . . ., began to feel the pangs of regret but found himself trapped, so that [at first] he saw no choice but to stand his ground, but then thought it better to retreat. . . .

A number of [Sultan Abu Saʿid's] Chaghatayid amirs, who with full sincerity of heart and purity of intent had accepted the yoke of subservience upon their neck and bound the sash of devotion about their waist, entrusted the face of their hopes to the royal threshold [of Uzun Hasan]; [these deserters] all were given their share of the abundant spoils, sufficient for noble and commoner alike. And the supreme *padishah*'s heir—scion of the mightiest monarchs of Persia (*akābir al-mulūk fī l-ʿAjam*) and progeny of the world's sultans, secure in the protective care of the Eternal Monarch—ʿAẓud al-Dīn Yādigār Muḥammad Mīrzā (God lengthen his life), grandson of the late *padishah* [, the son of Shah Rukh] Bāysunghur Mīrzā and fast among the cavalries of victory, we appointed governor of Transoxania (*Māwarāʾ al-Nahr*) and Khurasan and sent him thence, and invested the ruler (*shāh*) of Sistan and Badakhshan, the lords (*sādāt*) of Amul and Sari, the monarchs (*malikān*) of Mazandaran, Astarabad, Tabaristan and their ilk with royal robes of honor (*khilʿat*) and sent them back to their respective dominions. Thus with the help of divine protection and the glad fortune of His grace we took full control over all the dominions (*mamālik*) of Azarbayjan, Iraq, Fars, Kirman and Jarun. <<Praise be to God Who has fulfilled His promise and given us to inherit the earth [Quran 39, 74]>>.[4]

2 Turkmen conquest practices and dynastic formations

2.1 Uzun Hasan's Aq Qoyunlu conquest practices

In the domains of Azerbaijan, annexed—as announced in the above letter—by Uzun Hasan in 1467 and unsuccessfully claimed by Sultan Abu Sa'id in 1469, and in the wider frontier zone between the Cairo Sultanate and its Syro-Egyptian domains, the Ottoman Sultanate in western Anatolia, and the Timurid leaderships of Khurasan and Transoxania, instability and shifting relationships of power continued to represent a constant reality after Timur's passage. As suggested above, in the regions between the Caucasus and the Euphrates, Turkmen in particular—pastoral nomadic and Turkic-speaking Muslims, claiming origins in the Oghuz Turkish westward migrations of the 11th century—filled the vacuums left by, especially, the dislocation of Mongolian nomadic leaderships with the Jalayrid transformations of the 14th century. From the middle of this century onwards at latest, Turkmen leaderships appeared as ever more central in unstable configurations of local, regional, and trans-regional power and resources, and of symbiosis with small urban and rural communities and their commercial or agricultural activities. Above all, in this frontier zone of West-Asia's polycentric but stabilizing landscapes of power, Timur's example of charismatic conquest and leadership building, of personal trans-regional rule and ambitious claims to sovereignty, and of unsteady legacies continued to be emulated—mainly in a reversed, eastward direction, however—by such formidable Turkmen as Sultan Abu Sa'id's nemesis, Uzun Hasan (r. 1453–1478).

In fact, it was two rivalling configurations of Turkmen pastoral nomads and their leaderships that appeared as most prominent in this frontier zone's complex history between the later 14th and early 16th centuries. Uzun Hasan himself was a member of the Aq Qoyunlu ('the Clan of the White Sheep') leadership. Before Uzun Hasan's adventures in the middle of the 15th century, his predecessors and their followers had been migrating since at least the middle of the 14th century between summer pastures in eastern Anatolian, or Armenian, highlands and winter pastures in the lowlands of the northern Jazira. From these grazing grounds and migration routes, they had managed to present themselves mostly as overlords and protectors of local towns and routes, and as useful allies and vassals for more ambitious others. In the latter capacities, Aq Qoyunlu leaders had provided support and nomadic manpower to Timur and later also to his son Shah Rukh in their campaigns in Azerbaijan and Anatolia, and they had nurtured unsteady bonds with the Cairo Sultanate and its local military agents, wavering between 'submission and defiance', as one modern historian described the wide range of relationships between Cairo and the Aq Qoyunlu, from occasional displays of the Sultanate's coercive force in Aq Qoyunlu territories to the maximization of Turkmen autonomy.[5] The Aq Qoyunlu leadership operated especially as a useful local ally for these more ambitious others in the latters' more regular confrontations and more extensive competition with the other, similar constellation of Turkmen and its particular leadership in the regions between the Caucasus and the Euphrates. This other configuration of pastoral nomads is known as the Qara Qoyunlu ('the Clan of the Black Sheep') and it had simultaneously appeared, even more prominently, on the equally rich pastures of Azerbaijan, first as useful manpower in the context of the Jalayirid internecine warfare of the 1370s and 1380s, and eventually also as major, and effective, opponents for Timur's and Shah Rukh's claims to the Jalayirid territorial legacies between the Caucasus and the Euphrates.

Initially, after their remarkable survival of Timur's onslaught and after their aforementioned capture of Tabriz and execution of the last Jalayirid Sultan Ahmad in August 1410, the Qara Qoyunlu appeared as the central power brokers and main competitors for Shah Rukh

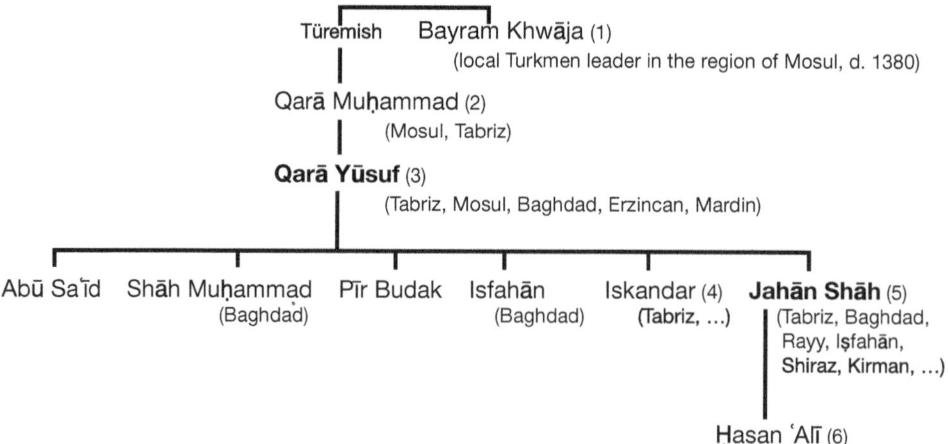

Dynastic Table 10 Simplified table of Qara Qoyunlu Turkmen dynastic leadership (with reference to the urban centers of their authority)

in these lands. Their history during this first half of the 15th century was defined by nomadic migration between winter and summer pastures and this pastoral pattern's regular disruption by campaigns of violence and conquest, and by movements east- and westwards as a result of victories as well as defeats. In these particular contexts the Qara Qoyunlu Turkmen were commanded by an illustrious and charismatic lineage of Turkmen leaders, represented especially by Qara Yusuf (r. 1389–1400, 1406–1420) and his sons Iskandar (r. 1420–1438) and Jahan Shah (r. 1439–1467). Upon the death of Shah Rukh in 1447 and the diminishing cohesion and loss of effective pull of Timurid leaderships, Jahan Shah even managed to reverse roles, advance eastwards, and deploy his own Turkmen practices of conquest in the regions of Iran, eventually—in 1458—even briefly occupying the Timurid center of Herat in Khurasan. In cooperation with local elites in many of these regions, he soon proved a formidable opponent for the aforementioned Timurid Sultan Abu Saʿid. Jahan Shah coerced many leaderships in these regions to submit to, or at least to acknowledge, the charismatic authority that he was now claiming—in a language and style reminiscent of the Jalayrids—from his seat of power at Tabriz in Azerbaijan, and thus transformed into a new, Turkmen sovereign claiming centrality in a territory that stretched from eastern Anatolia and Iraq deep into Iran.

From the 1460s onwards, however, Turkmen rivalry undermined Jahan Shah's claims to trans-regional sovereignty. The Aq Qoyunlu Turkmen leadership, headed by Uzun Hasan (r. 1453–1478), grandson of an equally notorious Turkmen chief and longstanding Qara Qoyunlu foe, ʿUthman Beg Qara Yuluk (r. 1402–1435), started moving beyond its traditional migration routes and pastures in northern Jazira and Armenia, in pursuit of its own charismatic practices of eastward conquest. Uzun Hasan's endless campaigning eventually culminated in his confrontations with Jahan Shah and with Sultan Abu Saʿid in Azerbaijan and subsequently in his taking 'full control over all the dominions of Azarbayjan, Iraq, Fars, Kirman and Jarun', as announced in Uzun Hasan's aforementioned boastful victory letters to the sultans of Egypt and Anatolia. The ultimate confrontation with Jahan Shah in 1467 ended with the death of the latter and the Aq Qoyunlu annexation of Azerbaijan, the elimination and integration of wider Qara Qoyunlu leaderships, and the installation of Uzun Hasan's own court in Tabriz. Uzun Hasan's victory of 1469 ended, as explained, with Sultan Abu Saʿid's head being sent to Cairo, Timurid claims to most Iranian lands and urbanities definitely being forfeited, the Timurid center of Herat in Khurasan once again being briefly occupied in Uzun Hasan's name, and an eventual settlement in which the new Timurid strongman in Herat, Sultan Husayn Bayqara (r. 1469–1506), accepted to at least acknowledge Uzun Hasan as his overlord in his public communication.

With the Aq Qoyunlu leadership, Uzun Hasan established therefore yet another Turkmen sovereignty claiming centrality and generating stabilization in a complex and wide-ranging web of networks of leadership, articulations of authority, and circulation of resources that stretched from eastern Anatolia and Iraq deep into, and even beyond, the regions of Iran. Further attempts to expand the reality of these Aq Qoyunlu claims to trans-regional centrality and sovereignty followed and appeared to be especially oriented in a westward direction. As already enigmatically announced in his letters of victory of 1469, the series of campaigns of conquest that followed were especially directed against Uzun Hasan's former nominal overlord, the Cairo sultan, and against his ever more powerful Ottoman peer in western and central Anatolia. In both cases, further missives and correspondence from Tabriz, basically now calling for acknowledgment of Uzun Hasan's superiority and for submission to his sovereignty, preceded actual displays of violence, as full symbolic components of the coercive apparatus that had been making for the era's practices of conquest since the days of Chinggis Khan. Interestingly, in one of the Arabic letters sent to a local military agent of the Cairo sultan in southeastern Anatolia, Uzun Hasan's actions against the sultan and his representatives were explained as a necessary consequence of the latter's unfree origins (see Chapter 10), as made explicit in the following appeal to legal argumentation:

> Freedom (*al-ḥurriyya*) is the prerequisite for command and authority (*al-amāra wa-l-ḥukūma*) according to sacred law and customary practice (*sharʿan wa-ʿurfan*). It is clear that this criterion is lacking in the sultans of Egypt and the rulers of Syria (*salāṭīn Miṣr wa-ḥukkām Bilād al-Shām*). . . . For this reason, it is incumbent upon every man of power to suppress the rule of unfree servants (*tasalluṭ al-ʿabīd*), and thus eliminate this outlandish innovation (*al-bidʿa al-baʿīd*) from among the Muslims.[6]

Uzun Hasan's actions in these westward directions, however, proved all but successful. His westward practices of conquest actually culminated in 1473 in no less than two unexpected, but decisive defeats. A first one occurred in March near Birecik on the northern Euphrates, where one of Uzun Hasan's sons and the rear-guard of his army were routed by a Syro-Egyptian host sent from Cairo. The second followed in August near Bashkent, in eastern Anatolia, where Uzun Hasan himself and his main forces were overrun by the aforementioned Ottoman sultan Mehmed II (r. 1451–1481) and his Anatolian vassals and allies. In hindsight, Uzun Hasan's defeats at Birecik and Bashkent and his failure to consolidate and expand his conquest practices in northern Syria, the Jazira, and eastern Anatolia actually confirmed—even stabilized—the frontier status of the eastern Anatolian and Jaziran regions between distinct leadership networks and Muslim sovereignties in the east and west of Islamic West-Asia for many more centuries to come.

Uzun Hasan continued to reign from Tabriz in Azerbaijan until his death in 1478. In the years after as well as, especially, before his defeat near Bashkent, he had actually succeeded in integrating local and regional networks of urban elites, their expertise, and their access to various resources into the new trans-regional power constellation that was, especially from the later 1460s, emanating from his household and court (see also next chapter). Many of these networks in Tabriz and in other major urban centers of Azerbaijan, Iraq, and western Iran had in fact similarly served their mediating and stabilizing purposes for Uzun Hasan's Qara Qoyunlu predecessors Jahan Shah and his brother and father (as well as for various Timurids). In this symbiosis between Arabo-Persian 'Tajiks' and Turkmen wielders of violence and patronage—as ever mainly mediated via households and courts and via *waqf*-related religious urban infrastructures—a continuity of organizational practices and articulations of dynastic identities was maintained that arguably went back to the aforementioned Jalayirid constructive interaction with the heirs of regional Arabo-Persian networks in Azerbaijan and western Iran, such as those of the aforementioned Hülegüid administrator Rashid al-Din Fadl Allah and his son.

This played out most explicitly and most clearly in the aforementioned victory letters. In these and in all kinds of related forms of courtly correspondence, the entourage and agents of Uzun Hasan proved their more than sufficient versatility in the complex requirements of Arabic and Persian letter-writing to convey his messages to not just the courts in Cairo and Constantinople, but also to Timurid courts in the east, to many local and regional rulers and elites, and even to European powers and allies, especially the Venetians. They actually managed to do so not only by creatively casting Uzun Hasan's announcements and claims in the formal requirements of the genre of leadership correspondence. In addition, they also showed their creativity and ingenuity in their formulations of a proper imagination of those ever grander claims to sovereignty and superiority, in constructive interactions with an age-old and equally complex discursive landscape of ancient, late antique, post-Abbasid, post-Seljuk, post-Hülegüid, Timurid, and other charismatic, even millenarian and apocalyptic, explanations of power and authority. As the leading modern historian of Aq Qoyunlu history, John Woods, argued many years ago, two of the era's most important religious scholars and philosophers, both active in Shiraz in Fars, identified Uzun Hasan in the mid-1470s in this vein as no less than 'the envoy of the fifteenth century' and as 'the renewer of the practices of the monotheist religion and faith, the reviver of the achievements of the ʿAbbasid dynasty, the promised one of the fifteenth century'. One of these scholars, furthermore, dedicated a Persian treatise on political ethics, first composed by the court's request in about 1475, to Uzun Hasan and one of his sons. As illustrated in the following passage, this treatise ingeniously represented Uzun Hasan along the ancient model of royal justice and welfare, the Inner-Asian model of dynastic fortune and divine blessing, and the Islamic model of the Caliphate.

> The ruler is a person distinguished by divine support so that he might lead individual men to perfection and order their affairs. The [antique] philosophers designate this person 'the absolute monarch' (*mālik ʿalā l-iṭlāq*) and his ordinances 'the craft of kingship' (*ṣanʿat-i mulk*). The 'moderns' call him 'the *Imām*' and his function 'the imamate'. Plato terms him 'organizer of the world' while Aristotle names him 'the civic man', that is, he who efficiently discharges the duties of state. When the control of affairs rests in the hands of such an exalted personage, good fortune and prosperity accrue to the entire country and all the subjects. Thus, by the grace of God and in accordance with the proverb: 'Give the bow to its maker', the regulation of welfare of mankind has been placed in the mighty grip of the victorious *padishah* [Uzun Ḥasan] . . .
>
> The first concern of the organizer of the world is the maintenance of the injunctions of the Sacred Law. In specific details, however, he retains the power to act in accordance with the public interest of his age (*maṣlaḥat-i vaqt*] as long as his actions fall within

> the general principles of the Sacred Law. Such a person is truly the Shadow of God, the Caliph of God, and the Deputy of the Prophet (*ẓill Allāh va-Khalīfat Allāh va nā'ib al-Nabī*).[7]

This circulation and innovative mixing of people and ideas around the wielding of violence, the charismatic authority, and the claims to sovereignty of Uzun Hasan, or for that matter of the Qara Qoyunlu ruler Jahan Shah before him, not only informed sophisticated engagements with contemporary discourses and articulations of West-Asian power and leadership. This creative heterogeneity also manifested itself in the organization of, and continuous performance of rulership claims at, Uzun Hasan's court, either in Tabriz or in his winter and summer encampments. One description, retold in a 16th century Persian chronicle of Aq Qoyunlu history, demonstrates how the workings of Uzun Hasan's court, and his performance within it, not only as a guarantor of its hierarchies of Turkmen and Tajik authority and agency and as a dispenser of universal justice, but also as a charismatic ruler whose physical comportment and appearance conformed to the requirements of Islamic and spiritual—even Sufi—leadership, were represented and remembered.

> When Uzun Hasan had finished the morning prayer, the 'drum of justice' would be sounded to indicate the convening of the court of appeals. There he would appear in person clothed in dervish attire consisting of a camel's wool waistband and a plain, leather-trimmed lamb's wool jacket. He would seat himself on a golden dais while his relatives and amirs took their places on the right and on the left. Needy, indigent plaintiffs were then summoned to present their suits through a public official who acted as their advocate and intermediary. Cases would be settled immediately and the secretaries (*kuttāb*) in attendance would draft and issue the orders. The plaintiffs would leave the court with firm decisions not subject to change or alteration.[8]

Uzun Hasan died in his winter encampment near Tabriz in January 1478, after an illness that is often related to his defeats in 1473, and to its effects not only on the charismatic appeal of his leadership, but also on his physical condition. After his death his dynastic configuration of Aq Qoyunlu leadership remained dominant throughout these regions for two more decades. This continued centrality of his sons and grandsons and their followings in the networks of Aq Qoyunlu Turkmen leadership and of wider nomad and urban elites and resources, stretching from the upper Euphrates in the west to Kirman in the east, actually happened in spite of the dynastic and wider Turkmen rivalries and internecine warfare that remained ongoing until the end of the century. Even during the slowly re-stabilizing reign of Uzun Hasan's son Ya'qub (r. August 1478–1490) and the eventual alignment of interests, from 1481 onwards, between his household (presided over especially by Ya'qub's mother, Seljukshah Begum, who had been Uzun Hasan's chief wife, as well as by his cousin) and court in Tabriz and some of the key 'Uzunhasanid' and related Aq Qoyunlu leaders and their Turkmen followers in and beyond Azerbaijan, that centrality and cohesion of Uzun Hasan's dispensation remained contested. This contentious search for a new Turkmen balance of leadership interests proceeded in a destructive as well as creative manner that was not dissimilar to what had already happened in the Timurid east after Shah Rukh's death. On the one hand, competing leaderships continued to stake their claims through extensive patronage of the arts and sciences, which contributed substantially to the efflorescence of Arabo-Persian cultural practices. On the other hand, Uzun Hasan's configuration of Aq Qoyunlu leaderships became ever more contested between rivalling groups of his descendants and

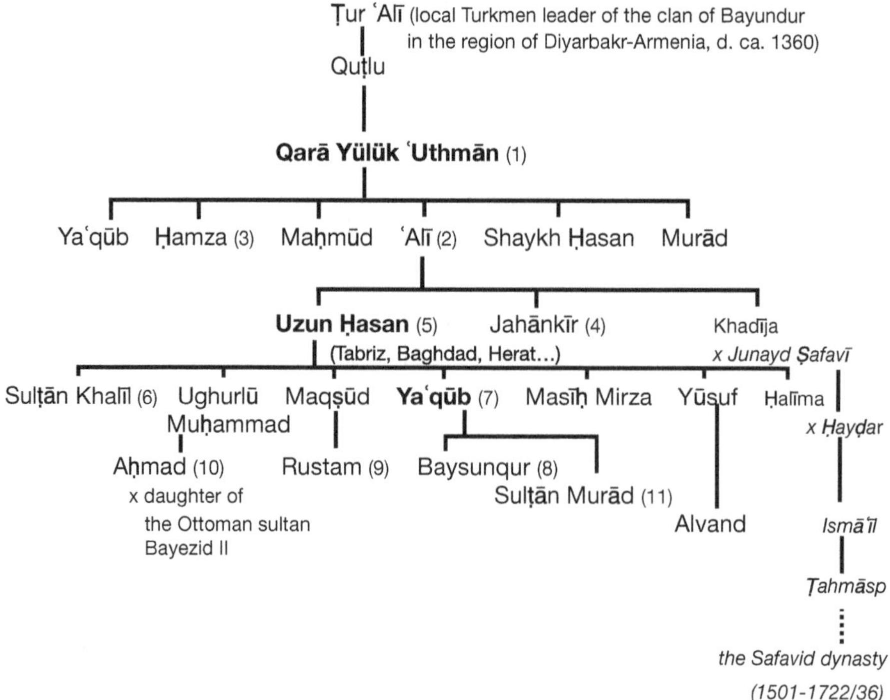

Arabic numbers = succession of Aq Qoyunlu sovereign dynasts

Bold = key Aq Qoyunlu sovereign rulers

Italics = Ṣafaviyya/Safavid dynastic leadership

Dynastic Table 11 Simplified table of Aq Qoyunlu Turkmen dynastic leadership (with reference to the urban centers of their authority), including identification of Safavi connections

cousins and of their allies among the Aq Qoyunlu strongmen, many of whom were often operating autonomously in regions assigned to their control, or were empowered through interactions with Ottoman and Cairo sultans in the west, or with Timurids in the east. This long episode of internecine warfare and violent disintegration continued until, in the summer of 1500, Uzun Hasan's former territories were formally divided in a treaty. This so-called 'Treaty of Partition'[9] split Uzun Hasan's legacy between two of the main claimants among his grandsons and their respective Aq Qoyunlu allies and supporters: Alvand ibn Yusuf ibn Uzun Hasan (d. 1505) reigned between the Caucasus and the Jazira, and Yaʿqub's son Sultan Murad (d. 1514) was granted the regions of western Iran, Iraq, Fars, and Kirman to control.

2.2 *Ismaʿil's conquest practices and early Safavid dynastic formation*

In this context of late-15th-century partition, and disintegration, new opportunities for empowerment arose within the wider dispensation of Aq Qoyunlu leadership, beyond the particular lineage of Uzun Hasan's direct male descendants. Among the new leaders who emerged more prominently, one stood out in particular, and in hindsight he would prove to represent yet another powerful individual—after Jahan Shah and Uzun Hasan in the 1450s to 1470s—who managed to unite the ranks of many Turkmen leaderships around his own charismatic practices of eastward conquest. In about 1493, this Isma'il Safavi (d. 1524), at that time only seven years old, had become the head (*pir*) of the so-called Safaviyya movement after the violent deaths of his two predecessors—his father on a Turkmen battlefield in the Caucasus and his brother in an Aq Qoyunlu prison in Azerbaijan. In the course of the 14th and 15th centuries, this movement of the followers of the Sufi *shaykh* Safi al-Din (d. 1334) and of his direct descendants—including eventually the young boy Isma'il—had been successful in establishing itself in and around Ardabil and the wider region of Azerbaijan as a central network of tentatively Sunni practices of spiritual leadership and worship, and of related infrastructures and substantial resources. From the mid-15th century onwards, due to the militant agency of Isma'il's grandfather, the Safaviyya had also begun to appear as an increasingly powerful local, regional, and trans-regional leadership, which included among its followers growing numbers of highly devoted Turkmen supporters from Azerbaijan as well as from eastern Anatolia and northern Syria. Different Turkmen groups that became, in the course of the 15th century, the military mainstay of the Safaviyya were identified as the Qizilbash, the 'red heads', after the distinctive headgear that they all adopted. Eventually, so later reports claim, their ranks were composed of twelve different Turkmen leaderships and their followers, and included longstanding participants in originally Aq Qoyunlu local and regional power, such as the Afshar and the Qajar (members of both of whom were to continue to play a key role in these regions' histories for many centuries to come [see Chapter 14]).

Figure 12.4 Ardabil (Iran): mausoleum of Shaykh Safi al-Din, Sufi master and ancestor of the Safavid dynasty

Source: Image Professionals GmbH/Alamy Stock Photo

In the course of this empowerment of *shaykh* Safi al-Din's descendants, Aq Qoyunlu leaderships had thus also been drawn to the powerful appeal of these descendants. This happened especially from the time of Isma'il's grandfather onwards, who had been active in warfare, resource management and spiritual guidance in northern Syria and eastern Anatolia before taking over leadership of the Safaviyya in Azerbaijan. In fact, Uzun Hasan himself also became tied up with this ever more militant version of the Safaviyya, as also illustrated by the marriages that were arranged between Isma'il's grandfather and a sister of Uzun Hasan and later also between one of Uzun Hasan's daughters and Isma'il's father. The latter had, furthermore, been raised at Uzun Hasan's court before succeeding Isma'il's grandfather as the spiritual leader of the Safaviyya. In the internecine warfare that followed Uzun Hasan's death in 1478, however, this deep entanglement of Uzunhasanid and Safaviyya networks radically transformed, and after the violent deaths of his father and brother, the young Isma'il was forced to seek refuge from Aq Qoyunlu aggression in the adjacent region of Gilan, on the southwestern Caspian coast. Eventually, amidst Aq Qoyunlu fragmentation and partition at the turn of the 15th to 16th centuries, the young Isma'il proved himself a very charismatic and militant figure in his own right, who inspired the expanding ranks of his Turkmen followers to follow and generate yet another charismatic and dynastic constellation of power and resources. As such, the latter new constellation became active in regions that at one point in Isma'il's own spectacular career of conquest once again stretched from eastern Anatolia and the Euphrates in the west to Khurasan and briefly even Samarqand in Transoxania in the east.

The very young Isma'il—he was only about fourteen when, in 1501, after a first series of successes, he was crowned the new sovereign in Tabriz—certainly achieved this as a result of the raw realities of successful violence wielding and profitable plundering that marked the first ten years of his leadership. Together with the conclusion of marriage alliances, the awarding of titles and benefits, and the allocation of control over newly acquired lands, these realities of successful conquest practices bound his Turkmen Qizilbash followers in ever growing and ever more forceful and loyal numbers to his claims. In addition, and building on the eclectic apparatus of sovereignty claims of predecessors at the head of the Safaviyya or of the 'Uzunhasanid' dispensation, Isma'il's expanding territorial and Turkmen centrality—even the veneration for his person—also followed from the successful articulation around his leadership of messianic and millenarian ideas and from the making of successful appeals to his blessed and even divine status. These ideas of divinely guided and apocalyptic leadership were also expressed in his own active production of Turkic poetry for his Turkmen followers, and reportedly already from 1501 onwards also in the propagation from his court of Imami Shi'ism—and its belief in the divine guidance of the Prophet's nephew 'Ali and of 11 of his designated descendants—as his and his entourage's preferred creed. The re-orientation of Iran towards Imami—or Twelver—Shi'ism that began here, in the entourages and claims of Isma'il, was, however, all but predestined to become intrinsically linked with the later dynastic claims of his successors, or to become dominant among Iranian communities until the present day. In fact, as scholarship in recent years has established, a rather rudimentary understanding of Twelver Shi'ism remained the norm throughout most of the 16th century. In fact, it represented only one component in a far wider and highly eclectic mix of claims to sovereignty and theocratic order that, much as had been the case for Uzun Hasan, were creatively articulated to explain Isma'il's successes and the expanding ranks of participants and successors in his power and authority. As one modern historian of Safavid history, Colin Mitchell, explained, while it would be wrong "to deny the centrality of Twelver-Shi'ism to the Safavid imperial project", it is also important to acknowledge that:

> There was a panoply of important religious, ethnic, and political constituencies in play during the sixteenth century. Indeed, . . . Safavid ideological pretensions in the sixteenth century were reflections of this unparalleled heterogeneity, and . . . this malleability allowed them to survive the transition from parochial mystical movement to political empire and emerge as a viable, premodern Islamic state. During this period, the Safavid shahs relied on an impressively variegated range of legitimization, which included ʿAlid messianic rhetoric (to mobilize their zealot nomadic adherents); Turco-Mongol symbols and apocryphal legends (to accentuate martial traditions and a sense of loyalty to [the] Steppe); legalistic and orthopraxic aspects of Twelver Shi'ite doctrine; ancient pre-Islamic notions of divine kingship and statecraft; and, lastly, a vigorous commitment to citing Abrahamic Prophetic history.[10]

The construction of this "panoply of . . . constituencies" and "unparalleled heterogeneity" was, as suggested, very much again the effect of conquest practices and their impact. Between Ismaʿil's enthronement in Tabriz in 1501 and his capture of Herat in Khurasan in 1510, these practices generated for Ismaʿil an endless series of victories, an accruing aura of good fortune and divine blessing—if not of messianic divinity—and a transfer and accumulation of charismatic authorities, especially from his 'Uzunhasanid' Aq Qoyunlu cousins in western Iran and the Jazira and from Shaybanid Uzbek rivals in Khurasan and Transoxania. In December 1510, the aforementioned Uzbek leader Muhammad Shaybani was actually killed in battle in Khurasan. In the period 1511–1512, support was thereafter given to the aforementioned Timurid warlord Babur (d. 1530) to take Samarqand in Transoxania from the Uzbek Shaybanids. Eventually, this proved a futile effort and a frontier zone subsequently stabilized on the Oxus river, or Amu Darya, between the Uzbek Shaybanids in Transoxania and Khwarazm (today still central components of 'the Land of the Uzbeks', Uzbekistan) and Ismaʿil's Qizilbash agents and their Turkmen followers in Khurasan (the northern part of which conforms to the present day 'Land of the Turkmen', Turkmenistan).

In the western parts of Ismaʿil's newly conquered territories, a frontier zone similarly stabilized in the 1510s, but this time even more in an unexpected reversal of his conquest practices, and allegedly with devastating effects for his aura of invincibility, especially among the Turkmen of eastern Anatolia and Azerbaijan. Rivalries and competition between the expansionist ambitions of the Ottoman sultan and the local interests of especially Turkmen leaderships, combined with Qizilbash campaigning in eastern Anatolia in the early 1510s, culminated in 1514 in an enormous Ottoman army marching against Azerbaijan. This army inflicted defeat and heavy losses on Ismaʿil and his Qizilbash leadership at the battle of Chaldiran, and very briefly occupied Ismaʿil's headquarters at Tabriz. Although the Ottoman sultan quickly withdrew from Azerbaijan, until his death in 1524, Ismaʿil—as with his grandfather Uzun Hasan after his defeats in 1473—reportedly abandoned any new participation in further campaigns against his rivals, especially the Uzbek Shaybanids, who regularly returned to Khurasan. Above all, the defeat at Chaldiran meant the loss of access from Tabriz to networks of Turkmen supporters and the resources they commanded in eastern Anatolia, and the start of a gradual 16th-century re-orientation—stimulated by further Ottoman aggression—of Safavid centrality from the Turkmen pastures in eastern Anatolia and Azerbaijan to the ancient urban centers of the Iranian plateau.

This shift also illustrated the ever-wider participation of other "constituencies" in the performance of Ismaʿil's power and authority. As with his 'Uzunhasanid' predecessors, Ismaʿil as well as his successors were tied up with growing numbers of other local and regional experts in their pursuits to eliminate rivals, protect clients, secure their reproduction, and

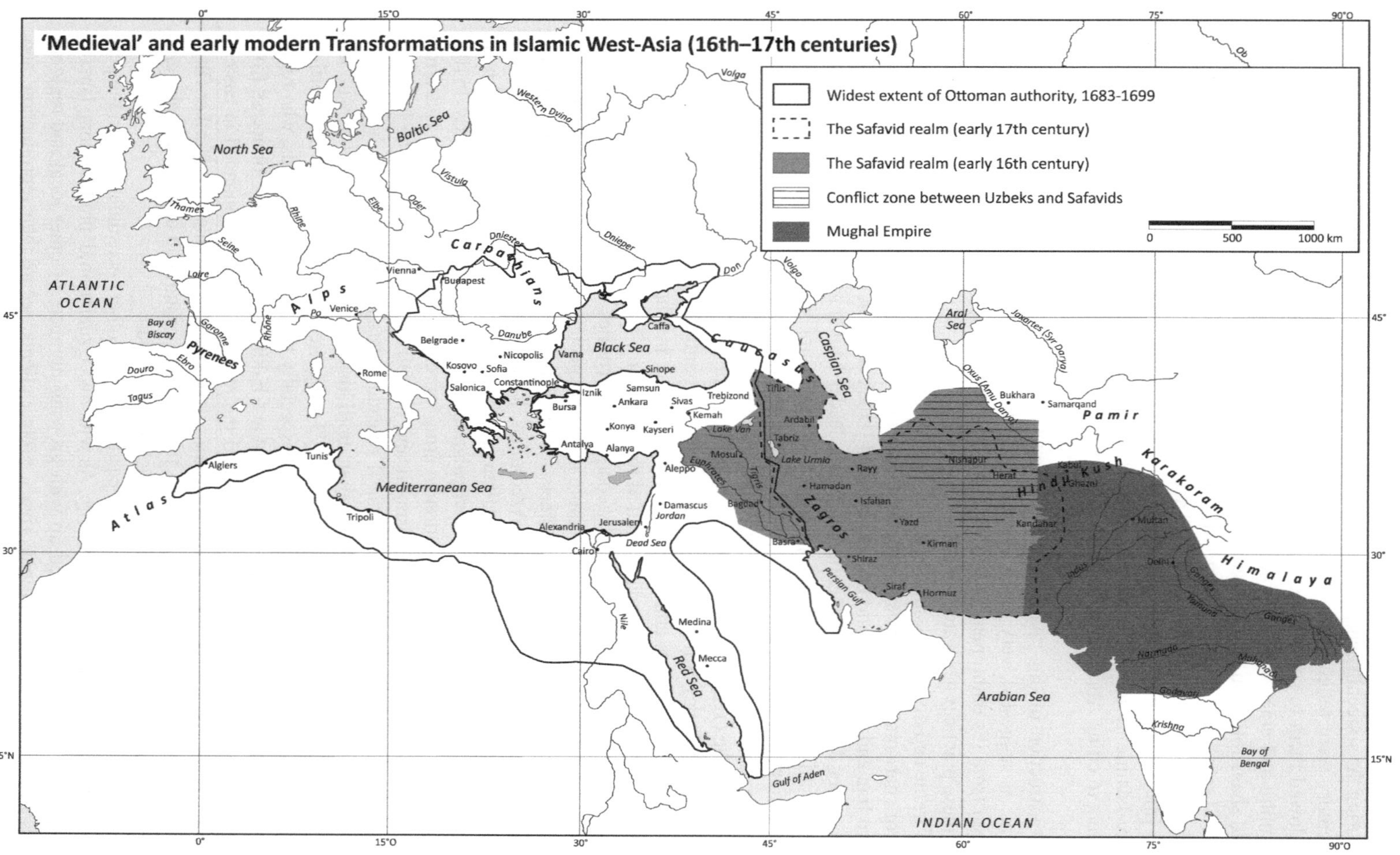

Map 11 'Medieval' and Early Modern Transformations in Islamic West-Asia (16th–17th centuries)

accumulate resources to achieve these ends. In the latter contexts of social reproduction and resource accumulation in particular, the long-standing symbiosis was continued between Arabo-Persian 'Tajiks' and Turkmen wielders of violence and patronage—as ever mainly mediated via households and courts and via *waqf*-related religious urban infrastructures. In fact, many of the 'Tajiks' who had run the courts of various 'Uzunhasanids' were quickly employed in Isma'il's service too, and the same seems to have happened with formerly Timurid agents in the east. As such, in these areas of courtly organization, too, a continuity of administrative practices and articulations of dynastic identities was maintained. This continuity connected not just Uzun Hasan's household, but also his aforementioned court with those of his grandson Isma'il and his successors, and arguably went back to the by now two-centuries old constructive interactions between successive trans-regional leaderships and the equally powerful heirs of local and regional Arabo-Persian networks in, especially, the many urban centers of Azerbaijan, Iran, and Khurasan. In fact, to any remaining ones of those ancient networks of urban elites, infrastructures, and resources, more layers of parallel leadership were only added in Ismail's service, via the longstanding experiences of the Safaviyya Sufi movement, as well as via the integration—or the elimination and appropriation—of similar autonomous, oft-overlapping networks of spirituality and millenarianism and, more in general, of particular traditions of knowledge, expertise, and resource management. The aforementioned Colin Mitchell again tellingly equals this even wider "unparalleled heterogeneity" of the social and cultural realities of crisscrossing urban and rural networks of power and resources, now clustering around the courts and infrastructures of power of Isma'il and of his subsequent dynastic formation, as a most complex chemical compound generating something new from the highly powerful mix of the many 'medieval' West-Asian practices that had so far preceded it, and that had originated in regions stretching, since Chinggisid times, from Asia Minor in the west to the Inner-Asian Steppes in the east.

> Examining early Safavid bureaucratic standards is similar to a chemist analyzing a complex chemical compound to isolate its individual elements. The Safavids subscribed to a long-standing, highly developed body of Perso-Arabic literary and religious traditions; at the same time, they inherited a collection of Turco-Mongolian traditions with their own distinct diplomatic, judicial and bureaucratic standards. The conquests of Chingīz Khān and Tīmūr, along with the resulting suzerain states in eastern Anatolia, Iran, and Central Asia, had fused Chingizid and Chaghatā'ī elements into the Persian bureaucratic culture as well as its use of terminology, seals, and symbols. While eastern Iran, notably Khurāsān, adhered to Timurid chancellery practices, Anatolian and western bureaucratic Iranian practices experienced further changes under the Türkmen dynasties of the Qarā Qoyūnlū and the Āq Qoyūnlū. Certainly, we cannot discount the influence of the neighbouring and relatively more established Ottoman empire. The Safavid dynasty, then, was not the recipient of a singular, linearly developed chancellery culture, but rather a complex and shifting nexus of different bureaucratic practices, which reflect the ethnically fragmented and politically decentralized history of the Turco-Mongolian world between 1300 and 1500.[11]

When Isma'il died in 1524, this mixing of 'Tajik', Turkmen, and many other leaderships, practices, and ideas continued. It actually did so even despite the repetition of the pattern of intense rivalry, fragmentation, and internecine warfare that also re-emerged within his household and entourage, as it also had in these eastern regions of Islamic West-Asia with each of his Timurid and Turkmen predecessors. In this particular case of Isma'il's succession, the main protagonists were not so much his four sons—all too young to really participate, with the oldest, Tahmasp, only ten years old at his father's sudden demise and his accession to the throne in Tabriz—but rather alternating sets of Qizilbash Turkmen leaders. From their appanages, from those of Isma'il's sons, or, especially, from their leading positions in Isma'il's household and at his court, all vied to win sufficient support, outdo their opponents, and operate as a kind of *atabeg* for the young successor of Isma'il, Tahmasp (r. 1524–1576). This continued for almost a decade until Tahmasp, in 1533, managed to take matters in his own hands. At least, by that time, the ranks of Qizilbash leaderships at the center of his authority were sufficiently purged and remolded for the ruler himself to formally come of age and to partake more actively and decisively in the creation and maintenance of balances of power and interests in his household and at his court. For more than four decades thereafter, Tahmasp would continue to do so rather successfully. Despite the ongoing presence of rivalling Qizilbash leaderships and their forceful Turkmen followers, charismatic authority accrued not only from the claims that came with Tahmasp's Safavid personality, but also from his successful empowerment in the 1520s and 1530s as well as simply from the remarkable longevity of his rule. These all at least proved strong integrative factors that contributed substantially to the dynastic and increasingly patrimonial formation of his power, authority, and centrality in local, regional, and trans-regional networks of leadership and resources.

Another contributing factor in this integrative formation was also related to the ways in which ongoing rivalries with the Ottoman sultan in the west and with the Shaybanid khans in the east continued to play out. Between Tahmasp's accession in 1524 and his assumption of personal authority in the 1530s, the latter Shaybanids and their Uzbek allies crossed the Oxus River (Amu Darya) and invaded and raided the region of Khurasan at least five times, occupying the regional center of Herat more than once. The fragmented nature of Uzbek leadership, however, meant that these Shaybanid campaigns of conquest—often in alliance with Qizilbash or local leaders or even with one of Tahmasp's brothers, posing as a Safavid pretender—never had any permanent effects. Uzbek activities continued to be centered on Transoxania and Khwarazm, Tahmasp and his forces time and again managed to reclaim Khurasan, and by the early 1540s, the frontier zone once again stabilized on the Oxus River lands. On the western front, the relationships with the Ottoman sultan were even more vexed and more deeply intertwined with Qizilbash Turkmen and Safavid dynastic rivalries. Between the mid-1530s and the mid-1550s, a handful of full-scale campaigns of conquest were organized from the Ottoman west, which invaded especially the Safavid heartlands of Azerbaijan and culminated once more in the taking of Tabriz. Reportedly, it was especially the scorched-earth policy that was applied by Tahmasp and his military agents in Azerbaijan that every time again obliged the Ottoman sultan and his military forces—apparently both in numbers and in equipment and training far superior to Tahmasp's mainly Turkmen cavalry forces—to withdraw and winter in eastern Anatolia and that time and again allowed Tahmasp to return to Azerbaijan and Tabriz. The treaty that was eventually concluded in 1555 between both sovereigns, known as the 'Treaty of Amasya', established a kind of status quo for subsequent decades, confirming the permanent Safavid loss of Iraq and the Jazira to the Ottoman sultan, but also the remaining of Azerbaijan within the reach of Tahmasp's authority, and even coinciding with further expansions into the Caucasus.

One of the consequences of the latter Ottoman pressures between the 1530s and 1550s may have been the permanent shift of Tahmasp's court and center of power southeastwards, away from the 'medieval' center of West-Asian sovereignty *par excellence*, Tabriz, and towards the Iranian plateau, to the urban center of Qazvin in particular. This remarkable territorial shift was perhaps even more related to a wider shift away from inherently unstable

Turkmen leadership contexts that occurred in the expanding apparatus of Tahmasp's centrality and that also manifested itself in the further widening of participation by other "constituencies" in the performance of Tahmasp's power and authority. This 16th-century transition to post-nomadic realities of rule actually involved the successful rise of new groups and the empowerment of specific non-Qizilbash and non-Safaviyya actors and agents in Tahmasp's entourage, next to the ongoing convergence of Turkmen and Arabo-Persian networks of amirs and viziers. This was in Tahmasp's case mediated especially via his court, first in Tabriz and eventually in Qazvin, where investments in entirely new court-related infrastructures and facilities transformed the urban texture and generated enormous opportunities for, especially, artists and literati and their cultural production. The mechanisms of distribution and patronage that these courts commanded continued Turkmen and especially Timurid precedents, and once more left a huge imprint—including in the format of Tahmasp's own extant memoirs, constructed around an anthology of seminal Persian and Turkic poetry and completed in 1561—on West-Asia's cultural landscapes. One of the many Persian chronicles produced during and shortly after Tahmasp's reign by some of the many participants in this courtly practice of cultural efflorescence tellingly described this cultural dimension not just as a central component of Tahmasp's leadership qualities, but even more importantly as usefully mediating relationships with agents from different Iranian urban elites, all partaking in this way in articulations and performances of different imaginations of Tahmasp's claims to sovereignty:

> [Tahmasp] was inclined towards calligraphy and art, and brought those singular masters who were without comparison in each of their own art. Of the calligraphers: Mullā ʿAbdi Nishāpuri, Ustād Shāh Maḥmūd Nīshāpuri, and Mullā Rustam ʿAlī Haravi. Of the artists: Ustād Sulṭān Muḥammad Muṣawwar, Ustād Bihzād Muṣawwar, Ustād Mirak Iṣfahāni, Mir Muṣawwar, and Dust Divāna. The *shah* paid absolute patronage and attention to these groups.[12]

This process of post-nomadic patrimonial formation and Safavid stabilization of trans-regional relationships and claims of power is traditionally considered to have manifested itself especially during the long reign of Tahmasp in the foregrounding of ideas and adherents of a particularly Safavid interpretation of Twelver Shi'ism. A leading role in the original articulation of Safavid Shi'ism—including the, for many contemporaries, controversial formulation of Safavid claims of ʿAlid lineage and direct descent from the seventh *imam*—is famously attributed to Nur al-Din ʿAli Karaki (1466–1534). An Arabic Twelver Shi'ite scholar from the Syrian region of Baʿlbakk and Jabal ʿAmil, Karaki already appeared as a powerful, resourceful, and controversial figure in Azerbaijan and Iraq at the time of Tahmasp's father Ismaʿil. At Tahmasp's court, he became deeply involved in the rivalries between different Qizilbash groups that marked the first decade of Tahmasp's reign. Karaki eventually emerged, with his own network of students and supporters, among the contested survivors, if not the winners, of these unstable years, as most famously suggested in a royal decree (*firman*) that was issued by Tahmasp in 1533. This decree, extant in an alleged copy from the original, described Karaki with highly controversial terms of singular religious authority, such as "the highly positioned seal of the legal experts", "the exemplar of expert *ʿulama*'", "the proof of Islam" and even "the deputy of the [Twelfth] Imam". The text of the decree itself delegated to Karaki full authority over affairs of religion and obliged all of Tahmasp's agents and representatives—duly identified in their different military, religious, administrative, and related categories—to submit to Karaki's authority.

> We decree that the great *sayyid*s and the lords and the honorable nobles and the commanders and the ministers and other pillars of the sacred dynastic reign (*dawlat-e qudsi*) consider the above-mentioned their guide and leader, offer him obedience and submission in all affairs, carry out what he orders and refrain from what he forbids. [They should consider] dismissed whomever he dismisses among the office-holders of the religious affairs of the [God-]protected realms and the victorious military, and appointed whomever he appoints.

The decree finally also bestowed *waqf* estates and tax-exempted properties in Iraq as well as various other benefits and privileges upon Karaki, and clarifies that the diverse fiscal rights and income from these are "to be handed over to his deputies" and "to his agents" and that "the thanks and complaints of his deputies and agents are to be given great weight". The decree ends with a confirmation of its date of issuance: "written on 16 Dhu l-Hijja 939 AH [9 July 1533]", and is authenticated in the margins in the following manner:

> The above order and all the orders regarding the above-mentioned Guide of the People [ʿAlī Karaki] is to be considered signed and effective, the offender cursed and banished. Ṭahmāsp.[13]

For a long time, modern scholarship has made much of this decree and of historiographical reports about Karaki's subsequent commands to create an exclusively Safavid Twelver Shiʿi trans-regional order and generate a wide-scale conversion of local populations. By now, however, it has become widely accepted, as argued amongst others by Safavid historian Andrew Newman, that the impact of Karaki and this decree upon contemporaries should not be overstated, especially not, in hindsight, from the perspective of the preponderance, in subsequent centuries, of Twelver Shi'ism and its clerical representatives in Iran. "Both the issuance of the *firman* and the substance of the *firman* itself", Newman argued, "represented less resounding evidence of the strength of al-Karaki's authority at the court or within the Twelver community than might seem to be the case."[14] Above all, this *firman* illustrates how one group in particular at Tahmasp's court, in this case Karaki and his network of students, supporters, and agents and their particular, contested, articulations of Safavid sovereignty and of the privileged relationship of Twelver Shi'i scholars with that sovereignty, successfully established itself in an active and resourceful partnership with Tahmasp and his trans-regional authority. Also, after Karaki's death, his students as well as his sons and descendants continued to occupy important positions at Tahmasp's court, and at the courts of his successors, at least until the end of the century. They continued to do so, however, in highly competitive contexts of expanding patrimonial authority, in which their positions were permanently challenged—even again more successfully after Tahmasp's death in 1576—by other groups of courtiers and by other intellectual networks of Shi'ite as well as of Sunni and Sufi scholarship, all of which together continued to make for the "panoply of constituencies" and the "unparalleled heterogeneity" of Safavid power and patronage throughout the 16th century. In fact, as one modern scholar recently confirmed, until the end of the 16th century "a Shi'i-Sufi-occultist amalgam was still the engine of Safavid imperial ideology", and only in the subsequent, 17th century (see Chapter 14) would this "amalgam" of dynastic ideas and ideals as well as of the competing or overlapping networks of their experts, infrastructures, and resources "eventually give way to a newly constructed Twelver Shi'i orthodoxy".[15]

The case of Karaki and his prevailing network of supporters and resources illustrates above all how during the very long reign of Tahmasp, the Safavid household, court, and entourages were gradually stabilized at the center of relationships of power in, especially, the regions of Iran, and how these relationships were simultaneously transformed by the addition and integration of all kinds of old and new local and regional (and external, including not just Ottoman and Uzbek, but also wider Asian and European) actors, agencies, and interests. The impact of traditional Safavid supporters and allies, especially of the Turkmen Qizilbash leadership, gradually diminished within the growing complexity and reach of the apparatus of Tahmasp's power and authority, even though they were never to entirely disappear. Other players that emerged more prominently, next to Karaki and his students and their Shiʿi, Sufi, occultist, and other intellectual competitors and peers, certainly included longstanding 'Tajik' experts, such as Qadi Jahan Qazvini, who was Tahmasp's all-powerful vizier from 1535 to 1551, and for whom the court's move to Qazvin was not just a kind of homecoming, but also a confirmation of his own network's powerful position at Tahmasp's court. Furthermore, from the 1540s and 1550s onwards, entirely new groups, particularly formerly Christian Georgians and Circassians, were introduced into the center of Safavid power and authority. This resulted mostly from military campaigning against Christian leaderships and communities in the Caucasus regions, and the resettlement or even re-employment of tens of thousands of prisoners of war from these regions in Tahmasp's service, in the royal harem

Figure 12.5 Folio with a painting representing Shah Tahmasp by Farrukh Beg (*c.* 1580–1619) (India, c. 1620) ('Shah Tahmasp in the mountains') (Freer Gallery of Art)

Source: Freer Gallery of Art and Arthur Sackler Gallery, Smithsonian Institution, Washington, D.C. Charles Lang Freer Endowment, F1939.47a

and household, at the court, and in his personal bodyguard. In these contexts of Tahmasp's household and court, much as with their aforementioned counterparts in 15th and 16th century Ottoman palace service, they were "religiously Islamicized, linguistically Turkified, and culturally" 'Safavidized' and thus prepared to counter the amalgam, heterogeneity, and panoply of constituencies that was defining and circumscribing Safavid power and authority. From the 1570s onwards, especially, these entirely new Safavid agents, and especially their descendants, at the Safavid center—even within Tahmasp's own Safavid family—began to play an increasingly prominent role in ways that remind of similar patterns of dynastic integration, representation, and empowerment via the mechanisms of unfreedom and patrimonial service in many other regions and episodes of Islamic West-Asia's history.

When Tahmasp died, in 1576, the relative stabilization, centralization, and post-nomadic patrimonial transformation of relationships of power and patronage that he and his supporters had achieved during at least a handful of decades in the regions between Azerbaijan and Khurasan once again relapsed into their opposites. As ever, lack of any clear succession arrangements, the continued dominance of the ancient notion of corporate dynastic sovereignty, and the remaining centrality of Qizilbash leaderships in different dynastic appanages re-created the difficult and unstable conditions that had also marred Tahmasp's own accession in the 1520s—and, for that matter, most other moments of dynastic transition in the eastern lands of Islamic West-Asia between the 13th and 15th centuries. The period between 1576 and 1587 was again marked by internecine warfare involving Tahmasp's three sons, other male and female members from his household, their Georgian and Circassian supporters at the court in Qazvin, and their Qizilbash allies in various parts of the realm. As a result, this period witnessed the dissolution of the trans-regional coherence and relative stability of Tahmasp's reign and the return of major territorial pressures on Safavid territorial claims in both west and east from Ottomans and Uzbeks. All of this meant that the stabilization and territorial integrity of Tahmasp's reign appeared for ever lost to many contemporaries, and that once more new realities and constellations of conquest and charismatic leadership seemed to loom on the horizon. Eventually, however, this 'medieval' pattern of leadership in eastern Islamic West-Asia was somehow broken when Tahmasp's territorial, charismatic, and patrimonial legacies were eventually left for one of his own grandsons to inherit. This was ʿAbbas (r. 1587–1629), in whose name a Qizilbash leader from Khurasan successfully marched on Qazvin in 1587. As will be detailed in Chapter 14, this pursuit quickly transformed in a true re-invention and re-orientation of those legacies, operating on a trans-regional and even truly globalizing—and therefore, early modern—scale that transcended by far what Tahmasp, Ismaʿil, or, for that matter, any of their Turkmen or Turko-Mongol predecessors in these regions had achieved before.

Notes

1 Manz, *The Rise and Rule of* Tamerlane, 147.
2 Manz, *Power, Politics and Religion in Timurid Iran*, 2.
3 Hodgson, *Venture of Islam*, 2: 490. See also Binbaş, *Intellectual Networks in Timurid Iran. Sharaf al-Dīn ʿAli Yazdī and the Islamicate Republic of Letters*.
4 See Keçik, *Briefe und Urkunden aus der Kanzlei Uzun Hasans*; translation from Melvin-Koushki, "The Delicate Art of Aggression: Uzun Hasan's *Fathnama* to Qaytbay of 1469", 205–9.
5 See Wing, "Submission, Defiance, and the Rules of Politics on the Mamluk Sultanate's Anatolian Frontier".
6 Translation from Woods, *The Aqquyunlu*, 116, 264 fn. 126, who translated it from a copy of this letter preserved in the archives of Topkapi Saray, Istanbul.

7 Jalāl al-Dīn Muḥammad Dāvānī (1427–1503), *Akhlāq-i Jalālī* ['The Ethics of Jalāl (al-Din Dāvānī)']; translation from Woods, *The Aqquyunlu*, 105.
8 Budāq Munshī Qazvīnī (fl. 1577), *Javāhir al-Akhbār* ['Exquisite Specimens of Historical Reports']; translation from Woods, *The Aqquyunlu*, 109.
9 Woods, *The Aqquyunlu*, 161.
10 Mitchell, *The Practice of Politics in Safavid Iran: Power, Religion and Rhetoric*, 5.
11 Mitchell, *The Practice of Politics in Safavid Iran: Power, Religion and Rhetoric*, 199.
12 Budāq Munshī Qazvīnī (fl. 1577), *Javāhir al-Akhbār* ['Exquisite Specimens of Historical Reports']; translation from Mitchell, "Ṭahmāsp I".
13 Translation after Arjomand, "Three Decrees of Shāh Ṭahmāsp on Clerical Authority and Public Law in Shiʿite Iran", 156–9.
14 Newman, "The Myth of the Clerical Migration to Safawid Iran: Arab Shiite Opposition to ʿAlī al-Karakī and Safawid Shiism", 101.
15 Melvin-Koushki, "Early Modern Islamicate Empire: New Forms of Religiopolitical Legitimacy", 365.

Selected readings

Abu Lughod, J. *Before European Hegemony: The World System, A.D. 1250–1350* (Oxford, 1989)

Aigle, D. *The Mongol Empire between Myth and Reality: Studies in Anthropological History* (Leiden, 2014)

Allsen, T.T. *Culture and Conquest in Mongol Eurasia* (Cambridge, 2001)

Amitai, R. *Holy War and Rapprochement: Studies in the Relations between the Mamluk Sultanate and the Mongol Ilkhanate (1260–1335)* (Turnhout, 2013)

Amitai, R. *Mongols and Mamluks: The Mamluk-Ilkhanid War, 1260–1281* (Cambridge, 1995)

Amitai, R. *The Mongols in the Islamic Lands: Studies in the History of the Ilkhanate* (Aldershot, 2007)

Arjomand, S.A. "Three Decrees of Shāh Ṭahmāsp on Clerical Authority and Public Law in Shiʿite Iran", in S.A. Arjomand (ed.), *Sociology of Shiʿite Islam. Collected Essays* (Leiden, 2016), pp. 151–65

Babinger, F. *Mehmed der Eroberer und seine Zeit: Weltenstrürmer einer Zeitenwende* (München, 1959)

Barkey, K. *Bandits and Bureaucrats: The Ottoman Route to State Centralization* (Ithaca, 1994)

Barkey, K. *Empire of Difference: The Ottomans in Comparative Perspective* (Cambridge, 2008)

Barkey, K. "The Ottoman Empire (1299–1923): The Bureaucratization of Patrimonial Authority", in P. Crooks, T.H. Parsons (eds.), *Empires and Bureaucracy in World History: From Late Antiquity to the Twentieth Century* (Cambridge, 2016), pp. 102–26

Binbaş, İ.E. "A Damascene Eyewitness to the Battle of Nicopolis: Shams al-Dīn Ibn al-Jazarī (d. 833/1429)", in N.G. Chrissis, M. Carr (eds.), *Contact and Conflict in Frankish Greece and the Aegean, 1204–1453: Crusade, Religion and Trade between Latins, Greeks and Turks* (Farnham, 2014), pp. 153–75

Binbaş, İ.E. *Intellectual Networks in Timurid Iran: Sharaf al-Din 'Ali Yazdi and the Islamicate Republic of Letters* (Cambridge, 2016)

Boyle, J.A. *The History of the World Conqueror* (Manchester, 1958)

Clot, A. *Suleiman the Magnificent* (London, 2005)

Faroqhi, S. and Fleet, K. (eds.), *The Cambridge History of Turkey. Vol. 2. The Ottoman Empire as a World Power, 1453–1603* (Cambridge, 2012)

Finkel, C. *Osman's Dream: The Story of the Ottoman Empire 1300–1923* (London, 2005)

Fleet, K. (ed.). *The Cambridge History of Turkey, Vol. 1. Byzantium to Turkey, 1071–1453* (Cambridge, 2009)

Freely, J. *The Grand Turk: Sultan Mehmet II – Conqueror of Constantinople, Master of an Empire and Lord of Two Seas* (London, 2012)

Godard, Y.A. "Bassin de cuivre au nom de Shaikh Uwais", *Āthār-é Īrān: Annes du service archéologique de Iran* 1 (1936): 371–73

Hodgson, M.G.S. *The Venture of Islam: Conscience and History in a World Civlization. 2. The Expansion of Islam in the Middle Periods* (Chicago, 1974)

Hope, M. *Power, Politics, and Tradition in the Mongol Empire and the Īlkhānate of Iran* (Oxford, 2016)

Imber, C. *The Ottoman Empire, 1300–1650. The Structure of Power* (New York, 2002)

Inalcik, H. *The Ottoman Empire: The Classical Age, 1300–1600* (London, 2000)

Inalcik, H. with Quataert, D. (eds.). *An Economic and Social History of the Ottoman Empire, 1300–1914* (Cambridge, 1994)

Işıksel, G. "Ottoman-Habsburg Relations in the Second Half of the 16th Century: The Ottoman Standpoint", in A. Strohmeyer, N. Spannenberger (eds.), *Frieden und Konfliktmanagement in interkulturellen Räumen: das Osmanische Reich und die Habsburgermonarchie in der Frühen Neuzeit* (Frankfurt, 2013), pp. 51–61

Jackson, P. *The Mongols and the Islamic World: From Conquest to Conversion* (New Haven and London, 2017)

Kafadar, C. *Between Two Worlds: The Construction of the Ottoman State* (Berkeley, 1995)

Kastritsis, D. (transl.). *An Early Ottoman History: The Oxford Anonymous Chronicle (Bodleian Library, Ms Marsh 313). Historical Introduction, Translation and Commentary* (Liverpool, 2017)

Kastritsis, D. *The Sons of Bayezid: Empire Building and Representation in the Ottoman Civil War of 1402–13* (Leiden, 2007)

Katouzian, H. *The Persians: Ancient, Mediaeval and Modern Iran* (New Haven, 2009)

Keçik, M.S. *Briefe und Urkunden aus der Kanzlei Uzun Hasans* (Freiburg, 1976)

Kolbas, J.G. *The Mongols in Iran: Chingiz Khan to Uljaytu, 1220–1309* (London, 2007)

Lane, G. *Early Mongol Rule in Thirteenth-Century Iran: A Persian Renaissance* (London, 2003)

Lewis, B. "The Mongols, the Turks and the Muslim Polity", *Transactions of the Royal Historical Society* 18 (1968): 49–68

Lowry, H.W. *The Nature of the Early Ottoman State* (New York, 2003)

Manz, B.F. *Power, Politics and Religion in Timurid Iran* (Cambridge, 2007)

Manz, B.F. *The Rise and Rule of Tamerlane* (Cambridge, 1989)

Melville, Ch. "The *Keshig* in Iran: The Survival of the Royal Mongol Household", in L. Komarovff (ed.), *Beyond the Legacy of Genghis Khan* (Leiden, 2013), pp. 135–64

Melvin-Koushki, M. "The Delicate Art of Aggression: Uzun Hasan's *Fathnama* to Qaytbay of 1469", *Iranian Studies* 44/2 (2011): 193–214

Melvin-Koushki, M. "Early Modern Islamicate Empire: New Forms of Religiopolitical Legitimacy", in A. Salvatore, R. Tottoli, B. Rahimi (eds.), *The Wiley-Blackwell History of Islam* (Hoboken, 2018), pp. 353–75

Meyvaert, P. "An Unknown Letter of Hulagu, Il-Khan of Persia, to King Louis IX of France", *Viator* 11 (1980): 245–60

Mitchell, C.P. *New Perspectives on Safavid Iran: Empire and Society* (Abingdon, 2011)

Mitchell, C.P. *The Practice of Politics in Safavid Iran: Power, Religion and Rhetoric* (London, 2009)

Mitchell, C.P. "Ṭahmāsp I", in *Encyclopaedia Iranica* (2009)

Morgan, D. *Medieval Persia, 1040–1797* (New York, 1988)

Morgan, D. *The Mongols* (Oxford, 1986)

Murphy, R. *Ottoman Warfare, 1500–1700* (London, 1999)

Newman, A.J. "The Myth of the Clerical Migration to Safawid Iran: Arab Shiite Opposition to ʿAlī al-Karakī and Safawid Shiism", *Die Welt des Islams* 33/1 (1993): 66–112

Newman, A.J. *Safavid Iran: Rebirth of a Persian Empire: Persia between the Medieval and the Modern* (London, 2006)

Pfeiffer, J., Quinn, Sh. A. (eds.), *History and Historiography of Post-Mongol Central Asia and the Middle East: Studies in Honor of John Woods* (Wiesbaden, 2006)

Quataert, D. *The Ottoman Empire. 1700–1922*. Second Edition (Cambridge, 2000)

Skinner, Q., Price, R. (eds. and transl.). *N. Machiavelli: The Prince* (Cambridge, 1988)

Stolz, B., Soucek, S. (eds. and transl.). *Konstantin Mihailović: Memoirs of a Janissary* (Ann Arbor, 1975)

Subtelny, M.E. *Timurids in Transition: Turko-Persian Politics and Acculturation in Medieval Iran* (Leiden, 2007)

Wing, P. "The Decline of the Ilkhanate and the Mamluk Sultanate's Eastern Frontier", *Mamlūk Studies Review* 11/2 (2007): 77–88

Wing, P. *The Jalayirids: Dynastic State Formation in the Mongol Middle East* (Edinburgh, 2016)

Wing, P. "Submission, Defiance, and the Rules of Politics on the Mamluk Sultanate's Anatolian Frontier", *Journal of the Royal Asiatic Society* 25/3 (2015): 377–88

Woodhead, C. (ed.). *The Ottoman World* (Abingdon, 2011)

Woods, J. *The Aqquyunlu: Clan, Confederation, Empire*. Revised and Expanded Edition (Salt Lake City, 1999)

13 'Medieval' symbiotic transformations in Islamic West-Asia

The construction of heterogeneous urbanities, ambiguous authorities, and dynastic courts (12th–16th centuries)

Introduction: norms, ideals, and discourses of power and belonging in 'medieval' West-Asia

'Medieval' Islamic West-Asia's post-Seljuk landscapes of leadership as discussed so far, from the post-nomadic stabilizations in the Euphrates-to-Nile zone, eventually extending into Asia Minor, to the returning instabilities of nomadic conquest and dynastic formation in the enormous Euphrates-to-Jaxartes-and-Indus zone, did not—as so often continues to be assumed in popular and generalist discourses—feed on sociocultural wastelands that lacked genuinely creative or sophisticated capacities. As the physical and temporal gap with Late Antique and even post-Abbasid achievements widened, no so-called 'post-Classical' dark ages, craving for a conservation of what was definitely lost, set in. On the contrary, as already announced in this second part's opening chapter, yet another, entirely different complex multitude of networks of people, ideas, and objects, enriched by intense Afro-Eurasian connections, and stimulated by the opportunities offered by—or the regular solutions required from—default dynastic transformations, rivalries, and migrations, soon came to replace any post-Abbasid remnants. This occurred throughout Islamic West-Asia along extremely diverse trajectories that were not entirely dissimilar from the era's and regions' oft-sweeping conquest practices and that in many creative ways continued to build on solutions and arrangements that had first emerged in the 11th and 12th century Seljuk and post-Seljuk contexts that were discussed in Chapter 8.

The extremely rich social and cultural lives of people, movements, and intellectual traditions, of artistic and literary currents, of architectural innovations and eclectic knowledge practices, of commodity chains and communication flows, and of many more 'medieval' phenomena have long been neglected, or they have at best only been accepted as exceptions to a more general rule of overall decadence, ossification, and decay. Today, the opposite is true, especially in specialist scholarship, even though only the already extremely rich tip of an enormous and highly complex 'medieval' iceberg has so far been uncovered, and a lot more research remains to be done to enhance understandings of this complexity—transcending by far that of the previous chapters and its different 'medieval' power elites—and of its many contemporary as well as modern meanings. This chapter will engage, therefore, with this tip of that 'medieval' iceberg, aiming both to add some more color and depth to the preceding chapters and to offer a means to start appreciating the rich post-Seljuk textures of that color and depth. Within the scope of this book, however, this can only be done from a generalizing and selective perspective, and no claims can be made that this generalization can possibly represent the full scope of those many 'medieval' textures, or that its necessary selectiveness could not just as easily have allowed for the development of multiple other narratives. In fact, it is these qualities of rich diversity, heterogeneity, ambiguity, and fluidity, and their oft-experimental interaction, that mark this post-Seljuk 'medieval' period in Islamic West-Asia's history above all, and that this chapter can only endeavor to leave an equally ambiguous impression of.[1]

Intellectual networks of 'medieval' normativity and heterogeneity

As referred to on several occasions in the preceding chapters, beneath the surface of the sheer endless process of 'medieval' dynastic fragmentations, transformations, and regular discontinuities across Islamic West-Asia, an accommodating resilience of people and interests and their local, regional, and trans-regional networks continued to occur, simultaneously generating a somewhat paradoxical resilience of many connectivities and continuities. In fact, throughout these long centuries between the 12th and 16th centuries, and despite the inherent tendency for competition, violence, and conquest, the appearance of cultural, social, and economic coherence across one imagined community of the Islamic *umma* acquired far more widely and deeply shared validity than ever before. This remarkably more integrated *umma* manifested itself certainly in the format of expanding connections, as a result of a second, slower 'medieval' wave of conversion that, mostly in the wake of spiritual and economic flows of people, ideas, and commodities, further expanded the boundaries of the world of Islam, especially towards Sub-Saharan Africa and southeast Asia. The new realities of *umma* also emerged from the ever more widely shared ways in which particular ideas of theocratic order and prophetic normativity became meaningful. In fact, the Islamic world of today still derives many of its most important dynamics from this new appearance of trans-regional interconnectivity. Perhaps most importantly, it was only in the course of this post-Seljuk 'medieval' period that the Sunni tenet within Islam is considered to have emerged as a more clearly and explicitly circumscribed theological and practical formulation of normative order, with which a majority of Muslims increasingly began to identify.

At the same time, even the polycentric reality of ongoing inter- and intra-dynastic fragmentation and competition became for many part of the idea of one Islamic world order, as willed, led, and confirmed by God and as guaranteed by the sovereignty of the successor of His prophet, the Abbasid caliph in Bagdad (and in Cairo from 1261). As explained in the preceding chapters, the authority of this caliph—first in Bagdad, then in Cairo, eventually in Constantinople—remained territorially limited or even non-existent throughout this period. Nevertheless, many old and new leaderships in these regions continued to pursue the confirmation and delegation of any of their claims to power from the notion of a prophetic link via the caliphate. The inclusion of the era's violent leadership practices into an explanatory framework of delegation of theocratic sovereignty via divinely inspired forms of mediation—such as the caliphate—was, moreover, an integral component of the symbiotic practices of elite accommodation and cooperation, and of dynastic patronage in return for theocratic integration, that determined 'medieval' elite life and that informed the continuous exchanges of elite resources that were facilitated by the era's many courts and *waqf*-related urban infrastructures. This even went so far that, from at latest the mid-13th century onwards—after the Chinggisid destruction of the Caliphate of Bagdad in 1258 and the contested restoration thereof by sultan Baybars in Cairo in 1261—the imagination of the relationship between nomadic and post-nomadic power and Islamic sovereignty, and between dynastic and theocratic order more in particular, was—and continued to be—rethought, contested, reconsidered, and reinvented by many scholars and intellectuals. One dominant trend, formulated within one of the main 'schools' of Sunni legal thought, accepted the notion—related to the aforementioned contemporary Chinggisid notion of leadership as blessed by 'good fortune' (*qut*) due to divine intervention—that prevalent conquest practices, and thus the coercive assumption of power in one or more regions, automatically allowed for a strongman to be accepted as a sovereign leader (*imam*) in the theocratic order of the Islamic religious community. Whatever the circumstances, the success of that coercive power was easily considered only to have been bestowed upon such a strongman as a result of divine will. In the early 14th century, in a treatise on the ethics of sovereign power, dedicated to the Cairo sultan and authored by a leading Shafiʿi legal scholar, the Egyptian chief judge Ibn Jamaʿa (1241–1333), this particular view on Islamic leadership and sovereignty—referred to here as the 'imamate' instead of the caliphate—was formulated in the following defining terms:

> At a time when there is no *imām* and an unqualified person seeks the imamate and compels the people by his power and his armies, without any formal oath of allegiance or succession, then his oath of allegiance is validly contracted and obedience to him is obligatory, so as to maintain the unity of the Muslims and preserve agreement among them. This is still so, even if he is barbarous or vicious, according to the best opinion. When the imamate is thus contracted by force and violence to one, and then another arises, who overcomes the first by his power and his armies, then the first is deposed and the second becomes *imām*, for the welfare of the Muslims and the preservation of their unity, as we have stated. It was for this reason that the son of ʿUmar said at the battle of Ḥarra, "We are with the victors".[2]

As is illustrated here, articulations of leadership and authority remained highly contested. This, by the way, of course also included this author Ibn Jamaʿa's own authority as Egyptian chief judge. As this derived entirely from the sultan who had appointed him, the latter had to be demonstrated to have the authority to do so in the interest of Ibn Jamaʿa's own religious persona, the soundness of his rulings, and the validity of his commands and advices to his agents, supporters, and followers. In this arena of contested articulations of leadership and sovereignty, the intellectual spectrum of options to argue with opened up increasingly, beyond any traditional and strict principles of membership of the Prophet's family or clan. Instead, different alternatives acquired prominence, often combining in creative ways the argument of divine providence with all kinds of variations of charismatic leadership narratives and strategies (including not least also messianic and divinatory ones).

In many, if not most, circles of Islamic intellectuals and elites, as illustrated by Ibn Jamaʿa's argumentation, there emerged, moreover, the normative idea of the absolute primacy, whatever the means and circumstances, of a social order in which the observance of God's Will (*shariʿa*) was ensured, in accordance with its practical application as based on the teachings of the so-called 'schools of law', the *madhhabs*, and their experts' engagements with Quran and Prophetic Sunna. In fact, as already mentioned in Chapter 8, this trans-regional process of an apparent post-Abbasid closing of the ranks of religious scholarship around a particular body of knowledge has been traditionally subsumed under the notion of a Sunni revival, a Sunni re-centering, or a Sunni centralization. It tends to be directly related to the spread and mushrooming across Islamic West-Asia of *madrasas* and related infrastructures and practices of Sunni Islamic learning and scholarship, as epitomized by the intellectual contributions of the aforementioned Seljuk-Nizamiyya scholar from Iran al-Ghazali (d. 1111). With the circumscribing of that learning and scholarship within, as it were, the walled spaces, textual practices, and scholarly positions of elite sponsored Sunni urban infrastructures, so it often tends to be argued, more delineated and especially traditionalist religious and legal knowledge turned increasingly into a hegemonic and universal norm in the era's knowledge practices. This intellectual crystallization of, and sociocultural centralization around, a shared Sunni form (and norm) of knowledge is then contained in a set corpus of some sixty or seventy key texts only (including al-Ghazali's) and the scholastic methods of extensive commentary traditions on these key texts. It was also shaped by the social relationships of a handful of closely connected and, from the later 12th century onwards, (mostly) mutually tolerant intellectual communities of teachers, students, and practitioners, all defined by the adherence to the primacy of divine law (*shari'a*) and Prophetic norm (*sunna*).[3]

However, by now it is becoming increasingly clear that although very dominant, if not hegemonic, in urbanized parts of regions such as Iraq, Egypt, and Syria, Sunni traditionalism remained highly contested, and the body of knowledge defined as affected by a crystallization and centering process remains highly dynamic—if not, from the 13th century, ever more heterogeneous—throughout these 'medieval' times. This happened from within the Sunni fold of legal communities and their competing views on the value and validity of traditionalism, as well as beyond that fold—far less strictly delineated than generally tends to be assumed—in Islamic West-Asia's western regions as well as anywhere else. In fact, for one of the discursive cornerstones of the so-called Sunni centralization—the 12th-century reorientation and intensification of *jihad* championship, closing the ranks of post-Seljuk leaders and scholars in a collective duty to take up arms against non-Muslims—it has recently been demonstrated by historian Kenneth Goudie that this represented only one, juristic narrative in the contemporary discourse of *jihad*. Other, non-juristic counter-narratives not only existed side-by-side with a dominant legal understanding of collective violent duty, but these different narratives were continuously formulated, interwoven, and reformulated to maintain a coherent discourse that was adapted to both changing contexts and changing intentions. "Alongside of the [legal narrative] and in reaction to it", Goudie explains, "counter-narratives developed and evolved . . . [including] the frontier discourse of *jihad* presented in such works as the 'Kitāb al-Jihād' of Ibn al-Mubārak, and the discourse of mujāhada, as espoused by Sufis such as al-Ghazālī".[4]

Just as the 'medieval' discourse of *jihad* was a never-ending creative process of formulation, contestation, adaptation, accommodation, and even reinvention, therefore, the wider juristic discourse of traditionalism, and of a 're-centering' Sunni Islam more in general, did not just spread in ever more dominant forms from, especially, 12th century Bagdad and Iraq to Egypt and Syria and then, from the 14th century onwards, back eastwards. It, at the same time, also remained one among several 'narratives' in Sunni Islamic discourse, and one among an expanding range—especially from the 13th century onwards—of normative Islamic discourses and their varying narratives more in general. As a result, it can be argued somewhat unconventionally, that the 16th-century Safavid context of experimentation with Twelver Shi'ism (see Chapter 12) may well be considered highly representative for 'medieval' intellectual and even ideological conditions, rather than any radical departure from those conditions. As explained before, Twelver Shi'ism became a central discourse in leadership claims articulated for Isma'il (r. 1501–1524) and especially for his son Tahmasp (r. 1524–1576), but it simultaneously continued to have to operate amidst what has been described as an "unparalleled heterogeneity" and an "impressively variegated range of legitimization" that allowed for substantial "malleability" and adaptation to the "panoply of important religious, ethnic, and political constituencies [that were] in play during the sixteenth century".[5] The relationship between the Sunni center and many—including Shi'ite—forms of heterogeneity was anything but different across the entirety of 'medieval' Islamic West-Asia, and competing discourses and narratives—claiming to pertain to that Sunni center or not—as well as their reformulations, adaptations, or even reinventions were as much part of West-Asia's diverse landscapes of leadership as practices of conquest and of dynastic, patriarchal, and patrimonial formation were. This perspective of widespread heterogeneity, and even fluidity, of competing discourses and, simultaneously, of their many adherents, explains at least how, as modern intellectual historian Matthew Melvin-Koushki has argued, "a Shi'i-Sufi-occultist amalgam was still the engine of [16th century] Safavid imperial ideology", and how at the same time "Ottoman elite enthusiasm for this science [of letter divination] of the [Shi'ite] *imam*s well into the 16th century" could be part of "the continued prevalence of Sunni imamophilia".[6] Both these 16th-century realities illustrate above all the complexity and ambiguity—for, in these particular cases, neither distinctly Sunni nor Shi'ite—of 'medieval' intellectual landscapes.

Social networks of 'medieval' heterogeneous and multiple identities

From at latest the middle of the 13th century onwards, complex networks of Muslim (and non-Muslim) scholars, artists, spiritual leaders, and messianic figures, each with their own students and followers, appeared increasingly prominent around these contested discourses and the resources they gave access to. Particular local, regional, or trans-regional branches of Sunni (or even Shi'ite) *madhhab*s, of traditionalist or speculative schools of theology, and of Sufi movements (also referred to as 'brotherhoods', *tariqa*s) were some of the—for later observers at least—more visible 'medieval' forms in which these networks manifested themselves. But there were also many others, operating in entirely autonomous, in equally overlapping and intersecting, and in continuously competing ways. The networks of coercive leadership, dynastic formation, Islamic sovereignty, and resource accumulation that clustered around the courts and *waqf*-related urban infrastructures of Cairo, Bursa, Edirne, and Constantinople, of Tabriz and Qazvin, or of Samarqand and Herat were often—but not always and never necessarily—actively involved in many of these networks and flows of people and resources. This was certainly also true for many other urban and even rural and nomadic elites in the vast and varied geographical landscapes of Islamic West-Asia, from the networks of people, infrastructures, and resources clustering around the aforementioned Arabo-Persian Hülegüid vizier Rashid al-Din Fadl-Allah Hamadani (d. 1318) and his descendants, over those of the Safavid Twelver Shi'i scholar Karaki (d. 1534), to those of the Mongolian and Turkmen leaderships of the Jalayrids, the Qara and Aq Qoyunlu, the Qizilbash, and the Uzbeks. In these and many more heterogeneous and fluid 'medieval' forms of belonging and identity, complex sets of dynamic networks of people, practices, objects, infrastructures, and ideas continued to intensively connect Transoxania and Khurasan to Asia Minor, Syria, and Egypt.

Those movements and groups that appear as more special, if not extreme, and therefore, also highly impactful and equally representative for the 'medieval' panoply and amalgam across all kinds of boundary definitions, were those that clustered around charismatic ideas of millenarianism and messianism. One of these was the aforementioned Safaviyya. Originating in an early 14th-century Sufi dervish context and generating substantial *waqf*-related and thus tax-exempted resources and estates around Ardabil in Azerbaijan, the Safaviyya transformed into a militant and apocalyptic movement in the mid-15th century in northern Syria and eastern Anatolia as well as in Azerbaijan. Eventually, it successfully integrated Turkmen leaderships and coercive force in its own relationships of total devotion to Safavid dynastic charisma, and of articulations of that charisma as not just a creative re-interpretation of the imamate, but as practically divine (see Chapter 12). Another set of these networks was that of the aforementioned Nizari Isma'ilis—also known as the 'sect of the Assassins'—which developed around messianic and related charismatic Shi'ite leaderships in some remote areas and strongholds in Syria and Iran. Widely feared mainly for their various assassinations and attempted murders of Seljuk, post-Seljuk, and other rivals and opponent, they were eliminated in the mid-13th century by the Chinggisid campaigns of West-Asian conquest. These Safaviyya and Nizariyya may appear as two rather extreme examples of 'medieval' heterogeneity, symbiosis, and charismatic force, and such an assessment may well be correct. At the same time, the 15th and 16th century Safaviyya and the 12th and 13th century Nizariyya are quite central in the making of that 'medieval' landscape, and they are in fact all but exceptional in their intellectual and practical trajectories. These trajectories involved their engagement in—or succumbing to—often violent rivalries with competitors, nurturement of the coercive force of followers and allies, accumulation of resources, and pursuit of strategies of spiritual as well as practical reproduction. All networks, movements, and groups iterated these trajectories, in more and especially less visible and violent manners, and many—if not increasingly more—coalesced around the charisma of similar apocalyptic visions. Other highly representative and impactful examples of these phenomena that deserve brief mention here are the so-called Hurufiyya and the Musha'sha'. The Hurufiyya basically refers to a network of various groups of dervishes, occult scientists, and lettrists operating between Cairo, Bursa, and Constantinople, and Tabriz and Isfahan. They first emerged in later 14th century Azerbaijan, and Hurufi clusters of adherents, lettrist divinatory practices, and messianic ideas continued to appear in multivalent capacities of alliance, integration, subversion, or prosecution at all of these urban center's royal courts throughout the 15th and 16th centuries. The Musha'sha' represents a related, but yet very different phenomenon, originating in their own set of messianic and dynastic claims, an amalgam of Sufi, Shi'ite, and Sunni ideas and practices, and militant action pursued especially among Arabian communities in southern Iraq and southwestern Iran (Khuzistan). As a result of the successful deployment of violent anti-Timurid and anti-Turkmen action in these regions, an autonomous space emerged for this movement's messianic leadership, its adherents and followers, and their descendants. Whereas in the course of the 16th century, this Musha'sha' leadership was integrated in the Safavid trans-regional order, it continued to appear as a local and often highly autonomous Safavid vassal and ally, and even remained a powerful local or regional player for many centuries more.

Dynastic networks of 'medieval' value systems

As the increasing visibility and even centrality of the latter messianic and millenarian examples suggest, equally heterogeneous and innovative 'medieval' value systems and imaginations of theocratic order and normativity contributed to the constitution and explanation of these networks, their practices and actions, and their relationships and hierarchies. Many aforementioned references actually shed more light on those equally determining value systems, including not least the doctrine of the imamate by coercion of the Egyptian chief judge Ibn Jama'a. As suggested in the preceding chapters, the Ottoman sultan was also described in a late 14th-century Arabic eyewitness report of his encounter with 'crusaders' near Nikopolis in related terms of both Islamic and coercive sovereignty, as 'the sultan Bayezid, whose justice spread far and wide afterwards, son of the Monarch of the Holy Warriors Murad, son of the Monarch of the Holy Warriors Orkhan, son of Osman.' One of the main post-Hülegüid Jalayirid rulers of Tabriz and Bagdad was at one point styled no less than 'Master of the people of all obediences' and 'Shadow of God in the World'. A Persian treatise on political ethics, composed in the 1470s, presented the Turkmen ruler Uzun Hasan along the ancient—but by this time clearly once more predominant—model of royal justice and welfare,[7] the Inner-Asian model of dynastic fortune and divine blessing, and the Islamic model of the Caliphate, styling him not just "the Shadow of God", but also no less than "the Caliph of God and the Deputy of the Prophet".[8] This also brings to mind how the aforementioned Twelver Shi'i scholar Karaki (d. 1534) was not only ambitiously styled 'the Proof of Islam' at the Safavid court of Tahmasp (r. 1524–76), but was also a leading articulator of Safavid dynastic claims of ʿAlid lineage and direct descent from the seventh *imam.*

One important returning element in many of these eclectic formulations of sovereignty, furthermore, is not just the many references to its direct relationship with notions of justice, but also the central role that tends to be awarded to custom-based rulings as formulated by the dynastic ruler. What tends to be identified as 'dynastic law'—with its origins often referring back to legal customs on the Inner-Asian steppes, and especially to the rulings and agreements formulated by Chinggis Khan and joined together in his famous law code, the *Yasa*—appears as increasingly central, often in juxtaposition to religious law (*shariʿa*), if not equally often superior to it, in many references to, formulations of, and actions inspired by dominant practices of social justice, from Transoxania to Asia Minor. In the late 15th-century Persian treatise on political ethics from Tabriz, this complex relationship between different normative authorities is described as follows:

> The first concern of the organizer of the world is the maintenance of the injunctions of the Sacred Law. In specific details, however, he retains the power to act in accordance with the public interest of his age (*maṣlaḥat-i vaqt*) as long as his actions fall within the general principles of the Sacred Law.[9]

In the 16th-century Ottoman context, this complex relationship had most clearly stabilized in favor of so-called dynastic law, which is one of the reasons why sultan Suleiman is best known by the title of *Kanuni*, the Lawgiver. Discussions in modern scholarship continue on the wider significance of this Ottoman prioritization of the sultan's legal authority. It seems, in any case, very clear that already in 15th-century Tabriz, Herat, and Cairo, balances in the ongoing competition between proponents of the priority of either type of discursive authority—in Cairo following on also from Ibn Jamaʿa's much earlier perspective on the imamate of the sultan—had similarly been tipping ever more clearly in favor of the dynastic counter-narrative. In 16th-century Constantinople, a leading role in this typically 'medieval' process of experimental mixing and competing of narratives and discourses was played by one of the most prominent Ottoman legal experts, Ebu l-Suʿud (*c.* 1490–1574). One of Ebu l-Suʿud's most important contributions to the development of the Ottoman normative system is considered to have been his theoretical-religious redefinition of the Ottoman sultan's (mainly fiscal) legislative activities, through ordinances in the form of *kanun*, as not merely complementary to God-given law, but as an integral and completely legitimate part of it.[10]

Dynastic networks of 'medieval' infrastructures

The 16th-century Ottoman sultan Suleiman is not just styled 'the Lawgiver', but also 'the Magnificent', as token of the cultural efflorescence that was generated by the enormous investments in the arts and sciences that he and his court are credited with. A late 15th-century Turkish chronicle provides the following description of this royal quality of cultural patronage, mediated through the ruler's court and his *waqf*-related investments, and often also linked to the qualities of justice, charity, and well-being, for Suleiman's forefather Murad II (r. 1421–1451):

> A description of the buildings constructed by Sultan Murad
>
> The pious foundations of the Sultan of Islam and of the Muslims, Sultan Murad, know no bounds. One of the many is the bridge over the Everge river, in what had previously been a forest. In the winter, the place would become muddy and the Muslims would be unable to pass. It would become a lair for brigands, and much evil would take place. So Sultan Murad took great pains to clear the forest and build a large bridge there, founding towns on either side as well as an *imaret* [=a hospice and public soup kitchen]. He went there in person to cook the *imaret*'s stew and distribute it to the poor, granting many other favors as well. Moreover, in Edirne he built a large Friday mosque and two *madrasa*s, one for the study of *Hadith*. There he also built an *imaret* and a lodge for dervishes of the Mevlevi [Sufi] order. He assigned *vakıf* (=*waqf*) property to these, so that every day his bounty reaches many poor people. Furthermore, in Bursa he built an *imaret*, and next to that a *madrasa* and a mausoleum intended as his own resting place. His pious foundations are without end.[11]

As suggested at various occasions in the preceding chapters, Suleiman's reputation and Murad's cultural patronage are all but exceptions in Islamic West-Asia's post-Seljuk and post-Mongol landscapes of power. In the 15th-century Timurid context, it was already explained that the Russian scholar Vasiliy V. Barthold (1869–1930) identified a remarkable, Timurid efflorescence of the arts and sciences, which was for modern historian Marshall Hodgson the result of the simple fact that "the descendants of Timur . . . stand out in Islamicate history for their high personal cultivation and their patronage of arts and letters".[12] In fact, Hodgson's well-intended judgement of Timurid exceptionalism is illustrative of traditional, rather negative, appreciations of cultural patronage by most 'medieval' leaderships. It is by now far more accepted to consider that, rather than standing out, Timur's descendants fit in very well with a wider pattern of intensive interest and investment in all kinds of cultural and intellectual expression and sophistication. In the case of the Cairo Sultanate and one of its periods most explicitly connected with an age of similar efflorescence, during the triple reign of the Qalawunid sultan al-Malik al-Nasir Muhammad (r. 1293–1294, 1299–1309, 1310–1341), it has in fact been argued that

> there was greater interconnectedness between al-Nasir Muhammad's household, Egypt's and Syria's governing elites, the [Qalawunid dynasty]'s bureaucratic and military [apparatus], normative ideas of social order, and cultural aesthetics than ever before in the Sultanate's history. As a result, al-Nasir Muhammad's [dynastic reign] was not only culturally produced by the sultan and his agents but was also reproduced by the elites who were emerging around him, joining forces in the fourteenth-century Qalawunid project and using the same language of power that served their common interests so well (at least as long as they managed to negotiate the sultan's favor).[13]

The 'medieval' panoply of local, regional, and trans-regional dynastic formations and the 'medieval' heterogeneity of imaginations, representations, and performances not just of Islamic legal normativity, but of much wider theocratic, eschatological, intellectual, social, and aesthetic order were almost everywhere deeply interrelated in often surprisingly multivalent ways. For the 15th-century Syro-Egyptian context, modern historian Carl Petry actually refers to no less than the rendering by these symbiotic interactions of a 'medieval' 'Silver Age' of scholarship. Extrapolating from Petry's focus on the Cairo Sultanate, it may be argued that an exceptional age of cultural efflorescence, intense circulation, dynastic formation, and local accommodation is indeed what West-Asia's many centers of power, trade, discourses, arts, and sciences experienced and connected during these 'medieval' times. As Petry summarily explains below, furthermore, these were all generated by practices of conquest and competition as much as by the mediating infrastructures of households and courts, and of *waqf*-related urban madrasas, mosques, khanqahs, mausolea, hospitals, and even Ottoman *imaret*s, or soup kitchens:

> In fact, the majority of [the leadership's] wealth was recycled back into [local] society via maintenance of great households with swarms of retainers and artisans, requisition expenditures to outfit military campaigns, and massive endowments (*waqfs*) made to found religio-academic institutions. By the ninth/fifteenth century, this latter propensity had created a network of more than two hundred mosques, colleges, and Sufi hospices in the capital [of Cairo] alone, each supporting a core staff of clerics or faculty, instructional deputies of various specialties, and students whose needs were met out of *waqf* proceeds [. . .]. The senior faculty, who held chairs in the Koranic sciences, Prophetic traditions, or Shari' jurisprudence, delivered formal lectures and certified the expertise of advanced students who presented themselves for disputation and examination. Their mentors signed authorisations attesting to textual proficiency, which facilitated a novice's entry into the courts and/or academies. Since junior instructors handled the bulk of routine pedagogy, these senior scholars, most of whom had achieved prior renown as clerics or jurists, were left free to pen the corpus of treatises, which rendered the [later 'medieval] era a "Silver Age" of Islamic scholarship.[14]

In the early 15th century, one active participant in, and observer of, this highly dynamic order of crisscrossing, overlapping, and competing bonds of loyalty, obligation, resources, and reputation, the Cairene scholar and historian Ahmad ibn ʿAli al-Maqrizi (d. 1442), penned down in a text of economic and monetary advice for the Cairo sultan a rather unique and insightful abstraction of two key aspects of this highly complex 'medieval' social constellation: the division of labor and the distribution of resources. In fact, al-Maqrizi assumed these aspects in his homeland of Egypt to be not only functionally revolving and clustering around those different infrastructures of power, accommodation, and efflorescence, but actually as being integrated and empowered by them. This idealized reflection on social roles, categories, and infrastructures will actually be used in the continuation of this chapter as a most useful starting point for an organized further discussion of some main components of these complex networks of theocratic ideas, multiple identities, dynastic value systems, and mediating infrastructures in Egypt as well as elsewhere across Islamic West-Asia.

> Know—May God guard you with His sleepless eye and His fearsome might—that the people of Egypt on the whole consist of seven categories. The first category are those who perform the dynastic reign (*ahl al-dawla*). The second [is formed of] the rich merchants and the wealthy who lead a life of affluence. The third [encompasses] the retailers, who are merchants of average means, and who are referred to as the cloth merchants. To them are also added the foodsellers, who are the small shopkeepers. The fourth category embraces the peasants, those who cultivate and plow the land and who live in the villages and on the countryside. The fifth category is made up of those who

receive a stipend (*al-fuqarā'*), consisting of most legal specialists (*al-fuqahā'*) and of the students (*ṭullāb al-'ilm*). [It is also made up of] many foot soldiers and their like. The sixth category [corresponds to] the artisans and the salaried persons who possess a skill. The seventh category [consists of] the needy and the paupers; and these are the beggars, who solicit charity from the people and who are fed by them.[15]

Obviously, this taxonomy was informed more by prescriptive than by descriptive intentions, and in line with the above-mentioned fluid boundaries of groups and identities, these categories represent, as will also become clear below, 'open' social roles in which—perhaps even platforms of infrastructural rights and obligations on which—communities, networks, and discourses met and interacted, rather than socioeconomic classes in any strict, closed, or self-conscious sense. Information on the majority of those engaging with many of these roles in Egypt, or elsewhere in Islamic West-Asia, moreover, remains very limited to almost non-existent due to the very specific and mainly Muslim elitist bias of the majority of the extant source material. It is above all for the courtly, intellectual, and, to a lesser extent, commercial urban elites of Islamic West-Asia, engaging with the first, second, third, and fifth categories of al-Maqrizi's list, that sufficient information has survived that allows for a discussion that can claim to reconstruct—in a generalizing fashion—some of the complexities and contradictions of 'medieval' West-Asia's social formations. While, following al-Maqrizi's taxonomy, the 'medieval' regions of Egypt and Syria will operate as central axes for this chapter's further discussions, many other parts of 'medieval' Islamic West-Asia—from Asia Minor to Transoxania—will be taken into consideration wherever relevant and possible.

1 'Medieval' urbanities in flux

1.1 Networks of exchange, chains of commodities, and everyday experiences

The heterogeneous experimentality and competitive agency just described as key characteristics for 'medieval' Islamic West-Asia's history certainly similarly marked the numerous trade networks that intensely connected these many regions. The range of these networks, with the commercial elites of urban centers, towns, and ports as its many nodes, extended from the galleys of the *Serenissima Repubblica* of Venice and the tax collectors of the post-Seljuk Rasulid rulers of Yemen in Sana'a to all kinds of entrepreneurial groups autonomously operating as Venetian, Rasulid, or their many peers' agents, contractors, and intermediaries, or simply as representatives of their own interests in the many margins of these complex trans-regional networks. The latter entrepreneurial groups included, most prominently perhaps, those listed as the second category in al-Maqrizi's socioeconomic taxonomy—'the rich merchants and the wealthy who lead a life of affluence'. Numerous land and sea routes actually crossed the regions of Islamic West-Asia, and allowed for these groups to remain strongly interconnected, and for the many nodes on these routes to operate as vital as well as resourceful points of negotiation, partnership, and infrastructural support with the movements, practices, and interests of local, regional, and trans-regional strongmen and their entourages. The most important among these many crisscrossing and regularly changing routes were the so-called silk routes, which ran from East Asia via Transoxania and Iran to Asia Minor and Syria, and the maritime east-west routes, which linked, via the ports of the Persian Gulf and the Red Sea, the ancient and rich worlds of the Indian Ocean and of the Mediterranean. Other important land and sea routes ran from the north to south and connected the many regions bordering the Black, the Caspian, and the Aral Seas, including the Pontic-Caspian steppes in the north, with the urban markets of Anatolia, Syria, and Egypt, and of Azerbaijan, Iraq, Iran, Fars, Kirman, and Khurasan.

On these and many other routes, trade took place in a great variety of commodities, from ordinary local merchandise and food wares to a wide array of highly valued products, including, not least, slaves, furs, and metal ware. Especially the pepper and spice trade represented a high-end and complex field of interactions between Southeast and West-Asia. For many 'medieval' centuries the ever more intensely used spice routes between India and Egypt, for instance, were dominated by a group of specialists known as the Karimi merchants. This maritime trade route ran via the Red Sea, and its dynamics were entirely determined by the monsoon winds. For centuries, its major transit points in the west were the ports of Yemen and the Syrian coasts and the Egyptian delta. Particularly Alexandria, where Italian and other Latin traders—first and foremost those from Genoa and Venice—purchased and transported loads of pepper for the growing European market, played an important role in these trade networks. In the early 15th century, an important change occurred in the route, which caused the ports of the Hejaz, especially Jeddah, and transit points in the interior of Syria, first and foremost Damascus, to start playing a significant role. The shift towards Jeddah also appears to have given the sultan's court in Cairo more direct access to this commercial route, and it largely enabled the sultan's fiscal and commercial agents to take over the central role of the Karimi merchants. Among other things, a new network of traders, known as the Khawajakiyya, appeared more prominently in this interregional spice trade as privileged commercial entrepreneurs and, at the same time, as exclusive representatives of the court. This had beneficial consequences for these traders themselves, but certainly also for the Sultanate's revenues.

Another highly priced commodity was represented by unfree men and women, brought to Islamic West-Asia from all over the Afro-Eurasian continents as a result of raiding, warfare, and tributary arrangements. Slave merchants with expertise in particular routes and provenances—from the Inner-Asian Steppes, the Caucasus, the Balkans, and Asia Minor, from the Mediterranean and Indian Ocean worlds, and from the African continent—brought their wares along regular rhythms of acquisition, long-distance travel, and sale on West-Asia's urban slave markets. The labor of unfree men and women in households and with families, for agricultural production, in commercial enterprises and networks, and also as fighters and military manpower was a central building block of everyday life across Islamic West-Asia, in elite urban households as much as in their more modest urban and non-urban counterparts. It even was a constitutive component of the social bonds of loyalty, obligation, and kinship that regulated household and family life. However, the majority of these men and women, their diverse relationships with merchants, masters, and peers, and their careers of forced labor have remained largely invisible in the era's source material. Only when some of them managed to become powerful patrimonial agents—and occasionally even masters and slave owners in their own right—was some more information about the economic and commercial conditions of their arrival and preparation for a life of service available. This was to some extent the case for the many Georgians and Circassians who were enslaved and employed by the Safavid ruler Tahmasp in mid-16th-century Qazvin. It applied especially to the Ottoman sultan's 'Servants of the Palace' in Constantinople (see below) and to the *mamluks* and 'Turko-Circassians' in Cairo. An insightful brief description of this arrival and preparation of *mamluks*—most likely representative for the trajectory imposed on many unfree men and women destined for elite household service in Cairo or in Damascus—was penned down by a late 14th-century historian in Egypt, alluding at the same time to how, for this scholar at least, this concerns a highly valued and even emancipatory rags-to-riches story, typically represented as an integral component of the theocratic order of things.

> The slave merchants bring [*mamluks*] to Egypt in batch after batch, like sand grouse flocking to watering places. The rulers have them paraded and bid against one another to pay the highest price for them. The purpose of their purchase is not to enslave them but to intensify their group solidarity and strengthen their prowess and their inclination towards [developing] a group solidarity that protects [their master]. . . . Then the rulers lodge them in the . . . [citadel of Cairo], foster their loyalty, and give them a careful upbringing, including the study of the Quran and other subjects of instruction, until they become proficient in these things. Then they train them in the use of the bow and the sword, in riding in the hippodromes, in fighting with the lance, until they become tough and seasoned soldiers and these things become second nature to them. When the rulers are convinced that they are prepared to defend them and to die for them, they multiply their pay and augment their fiefs. Then, they impose upon them the duties of perfecting themselves in the use of weapons and in horsemanship, as well as of increasing the number of men of their own races [in the ruler's service] for the same purpose. Then they appoint them to high offices. Even sultans are chosen from among them, who direct the affairs of the Muslims, as had been ordained by the Providence of Almighty God and out of His benevolence to His creatures. Thus one group [of *mamlūks*] follows another and generation succeeds generation and Islam rejoices in the wealth which it acquired [by means of them] and the boughs of the regime are luxuriant with the freshness and verdure of youth.[16]

In the relatively limited extant source material that informs us about the activities of these slave merchants and of many related specialists of trans-regional trade, the fabulous riches of some of them emerge as particularly captivating. This incited al-Maqrizi to identify them all as "the rich merchants and the wealthy who lead a life of affluence", and in al-Maqrizi's chronicles as well as in those of many of his contemporaries, occasional allusions are made to how it was crucial for them all to engage in extensive networks of credit that occasionally even involved West-Asia's central courts. These sophisticated and widespread networks of credit were constructed around wider social bonds of trust (organized around practices of loyalty and obligation referred to as *suhba*—'companionship') and trade contacts that enabled the most ambitious and successful of these merchants and their partners to be active in complex relationships of exchange across Afro-Eurasia. This was also the case for Jewish trading communities of Islamic West-Asia and North Africa. The activities of these communities are, in fact, much better known than those of many other commercial networks because of the 19th-century discovery of a huge Jewish archive in the storage space (*geniza*) of a synagogue near Cairo. The painstaking academic research that, since many decades, has been devoted to the many tens of thousands of private and public texts and documents of this archive considers these Jewish trading communities as a highly integrated and closely connected 'Mediterranean Society'—intensely exchanging correspondence, commodities, and assets across geographical obstacles and dynastic boundaries—which was, at the same time, deeply embedded in the commercial and sociocultural practices of its wider 'medieval' world.[17]

The traditional urban centers of these regions were predominantly organized around these trading communities and their varied commercial activities, particularly around the many public markets along open-ended streets (the *suqs*) where especially al-Maqrizi's "retailers, . . . merchants of average means, . . . cloth merchants, . . . food sellers, [and] small

Figure 13.1 Cambridge: Solomon Schechter at work in the Taylor-Schechter Geniza collection of Cambridge University, in 1898. Schechter was the scholar who, in 1896, acknowledged the historical value and academic potential of this ancient archive of the Jewish community of Fustat (Cairo); he had most of it—about 140,000 handwritten documents and texts—transferred to Cambridge for research

Source: Reproduced by kind permission of the Syndics of Cambrige University Library, Views BB 53.2.89.17

shopkeepers" were active. One leading modern historian, Jonathan Berkey, describes very aptly how in current academic research this strikingly commercial arrangement of urban centers is actually regarded as defined by the same 'medieval' heterogeneity, fluidity, and even ambiguity that made for most of the era's practices and discourses:

> In [the] analysis [of the modern historian Ira Lapidus] the entire city took the form of a 'bazaar,' characterized by a 'fluid pattern of social interchange and of daily living', in which religious institutions, baths, and commercial establishments were mixed together because the individuals who used them passed easily from prayer and study to work and business, and thence to social interaction and relaxation.[18]

We find this fluidity and mixing of commercial and other activities not just in the context of urban markets and small shopkeepers, but also in the organization and arrangement of strategically located, semi-closed commercial infrastructures. These were the caravanserais (known as *khans*, *funduqs*, or *wikalas*) in which commerce in luxury goods as well as in more mundane merchandise was organized. While many caravanserais were established along the trade routes of Islamic West-Asia in or near small towns or villages, as stopping points and resting places for caravans and traveling merchants, in the urban centers, these buildings also served many other social functions.

This is certainly also suggested in the following contemporary detailed description of the life and times of such a caravanserai, constructed in the first half of the 14th century by an enterprising amir along one of Cairo's main arteries:

> In this *wikāla* . . . there are staying merchants trading in Syrian commodities such as olive oil, sesame oil, soap, molasses, pistachio nuts, walnuts, almonds, carob, fruit pulp and similar items. On its terrain between the congregational mosque of al-Ḥākim and the Sa'īd al-Su'adā' *khanqah* there used to be a house . . . which was demolished together with any adjacent infrastructures by [order of] the amir Qūṣūn. He had [this *wikāla*] made as an enormous warehouse with lodgings (*funduq*) and with a series of storerooms (*makhāzin*) surrounding its [courtyard]. He stipulated that every storeroom could only be let for five silver coins, with no increments, and that no one could be expelled from it. Due to these low rents and profitable conditions these storerooms came to be inherited from generation to generation. I visited this *wikāla* long time ago, and at that occasion I saw that from the inside as well as from the outside it looked truly breathtaking, because of the quantity of all kinds of merchandise that were there, its being packed with people, and the loud yelling of carriers bringing goods and taking them away for whomever had bought them. Later, however, its business was ruined due to Syria's destruction in the year 1400 by the hands of Timur Lank. Nevertheless, until now [*c*. 1428] [some business] remains ongoing there.
>
> The top floors of this *wikāla* are taken up by large tenement structures (*ribā'*), consisting of three hundred sixty living units (*bayt*), for which I was able to determine that they were all inhabited. They can roughly house some four thousand souls, men and women, young and old. But when the misfortunes of the years 1403–1404 occurred, many of these living units got in disarray, even though many others continued to be inhabited and populated.[19]

This detailed description of the history of this *wikala* of the Qalawunid amir Qusun al-Nasiri (d. 1342), once again from the pen of al-Maqrizi, also suggests how trade, commerce, and urban life more in general were sometimes seriously affected by both the practices of conquest—topped in the recollection of many inhabitants of Syria and Egypt by those pursued by Timur—and the other calamities that regularly affected communities and their everyday lives across Islamic West-Asia. The latter consisted especially of the devastating effects of drought and failed harvests, and more in general also of epidemics such as plague and pestilence. Especially from the middle of the 14th century onwards, amidst the dissolution of the Hülegüid dynastic formation in the regions between Anatolia and Khurasan, conditions of travel as well as of urban life seem to have continued to be seriously hampered by a combination of these factors. After the end of Hülegüid threats against Syria in the early 14th century, ongoing realities of violence and warfare between rivalling leaderships eventually only became really disastrous again by the end of the century, in the shape of the raiding parties of Timur's armies. In the meantime, however, even more disruptive, perhaps, was the mid-century pandemic of the Black Death. This worldwide epidemic of the bubonic plague, which originated in the Inner-Asian Steppes, reached first Egypt and then Syria in 1348

Figure 13.2 Cairo: view from the internal courtyard on various commercial and residential amenities of the caravanserai (*wikala*) of sultan Qanisawh al-Ghawri (*c.* 1505)

Source: © Ashmolean Museum, University of Oxford

via the trade routes that connected the Sultanate with the Black Sea and the Pontic Caspian Steppes. According to most contemporary stories, the Egyptian port of Alexandria was the first to be confronted with the deadly consequences.

> A ship arrived in Alexandria. Aboard it were thirty-two merchants and a total of three hundred people—among them traders and slaves. Nearly all of them had died. There was no one alive on the ship, save four of the traders, one slave and about forty sailors. These [forty-five] survivors [soon] died in Alexandria.[20]

The epidemic spread very quickly inland and wreaked serious havoc in Cairo as well. Its particularly mortal appearance in 1348, and the regular return of pneumonic plague in subsequent decades, not only decimated these regions' populations, but also prevented them from recovering. This seriously affected life in Cairo, as in many of West-Asia's other urban centers. The regularly returning apocalyptic horrors of omnipresent death are represented, in hindsight, in many reports, as in the following attempt in one of al-Maqrizi's main chronicles to quantify the Black Death's devastating impact on Cairo's urban population.

> It is said that the number of deaths in one day amounted to twenty thousand, and that between November and December 1348 there were counted nine hundred thousand

> funerals just in Cairo. It turned out that there were not enough piers, even though there were fourteen hundred of them. That is why the dead were transported on mazes, doors of shops, and wooden panels. Eventually carriers even had to transport two or three deaths on just one panel.[21]

The Black Death and subsequent cycles of pestilence also affected in unprecedented ways al-Maqrizi's "fourth category [of Egyptians], embracing the peasants, those who cultivate and plow the land and who live in the villages and on the countryside". As a result, the traditional tributary and fiscal system of Egypt (see below), entirely organized around very labor-intensive agriculture, was severely disrupted, and would remain so for a very long time. The general effects of all this—on rural and urban populations as well as on their leaderships—combined with regular warfare and raiding, including eventually Timur's trans-regional raiding campaigns, made the regions of Egypt and Syria, by the end of the 14th and early 15th century, especially vulnerable to famine and social unrest, as also suggested in al-Maqrizi's above-mentioned description of a caravanserai's life and times. Even al-Maqrizi's own life was seriously affected by the losses of friends and family that followed from these insecure, if not indeed apocalyptic, circumstances. In a treatise written in the period 1405–1406 to analyze and better understand his and his contemporaries' dire socioeconomic situation, he vividly expressed the despair and insecurity that belonged to the conditions of 'medieval' life in Egypt, and in Islamic West-Asia more in general, and that go a long way to also explain the widespread prevalence—in small villages and pastoralist communities as well as at the 'medieval' courts of sultans and padishahs—of apocalyptic, messianic, millenarian, and divinatory practices, ideas, leaderships, and movements.

> In the middle of Shawwāl 801 [20 June 1399] there was the death of [sultan] al-Ẓāhir Barqūq. On that date, in Cairo, one *irdabb* of wheat sold for less than thirty dirhams. The next day its price reached forty dirhams. Prices continued to rise until one *irdabb* [of wheat] sold for more than seventy dirhams in the year 802 [1399–1400]. Wheat prices remained at this level until the Nile failed to reach its plenitude in 806 [1403–1404]. This led to a calamity: prices soared so high that the price of one *irdabb* of wheat exceeded four hundred dirhams. Prices of other commodities, such as foodstuffs, drink, and clothing, followed a similar trend, thus causing an increase unheard of in recent times in the wages of such persons as construction workers, laborers, craftsmen, and artisans. Finally, succor came from Almighty God in the year 807 [1404–1405]: the level of the Nile rose greatly, and the entire land benefited from this; thus, the people were in need of seed. At that time, abundant quantities of grain were under the control of high officials and other influential persons. This [grain shortage] was due to two factors; first, the dynasty's monopoly kept foodstuffs out of the reach of the people unless they agreed to pay the prices set by the officials; second, the increase in grain [prices] in the year 806 [1403–1404], which was unparalleled in living memory. Because of these factors, as well as others that will be mentioned later, the situation became critical; conditions became perilous, disaster was widespread and calamity universal, to the degree that more than one-half of the population of the land [of Egypt] died of hunger and cold. Death was so prevalent that even the animals perished in the years 806 [1403–1404] and 807 [1404–1405]. They became so scarce that their prices reached levels that we are embarrassed to mention. We are presently at the beginning of the year 808 [1405–1406], and because of the fluctuation of the currency, the scarcity of the necessities of life, and malfeasance and poor judgment [on the part of the officials], the situation is continually worsening due to greatly distressed and abominable conditions.[22]

1.2 Networks of scholars and men of religion

The most prominent and well-known as well as heterogeneous component of the many urbanities of 'medieval' Islamic West-Asia undoubtedly is represented in al-Maqrizi's Egyptian taxonomy by "the fifth category . . . of those who receive a stipend, consisting of most legal specialists and of the students seeking knowledge". This vague definition, often paralleled to the equally vague and comprehensive notion of the *ʿulamaʾ*, represents a very open social category, to which—as suggested before—many different communities, networks, and individuals contributed and which was made up not only of erudite and authoritative teachers, writers, judges, and scholars, but also of poorly educated prayer leaders active in small neighborhoods or villages, of popular storytellers and unskilled street preachers, and of all kinds of small-time religious associates, assistants, and students.

The diversity of roles and responsibilities that was taken up by, or awarded to, "those who receive a stipend" is in fact very clearly illustrated in an extant version of a legal document that organized the religious endowment, or *waqf*, set up by sultan al-Malik al-Ashraf Barsbay (r. 1422–1438) for his religious complex of a mosque, a *madrasa*, and a mausoleum in the center of Cairo. Legal documents such as these stipulated in minute detail the estates and income that were transferred to their endowment, as well as the stipends that were to be paid from these assets, and the services for which they were meant to cater. The potentially wide range of those services and stipends, most of them involving different groups of *ʿulamaʾ* of diverse expertise and standing, are detailed in this document from 1428 as follows:

> To the prayer leader (*imām*) of this mosque there should be paid every month 1,000 silver coins, and every day three units of bread; to the preacher (*khaṭīb*) every month 500

Figure 13.3 Sivas (Turkey): remains of the Çifte Minareli Medrese (1271), a *madrasa* constructed under the patronage of a daughter of the Rum Seljuk sultan Kayqubad (r. 1220–1237)

Source: SALT research, Ali Saim Ülgen Archive; Wikimedia reference

silver coins, and every day three units of bread; to the warden every month 100 silver coins; to nine muezzins every month 1,800 silver coins, and every day 27 units of bread; to the timekeeper (*muwaqqit*) 300 silver coins, and three units of bread; to a Hanafi teacher (*mudarris*) every month 300 silver coins, and every day six units of flatbread; to a Maliki teacher every month 50 silver coins, and every day six units of flatbreads, and the same to a Hanbali teacher; to a Shafiʿi teacher 100 silver coins and six units of flatbread; to 65 students (*ṭullāb*) every month 7,500 silver coins and every day 95 units of bread; to two servants for the students who also take care of the spreading of the prayer rugs, every month 200 silver coins, and every day six units of bread; to the scribe (*kātib*) who records absences 300 silver coins and three units of bread; to nine readers (*qurrāʾ*), to recite the Quran daily in the prayer room, every month 1,000 silver coins, and every day 27 units of bread; to the keeper of the books in the prayer room 300 silver coins and three units of bread; to five people in charge of the rugs 800 silver coins and 15 units of bread, to two people in charge of lighting the candles and lamps 400 silver coins and three units of bread, and the same to the one in charge of the waterwheel; to the sweeper who has to sprinkle water in front of the prayer room 300 silver coins and three units of bread; and for the price of lamp oil every month 1,000 silver coins, and for the fodder of the oxen who drive the waterwheel, the buckets and their like every month 600 silver coins; and for the 30 orphans in the primary school of the mosque every month 2,000 silver coins, and every day 90 units of bread; and for their teacher every month 300 silver coins and every day three units of bread, and for the one in charge of keeping the drinking water cool every month 500 silver coins, and every day three units of bread.[23]

Particular practices of education, employment, communication, and association, moreover, made the environment of scholars anything but a parochial, closed, or static community. The westward migration of people, infrastructures, and ideas from Seljuk and post-Seljuk Transoxania and Khurasan that had given rise to new scholarly elites in Zengid Iraq and Syria, and eventually in Ayyubid Egypt as well, in general managed to sustain those trans-regional Asian connections. As a consequence, from at latest the first decades of the 14th century onwards, Cairo, Bursa, Tabriz, and many other urban centers remained connected in many ways as post-Seljuk and post-Mongol hubs of knowledge. Prose and poetry in Arabic, Persian, and, from about the 15th century onwards, Turkic, moreover, became a substantial, integrated, and equally normative channel of communication in the lives of cultural and intellectual elites, who were thus always trained as—and who were thus always expected to perform as—both *ʿalim*, religious intellectual, and *adib*, one of the *literati*. Moreover, these cultural changes were not limited to these Arabic, Arabo-Persian, and Turko-Persian Muslim elites, but also involved other social groups (including also various non-Muslim Christian and Jewish ones) in a complex trans-regional cultural context that was created as a common framework within which people, groups, and ideas met, communicated with each other, and further transformed that framework. In fact, in the course of the 14th century, no less than a process of 'popularization' of reading and textual practices has been identified for intensely interconnected West-Asian regions such as Egypt, Syria, and Anatolia, in which more urban groups and individuals than ever sought and found direct access to texts and to diverse sets of textual traditions and practices, and also contributed increasingly actively to their production and reproduction.

These varied knowledge practices and discourses were organized, preserved, and transmitted through personal relations of loyalty, obligation, and kinship rather than in any formal institutional context. The most paramount and defining among these personal bonds were those that took the hierarchical format of teacher-student relationships. In most knowledge contexts, these were formalized by an individual teacher, or *shaykh*, attesting a pupil's mastery of a particular text, often by the awarding of a kind of certificate (*ijaza*), or confirming the pupil's attainment of a particular level of training. This was a standard procedure which was first and foremost an expression of a successful relationship of knowledge transmission and which gained its relative value through the quality and quantity of such certified relationships of a pupil with specific masters. Many scholars kept, and even published, personal lists, often referred to as *mashyakha*s ('shaykh lineages') or *silsila*s ('chains'), of their teachers and of the nature of their relations with them. They thus communicated on quantitative as well as on qualitative grounds the trans-regionally embedded social as well as cultural value, or capital, that they claimed for themselves, for their masters and peers, and for their knowledge communities.

Acquiring an authority and a reputation for knowledge was not just a challenging intellectual and academic endeavor. They concerned practices that also carried great socioeconomic value because they gave access to opportunities of salaried employment, as in the complex of sultan Barsbay in Cairo, or also in positions of teaching or of legal advice in household and court service. Above all, acquiring knowledge and intellectual authority always remained a relational affair, involving an entry into, and an accumulation of, endless chains of master-student relations, first as a student, but in due time, also as a master. The omnipresent ideal of the pursuit of knowledge, therefore, also constantly required an intensive physical search for masters (and for the consensual products of these masters' value on the Islamic knowledge market: their scholarly authorities and reputations, as defined in no small measure by this factor of student demand) in the major towns and urban centers of the 'medieval' Islamic world. As a result, the networks and imagined communities of teachers and students that appeared around diverse sets of knowledge practices made for the prime performers of the 'medieval' processes of discursive integration and—as suggested above—simultaneous contestation, transformation, and even reinvention, on a remarkably intensely connected trans-regional scale.

A good example of these fluid processes of both intellectual and social integration, contestation, and innovation is the life of the famous scholar ʿAbd al-Rahman Ibn Khaldun (1332–1406), referred to also in the introduction to this book. This widely reputed scholar made his career as a secretary and vizier of the various dynasties that were in power in North Africa and al-Andalus in the 14th century, before somewhat unexpectedly ending up in Egypt in 1382. He lived in Cairo, mostly as an active member of the courts of sultan al-Malik al-Zahir Barquq and his two sons (r. 1382–1412) until his death in 1406. In Egypt, Ibn Khaldun fulfilled teaching assignments at various *madrasas*, regularly served at the sultan's court as Egyptian chief judge of the Maliki school of law, and was actively involved in many of his time's scholarly and courtly controversies and debates. He also left a famously complex and innovative work of historical theory, Islamic history, and autobiography. Among many other things he also reported in this work about his meeting and sophisticated debates with the Turko-Mongol ruler Timur (r. 1370–1405), when Ibn Khaldun was invited to the mobile court in the latter's encampment while his troops were raiding Syria and besieging Damascus.

A younger contemporary, student, and admirer of Ibn Khaldun was the aforementioned Cairene historian, Ahmad ibn ʿAli al-Maqrizi (*c.* 1365–1442), whose family came from Baʿlbakk in Syria, but who was himself born and raised in Cairo. Al-Maqrizi's background and career, in fact, sublimely illustrate how the fluidity of social and cultural boundaries seemed to increase in the course of the 13th and 14th centuries. Although al-Maqrizi's father and grandfather are known as traditionalist Hanbalite scholars, and although his maternal grandfather was a leading Hanafi scholar in Damascus, al-Maqrizi himself is said to have exchanged, at the age of twenty, the Hanafi legal allegiance of his youth for a Shafiʿi one, predominant in Egypt since the late 13th century. He is known to have served as a secretary (*katib*) at the highly diversely composed and widely connected court of, again, sultan al-Malik al-Zahir Barquq (r. 1382–1399), as an assistant judge and as a preacher (*khatib*) in several mosques in Cairo, and on a handful of brief occasions also as a *muhtasib*, appointed by the sultan and responsible for moral order in Cairo's streets and on its markets. When al-Maqrizi reached his mid-forties, however, the aforementioned apocalyptic context of late 14th- and early 15th-century crises and subsequent Turko-Circassian leadership transformation in Cairo turned out quite badly for him, as he had to make way in royal service for more ambitious and better-connected colleagues. Switching thereupon to an equally involved full-time writer's existence (during which he mostly remained in Cairo, but also stayed in Damascus and in Mecca during some periods), al-Maqrizi produced—as visible from the many references in this chapter—some of the most detailed and insightful Arabic chronicles, treatises, and collective biographies for today's knowledge about the history of this region and time.

A prominent colleague of al-Maqrizi was Ahmad Ibn Hajar al-ʿAsqalani (1372–1449), an authoritative religious scholar who gained worldwide name and fame (lasting to this present day) through his lectures and teaching sessions in various mosques and madrasas in Cairo and his many, extensive writings about the Prophetic Sunna and *hadith*. Ibn Hajar was born and raised in Cairo and, as a student, led a traveling existence in search of knowledge and teachers, bringing him to places as wide apart as Alexandria, Jerusalem, Damascus, Mecca in the Hejaz, and Zabid in Yemen. In Cairo, Ibn Hajar eventually obtained numerous important and beneficial posts as a teacher, as the head of a *khanqah*, as a jurisconsult (*mufti*), and for many years also as the court's Shafiʿi chief judge, the formal leader of the Shafiʿi community of scholars and judges in Egypt. What is most striking about Ibn Hajar's case, however, is not just his successful career and the intense, widespread impact of his intellectual and literary legacy—considered a pinnacle and culmination point of centuries of Sunni *hadith* scholarship and traditionalism, which caused both the Timurid Shah Rukh (r. 1405–1447) in Herat and the ruler of Tunis to approach sultan Barsbay (r. 1422–38) in Cairo and request a copy of Ibn Hajar's most important book, entitled *Fath al-Bari* ('Unlocking the Divine Wisdom'), a highly authoritative commentary on one of the six canonical works of Sunni *hadith* from the 9th and 10th centuries. What is at least as important, in terms of social permeability and fluidity of boundaries, is that Ibn Hajar could develop himself and his scholarship in ideal socioeconomic circumstances, since he was closely related to very important Karimi merchant families with (probably) Yemeni roots, who are said to have left him a substantial fortune.

A final example that should be mentioned here as an extremely famous witness to, and equally representative product of, this 'medieval' connectivity, permeability, and fluidity is the scholar and worldwide traveler Muhammad Ibn Battuta (1304–1368/1377). As already mentioned in the introduction of this book, Ibn Battuta turned his pilgrimage from his North African hometown of Tangier to Mecca in the 1320s into more than three decades of wanderings throughout many of the worlds of 14th-century Afro-Eurasia. The literary account of Ibn Battuta's travels impressively illustrates how the appearance of a shared and inclusive socio-religious identity and an ambiguous sense of globalizing Islamic belonging had become a central integrative force in these highly diverse and heterogeneous worlds. It shows how a familiar connectivity of ritual, legal, and social practices and their meanings—from name giving over the organization of time to the appreciation of Islamic, and especially prophetic Sunna-related, forms of knowledge and normativity—enabled a scholar of Arabized Amazigh origins from Tangier to travel relatively easily in between and beyond the 'medieval' worlds of the Mediterranean and Indian Ocean, without ever really being considered, or considering himself, a total stranger and an outsider, even in places as far apart as Granada, Fez, and Timbuktu in the west and Delhi, the Maldives, East African Mogadishu, or perhaps even Chinggisid Khanbaliq in present-day Beijing in the east.

As suggested in the introduction to this chapter, representative examples of the fluid processes of both intellectual and social integration, contestation, and innovation that marked the lives of scholars and all kinds of related urban elites should not be limited to the fluid networks and discourses of these Arabic-speaking champions of Sunna-related forms of knowledge and normativity. Across Islamic West-Asia, many others were similarly widely connected and active participants in these intense 'medieval' practices of exchange, circulation, and confrontation of ideas, texts, students, teachers, opportunities, and disasters. Especially from the 14th century onwards, numerous, and often overlapping, networks of legal scholars and *hadith* specialists, of ascetics and Sufis, of philosophical theologians, of specialists of medicine, the science of the stars and the occult sciences, and of all kinds of other merchants in the charisma of ideas, values, and norms, from Transoxania and Khurasan, from Iran and Azerbaijan, and from Anatolia, Egypt and Syria tended to be similarly gripped by the allure of intellectual hubs such as Cairo, Damascus, or Mecca, and to blend in with various local networks of Arabic-, Persian-, and Turkic-speaking peers. Influential traditions of post-Avicennan philosophy and Sufism that originated in the Islamic west, among Andalusian thinkers such as the philosopher Ibn Rushd (Averroes, 1126–1198) and the Sufi master, philosopher, and monist thinker Ibn ʿArabi (1165–1240), fused in these creative contexts in complementary, accommodating, or competing ways with Arabo-Persian wisdoms of philosophical Sufi theologians such as al-Ghazali (1058–1111) and of controversial Sufi leaders such as the illuminationist al-Suhrawardi (1153–1191).

To these highly mobile and interconnected ranks should above all be added the even more diverse, contested, and trans-regionally connected ranks of highly influential spiritual and Sufi masters. Many generations of their followers, students, and successors as well as the distinctive sets of ritual and knowledge practices that they jointly created, eventually, in the course of the 14th to 16th centuries, transformed into some of the most important trans-regional movements and communities of Sufis, referred to as the 'brotherhoods' (*turuq* or *tariqa*s). The ranks of these masters included most prominently—next to the aforementioned extremely influential Sufi masters Ibn ʿArabi and al-Suhrawardi—the Bagdadi Hanbali theologian and Sufi master ʿAbd al-Qadir al-Jilani (d. 1166); the Maghribi *shaykh* Abu l-Hasan ʿAli al-Shadhili, who eventually settled in Alexandria and died in Upper-Egypt in 1258 on his way to perform the pilgrimage in Mecca; Najm al-Din Kubra from Khwarazm, who studied in Cairo and Tabriz, built up his own Sufi following of pupils in Khwarazm, and reportedly died while heroically fighting the Chinggisid invasion in 1220; the mystic and miracle worker Ahmad al-Rifaʿi (d. 1182), who was active and revered in the lower Iraqi regions of Wasit and Basra; the Sufi *shaykh* from Bukhara Bahaʾ al-Din Naqshband (1318–1389), popular among Transoxania's Turko-Mongols and Persians alike and preaching sobriety and Sunni conformity with God's law (*shariʿa*); and ʿAbd al-Rahman al-Bistami (d. 1454), most well known as a Hurufi scholar of the occult 'science of letters and divine names', who was born in Antioch, studied in Egypt (including again at the court of sultan al-Malik al-Zahir Barquq [r. 1382–1399]), Syria, and the Maghrib, and who eventually became a famous Sufi master and proponent of Ibn ʿArabi's thought at the Ottoman court in Bursa. Equally notable eponyms of this creative and constitutive 'medieval' landscape of intellectual development and transforming knowledge practices are the Jewish philosopher, theologian, and scientist Musa ibn Maymun al-Qurtubi, also known as Moses Maimonides (1135–1204), who was born in Andalusian Cordoba and died in Fustat in Egypt, after having been a court physician for one of the Ayyubids, a *nagid* or leading spokesman for his community (a position maintained by his family into the 14th century), and a prolific author who also engaged in very creative ways with the legacies of Islamic thinkers such as al-Farabi and al-Ghazali; the mathematician, philosopher, theologian, adept in the science of the stars, and Persian Shi'ite scholar Nasir al-Din al-Tusi (d. 1274), active in the service of the Nizari Isma'ilis in their stronghold of 'Alamut and in Tus, Nishapur, and Bagdad, companion of the Chinggisid leader Hülegü, founder of a famous observatory at Maragha in Azerbaijan, and remembered as 'the third master' (after the Greek philosopher Aristotle and the 10th-century Islamic philosopher al-Farabi); Ibn al-Shatir (1304–1375), a timekeeper in Damascus' Great Mosque, famous for both making his own timekeeping instruments and for successfully continuing al-Tusi's highly important and complex revisions of Ptolemaic planetary theory; and the Turka family of religious scholars, who appear to have been related to the aforementioned networks of both the Khujandis (and thus the Nizamiyya) of post-Seljuk 12th-century Isfahan and the former Jewish physician and convert Hülegüid vizier Rashid al-Din Fadl-Allah Hamadani (*c.* 1247–1318), who monopolized the position of Shafi'i chief

Figure 13.4 Samarqand (Uzbekistan): restored remains of the astronomical observatory (*rashd-khaneh*) of the Timurid ruler Ulugh Beg (1394–1449) (1428). This structure in the shape of a cylinder with three floors and a subterranean part consisted among other things of a sun clock and a gigantic sextant with a diameter of more than 40 meters, designed to map stellar constellations. The observatory was destroyed in 1449, by order of Ulugh Beg's son and successor; it was rediscovered in 1908 by a Russian archaeologist

Source: Melvyn Longhurst/Alamy Stock Photo

judge of, especially, Isfahan for most of the period between the 14th and 16th centuries, and who engaged very prominently in the highly influential and heterogeneous strand of Islamic philosophical-theological thinking that was related to Ibn ʿArabi's monism, al-Tusi's thought, the revolutionary emergence of neo-Pythagorean sciences, the formulation of what has been termed "lettrist metaphysics . . . as the most effective means of conceptualizing and celebrating [Islamic] writerly culture",[24] and the activities of millenarian and apocalyptic movements of Sufi signature.

A final, highly relevant case of this 'medieval' connectivity, heterogeneity, and even ambiguity that bound West-Asia's elites above all else, and that widely transcended, and eventually also accommodated, the hegemonic practices of Prophetic Sunna-related forms of knowledge and normativity, was that of the (in)famous *shaykh* Badr al-Din Mahmud, born in 1359 across the Bosporus and Sea of Marmara, in the Greek region of Thrace, near the Ottoman urban center of Edirne. Badr al-Din's father seems to have been a local Hanafi judge, while his later hagiographers claim that his mother was a Greek convert to Islam. In his own pursuit for knowledge, *shaykh* Badr al-Din is said to have travelled from Edirne to study with famous teachers in Konya, Jerusalem, and Cairo, where he ended up as a tutor of sultan al-Malik al-Zahir Barquq's son and later successor Faraj (r. 1399–1412). In Cairo, *shaykh* Badr al-Din also became a follower and student of one of the most influential Sufi masters of his age, Husayn Akhlati (d. *c.* 1402), whom he eventually also succeeded as a local leader in Cairo in a particular Arabo-Persian branch of the aforementioned Hurufi network of millenarian and lettrist knowledge practices. In the meantime, moreover, he also seems to have spent some time in Tabriz, where he is said to have participated—just as Ibn Khaldun did outside the besieged walls of Damascus—in debates at Timur's court. Eventually, however, *shaykh* Badr al-Din returned from Cairo to Anatolia, where he gained quite a reputation (and a popular following among various local communities) due to his active engagement with a particular set of ideas revolving around extreme interpretations of sociopolitical egalitarianism and of Ibn ʿArabi's monist notion of unity of being (*wahdat al-wujud*). *Shaykh* Badr al-Din simultaneously became deeply embroiled as an Ottoman official and judge in the internecine warfare that almost destroyed the Ottoman Sultanate after Timur's victory over the sultan at the battle of Ankara in 1402 (see Chapter 11). In the course of this Ottoman succession conflict he was first exiled with his family from Edirne to northwestern Anatolia and later fled with many of his followers to the area of Bulgaria. Eventually, in 1416, following an anti-Ottoman rebellion in Anatolia that is believed to have been inspired by—some say even led by—*shaykh* Badr al-Din's charismatic personality and controversial thinking, he was captured and executed in Macedonia by order of the Ottoman sultan Mehmed I (r. 1412–1421).

Even though *shaykh* Badr al-Din's story, remembered until today in different more or less hagiographic ways, certainly displays many exceptional and unusual characteristics, the base lines of his life story—connecting, at the turn of the 14th and 15th centuries, in highly creative ways the competing courts of Cairo, Ottoman Edirne, and Timurid Tabriz, equally diverse sets of ideas and knowledge practices, and even more diverse networks of Arabic, Persian, and Anatolian scholars, mystics, and strongmen—should be considered all but exceptional. In similarly intense and fluid ways, this mix of traditions, infrastructures, and people formed fertile ground for the rich, contested, creative, and highly diverse—but still too often undervalued—scientific, spiritual, and aesthetic (Muslim, but also non-Muslim) knowledge practices, discourses, and artistic achievements that continued to characterize 'medieval' Islamic West-Asia. Many, if not most, of these practices, discourses, and achievements began in the social margins, in anarchist, reformist, and even apocalyptically inspired circles. Some, like many Sufi traditions and especially also the occult sciences, evolved from these margins to move in a striking way to the contested centers of claims to orthopraxy, normativity and sovereignty, where they assumed leading and influential roles.

The Hurufiyya and its even wider lettrist and Kabbalistic teachings and ideas of theocratic order and relationality are one powerful example of this phenomenon that has already been mentioned in this chapter. The same is true in overlapping and equally powerful ways for the remarkable 15th-century empowerment of the Safaviyya brotherhood and its Qizilbash Turkmen, the claims to messianic authority and divinity of Isma'il, and then the beginnings of a Twelver Shi'i and Safavid dynastic fusion at the court of Tahmasp in 16th-century Azerbaijan and Iran (see Chapter 12). Similar anarchist, reformist, or apocalyptic notions must have also played their part among the Greek and Turkmen marcher lords and frontier warriors of northwestern Anatolia who joined in the raiding parties of Turkmen leaders, such as the son and descendants of Osman, and later styled, or at least remembered, themselves as 'holy warriors', *ghazi*s. That all of this happened in an open rather than closing context of accommodation, contestation, cross-fertilization, and deepening complexity is finally suggested by one of the most illustrative instances of the many and ongoing effects of these 'medieval' practices: an intellectual contest organized in mid-15th-century (newly conquered) Ottoman Constantinople. This contest, as 16th-century reports explain, and as surviving manuscript texts and commentary traditions confirm, was set up by the Ottoman sultan Mehmed II (r. 1451–1481) as an argumentative competition between the Hanafi judge, legal scholar, and teacher from Bursa Khojazada (d. 1488) and the philosophical theologian and Sufi adept from Timurid Samarqand 'Ala' al-Din Tusi (d. 1472/1482). Its objective was to once and for all decide a famous polemic between al-Ghazali from Seljuk Iran and Ibn Rushd from al-Andalus regarding the soundness of Avicenna's philosophical argumentation, as expressed in their respective Arabic texts 'the Stumbling of the Philosophers' (*Tahāfut al-Falāsifa*) and 'the Stumbling of "the Stumbling"'. Even though Khojazada is said to have been considered most convincing with his pro-Ghazali argumentation, what really won him his victory seems to have been his success at simultaneously acknowledging and engaging with the value of Ibn Rushd's thinking and of that of some of his philosopher peers and successors, and thus of bringing the different narratives and counter-narratives of this discourse to a new state of balance. Indeed, as has recently been argued,

> the discourse as a whole had moved far beyond the level it was at in the eleventh century, when Ghazālī was writing, and both Khojazāda and 'Alā' al-Dīn Ṭūsī seem determined not to turn back the clock on these discussions but instead bring the discussion of the problems Ghazālī included in his *Tahāfut* to the standards of the fifteenth century.[25]

As such, this occasion illustrates above all how 'medieval' knowledge practices, and intellectual discourses and their contested narratives in particular—in this case, on the theologically vexed issue of the value of post-Abbasid Avicennan philosophy—continued to be arenas of vivid rivalry, adaption, sophistication, and reinvention by different generations of great diversities of specialists.

2 'Medieval' courts and courtiers between dynastic flux and stabilization

'Medieval' Islamic West-Asia's post-Seljuk landscapes of leadership between the post-nomadic stabilizations in the Euphrates-to-Nile zone, eventually extending into Asia Minor, and the returning instabilities of nomadic conquest and dynastic formation in the enormous

Euphrates-to-Jaxartes-and-Indus zone, also represented itself—in spite of all the Turkish, Mongol, Turko-Mongol, and Turkmen discontinuities—as a complex multitude of deeply interrelated networks of people and infrastructures of power. These continued to be organized everywhere around the post-Seljuk, Hülegüid, Timurid, and Turkmen practices and appearances of royal households and personal guards (*keshig*) and to be stimulated by the distinguishing demands of endless competition and rivalries. These nomadic and post-nomadic power elites, from the era's padishahs and sultans with their elaborate urban courts to the many warlords and their closely-knit bands of experienced fighters and followers (*nöker*), were far more connected in shared practices, infrastructures, and imaginations of power and authority than often tends to be acknowledged. Those that dominate al-Maqrizi's first category and 'perform the dynastic reign (*ahl al-dawla*)' are actually widely connected in their non-urban and even non-West-Asian nomadic origins, the violent and pragmatic nature of their political action, the creative set of shared forms and meanings with which these strongmen and their entourages were able to explain this strangeness and violence, and more in general in the different forms of Inner-Asian Turkish-ness that—linguistically as well as socially—often proved a central factor in those explanations. Most also have the successful combined deployment of charisma and dynasty in any local, regional, or trans-regional power struggle in common, as well as patriarchal appanage practices to organize the distribution of power and wealth within leading kinship groups. In addition—based on these first two characteristics—these Turkic- or Mongolian-speaking strongmen also had an extremely complex, even problematic, practice of social reproduction in common that continuously jeopardized this power, the control over these resources, and the hierarchies and leadership relations that ensured them. In fact, between the 14th and 16th centuries, the endless process of the integration and disintegration of different transregional balances of leadership, sovereignty, and resources into, and out of, powerful local, regional, or external constellations only very slowly stabilized in more sustained centripetal patterns. As detailed in the preceding chapters, this happened especially in the west around the non-dynastic court in Cairo and then also around the tenacity of the Ottoman dynasty, in particular from its mid-15th-century capture of Constantinople and early 16th-century integration of the Cairo Sultanate onwards.

At the same time, under the rough surface of integration, disintegration, conquest practices, and dynastic or even patrimonial formation, not just in practical but also in social terms far less change, difference, and discontinuity should be assumed than the 'medieval' landscape of power at first sight suggests. Everywhere, often longstanding local and regional leaderships and their networks of expertise and local resources played an equally important role in dynastic successes of this or that warlord and his relatives and supporters. The example of Nizam al-Mulk and his own extensive network of family, representatives, infrastructures, and resources—the Nizamiyya—discussed in Chapter 8, is, therefore, not so much an exception, but rather a high-end example illustrative of many who followed in his footsteps. For centuries, these regions continued to draw upon not only the fresh strength of new rulers and outsiders, but also the experiences and creative involvement of many 'inside' elites and powerbrokers with much longer histories, and often also substantial amounts of followers of their own. The latter are generally identified as the region's genuine urban leaders, or the *a'yan*, and their highly diverse ranks included not just administrative (Muslim and non-Muslim) experts and related local urban notables, but also Arabian, Turkmen, Kurdish, and other pastoralist leaderships, and many of the above-mentioned reputed or charismatic *'ulama'*, *shaykh*s, and popular preachers. The social and functional boundaries between these distinct sociopolitical groups (also often idealized in contemporary texts as a triumvirate of 'the lords of the swords, the lords of the pens, and the lords of the turbans', or in many Persianate parts of West-Asia also as a duumvirate of violence-wielding 'Turks' and 'Tajik' bureaucrats) remained always rather fluid and permeable, especially when dynastic formation had brought more stability and organizational complexity, and thus more mechanisms and opportunities for participation and empowerment for these urban elites and their own households and bands of followers. The aforementioned contested 'Tajik' influence, resources, and even manpower of the former Jewish physician and convert Hülegüid administrator Rashid al-Din Fadl-Allah Hamadani (*c.* 1247–1318) in Tabriz and Azerbaijan, of at least one of his sons after him, and perhaps even of their descendants are a powerful example of these local and regional leadership continuities. The employment of another Jewish physician and converted bureaucrat from Tabriz, Fath Allah al-Tabrizi (d. 1413), in a similarly leading position of authority at the courts in Cairo of Sultan al-Malik al-Zahir Barquq (r. 1382–1399) and of his son, Sultan al-Malik al-Nasir Faraj (r. 1399–1412), may well represent a remarkable extension and transfer of that network, pushed to Cairo by Jalayrid and Timurid warfare in Azerbaijan. Another typical and anything but unusual example can be found in the lives of Ghiyath al-Din Pir-Ahmad Khwafi (d. 1453) and his son Majd al-Din Muhammad Khwafi (d. 1494). Ghiyath al-Din stood at the head of the financial administration of the Timurid ruler Shah Rukh (r. 1405–1447) between 1417 and 1447, and subsequently, he served several other Timurid princes in a similar way. His son Majd al-Din was chief administrator at the court of the Timurid ruler Sultan-Husayn (r. 1469–1506) ever since its installation at Herat in 1469. He orchestrated the expansion of that court's centralizing patrimonial power in subsequent years, and he was eventually murdered in 1494 due to court intrigues between 'Turkish' opponents and 'Tajik' proponents of such centripetal arrangements. Father and son, each with their own personal following, entourage, and resources, thus significantly dominated the courts of Timurid rulers for most of the 15th century. In fact, even though further research in this phenomenon remains wanting, many more peers of father and son Khwafi may have managed to achieve similar power and longevity at the Turkmen, Timurid, Ottoman, and Safavid courts of Islamic West-Asia than tends to be acknowledged. Their ranks definitely included a dozen of Syrian and Egyptian families who monopolized court positions in 15th-century Cairo, and also many of those Persianate bureaucrats who had first been operating in Aq Qoyunlu service in Azerbaijan and who were subsequently enlisted among several competing groups of experts charged with the organization and consolidation of the court of Uzun Hasan's grandson Isma'il, upon his enthronement in Tabriz in 1501.

2.1 'Medieval' dynastic courts

The courts of 'medieval' West-Asia's polycentric landscapes of nomadic as well as post-nomadic leaderships were—unlike in the Abbasid cases—no longer situated in vast palaces in urban centers, but close to those urban centers, in nomadic summer and winter camps, hunting encampments, or a new military infrastructure, the court citadel. In these 'medieval' royal encampments and strongholds, the organization of the court was directly intertwined with the organization of the ruler's armed forces.

An aforementioned description of the court of Uzun Hasan, retold in a 16th-century Persian chronicle that rendered Aq Qoyunlu history meaningful for the Safavid court of Tahmasp, demonstrates the workings of the court—in an ideal Aq Qoyunlu setting undoubtedly also articulating Safavid ideals—as tied up with clear-cut hierarchies. It describes how, on the one hand, Uzun Hasan "would seat himself on a golden dais while his relatives and amirs took their places on the right and on the left" and how, on the other hand, Tajik officials and secretaries "acted as [plaintiffs'] advocate" and "would draft and issue [Uzun Hasan's]

Figure 13.5 Representation of a banquet at the court of a Chinggisid/H ülegüid ruler; illustration from a manuscript of the first part of the Jamiʿ al-Tawarikh ['The Compendium of Histories'] by Rashid al-Din (Tabriz [?], first half 14th century) (Staatsbibliothek zu Berlin, Diez A, fol. 70, S. 22)

Source: © 2019. Photo Scala, Florence/bpk, Bildagentur fuer Kunst, Kultur und Geschichte, Berlin

orders". At the same time, this passage brings once more to mind how the court is first and foremost also a mediator of structured relationships with the wider world, and with the articulation of the ruler within that wider world as a just and benevolent Islamic sovereign, for whose presiding of "the court of appeals" "the 'drum of justice' would be sounded" and whose rulings represented "firm decisions not subject to change or alteration".[26]

In Constantinople, which was converted into the new center of Ottoman power in 1453, a true imperial urban complex of inner and outer courts—the 'Porte'—was set up around the Ottoman sultan, his family, and his new palace complex (since late in the 18th century known as Topkapi Saray) in the same trend of hybrid and continuous traditions and practices. At least from that middle of the 15th century onwards, an impressive, patrimonial apparatus of violence, communication, and revenue accumulation (also known in discourses of Ottoman patrimonial organization as the *Seyfiye*, the Men of the Sword, and the *Kalemiye*, the Men of Pen) gradually developed. This apparatus was led by the grand vizier and the central *divan*, organized in increasingly complex and professionalized ways, and to an ever more efficient and autonomous extent capable of defending the interests of the dynasty and its agents. This apparatus and its functioning are relatively well known, since from the 16th century onwards, a particularly intensive—at least in the context of Islamic history—bureaucratic tendency towards (especially fiscal) registration, documentation, and archiving appeared, which has left massive traces to this date and, therefore, created unique possibilities for modern historical research. Both qualitatively and quantitatively, however, these Ottoman archives continue to place researchers before a number of challenges, and the last word on this is by no means said.

The other well-known examples of these 'medieval' courts and their apparatus undoubtedly concern those of the Sultanate in the Citadel of Cairo. As argued above, they are in their own distinctive forms and meanings deeply interconnected with Safavid renderings of Uzun Hasan's court, or for that matter, with any other Turko-Mongol ruler's court, all harking back to post-Abbasid, post-Seljuk, and even post-Hülegüid precedents. In the following excerpt from a report about the identities of the court's officials at the start of the year 1433, a related distinction, as in the case of Uzun Hasan's court between, first, the amirs and, secondly, the bureaucrats, can be discerned, with the further addition in Cairo's case of an explicit reference to the four chief judges as representatives of the centrality and authority of Sunni Islam in the Sultanate.

> The grand amir is Sūdun min ʿAbd al-Raḥmān; the amir of arms is Aynāl al-Jakamī, the amir of the council is Aqbughā al-Timrāzī, the head of guards is the amir Timrāz al-Qirmishī, the amir of the horse is Jaqmaq, the executive secretary is Urkmās al-Ẓāhirī, and the grand chamberlain is Qurqmās.
>
> The vizier and major-domo is Karīm al-Dīn ʿAbd al-Karīm Ibn Kātib al-Manākh, the confidential secretary is Kamāl al-Dīn Muḥammad ibn Nāṣir al-Dīn Muḥammad Ibn al-Bārizī, the controller of the army is the *qāḍī* Zayn al-Dīn ʿAbd al-Bāsiṭ—he is the mighty effective manager of the resources of the reign (*dawla*)—, and the controller of the privy funds is Saʿd al-Dīn Ibrāhīm Ibn Kātib Jakam. The chief judges [of the four schools of law] remained [as before].
>
> The viceroys and the rulers of the different regions [in Egypt, Syria, the Hejaz, and beyond] are as they have been mentioned for the preceding year.[27]

Figure 13.6 Representation of the reception of a Venetian embassy (dressed in black) by the sultan's delegate in Damascus (dressed in white, with a turban) and his court (Venice?, 1511) (Musée du Louvre-Lens, 'Réception d'une delegation vénitienne à Damas. Huile sur toile. Collection du roi de France Louis XIV [1643–1715])

Source: Peter Horree/Alamy Stock Photo

The seven amirs that are mentioned here were not just privileged with a position in the sultan's household, and thus at the center of his court. They all also were enlisted in the—in theory of at least—strict military organization of the Sultanate, where an elaborate military hierarchy of *amirs* was subdivided according to the number of troops (10, 40, or 100) that they were allowed to have in service. From this hierarchy, senior *amir*s of 100 or 40, as in the seven cases mentioned in this list for 1433, were also charged with responsibilities in the household or at the court of the sultan, or as his representatives in the different urban centers and regions of the Sultanate. At the court, all were closely involved in the ceremonies and rituals organized there, including the ceremonial procession through Cairo (*mawkib*) and the public service (*khidma*) in the audience hall (*iwan*) where the sultan also—just as happened at Uzun Hasan's court—performed his authority to counter any injustices and apply dynastic law to that effect (*mazalim*).

2.2 'Medieval' royal households

The extended household (*bayt*) of the Cairo Sultan was housed in the so-called Citadel of the Mountain, southeast of the historical center of Cairo. It mainly consisted of the sultan's military family—his personal elite troops of *mamluks* and *mamluks*-in-training—and of his actual kin and harem. Each were housed in a private and enclosed part of the citadel, where they were served and guarded by eunuchs. This harem of the Sultan actually underwent a significant transformation in its composition, which was perhaps not entirely disconnected from the powerful social, cultural, and political roles that were regularly played in 'medieval' Islamic West-Asia by many female members of Mongolian, Turko-Mongol, and Turkmen families, dynasties, and elite households. In Cairo, this royal harem's composition was for a long time defined by conscious polygamy, involving political marriages, especially with Chinggisid princesses in the 14th century, and in the course of the 15th century especially with widows of predecessors. It also witnessed a sustained presence of substantial numbers of concubines. Eventually, from the mid-15th century onwards, concubines remained, but marriages became limited to one wife only. In that process, a greater variety of spouses made its appearance in the 15th century. Many of these spouses still had outsider origins (including, at one point, Ottoman and Circassian princesses), but some also belonged to different local urban elites and networks, which allowed them to acquire a substantial and undeniably powerful amount of economic, cultural, and political agency.

As far as the integration and reproduction of the Ottoman household and dynastic center are concerned, until the early 16th-century, marriages appear to have been instrumental for linking friendly or rival leaders in Anatolia or in the Balkans to the Ottoman dynasty, and thus for having the sovereignty of the latter accepted. Sultan Bayezid I (d. 1402) was thus married to the daughters of two powerful Anatolian *beys* and to a Serbian and a Byzantine princess. The three wives of Mehmed I (d. 1421) were daughters of Anatolian *beys*. Murad II (d. 1451), his son Mehmed II (d. 1481), and his grandson Bayezid II (d. 1512) also married Anatolian princesses (Murad married a Serbian princess as well), which greatly supported the complex process of the 15th-century integration of various Turkish-Anatolian *beylik* dynasties and their followers into the orbit of Ottoman political leadership. The reproduction of the Ottoman lineage, however, was ensured not only through these and many more marriages, but also through concubines. According to most reports, most Ottoman sultans—from Bayezid I in the 14th to his great-great-grandson Bayezid II in the 15th century and again from Suleiman in the 16th century onwards—were themselves sons of their fathers' unfree concubines. Only Selim was an exception to this rule, being born in *c.* 1470 to Bayezid and

Figure 13.7 Representation of a ruler and his court, on the opening page of an illustrated manuscript of a popular 11th-century Arabic 'trickster romance', the *Maqamat* of al-Hariri (1054–1122). This manuscript was produced in 1334 in Cairo, at the Qalawunid court of sultan al-Nasir Muhammad, and in its mix of Turko-Mongol, Persian, and Egyptian imagery it illustrates the heterogeneous aesthetic norms and socio-cultural realities of that court

Source: Österreichische Nationalbibliothek, Handschriftensammlung, Cod. A.F. 9, f. 1r

his wife 'Ayshe, who was the daughter of a southeast-Anatolian ruler of strategic importance to the Ottomans. In fact, however, this alliance between Bayezid and 'Ayshe is the last known Ottoman marriage of this political nature.

The disappearance of Ottoman marriages appears to have coincided with various other transformations in the Ottoman harem membership and organization. This concerned, in particular, the position of concubines. In fact, it was above all with Suleiman's concubine and later wife Hürrem Sultan (*c.* 1502–1558)—also known as Roxelana—that this marked change came about. According to some accounts the daughter of a Ukrainian Orthodox priest who was robbed and sold as merchandise, Hürrem Sultan wound up in Suleiman's harem already before 1520. There, she eventually acquired the leading status of the sultan's favorite partner (*haseki sultan*), and she gained numerous privileges that were unheard of for Ottoman concubines (and often presented as shocking to contemporaries). She gave birth to a total of seven of Suleiman's children (including his successor Selim II, who was born in 1524), continued to live at the court of Constantinople, was manumitted, and in 1533 even married the sultan. In this way, she became one of the most powerful figures at the court, and a well-known (and diplomatically well-connected) representative of the dynastic power that royal women managed to acquire across 16th-century Eurasia. In the following decades, the new precedent that was thus created culminated in the phenomenon of the powerful queen mother (*valide sultan*) who tended to play an important political role from the harem during the reign of her son. After Hürrem's death in 1558, the concubine of her son, sultan Selim II, Nurbanu Sultan (d. 1583)—originally a girl of Venetian noble descent who was captured, enslaved, and forced into the royal harem, and whom Selim eventually married—played a similar role at his court, as well as at that of their son Murad III. Ultimately, this active political role was taken over by Safiye Sultan (d. 1605), a concubine of Albanian origin and the favorite partner of Murad III, who fathered more than twenty sons with numerous concubines, but who was succeeded in 1595 by Safiye's son Mehmed III (r. 1595–1603).

2.3 'Medieval' non-royal households

In the many strongholds and palaces in Cairo and in the other urban centers of the realm of the sultan of Cairo (Damascus, Aleppo, Tripoli, Hama, Jerusalem, Alexandria), all built or occupied by the Sultanate's senior leadership such as the seven senior courtiers and amirs mentioned above, a very similar type of organization was found. In this particular urban embedding of that leadership, the reality comes to the fore of the Sultanate's organization around a particular, contested selection of military households and their specific configurations, connections, resources, and interests, balanced and kept in check by the most powerful household among them, which was at least formally that of the sultan in the citadel. This is evident from the description of this organization in one of the most important contemporary handbooks of court organization and protocol, compiled in Cairo at the beginning of the 15th century:

> You should know that in general every amir of one hundred and [every amir] of forty is like a miniature sultan. Every one of them has specifically dedicated service units, just like the sultan has, such as for metal ware, textiles, riding gear, weapons, cooking, and music. . . . Every one of these units has a supervisor responsible for its business and in charge of men and servants each of which has a specific task. [Every amir also] has from among his troopers [office holders such as] a majordomo, a head of the guard, a pen box holder, a commander of the public session, a master of the robe, a stable master, a kitchen master, and a comptroller.[28]

Modern academic research of the elaborate socioeconomic organization of these amirs and their strikingly autonomous military entourages also demonstrates how they claimed their place and status in the urban space and at the court through a distinctive symbolic apparatus that was derived from this household organization. One of the pioneers of this field of study, David Ayalon, long time ago aptly summarized this as follows:

> As for the amir's court, it was a copy on a reduced scale of the court of the sultan. He had a coat of arms, with a special design serving as his emblem, such as a cup, an inkwell, a napkin, a *fleur-de-lis*, and the like. This coat of arms, which bore a color of the amir's choice, was painted on the gates of his house and his other possessions, such as the grain storehouses, the sugar refineries, the ships, as well as on his sword, his bow, and the caparisons of his horses and camels. When the amir rode out of his house, the important members of his corps would escort him as follows: the *ra's nawba* [in charge of his personal guard of *mamluks*], the *amir* of the council, and other key officeholders

> [in his household] would precede him; the *jamdariyya* [that is, the *mamluks* in charge of his wardrobe,] would follow him, and the *amir akhur* [in charge of his stable] would come last, leading the reserve horses. The sultan rode in the same manner.[29]

Resources for these complex and devolved personal entourages of agents and representatives were acquired through direct granting of the right to tributes and other fiscal revenues, both in cash and in kind, from well-defined commercial or (mainly) agricultural surplus. As mentioned before, this *iqta*ʿ practice of revenue apportionment had a long history in Islamic West-Asia before its further development by Syro-Egyptian post-Seljuk leaderships. Closely related to the patriarchal appanage systems of post-Abbasid and Seljuk times, this particular arrangement of revenue apportionment continued to organize the more structured and centralized forms of resource accumulation that were favored whenever Turkish, Mongolian, Turkmen, or Turko-Mongol leaderships across Islamic West-Asia stabilized. It emerged in the adapted appanage format of the tax-exempted estates of the *soyurghal*, distributed to leaderships and elites in Hülegüid, Turkmen, and Timurid service. In the Anatolian lands of the Ottoman sultans of Bursa and Edirne, it appeared in the equally particular format of the *timar* (see above). Everywhere in 'medieval' West-Asia, these fiscal practices connected in

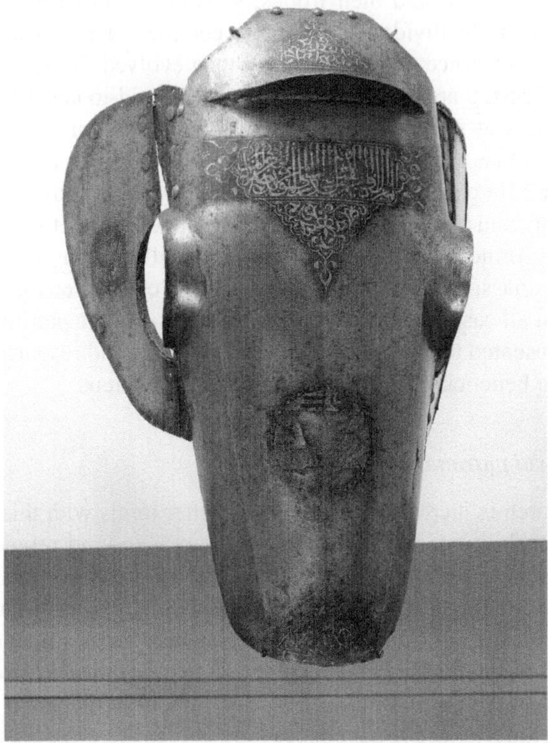

Figure 13.8 Richly decorated metal headgear for a horse, with calligraphic inscription and heraldic emblem (round medal divided in three sections: a small and a large cup below the symbol of the penbox); the inscription identifies the owner as the amir Muqbil al-Husami (d. 1433), Master of the Penbox of sultan al-Malik al-Muʾayyad Shaykh (r. 1412–1421) (Cairo?, ca. 1419)

Source: Musée des Beaux Arts, Lyon, D377

parallel distributive ways all kinds of military leaders and their violent merits to numerous local flows of resources on the one hand, and to the regional and trans-regional needs and ambitions of central leaderships on the other. Everywhere, too, this mixing and transformation of post-Abbasid and Inner-Asian appanage and apportionment practices were shaped by administrative and territorial modalities that could differ substantially depending on context, time, and place.

In Egypt and Syria, the last major restructuring of the court's *iqta*ʿ practice took place between 1313 and 1326, in the form of *al-rawk al-Nasiri*, the land registration and fiscal reformation directed by the Qalawunid sultan al-Malik al-Nasir Muhammad (r. 1293–1341). This particularly involved a remarkable shift of the division—expressed in extant literary sources in abstract fiscal terms—of the income from agricultural surplus between the sultan and his amirs in favor of the former. The sultan thus increasingly empowered his own patrimonial apparatus of power to serve the interests of his own Qalawunid court and household. From this period onwards, the principle was established that 5/12 of all fiscal income generating activities in Egypt and Syria—mainly collected in the form of traditional *kharaj*, now referring mostly to a tithe on agricultural production—should contribute directly to the financing of the household of the sultan, including the maintenance of his personal guard, the sultan's *mamluks*. The remaining 7/12 were destined for the few hundred *amirs*, other (semi-) professional military, and their troops, which constituted the patrimonial military elites of the Sultanate, to be divided according to complex hierarchical principles of merit, privilege, and royal preference. How the system then evolved further remains a subject for further research. At least, it appears that the crises of the mid-to late-14th century, including the long-lasting effects of the above-mentioned Black Death pandemic, put a heavy strain on *iqta*ʿ income, and that creative experiments were carried out in the search for alternatives throughout the 15th century. These materialized in the form of a commercialization of the political economy and also of a reorientation of that economy towards (or, according to many researchers, a further undermining of that political economy by) the structural flows of revenue that the massively expanding *waqf* system of religious endowments was still able to guarantee. In all cases, Cairo's successive sultans and the patrimonial apparatus that performed and represented their claims to power, authority, and resources continued to participate as important beneficiaries in these many transformations.

2.4 'Medieval' royal patronage

While modern research is increasingly coming to better terms with this expanding fluidity, mingling, and permeability of resources from military *iqta*ʿ and religious *waqf* in central leadership's pursuance of resource accumulation, the permeability of boundaries between violence wielding and religious or wider intellectual action by dynastic and royal leaderships and their military courtiers in Cairo as well as elsewhere across 'medieval' Islamic West-Asia is, since some time, similarly being revalued. In fact, in modern understandings of these crossover dynamics, it is becoming clear that the cultural participation of Turkic-speaking elites has, for a long time, tended to be reduced too easily to mere material and social involvements and actions, such as those by sultan al-Malik al-Ashraf Barsbay (r. 1422–1438) for his religious complex in the center of Cairo—stipulating as quoted above in detail the use of *waqf* assets in his complex' working—and by his contemporary, the Ottoman sultan Murad II (r. 1421–1451), who is—as detailed above—especially remembered for having endowed not just mosques, madrasas, and khanqahs in Edirne and Bursa, but also highly functional and widely appreciated bridges, soup kitchens, and even entire towns. Both cases are certainly illustrative, and even representative, of leadership's vital 'medieval' practice to mediate elite integration, accommodation, and competition not only via dynastic households and courts, but also—and in fact, as patrimonial transformations furthered, in increasingly more deeply entangled courtly ways—via *waqf*-related urban infrastructures. However, this practice and its very tangible transformative effects on urban landscapes and cultural forms of expression should never be disconnected from the wider, theocratic imaginations and related contested discourses and narratives of order that defined these actions and intentions, and that made them into more than mere financial and social practices of patronage of certain favorites or trans-regional communities. The example of Barsbay's detailed *waqf* stipulations is, therefore, not just representative of investment practices, but even more for how these practices participated in the ongoing contested and ambiguous formation of religious, scientific, intellectual, and normative discourses discussed in the introduction of this chapter. In this particular case, Barsbay and his agents interfered directly in the very central juristic discourse of Sunni legal practice, intensely contested in Cairo between proponents of Arabic Shafiʿi priority and their Persianate Hanafi opponents, and with Barsbay, following the example of many of his Turkic-speaking royal peers, favoring the latter and therefore stipulating that the teacher of Hanafism at his *madrasa* should receive a salary that was thrice the amount of the salary awarded to his Shafiʿi colleague, and even six times the amount set aside for their Maliki and Hanbali peers. This direct interference in the practices as well as the narratives and counternarratives of juristic discourse are today actually considered to have culminated, in the course of the 16th century, in an even more direct, dynastic intervention. On the one hand, the Ottoman sultan and his agents not only far more forcefully prioritized Hanafism, but even "shaped and regulated the structure of the specific branch within the Hanafi school of law [they] adopted" to accommodate the priority of Ottoman dynastic law.[30] On the other hand, Ismaʿil and Tahmasp—with the support of individuals such as the aforementioned ʿAli Karaki (d. 1534) and his students—similarly worked hard to prioritize, shape, and regulate a particular branch of Twelver Shi'ism that accommodated their understandings of Safavid sovereignty and theocracy.

Very often, an even more direct and involved intellectual participation also was the case, as is well illustrated by the example of the Syro-Egyptian Qalawunid *amir* Taybugha al-ʿUmari al-Hanafi al-Faqih (d. 1373). He was not only a rather insignificant low ranking *amir* in Cairo, but—as his name suggests—he also acquired some reputation and standing as a legal specialist (*faqih*) for the Hanafi school of law in his own right.[31] That this was not necessarily an exception in the history of the Cairo Sultanate is suggested by the unusual story of the *amir* Sanjar al-Jawuli (1255–1345), who was captured at a very young age in Hülegüid confrontations in the Jazira and then educated and raised as a *mamluk* in numerous royal and other households in Egypt and Syria. Growing up to become one of the most important leaders of the mid-14th-century Qalawunid Sultanate, he gained prominence not just due to the *madrasa* and mosque he built in the Syro-Palestinian town of Gaza, but also because of the important role he played as a *hadith* scholar, a *mufti*, and an author—in his case for the Shafiʿi school of law.[32]

In many ways, it may actually be argued that this integrative, sociocultural participation of Turkic-speaking leaderships coincided in mutually constitutive ways with discourses that portrayed some of the era's Hülegüid, Qalawunid, Jalayirid, Timurid, Ottoman, Turkmen, and Turko-Circassian rulers with the ancient ideals of the philosopher-king or the scientist-king, and—as explained in this chapter's introduction—as paragons of Islamic justice and erudition. In fact, this was not just a discursive return of royal favor by a diverse group of Arabic-, Persian-, and Turkic-speaking scholars, but a representation of an actual symbiotic reality of wide intellectual interests, creativity, and participation, and of active engagements in cultural practices such as literary salons, intellectual debates, and authorship, pursued and organized at many of Islamic West-Asia's courts. This is at least suggested by well-known and wide-spread examples of these phenomena, such as the Ottoman sultan's aforementioned organization of a competition over the polemic between al-Ghazali and Ibn Rushd in mid-15th-century Constantinople, by the active patronage of state-of-the-art observatories near Maragha and Samarqand by the Chinggisid ruler Hülegü in the mid-13th century and by the Timurid ruler Ulugh Beg in the first half of the 15th century, by the Turko-Circassian Sultan Qanisawh's hosting of gatherings of learned men at his court in Cairo to debate all kinds of thorny theological, legal, philosophical, and related issues, and by the same early 16th-century sultan's compilation of, and original contributions to, an anthology of Turkic poetry, just as was done by his Safavid peers Isma'il and Tahmasp in 16th-century Tabriz and Qazvin.

Notes

1 On these 'medieval' ambiguities and their modern meanings, see especially Ahmed, *What is Islam? The Importance of Being Islamic*; Bauer, *Die Kultur der Ambiguität. Eine andere Geschichte des Islams*.
2 Ibn Jamā'a (1241–1333), *Taḥrīr al-aḥkām fī tadbīr Ahl al-Islām* ['The Formulation of the Rules Regarding the Organization of the Muslims']; translation from Lewis, *Islam from the Prophet Muhammad to the Capture of Constantinople. Volume I: Politics and War*, 179.
3 See Berkey, "A Sunni 'revival'?"
4 Goudie, *Reinventing* Jihād, 201.
5 Mitchell, *The Practice of Politics in Safavid Iran: Power, Religion and Rhetoric*, 5.
6 Melvin-Koushki, "Early Modern Islamicate Empire: New Forms of Religiopolitical Legitimacy", 365.
7 See Darling, *A History of Social Justice and Political Power in the Middle East: The Circle of Justice from Mesopotamia to Globalization*.
8 Jalāl al-Dīn Muḥammad Dāvānī (1427–1503), *Akhlāq-i Jalālī* ['The Ethics of Jalāl (al-Din Dāvānī)']; translation from Woods, *The Aqquyunlu*, 105.
9 Jalāl al-Dīn Muḥammad Dāvānī (1427–1503), *Akhlāq-i Jalālī* ['The Ethics of Jalāl (al-Din Dāvānī)']; translation from Woods, *The Aqquyunlu*, 105.
10 See Imber, *Ebu's-Su'ud: The Islamic Legal Tradition*; Burak, "The Second Formation of Islamic Law".
11 Translation from Kastritsis, *An Early Ottoman History. The Oxford Anonymous Chronicle*, 170.
12 Hodgson, *Venture of Islam*, 2: 490. See also Binbaş, *Intellectual Networks in Timurid Iran. Sharaf al-Dīn 'Ali Yazdī and the Islamicate Republic of Letters*.
13 Flinterman, Van Steenbergen, "al-Nasir Muhammad and the Formation of the Qalawunid State", 108.
14 Petry, "Scholastic Stasis in Medieval Islam Reconsidered", 324 (slightly adapted).
15 Al-Maqrīzī (1364–1442), *Ighāthat al-Umma bi kashf al-ghumma* ('Saving the community by examining its distress'); translation from Allouche, *Mamluk Economics*, 73.
16 Ibn Khaldūn (1333–1406), *Kitāb al-'Ibar* ['The book of examples']; translation from Ayalon, "Mamlūkiyyāt: (B) Ibn Khaldūn's view of the Mamlūk Phenomenon", 345–6.
17 See Goitein (1900–1985), *A Mediterranean Society: The Jewish Communities of the Arab World as Portrayed in the Documents of the Cairo Geniza*.
18 Berkey, "Culture and Society during the Late Middle Ages", 397; referring to one of the seminal pioneering contributions to the modern study of the 'medieval' history of Islamic West-Asia: Lapidus, *Muslim Cities in the Later Middle Ages*, 144.
19 Al-Maqrīzī (1364–1442), *Kitāb al-Mawā'iẓ wa-l-I'tibār fī Dhikr al-Khiṭaṭ wa-l-Āthār* ['The Book of Admonitions and Contemplations on the basis of the Stories of the Neighbourhoods and Monuments (of Cairo)].
20 Al-Maqrīzī (1364–1442), *Kitāb al-Sulūk li-Ma'rifat Duwal al-Mulūk* ['The Book Guiding towards the Knowledge of the Reigns of the Kings']; translation from Borsch, *The Black Death in Egypt and England*, 1.

21 Al-Maqrīzī (1364–1442), *Kitāb al-Sulūk li-Ma'rifat Duwal al-Mulūk* ['The Book Guiding towards the Knowledge of the Reigns of the Kings'].
22 Al-Maqrīzī (1364–1442), *Ighāthat al-Umma bi kashf al-ghumma* ['Saving the Community by Unveiling (the Causes of) its Despair']; translation from Allouche, *Mamluk Economics*, 51–2.
23 *Waqfiyya Jāmi' Barsbāy* ['Endowment Document of the Mosque of Barsbāy'] (Cairo, 1427–28).
24 See Melvin-Koushki, "Of Islamic Grammatology: Ibn Turka's Lettrist Metaphysics of Light", 42.
25 Van Lit, "An Ottoman Commentary Tradition on Ghazālī's *Tahāfut al-Falāsifa*", 393.
26 Budāq Munshī Qazvīnī (fl. 1577), *Javāhir al-Akhbār* ('Exquisite Specimens of Historical Reports'); translation from Woods, *The Aqquyunlu*, 109.
27 Al-Maqrīzī (1365–1442), *Kitāb al-Sulūk li-Ma'rifat Duwal al-Mulūk* ['The Book Guiding towards the Knowledge of the Reigns of the Kings']; translation from Van Steenbergen, "Re-reading 'the Mamluks' with Ibn Khaldun (d. 1406)".
28 Al-Qalqashandī (1355–1418), *Ṣubḥ al-A'shā fī ṣinā'at al-inshā'* ['Dawn for the Night-Blinded Concerning the Chancery Practice'].
29 Adapted from al-Qalqashandī (1355–1418), *Ṣubḥ al-A'shā fī ṣinā'at al-inshā'* ['Dawn for the Night-Blinded Concerning the Chancery Practice'] by Ayalon, "Studies on the Mamluk Army – II", 461–2. Translation after Ayalon and Flinterman, Van Steenbergen, "al-Nasir Muhammad and the Formation of the Qalawunid State", 108.
30 Burak, "Between the *Ḳānūn* of Qāytbāy and Ottoman *Yasaq*: A Note on the Ottomans' Dynastic Law", 23.
31 Al-Kutubī (d. 1363), *'Uyūn al-Tawārīkh* ['The Sources of History'].
32 Ibn Qāḍī Shuhba (d. 1470), *Tārīkh* ['History'].

Selected readings

Ahmed, Sh. *What Is Islam? The Importance of Being Islamic* (Princeton, 2016)

Allouche, A. *Mamluk Economics: A Study and Translation of al-Maqrīzī's Ighāthah* (Salt Lake City, 1994)

Apellániz Ruiz de Galarreta, F.J. *Pouvoir et finance en Méditerranée pré-moderne: le deuxième Etat mamelouk et le commerce des épices (1382–1517)* (Barcelona, 2009)

Ashtor, E. *Levant Trade in the Later Middle Ages* (Princeton, 1983)

Ayalon, D. "Mamlūkiyyāt: (A) A First Attempt to Evaluate the Mamlūk Military System; (B) Ibn Khaldūn's View of the Mamlūk Phenomenon", *Jerusalem Studies in Arabic and Islam* 2 (1980): 321–49

Ayalon, D. "Studies on the Structure of the Mamluk Army", *Bulletin of the School of Oriental and African Studies* 15; 16 (1953; 1954): 203–28, 448–76; 57–90

Bauer, Th. *Die Kultur der Ambiguität. Eine andere Geschichte des Islams* (Frankfurt, 2011)

Bauer, Th. "Mamluk Literature as a Means of Communication", in St. Conermann (ed.), *Ubi Sumus? Quo Vademus? Mamluk Studies – State of the Art* (Bonn, 2013), pp. 23–56

Behrens-Abouseif, D. *Cairo of the Mamluks: A History of the Architecture and Its Culture* (London, 2007)

Berkey, J.P. "Culture and Society during the Late Middle Ages", in C.F. Petry (ed.), *The Cambridge History of Egypt. Vol. 1: Islamic Egypt, 640–1517* (Cambridge, 1998), pp. 375–411

Berkey, J.P. "A Sunni 'Revival'?", in J.P. Berkey (ed.), *The Formation of Islam: Religion and Society in the Near East, 600–1800* (Cambridge, 2003), pp. 189–202

Berkey, J.P. *The Transmission of Knowledge in Medieval Cairo: A Social History of Islamic Education* (Princeton, 1992)

Binbaş, İ.E. *Intellectual Networks in Timurid Iran: Sharaf al-Din 'Ali Yazdi and the Islamicate Republic of Letters* (Cambridge, 2016)

Borsch, S.J. *The Black Death in Egypt and England: A Comparative Study* (Austin, 2005)

Burak, G. "Between the *Ḳānūn* of Qāytbāy and Ottoman *Yasaq*: A Note on the Ottomans' Dynastic Law", *Journal of Islamic Studies* 26/1 (2015): 1–23

Burak, G. *The Second Formation of Islamic Law: The Hanafi School in the Early Modern Otoman Empire* (Cambridge, 2015)

Burak, G. "The Second Formation of Islamic Law: The Post-Mongol Context of the Ottoman Adoption of a School of Law", *Comparative Studies in Society and History* 55/3 (2013): 579–602

Chamberlain, M. *Knowledge and Social Practice in Medieval Damascus, 1190–1350* (Cambridge, 1994)

Christ, G. *Trading Conflicts: Venetian Merchants and Mamluk Officials in Late Medieval Alexandria* (Leiden, 2012)

Coulon, D. *Barcelone et le grand commerce d'Orient au Moyen Âge: un siècle de relations avec l'Egypte et la Syrie-Palestine (ca. 1330–ca. 1430)* (Madrid and Barcelona, 2004)

Darling, L. *A History of Social Justice and Political Power in the Middle East: The Circle of Justice from Mesopotamia to Globalization* (New York, 2013)

Elbendary, A. *Crowds and Sultans: Urban Protest in Late Medieval Egypt and Syria* (Cairo, 2015)

Eychenne, M. *Liens personnels, clientélisme et réseaux de pouvoir dans le sultanat mamelouk (milieu XIIIe-fin XIVe siècle)* (Damas-Beyrouth, 2013)

Flinterman, W., Van Steenbergen, J. "al-Nasir Muhammad and the Formation of the Qalawunid State", in A. Landau (ed.), *Pearls on a String: Art in the Age of Great Islamic Empires* (Baltimore and Seattle, 2015), pp. 101–27

Goitein, S.D. *A Mediterranean Society: The Jewish Communities of the Arab World as Portrayed in the Documents of the Cairo Geniza. Vol. 1 Economic Foundations; Vol. 2 The Community; Vol. 3 The Family; Vol. 4 Daily Life; Vol. 5 The Individual* (Berkeley, 1967–88)

Golombek, L., Subtelny, M. (eds.). *Timurid Art and Culture. Iran and Central Asia in the Fifteenth Century* (Leiden, 1992)

Goudie, K. *Reinventing Jihād: Jihād Ideology from the Conquest of Jerusalem to the End of the Ayyūbids (c. 492/1099–647/1249)* (Leiden, 2019)

Hirschler, K. *Medieval Damascus: Plurality and Diversity in an Arabic Library. The Ashrafīya Library Catalogue* (Edinburgh, 2016)

Hirschler, K. *A Monument to Medieval Syrian Book Culture: The Library of Ibn ʿAbd al-Hādī* (Edinburgh, 2020)

Hirschler, K. *The Written Word in the Medieval Arabic Lands: A Social and Cultural History of Reading Practices* (Edinburgh, 2012)

Hodgson, M.G.S. *The Venture of Islam: Conscience and History in a World Civlization. 2. The Expansion of Islam in the Middle Periods* (Chicago, 1974)

Igarashi, D. *Land Tenure, Fiscal Policy and Imperial Power in Medieval Syro-Egypt* (Chicago, 2015)

Imber, C. *Ebu's-Su'ud: The Islamic Legal Tradition* (Edinburgh, 1997)

Karamustafa, A.T. *Sufism: The Formative Period* (Berkeley and Los Angeles, 2007)

Kastritsis, D. (transl.). *An Early Ottoman History: The Oxford Anonymous Chronicle (Bodleian Library, Ms Marsh 313). Historical Introduction, Translation and Commentary* (Liverpool, 2017)

Lapidus, I.M. *Muslim Cities in the Later Middle Ages* (Cambridge, MA, 1967)

Loiseau, J. *Reconstruire la Maison du Sultan. 1350–1450. Ruine et Recomposition de l'ordre urbain au Caire*. 2 Volumes (Le Caire, 2010)

Martel-Thoumian, B. *Délinquance et ordre social. L'état mamlouk syro-égyptien face au crime à la fin du IXe–XVe siècle* (Bordeaux, 2012)

Martel-Thoumian, B. *Les civils et l'administration dans l'état militaire mamlūk (IXe/XVe siècle)* (Damascus, 1992)

McGregor, R.J.A., Sabra, A.A. (eds.). *Le développement du soufisme en Egypte à l'époque mamelouke* (Cairo, 2006)

Melvin-Koushki, M. "Early Modern Islamicate Empire: New Forms of Religiopolitical Legitimacy", in A. Salvatore, R. Tottoli, B. Rahimi (eds.), *The Wiley-Blackwell History of Islam* (Hoboken, 2018), pp. 353–75

Melvin-Koushki, M. "Of Islamic Grammatology: Ibn Turka's Lettrist Metaphysics of Light", *Al-ʿUṣūr al-Wusṭā* 24 (2016): 42–113

Mitchell, C.P. *The Practice of Politics in Safavid Iran: Power, Religion and Rhetoric* (London, 2009)

Miura, T. "Administrative Networks in the Mamluk Period: Taxation, Legal Execution, and Bribery", in Ts. Sato (ed.), *Islamic Urbanization in Human History: Political Power and Social Networks* (London and New York, 1997), pp. 39–76

Peacock, A.C.S. *Islam, Literature and Society in Mongol Anatolia* (Cambridge, 2019)
Peirce, L.P. *The Imperial Harem: Women and Sovereignty in the Ottoman Empire* (New York, 1993)
Petry, C.F. *The Civilian Elite of Cairo in the Later Middle Ages* (Princeton, 1981)
Petry, C.F. *The Criminal Underworld in a Medieval Islamic Society. Narratives from Cairo and Damascus under the Mamluks* (Chicago, 2012)
Petry, C.F. "Scholastic Stasis in Medieval Islam Reconsidered: Mamluk Patronage in Cairo", *Poetics Today* 14/2 (1993): 323–48
Pfeiffer, J. (ed.). *Politics, Patronage and the Transmission of Knowledge in 13th–15th Century Tabriz* (Leiden, 2014)
Rabbat, N. *The Citadel of Cairo: A New Interpretation of Royal Mamluk Architecture* (Leiden, 1995)
Rapoport, Y. *Marriage, Money and Divorce in Medieval Islamic Society* (Cambridge, 2005)
Rapoport, Y. *Rural Economy and Tribal Society in Islamic Egypt: A Study of al-Nābulusī's Villages of the Fayyum* (Turnhout, 2018)
Raymond, A. *Cairo: City of History* (Cairo, 2000)
Sabra, A.A. *Poverty and Charity in Medieval Islam: Mamluk Egypt, 1250–1517* (Cambridge, 2000)
Stilt, K. *Islamic Law in Action: Authority, Discretion, and Everyday Experiences in Mamluk Egypt* (Oxford, 2011)
Tabbaa, Y. *The Transformation of Islamic Art During the Sunni Revival* (Seattle, 2001)
Talmon-Heller, D. *Islamic Piety in Medieval Syria: Mosques, Cemeteries and Sermons Under the Zengids and Ayyūbids (1146–1260)* (Leiden, 2007)
Vallet, E. *L'Arabie marchande. Etat et commerce sous les sultans rasulides du Yémen (626–858/1229–1454)* (Paris, 2010)
van Lit, L.W.C. "An Ottoman Commentary Tradition on Ghazālī's *Tahāfut al-Falāsifa*. Preliminary Observations", *Orients* 43 (2015): 368–413.
Van Steenbergen, J. *Caliphate and Kingship in a Fifteenth-Century Literary History of Muslim Leadership and Pilgrimage. A Critical Edition, Annotated Translation, and Study of al-Maqrīzī's al-Ḏahab al-Masbūk fī Ḏikr man ḥağğa min al-Ḫulafā' wa-l-Mulūk* (Leiden, 2016)
Van Steenbergen, J. "Re-reading 'the Mamluks' with Ibn Khaldun (d. 1406): *'Aṣabiyya*, Messiness, and 'Mamlukization' in the Sultanate of Cairo (1200s–1500s)" (2020)
Verlinden, Ch. *Le commerce en Mer Noire des débuts de l'époque byzantine au lendemain de la conquête de l'Egypte par les Ottomans (1517)* (Moscou, 1970)
Walker, B.J. *Jordan in the Late Middle Ages: Transformation of the Mamluk Frontier* (Chicago, 2011)
Woods, J. *The Aqquyunlu: Clan, Confederation, Empire*. Revised and Expanded Edition (Salt Lake City, 1999)

14 Early modern dynastic formations

(Post-)Safavids, Ottomans, and many others (17th–18th centuries)

Introduction: situating early modernity, 'gunpowder empires', and narratives of decline

Throughout Islamic West-Asia, the 16th century coincided with particular moments of successful trans-regional conquest practices and dynastic formation that, in hindsight, appear as turning points for the stabilization of relationships of power and for the disciplining of all kinds of heterogeneities in the so-called early modern period. This stabilization and disciplining occurred in the well-known format of three post-nomadic dynastic formations and their distinct Turko-Persian dynastic as well as Sunni or Shi'i Islamic identities. These seemed once again, as it were, to unite the Islamic *umma* in a more homogeneous apparatus of trans-regional power and authority, reminiscent for many—not least dynastic agents themselves—of late antique Abbasid imperial achievements. In the far east of the Islamic world, in the regions of the Indian Peninsula, this happened under the leadership of the descendants of the aforementioned Timurid warlord Babur (d. 1530), who transformed into the dynasty of the Mughals (1526–1857) especially with the long reign of Babur's grandson Akbar (r. 1556–1605). In the regions of Iran, Azerbaijan, and Khurasan, the dynasty of the Safavids (1501–1722), which had emerged with the aforementioned Isma'il and his son and successor Tahmasp, transformed into a new and stable post-nomadic dynastic formation especially in the reign of Tahmasp's grandson 'Abbas I (r. 1588–1629). In the western lands of Islamic West-Asia, eventually extending into North Africa and eastern Europe, the Ottoman Sultanate had been transforming since the early 14th century, and eventually did so on an equally expansive and stabilized scale that was reimagined and even reorganized as a so-called "second Ottoman empire", as has recently been argued, from the end of the 16th century onwards.[1]

In traditional scholarship, each of these three major dynastic formations are represented as full participants in an early modernity of globalizing dimensions—but European construction—that would have included historical dynamics in Islamic West-Asia ranging from the Ottoman conquest of Constantinople in 1453 and the enthronement of Shah Isma'il in Tabriz in 1501 to Babur's victory over the Delhi sultan at the battle of Panipat in 1526. As convenient—and valid—an early modern starting point as these new dynastic beginnings may well be, however, as suggested in the preceding paragraph, any more stabilized patrimonial-bureaucratic dimensions for these trans-regional dynastic formations remained wanting until the later 16th century. 'Medieval' conquest practices, appanage-related dynastic rivalries, and in certain cases, even nomadic warfare remained very much at the core of each of these highly personalized 15th- and 16th-century achievements, as did competing and contested discourses of sovereignty, normativity, and ambiguity. It has made, therefore, much more sense for this book's second part to discuss and explain these only very slowly stabilizing 16th-century dynamics of West-Asian power and belonging as part and parcel of 'medieval' realities and imaginations, and to shift the analytical boundary of the beginnings of early modernity and of its stabilizing and globalizing dynamics—at least for the purpose of this book and its West-Asian subject matter—forward, towards the turn of the 16th to 17th centuries and the emergence of more stabilized dimensions for these trans-regional dynastic formations, both as a direct continuation and as a radical departure from those 'medieval' realities.[2]

As far as these continuities are concerned, everywhere elite households and their entourages, constituted around bonds of loyalty, obligation, and kinship and including personal troops and assets, remained central building blocks of reconfigurations of early modern power, as did the often brutal competition between these households. More in general, the coercive force of impressive cavalries with Turkish, Turkmen, and Turko-Mongol roots equally remained among the main ingredients for successful dynastic expansion and trans-regional hegemony. Especially in the Ottoman west, however, this was accompanied by the expansion of the ranks and centrality of infantry units, as well as of their intense use of firearms, canons, and handguns, to consolidate the priority and sovereignty of the sultan and his household's and court's centralizing power. In fact, although the Mughals, Safavids, and Ottomans have all been referred to for genuine reasons—since the writings of the aforementioned historian Marshall Hodgson in particular[3]—as the 'gunpowder empires', it is mainly the Ottoman Sultanate that can truly justify a claim to such a title.

The real early modern departure from 'medieval' realities is, therefore, perhaps not so much represented by changing technologies of warfare—which were already around since the mid-15th century—but rather by their more effective and sustained uses, in far more stabilized contexts of long, drawn-out frontier warfare and by new experts and providers who, as a result, managed to penetrate ever deeper in the multiple logistics of dynastic court rivalries. Indeed, from the second half of the 16th century onwards, each of these new early modern dynastic formations significantly managed to draw its expanding and integrating power and authority from the capacity to use the early modern period's substantially transforming, and globalizing, mechanisms, infrastructures, and agencies of power to pursue the

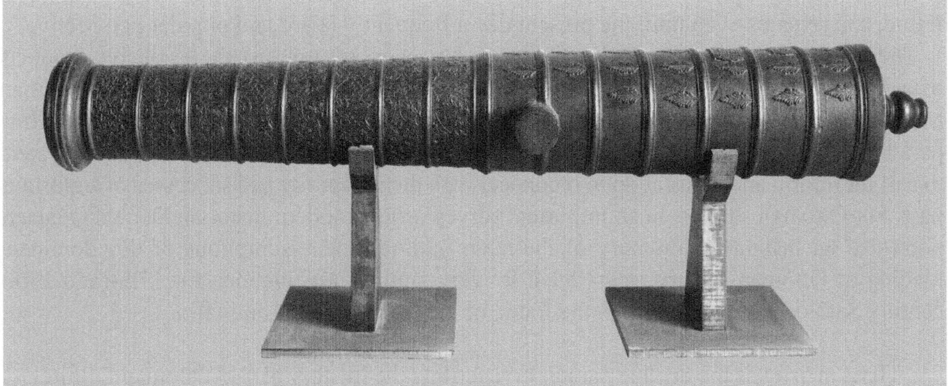

Figure 14.1 Ottoman canon

Source: Photo (C) Paris—Musée de l'Armée, Dist. RMN-Grand Palais/Emilie Cambier

elimination of its rivals, the protection and involvement of its partners and clients, the accumulation of sufficient resources to enable such pursuits, and the organization of stabilizing mechanisms for the reproduction of the centralizing power of dynastic households and courts. As a result, a much more complex and, once again, patrimonial-bureaucratic organization emerged around the courts of Ottoman Constantinople, Safavid Isfahan, and Mughal Agra, and around mutually constitutive and intensely interconnected Sunni Ottoman Turkish, Shi'ite Safavid Irano-Persian, and Mughal Indo-Persian identities. As one of the main proponents of this early modern Asian model of the patrimonial-bureaucratic dynastic formation, the modern specialist of Indian history Stephen Blake, claims for the latter Mughal case, it was indeed nothing less than the achievement of Babur's grandson Akbar, in the second half of the sixteenth century,

> to develop, refine, and systematize the elements of state organization he had inherited from India and West and Central Asia. . . . Akbar synthesized these elements into the coherent, rational system of government that . . . gave the patrimonial bureaucratic empire in India its most systematic, fully developed, and clearly articulated form.[4]

From these three early modern patrimonial bureaucratic formations, only the West-Asian ones will be central to this chapter. Traditionally, these Ottoman and Safavid-Iranian formations and their early modern patrimonial bureaucratic transformations have actually tended to be interpreted negatively. They have been understood as losses of dynastic power to outsiders, as the dissolution of longstanding and successful elite configurations, and even as functions of inevitable decay and disintegration, of Ottoman decline and "the long fall of the Safavid Dynasty".[5] For a long time, this 'decline' thinking has actually remained a dominant explanatory model, used since at latest the 19th century by both European policymakers and historians to understand the course of the (early modern and modern) history of West-Asia and North Africa. 19th-century framings of the Ottoman sultan as 'the sick man of Europe' and of Iran as a "bedraggled, backward country of ruined towns inhabited by impoverished, ignorant people who seemed in dire need of Western tutelage"[6] became common images that determined dominant European geopolitical and historiographical discourses. The idea that the Islamic cultural and intellectual world would have lost all its capacity for creativity, innovation, and progress, even already since at latest the 13th-century destruction of the Abbasid caliphate of Bagdad, and that it had since fallen into 'dark times', pertains to this same frame, and remains even until the present day a frequently heard and popular perspective.

These value-driven and negative framings, however, are not just the exclusive products of a Eurocentric mindset. In the 17th and 18th centuries, the writings of many Ottoman and (post-)Safavid contemporary observers started situating themselves in a similar 'decline paradigm' to interpret their contemporary history, to consider it as a time of moral decay, and to call for reform and restoration to reconnect with the prosperity and successes of a glorious past. For Ottoman studies, in an important survey article modern historian Donald Quataert presented an insightful summary of the main outlines and assumptions of this dominant reading of Ottoman history—paralleled by very similar imaginations for 17th- and 18th-century Safavid history—through the frame of inevitable decline and fall:

> Here, in brief, is the decline paradigm regarding the [history of the] Ottoman Empire. . . . Between 1300 and 1566, the Ottoman Empire expanded steadily under the guidance of ten sultans who were remarkable for their warrior and/or administrative skills. Decline set in at the apex of Ottoman power, under Sultan Suleyman the Magnificent (1520–66),

CONSULTATION ABOUT THE STATE OF TURKEY.

Figure 14.2 Cartoon representing the great powers Great Britain and France as two well-known politicians deliberating the future of a mortally ill Ottoman Empire (J. Leech, wood engraving, 1854)

Source: Punch Cartoon Library/Topfoto

> who foolishly allotted power to a concubine who became his wife, with devastating effects on the Empire. The accession of his son, Selim "the Sot", affirmed the maxim "the fish begins to rot from the head" and the rule of the harem only made things worse. Coupled with the price revolution triggered by the [early modern] influx of American silver, the foundations of Ottoman power were permanently shaken. . . . In the 17th century, incompetent, sex-crased, or venal rulers were incapable of maintaining control. The disastrous defeat of the Ottoman army before the walls of Vienna in 1683 made the decline visible to all and the Empire subsequently staggered from one defeat to the next. Crowned with the title "The Sick Man of Europe", the Empire survived because of divisions among its enemies. In the 19th century, possible salvation appeared in the form of westernisation, as Ottoman leaders sought to import military and administrative models from Europe. But the changes made were incomplete, both too few and too late. Ineptitude and retardation permitted nationalism to spread among the subject peoples; the imperial structure, thus unable to adjust, was torn apart from within. The last of the groups to gain national identity, the Turks, administered the final blow in 1922 and the Turkish Republic was born in 1923. Having eagerly sought to end the Ottoman "yoke", the Turkish and other successor states then struggled to eliminate its legacy and achieve modern nation-statehood.[7]

Quataert's survey article is, in fact, a strong wake up call to appreciate recent Ottoman studies that manage to move beyond the assumptions inherent in this particular, negative reading of six centuries of Ottoman dynastic history. Since several decades, this traditional and widespread way of thinking and explaining West-Asia's age of early modernity has indeed become the subject of ever more debate, both among the growing number of Ottoman historians and in the more limited academic circles of Iranian early modern historiography. More specifically, it is by now certainly clear that the negative analyses of contemporary Ottoman and (post-)Safavid observers must primarily be understood as the moralizing assessment of a traditional elite for whom the impact of early modern changes appeared as a threat to vested interests and hierarchies, making them, therefore, argue for a return to the norms and values of an idealized past in which their status and privileges had appeared beyond question. As far as modern political and historical analyses are concerned, it has by now been demonstrated in equally convincing ways how these analyses in turn were determined by a specific normative historical way of thinking, in which the formation of European nation states, the European economic world system, and the European Enlightenment were long considered the only redemptive trajectory for historical progress. In this equally value-driven historical imagination, any deviations from this allegedly natural model of development and self-improvement were seen as wrong and without a future, and thus as a sick man's trajectory of decline and imminent disintegration, crisis, and downfall.

Value-driven descriptions and analyses that were (and continue to be) determined by that early modern Ottoman and Safavid conservativism or by this Eurocentric 'modernization theory' of progress have presently largely been revised, nuanced, and contradicted by new approaches in early modern West-Asian historical research. One of these approaches, actually, wishes to consider the changes of the 17th and 18th centuries on their own, regardless of any moralizing comparison with previous periods or any measuring against a European ideal of modernization and progress. Especially for the long and continuous history of the Ottoman dynastic formation, an entirely different narrative of change, flexibility, and adaptation thus appears—as in the aforementioned case that has been made by modern historian Baki Tezcan for considering early modern Ottoman history as that of an entirely reconfigured and even reinvented "second Ottoman empire".[8] This new narrative of endless transformation and reconfiguration is certainly far better equipped to capture, and understand, the centuries-long and ever-changing Ottoman reality than any discourse of more than three centuries of Ottoman passivity and inability to deal with changing realities after the turn of the 16th to 17th centuries may be. Quataert, therefore, aptly clarifies the current academic imagination of Ottoman history as driven by six centuries of transformation and reconfiguration, in radical contradistinction from traditional Ottoman scholarship determined by the paradigm of decline that was quoted above, as follows:

> The emerging new scholarship is revealing an Ottoman state (society and economy) in the process of continuous transformation, rather than a decline or fall from idealised norms of the past or a failure to successfully imitate the West. In this new understanding, the Ottoman state underwent continuous modifications in its domestic policy, an ongoing evolution in which there is no idealised form, since change itself is understood as the norm. Take the role of sultans in the Ottoman political structure. They began as *primus inter pares*—first among equals—in the early days of the state; but then, between *c.* 1453 and the later 16th century, sultans ruled as true autocrats. Subsequently, others in the imperial family and members of the palace élites—often in collaboration with provincial élites—took real control of the state until the early 19th century. Thereafter, bureaucrats and sultans vied for control of the state. In sum, the sultan presided over the imperial system for all of Ottoman history but actually, personally, ruled only for portions of the 15th, 16th, and 19th centuries. And so, rather than looking for sultanic despotism as the norm and deviation from it as decline, scholarship is revealing a constantly shifting locus of power.[9]

In modern Safavid history writing—more heavily determined by the reality of the Safavid sovereign order's quick implosion in the 1720s, and of an unstable post-Safavid polycentric order of highly mobile and violent leaderships during the remainder of the 18th century (see below)—the validity of exchanging decline for transformation remains much more debated. In this context, modern Safavid historian Rudi Matthee actually calls for a nuanced approach that circumscribes the notion of Safavid decline more explicitly as value-driven and reductive amidst complex realities, but nevertheless, for lack of a better term, as "appropriate for this [early modern] period and these [early modern Safavid] conditions".[10]

There are, in fact, many parallels in patrimonial-bureaucratic stabilization between the early modern Ottoman and Safavid cases, especially in the shifts of the locus of dynastic power relationships, from the ruler's centrality, over that of his household and then that of contested constellations of household members and many other courtiers and their followers, to a trans-regional proliferation of these polycentric realities. The current chapter will therefore proceed from a shared perspective of substantial transformation, rather than in search of factors of change in the Ottoman case and of inevitable crisis in the Safavid one. Instead, as in previous chapters, such a subtext of linear trajectories of causality—in which past and present are interconnected as in a cascade of inevitabilities—will be exchanged for an acknowledgement of the multiplicity, multi-directionality, and many ups and downs that mark any phenomenon's historical trajectory. Ottoman resilience and Safavid disappearance will therefore be understood in even more generally conceptualized, processual terms, as two variations of trans-regional West-Asian leadership configurations pursuing an endless process of becoming. In fact, what has been identified as the 'loosening' of Ottoman trans-regional leadership arrangements in the 18th-century moment of this process remarkably—quite exceptionally, in fact, from the *longue durée* perspective of this 2nd wave's long West-Asian history—continued to situate itself within an appearance of Ottoman theocratic order, while, at the same time, the parallel Safavid process of disintegration only slowly re-assembled in the format of a post-Safavid order.

As announced before, these two variations of West-Asia's process of early modern dynastic formation, with strikingly parallel as well as revelatory distinct effects, will be surveyed in this chapter. The dynamics of changing Ottoman sovereignty, centrality, and dynastic identities in the 17th and 18th centuries will be detailed in this chapter's second part. The even more complex Safavid and post-Safavid versions of this story of dynastic formation and leadership reconfigurations will be considered first.

1 Early modern dynastic formation from Azerbaijan to Khurasan

1.1 Safavid dynastic formation (1587–1722)

As suggested in this chapter's introduction, it was only during the reign of Tahmasp's grandson Shah ʿAbbas I (r. 1587–1629) that the dynastic power and the Twelver Shi'ite sovereignty of the Safavid dynasty began to be effectively stabilized. This contributed substantially to the dynasty's continued centrality into the early 18th century, and to its referential status as an ideal of West-Asian sovereignty for many decades thereafter. Further expansion of the dynastic apparatus of power, including the local penetration of Safavid power relations across Iran, as well as military and diplomatic successes, investments in commerce and globalizing trade relations, and an active patronage of religious practices in Twelver Shi'ite shrine centers, such as Qum in central Iran and Mashhad in Khurasan as well as in the new Safavid urban center of Isfahan, made Shah ʿAbbas one of the most powerful and globally connected rulers of his time.

In each of these areas of leadership practices and integration of people and resources, ʿAbbas successfully negotiated Safavid balances between 'Turks', 'Tajiks', and various new elites at his court and between Ottomans in the west, Uzbeks in the northeast, and many other players on the expanding world stage. In the Safavid apparatus, new types of dynastic manpower—particularly renewed ranks of *ghilman* of unfree Georgian and Circassian origins, but also allied or mercenary leaderships and their free associates and troops of Arabian, Irano-Persian, and Kurdish origins—represented an even ever more important and effective counterweight to the traditional Qizilbash Turkmen leaderships, or khans. Traditionally operating from major appanages that were awarded to them and their followers as tax-exempted land grants (*tiyul*) in return for military services, their ranks and relationships of mutual interdependence were complemented by these new types of manpower in highly competitive constellations ever more directly controlled by ʿAbbas himself. At the same time, however, some Qizilbash leaders appeared as important supporters in the balancing act that represented the new patrimonial apparatus, even for a forceful personal ruler such as ʿAbbas. An example of the latter was one Ganj ʿAli Khan, a Qizilbash leader as well as a close household associate of ʿAbbas, who eventually received the region of Kirman as his appanage to administer, allowing him to set up his own household and court in parallel to that of ʿAbbas in Isfahan. Similar favors were bestowed upon particular members of ʿAbbas' *ghilman*, such as Allah Virdi Khan, who with his descendants received Fars as an appanage to rule for ʿAbbas and who was also appointed as the effective chief commander of his joined armies, composed of *ghilman*, Qizilbash, and various other forces. Finally, there was the Armenian *ghulam* Qarachaqay Khan, who was given Khurasan as an appanage to rule and

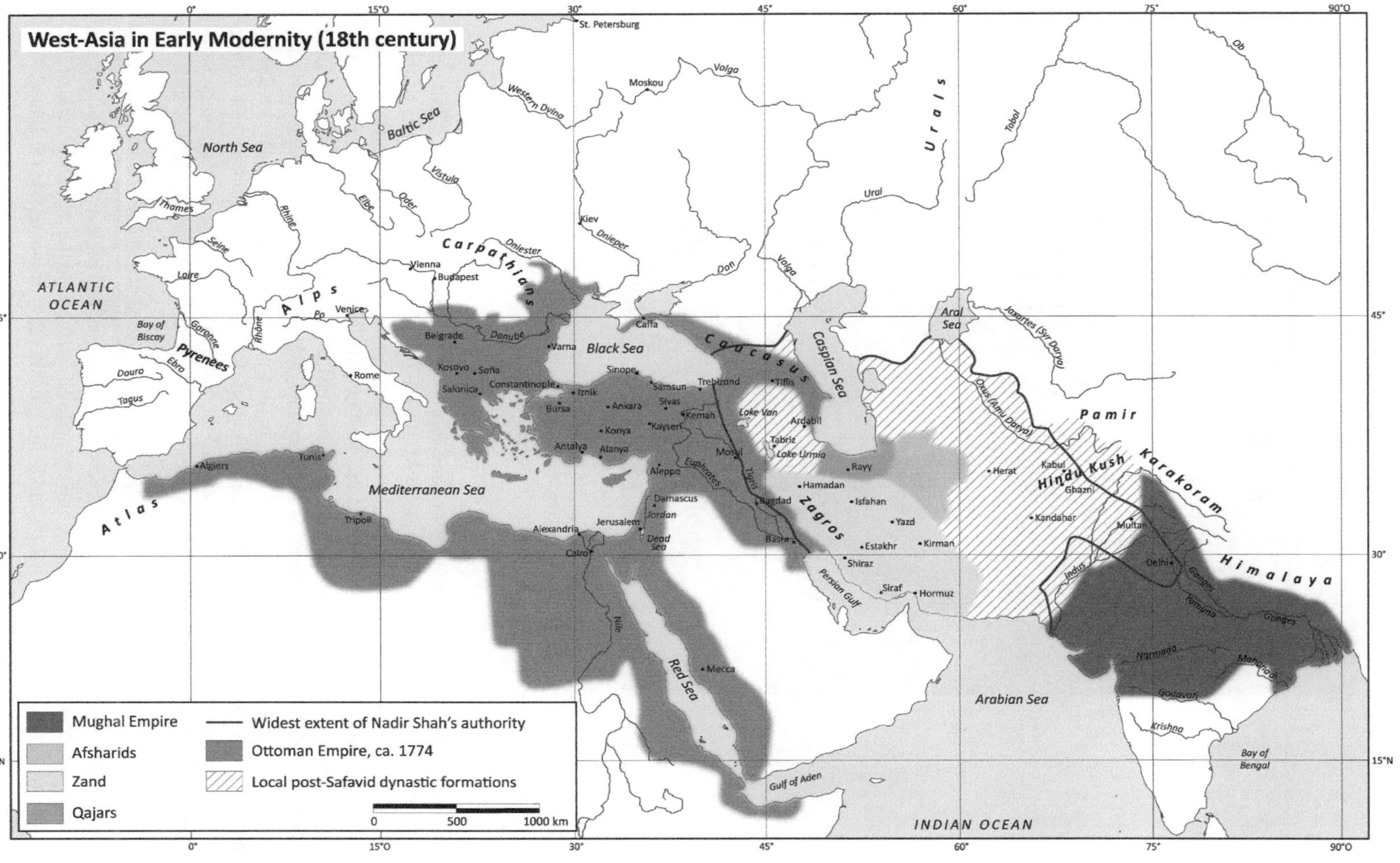

Map 12 West-Asia in Early Modernity (18th century)

Figure 14.3 Folio with a painting representing Shah ʿAbbas (central right) receiving, in 1618, an envoy from the Mughal court (painter unknown) (British Museum)

Source: UtCon Collection/Alamy Stock Photo

whose descendants continued to perform and represent Safavid authority from Khurasan's ever more central Twelver Shi'ite shrine of Mashhad. The centrality and autonomy of these and similar household members and patrimonial agents in the Safavid constellation of power expanded especially from the middle of the 17th century onwards, when, allegedly, some 1,000 *ghilman* and no less than some 3,000 eunuchs of similar unfree origins populated the Safavid palace courts in Isfahan. Simultaneously, many of them were not just awarded appanages to administer in the name of their master and ruler, but also given the formal control over the Turkmen residing in these appanages, transferring the status of their former Qizilbash leaders to these patrimonial agents of the Safavid center. One contemporary Safavid court historian explained this process of far-reaching *ghilman* empowerment as follows:

> Since some of the tribes (*oymaq*) did not possess qualified candidates to take on high posts once their Qizilbash generals (*emirs*) and governors had died, a slave (*ghulam*) was appointed, due to his justice, skill, bravery and self-sacrifice, to the rank of general of that clan (*il*), army (*qushun va lashkar*) and to the governorship of that region (*hukumat*).[11]

In addition to this remarkable diversification of personal relationships of power, authority, and patronage, another measure that ʿAbbas took to stabilize his rule and balance the devolved authorities of these Qizilbash leaders was pursued via the members of his own family, eventually resulting also in the massive expansion in the numbers and roles of court eunuchs. Before his enthronement, the young ʿAbbas himself still had to be sent away from the Safavid court at Qazvin to one of the dynastic appanages to start acquiring his own household and training. As this always involved arrangements of guardianship for Qizilbash leaders, ʿAbbas himself, as with many other young members of the Safavid line, had become a pawn in Qizilbash hands in the powerplay and internecine warfare that had defined the succession of his grandfather Tahmasp. To counter these destabilizing realities, from the 1590s onwards, ʿAbbas' sons and grandsons were no longer given any appanages, but were secluded in the harem, in his new palace in Isfahan. ʿAbbas eventually even had one of his sons murdered on suspicion of rebellion and two others blinded—considered an effective practice to disqualify anyone for rule. When ʿAbbas eventually died, in 1629, therefore, the only qualified person to succeed him was a grandson, who succeeded him as Shah Safi (r. 1629–1642).

Combined with the longevity of the reigns of ʿAbbas and of his successors—numbering only five Safavids between 1587 and 1722—this seclusion of Safavid princes in the inner spaces of the patriarchal household and court made that neither internecine warfare nor Qizilbash interference ever destabilized Safavid centrality again. At the same time, it also made that from the accession of Shah Safi onwards, Safavid centrality continued invariably to be performed from the secluded spaces of the harem in the Isfahan palace. As a result, the locus of stabilizing Safavid power shifted from the person of the Safavid ruler—where it had come to reside when ʿAbbas had managed to marginalize the Qizilbash leaders—to the wider membership of his patriarchal household, especially to the eunuchs and the royal concubines, the queen mother among them in particular. Especially during Shah Safi's reign, and in the first few years of that of his young son, Shah ʿAbbas II (b. 1633, r. 1642–1666), eunuchs and concubines pulled many strings. Central Safavid powerbrokers in these years appear to have been the eunuch, administrator of the region of Mazandaran for ʿAbbas I, and eventually grand vizier Saru Taqi (d. 1645), and the mother of ʿAbbas II, a concubine of alleged Circassian origins and known as Anna Khanum (d. 1647). A French merchant who lived in Isfahan in the 1660s and 1670s and left one of the most detailed contemporary accounts of Safavid history was later informed about this powerful *entente* between the grand vizier and the queen mother, which he described in the following generalizing terms, as much inspired by what he observed in his own days as by how this *entente* continued to be remembered:

> The power of the mothers of Persian kings looms large when they are at a young age. Abbas II's mother had much influence, which was absolute. [The queen-mothers] were in close contact with the prime minister and would help each other mutually . . . Saru Taqi was the agent and confident of the queen-mother; he would gather immense fortunes for her. She governed Persia at her will through her minister.[12]

Commercial entrepreneurship and extensive cultural patronage were, furthermore, some of the most important—and most visible—instruments for Shah ʿAbbas to deepen relationships of loyalty and obligation and provide his complex configuration of diverse Safavid leaderships with a growing flavor of coherence and stability. Active participation in the further expansion of what has been termed a 'Persian cosmopolis' of literary and intellectual production and reproduction was a central building block of his patronage, as mediated by

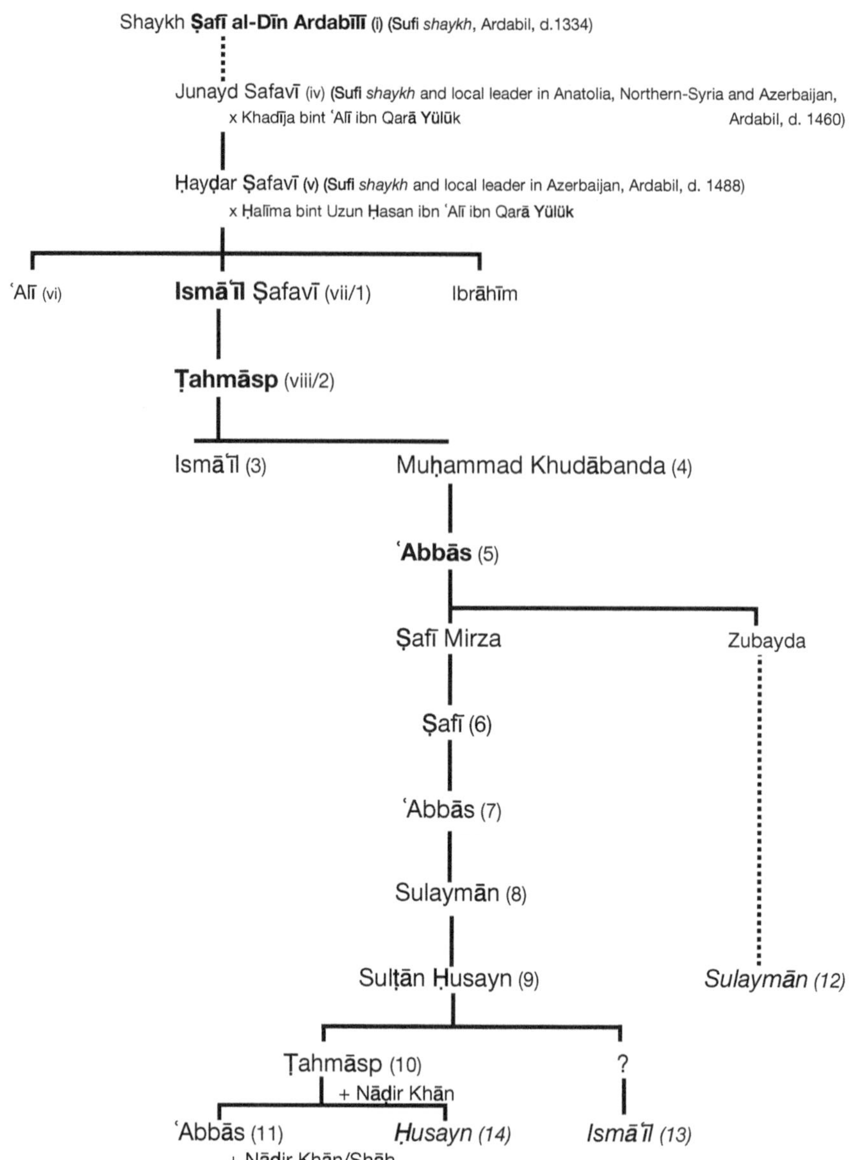

Roman numbers: succession of Ṣafaviyya *shaykh*s

Arabic numbers: succession of Ṣafaviyya-*shāh*s

Dynastic Table 12 Simplified table of Safavid dynastic leadership

his new court in Isfahan. Intense trans-regional competition for highly mobile artists, intellectuals, and their cultural products with the courts of Safavid peers in India and in Anatolia was also pursued by Shah ʿAbbas' patrimonial agents in Fars, Kirman, Khurasan, and elsewhere. It was even more intensely pursued by most of Shah ʿAbbas' successors, and as such bespeaks the enormous reach as well as continued diversity and refinement of the shared Persianate linguistic and cultural idiom in this early modern period. Via a dynastic monopoly on the silk trade, a growing trans-regional and even Eurasian appreciation for Iranian ceramics and gold- and silver-thread silk carpets, and the forced transfer to Isfahan and employment in court service of groups from the very globally oriented Christian Armenian trading community, an even more extensive and successful web of commercial and diplomatic networks was simultaneously developed around the Safavid court. In this web, among others, Ming China, Mughal India, the Ottoman Sultanate, and Elizabethan England met in Shah ʿAbbas' center of Isfahan. Enormous investments by the Shah and by various members of his court and entourage in Persianate arts and sciences and in urban religious infrastructures provided an important further support for the local integration of the dynasty and of Twelver Shiʾism and its intellectual and authoritative proponents. One of the many results of all this was that ʿAbbas and his armies succeeded in recapturing important territories, such as Azerbaijan and Bagdad in the west from the Ottomans, and Mashhad and Kandahar in the east from the Uzbeks. His reign thus also substantially contributed to the stabilization of frontier zones in east and west that, especially from the 1640s onwards, became a remarkable and long-sustained West-Asian reality.

After the enormous political, economic, and cultural accomplishments of Shah ʿAbbas, the Safavid dynastic configuration therefore experienced its own, largely unrivalled, process of early modern dynastic formation throughout the relatively stable 17th century. As modern historian Rudi Matthee summarizes some of the main trends for this entire period:

> for decades after the death of Shah ʿAbbas I in 1629, foreign visitors continued to find Iran a safe and agreeable place, and especially the reign of his great-grandson, Shah ʿAbbas II (1642–66) earned a reputation for relative peace and prosperity . . . The shah continued to make efforts to stay on top of competing bureaucratic interests. The turnover rate of high-ranking officials remained comparatively low. Politically, matters were far less chaotic than in the Ottoman Empire or Mughal India—and much more stable than in the sixteenth century. . . . Between 1624 and 1720 Safavid shahs were served by ten grand viziers, one of whom, Shaykh ʿAli Khan Zanganah, was in office for a full twenty years. Several were dismissed but only Mirza Abu Talib Khan Urdubadi (1634) and Mirza Muhammad 'Saru' Tapi (1645) met a violent death at the shah's orders. . . . Jean Chardin . . . made a famous claim that Iran's peasants were better off than their French counterpart; and his equally telling observation that, at least until the end of Shah ʿAbbas II's reign, its roads remained relatively safe, epitomizes this tranquility.[13]

At the same time, however, especially after the forceful personal rule of Shah ʿAbbas II in the middle of the century, the locus of power shifted further, to the wider scale of the patrimonial and therefore, also bureaucratic apparatus, and its many different memberships, from the sultan over the harem and the *ghilman*, to 'Tajik' bureaucrats and remaining Qizilbash khans as well as, not least, ever more active groups of Twelver Shiʾite scholars. These substantial transformations of leaderships and their relationships at the Safavid center as well as in many of its peripheries were also accompanied by an impressive reorganization of the flows of income. As a result of the gradual 17th-century transformation of dynastic and

Qizilbash appanages into crown land (*khassa*), the administration and integration of these lands and their resources had been radically altered. This happened especially via tax farming auctions, in which pledges of advance payments were made and a locality's administration and resource accumulation were outsourced to the highest bidder, especially courtiers and their entourages. As the 17th century proceeded, ever more competitors emerged to claim access to these and related resource flows, while at the same time, control over this redistribution of resources slipped from the hands of the Shah and his direct agents. Not just outsourcing revenue rights via tax farming arrangements, but also practices and discourses of corruption and over-taxation appeared in this Safavid context. Together, they were above all a function of the dissemination of central power across an ever more expansive and divided patrimonial-bureaucratic apparatus. Equally important socio-economic changes that have been noted in this context of patrimonial bureaucratic formation concern the difficult adaptation of resource flows to lowering demands on European markets for Persian silk, and an increasing demand in Persia itself for spices supplied from India by European traders.

All this is suggested to have weakened the mechanisms of central cohesion and resource accumulation in drastic ways. From the end of the 17th century, the most important consequence of this difficult situation seems to have been a marked weakening of the Safavid dynasty's coercive force, as it experienced ever more difficulties in maintaining its professional armies and coercive apparatus. A specific ideological shift, revolving around new, more deeply integrated generations of Twelver Shi'ite *ulema*, in which the Twelver Shi'ite identity of the dynasty, the court, and their representatives was emphasized more than ever, simultaneously undermined the cohesion of the diverse landscape of people and communities over which the Shah continued to rule. Around 1700, large parts of Iran's populations were genuinely Shi'ite, but at the same time, particular leaderships and their followers, active at the center and in the many peripheries of Safavid power, continued to be Sunni, or at least non-Twelver Shi'ite, and as a result of this, many of them were rapidly estranged, if not prosecuted. The combination of these factors goes a long way to explain how in 1722, in a context of uprisings in various frontier areas, the Safavid army was defeated when the center of Isfahan fell victim to a military siege by a (Sunni) coalition of Afghan leaderships led by the Afghan warlord Mahmud of Kandahar. Eventually, on 23 October 1722, after six months of siege, famine, and military incapacity, the last Safavid Shah Sultan Husayn (r. 1694–1722, d. 1726) found himself forced to surrender and accept the end of the dynasty.

1.2 Post-Safavid disintegration, conquest practices, and the rise of alternative leaderships

Twelver Shi'ite *ulema* had originally mostly been residing in urban centers beyond Iran and had only indirectly or at best temporarily been related to Safavid authority. In the course of this long 17th century, however, discussions appeared to intensify about their relationship with the Safavid sovereign order and its claims—inspired by the aforementioned early 16th-century scholar and Safavid powerbroker ʿAli Karaki (d. 1534) and his 16th-century network of students and successors—to represent Twelver Shi'ism. Intense and strategic Safavid uses of the mechanisms of court patronage and of *waqf*-related urban infrastructures of mosques, mausolea, and their like since the days of ʿAbbas I not only generated the ever deeper local penetration of a Safavid strand of Twelver Shi'ism, but also ever stronger links with Twelver Shi'i scholarship, and ever more heated debates about Safavid claims to authority. In due course, new central spaces of Twelver Shi'ite thought and practice emerged within the Safavid-controlled lands—in Isfahan, as well as in the shrine centers of Mashhad and Qum—and both Safavid claims as well as certain groups within Twelver Shi'ite scholarship found ways of accommodation. Eventually, with the disappearance of Safavid sovereignty in the early 18th century, the latter groups appeared as increasingly more central, powerful, and resourceful actors and agents in the regions of Iran, especially during the instability of the 18th century so-called 'age of warlords' (see below).

The 18th-century disappearance of Safavid claims to Twelver Shi'ite order, and even sovereignty, actually created even more space for Shi'ite scholars to emerge as central power brokers and highly authoritative figures. An important change that contributed to the shaping of new configurations of these scholars—partly due to the contributions of Muhammad Baqir Behbahani (1706–1791), a leading Twelver Shi'ite scholar mostly active in Najaf in Iraq—arose from the settlement of the so-called *akhbari-usuli* controversy within Twelver Shi'ite discourse. This long-raging controversy was eventually settled in favor of the *usuli* narrative, which supported the qualified scholar's ability to pursue his own interpretations (*ijtihad*) in formulations of theocratic normativity, and the view that all Twelver Shi'ite believers should follow whom they consider the most learned of these qualified scholars. From discursive as well as wider social and intellectual competitive realities such as these, the Twelver Shi'ite religious establishment emerged as the new stabilizing factor of legitimate leadership in the complex 18th-century context of Twelver Shi'ite Islam, as it continued to exist and grow in intellectual as well as popular terms between Iraq and Khurasan. The expanding authority, autonomy, and popularity of this establishment then translated into the appearance of its own, powerful hierarchy of authoritative figures who could, and would continue to, claim autonomy, power, and resources in the complex Iranian landscape of competing leaderships and stabilizing Twelver Shi'ite theocratic order, especially beyond the early modern period.

The rivalling Twelver Shi'ite establishments of Iraq, Iran, and Khurasan were not, however, the only leaderships that emerged and thrived amid the sudden post-Safavid autonomy that the fall of Isfahan in 1725 had created. After the abdication of the last Safavid Shah, the Sunni Afghan leader Mahmud not only took over power in Isfahan, but also claimed a post-Safavid type of authority from Azerbaijan to Khurasan, as Shah Mahmud (r. 1722–1725). He and other similar strongmen, however, never succeeded in having their new Afghan leadership accepted. This followed above all from the fact that his newly claimed authority was immediately challenged by a son of Sultan Husayn, Tahmasp II (r. 1722–1732), who eventually temporarily succeeded in restoring Safavid power, first in Qazvin, then in Tabriz, and eventually back in Isfahan. This was especially the accomplishment of Tahmasp's main military supporter, a Qizilbash Afsharid khan who styled himself Nadir Khan (d. 1747). Nadir Khan, however, soon proved at least as ambitious as the Afghan leadership that he had defeated. Eventually, in 1736, he appropriated the power, Safavid claims, and title of Shah from Tahmasp's young son and successor, ʿAbbas III (r. 1732–1736). This actually continued the relapse of the regions' landscapes of power, announced by the Afghan campaigns and claims to the Safavid authority of Shah in the 1720s, into a dominance of charismatic conquest practices and highly unstable nomadic military leadership arrangements. In a career of endless campaigns and conquests that is once more remembered as particularly violent and destructive, the new Nadir Shah soon consolidated his authority across Iran and Azerbaijan, culminating in the early 1730s in his unsuccessful siege of Ottoman Bagdad and the recapture of western and northern territories taken, upon the Safavid collapse in the 1720s, by Ottomans and Russians. Subsequently, Nadir Shah equally swiftly extended his networks of coercive subordination and raiding to Afghan-dominated Khurasan (where subsequently he would re-settle his headquarters in Mashhad) and to Uzbek Transoxania. At around the same period, in 1739, he engaged in a violent rampage through the northern Indian domains of the Mughals, which culminated in his sacking of Mughal Delhi and his appropriation of the famous Peacock Throne of the Mughal emperors. In 1747, however, Nadir Shah was murdered by some members of his own Qizilbash entourage. When no one proved capable to succeed him in any similarly powerful and charismatic way, most of Nadir Khan's violently constructed network of trans-regional leadership disintegrated into various groups and parties led by some of his main Turkmen, Afghan, and Iranian agents.

Afsharid Qizilbash leadership remained dominant in Mashhad and Khurasan for many more decades. In the regions of Iran, the leaders from an Iranian community of pastoralists from the Zagros mountains in western Iran, the Zand, led by a former commander in Nadir Shah's army, Karim Khan Zand (r. 1754–1779), successfully contested for regional power and control over resources with various other similar Iranian, Afghan, and Turkmen pastoralist leaderships. Karim Khan actually did so while situating his authority explicitly within the fictive symbolic dimensions of a Safavid order of sovereignty. Unlike Nadir Shah Afshar, Karim Khan refrained from ever exchanging his regional title of Khan for the Safavid one

Figure 14.4 Folio with a painting representing Nadir Shah, based on an 18th-century drawing

Source: Freer Gallery of Art and Arthur M. Sackler Gallery, S1986.439, https://archive.asia.si.edu/collections/edan/object.php?q=fsg_S1986.439

of Shah. Instead, in 1757, just as Nadir first had done, he put another infant grandson of the Safavid Shah Sultan Husayn, Isma'il III (r. 1757–1773), on the throne—now set up in Shiraz in Fars—nominated himself the Shah's 'deputy' (*wakil*), and engaged again in lavish patronage of, especially, Twelver Shi'ite Islam and its scholarship.

Despite these attempts by Karim Khan and also later Zand rulers to uphold a post-Safavid fiction of Safavid sovereignty and theocratic order, and to re-create the Safavid dynasty with its few remaining members as an infrastructure of empowerment and distinction in its own right, internecine warfare, raiding, and unstable local and regional leadership arrangements remained dominant features, especially after the death of Karim Khan in 1779. These persistent practices of violence explain the identification of this period as Iran's 'era of warlords'. It was not until the end of the 18th century that one Agha Muhammad Khan (r. 1794–1797), a leader of another ancient Turkmen Qizilbash family of relatively successful Safavid service, the Qajar, succeeded in uniting the regions of Iran and Khurasan once again under his authority. His successor Fath 'Ali Khan (r. 1797–1834) then managed to repeat and consolidate his murdered uncle's short-lived Qajar achievement, and he did so once again by styling himself—in the post-Safavid fashion of Nadir Shah—Shah. Fath 'Ali Shah subsequently generated a renewed moment of Iranian dynastic formation under Turkmen Qajar leadership (1785–1925). Building their own dynastic constellation of people, practices, and resources after the Safavid model, Fath 'Ali Shah and his successors were successful in doing so not least in their introduction of a yet entirely new—and equally complex and daunting—chapter in the history of Iran. With the violent expansion of Qajar leadership across the ancient Safavid lands, therefore, the early modern period of Safavid stabilization and post-Safavid fragmentation and accommodation came to its end, and subsequent entirely alternative confrontations and relations, with different European powers and agents in particular, announced a radical departure from early modern dynastic realities.

2 Early modern Ottoman dynastic formation from Constantinople to Cairo

2.1 Dynastic formation in a changing Eurasian world

In the 17th and 18th centuries, the balances of power and interests on the extended landscape of Eurasian trans-regional leaderships witnessed radical transformations that did not just affect relationships of elites and resources between Azerbaijan and Khurasan in mutually constitutive ways. In Islamic West-Asia's western zone, similar changes of even more sustained stabilization, and even reinvention, affected the 'medieval' dynastic and highly charismatic apparatus of Ottoman dynastic power in equally transformative and mutually constitutive ways. A crucial vector of early modern dynastic transformation actually was the reality that the charismatic practices of continuous expansion and coercive dynastic formation gradually had to accommodate increasing practical, physical, and mental barriers to any continued investments in these practices. These barriers were related to the ever more successful integration of the Ottoman domains—at least as these were imagined by in- and outsider contemporaries, such as Machiavelli and his aforementioned statement (see Chapter 11) that the sultan's realm "is divided into sanjaks, to which he sends various administrators, whom he changes and moves as he pleases".[14] These emerging barriers were also related to the territorial stretch of the Ottoman domains, and the subsequent stabilization of its main frontier zones (see Chapter 11), in the regions of eastern Anatolia, the Jazira, Iraq, and the Persian Gulf and Red Sea in the Asian east; on the Adriatic coast, in the Hungarian lands bordering the Danube and in the vassal realms of the Transylvanian and Moldavian principalities and of the Crimean Khanate in the European north and northwest; and along the North African coast, between Tunis, Algiers, and Oran in the Mediterranean southwest. This stabilization did not end practices of conquest and realities of further expansions, which remained ongoing until the last quarter of the 17th century, and even persisted in other formats through the first half of the 18th century. As a result of these emerging barriers of distance from the center of Ottoman power, however, already from the later 16th century onwards, a significant slowing down was noticeable in the regularity as well as in the success rate with which these practices had been pursued during the preceding two centuries. Basically, the return on conquest investments, which had served the Ottoman dynasty so well since the 14th century—in charismatic as well as in territorial and, especially, economic terms—was less and less consistent. This invited for the adoption of alternative solutions to safeguard the Ottoman center's interests against internal and external rivals, to protect the interests of its clients, vassals, and allies, to continue to generate sufficient resources to pursue these ends, and to ensure the reproduction of dynastic and related central power relationships.

This slowing down—in modern Ottoman studies, also usefully identified as a 'change of pace' in Ottoman practices of warfare and realities of expansion—[15] manifested itself first and foremost in the organization of the Ottoman frontier zones in the Safavid east and the Habsburg west, and in their more direct integration in the apparatus of Ottoman dynastic power. In the west, Hungary was divided into a number of centrally administered Ottoman regional units (*eyalet*), the Ottoman vassal principalities of Upper Hungary and Transylvania, and the Habsburg region of the Kingdom of Hungary. The exact contours of these administratively divided territories, however, and of the various sovereignty claims over them, remained an issue of fierce competition with the Austrian Habsburg royal house. In this early modern period, this competition acquired, moreover, the unprecedented format of a state of war and confrontation that lasted for years and that mainly involved this frontier zone only. This was very different from the annual seasonal campaigns that until then used to depart from the Ottoman center. These always involved the deployment of central Ottoman forces, especially the Turkish *sipahi* cavalry, and very often were led by the Ottoman sultan himself, supported by the select infantry forces of his palace guards, including the Janissaries—a default practice almost epitomized by the aforementioned death of old age of sultan Suleiman in 1566 in his royal encampment during the siege of the rebellious Hungarian fortress of Szigetvár (see Chapter 11).

Before considering the total transformation of the Ottoman center and its dynastic chains of authority and agency effected by, and affecting, this change of pace in early modern Ottoman practices of warfare and trans-regional competition, particular moments in the latter new forms of competition will first be briefly reviewed here. These revolve especially around moments of marked intensification of trans-regional relationships and rivalries, to be situated loosely around the turn of the 16th to 17th centuries, around the turn of the 17th to 18th centuries, and in the middle of the latter century. These moments of intensification involved shifting frontier relationships with the Habsburg and European west, including in the Mediterranean, and also related transformations that occurred in the Asian east. The many shifts in trans-regional balances that they represented, furthermore, mostly materialized in a number of famous early modern truces and treaties that contributed to the re-creation and restabilization of some of the most central frontier zones of early modern Eurasian history. As suggested below, these settlements of often long-lasting and resource-intensive military operations and confrontations appear above all to confirm the gradual early modern loss of power, authority, and territories for the Ottoman Sultanate, and thus the narrative of decline that has, as mentioned above, pervaded analyses of Ottoman contemporaries as well as of modern observers ever since their conclusion. Nevertheless, the shifts that unmistakably occurred never did so uniformly across all of the Ottoman frontier zones, and the directions that they took were always multiform, often serving interests of particular groups within the complexity of central Ottoman leadership as much as those of outsiders and opponents. In many ways, one could argue that these early modern transformations also acted as accommodations to recurring confrontations with realities of Ottoman logistical overstretch, and that their main effects were not only destructive in Ottoman territorial terms, but also constitutive both for the sustained integration of multivalent relationships and resources of power around the Ottoman dynastic center and for that center's equally sustained successful claims to transcendent forms of Sunni Islamic sovereignty. The early modern Ottoman trans-regional configuration of power, authority, and resources was a very different one from before. However, even by the end of the 18th century, it was not necessarily less forceful and effective in the pursuance of the interests of its many dynastic and non-dynastic stakeholders, even in spite—or perhaps rather as an effect—of its territorial shrinkage and of its obvious loss of priority in the early modern hierarchy of great Eurasian powers.

The Ottoman-Habsburg 'Long War' (1593–1606) represents a first major moment of confrontation with the changing early modern format of trans-regional competition. This long, drawn-out frontier war was ended only by a laboriously negotiated treaty concluded in November 1606 in Zsitva Torok—situated in the Hungarian frontier zone on the Danube—and in which the Ottoman domination in Hungarian lands, including east of the Danube, was once again confirmed. Another shift occurred when, from the reign of Sultan Murad IV (r. 1623–1640) onwards, frontier zones in west and east further stabilized, and competition was at least for some time in the middle of the century mostly reduced to local frontier conflicts only. At that time, it seems that Ottoman attention was again directed towards the Mediterranean zone, where Ottoman forces made Venice withdraw from Crete in the long Cretan War (1645–1669), after which this island was made a directly administered Ottoman *eyalet*. Another zone of intense transregional interaction that simultaneously affected ever more Ottoman dynastic interests—as also happened in the Safavid context—concerned different sets of globalizing commercial networks, very often revolving around European-centered sets of actors and commodity flows. The port of Izmir in western Anatolia actually became an important commercial center. The vibrant trade market in this regional Ottoman center was even occasionally opened up for European connections. Especially English, French, Venetian, and Dutch traders (under the protection of so-called 'capitulations' and each represented with its own consulate in Izmir) traded here silver from the 'New World' for numerous local and other goods (including not least cotton) from the Asian continent.

In the last quarter of the 17th century, Ottoman central leadership again assumed a more aggressive stance, especially in its relations with the Austrian Habsburg royal house. Eventually, in 1683, this resulted in nothing less than a second siege of the Habsburg capital of Vienna, which failed. Unlike with the siege of Vienna in 1529, when adverse weather conditions reportedly were to blame, this time, Ottoman failure was mostly due to strategic errors of the commanders of the besieging Ottoman armies. This heralded another long war with European powers, in which a series of military defeats made the Ottoman dynastic center eventually lose control of the whole of its Hungarian lands. At long last, the Ottoman sultan was forced into a new peace treaty and made to accept conditions imposed by the Holy League of Habsburg, Poland-Lithuania, Venice, and Russia. This treaty of Karlowitz (26 January 1699) effectively ended Ottoman control over European regions north of the

Danube and Sava rivers, but importantly also confirmed Ottoman sovereignty in most of the Balkans, to the south of that natural boundary.

In subsequent years Habsburg military pressures in the Balkans persisted, and some further European territories were lost as a result of new defeats, including Belgrade on the Danube in 1718. In other cases of competition with European rivals, however, the opposite was true, and Ottoman successes were also achieved, as with the retaking of the Greek Peloponnesus. The collapse of Safavid sovereignty in 1722, furthermore, turned out to offer numerous new opportunities in the Asian east, which eventually also materialized in renewed expansions in the directions of the Caucasus and the Persian Gulf.

One of the most important major stakeholders in this mixed story of the 18th-century's ups and downs of Ottoman trans-regional power and authority was the Russian imperial leadership of Peter I the Great (r. 1682–1725) and especially of Katharina the Great (r. 1762–1796). This early modern great power in the making actually rivalled ever more forcefully with the Ottoman center for control over areas in eastern Europe, around the Black Sea, and in the Caucasus. The Russian empire became particularly active from the second half of the 18th century onwards, and in 1768, it even entered into a head-on confrontation with its Ottoman neighbors, which lasted for several years. This Russian-Ottoman war (1768–1774)—pursued on many different fronts, from the Crimea to the Mediterranean coasts of Anatolia

Figure 14.5 Painting representing the Ottoman siege of Vienna (Pierre-Denis Martin [1663–1742], 'The Battle of Vienna [1683]', Staatgalerie im Neuen Schloss, Schießheim)

Source: The Picture Art Collection/Alamy Stock Photo

and Syria—was begun by anti-Russian aggression of the Ottoman leadership itself, but soon demonstrated how that leadership underestimated the force and resources of Russian empress Katharina. Reportedly, the result was a success 'like Russia never achieved before' and considered by many a total humiliation for the Ottoman sultan and his associates. In the negotiations of the treaty that ended this war—concluded in 1774 at the Bulgarian place of Küçük Kaynarca—all European 'Great Powers' were involved (in addition to Russia also France, England, Austria, and Prussia) to consolidate the newly emerging but precarious trans-regional balance of interests. The conditions stipulated in this treaty represented a huge infringement of Ottoman territorial integrity and sovereignty, with lasting consequences for the configuration of Ottoman leadership and of its relations with European Great Powers throughout the long 19th century. Russia was ensured secure access to the Black Sea, through the once again autonomous Crimean Khanate (in 1783, however, the peninsula was permanently annexed by Russia), and free passage was to be granted to Russian merchants who wished to be active in the Ottoman lands and in the Mediterranean. Direct Russian interference in Ottoman affairs was further assured by the establishment of consulates and by the granting to Russia of responsibility for the well-being of the Orthodox Patriarchate of Constantinople, and thus of the large Orthodox Christian community in, especially, the European parts of the Ottoman territories.

Eventually the Ottoman domains were even more deeply involved in the turmoil that affected the balances of Europe's Great Powers at the turn of the 18th to 19th centuries, specifically when, in 1798, the French general (and future Emperor Napoleon) Bonaparte (r. 1799–1814, 1815, d. 1821) and his army landed in the Ottoman *eyalet* of Egypt and defeated its leadership. When the sultan's agents and armies only managed to respond to these entirely new French practices of conquest with British maritime assistance, new realities announced themselves. These would consist not least of expanding European impact on, and even involvement in, Ottoman relations of local, regional, and trans-regional power. A token of wider Eurasian reconfigurations of powers, these realities represented therefore radical departures from the balances that had made for the early modern period as discussed here.

2.2 Dynastic formation in a changing Ottoman World

One of the main consequences, and at the same time one of the main catalyzers, of the stabilization of Ottoman frontier zones and of the radical transformation of Ottoman realities of warfare since the later 16th century was the equally radical reconfiguration of the Ottoman dynastic and patrimonial apparatus and of its relationships of power and authority. Most importantly, this apparatus was now fully 'Ottomanized' and populated by ever more elites whose interests were directly tied up with those of the Ottoman dynastic center and were pursued in competitive contexts that proceeded along ever more centripetal Ottoman trajectories. This stabilization of Ottoman centrality—but not necessarily of balances of power within that centrality—manifested itself further in a renegotiation of the chains of agency and authority that connected the great varieties of local and regional elites and resources to that Ottoman center and its agents and representatives. Especially from the turn of the 17th to 18th century onwards, those chains of the Ottoman dynastic constellation experienced what has been usefully identified by modern Ottoman historian Suraiya Faroqhi as "a gradual 'loosening' of the structures which had seemed so much more solid in the second half of the sixteenth century".[16] A newly complex and highly devolved configuration of internal Ottoman trans-regional power relationships emerged. This transformed configuration consisted of an occasionally very abstract framework of dynastic sovereignty that allowed for the trans-regional diversity of center-periphery connections and for the occasionally extensive autonomy of certain local or regional elites to continue to be bound to, and by, shared imaginations of Ottoman order.

This early modern re-arrangement—even total renewal—of Ottoman leadership relationships in the dynastic center as well as in its many and diverse dynastic peripheries mainly resulted in a gradual marginalization of the power and authority of traditional Ottoman groups, who had originally been empowered, or integrated, through the 'medieval' practices of conquest and dynastic formation. These included first and foremost the, since many centuries, central martial personality of the Ottoman sultan himself, and eventually also other members of his dynastic household. Others who were similarly marginalized were the *sipahis*, the traditional Turkic-speaking elite of horsemen, whose leading members had already come under increasing pressure from the sultan's patrimonial agents from the turn of the 15th to 16th centuries onwards (see Chapter 11), and whose involvement in Ottoman leadership practices and rewards were further reduced in the course of the early modern period. This occurred especially when new practices of warfare and different valorizations of leadership empowered new groups and elites and substantially expanded the Ottoman apparatus of power. In the transforming and, especially, slowing down landscape of military action and expansion, the importance of professional infantry units to guard the ever more permanently defined frontiers grew substantially. This in turn increased the need for new mechanisms of resource accumulation to enable the recruitment and deployment of these standing army units, their engagement in protracted situations of frontier warfare, and the absorption via new sources of revenues of the absence of booty as well as of recurring realities of defeat. A central novelty in these new mechanisms appears to have been represented by a new group of tax farmers among, especially, the palace officials, who from the end of the 17th century onwards, also appropriated military and administrative responsibilities within the tax farms (*iltizam*) awarded to them—often for a lifetime (in which case a tax farm was called a *malikane*) and sometimes even in a hereditary fashion. In such areas, spread all over the Balkans, Anatolia, and the Arabian lands, the implementation of new tax farming arrangements usually occurred at the expense of traditional military leaders, such as the *sipahis* and the *sanjaq beys*, and their revenues from *timar* arrangements. These new arrangements in dynastic—or *miri*—lands originally apportioned as *timar* to *sipahi*s and *bey*s in return for active participation in practices of conquest also meant that any further direct involvement of the sultan's agents in these areas was reduced to a minimum. As a result, these tax farming arrangements—which were sold to the highest bidder in regular auctions and arranged for advance payments by tax farmers to the central or provincial treasuries, and thus, at least in theory, secured sufficient funds for the treasury to pay for the standing infantry army—contributed to the aforementioned relative loosening of patrimonial arrangements in many Ottoman territories, or in this case also the addition of new layers of leadership arrangements over and against traditional ones.[17]

2.2.1 Ottomanization and bureaucratic-patrimonial formation in the dynastic center

At the center of Ottoman power, it was above all a patrimonial-bureaucratic stabilization in the Ottoman apparatus of power and authority that made that most sultans who ascended the throne in the 17th and 18th centuries needed to consider the contested interests and agencies of ever more layers of dynastic agents and representatives at or near the different courts of the palace complex in Constantinople. Such increasingly autonomous and powerful appearances of different interest groups in the extremely complex Ottoman power apparatus in the dynastic center manifested itself, in the first place, in the growing centrality of the sultan's household members and agents. In due course, however, not just Ottoman household members, but all kinds of court agents and representatives, each defending the interests of their own households, entourages, and networks of supporters and resources, became the main agents of Ottoman leadership. In these shifts of the Ottoman locus of power from the Ottoman household to the court at large, new practices of collective patrimonial-bureaucratic leadership under an Ottoman dynastic umbrella gradually emerged.

This new collective leadership involved especially—in direct contrast with conquest oriented 'medieval' social realities, dominant into the 16th century—the rise to Ottoman central prominence of non-military leaders from the ever more complex administrative hierarchy of Ottoman agents, agencies, and authorities. This manifested itself also in the gradual marginalization of the sultan's personal 'servants of the Porte' and in the slow disappearance from the early 17th century onwards of the child levy practice of the *devshirme*. Instead, in the course of the 17th century, the ever expanding ranks of court servants—numbering no less than 1,000 *Kalemiye* employees just in the court bureaus responsible for revenue management and communication during most of the 17th and 18th centuries—came from an equally ever greater variety of origins. New specialists of court service were introduced via other powerful courtiers who acted as patrons and increasingly powerful brokers of court resources, and who as such began to construct their own households of relatives, unfree servants, clients, and allies as true breeding grounds for courtship and for courtly competition with peers and rivals.

Another intrinsic component of this patrimonial-bureaucratic shift in the Ottoman apparatus of power was the emergence of a more clearly circumscribed, structured, and hierarchal organization of Sunni Islamic law and jurisprudence, education, and knowledge practices, and of religious and spiritual experience, within a normative framework that was identified as both an Ottoman dynastic and a Sunni orthodox order. Diversity (including in regions with a predominantly Christian population) and heterogeneous ambiguity certainly persevered, but the centering impact of this integration of Sunni Islamic infrastructures and authorities of normativity into the Ottoman apparatus, and of the growing participation of its *ulema* as courtly brokers and grandees in their own right, became at least as striking. An important initial role in this process was reserved for the aforementioned Ottoman jurist Ebu l-Suʿud (*c.* 1490–1574) (see Chapter 13). During his long career in the Ottoman legal apparatus, he ultimately became a chief justice (*kadi ʿasker*) (1537–1545) and subsequently grand mufti of Istanbul (1545–1574). His scholarly authority and long tenure as grand mufti paved the way for this position to become equated with that of *shaykh ül Islam* at the head of the equally rapidly expanding so-called *ʿilmiyye* hierarchy of Sunni Islamic scholarship, learning and justice.

The sultan himself became at best only one of the participants in this contested Ottoman collective leadership. This manifested itself especially in the remarkable stabilization in succession practices. In fact, the aforementioned violent practices of internecine warfare and fratricide (see Chapter 11) gave way, from the early 17th century onwards, to the fully pacified practice of succession by the oldest male member of the royal family (*ekberiyet*). From 1617 onwards, therefore, and the death of Sultan Ahmed I (r. 1603–1617), brothers, or even uncles, succeeded a deceased sultan. From the early 1620s onwards, furthermore, the related 'gilded cage' practice (*kafes*) entered the palace. According to this practice, Ottoman male relatives were allowed to stay alive upon the succession of one of them, but they were, at the same time, forced to bide their time in the secluded palace grounds of the harem, without any right to father children. Ottoman sultans who all emerged from this 'gilded cage' of the harem became thus ever less well prepared, connected, and empowered characters at the wider palace courts. At the same time, however, their role continued to be considered of primordial importance for supporting the apparatus' and its agents' claims to continued sovereignty and trans-regional authority and for commanding related relationships of loyalty and obligation, which continued to bound the complex and diversely constructed trans-regional whole to the sultan's Ottoman dynastic charisma. One of the most important research essays of the recent decades that considered this transformation, Abou-el-Haj's *Formation of the Modern State*, aptly summarized this total reconfiguration of the early modern Ottoman constellation of leadership as follows:

> Seventeenth century Ottoman rulers ruled in only a limited sense; their presence was necessary so that bureaucratic commands could be appropriately legitimised. Mehmed IV (1648–1687) for example, was a child during a considerable part of his reign, yet the state apparatus functioned adequately without him. The sultans of the seventeenth century did participate in politics, and a major political mistake could and occasionally did, cost them their throne. But basically, the Empire was governed by bureaucrats who were based in the palace or the grand vezir's office, and the major officeholders used their households as a means for the recruitment and training of new personnel.[18]

The Ottoman dynasty itself, therefore, transformed as it were into an abstract as well as highly stable infrastructure of sovereignty. It mediated relationships of different sets of leadership and resources, and empowered those who best managed to manipulate, or at least to negotiate, the arrangements and mechanisms that performed Ottoman power in the dynastic center of the court as well as beyond that center, among the many and diverse networks of dynastic agents, tax farmers, autonomous elites, and their like in the many Ottoman peripheries. The unstable balances of power that thus arose within this strongly Ottomanized patrimonial-bureaucratic leadership of administrators, household members, and court servants, and their many entourages, actually display remarkably coherent shifts in the main locus of the dynastic performance of Ottoman power. These alternative manifestations of the stabilization of Ottoman patrimonial-bureaucratic leadership actually make it possible to add more nuance to the long narrative of that Ottoman collective leadership in the 17th and 18th centuries.

As a follow-up to the aforementioned achievements of the Ottoman concubine spouses and queen mothers of the 16th century (see Chapters 11 and 13), the first half of the 17th century was characterized by the even greater power and autonomous centrality of the *valide sultan*. One of the most notorious and powerful of these early modern Ottoman harem women was undoubtedly Kösem Sultan (*c.* 1589–1651), a concubine of Greek origin, favorite partner and later wife of Sultan Ahmed I (r. 1603–1617), mother of Murad IV (r. 1623–1640) and Ibrahim I (r. 1640–1648), and grandmother of Sultan Mehmed IV (r. 1648–87). She officially acted as a regent for her underage son Murad, and later again for Mehmed. Her eventual murder in the Ottoman harem allegedly happened on the orders of Mehmed's own mother, Turhan Hatice Sultan (1627–1683), reportedly when rumors about the imminent enthronement of another one of Kösem's grandsons began to circulate in the harem. Turhan Hatice Sultan then took over the role of regent for her underage son, and reportedly continued to rule in his name until her death, even after he reached the age of majority.

The stability and relative prosperity of the mid-17th-century reign of sultan Mehmed IV was, however, mainly due to the fact that mother and son left the performance of Ottoman central power and authority largely to their grand vizier Köprülü Mehmed Pasha (r. 1656–1661)

Figure 14.6 Portrait of Kösem Sultan and one of her sons (sultan Murad IV or sultan Ibrahim) (unknown artist, Austrian School, second half of 17th century)

Source: Private Collection/Photo © Christie's Images/Bridgeman Images

and the members of his Köprülü family. This family of Albanian origins, introduced to the court through the *devshirme* tributary collection mechanism, which had condemned the young Mehmed to the loss of his freedom but also to strongly Ottomanized court service, provided a total of six grand viziers and several other senior court and military officials. Among other things, members of this Köprülü family achieved the widest territorial expansion that the Ottoman dynastic formation ever reached through the conquest of Podolia in 1676 and Crete in 1669. Mehmed's stepson and son-in-law Kara Mustafa Pasha, grand vizier from 1676 to 1683, eventually commanded the failed siege of Vienna (where he also died) in 1683. A revolt of Janissaries in 1703, ending in the deposition of Sultan Mustafa II (r. 1695–1703), ultimately meant the end of the enormous power of the Köprülü family in the service of the Ottoman dynasty and, at the same time, of their own Ottoman viziral dynasty.

After the fall from central Ottoman power of the Köprülü family, different viziers and pashas, each with their own households, and occasionally also the sultan himself, acquired centrality in the course of the 18th century. One of the most successful sultans in this period was undoubtedly Sultan Ahmed III (r. 1703–1730). Due especially to the actions of his son-in-law and grand vizier, Nevshehirli Ibrahim Pasha (*c.* 1662–1730), the latter part of the reign of Ahmed III is identified with the so-called Tulip period (1718–1730). This is a term used to refer to a particular period of exceptional artistic and cultural production for, and consumption by, the Ottoman elites. The shared sense of taste as well as the enormous investments of resources that this culture of splendor, lavish patronage, and courtly distinction stimulated—epitomized by the highly appreciated but rare and therefore extremely expensive tulip flower—integrated the Ottoman palace elites strongly into the redistributive mechanisms of wealth and authority that revolved around the sultan and around his grand vizier.

2.2.2 Ottomanization and 'autonomization' from Bagdad to Cairo

In the Ottoman regions that were further removed from the center of dynastic authority, the early modern reconfiguration of power relationships manifested itself in often highly maximized manifestations of the aforementioned gradual loosening of Ottoman patrimonial arrangements. More specifically, in these peripheries, this loosening occurred above all in the creation, or at least reconfiguration, of parallel layers of leadership arrangements. Much as in the center of Ottoman leadership, these new arrangements and their actors were actually added to, mostly in overlapping and intersecting ways, Ottoman *eyalet* arrangements. Between the later 16th and early 17th century, the Ottoman territories had been divided into more uniformly organized and more directly administered units, called *eyalet*s. Their number rose steadily to no less than thirty-two in the early 17th century, including Abyssinia and Yemen around the Red Sea; Adana, Maraş, Erzurum, Van, Diyarbakir, Trebizond, and Sivas in Anatolia; Sharazor, Mosul, al-Raqqa, Aleppo, Tripoli, Syria, Bagdad, Basra, and Egypt; and Algiers, Tunis, and Tripolitania in North Africa. These *eyalets* were administered in the sultan's name by Ottoman military officials with the high court rank of *pasha*, with extensive military and administrative powers and responsibilities. These pashas, as well as various *qadi*s, Janissaries, and many similar Ottoman agents used to be sent from the court in Constantinople to these *eyalet*s to negotiate, if not enforce, locally the Ottoman sultan's interests.

In the course of the 17th century, however, this patrimonial integration and circulation of dynastic agents and resources around the Ottoman center of gravity shifted from collecting resources and men for conquests and for punitive expeditions to maximizing revenue for maintaining integration, funding frontier warfare, and securing elite reproduction. In this early modern process of transformation, the intensity of this circulation and of these flows of people and resources slowed down substantially. As the modern historian of Ottoman Egypt, Jane Hathaway, summarily explained:

> The Ottoman Empire's shift from a military conquest state to a bureaucratic, revenue-collecting state in the course of the seventeenth century was characterized by the localization of the empire's servants in the provinces.[19]

Even when this 'localization' occurred, however, including in more distanced regions, the subsequent prioritization of local or regional layers of leadership arrangements continued to coincide—again much as in the center of Ottoman leadership—with some, even if only highly symbolic and titular, forms of relevance for the infrastructure of Ottoman dynastic sovereignty. This often highly symbolic and particularly imagined infrastructure, represented above all by bureaucratic forms and meanings that appear as residual abstractions of loosening local patrimonial arrangements, continued to mediate particular relationships of locally or regionally constructed leadership, enhancing their status, aura, or even access to resources vis-à-vis any local or regional rivals or competitors. This particular kind of Ottoman stabilization of many center-periphery relationships, in fact, resulted in the 18th century in particular in the substantial 'autonomization', or even new emergence, of powerful and varied local and regional elite groups. These basically consisted of centrally appointed local or regional administrators and their entourages, agents, and supporters, many of whom shared local roots; local notables and leaders who rose to prominence mostly by their own actions and in contexts of leadership that were not related to Ottoman infrastructures of power; and military leaders of *mamluk*, mostly Caucasian, origins, who actually in many ways had come—or continued—to play roles similar to the latter group of local leaders in the regions of, especially, Bagdad, Mosul, and Egypt. "Whole sections of the empire fell under the political domination of provincial notable families", modern historian Donald Quataert summarized, continuing with a brief survey of 18th-century Ottoman leaderships beyond the dynastic center:

> For example, the families of the Karaosmanoğlu, Çapanoğlu, and Canıklı Ali Paşaoğlu respectively dominated the economic and political affairs of west, central, and north-east Anatolia; in the Balkan lands, Ali Pasha of Janina ruled Epirus, while Osman Pasvanoğlu of Vidin controlled the lower Danube from Belgrade to the Sea. And, in the Arab provinces, the family of Süleyman the Great ruled Baghdad for the entire eighteenth century (1704–1831) as did the Jalili family in Mosul, while powerful men such as Ali Bey dominated Egypt.[20]

Some more detailed examples will be presented below of these three types of centrally appointed administrators, local leaderships, and *mamluk* commanders for the regions of North Africa, Syria, and Egypt in particular. In each of these regions, these different types of novel leaderships managed to newly negotiate, or renegotiate, the exact extent and nature of their 'Ottoman-ness', and of their bonds of loyalty and benefit with the sovereign Ottoman order that continued to emanate from the dynastic infrastructures in Constantinople.

In each of North Africa's main Ottoman urban centers of Algiers, Tunis, and Tripoli, new power groups developed from the amalgam of diverse local urban elites and the leaders and descendants of, especially, regiments of 'Islamized', 'Turkified', and 'Ottomanized' Janissaries that, since the later 16th century, had been stationed in these regions to represent, and if necessary, locally enforce Ottoman centralizing interests. From the later 17th century onwards, in particular, different groups of local urban leaderships emerged almost simultaneously in each of these North African centers. They acquired such a large degree of autonomy that the relationship with Constantinople was eventually everywhere reduced to Ottoman titles and the mere payment of a (often very limited) annual tribute from local revenues, as fictional tokens of continued Ottoman sovereignty. Algiers thus came to be ruled by different sets of local leaders, styled as Ottoman *deys* (1689–1830), but actually appearing especially as representatives of local elite groups and power balances, who were every time again elected for life by the local military, administrative, and religious leaderships of Algiers and its hinterlands. In Tunis, a similarly Ottoman-styled *bey* (clearly formally distinguished from the *dey* of Algiers) was in power, but here this position continued to be monopolized by one dynastic lineage. These were the long-reigning Husaynids (1705–1956), the descendants of the Tunisian *bey* Husayn ibn ʿAli (r. 1705–1735) who was, in fact, the son of one ʿAli al-Turki, a 'Turkified' Ottoman Janissary of Greek Cretan birth. In Tripoli, another newly constructed Ottoman-local dynasty similarly retained autonomous Ottoman power until the first decades of the 19th century. This was the Karamanli dynasty (1711–1835) of Tripoli, who had risen to local prominence with the violent takeover of leadership by one Ahmed Karamanli (r. 1711–1745), an Ottoman military *sipahi* commander and *pasha*, who himself was a descendant of the 'medieval' South Anatolian *beylik* of the Turkmen Karamanids of Konya.

In Syria, things changed somewhat differently, and ties with the Ottoman center remained somewhat stronger and real. In many parts of this region, prominent families of mainly local landowners succeeded in transforming into dynasties of successful Ottoman administrators. They continuously presented themselves as loyal and subordinate to Ottoman leadership, but at the same time, also strived for the greatest possible autonomy within this more direct presence of the Ottoman order of sovereignty. Damascus and its hinterlands were thus dominated

Figure 14.7 Portrait of the *dey* of Algiers. By G. M. Brighty—G. A. Jackson, *Algiers—Being a complete picture of the Barbary States*, London 1817

Source: Public Domain, https://commons.wikimedia.org/w/index.php?curid=37180724

Figure 14.8 Damascus: palace of the ʿAzm family (1750), constructed by Asʿad Pasha al-ʿAzm, Ottoman *pasha* of Damascus

Source: Photo by K.A.C. Creswell. Creswell Archive, Ashmolean Museum, University of Oxford, neg. EA.CA.5619

by the Arabian ʿAzm family, with various members acting in the course of the 18th century as Ottoman *pashas* and local administrators in various Syrian localities. This happened for the area of Damascus itself (1725–1783) (including during the term of office of Asʿad Pasha al-ʿAzm, r. 1743–1757), but also in other *eyalets* of the region (Sidon, Tripoli, Hama, and Aleppo).

Yet another story was that of Ottoman bonds with the Syro-Palestinian area that stretched between Tiberias, Galilee, and Acre, which were completely severed in the course of the 18th century, and eventually only restored with direct and violent Ottoman interference. From the 1730s onwards, a local Arabian chief, Zahir Al ʿUmar (*c.* 1690–1775), and his Zaydani allies, supporters, and followers were able to extend and develop their local leadership completely autonomously from any Ottoman connection. Zahir Al ʿUmar was supported in this long-lasting endeavor of local empowerment by rich revenues generated from commercial activities (particularly trade in cotton and olive oil) in the ports of Acre and Haifa, and eventually, in the 1770s, managed to violently extend his authority along the wider Syro-Palestinian coast to Beirut in the north and to Gaza in the south. Only in 1775, Ottoman armed forces were able to restore the local Ottoman order by the siege and capture of Acre, at which occasion Zahir Al ʿUmar himself was killed.

Zahir Al ʿUmar's mid-18th-century territorial successes were in no small part due to the support he had received from his peer and ally in Egypt ʿAli Bey al-Kabir (*c.* 1728–1773), allegedly also known as a result of his boundless ambition as, in Arabic, 'ʿAli the Devil' (*Jinn ʿAli*) and, in Turkic, 'the Cloud-Catcher' (*Bulut Kapan*). This ʿAli was a *mamluk* of Georgian origins, offered as a gift to one of Egypt's leading figures in the early 1740s, and then made a career of military service until he rose to the status of *sancak bey*, or tax farmer in this particular Egyptian context. At that time, Ottoman-styled military officials and *beys*, often just as ʿAli Bey of *mamluk* or *mamluk*-related origins, dominated the highly competitive Egyptian landscape of power and resources with extended military households of mixed Ottoman-Egyptian origins. These competing households were deeply entangled with the ranks of local Janissary and similar regiments and resources of Ottoman making, and reproduced across diverse *mamluk* and kin relationships. Most central and powerful of these complex households until the later 18th century was that of the Qazdughli, whose *beys* or *amirs* became some of the most important supporters and eventually also opponents of ʿAli Bey. In 1760, he acquired with Qazdughli support the position of *shaykh al-balad*, administrator of the urban center of Cairo and senior of all the *beys* in the Ottoman *eyalet* of Egypt. Thereupon, ʿAli Bey embarked upon his own career of household building and violent confrontation with rivals, including Egyptian *beys* as well as Ottoman agents, especially the senior Ottoman administrator of Egypt, the *pasha*. In 1768, he managed to depose the Ottoman *pasha* and to take his place as a local sovereign substitute (*qa'im-maqam*), and eventually declared himself autonomous of Constantinople, refusing to send any of the annual Egyptian tribute to Constantinople.

From 1770 onwards, ʿAli Bey al-Kabir also became active beyond the Ottoman boundaries of the *eyalet* of Egypt in the Hejaz and the Red Sea and also in Syria. In these contexts, he is seen to have started to explore the very margins of his tenuous relationship with the Ottoman center, styling himself 'Sultan of Egypt' (*Sultan Misr*) and 'Commander of the Two Seas' (*Amir al-Bahrayn*), setting up direct commercial relationships with European powers in the Red Sea, and minting coins with competing references to his and the Ottoman sultan's sovereignty. One contemporary historian actually even claims that ʿAli Bey read all about the Cairo Sultanate that preceded the Ottoman presence in Egypt and was keen to restore it, through his leadership, to its former glory. The latter context is often provoked to explain why he eventually started, together with the aforementioned Zahir Al ʿUmar, a campaign of conquest of southern Syria, even though—as with the Hejaz—the commercially strategic control of the 'Two Seas', the eastern Mediterranean and Red Sea, may also have been an important issue. In the course of this at first highly successful campaign, however, ʿAli Bey was confronted with resistance among his own military leaders. As a result, he was overturned, had to flee to Zahir Al ʿUmar in Syria, and was eventually mortally wounded in a confrontation with his former allies of the Qazdughli household. He eventually died in Cairo in early May 1773, and was succeeded by the the leaders of the latter household. This involved the installation of a new Ottoman *pasha* in Cairo's Citadel of the Mountain, but actual power and leadership—especially represented by the position of *shaykh al-balad*—as well as control over Egypt's resources remained mainly contested between Qazdughli *beys* of Georgian *mamluk* origins.

Most prominent among these *beys*, from 1775 onwards, were *shaykh al-balad* Ibrahim Bey (1735–1816) and his associate and competitor Murad Bey (d. 1801). Murad Bey actually soon followed in ʿAli Bey al-Kabir's footsteps and attempted with mixed successes to severe as many ties as possible with Constantinople. Despite repeated attempts to increase Ottoman interference in Egypt, for most of the period between the mid-1770s and the French invasion of 1798, Ibrahim and Murad Bey and their competing entourages continued to represent the dominant force in the region. They at the most tolerated a symbolic Ottoman presence in the form of powerless *pasha*s sent by Constantinople. They are especially remembered for depleting Egypt's resources, allegedly in the interests of their household rivalries, in retaliation for Ottoman attempts to join forces with opponent Qazdughli *bey*s and various other urban groups and merchant communities, and even in association with—through the regularly reactivated Georgian connection of their *mamluk* origins—Ottoman's main adversary at the time, Russia. At least as impactful for the remarkably negative spiral of violence and death that is recorded to have marked the 1790s in Egypt's history, and that is said to have generated another moment of substantial depopulation and shrinkage, are a series of very short cycles of plague, epidemics, and famine, to which eventually, in 1801, also Murad Bey succumbed. At that time, however, he, Ibrahim and their followers had been chased from Cairo by the French forces of Bonaparte.

In fact, the particularly bad press that Murad, Ibrahim, and other 18th-century Egyptian *bey*s have tended to receive may be as much due to their tense relationship with the Ottoman center and to the more general adverse socioeconomic conditions of the later 18th century as to how their defeat and the French victories in Egypt, culminating in July 1798 in the so-called 'Battle of the Pyramids', was framed. They received this bad press in both Ottoman and Egyptian later renderings of these events as well as in contemporaneous French

Figure 14.9 Portrait of Murad Bey (d. 1801) by A. Dutertre (1753–1842) in *Description de l'Égypte*, 1809

Source: Heritage Image Partnership Ltd/Alamy Stock Photo

declarations, statements, and correspondence aiming to support Bonaparte's campaign of Egyptian conquest. Upon his arrival in the Egyptian port of Alexandria, Bonaparte actually issued the following famous statement, defining for the future the particular—later identified as 'orientalizing'—imagination of both Egypt's early modern history and the French imperial mission:

> Bonaparte, member of the National Institute, General-in-chief:
> For a long time, the Sanjak [Beys] governing Egypt have insulted the French nation and its traders. The hour of their punishment has come.
> For too long, this assortment of slaves bought in Georgia and the Caucasus has tyrannized the most beautiful part of the world; but God, on whom all depends, has ordained that their empire is finished.
> People of Egypt, you will be told that I have come to destroy your religion; do not believe it! Reply that I have come to restore your rights, to punish the usurpers, and that more than the Mamluks I respect God, his Prophet, and the Quran. . . . Of old, there used to exist here, in your midst, big cities, big canals, a thriving commerce. What has destroyed all this, but Mamluk avarice, injustice and tyranny?
> . . . Have we not been for centuries the friends of the Grand Seigneur (may God fulfill his wishes!) and the enemies of his enemies? Have not the Mamluks, on the contrary, always revolted against the authority of the Grand Seigneur, whom they still ignore? They do not but satisfy their own whims.
> Thrice happy are those who join us! . . . But unhappiness, threefold unhappiness, to those who arm themselves for the Mamluks and fight against us! There shall be no hope for them; they shall all perish.[21]

The ranks of Egyptian leaderships were violently shaken and totally reconfigured due to this sudden and entirely unfamiliar interference from external agents and practices of conquest. As a result, entirely new realities announced themselves in the landscapes of power and resource management of Egypt, of its adjacent regions, and of the wider—now substantially challenged—early modern order of Ottoman theocratic sovereignty. As announced in strongly propagandistic terms in Bonaparte's 'proclamation to the Egyptians', these new realities were bound to include particular, negative imaginations of these regions' past leaderships, as well as related, powerful 'orientalizing' discourses of decline and the need for European salvation and nation building. In many ways, therefore, Bonaparte's claims and campaigns not only illustrate how Egyptian leadership arrangements and a sovereign Ottoman dynastic order had found particular and variously contested early modern balances. They also represent an unwarranted intrusion on those balances, on their many actors, and on their endless, often violent, Egyptian and occasionally even Syrian negotiations. These impactful and destabilizing infringements from outside upon local and regional arrangements as well as on widely shared Ottoman notions of theocratic sovereignty, therefore, introduced no less than the coming of radical departures from Islamic West-Asia's early modern period.

2.3 Ottomanization, stabilization, and a preview of the challenges of modernity

Just as these diversely operating local and regional Ottoman rulers, from the *dey* of Algiers to the *pasha*s of Aleppo, Mosul, and Bagdad, the extremely diverse landscape of people and groups active, on the eve of the 19th century, in the center or in the many peripheries of the Ottoman sovereign order actually continued to be characterized by striking degrees of not only variety and heterogeneity, but also autonomy within a shared order of Ottomanized stability. In this whole of diverse relationships and multiple identities, the flux and fluidity of the 'medieval' period had, by the 18th century, been exchanged, as it were, for a much higher degree of structuration, less permeable boundaries of 'otherness', and more explicit discursive hierarchies that distinguished narratives from their counter-narratives. Modern scholarship has stressed, in a more generalizing fashion, how various local and regional groups and their leaderships and resources actually lived side by side as though in a mosaic of highly diverse and self-regulating communities, with wider social interactions or social mobility beyond the well-defined boundaries of one's own milieu or environment being practiced in very particular and organized ways. Especially the leaders, representatives, and spokesmen of these diverse groups and discursive positions—mostly identified as the notables (*aʿyan*) of the villages, urban neighborhoods, professional associations, Sufi brotherhoods, law school and other religious communities, and other types of social movements in the many Ottoman regions of West-Asia and North Africa—defined the local or regional configuration of symbiotic and competitive leadership arrangements, resource distribution, and authority claims, including through negotiations with the households and courts of local or regional rulers and with agents of the Ottoman theocratic order. In this particular context, the Ottoman sultan, or rather his representatives, had become no more than just one of the many actors that were involved with the course of local events. Across the realm, they were so in a wide variety of ways, and sometimes even—as also suggested by some of the regional cases mentioned above—in extremely minimalist capacities. Continually, these representatives had to negotiate—occasionally with the backing of physical or symbolic violence, usually through strategies of diplomacy—the degree of Ottoman involvement with the wide range of *aʿyan*, even despite the fact that, as a principle, that involvement itself was never really questioned, nor was the overall framework of Ottoman and Islamic theocratic sovereignty. A strong metaphor that was formulated some decades ago in modern historical research to interpret the complex reality of this specific and multi-dimensional 18th-century Ottoman sovereign order is that of an Ottomanized line-up of different blocks of flats. In each of these blocks, variously defined and constituted social groups, including the Ottoman dynastic center's local agents, occupied different flats of varying sizes and facilities as autonomous living units and they only met each other in the block's corridors via the agency of their leaders, representatives, and *aʿyan* notables. Only the latter negotiated, in these corridors, the continuously changing ways in which these flats and their different constituents and resources interacted with each other and with the symbolic guardians of the entire block, the Sunni Muslim judges and scholars of the Ottoman *ʿilmiyye*. At the same time, the latter contributed substantially to the Ottomanized discursive imagination of the whole block and wider line-up as directly related to a stabilized normative theocratic order that was emanating from the Ottoman palace in Constantinople. One modern historian aptly evokes this image in the following insightful way:

> The Muslim ideal of a stable society, based on justice and composed of the four classical pillars—bureaucrats, soldiers, merchants and artisans, and peasants—bore little relation to the reality of Near Eastern society in 1800. Near Eastern society has been described as a block of flats in which the inhabitants met only in the corridors. It is right to emphasize the compartmentalised nature of the society but it is important also to understand the significance of the traffic in the corridors. Each compartment had its hierarchy and the leaders of those hierarchies transacted much business together. It was the people who bridged the compartments, *qāḍīs* and notables, who made the system work.[22]

In the 21st century, Islamic West-Asia and the Middle East more in particular are characterized by various sets of dynastic and non-dynastic leaderships, wide-ranging configurations of people and resources, and many conflicting imaginations of sovereignty and belonging that appear, just as elsewhere in the contemporary world, as entirely disconnected from the Ottoman or post-Safavid worlds of the end of the 18th century. The dynamics of change that brought about this third complete transformation—after the late antique Arabian and the 'medieval' Inner-Asian ones—of West-Asia's ancient landscapes of power, elites, and arrangements of leadership and resource distribution was the consequence of another set of destabilizing processes of conquest and infiltration, and of both globalizing and localizing transformations in the wake thereof. This was as disruptive a set of processes as those of the late antique and 'medieval' ones were. In an oversimplifying way, one could argue that in many regions of Islamic West-Asia and North Africa, the creative as well as destructive forces of this third set of disruptions continue to be in a contested state of flux and of competitive recalibrations between winners, losers, and their intermediaries. As in preceding centuries, in many contexts, such disruptive processes have also continued to result in varying reactions of accommodation, manipulation, and resistance. Until today, the more extreme trends among the latter forms of resistance, in particular, often continue to be fed by traditional as well as modern variants of the eschatological, millenarian, and messianic ideas that similarly motivated many moments of late antique or 'medieval' militant action, and they continue to do so in equally horrifying variations of violence wielding, utter destruction, and counter-narratives of salvation. Simultaneously, the long-term effects of modern dynamics of accommodation or manipulation—in the form of processes of industrialization, urbanization, secularization, constitutionalization, globalization, neo-liberalization, or even disambiguation and related aspects of (post-)modernization—have not necessarily proven more constructive for many inhabitants of these regions, and equally instrumental narratives of progress, westernization, nationalization, democratization, or islamization have certainly not resulted in any more stabilization or, for that matter, salvation.

Overall, these and all kinds of related current unbalances and predicaments are part and parcel of a thoroughly modern and globally connected world of actors, agencies, and authorities that cannot, and should not, be reduced to any premodern West-Asian roots. They deserve to be understood by themselves as another 'Khaldunian' wave of power dynamics and relational transformations. Nevertheless, updated general understandings of late antique and 'medieval'-early modern West-Asian transformations as enormously complex as well as highly interconnected, and more in general of Ibn Khaldun's waves of disruption and gradual stabilization as iterative, if not cyclical, may offer refreshing perspectives on many more patterns of constructive and creative interaction in these regions' histories of leaderships and identities than generally tends to be acknowledged. Understandings such as those presented in this book may at least offer some more valid points of reference for appreciations of the disruptive impacts of modern and contemporary transformations, by identifying these points as not simply precursors of modernity, but as creative solutions to substantial challenges to leadership configurations, practices of power, and discourses of belonging in their own right.

Notes

1 See Tezcan, *The Second Ottoman Empire. Political and Social Transformation in the Early Modern World.*

2 Many parallel adaptations of these early modern chronological boundaries abound, confirming above all their malleability and permeability, depending on context and perspective; for a slightly

more conservative adaptation in, above all, an equally valuable and valid opposite 'medieval' direction favoring the prehistory of the 1450s by "arguing that the 'early modern' in Eurasia and Africa at least . . . would extend from the middle of the fourteenth to the middle of the eighteenth century, with a relatively greater emphasis on the period after about 1450" (p. 736), see Subrahmanyam, "Connected Histories: Notes towards a Reconfiguration of Early Modern Eurasia".

3 See Hodgson, *The Venture of Islam. Vol. 3 The Gunpowder Empires and Modern Times.*

4 See Blake, "The Patrimonial-Bureaucratic Empire of the Mughals", 82; the model was repeated, extended, and revised more recently in Blake, "Returning the Household to the Patrimonial-Bureaucratic Empire: Gender, Succession, and Ritual in the Mughal, Safavid and Ottoman Empires".

5 See Foran, "The Long Fall of the Safavid Dynasty: Moving Beyond the Standard Views"; especially Lockhart, *The Fall of the Safavi Dynasty.*

6 Matthee, *Persia in Crisis: Safavid Decline and The Fall of Isfahan*, xviii; referring – so it is explained by Matthee elsewhere – to "an imperialist mindset" and "the verdict of Westerners visiting Iran after the fall of the Safavids" (Matthee, "A Comment on Kioumars Ghereghlou's Review of R. Matthee, *Persia in Crisis*", 426).

7 Quataert, "Ottoman History Writing and Changing Attitudes towards the Notion of 'Decline'", 1–2.

8 See Tezcan, *The Second Ottoman Empire. Political and Social Transformation in the Early Modern World.*

9 Quataert, "Ottoman History Writing and Changing Attitudes towards the Notion of 'Decline'", 4–5.

10 Matthee, *Persia in Crisis: Safavid Decline and The Fall of Isfahan*, xxviii–xxix.

11 Iskandar Beg Munshi (*c.* 1560–1633), *Tarikh-i alam ara-yi Abbasi* ['The World Illuminating History of [Shah] ʿAbbas']; translation from Babaie et al., *Slaves of the Shah. New Elites of Safavid Iran*, 31.

12 Jean Chardin (1643–1713), *Journal du voyage du Chevalier Chardin en Perse & aux Indes Orientales, par la Mer Noire & par la Colchide*; translation from Babaie et al., *Slaves of the Shah. New Elites of Safavid Iran*, 44.

13 Matthee, *Persia in Crisis: Safavid Decline and The Fall of Isfahan*, xxiii–xxiv.

14 Niccolò Machiavelli (1469–1527), *Il Principe* ['The Prince']; translation from Skinner, Price, *The Prince*, 15.

15 See Faroqhi, *The Ottoman Empire and the World Around It.*

16 See Faroqhi, *The Ottoman Empire and the World Around It.*

17 See Barkey, "The Ottoman Empire (1299–1923): The Bureaucratization of Patrimonial Authority".

18 Abou-el-Haj, *The Formation of the Modern State. The Ottoman Empire, Sixteenth to Eighteenth Centuries.*

19 Hathaway, *The Politics of Households in Ottoman Egypt: The Rise of the Qazdağlıs*, 14.

20 Quataert, *The Ottoman Empire. 1700–1922*, 46.

21 "Napoleon's Proclamation to the Egyptians. 2 July 1798"; translation from the French text in Napoleon I, *Correspondance*, 4: 191–2.

22 Yapp, *The Making of the Modern Near East. 1792–1923*, 9–10.

Selected readings

Abou-el-Haj, R.A. *The Formation of the Modern State: The Ottoman Empire, Sixteenth to Eighteenth Centuries*. Second Edition (New York, 2005)

Axworthy, M. *The Sword of Persia: Nader Shah, from Tribal Warrior to Conquering Tyrant* (London, 2009)

Babaie, S., Babayan, K., et al., *Slaves of the Shah: New Elites of Safavid Iran* (London, 2004)

Barkey, K. "The Ottoman Empire (1299–1923): The Bureaucratization of Patrimonial Authority", in P. Crooks, T.H. Parsons (eds.), *Empires and Bureaucracy in World History: From Late Antiquity to the Twentieth Century* (Cambridge, 2016), pp. 102–26

Bérenger, J. *La paix de Karlowitz, 26 janvier 1699: les relations entre l'Europe centrale et l'Empire Ottoman* (Paris, 2010)

Blake, S.P. "The Patrimonial-Bureaucratic Empire of the Mughals", *The Journal of Asian Studies* 39/1 (1979): 77–94

Blake, S.P. "Returning the Household to the Patrimonial-Bureaucratic Empire: Gender, Succession, and Ritual in the Mughal, Safavid and Ottoman Empires", in P.F. Bang, C.A. Bayly (eds.), *Tributary Empires in Global History* (New York, 2011), pp. 214–26.

Blow, D. *Shah Abbas: The Ruthless King Who Became an Iranian Legend* (London, 2009)

Edhem, E., Goffman, D., Masters, B.A. *The Ottoman City between East and West: Aleppo, Izmir and Istanbul* (Cambridge, 2005)

Erimtan, C. *Ottomans Looking West? The Origins of the Tulip Age and Its Development in Modern Turkey* (London, 2008)

Faroqhi, S. *The Cambridge History of Turkey. Vol. 3. The Later Ottoman Empire, 1603–1839* (Cambridge, 2006)

Faroqhi, S. *Coping with the State: Political Conflict and Crime in the Ottoman Empire, 1550–1720* (Istanbul, 1995)

Faroqhi, S. *The Ottoman Empire and the World Around It* (London, 2006)

Foran, J. "The Long Fall of the Safavid Dynasty: Moving Beyond the Standard Views", *International Journal of Middle East Studies* 24 (1992): 281–304

Hathaway, J. *Beshir Agha: Chief Eunuch of the Ottoman Imperial Harem* (Oxford, 2005)

Hathaway, J. *The Politics of Households in Ottoman Egypt: The Rise of the Qazdağlis* (Cambridge, 1997)

Hodgson, M.G.S. *The Venture of Islam: Conscience and History in a World Civlization. 3. The Gunpowder Empires and Modern Times* (Chicago, 1977)

Lockhart, L. *The Fall of the Safavī Dynasty and the Afghan Occupation of Persia* (Cambridge, 1958)

Marcus, A. *The Middle East on the Eve of Modernity: Aleppo in the Eighteenth Century* (New York, 1989)

Matthee, R. "A Comment on Kioumars Ghereghlou's Review of R. Matthee, *Persia in Crisis*", *International Journal of Middle East Studies* 48 (2016): 425–27

Matthee, R. *Persia in Crisis: Safavid Decline and The Fall of Isfahan* (London, 2011)

Quataert, D. "Ottoman History Writing and Changing Attitudes Towards the Notion of 'Decline'", *History Compass* 1 (2003): 1–9

Quataert, D. *The Ottoman Empire: 1700–1922*. Second Edition (Cambridge, 2000)

Rogan, E. *The Arabs. A History* (New York, 2009)

Subrahmanyam, S. "Connected Histories: Notes Towards a Reconfiguration of Early Modern Eurasia", *Modern Asian Studies* 31/3 (1997): 735–62

Tezcan, B. *The Second Ottoman Empire: Political and Social Transformation in the Early Modern World* (Cambridge, 2010)

van Leeuwen, R. *Waqfs and Urban Structures: The Case of Ottoman Damascus* (Leiden, 1999)

Wolf, J.B. *The Barbary Coast: Algiers under the Turks, 1500 to 1830* (New York, 1979)

Yapp, M.E. *The Making of the Modern Near East. 1792–1923* (London, 1987)

Selected readings (general)

Ansary, T. *Destiny Disrupted: A History of the World through Islamic Eyes* (New York, 2010)
Berkey, J.P. *The Formation of Islam: Religion and Society in the Near East, 600–1800* (Cambridge, 2003)
Bianquis, T., Garcin, J.-C., et al. (eds.). *États, sociétés et cultures du monde musulman médiéval: Xe–XVe siècle* (Paris, 1995–2000)
Choueiri, Y.M. (ed.). *A Companion to the History of the Middle East* (Chichester, 2005)
Egger, V.O. *A History of the Muslim World to 1405: The Making of a Civilization* (Upper Saddle River, 2004) & *A History of the Muslim World since 1260: The Making of a Global Community* (Upper Saddle River, 2008); republished as *A History of the Muslim World to 1750: The Making of a Civilization* (New York, 2018)
Endress, G., Hillenbrand, C. (vert.). *Islam: An Historical Introduction*. Second Edition (Edinburgh, 2002)
Gordon, M.S. *The Rise of Islam* (London, 2005)
Hodgson, M.G.S. *The Venture of Islam. Conscience and History in a World Civilization. 1. The Classical Age of Islam; 2. The Expansion of Islam in the Middle Periods; 3. The Gunpowder Empires and Modern Times* (Chicago, 1974–77)
Holt, P.M. *The Age of the Crusades: The Near East from the Eleventh Century to 1517* (London, 1986)
Hourani, A. *A History of the Arab Peoples* (London, 1991)
Humphreys, R. St. *Islamic History: A Framework for Inquiry* (London, 1991)
Kennedy, H. *The Prophet and the Age of the Caliphates*. Second Edition (London, 2004)
Lapidus, I.M. *Islamic Societies to the Nineteenth Century: A Global History* (Cambridge, 2012)
Lewis, B. (ed. and transl.). *Islam from the Prophet Muhammad to the Capture of Constantinople. Volume I: Politics and War* (Oxford, 1987)
Morgan, D. *Medieval Persia, 1040–1797* (New York, 1988)
Robinson, Ch.F. (ed.). *The New Cambridge History of Islam*. 6 Volumes (Cambridge, 2010)
Robinson, F. (ed.). *The Cambridge Illustrated History of the Islamic World* (Cambridge, 1996/2009)
Salvatore, A., Tottoli, R., Rahimi, B. (eds.). *The Wiley-Blackwell History of Islam* (Hoboken, 2018)
Silverstein, A.J. *Islamic History. A Very Short Introduction* (Oxford, 2010)
Sonn, T. *A Brief History of Islam* (Oxford, 2004)
Sonn, T. *Islam: History, Religion, and Politics*. Third Edition (Chichester, 2015)

Glossary

abna' al-dawla (abnā' ad-dawla) 'sons of the [Abbasid] dynasty'—name for the main early Abbasid forces in Iraq, sharing an origin in Khurasan and in the process of Abbasid empowerment during the mid-8th century

adab 'habit', 'culture', 'literature'—refined ethical and esthetic norms, values, and qualities; a complex whole of individual qualities that inform of a person's erudition, his cultural refinement and skills, and his active participation in an elitist urban lifestyle

adib (adīb) an individual of refined cultural qualities and skills, who endeavors to distinguish himself by, especially, composing and reciting high-quality Arabic prose and poetry

'ahdname ('ahdnāme) 'capitulation treaty' (Turkic)—an order from the Ottoman sultan that stipulates the rights and duties of a minority community that resides under Ottoman authority

ahl al-bayt 'the people of the [Prophet's] household'—the direct relatives and descendants of the Prophet Muhammad

akhbar (akhbār) 'reports', 'stories'—including about the Prophet, and especially about major figures among his descendants, the *imam*s, and therefore, a defining component of the Shi'ite religious tradition (see also *khabar*)

akhbaris (akhbāriyya) 'traditionalists'—Twelver Shi'ite scholars who, especially in the early modern period, awarded priority to the authority of *akhbar* in the formulation of their doctrines (see also *usuli*s)

amir (amīr) 'commander'—a wielder of coercive force leading his own band of armed retainers; title of a regional or local leader and administrator

amir al-mu'minin (amīr al-mu'minīn) 'commander of the believers'—a title of universal Islamic monotheist aspiration, on a par with the later title of caliph

amir al-umara' (amīr al-umarā') 'commander of commanders'—title of the chief *amir* in the Abbasid apparatus of power, used especially in the 10th and 11th centuries

amsar (amṣār) see *misr*

ansar (anṣār) 'helpers'—the original inhabitants of the oasis of Yathrib/Medina in the Arabian Hejaz, who welcomed Muhammad and his followers in 622; they are mostly considered to have belonged to two Arabian tribal formations (the Banu Khazraj and the Banu Aws)

ashraf (ashrāf) 'nobles'—collective referring to the leadership lineages of the Arabian Peninsula and Syrian desert that appeared as dominant in the pre-Islamic and early Islamic periods

'askeri ('askeri) the 'military' (Turkic)—a wide-ranging collective denoting all members of the Ottoman apparatus of power who received an income from the sultan in exchange for their military and non-military services

'ata' ('aṭā') stipend for services rendered to the *umma* in the early Islamic period; salary in exchange for military service

atabeg 'father of the prince' (Turkic)—royal guardian, or regent, for Seljuq and post-Seljuq minor rulers

atrak (atrāk) (*sing. *turk) 'Turks'—collective for diverse nomadic groups and political formations on the Inner-Asian steppes that, since at latest the beginning of the first millennium CE, had particular sets of linguistic features, relationships, practices, and values in common; horsemen from diverse Inner-Asian nomadic origins in the service of Islamic leaders, mostly sharing an individual history of unfreedom, islamization, and employment as coercive force; (in the 'medieval' and early modern periods) distinctive collective identity of leaderships and their armed retainers in Islamic West-Asia

a'yan (a'yān) 'notables'—an informal category referring to a social group's elite membership, especially in 'medieval' and 'early modern' West-Asian urban contexts

Bahriyya (Baḥriyya) elite corps of several hundreds of armed horsemen selected from the personal guard of royal *mamluk*s of the Ayyubid sultan al-Salih Ayyub (r. 1240–1249) (see Salihiyya); named after their headquarters on an island in the Nile (referred to as *al-bahr*, 'the sea', in the region)

banu (banū) 'the Sons of'—clan, tribe

bayt 'house'—household, extended (elite-)family

Bayt al-Hikma (Bayt al-Ḥikma) 'House of (Ancient) Wisdom'—the early Abbasid palace library and repository of ancient books in Baghdad, with Perso-Sasanian roots and expanded from the early 8th century onwards to also include many specimens of Greek and Hellenistic knowledge and related practices, including not least translation to Arabic

beylerbeyi 'commander of commanders' (Turkic)—Ottoman military official with the high court rank of *pasha*, who wielded extensive military and administrative powers and responsibilities in an *eyalet* (until the 16th century known as a *beylerbeylik*) and who was always appointed by the Ottoman grand vizier

beylik 'lordship' (Turkic)—configuration of power, especially in 'medieval' Asia Minor, organized around a charismatic wielder of violence and authority claims of Turkmen background and/or his descendants

caliph (*khalīfa*) 'successor', 'deputy'—title of sovereign Islamic leadership expressing claims to succession of the Prophet at the head of the *umma*, wielding an authority that was political as well as religious (as an instrument of God's will) and increasingly also spiritual (as an agent of sacral charisma); for many centuries, this title and its claims were closely tied up with trans-regional leaderships of Meccan origins (the Umayyad and, especially, Abbasid imperial dynasties) as well as, eventually, with the idea of the *umma* as a rightly guided Sunni community

dargah 'court'—the court of a Seljuk ruler

dawla 'dynasty', 'reign', 'state'—complex politico-religious concept that refers to the era within which the power configuration with which, and the apparatus of power by which, an individual, a family, or a group successfully claims legitimate, God-given sovereignty

Dawla (al-Dawla) the Abbasid dynasty

devshirme *(devşirme)*: 'the collection' (Turkic)—child levy, the regular collection of a tribute of young boys from among Christian communities on the Balkans and in Anatolia and their selection for education and training for military and/or administrative Ottoman palace service, as members of the 'servants of the Palace' (*kapıkulları*)

dihqan the local elite families of landholders and landed gentry in the Sasanian empire

***diwan (dīwān* [Ar.], *dîvân* [T.])** (in the early Islamic period) a regional center's register of names identifying entitlement to income from spoils, tribute, and taxes; (general) a branch of particular expertise and related tasks in an Islamic court's apparatus of power, populated by *kuttab* and mostly engaging with the management of resource flows, with matters of correspondence and representation, and with the reception of visitors; (in literature) a collection of poems

Early Modern Period the historical period of the 17th and 18th centuries (as defined here; mostly, however, defined as the period between the 16th and 18th centuries)

eyalet (eyâlât) 'province' (Turkic)—major unit in the central patrimonial domains of the Ottoman territory, directly administered by leading Ottoman officials, especially the *beylerbeyi*

fitna 'chaos', 'trial', 'competition'—(general) a moment of discord, violent competition, and disruption in the *umma*'s history and in its imagination as progressing towards salvation, used especially to refer to four moments of widespread violence and contestation of legitimate leadership in early Islamic history (656–661; 680–693; 746–750; 809–819); (in the 'medieval' period) the patronage-related social practice of competition for resources, appointments, gifts, status, and related benefits

futuh (futūḥ) 'opening'—the full set of territorial changes of the 7th and 8th centuries, 'opening' up the Late Antique world for violence-wielding networks of Arabian leadership and involving a wider process of integration of these networks, new territories, and local elites in the new, early Islamic configurations of power and belonging

geniza (genīzah) 'storage' (Hebrew)—storage space (e.g. in a synagogue) where a Jewish community kept old letters, documents, books, and other texts that, for religious reasons, could not be destroyed

***ghazi (ghāzī* [Ar.], *gâzî* [T.])** 'holy warrior'—fighter in the name of Islam, conceptualized within a legitimating ideological framework of Holy War (*ghaza* or *jihad*); especially encountered in an Ottoman context of westward expansion against different Christian opponents in Anatolia and the Balkans

ghazw 'raiding'—practice of violence wielding for booty and plunder that defined life of Arabian leaderships and their followers in the pre- and early Islamic periods

***ghilman (ghilmān)* (sing. *ghulam*)** 'youths'—a leader's personal entourage of armed retainers, made up of men of especially non-local and unfree origins (including especially *atrak*)

hadith (ḥadīth) 'story'—collective for the orally transmitted accounts about the Prophet Muhammad's actions, thinking, intentions, commands, or prohibitions that, as a key component of the Prophetic Tradition (Sunna), came to be considered as ethically and legally normative

haram (ḥaram) 'sanctuary'—a sacred place

***harim (ḥarīm)* (sing. *huram*)** 'what is untouchable, 'harem'—female members of a household and family that are considered to have to be protected against illicit relationships and contacts; the closed spaces in an elite residence or palace dedicated to housing the women of the family and only accessible to select groups of family members, servants, and visitors

haseki sultan (ḫâsekî sulṭân) 'the sultan's favorite' (Turkic)—leading partner/spouse of the Ottoman sultan, who was in charge of the harem and often wielded substantial power and influence

hijra 'migration'—the journey of Muhammad and his followers from the inimical environment of Mecca to the hospitable oasis of Yathrib/Medina in 622; considered the start of the new era of the *umma* and therefore, also of the Islamic lunar calendar (hence also known as the *hijra* calendar and often referred to with the Latin abbreviation AH [*anno hegirae* ('since the year of the *hijra*')])

ijaza (ijāza) 'permission'—formal confirmation by a teacher of a pupil's mastery of a particular textual tradition, or more in general, of his attainment of a particular level of understanding and intellectual training

ijtihad (ijtihād) interpretation on the basis of one's own rational capacities in the formulation and imagination of ideas, concepts, and rules of theocratic normativity

Il-Khan 'sovereign Khan'—rulership title claimed for the Mongol Chinggisid dynasty of the Hülegüids and some of their post-Mongol successors in Islamic West-Asia (13th–14th centuries)

ʿilm 'knowledge'—especially knowledge of Quran and Prophetic Tradition, and of any related domains of monotheist knowledge and of its theoretical and practical particularities

ʿilmiyye 'those who are knowledgeable' (Turkic)—the hierarchically organized community of Sunni religious scholars, teachers, and officials that, in the early modern, was an integrated component of the Ottoman dynastic apparatus of power

imam (imām) 'precursor', 'leader'—(general) the person who precedes in ritual prayer; (specific) the individual who leads the *umma* on God's path to salvation. For those Muslims who eventually identify themselves as Sunnis, this refers to the Abbasid caliphs and those rulers who later followed in their footsteps. For Shi'ites, this title and its claims are the prerogative of the descendants of Muhammad, beginning with his nephew and son-in-law ʿAli, succeeding each other via the designation by an *imam* of his successor, and including qualities of divine inspiration and infallibility; main Shi'ite sectarian groups are those that believe that either the fourth, the seventh, or the twelfth *imam* had gone into hiding only to return at the end of time to save his community of believers

imamate the divinely inspired and infallible status that, according to Shi'ite doctrine, distinguishes the *imams* and that allows them to guide the *umma* along God's path towards salvation (see also *imam*)

iqtaʿ (iqṭāʿ) 'apportionment'—a kind of prebendal allotment in return for military or administrative service; especially widespread in the 'medieval' period and consisting of the assignment to an *iqtaʿ* holder of the (mostly) temporary and revocable right to directly collect tribute and other (fiscal) income in cash and kind from well-defined commercial and (especially) agricultural activities and estates

Ismaʿilis (*Ismāʿīliyya*—Sevener Shi'is) the diversely composed Shi'ite community of believers and scholars that, from the 8th century onwards, organized itself increasingly explicitly (also politically) around the doctrine of a specific lineage of *imams* that adhered to claims of Muhammad ibn Ismaʿil to be the seventh *imam*, and to related claims of the divine guidance of at least some of his descendants; Isma'ili thought developed, especially from the 10th century onwards, strong ties with gnostic and neoplatonic systems of thought

iwan (īwān) vaulted open hall with public functionalities (e.g. as an audience hall) used in palaces as well as in *madrasas* and related infrastructures

jahiliyya (jāhiliyya) 'era of ignorance'—collective used in Islamic scholarship to identify the time before Muhammad's Prophecy, especially on the Arabian Peninsula, as an era that was ignorant of God and His pathway to salvation

Jazira (al-Jazīra) 'the Island'—today's region of northern Iraq and northeastern Syria, between the upper Euphrates and the upper Tigris

jihad (jihād) 'struggle (on God's path)'—complex concept revolving in varying interpretations around the efforts required from Muslims to do good and avoid bad things, which is generally considered a constant struggle with the self as well as with (variously defined) others

jizya 'poll tax'; (in the early Islamic period) one of the names for the diverse types of taxes that were levied (see also *kharaj*); (general) a *per capita* tax that all Christians and Jews had to pay in exchange for their protected socio-juridical status (*dhimma*)

julban (julbān) 'young trainees'—the most recently acquired generations of *mamluk* horsemen in the elite corps of the sultan of Cairo

kadi ʿasker (ʿkâdî ʿasker) 'army judge' (Turkic)—Ottoman chief judge (see also *qadi*)

kapi kullari (kapı kulları) 'servants of the palace' (Turkic)—the personal manpower of the Ottoman sultan, serving him as members of his elite guard corps, as palace staff, or as administrators, and consisting between the 15th and 17th centuries exclusively of especially selected and trained unfree men, recruited via the *devshirme* and from the ranks of war captives

Karimi (Kārimiyya) name for an extended network of Islamic families with Yemeni roots and specific commercial expertise who, between the 12th and the 15th centuries, dominated the maritime spice trade routes between the West Indian coasts and, especially, the Red Sea

keshig 'royal household'—(in the 'medieval' period) the entourage and personal guard of a Mongol leader

khabar 'story', 'report'—account from the life story of the Prophet Muhammad that did not necessarily have normative meaning (unlike *hadith*) (see also *akhbar*)

khan ***(khān, khāqān)*** 'chief' 'ruler'—Inner-Asian title of leadership

khanqah (khānqāh) 'Sufi hospice'—urban infrastructure for the housing of Sufi adherents and/or the facilitation of Sufi rituals and practices

kharaj (kharāj) 'land tax'—(in the early Islamic period) one of the names for the diverse types of taxes that were levied (see also *jizya*); (general) a tithe on agricultural production owed by all agricultural producers to the legitimate Islamic sovereign

kharijites (khārijiyya) 'those who move away'—an Islamic sec, the origins of which lay in the 1st *fitna* and disagreement with ʿAli's course of action, and organizing itself especially around a particular set of doctrines, including that of absolute egalitarianism, which made any believer a legitimate candidate for leadership of the *umma*, and that of a very strict and violent view on diversion from God's path and its consequences for the status of a believer; in the course of its long history, this sect soon fragmented in various smaller, local, and often rather isolated communities and groups, each with its own set of doctrines and views; today, its most important direct heirs are the Ibadites, who remain especially active in North Africa (Algeria)

khatib (khaṭīb) 'preacher'—the religious official who is formally appointed by a ruler, patron, or local community to deliver the weekly Friday sermon (*khutba*) from the pulpit (*minbar*) in a congregational mosque (*jamiʿ*)

Khurasaniyya (*khurāsāniyya*) one of the groups that wielded violence on the battlefields of the later 8th and early 9th centuries as agents of the early Abbasids, originating from the region of Khurasan and especially renowned as a heavy cavalry unit

Khwarazmians (*khwarazmiyya*) groups of raiding Turkic-speaking mercenaries who originated from the entourage of the last Khwarazm Shah and who, upon the latter's defeat by the Mongols in 1231, moved westward and offered their services to, amongst others, the Ayyubid sultan of Egypt and southern Syria al-Malik al-Salih Ayyub (r. 1240–49)

***kuttab (kuttāb)* (sing. *katib*)** 'writers', 'clerks'—collective referring to the specialists of administration and organization, often with local and non-Islamic roots, who populated the apparatus of power (especially the *diwan*s) of all Islamic dynasties and leaderships; communication and resource management were traditionally their main areas of expertise

Late Antiquity the historical period between the 4th and 10th centuries (or, according to many, between the 4th and 8th centuries only)

***madhhab* (pl. *madhahib*)** 'method', 'tradition', 'school' (of Islamic law)'—method of Islamic jurisprudence, which gave shape to an institutionalized practice and an imagined community of followers and practitioners of this method among legal scholars and believers, and the origins of which is always situated with an early Islamic pioneer; in the course of the 10th to 12th centuries, four *madhahib* remained as dominant, equally valid, and ubiquitous for all Sunni Muslims, by then identified as the followers of Malik (the Malikites), of Abu Hanifa (the Hanafites), of al-Shafiʿi (the Shafiʿites), and of Ahmad ibn Hanbal (the Hanbalites); in due course, a geographic spread emerged in the relationships between these open legal communities of Sunni Muslims, with their demographic centers of gravity situated in, respectively, North Africa, Asia, the Middle East, and the Arabian Peninsula

madrasa 'college (of law)'—urban infrastructure for the housing of students and for the facilitation of education in, primarily, Sunni jurisprudence (*fiqh*) of one, two, or all four of the Sunni Islamic *madhhab*s

***malik* (al-Malik)** 'monarch'—part of the titles of royalty and kingship (*mulk*) awarded to local and regional rulers during, especially, the 'medieval' period

mamluk (mamlūk) 'property' '(military) slave'—trained fighter of unfree origins and/or status; especially used in the 'medieval' period to denote a (formerly) unfree armed horseman

***mawali (mawālī)* (sing. *mawla*)** 'clients' 'servants'—(in the early Islamic period) collective referring to non-Arabian Muslims of both freeborn and unfree origins and diverse status and occupation, capable of participating only by linking themselves to one of the early Islamic period's Arabian leaderships; (general) slaves, servants, and all kinds of (unfree) people related by bonds of clientage (*walaʾ*) to a master

Middle Period, 'Medieval' Period the historical period between the 11th and 16th centuries

mihna (miḥna) 'inquisition'—9th-century conflict of authority between the Abbasid caliphs and their imperial entourages on the one hand, and traditionalist Islamic scholars in Iraq and Syria on the other hand, culminating in the period between 833 and 849 in the violent enforcement of particular, non-traditionalist, doctrines; it is generally accepted that the traditionalists emerged victoriously from this conflict

military patronage state analytical model to understand dynamics of power, focusing on the highly personalized patriarchal and/or patrimonial politics of competing elite households, their leaders, and the military sources of their social power, and the integrative dynamics of their politics of resource accumulation and sociocultural patronage

miri (mīrī) 'dynastic lands' (Turkic)—land in the central Ottoman regions of, particularly, Rumeli (the Balkans) and Anadolu (Asia Minor) that were formally owned by the sultan, the usufruct of which was given to local farming communities, and the surplus proceeds of which were especially used for the remuneration of the Ottoman landed gentry (*sipahi*)

***misr (miṣr)* (pl. *amsar*)** strategically located regional centers of early Islamic Arabian power, emerging from the encampments of Arabian leaderships and from the practice of keeping their followers, supporters, and anyone who joined them from the Arabian Peninsula concentrated in them, and subject to swift processes of urbanization; most well known and successful of these centers were Kufa and Basra in Iraq, Fustat in Egypt, and Qayrawan in North Africa

muhajirun (muhājirūn) 'those who undertook the *hijra*' 'migrants'—the first believers from Mecca who were the first to accept Muhammad's message and left with him for the oasis of Yathrib/Medina in 622

muhtasib (muḥtasib) 'public supervisor'—religious official responsible for the supervision and maintenance of moral socioeconomic order (*hisba*) and just commercial practices in an urban center (also sometimes referred to in a more reductive fashion as 'market inspector')

patriarchal rule/authority analytical model to represent and understand relationships of power that are fully defined by traditional kin and kin-related ties and practices

patrimonial rule/authority analytical model to represent and understand relationships of power that appear as coherent historical apparatuses of wielders of violence and organizers of resource accumulation operating in the service of a patriarchal (or dynastic) power center

patrimonial-bureaucratic rule/authority analytical model to represent and understand relationships of power that appear as more complex and elaborate variants of patrimonial authority, with components that acquire greater autonomy as powerful cogs in a bureaucratic machinery with a logic and agency that can be distinct from that of its patriarchal/dynastic center

qa'id (qā'id) commander of a sizeable band of armed retainers who operated in Abbasid military service in return for Abbasid income and privileges

qadi (qāḍī) legal scholar authorized by an Islamic ruler or by relevant legal authorities to act as a judge

Qizilbash (*qizil-bâsh*) 'the red heads' (Turkic)—collective referring to the Turkmen followers and supporters of 15th-century Safaviyya leadership in Azerbaijan, eastern Anatolia, and northern Syria, eventually considered to have consisted of twelve different Turkmen leaderships and their followers, many of whom continued to play leading roles in these and adjacent regions' histories into the modern period

ridda 'apostasy'—(in the early Islamic period) the breaking of bonds with Medina and the *umma* by many Arabian leaderships upon the death of Muhammad in 632

sabiqa (sābiqa) 'precedence (in conversion)'—(in the early Islamic period) term that refers to seniority in conversion to Muhammad's message as a key component in claims to status and priority in the early Islamic *umma*

sadaqa (ṣadaqa) 'charity'—(in the early Islamic period) tributary contribution to the leadership of the *umma*; (general) voluntary charitable gifts to the needy and poor

sahaba (ṣaḥāba) 'companionship'—(in the early Islamic period) term that refers to the measure of a person's closeness and acquaintance with the Prophet Muhammad as a key component in claims to status in the early Islamic *umma*; those who possessed this quality of Prophetic companionship are known as the 'companions' (*ashab*)

salaf (al-salaf [al-ṣāliḥ]) 'the (pious) ancestors'—the three generations of the Prophet Muhammad's companions (*ashab*), their children, and the children of their children considered by their 'closeness' (*sahaba*) to the Prophet as possessing an exemplary and even normative quality for later generations of Muslims

Salihiyya (Ṣāliḥiyya) the extended household guard of personal *mamluk*s of the Ayyubid sultan al-Salih Ayyub (r. 1240–9)

sanjak bey 'banner commander' (Turkic)—Ottoman military leader and administrator of a military district (*sanjak*) in an *eyalet*, subordinate to a *beylerbey*

shah (shāh) 'king'—Persian title of kingship, also actively used by various Islamic rulers, especially the Safavids and their successors

shahanshah (shāhānshāh) 'king of kings'—ancient Persian title of imperial kingship which was equally claimed by various Islamic rulers

shaykh ül Islam 'master of Islam' (Turkic)—head of the hierarchically organized community of Sunni religious scholars, teachers, and officials in early modern Ottoman service (see *'ilmiyye*)

Shi'ites (*shī'at 'Alī*) 'the partisans of 'Ali'—(in the early Islamic period) diverse groups who only accepted the claims to legitimate leadership of Muhammad's son-in-law 'Ali and his descendants; (general) collective for diverse Islamic groups and communities who believe in the ethical and normative force of the imamate (see imamate)

***sipahi* (*sipâhî*)** 'horseman' (Turkic)—member of the traditional Turkic-speaking elite of cavalrymen in Ottoman service who received a *timar* in return for their and their retainers' military service and who became the Ottoman landed gentry; member of one of the six elite cavalry divisions in the Ottoman sultan's personal guard force

Sultan (*sulṭān*) 'force' 'governance'—general notion of effective rulership increasingly used as an individual ruler's title in the course of the 11th century and soon transformed into the traditional designation of the sovereign Islamic authority that was claimed for diverse—especially Turkish, Turko-Mongol, and Turkmen—dynastic leaderships in Islamic West-Asia

sunna 'custom' 'tradition'—referring especially to Prophetic Tradition, as preserved in specific collections of *hadith* that are considered authentic by Sunni Islamic authorities

Sunni/Sunnites (*ahl al-sunna*) 'traditionalists'—the majority sectarian community in Islam, believing in the ethical and normative force of the example of the Prophet Muhammad as transmitted, preserved, and interpreted by religious scholars in the format of the Prophetic Tradition (*sunna*)

tariqa (ṭarīqa) (pl. turuq) 'path' 'brotherhood'—a community of Sufi scholars and/or practitioners, organized around the teachings, practices, relationships, and charisma of Sufi masters and around related resources, infrastructures, and teacher-student hierarchies

timar 'care' 'attention' (Turkic)—a particular type of prebendal allotment in return for the military service of a cavalryman (*sipahi*) and his followers to the Ottoman sultan

turk see *atrak*

Turkmen (*turkumān* [Ar.], *türkmen* [T.]) 'Turk-like'—the name most commonly used to identify both diverse groups of Turkic-speaking and Muslim nomadic pastoralists that, from the 11th century onwards, roamed across much of Islamic West-Asia in search of pastures for their herds, and various dynastic leaderships that emerged from these groups as local and regional leaders in, especially, 'medieval' Islamic West-Asia

Twelver Shi'ism (*ithnā 'ashariyya*) the Shi'ite community of believers and scholars that, from the 10th century onwards, organized itself increasingly explicitly around the doctrine of a specific lineage of twelve *imam*s, ending with Muhammad al-Mahdi, who, according to the Twelvers, disappeared in 874 and will remain in hiding until the end of time

***'ulama' ('ulamā'* [Ar.], *ulema* [T.]) (sing. *'alim*)** 'those who have knowledge'—collective for Islamic scholars who are the makers, guardians, and transmitters of an enormous diversity of knowledge practices related to Quran, Tradition, and Islamic ethics and who derive social authority and status from that intellectual agency

umma 'community of believers'—the imagined collective of Muslims, the origin of which is the Prophet's migration from Mecca to Medina (*hijra*), the goal of which is the implementation and performance of God's Will, and the destination of which is salvation and paradise after God's judgement at the end of times; discussions and conflicts about the boundaries and leadership of the *umma* define its history from the moment of Muhammad's death in 632

usulis (uṣūliyya) 'rationalists' 'fundamentalists'—the (eventually dominant) group within the Twelver Shi'ite clergy that, especially in the early modern period, awarded priority to the authority of a structured form of rationalism and to explanation and interpretation (*ijtihad*) of the 'sources' (*usul*; Quran and especially *akhbar*) by qualified experts in the formulation of Islamic doctrines and regulations (see also *akhbaris*)

valide sultan (vâlide sulṭân) 'sultan's mother' (Turkic)—the Ottoman queen mother who, as a result of her strong connection with the Ottoman sultan, tended to wield substantial power and influence from the harem (especially from the mid-16th century onwards)

vizier (*wazīr* [Ar.], *vezîr* [T.]) 'deputy', 'minister'—title for a leading administrative and/or military advisor and agent of Islamic rulers, who often headed the apparatus that organized an Islamic dynasty's power

waqf 'dead hand' 'mainmorte'—Islamic legal instrument that allows for personal assets to be transformed into an inalienable, inviolable, and non-taxable endowment that can only be used to provide for all kinds of predetermined religious needs and services

wikala (wikāla) 'caravanserai'—semi-closed infrastructure combining commercial and residential functions

Index

Note: Key concepts and words that are defined in the glossary appear in **bold**.